A Companion
to Border Studies

The *Blackwell Companions to Anthropology* offers a series of comprehensive syntheses of the traditional subdisciplines, primary subjects, and geographic areas of inquiry for the field. Taken together, the series represents both a contemporary survey of anthropology and a cutting edge guide to the emerging research and intellectual trends in the field as a whole.

1. *A Companion to Linguistic Anthropology*, edited by Alessandro Duranti
2. *A Companion to the Anthropology of Politics*, edited by David Nugent and Joan Vincent
3. *A Companion to the Anthropology of American Indians*, edited by Thomas Biolsi
4. *A Companion to Psychological Anthropology*, edited by Conerly Casey and Robert B. Edgerton
5. *A Companion to the Anthropology of Japan*, edited by Jennifer Robertson
6. *A Companion to Latin American Anthropology*, edited by Deborah Poole
7. *A Companion to Biological Anthropology*, edited by Clark Larsen (hardback only)
8. *A Companion to the Anthropology of India*, edited by Isabelle Clark-Decès
9. *A Companion to Medical Anthropology*, edited by Merrill Singer and Pamela I. Erickson
10. *A Companion to Cognitive Anthropology*, edited by David B, Kronenfeld, Giovanni Bennardo, Victor de Munck, and Michael D. Fischer
11. *A Companion to Cultural Resource Management*, edited by Thomas King
12. *A Companion to the Anthropology of Education*, edited by Bradley A.U. Levinson and Mica Pollack
13. *A Companion to the Anthropology of the Body and Embodiment*, edited by Frances E. Mascia-Lees
14. *A Companion to Paleopathology*, edited by Anne L. Grauer
15. *A Companion to Folklore*, edited by Regina F. Bendix and Galit Hasan-Rokem
16. *A Companion to Forensic Anthropology*, edited by Dennis Dirkmaat
17. *A Companion to the Anthropology of Europe*, edited by Ullrich Kockel, Máiréad Nic Craith, and Jonas Frykman
18. *A Companion to Rock Art*, edited by Jo McDonald and Peter Veth
19. *A Companion to Border Studies*, edited by Thomas M. Wilson and Hastings Donnan

Forthcoming

A Companion to Moral Anthropology, edited by Didier Fassin
A Companion to Paleoanthropology, edited by David Begun
A Companion to Chinese Archaeology, edited by Anne Underhill

A Companion
to Border Studies

Edited by
Thomas M. Wilson
and Hastings Donnan

WILEY-BLACKWELL

A John Wiley & Sons, Ltd., Publication

This edition first published 2012
© 2012 Blackwell Publishing Ltd.

Blackwell Publishing was acquired by John Wiley & Sons in February 2007. Blackwell's publishing program has been merged with Wiley's global Scientific, Technical, and Medical business to form Wiley-Blackwell.

Registered Office
John Wiley & Sons Ltd, The Atrium, Southern Gate, Chichester, West Sussex, PO19 8SQ, UK

Editorial Offices
350 Main Street, Malden, MA 02148-5020, USA
9600 Garsington Road, Oxford, OX4 2DQ, UK
The Atrium, Southern Gate, Chichester, West Sussex, PO19 8SQ, UK

For details of our global editorial offices, for customer services, and for information about how to apply for permission to reuse the copyright material in this book please see our website at www.wiley.com/wiley-blackwell.

The right of Thomas M. Wilson and Hastings Donnan to be identified as the authors of the editorial material in this work has been asserted in accordance with the UK Copyright, Designs and Patents Act 1988.

Library of Congress Cataloging-in-Publication Data

A companion to border studies / edited by Thomas M. Wilson and Hastings Donnan.
p. cm.
Includes bibliographical references and index.
ISBN 978-1-4051-9893-6 (hardcover : alk. paper)   1. Boundaries.   2. Borderlands.   3. Political geography.   4. Human geography.   I. Wilson, Thomas M.   II. Donnan, Hastings.
JC323.C655 2012
320.1'2–dc23

2011049092

A catalogue record for this book is available from the British Library.

Set in 10/12.5 Galliard by Toppan Best-set Premedia Limited
Printed and bound in Singapore by Markono Print Media Pte Ltd

1   2012

Contents

Figures and Table

Notes on Contributors

Robert R. Alvarez, Jr is Professor of Ethnic Studies and the Director of the Center for Global California Studies at the University of California, San Diego. His research has focused on immigrant communities on the United States–Mexico border and global agriculture, especially transnational markets, entrepreneurs and the ethnic fruit trade. He has conducted research throughout Mexico, Panama and along the US–Mexico border, and participated in applied research and education in the US southwest, California, Micronesia, Hawaii, Belau and the Northern Marianas.

James Anderson is Professor Emeritus of Political Geography and Visiting Senior Research Fellow in Sociology in Queen's University Belfast. He is currently employed on an Economic and Social Research Council (UK) funded project, 2007–2012, on Conflict in Cities and the Contested State: Belfast, Jerusalem and Other Divided Cities (www.conflictincities.org) of which he is a grant-holder along with colleagues in Cambridge, Exeter and Queen's, having shared previous ESRC grants for work on Jerusalem with Exeter and Cambridge in 2003–2004 and 2005–2007. Recent and current research interests in political and urban geography include nationalism and national conflicts, territoriality and borders, state–city relations, political violence, European integration and transnational democracy. He is a founder member and co-director of Queen's University's Centre for International Borders Research (www. qub.ac.uk/cibr).

Anthony Ijaola Asiwaju is Emeritus Professor of History at the University of Lagos. He has published widely in the area of comparative African borderland studies, including *Western Yorubaland under European Rule, 1889–1945: A Comparative Analysis of French and British Colonialism* (1976); *Partitioned Africans: Ethnic Relations across Africa's International Boundaries, 1884–1984* (1985); *Boundaries and African Integration: Essays in Comparative History and Policy Analysis* (2003); *African Boundaries: Barriers, Conduits and Opportunities* (with Paul Nugent, 1996). He has also been the pioneer Commissioner (International Boundaries) of Nigeria's National Boundary Commission and a foundation member of the African Union Border Programme Steering Committee.

Pamela Ballinger is Fred Cuny Professor of International Human Rights and Associate Professor of History at the University of Michigan. She is the author of *History in Exile* (2003). Her research focuses on refugees, displacement, repatriation and memory, and has appeared in journals such as *Comparative Studies in Society and History*, *Current Anthropology*, *History and Memory*, *Journal of Modern Italian Studies*, and *Past and Present*.

John Borneman is Professor of Anthropology at Princeton University. He has done ethnographic fieldwork in Germany, Central Europe, Lebanon, and Syria, and been guest professor in Sweden, Norway, France, Germany, and Syria. He served on the executive board of the Internationales Forschungszentrum Kulturwissenschaften in Vienna, and currently sits on the boards of the Max Planck Institut-Halle and the Forum Psychoanalytischer Wissenschaften of the Berliner Institut für Psychotherapie und Psychoanalyse. His publications include *Belonging in the Two Berlins: Kin, State, Nation* (1992), *Syrian Episodes: Sons, Fathers, and an Anthropologist in Aleppo* (2007), *Being There: The Fieldwork Encounter and the Making of Truth* (as co-editor, 2009), and *Political Crime and the Memory of Loss* (2011).

Emmanuel Brunet-Jailly is Associate Professor of Public Administration at the University of Victoria, British Columbia, Canada, where he is also Jean Monnet Chair in European Urban and Border Region Policy and Director of the European Union Centre for Excellence. He is also co-director of the Local Government Institute and the editor of the *Journal of Borderlands Studies*. He is the author of many articles, chapters and books in urban and border studies.

Brenda Chalfin is Associate Professor of Anthropology at the University of Florida in Gainesville. She has conducted ethnographic research on neoliberal reform and state transformation in Ghana with a focus on border zones, with funding from the National Science Foundation and Wenner-Gren Foundation. These themes are the subject of her book *Neoliberal Frontiers: An Ethnography of Sovereignty in West Africa* (2010). She continues to research global transformations in border controls and security protocols within the late modern state in both Africa and Europe. With the support of a Fulbright Hays grant she is working on a comparative study of African portscapes as zones of special sovereignty emerging out of the uneven effects of global integration. She has been a member of the School of Social Science at the Institute of Advanced Study in Princeton, and was awarded a 2005–2006 Fellowship at the Woodrow Wilson International Center for Scholars in Washington, DC.

Mathew Coleman is Assistant Professor in Geography at the Ohio State University in Columbus, Ohio. He is a political geographer with a broad theoretical background in critical geopolitics, law and geography, immigration law and political economy. His current research funded by the National Science Foundation focuses on racial profiling and interior immigration enforcement in the US South. He has published widely in leading scholarly journals, including the *Annals of the Association of American Geographers*, *Antipode*, *Environment and Planning D: Society and Space*, *Geopolitics* and *Political Geography*.

David B. Coplan is the Professor and Chair in Social Anthropology at the University of the Witwatersrand in Johannesburg. He has been researching and writing about South African performing arts and media since 1976. He is the author of numerous publications in this field, including most notably *In Township Tonight! South Africa's Black City Music and Theatre* (1986), revised, enlarged and published in a second edition in 2007. Professor Coplan is also a specialist in the ethnographic history and performance culture of the Basotho of southern Africa. His related works include *In the Time of Cannibals: The Word Music of South Africa's Basotho Migrants* (1994) and the film *Songs of the Adventurers* (1986). His forthcoming social history of the Lesotho–South Africa border is entitled *Major Warden's Knife: Narrating Race and Place in a South African Borderland*. David Coplan appears frequently on South African radio and television as an arts, culture, and media commentator.

Hilary Cunningham is Associate Professor of Anthropology at the University of Toronto and has published widely on borders and the environment. She is currently working on what she calls "gated ecologies" in northern Ontario. Adopting a unique interdisciplinary framework that builds on anthropological insights into culture, power and history, she explores "nature" as entailing boundary-making; that is, as involving metaphysical, aesthetic and political practices that enact and enable particular human–nature interactions.

Nicholas De Genova has taught anthropology, migration studies, and ethnic studies at Columbia and Stanford Universities (USA) and the University of Bern (Switzerland), and has also held research positions at the University of Warwick (UK), the University of Amsterdam (Netherlands), and the University of Chicago (USA). He is the author of *Working the Boundaries: Race, Space, and "Illegality" in Mexican Chicago* (2005), co-author of *Latino Crossings: Mexicans, Puerto Ricans, and the Politics of Race and Citizenship* (2003), editor of *Racial Transformations: Latinos and Asians Remaking the United States* (2006), and co-editor of *The Deportation Regime: Sovereignty, Space, and the Freedom of Movement* (2010). He is completing a new book, titled *The Spectacle of Terror: Immigration, Race, and the Homeland Security State*.

Hastings Donnan is Professor of Anthropology at Queen's University Belfast. He is the author, editor or co-editor of nearly 20 books, including, most recently, *The Anthropology of Sex* (with Fiona Magowan, 2010), *Borderlands: Ethnographic Approaches to Security, Power and Identity* (with Thomas M. Wilson, 2010) and *Borders: Frontiers of Identity, Nation and State* (with Thomas M. Wilson, 1999, 2001). He is a Member of the Royal Irish Academy and a Founding Academician of the UK's Academy of Social Sciences.

Michele Ford is Associate Professor in the Department of Indonesian Studies at the University of Sydney, where she teaches about social activism and human rights in Southeast Asia. Her research focuses on the Indonesian labor movement, organized labor's responses to temporary labor migration in East and Southeast Asia, and the Singapore–Indonesia borderlands. She is the author of *Workers and Intellectuals:*

NGOs, Trade Unions and the Indonesian Labour Movement (2009) and the co-editor of *Women and Work in Indonesia* (2008); *Women and Labour Organizing in Asia: Diversity, Autonomy and Activism* (2008) and *Indonesia beyond the Water's Edge: Managing an Archipelagic State* (2009).

Jonathan Goodhand is Reader in the Department of Development Studies at the School of Oriental and African Studies at the University of London. Before taking up this position he managed humanitarian and development programs in conflict situations in Afghanistan, Pakistan and Sri Lanka, and has extensive experience as a researcher and advisor in South and Central Asia for a range of nongovernmental organizations and aid agencies. His research interests include the political economy of aid and conflict, NGOs and peace-building and "postconflict" reconstruction. He is author or co-author of *Aid, Conflict and Peacebuilding in Sri Lanka: Caught in the Peace Trap* (forthcoming), *Aiding Peace: The Role of NGOs in Armed Conflict* (2006) and *War Economies in a Regional Context: Challenges for Transformation*.

Sarah Green is Professor of Social Anthropology at the University of Manchester. Throughout her career, she has been interested in anthropological understandings of space, place and location, both within cities and in wider terms, such as the virtual spaces of the internet. Her interest in how location becomes involved in people's lives culminated in an enduring interest in borders. She has done fieldwork on the Greek-Albanian border and, more recently, in the Aegean, along and across the border area between Greece and Turkey. She is author of *Notes from the Balkans* (2005) and *Urban Amazons* (1997).

Alejandro Grimson received his PhD in anthropology from the University of Brasilia. His principal research interests are in migratory processes, border areas, social movements and political cultures. Among his principal publications are *On Argentina and the Southern Cone* (with Gabriel Kessler, 2005), *La nación en sus límites* (2003) and *Los límites de la cultura* (2011). He is currently a researcher at CONICET, the National Scientific and Technical Research Council of Argentina, and is Dean of the Institute of Social Studies of National University of San Martín in Argentina.

Josiah McC. Heyman is Professor of Anthropology and Chair of Sociology and Anthropology at the University of Texas, El Paso. Among his publications are *States and Illegal Practices* (1999), *Finding a Moral Heart for US Immigration Policy: An Anthropological Perspective* (1998) and *Life and Labor on the Border: Working People of Northeastern Sonora, Mexico 1886–1986* (1991). His research interests include migration and border control; states, bureaucracies and power; and engaged social science.

Nancy Hiemstra is a faculty Scholar in Residence at Emerson College's Institute of Liberal Arts and Interdisciplinary Studies. Her research interests focus on human mobility, migration policy-making and the role of the state in shaping daily life. Previous research examined Latino immigration to small-town Colorado. Current research focuses on impacts in Ecuador of international migration, migrant detention and deportation policies and practices in the US and the embodied consequences of immigration enforcement policies in countries of migrant origin. She has published articles in *Antipode, Geopolitics* and *Social and Cultural Geography.*

Robert J. Kaiser is Professor of Geography at the University of Wisconsin – Madison. His research explores the always politicized socio-spatial processes of place-making, identification and differentiation. Recently, his work has turned to developing an event ontology in human geography, primarily using Deleuze's philosophy of the event. He has long-standing interests in the political and cultural geographies of the USSR and postsocialist space.

Olivier Thomas Kramsch is Senior Lecturer in the Department of Human Geography, Radboud Universiteit, Nijmegen, The Netherlands, and a member of the Nijmegen Centre for Border Research (NCBR). He has written extensively on various dimensions of European transboundary regionalism, drawing on theories of cosmopolitanism, postcoloniality and nineteenth-century French anarchism, while eschewing, wherever possible, the word "scale." He believes it is possible, one day, to link the literatures on internal and external European Union borders within a single, coherent and convincing analytic frame.

Lenore Lyons is Research Professor in Asian Studies at the University of Western Australia. Recognized as the leading scholar on the feminist movement in Singapore, her book *A State of Ambivalence: The Feminist Movement in Singapore* was published in 2004. She recently completed a major study of citizenship, identity and sovereignty in the Riau Islands borderlands of Indonesia (with Michele Ford) and is currently working on a project that examines labor migration and human trafficking in Singapore, Indonesia and Malaysia.

Cathal McCall is Senior Lecturer in European Studies, School of Politics, International Studies and Philosophy, Queen's University, Belfast. He has published widely on the theme of cross-border cooperation and conflict transformation in the Irish border region. His book *Europeanisation and Hibernicisation: Ireland and Europe* (co-edited with Thomas M. Wilson) was published by Rodopi Press in 2010.

Allan K. McDougall is Professor Emeritus in Political Science at the University of Western Ontario and Adjunct Research Professor at the University of Alberta. His recent research addresses hegemonic transformation in regions of contested jurisdiction as state systems were imposed.

Nick Megoran is a political geographer and lecturer at Newcastle University. His main research interests are nationalism in Central Asia, Christianity in recent US-UK foreign policy contexts, classical and critical geopolitical theory, peace and nonviolence, and international boundaries. He has been fascinated by international boundaries since childhood.

Alison Mountz is Associate Professor of Geography at Syracuse University where she teaches courses on migration, and political, feminist and urban geography.

Her work explores struggles over border enforcement, asylum and detention. Mountz is the author of *Seeking Asylum: Human Smuggling and Bureaucracy at the Border*, which was awarded the 2011 Meridian Book Prize from the Association of American Geographers. She is now conducting research on detention facilities located on islands off the shores of North America, Australia and the European Union.

David Newman is Professor of Political Geography in the Department of Politics and Government at Ben Gurion University in Israel where he currently serves as Dean of the Faculty of Humanities and Social Sciences. His work focuses on the territorial dimensions of ethnic conflict and he has written extensively on issues related to borders and their significance in the contemporary world, and more specifically on border and territorial issues in Israel-Palestine. He is the editor of the international journal *Geopolitics*.

Paul Nugent is Professor of Comparative African History and Director of the Centre of African Studies at the University of Edinburgh as well as President of the Centre's European African Studies Association, AEGIS. He is also Chairman of the European Science Foundation-funded African Borderlands Research Network (ABORNE). He is the author of *Africa since Independence: A Comparative History* (2004, 2012) and of *Smugglers, Secessionists and Loyal Citizens of the Ghana–Togo Frontier: The Lie of the Borderlands since 1914* (2003). He is currently completing a monograph entitled *Boundaries, Communities and State-Making in the Senegambia and the Trans-Volta: The Centrality of the Margins, c. 1750 to the Present*.

Liam O'Dowd is Professor of Sociology at Queen's University Belfast and Director of the Centre for International Borders Research. His research has focused on state borders and border regions in the European Union and more recently on divided cities and the contested state. His recent publications include *Crossing the Border: New Relationships between Northern Ireland and the Republic of Ireland* (2007), *New Borders for a New Europe* (2003) and "From a 'Borderless World' to a 'World of Borders': 'Bringing History Back In,'" *Environment and Planning D: Society and Space* (2010).

Brendan O'Leary is Lauder Professor of Political Science at the University of Pennsylvania. His books include *How To Get Out of Iraq with Integrity* (2009), *Power-Sharing in Deeply Divided Places* (in press) and *Understanding Northern Ireland: Colonialism, Control, Consociation* (forthcoming). His research interests include ethnic conflict, political violence and power-sharing in deeply divided places. He has served as the Senior Advisor on Power-Sharing to the Mediation Support Unit of the United Nations.

Mathijs Pelkmans is Lecturer in Anthropology at the London School of Economics. He holds a PhD from the University of Amsterdam and worked as a research fellow at the Max Planck Institute for Social Anthropology from 2003 to 2006. He is the author of *Defending the Border: Identity, Religion, and Modernity in the Republic of*

Georgia (2006) and editor of *Conversion after Socialism: Disruptions, Modernisms, and Technologies of Faith in the Former Soviet Union* (2009).

Lisa Philips is Professor and Chair of the Department of Anthropology at the University of Alberta. Her research has focused on First Nations and state relations, both contemporary and historical. With Allan McDougall, she explores hegemonic processes, especially through the construction and reconstruction of political, legal and social identities.

Dan Rabinowitz is Professor of Anthropology at Tel-Aviv University and at Central European University and has held visiting professorships at the universities of Princeton, New York and Toronto. He is has published with many of the major university presses and in leading journals such as *American Ethnologist, Critical Inquiry, Man (Journal of the Royal Anthropological Institute), International Journal of Middle East Studies, Journal of Anthropological Research, Ethnic and Racial Studies, Identities, Annual Review of Anthropology, Environmental Justice* and more. He is a regular contributor to the op-ed page of *Haaretz*, Chair of the Israeli Association for Environmental Justice and Vice Chair of Greenpeace UK.

Timothy Raeymaekers is a lecturer in political geography at the University of Zurich. His research interests are in legal pluralism, economic anthropology, migration and borderlands. He currently works in Central Africa and Europe.

James Wesley Scott is Professor of Regional and Border Studies, Karelian Institute at the University of Eastern Finland and an Associate Professor of Geography at the Free University of Berlin. His principal fields of research include urban and regional development, border regions, regional and urban governance, metropolitan area problems, and European and North American geography. He currently coordinates the EUBORDERREGIONS project, financed by the European Union's Seventh Framework Programme for Research and Technological Development.

Alan Smart is Professor at the Department of Anthropology, University of Calgary. His research has focused on urban issues, housing, foreign investment, social change, food safety, zoonotic diseases, and agriculture in Hong Kong, China and Canada. He is author of *Making Room: Squatter Clearance in Hong Kong* (1992) and *The Shek Kip Mei Myth: Squatters, Fires and Colonial Rule in Hong Kong, 1950–1963* (2006), and co-editor (with Josephine Smart) of *Petty Capitalists and Globalization* (2005).

Josephine Smart is Professor of Anthropology at the University of Calgary, where she received a Distinguished Research Award in 2006 and a Distinguished Teacher Award in 2000. Her research and teaching interests are economic anthropology, food biosecurity and emergent infectious diseases, Bovine Spongiform Encephalopathy and social-economic impact in Canada, social and economic development in post-1978 China, Chinese international migration, globalization, immigrant entrepreneurs, and the international mobility of capital and labor. Author of *The*

Political Economy of Street Hawkers in Hong Kong (1989), she is also co-editor of *Petty Capitalists and Globalization: Flexibility, Entrepreneurship and Economic Development* (2005) and *Plural Globalities in Multiple Localities: New World Borders* (2001). Her current research project, a comparative study of the political economy of farming policies in Canada and China, is funded by the Social Sciences and Humanities Research Council of Canada (2009–2012).

Henk van Houtum is Associate Professor of Geopolitics and Political Geography and Head of the Nijmegen Centre for Border Research, Radboud University of Nijmegen in the Netherlands and Research Professor of Geopolitics at the University of Bergamo in Italy. He has written extensively on the ontology and (im)morality of borders and b/ordering, immigration regimes, (national) identity, regional and urban politics and cartography. He is editor of the *Journal of Borderlands Studies*.

Thomas M. Wilson is Professor of Anthropology and Chair of the Department of Anthropology in Binghamton University, State University of New York. Currently an Honorary Professor in the School of Sociology, Social Policy and Social Work in Queen's University Belfast, he is also a founder member and co-director of that university's Centre for International Borders Research. From 2008 to 2010 he was President of the Society for the Anthropology of Europe.

CHAPTER 1

Borders and Border Studies

Thomas M. Wilson and Hastings Donnan

There are more international borders in the world today than ever there were before. This is a significant fact when one considers the impact of these many borders on the ways in which the billions of people encompassed by them live, work and travel. As important a development as this multiplication in international borders is, however, it alone is not the guiding imperative behind the origin and evolution of comparative border studies in scholarship worldwide. The proliferation of borders, and the many forces that have created and fostered their development, together have drawn scholars from all the humanities and social sciences to a mutual interest in what happens at, across and because of the borders to nations and states, and in extension to other geopolitical borders and boundaries, such as those of cities, regions and supranational polities. Their interest has been as much in what happens at specific borders, frontiers and borderlands as it has been in what borders help us to understand of major forces of change that seem to be sweeping the globe, forces often included as aspects of globalization, but which may also be seen as neoliberalism, neo-imperialism, late modern capitalism, and supranationalism. Within these interests and perspectives, border studies scholars enter into dialogue with all those who wish to understand new liberties, new movements, new mobilities, new identities, new citizenships and new forms of capital, labor and consumption. Border studies have become significant themselves because scholars and policy-makers alike have recognized that most things that are important to the changing conditions of national and international political economy take place in borderlands – as they do in like measure almost everywhere else in each of our national states – but some of these things, for instance those related to migration, commerce, smuggling and security, may be found in border-lands in sharper relief. And some things of national importance can be most often and best found in borderlands.

This book, a collection of essays that represent views both of where border studies have come from and where they are going, reflects the current state of border

A Companion to Border Studies, First Edition. Edited by Thomas M. Wilson and Hastings Donnan.
© 2012 Blackwell Publishing Ltd. Published 2012 by Blackwell Publishing Ltd.

studies, or perhaps this might be better expressed as the current states of border studies. In particular, it shows how scholarly attention to political and social borders has grown apace with the growth in numbers of borders, states and the peoples who live in and cross borders, borderlands, frontiers and boundaries. Once principally the focus of geography, the study of territorial, geophysical, political and cultural borders today has become a primary, abiding and growing interest across the scholarly disciplines, and is related to changing scholarly approaches to such key research subjects and objects as the state, nation, sovereignty, citizenship, migration and the overarching forces and practices of globalization. All of these approaches to borders and frontiers have been complicated by various attempts to understand and express identities, an effort often related to the investigation of hybridity, creolization, multiculturalism, postcolonialism and many other central concerns of social theory today.

Scholarly and political interests are not alone in the recognition of the increasing prominence of borders in the lives of many people in all parts of the world. Borders have become a master narrative and hegemonic symbol in popular, commercial, youth and liberation cultures. Borders have captured the fancy of the peoples of the world and they function as a grand motif in everyday life, everywhere. This is true of some people all of the time, others just some of the time, and perhaps seldom for still others. It is difficult in today's world to avoid public debates over borders, or to ignore the many ways in which borders figure in a great deal of popular discourse. This is not just the result of a borders numbers game. While more borders than in years past frame our collective lives today as a consequence of the removal and strengthening of various state and other political borders, it has also been the mix of populations and the agencies of the state and others where countries and their peoples meet, and the metaphorical borderlands of hegemonic and minority identities, that spark so much popular interest. There is every indication that the scholarly fascination with this intersection of the metaphorical negotiations of borderlands of personal and group identity (in what has come to be known as "border theory") with the geopolitical realization of international, state and other borders of polity, power, territory and sovereignty ("border studies") has mushroomed of late and continues to grow.

This scholarly turn is not simply a reflection of ivory tower musings, but is provoked and challenged by real events that have affected us all over the last 20 years. A list of these events that revolve around changing borders would include, but be far from complete with, the fall of the Iron Curtain; the expansion of the European Union (EU); the rise of new and old ethnonationalisms; the creation of many new states and regional trading blocs to rival the EU and the United States; the rise of new global forces, from neoliberal economics to New World Political Orders; the clash of civilizations; and new engagements between developed and emerging countries and hemispheres. These have all made borders and borderlands new sites of empirical investigation, of processes of localization and globalization in the face of so many forces of change. Borders and frontiers are also elements in the transforming dimensions of culture, politics, society and economics at every level of social and political complexity, experience and expression across the globe. Recent events and ongoing dilemmas brought on by 9/11, the war on terror, and the new security, environmental, health and economic problems and opportunities of world populations on the move, all indicate that the related notions of borders, boundaries and frontiers will attract more attention in future from scholars, policy-makers and other peoples of the world who must negotiate and cross the barriers and bridges that borders represent (see Donnan and Wilson 2010).

The timeliness and relevance of border studies is one theme which runs through the essays in this volume, but there are other thematic motors which have driven us collectively. In the volume our authors show repeatedly that border theory, which seeks answers to questions about how identity, territory and the state are interrelated in the formation of the self and of group identification, has much to offer scholarship on the political economies of geopolitical entities that are encapsulated and in some instances defined by their geophysical borders. But the converse is true too, as our authors also show repeatedly, where the confluence of territory, power and the state is instrumental in many issues of identity and culture, locally and also farther afield. As our authors show through their historical case studies and historical framings of contemporary issues, border studies have proliferated along with borders, and the speed with which border studies are changing and expanding is both remarkable and significant.

This *Companion* is thus a freezing in time of what can best be described as mercurial: who knew in the 1980s how global political and economic order would change, and so drastically, and who knew in the 1990s that so many borders, new and old, in the world would be configured as they have been in the wake of so many epochal events in the global landscape. Some case studies here are offered to illustrate forces at work in those borderlands and in those regions which we anticipate will have corollaries elsewhere and will help to inform scholarship in more distant areas of the globe. Other essays in the volume take a much more explicitly comparative and theoretical view of borders. But we realize too that as soon as a volume like this presents "state of the art" essays, that the "state" and that "art" will change. Our task here is to try to make sense of where we are and where we have been in border studies, to offer some choices for those whose interests and works will make the future changes to the state and the art of border studies. Our introduction is thus both retrospective and prospective and locates the likely future trajectories of border studies within the themes and approaches of the present and the recent past.

In the remaining sections of the introduction we review some of the key features in the border studies which we entered in the early 1990s. These earlier border studies, which were particularly influential on us, were deeply entrenched in geography, but history, political science and sociology also contained much of interest to us, which helped us to formulate our own ideas and to chart our own path. This was especially beneficial to us when we began our assessment of border and boundary studies within our parent discipline, anthropology. But earlier border studies also helped us to fashion the beginnings of what we saw as an interdisciplinary, multidisciplinary, and perhaps even postdisciplinary approach to so much that mattered to scholars and others around us, most of which was related to the changing nature of the territorial dimensions to the state and the nation. In the final section of this introduction we examine what border studies are today. Using our authors as inspiration, we explore how contemporary border studies have in the main eschewed single case studies in favor of explicitly or implicitly comparative analyses, and have largely moved beyond the constraints of their own disciplinary borders to read widely and consider seriously the evidence and arguments offered by like-minded scholars in other disciplines and from other national traditions.

Border studies today are a "field" made up of many fields and yet no one field in particular. Border studies are akin to what we study: rooted in space and time they are also about process and fluidity. They reflect intellectual convergence as well as scholarly differentiation, and through them we can begin to see not only the interstices of nations and states, but those of a new world understanding of scholarship, where academics increasingly seek cooperation, collaboration and intellectual fellowship across those same borders we are drawn to study. But all of this, as far as we have seen since the 1990s, while quick in the making, has not been without its own variations. Before considering how border studies have changed over the last two decades, and to illustrate some of the difficulties to be faced by scholars in any discipline in their attempt to pursue scholarship at what might be seen by many to be the margins of their own discipline, we turn first to the anthropology of borders, then and now. We do so to offer an example of how border studies have evolved from individual cases seen through the lens of one scholarly discipline to a more comprehensive and comparative perspective on other borders and other intellectual traditions.

OF DISCIPLINES AND CASE STUDIES

In the 1990s when we began our collaboration in border studies, after we had each done separate ethnographic field research in borderlands, it was widely asserted in certain academic circles, associated with what has become known variously in scholarship as postmodernism, cultural studies and globalization, that the world had become smaller, time and space had been compressed, there had been a speeding up in global movement of almost everything significant, and the preeminent institutions of modernity were no longer as powerful and unassailable as they once were. Foremost among these waning institutions, so it was asserted by a host of scholars eager to chronicle and understand the seismic shifts in a globalizing world, was the national state, that is, that particular state conglomeration of government and governance dedicated to the creation and defense of its nation. The predicted withering away of the national state as the preeminent political structure of modernity also was believed to herald the end of institutions and actions dependent on the national state and the dissipation of the affective dimensions to national identities and state identifications. It was expected that the filtering down of these effects would dilute traditional political, social and cultural structures and associations within equally traditional and threatened territorial entities, such as nations and regions. These effects were expected to be devastating for some and liberating for others.

This sort of globalization and postmodernist rhetoric continues to capture the imagination of scholars and policy-makers alike. At times this rhetoric is also used to support scholarly treatments of neoliberalism, now just as pervasive a concept as globalization in the provision of oft-asserted but seldom demonstrated causes of so much that promises salvation or ruin to people (among them scholars) in the world today. Changes in individual and group loyalties, associations and identities have fueled the new politics of identity, in which the definitions of citizenship, nation and state vie with gender, sexual, ethnic, religious and racial identities for prominence if not preeminence in new national and world orders. Or at least vie with each other in the imaginations of scholars who study such things. The gist of much of this sort of approach to the nation and state as it affected the study of borders was that we were all living in a world where state borders were increasingly obsolete, where porous international borders no longer fulfilled their historical role as barriers to the move-ment of aliens and citizens, and as markers of the extent and power of the state.

While this sort of argument was heady and persuasive in the 1990s, and moved us in scholarly directions which have led us to this *Companion*, it also persists today in many areas of scholarship. This is so despite so much evidence to the contrary, namely that there are more states, more state institutions, more state intrusion into the daily lives of citizens and denizens (through the utilization of new technologies), and more state intervention into global political economy. Today there are still many scholars globally who argue that the state, as an ideal and abstraction, is weak and in decline. And while we are well aware that there are so-called failed states, the defi-nition of that failure must be held against some standard, some test case of success. The vast majority of states, in the real rather than the ideal, are successful, and there is unlikely to be any form of political and social integration to take the place of the national state for the foreseeable future. (As we write this, the eurozone crises are putting great stress on the European Union, in what may be the only model extant of a possible supranational successor to a world order of states.)

When we began our own foray into comparative border studies, we recognized that globalization and deterritorialization were alternative interpretative slants on politics and power in the contemporary world. We argued that the growing interest in the new politics of identity and transnationalism was incomplete (Donnan and Wilson 1994, 1999; Wilson and Donnan 1998). It needed the corrective offered by modernists and traditionalists, in geography, history, political science and sociology, to renew the commitment to the concrete manifestations of government and politics, at local levels and at the level of the state. In our neomodernist view, definitions of the "political" which articulated self, gender, sexuality, race and ethnicity within discussions of sign, symbol, contestation and representation risked underestimating the role the state continued to play in the everyday lives of its and other states' citi-zens. We recognized that the institutions and personnel of the nation and the state had been increasingly excluded from much anthropology (and also to some extent in cognate disciplines), but we concluded as well that the nation-state had been rather more successful in weathering the storms of postsocialism, postcolonialism, and glo-balization than many scholars had credited. As we moved into border studies, with an interest in what the lives of borderland peoples were like at the end of the twen-tieth century, we wondered why there were so few scholars, in our and in other disciplines, who were equally interested in investigating how the state sustained its historically dominant role as an arbiter of control, violence, order and organization for those whose identities were being transformed by world forces. We realized we were not alone in our interests in theorizing the intersections of borders, place, power, identity and the state, and that such interests had been pioneered before us by scholars in geography, history, politics, sociology and anthropology. But we were also aware that the end of the Cold War and the new globalization scholarship seemed to distract so many more scholars away from the political economy of territory.

It was our contention then, and it remains so today, that a globalized and deterritorialized world of identity politics is a world too of many more and, in some cases, stronger states, where the new politics of identity is in large part determined by the old structures of the state. The politics of representation and resistance, whether couched in national electoral terms or those of new social movements, need the state as their principal contextual opponent. In our view it has always been the intention of political anthropology to position symbolic politics alongside all other sorts of politics, to enforce the proposition that all politics is by definition about the use of power to achieve individual or group public goals. The symbolic of culture and identity is the symbolic of power, whether that power is found in interpersonal relations or in the hands of agents of the government. The physical structures of territory, government and state have not withered away in the face of the scholarly onslaught that asserts that people are now freer to slip the constraints of territorially based politics. Border studies in anthropology in the 1990s as we saw it needed to focus on the visible borders between states, on the symbolic boundaries of identity and culture which make nations and states two very different entities, and on the politics of the liminal and interstitial that rested both easily and uneasily between nation and state.

Many things have made an anthropology of borders distinctive. Anthropological ethnography focuses on local communities at international borders in order to examine the material and symbolic processes of culture. This focus on cultural constructions of everyday life which give meaning to the boundaries between communities and between nations was often absent in the perspectives to be found in other social sciences at the time. The anthropology of borders helped to remind social scientists in and outside of anthropology that nations and states are composed of people who should not be reduced to the images that are constructed of them by representatives of the state, the media and academics. We argued that the anthropological study of the everyday lives of border cultures was simultaneously the study of the daily life of the state, particularly through the implementation of economic and security policy in borderlands. When ethnographers study borderlanders, they narrate the experiences of people who are tied culturally to many other people in neighboring states. Thus, the anthropology of borders simultaneously explored the permeability and permanence of borders by focusing on the adaptability and rigidity of border peoples and states in their efforts to control the social, political, economic and cultural fields which transcend their borders. We cannot review the field comprehensively here or rehearse again the history of the anthropology of border studies. Substantial reviews exist elsewhere (Alvarez 1995; Donnan and Haller 2000; Donnan and Wilson 1999). But it is nevertheless important for our argument in this introduction that we sketch the broad parameters of approach, first in the anthropology of borders and subsequently in the other social science disciplines.

Early work in the anthropology of borders owed much to Fredrik Barth (1969), whose paradigmatic ideas on ethnic boundaries stressed their relational nature as socially constructed boundaries marking affective and identificatory as well as structural, organizational and sometimes territorial disjunctures. It was informed too by the historical anthropologists and ethnologists who examined how cultural landscapes transcend social and political divides (e.g., Bohannan and Plog 1967; Cohen 1965). But perhaps the first major milestone to focus explicitly on state borders was Cole and Wolf (1974). Their field site in the Italian Tyrol was specifically chosen because its successive historical partitions allowed them to explore the transformation of local political loyalties in relation to nation-building and thus to widen disciplinary perspectives by demonstrating the need to situate local communities within the larger polities of which they are a part. The anthropology of borders was transformed as a result and later anthropologists explored this relationship in various ways. Some studied border areas as a way of examining how proximity to an international border could influence local culture. Others focused on the voluntary and involuntary movement of people across borders as traders, migrants and refugees. And yet others concentrated on the symbols and meanings which encode border life. Regardless of theoretical orientation or locale, however, most of these border studies in anthropology focused on how social relations, defined in part by the state, transcend the territorial limits of the state and, in so doing, transform the structure of the state at home and in its relations with its neighbors. Such work demonstrated the growing importance of a border perspective in which the dialectical relations between border areas and their nations and states took precedence over local culture viewed with the state as a backdrop.

Despite such novel developments, a "localism" continued to influence the border anthropology of this early period so that the state and the nation and even the border were sometimes underplayed in the ethnographers' efforts to bound their "community" study. So too and for similar reasons comparison was often underutilized, in spite of its rhetorical centrality to the discipline more generally. A good example of this is early ethnographic research at the Mexico–US border, which was subject to the same limitations, although this was the one border at the time to have generated a systematic and sustained body of work. While many of the studies carried out there used the border to frame their focus, the border itself was rarely a variable in the analysis, nor was it compared to borders elsewhere. However, this did not preclude the Mexico–US border from becoming the touchstone for analyses of other borders, as a kind of "hyperborder" that epitomized processes that other borders seemed to share (Romero 2008). As the anthropology of borders began to grow (especially in Europe in response to post–Cold War EU expansion), border scholars looked to research on the Mexico–US border for theoretical and conceptual stimulation to such an extent that this border took on – and to a considerable degree still occupies – iconic status as *the* template for border studies in whatever part of the globe border research is carried out. A brief look at the number of entries for the Mexico–US border in the index to *Borders* (Donnan and Wilson 1999) will quickly bear this out. Yet the comparisons rarely flowed in the other direction and insights from European border studies, for instance, have only belatedly begun to inform systematically those conducted by anthropologists – as well as other social scientists – at the Mexico–US border, as Roberto Alvarez suggests in this *Companion*.

It was probably the early 1990s before the wider political and economic contexts of international borders featured in analyses of the Mexico–US border, where the issues of underdevelopment, transnationalism and the globalization of power and capital, among other aspects of culture, increasingly occupied the growing number of historically informed and wide-ranging ethnographic accounts (see Heyman in this volume). Much of this research focused on the implications of the economic asymmetry between the United States and Mexico, whose wage differentials continue today to draw labor migrants northwards and ensure the profitability of locating unskilled occupations on the Mexican side. Migration across and increasing urbanization along this border have both been major topics of study, particularly within applied anthropology, and have generated research on a broad range of related issues such as local labor markets, health, pollution, and the environment (Alvarez 1995: 454–456). Nevertheless, discussion frequently lapsed into straightforward description of the region and how it might develop economically, with researchers "constantly pulled toward the specific, the unique (sometimes the folkloric), and the problematic" (Fagan 1984: 271) and thus continuing to eschew comparison for a focus on more local and immediate concerns (Alvarez 1995: 463).

First generation studies in the anthropology of borders thus largely centered on a localized, particularistic and territorially focused notion of borders. This was in keeping with anthropology's hallmark emphasis on culture in its ethnographic study of society through long-term residential research. All of the work alluded to above emphasized the local setting and cultural context, stressing the meaning and experience of borders in the lives of those who lived and worked there. Above all else perhaps, anthropologists brought to the study of borders a sensitivity to the role of borders in daily life and to people's narratives of these meanings and the ways in which borders were marked in and through their everyday practice. It is in this emphasis on how borders are constructed, negotiated and viewed from "below" that the value and distinctiveness of an anthropology of borders arguably initially relied. It is not that these characteristics were wholly absent in the other social sciences – disciplinary boundaries have always been much less clear-cut than sometimes implied – but they were arguably less prominent there than other core themes, concepts and questions that animated research on borders in these disciplines, as we outline next. Not surprisingly, like anthropology the other social sciences largely concentrated on their particular disciplinary concerns and interests. And like anthropology, they too looked most often to the body of research on the Mexico–US border as their template and stimulus.

Geography, for instance, has been drawn to the study of the spatial dimension to borders and to the ways in which territory and the physical environment interrelate with the social, economic, political and cultural conditions of nations and states. Geographical research initially focused on the classification and function of different kinds of borders and on clarifying concepts such as "boundaries" and "frontiers" which were seen to separate territories that are subject to different sovereignty (see Prescott 1987). The analysis of "border landscapes" was one way in which geographers sought to move beyond simple description and categorization of borders to grapple with the complex relations between boundaries and the physical and human environments which shape them and which in turn are shaped by them. The concept of border landscapes – those areas contiguous to the state boundary which are molded by the human and physical environment, including the boundary itself, and which in turn shape the environment – spawned a range of different kinds of case study (Prescott 1987: 161–173). Although this generated an impressive set of themes, it did not lead to a major breakthrough in the role and importance of geographical border studies within the discipline of geography more generally, nor had it much influence beyond the discipline. The case study approach in political geography tended to fall into set categories, such as the study of disputed areas, boundary changes, the evolution of boundaries, boundary delimitation and demarcation, exclaves and tiny states, maritime boundaries, disputes over natural resources and internal boundaries (Minghi 1969). It remained descriptive and was not interested in understanding social and political process or in developing border landscape theory (Rumley and Minghi 1991: 1–4). By the 1990s a new border geography argued for a reorientation by border landscape geographers to wider comparative and theoretical issues, recognizing that "too little concern [had] been given to conceptual developments in the other social sciences which might have some relevance to an understanding of border landscapes" (Rumley and Minghi 1991: 4). This call for a reorientation has been answered by many scholars who have recentered border studies in geography and who continue to foster interdisciplinary approaches through their calls to modify their ways of "graphing the geo" (Sparke 2005; see also Amoore 2011).

While geographers wrangled with the spatial dimension to the definitions of borders and their roles in nation and state relations, in part in an effort to construct the beginnings of a comparative study of boundaries and frontiers, historical studies pursued similar objectives from a temporal perspective. Frederick Jackson Turner's 1920 essay on "The significance of the frontier in American history" (Turner 1977) is clearly a landmark in border studies, but it was not until much later that historians began to question how to mold the unique case studies that result from frontier histories into a framework for comparison, generalization and theory building. Here once again the Mexico–US border played a major part. Between 1930 and 1974 historians of this border had viewed it as a frontier and concentrated on its explorers, economic development, missionary activity, armies and fortifications, administrative structures and role in international relations (Almaráz 1976: 10). But like the geographers and anthropologists, by the 1990s historians were looking for ways to develop models of borderlands to facilitate regional and global comparison. Oscar Martinez (1994) was at the forefront of such scholars and his insightful history of the Mexico–US border recognizes how borders share functional commonalities with other borders worldwide because they are there to regulate, prevent and control the economic, political and social interactions between people in both states. Through his concept of the "borderlands" milieu, Martinez constructed a typology that distinguished four kinds of interaction at borders to facilitate comparison: alienated borderlands, coexistent borderlands, interdependent borderlands, and integrated borderlands (1994: 6–10).

Borderlands were understood here as the region bisected by the boundary line between states, which in comparative perspective is presumed to encapsulate a variety of identities, social networks and formal and informal, legal and illegal relationships which tie together people in the areas contiguous to the borderline on both of its sides. Analogous to geographers' border landscapes, this concept of borderlands provided a similar function in history as landscape did in geography, which was to focus on the border region and its people as active participants in their state and as important forces in their nation's and state's relationship to their territories (as

McDougall and Philips show here for the historical emergence of the US-British border).

As a tool to facilitate cross-cultural and international comparison, borderlands began to occupy a central place in the historical study of borders and to open up novel lines of inquiry. Other scholars, for example, pointed out that while much had been written on how states deal with their borderlands, "historians have paid much less attention to how borderlands have dealt with their states" (Baud and van Schendel 1997: 235). Some thus argued in favor of a new view of borders from the perspective of a state's periphery, a view which recognizes the active historical role and agency of borderlands and the ways in which they play a part in the formation and consolidation of the nation and the state (Sahlins 1989). By the 1990s these evolving relations between territory, identity and sovereignty emphasized by historians had also become the concern of political science.

Culture has not been a principal focus in political science analyses of power, territory and politics at international borders, although culture's role in facilitating cross-border political and economic cooperation, as well as its place in the definition, recognition and behavior of ethnic groups, have become important parts of recent political scholarship. This reflects the evolution of political science as a discipline, and in particular a turn toward a concern with history, locality, ethnicity and regionalism. At the Mexico–US border, the politics of international boundaries initially focused on political culture – the attitudes and values that enable individuals and groups to be socialized into the ways of their political system – while in Europe greater attention has always been paid to the policy implications of boundary making. Yet here too culture was recognized as a factor in transfrontier collaboration, even if it was regarded as subsidiary to the politics and institutional frameworks which allowed orderly and predictable forms of international cooperation (see Anderson 1982).

Since the 1970s these interests have coalesced around the notion of "border regions," a concept with evident similarities to both geography's border landscapes and history's borderlands. Case studies of border regions explored a range of cross-border policies, with studies on the environment, transportation and communication, immigration and border controls, policing crime and terrorism, and regional development. Border regions were recognized by political scientists as places and processes of identity and policy, including their making and meaning and, like geographers and historians, political scientists have become part of the wider theorizing about what culture can tell us about the role of borders in the shifting relationships among identity, territory and sovereignty. Although Anderson's *Frontiers* (1996) ranges far and wide in comparative and empirical scope, it is significant that it highlights the role of identities in understanding international borders, as well as the role borders play in shaping identities such as ethnic, local, class, religious and linguistic. This emphasis reflects intellectual processes in political science that have parallels in the other social sciences, where the precise correspondence between nation, state and territory that was once assumed is being challenged through concepts such as border regions, borderlands and border landscapes. Like other scholars, political scientists, often through consideration of new theories of constructivism, are having to grapple with the proliferation of identities in a postindustrial and globalizing world, one in which the meanings of national and ethnic identity and their relations to territory and sovereignty are no longer the self-evident givens that they were once taken to be. As part of these new initiatives, political scientists and political sociologists have turned to the consideration of multi- and interdisciplinarity (Brunet-Jailly 2005; Newman 2006a).

Sociologists have been subject to the same pressures to conform to the methods, theories and professional interests of their subject as have the proponents of the other social sciences. The study of social groups, institutions and movements has been the hallmark of international boundary studies in sociology. These studies are often framed as analyses of minority groups at and across state and subnational borderlines. This attention to minorities was due in part to the resurgence in ethnic identities in the 1960s and 1970s, and continues today as one of the major themes in the sociology of borders, although the ways in which minorities have been contextualized have changed. Earlier studies of assimilation, nation-building, migration, and ethnic conflict and accommodation have given way to studies of ethnic and national identity, the politics of identity, regionalism, the role of local social groups and institutions in cross-border cooperation, and border communities which straddle borderlines (for a review of perspectives in the sociology of international borders at this time, see Strassoldo 1989). The ambivalence of border life has been regarded by some sociologists as a defining feature of border societies (Strassoldo 1982: 152). Border people may demonstrate ambiguous identities because economic, cultural and linguistic factors pull them in two directions. This ambivalent border identity affects the role that border communities play in international cooperation and conflict.

Like other social scientists, sociologists have increasingly had to accommodate the fact that old definitions of sovereignty, which were dependent on the twin bases of state and territory, have given way to new ones which incorporate various versions of territory, statecraft, culture and identity (O'Dowd 2010). And as in the other disciplines so too in sociology, culture and identity have come to occupy a new prominence in the latest wave of border studies, reflecting their centrality in contemporary social research more generally (as may be seen in the work of Vila 2000, 2003, 2005 and Salzinger 2003; and in calls such as that of Turner 2007 to study the sociology of immobility in enclave societies; and of Burawoy 2003 to revisit ethnography). In fact, sociology has adopted ethnography as one of its principal methodologies to a degree that the boundaries between sociology and social anthropology across a wide range of interests are blurred, as may be witnessed in a review article on global ethnography in the *Annual Review of Sociology*, wherein much of the ethnography cited, especially in regard to borders, was done by anthropologists (Gille and Ó Riain 2002).

Disciplinary differences and similarities are not our prime focus here, however, because in our view the comparative study of borders need not concentrate on academic disciplines if the goal of research is to chronicle and understand how borders, and border cultures, societies, polities and economies, are not only changing due to major transformations in the global political economy, but also how borders often play key roles in these changes. We have focused so far in this introduction on the evolution of the anthropology of borders and the other social sciences over the last generation of scholarship as an example of how all of our scholarly disciplines have moved from a concentration on the discipline's major concerns, which often excluded the theories, methods and results of other academic disciplines, and on individual, sometimes iconic, case studies, to what we argue here is the current state of affairs in border studies. In border studies today there has been a convergence in theoretical and methodological interests on a more interdisciplinary pursuit of comparative border studies, whether these are explicit or implicit. In these ways border studies may provide a productive way forward in how the social sciences and humanities may truly build the synergy in research and practical application of academic work which now seems to be so important in policy and university circles.

We still hold that, when in 1994 (Donnan and Wilson 1994) and in 1998 (Wilson and Donnan 1998) we asserted that an anthropology of borders was distinctive in a number of ways, we were both correct and prescient. But our conclusions then must now be weighed against what was also happening in our cognate disciplines, most notably among sociologists and geographers, who were drawing closer to anthropology through the widespread adoption of ethnographic methods. But we also want to acknowledge that our claim for distinctiveness of an anthropology of borders was as much directed at anthropologists, many of whom in our view were moving away from studies of the political economy of nation, state and territory, as it was directed at other social scientists, in order to draw their attention away from their own disciplinary concerns to recognize what anthropologists were doing.

Our aim then as it is now was to stress that in the study of borders multiple perspectives are invaluable, if not essential. These perspectives require flexibility and adaptability, to respond better to the needs and concerns of multiple populations who live and work at and across borders, but also to those of many academic disciplines and scholarly approaches. Thus the multiple perspectives we invoke and which are represented in this volume often involve one or more of the following: an ethnographic sensibility that is simultaneously sensitive to political economic context; ethnographic and other methodological approaches that are holistic insofar as they can draw out the interconnections among border phenomena while remaining problem oriented; micro- and macro-comparisons, both narrow and broad, across space and through time; and a recognition of the limitations of a perspective whose starting point is a Euro-American understanding of borders and states. This multiplicity in approach is now largely taken for granted in much contemporary writing in border studies, but it was not always so. The dynamism of life and work at borders and among border peoples, and the changing dimensions of global political economy, have pushed border studies to challenge disciplinary compartmentalization. As a result, border studies today offer a heady mix of disciplinary concerns with multiple disciplinary perspectives, in a provocative fusion of theories, methods and comparison.

BORDER STUDIES TODAY

Up to and including the 1990s, while the other disciplines each in their way looked at borderlands, border regions and border landscapes in much the same way as anthropology focused on border identities and cultural contact and mixing, the social sciences had all adopted approaches to international borders which predominantly favored single case studies that reflected the theories and methodologies pertinent to that field. However, over the last decade or so there has been a shift in border studies, heralding a set of approaches less constrained by past disciplinary boundaries.

It would of course be misleading to draw this contrast too sharply, and prudent to indicate that elements characteristic of the different moments in the periodization we presented above are still present to varying degrees throughout border studies today. Thus, for example, and often for good reason, the emphasis on case studies of particular border localities persists and their analysis generally continues to be directed at discipline-specific questions and concerns. Similarly, and unsurprisingly, comparison was also a feature of border studies in the past, as we note above, if not perhaps to the same extent as at present. Thus we wish to stress that the evolution of border studies which we describe here has been both gradual and punctuated by growth spurts and slowdowns, wherein case studies of particular borders, border peoples and border programs and policies continue to provide much of the lifeblood of border studies, which after all are still driven by a desire to chronicle what happens in borderlands. But border studies are also equally driven by the desire not only to chronicle but to understand if not predict other changes in which borders are both caught up and instrumental, as for example in regard to such contemporary key issues as citizenship, migration and security, and hence the increasing emphasis in border scholarship on comparison. Therefore we have no cataclysmic event to show the before and after in border studies, within and across the disciplines. Rather, we examine instead early and emergent themes in border studies in order to reflect better the convergences that are represented in the following chapters of this *Companion*.

Nevertheless, it is possible to summarize in ideal typical terms the features of the first generation border studies outlined above, together with their core differences from the present approach. Thus, as we have seen, the emphasis of earlier studies was (1) on the Mexico–US border as main focus or chief comparator; (2) on the relation between nation and state; (3) on borders as geographical and political "peripheries"; and (4) on engaging the key issues of interest to the discipline concerned.

Now, however, the emphasis has shifted, with border scholars sharing a number of features which previously may have distinguished them. This entails a new cross-discipline adoption of a focus on (1) culture and, as a corollary, (2) an emphasis on ethnographic methods. It has also involved a shift in epistemology, with (3) borders seen as "process" as much as "product"; (4) states regarded as incomplete, fragmented and embedded through everyday practice; (5) border(ing) understood as within as well as at the edges; (6) and "margins" as the new "centers" (e.g., Horstmann and Wadley 2006). Furthermore, with the expansion of borders research, examples and case studies have been much more far-flung, and from the few iconic studies focusing on the Mexico–US border and some parts of the Middle East and Europe, we now have studies from throughout EU and non-EU Europe, Africa, South and Southeast Asia, North and South America, as well as of colonial, precolonial, indigenous and pre- and postsocialist borders. The conceptual approach does, though, still remain largely Eurocentric, but the chapters in this *Companion* certainly point some ways forward as to new approaches which may chip away at the Western-oriented ways in which border studies have developed.

If border studies are to be more than a collection of fascinating case studies, or more than a subfield within the parent disciplines of its practitioners, they must address a set of unified thematic, conceptual and theoretical concerns and questions. This does not necessarily mean a quest for a general theory of borders, an objective toward which some are rightly critical given the need to understand borders contextually (Newman 2006b: 156; Paasi 2005: 668). But it does imply an ability to be open to the work of others not in one's own field. The current openness toward cross-disciplinary conversations in border studies, if not indeed a new approach and perspective, suggests a willingness and readiness to engage global comparison and the work of other scholars that we maintain is clearly demonstrated by the contributors to this *Companion*.

The chapters here exemplify a range of types of comparison that are worth identifying. Some of the comparisons are implicit, evident only through their use of terminology and concepts developed in one setting to analyze another. But most are explicit, or a combination of implicit and explicit, and endeavor to compare at different levels and different scales. These include comparison of global border cities disembedded from their states as they become the hub of regional and international trade and the global flow of capital (Nugent; O'Dowd), as well as comparison at the level of the regional, national and the global. Thus some chapters in the *Companion* compare different borders within a single state (for example, the chapter by McCall), others compare borders within a region (Coplan; Pelkmans), and yet others draw comparisons between continents (Alvarez; Asiwaju; Brunet-Jailly; Coleman; Nugent) or more globally (Anderson; O'Dowd; O'Leary). Some chapters also range far and wide across both space and time, exploring the relationship between nationalism and imperialism by drawing historical comparisons between Europe and its colonies (Kramsch), by emphasizing the need for multilevel comparisons from social practice to the geopolitical (Scott), and by tracing the historical transformations of a single border through "border biographies" (Megoran) or through the border representations of academics and policy-makers (Rabinowitz).

Many of these use comparison for a similar end: to enhance description and facilitate analysis of a particular case rather than to generalize. The "cultural turn" across the social sciences has arguably loosened the grip of a style of comparison typical of positivistic social science, in which comparison is used to test hypotheses and identify functional correlations between societal and cultural variables as a means to generalization (Holy 1987). Nevertheless, the cultural turn has not weakened the enduring allure of this kind of comparison. The seductive promise of generalization coupled with policy and governmental interest in borders research which continues to expect some form of generalizing, and upon which research sponsorship may depend, have ensured that many scholars continue to practice it. As evidenced in these pages, some researchers thus continue to struggle with the methodological and technical challenges of devising a generalizing social science (of borders) that does not decontextualize the subjective, experiential and socially constructed nature of human social life. For interpretivist and constructivist social scientists this is particularly challenging, since relations of similarity and difference are not empirical givens but are created through the process of comparison in the first place, which classifies them as one thing or the other (Holy 1987: 16).

The chapters in this *Companion* also stress the value of cross-disciplinary dialogue. Anssi Paasi (1996: 5, 6) notes that the 1990s "witnessed a surprising interest in boundaries and frontiers within different academic fields" and a "new interdisciplinary interest in boundary studies." According to Paasi (1996), several factors stimulated this new interest: the "structural background," which he sees as the changing economic and political conditions created by increasing globalization, mobility and global flows; and the "intellectual background," which are the novel concepts generated by scholars who seek to interpret this changing world (concepts such as "time-space compression" and "disorganized capitalism"). Our contributors take Paasi's ruminations forward in several respects. One relates to the relationship he posits between social theory and empirical conditions. The early 1990s were tumultuous years for international borders and it would be easy to conclude that the former straightforwardly reflects the latter. From this perspective, early border perspectives might be seen as lagging far behind empirical circumstances and as being propelled by them to develop more innovative and imaginative approaches. For example, it could be argued that existing border concepts and theory were taken unawares by the collapse of socialism and were outpaced by the acceleration of world events.

In this sense, border studies were always running to catch up with how "real" borders were being modified and transformed (cf. Parker and Vaughan-Williams 2009: 586). The same might be said of the expanding interest in border surveillance, security and biometrics post–9/11, with technological developments of border control in the 2000s sometimes outrunning scholarly analyses of them (as in Cunningham and Heyman 2004). At other times, though, it is conceptual developments that drive the agenda, and while recognizing like Paasi that border studies may lag behind world events, the contributors here also note how progressive social theory may overtake them, anticipating what the issues might be and how conditions are likely to look in the future.

Paasi's review also raises a second issue of relevance to this *Companion*: the suggestion that the new interest in border studies in the 1990s was interdisciplinary. In the 1990s, borders began to feature more frequently as a topic of research among a greater range of disciplines. However, this often resulted in an uncritical accumulation or juxtaposition of different perspectives which in itself did not advance the study of borders very far. To be "interdisciplinary" the disciplines need to be receptive to one another and to reflect critically on their complementary but sometimes conflicting disciplinary perspectives on borders. In the 15 years since Paasi's review, the context for this exchange has often been provided by large-scale collaborative interdisciplinary research projects in border studies, especially in Europe where much of this research has been stimulated by EU funding (e.g., Leontidou et al. 2005; Meinhof 2002). While there have been attempts to do similar research across member states of other international and supranational arrangements, such as in MERCOSUR (Ferradás 2004, 2010; Grimson 2000, 2003; Gordillo and Leguizamón 2002) and in the North American Free Trade Agreement area (Cunningham 2004, 2010; Helleiner 2009, 2010; Sparke 2005), this work has not been financially supported to the same extent as in the EU, nor has it captured the imagination of policy-makers and other elites as it has in Europe. The chapters in this *Companion* exemplify this reflective interdisciplinary approach within which researchers strive not only to acknowledge different disciplinary perspectives but to engage, assess and incorporate them critically in order to advance conceptually, theoretically and methodologically the field of border studies.

The interdisciplinary ambitions of the contributors here are thus succinctly summarized by Marilyn Strathern's threefold definition of interdisciplinarity as "a *self-consciousness about the ability to mix knowledges*; a 'common framework shared across disciplines to which each contributes its bit'; and as *a tool (a means) to address* problems seen to lie athwart specialisms" (2005a: 127, emphases in original). It is the receptivity to other disciplines and the critical borrowing and dialogue with their concepts and understandings that distinguishes the essays in this *Companion* and that we maintain will be the future of border studies as a novel and magnetic field of study rather than just a mix of disciplines.

But there remain many reasons to be skeptical about interdisciplinary research in border studies, as in other fields. While scholars regularly reiterate that border studies is now an interdisciplinary field, they rarely explain precisely what this entails (e.g., Kolossov 2005). One risk is that interdisciplinarity becomes simply a re-citation of ideas from other disciplines, which are endlessly circulated with each new publication as a genuflection rather than engagement with whatever "big idea" on borders a particular discipline might have produced (e.g., borders as discourses, practices, as verb rather than noun). In other words, interdisciplinarity becomes a fashionable branding rather than an approach that significantly underpins border studies practice. It can also risk downplaying fieldwork by encouraging the production of texts by means of other texts, repeatedly recycling the ideas of colleagues rather than gathering new border material (cf. Paasi 2005: 668–669). Even knowing how to recognize that *interdisciplinary* research has actually taken place can be problematic, as too is identifying the evidence which confirms that the interaction has been valuable and productive: publications may be cited but "explanatory power, aesthetic appeal [and] comprehensiveness" are more rarely articulated (Mansilla and Gardner 2003: 1–2, cited in Strathern 2005b: 82–83). The processes through which certain disciplinary traditions come to occupy a central place in interdisciplinary thinking may also be obscured. Interdisciplinarity might mean little more than a weak or poorly represented discipline adopting the theoretical vocabulary from a stronger one. Interdisciplinarity might thus entail a "nesting" model of theoretical capacity whereby a theoretically weaker discipline "nests" within a more powerful one, which in turns nests within one more powerful still. Disciplinary hegemony and intellectual imperialism might be the outcome rather than mutually beneficial interdisciplinary exchange.

Although interdisciplinarity characterizes current scholarship in border studies, the multiple styles, motifs, methods and theorizing that may be associated with the relative convergence in border studies around certain themes lead us to see border studies as approaching a postdisciplinary state. The comparative turn which border studies have taken is a good example of this. As we have discussed above, contemporary scholarship on borders has adopted as a principal method of analysis and explication both explicit and implicit comparison, across sometimes long and wide times and spaces, in a manner that distinguishes it from the classic studies of borders and from many more discipline-based case studies conducted before the 1990s. This comparative turn reflects the other approaches we noted above as marking current scholarship, namely the emphases in border studies today on culture; various forms of ethnography; process rather than structure and institutions at borders; and new relations and processes of bordering, rebordering and "borderization" as aspects of changes in territorialization and marginalization that are particularly visible under regional integration (Scott; Grimson). It also reflects the pressing need to explore how borders are always an ongoing process socially, politically and epistemologically (Green).

But what has driven this new convergence around these themes and the widespread reliance on various forms of comparison? Real world events are key forces at work in all of the ways we now conceptualize borders, and scholarly approaches to borders are no exception to this. In an era of globalization theory and rhetoric it is not surprising that scholars should look globally for examples that are relevant and that capture the imagination of audiences eager to see local–global connections. The overall turn to culture as a relatively free-flowing aspect of (post)modern life also supports the scholarly questioning of borders and invites us to conceptualize them not just in terms of physical place but as spaces of struggle between inclusion and exclusion wherever such struggles are found (e.g., see the notion of "borderscape"; Rajaram and Grundy-Warr 2007). Several of our contributors thus rethink the classic associations between place and boundedness and their limitations for understanding and representing flows (Ballinger; van Houtum). In this view, borders are seen as processes, as floating signifiers, as waypoints and conduits in the flow of peoples, ideas, goods, capital and threats to the body politic. Seeing borders in these ways also liberates scholars from too close a reliance on the specificities of geography and history in their comparisons: one need only find a few points of comparison depending on the problem being raised. The correlated and apparent demise of the nation-state within certain ways of thinking about globalization – an assertion regarding the national state which we dispute, in line with scholars such as Michael Mann (2007), who insists that the state form of polity, and especially strong states, are more powerful and intrusive in the lives of citizens than ever before in history – also gives rise to comparisons of new forms of governance which shape the new forms of citizenship and identity that are carried by the many groups of people who are labeled as refugees, migrants, tourists and terrorists, all of whom are involved in important relations with borders. These new forms of belonging and nonbelonging include shifts in what border regimes allow in or keep out following what Borneman (this volume) refers to as the "victory of capitalism," as well as the deterritorialized zones of exception like the offshore detention centers described here by Mountz and Hiemstra. As Chalfin's chapter suggests, such developments are arguably the outgrowth of a free-flow "borderless" capitalism rather than a radical departure from it.

A global political economy, a new world order, the war on terror, new imperialisms and late-modern capitalism have also combined to create new forms of region and culture within recognizable and distinct geopolitical entities. One reason why the Mexico–US border no longer functions as the iconic border universally is because of the proliferation in the numbers and types of borders worldwide, but especially in Europe and Asia, where most of the new national states arose in the last 20 years or so and where the most successful experiment in supranationalism, the European Union, moves forward, despite its continual state of crisis. Indeed, European integration has been one of the defining features of a great deal of border studies, due to the emphasis in the EU on cross-border development, on the free flow of capital, goods and people across its internal borders, on the new forms of governmental and police cooperation to thwart crime and threats to national and continental security, and on the construction of new forms of European culture and identity which are meant both to transcend national borders and to create a new affective dimension to European citizenship and residence. These new forms of border and bordering in Europe have been seen by some scholars as creative of a new European identity and spirit, wherein many groups and institutions do the "borderwork" in regard to territorialization and sovereignty that was once presumed to be the almost sole domain of the state (Rumford 2006).

Martin Kohli (2000), for example, has looked to Europe's borderlands as the best hope for the fostering of a truly postnational European identity. The rhetoric of a borderless Europe is at the core of a similar rhetoric of a borderless world, but the examples of such a world keep us coming back to the EU. And while the borderless world has come in for some healthy criticism (for example, by one of our authors in this collection, O'Dowd 2010), Europe is still seen by many to be a space where rebordering and reterritorialization have created new niches for peoples on the move (as may be seen in the works of another of our authors, van Houtum 2005). In these ways the global ethos to be found in so much scholarship and media and government narratives has more concrete manifestations in the "unidentified political object" (in the words of Marc Abélès 2000) that is the EU, and as part of this ethos in Europe international borders have become of intense scholarly interest as if they too are unidentifiable political, economic, social and cultural objects.

The expansion of interest in multilevel governance, in multi-sited research and in multidisciplinarity might have a great deal to do with the professional and academic response to great global changes in capitalism and global politics, and to regional rearticulation of sovereignty and citizenship in experiments such as the EU, but the central thread running through both individual case studies and comparative approaches to borders is still that of the nation-state, whether that state be a relatively more homogeneous national state or a multinational and multi-ethnic one. Here, too, nations without states are also implicated, as they also have over time more or less sought the borders of homeland and statehood. And while the multiplication tables of scholarship seem to be working overtime in the theorizing of global, national, regional and local borders, there has been little change to the number and types of methodologies employed in border scholarship, wherein case studies and other more synthetic scholarly studies remain implicitly comparative.

However, as we have noted, much that is comparative in today's scholarship is far removed from the more controlled comparisons that supported model building and hypothesis testing of past generations of scholars. In its place we are often offered instead episodic story-byte comparisons. Yet border studies today rely on both approaches to comparison. The global study of the politics of identity has adopted the metaphors of borders and borderlands to understand the relations between people and territory in postmodern life. Approaches such as this in border theory vitalize and enrich any social science of borders precisely because so much that pertains to national and international culture and identity happens in stark relief in the interstices of nations and states. The use of "borderland" as an image for the study of cultures has opened up social and cultural theory (e.g., see Rosaldo 1989), but has often done so by underplaying changes in local and more global political economy.

This is why case studies of borders, as shifting, porous and mobile as they have been seen to become, are still at the center of comparative border studies (cf. Wastl-Walter 2011). National states are changing in this new global political economy – and here we repeat that changing does not necessarily mean dying – and these transformations lead to new relations of power between and among states. We agree with Josiah Heyman (1994: 46) who has argued that to address how dual but unequal state power operates at borders, and how cultural relations develop historically at frontiers, we must return to a localized and territorially focused notion of borders. But case studies of borders have become case studies of multiple borders, of multiple sites at the same borders, and of a multiplicity of experiences at those borders, which might just as easily be conceived as being at airports, floating customs and immigration checks, immigration and passport offices, armed service installations and internal revenue institutions, as being at the geopolitical lines agreed to in treaties between empires and states (cf. Balibar 2009). Indeed, immigration control, for instance, has come increasingly to be understood as a feature of governance in general, potentially enforceable everywhere and not just at the border itself, as many of the contributors argue (see Coleman; Ford and Lyons; De Genova).

The multiplication of borders on the world stage, and of sites and experiences of borders, has resulted too in a multiplicity of ways to inscribe and perform these same borders, by so many more people than the organs and the agents of the state, with whom it was once presumed those prerogatives lay. This is one reason why so much that we have discussed here as border studies is imbricated in border theory. But we must also not forget that the state remains the major player in border studies, and it too has a role to play in the performances of culture and identity. As Mark Salter has reminded us, "The border is a primary institution of the contemporary state, the construction of a geopolitical world of multiple states, and the primary ethico-political division between the possibility of politics inside the state and the necessity of anarchy outside the state" (2011: 66). And the state is still associated in most people's minds worldwide with their nations, so much so that in most places in the world today there remains a marked preference to have national solutions to national problems, including those related to securing borders (as Newman shows in this volume and as may be witnessed in recent European reactions to debt crises and to the changes in the governments of some non-European Mediterranean neighbors (Bialasiewicz 2011)). As building blocks and bulwarks of nation and state, borders require continual reinscription and reperformance, on the part of citizens, governments and other institutions and groups both within the state and beyond it. As Salter puts it, this necessitates three registers of border performativity, that of the *formal*, where borders are delimited and defended, the *practical*, where the processes of filtering people, goods and ideas occur at borders, and the *popular*, wherein the meanings of borders are disseminated and contested (Salter 2011: 66). If all the world is a stage, then borders are its scenery, its *mise en scène*, its ordering of space and action, wherein actors and observers must work at making borders intelligible and manageable, and must do so in order for the drama to proceed. It is not surprising then that some of our authors (Coplan; Kaiser) have approached borders along similar lines of performance, and have done so by treating them as "discursive/ emotional landscapes of social power" that are related to historically framed national practices, discourses and ideologies (Paasi 2011: 63). All of these appreciations of the performance of borders, at borders, must address the tensions inherent in the institutional, technical and emotive aspects of territory, state and sovereignty wherever and whenever geopolitical borders are encountered. And these encounters are as multidimensional, multivocal, and multisemic as anything that nations and states have ever fashioned for themselves. It is no wonder that border studies today have proliferated as quickly and as widely as have the subjects and objects of their interest.

CONCLUSION

In 2005 Anssi Paasi challenged border scholars "to reflect on our concepts of the theory rather than trying to develop a general theory of borders. This is best done in relation to other categories inherent to geography and the social sciences, such as region, place, space, territory, agency and power, to social practices such as politics, governance and economics and to cultural processes such as ethnicity or national socialisation (education)" (2005: 670). This *Companion* is testament that the inter- and multidisciplinary study of borders has come of age, in great part fulfilling Paasi's call to multiple forms of analysis and theorizing. So too comparative studies, or at least those which seek to be passively or implicitly comparative in aid of theorizing global and regional approaches to borders, have come of age. In border studies it is no longer sufficient or advisable to focus solely on a specific border locale, at least not without framing the analysis with reference to other borders and to theories and methodologies once associated with other scholarly disciplines. The engine of conceptual developments in border studies today is now both comparative and multidisciplinary.

Thus border studies represent what we suggest is a new postdisciplinarity, a convergence in approaches, theories, conceptualizations and methodologies that has been building steadily over the last decades. This is evidence that scholarship in the humanities and social sciences has much to benefit from transcending the boundaries of national intellectual traditions and national academic disciplines. We acknowledge, of course, the international character of scholarship which has molded all of our academic approaches: who could conceive of the social sciences without reference to the European classical theorists? And each of our disciplines has its own genealogy and origin myth, which traces itself back to other countries and various theories. Anthropology, for example, has shaped its own contemporary character largely through the dialectics among British, American, French and German anthropologies. But the border studies to which we draw attention in this introduction and volume show too that the European-North American nexus no longer needs to be the sole or even the main one in collaborative scholarship. Border studies show that all continents, all nations, all states have something to offer us in the quest to understand the changing nature of territory, power, governance and identity, within both national and more global frames of reference. They also show how resilient and adaptable borders themselves are, in ways sometimes that make them more successful at weathering the storms of global forces than other aspects of their nations and states. This is especially apparent when one considers that the processes of bordering that owed so much to the state institutionalization of geopolitical borders are now also largely found distant from the borderlines themselves, and are often in the hands of people divorced from or resistant to more hegemonic ideas and practices associated with nations and states.

As we have reviewed above, and as Amoore (2011) also sees it, borders are no longer the main or sole agents for disciplining citizens and aliens through various forms of prohibition, enclosure and proscription, precisely because borders must now facilitate movement in order to serve the interests of the nation. But the demands for movement must be matched against the needs of security, all of which reside in virtual space as much as they do in the landscapes that instantiated border studies in the past, and which regulate the flow of everything from bugs to thugs and drugs (Smart and Smart; Cunningham; Raeymaekers; Goodhand, respectively). Border studies then must expand their view, to look at but also to gaze away from the geopolitical borders that gave them their name and focus for so many years, to focus now too on other practices and sites as elements of a "novel modality of power" (Amoore 2011: 64). Border studies can no longer just ask us to "see like the state." Now we must see beyond and within the state to mark the extent of geopolitical borders, and to recognize the multiple forms of disciplining in the bordering work done within and between nations and states, and within and between other political, economic, social and cultural entities (van Houtum; Coleman; De Genova). It is no wonder then that the multidisciplining of border practices has led too to the multidisciplining within border studies, wherein many scholars search for more coherent interdisciplinary agendas, as in a recent suggestion by Corey Johnson and Reece Jones (2011) to focus this interdisciplinarity on the interconnected themes of place, performance, perspective and politics. These themes are both welcome and well represented in this volume, and may be found within the organizing themes of "sovereignty, territory and governance," "states, nations and empires," "security, order and disorder," "displacement, emplacement and mobility," and "space, performance and practice" that are offered here. But we are aware, and remind our readers, that as soon as a set of such themes is proffered others will spring to mind, as we in border studies seek to recognize and capture the mercurial nature of the geopolitical borders which many people still perceive as fixed in time and place, but which just as many others see as mobile and timeless.

Today, in border studies, concepts developed in one field, one discipline or one locale now inform work in other fields, and provide inspiration if not provocation to be less insular, less dogmatic and less introspective. Where once there was an iconic border or two, such as the Mexico–US border or the border between Israel and Palestine, today these are cases to be placed alongside so many more, to appreciate what borders are and what they represent in the lives of the millions of people who live at and cross them daily. This *Companion* offers a range of scholarly approaches to border studies and a variety of disciplinary and multidisciplinary ways to understand how borders work and function as causes and effects within regional, national and international contexts. But this *Companion* does not seek to provide a state of the art, full-scale compendium of all that is worthwhile in border studies. Rather, its authors offer their versions of the state of the art in their own border studies. It is our hope that these glimpses into the rich landscape of border studies will foster more global attention to the borders which separate and connect us all.

ACKNOWLEDGMENTS

We would like to thank all of our contributors for delivering so promptly and for so agreeably accommodating our editorial suggestions. Rosalie Robertson and Julia Kirk at Blackwell have been paragons of patience and fonts of good advice throughout. We also thank Ann Bone for her meticulous and sensitive copy-editing and Sue Leigh for efficient and careful proofing of the manuscript. As with all our work, the collection and this essay are the result of equal authorship irrespective of the order in which our names appear.

REFERENCES

Abélès, Marc. 2000. Virtual Europe. In Iréne Bellier and Thomas M. Wilson, eds, *An Anthropology of the European Union*. Oxford: Berg.

Almaráz, F.D., Jr. 1976. The status of borderlands studies: history. *Social Science Journal* 13 (1): 9–18.

Alvarez, Robert R., Jr. 1995. The Mexican-US border: the making of an anthropology of borderlands. *Annual Review of Anthropology* 24: 447–470.

Amoore, Louise. 2011. On the line: writing the geography of the virtual border. *Political Geography* 30: 63–64.

Anderson, Malcolm. 1982. The political problems of frontier regions. *West European Politics* 5 (4): 1–17.

Anderson, Malcolm. 1996. *Frontiers: Territory and State Formation in the Modern World*. Cambridge: Polity.

Balibar, Étienne. 2009. Europe as borderland. *Environment and Planning D: Society and Space* 27: 190–215.

Barth, Fredrik. 1969. Introduction. In Fredrik Barth, ed., *Ethnic Groups and Boundaries: The Social Organization of Culture Difference*. London: George Allen & Unwin.

Baud, Michel and van Schendel, Willem. 1997. Toward a comparative history of borderlands. *Journal of World History* 8 (2): 211–242.

Bohannan, Paul and Plog, F., eds. 1967. *Beyond the Frontier: Social Process and Cultural Change*. New York: Natural History Press.

Bialasiewicz, Luiza. 2011. Borders, above all? *Political Geography* 30: 299–300.

Brunet-Jailly, Emmanuel. 2005. Theorizing borders: an interdisciplinary perspective. *Geopolitics* 10: 633–649.

Burawoy, Michael. 2003. Revisits: an outline of a theory of reflexive ethnography. *American Sociological Review* 68 (5): 645–679.

Cohen, Abner. 1965. *Arab Border-Villages in Israel: A Study of Continuity and Change in Social Organization*. Manchester: Manchester University Press.

Cole, John W. and Wolf, Eric R. 1974. *The Hidden Frontier: Ecology and Ethnicity in an Alpine Valley*. New York: Academic Press.

Cunningham, Hilary. 2004. Nations rebound? Crossing borders in a gated globe. *Identities: Global Studies in Culture and Power* 11 (3): 329–350.

Cunningham, Hilary. 2010. Gating ecology in a gated globe: environmental aspects of "securing our borders." In Hastings Donnan and Thomas M. Wilson, eds, *Borderlands: Ethnography, Security and Frontiers. Lanham: University Press of America.

Cunningham, Hilary and Heyman, Josiah McC. 2004. Introduction: mobilities and enclosures at borders. Identities: Global Studies in Culture and Power 11 (3): 289–302.

Donnan, Hastings and Haller, Dieter. 2000. Liminal no more: the relevance of borderland studies. Ethnologia Europea 30 (2): 7–22.

Donnan, Hastings and Wilson, Thomas M. 1994. The anthropology of borders. In Hastings Donnan and Thomas M. Wilson, eds, Border Approaches. Lanham: University Press of America.

Donnan, Hastings and Wilson, Thomas M. 1999. Borders: Frontiers of Identity, Nation and State. Oxford: Berg.

Donnan, Hastings and Wilson, Thomas M., eds. 2010. Borderlands: Ethnography, Security and Frontiers. Lanham: University Press of America.

Fagan, Richard R. 1984. How should we think about the borderlands? New Scholar 9 (1–2): 271–273.

Ferradás, Carmen. 2004. Environment, security, and terrorism in the trinational frontier of the Southern Cone. Identities: Global Studies in Culture and Power 11 (3): 417–442.

Ferradás, Carmen. 2010. Security and ethnography on the triple frontier of the Southern Cone. In Hastings Donnan and Thomas M. Wilson, eds, Borderlands: Ethnography, Security and Frontiers. Lanham: University Press of America.

Gille, Zsuzsa and Ó Riain, Seán. 2002. Global ethnography. Annual Review of Sociology 28: 271–295.

Gordillo, Gastón and Leguizamón, Juan Martín. 2002. El río y la frontera. Aborígenes, obras públicas, y Mercosur en el Pilcomayo. Buenos Aires: Biblos.

Grimson, Alejandro. 2000. Fronteras naciones e identidades. La periferia como centro. Buenos Aires: Ciccus-La Crujía.

Grimson, Alejandro. 2003. La nación en sus límites. Contrabandistas y exiliados en la frontera Argentina-Brasil. Barcelona: Gedisa.

Helleiner, Jane. 2009. "As much American as a Canadian can be": cross-border experience and regional identity among young borderlanders in Canadian Niagara. Anthropologica 51 (1): 225–238.

Helleiner, Jane. 2010. Canadian border resident experience of the "smartening" border at Niagara. Journal of Borderlands Studies 25 (3, 4): 87–103.

Heyman, Josiah McC. 1994. The Mexico–United States border in anthropology: a critique and reformulation. Journal of Political Ecology 1: 43–65.

Holy, Ladislav, ed. 1987. Introduction: description, generalization and comparison: two paradigms. In L. Holy, ed., Comparative Anthropology. Oxford: Blackwell.

Horstmann, Alexander and Wadley, Reed L., eds. 2006. Centering the Margin: Agency and Narrative in Southeast Asian Borderlands. Oxford: Berghahn.

Johnson, Corey and Jones, Reece. 2011. Rethinking "the border" in border studies. Political Geography 30: 61–62.

Kohli, Martin. 2000. The battlegrounds of European identity. European Societies 2 (2): 113–137.

Kolossov, Vladimir. 2005. Border studies: changing perspectives and theoretical approaches. Geopolitics 10 (4): 606–632.

Leontidou, Lila, Afouxenidis, Alex and Donnan, Hastings. 2005. Exclusion and difference along the EU border: social and cultural markers, spatialities and mappings. International Journal of Urban and Regional Research 29 (2): 389–407.

Mann, Michael. 2007. The age of nation-states is just beginning. Paper, Beyond the Nation conference, Queen's University, Belfast, Sept. 12.

Mansilla, Veronica Boix and Gardner, Howard. 2003. Assessing interdisciplinary work at the frontier: an empirical exploration of "symptoms of quality." In C. Heintz and G. Origgi, moderators, Rethinking Interdisciplinarity. At www.interdisciplines.org.

Martínez, Oscar J. 1994. *Border People: Life and Society in the US–Mexico Borderlands.* Tucson: University of Arizona Press.

Meinhof, Ulrike H., ed. 2002. *Living (with) Borders: Identity Discourses on East–West Borders in Europe.* Aldershot: Ashgate.

Minghi, J.V. 1969. Boundary studies in political geography. In R.E. Kasperson and J.V. Minghi, eds, *The Structure of Political Geography.* Chicago: Aldine. First publ. 1963.

Newman, David. 2006a. Borders and bordering: towards an interdisciplinary dialogue. *European Journal of Social Theory* 9 (2):171–186.

Newman, David. 2006b. The lines that continue to separate us: borders in our "borderless" world. *Progress in Human Geography* 30 (2): 143–161.

O'Dowd, Liam. 2010. From a "borderless world" to a "world of borders": "bringing history back in." *Environment and Planning D: Society and Space* 28: 1031–1050.

Paasi, Anssi. 1996. Inclusion, exclusion and territorial identities: the meanings of boundaries in the globalizing geopolitical landscape. *Nordisk Samhällsgeografisk Tidskrift* 23: 3–17.

Paasi, Anssi. 2005. Generations and the "development" of border studies. *Geopolitics* 10 (4): 663–671.

Paasi, Anssi. 2011. Borders, theory and the challenge of relational thinking. *Political Geography* 30: 62–63.

Parker, Noel and Vaughan-Williams, Nick. 2009. Lines in the sand? Towards an agenda for critical border studies. *Geopoltics* 14: 582–587.

Prescott, J.R.V. 1987. *Political Frontiers and Boundaries.* London: Unwin Hyman.

Rajaram, Prem K. and Grundy-Warr, Carl. 2007. Introduction. In Prem K. Rajaram and Carl Grundy-Warr, eds, *Borderscapes: Hidden Geographies and Politics at Territory's Edge.* Minneapolis: University of Minnesota Press.

Romero, Fernando. 2008. *Hyperborder: The Contemporary US–Mexico Border and Its Future.* Princeton: Princeton Architectural Press.

Rosaldo, Renato. 1989. *Culture and Truth: The Remaking of Social Analysis.* Boston: Beacon Press.

Rumley, D. and Minghi, J.V. 1991. Introduction: the border landscape concept. In D. Rumley and J.V. Minghi, eds, *The Geography of Border Landscapes.* London: Routledge.

Rumford, Chris. 2006. Theorizing borders. *European Journal of Social Theory* 9 (2): 155–169.

Sahlins, Peter. 1989. *Boundaries: The Making of France and Spain in the Pyrenees.* Berkeley: University of California Press.

Salter, Mark. 2011. Places everyone! Studying the performativity of the border. *Political Geography* 30: 66–67.

Salzinger, Leslie. 2003. *Genders in Production: Making Workers in Mexico's Global Factories.* Berkeley: University of California Press.

Sparke, Matthew. 2005. *In the Space of Theory: Postfoundational Geographies of the Nation-State.* Minneapolis: University of Minnesota Press.

Strassoldo, Raimondo, ed. 1982. Boundaries in sociological theory: a reassessment. In R. Strassoldo and G. Delli Zotti, eds, *Cooperation and Conflict in Border Areas.* Milan: Franco Angeli.

Strassoldo, Raimondo. 1989. Border studies: the state of the art in Europe. In A.I. Asiwaju and P.O. Adeniyi, eds, *Borderlands in Africa.* Lagos: University of Lagos Press.

Strathern, Marilyn. 2005a. Anthropology and interdisciplinarity. *Arts and Humanities in Higher Education* 4 (2): 125–135.

Strathern, Marilyn. 2005b. Experminents in interdisciplinarity. *Social Anthropology* 13 (1): 75–90.

Turner, Bryan S. 2007. The enclave society: towards a sociology of immobility. *European Journal of Social Theory* 10 (2): 287–303.

Turner, Frederick Jackson. 1977. The significance of the frontier in American history. In *The Frontier in American History.* Franklin Center, PA: Franklin Library. First publ. 1920.

van Houtum, Henk. 2005. The geopolitics of borders and boundaries. *Geopolitics* 10: 672–679.

Vila, Pablo. 2000. *Crossing Borders, Reinforcing Borders: Social Categories, Metaphors, and Narrative Identities on the US–Mexico Frontier.* Austin: University of Texas Press.

Vila, Pablo. 2003. Conclusion: the limits of American border theory. In Pablo Vila, ed., *Ethnography at the Border*, pp. 306–341. Minneapolis: University of Minnesota Press.

Vila, Pablo. 2005. *Border Identifications: Narratives of Religion, Gender, and Class on the US–Mexico Border.* Austin: University of Texas Press.

Wastl-Walter, Doris, ed. 2011. *Ashgate Research Companion to Border Studies.* Farnham: Ashgate.

Wilson, Thomas M. and Donnan, Hastings. 1998. Nation, state and identity at international borders. In Thomas M. Wilson and Hastings Donnan, eds, *Border Identities: Nation and State at International Frontiers.* Cambridge: Cambridge University Press.

PART I Sovereignty, Territory and Governance

CHAPTER 2 Partition

Brendan O'Leary

Partition, in a general sense, is the division of an entity into parts. It may be analytical: a mathematician partitions one side of an expression; it may be actual: a physical object is divided, as when a butcher dismembers a sheep's body. A political partition has generally been considered as an objective description. A previously unified territorial entity is divided into two or more parts, and each part is demarcated, perhaps with fences, walls, paint or barbed wire, and official posts, where passes may be demanded; but reactions to a political partition are also subjective. One sees a homeland sadly broken up, another denies it was ever a shared homeland.

Partition should be distinguished from secession. Metaphorically speaking, secession "unfastens," whereas partition "cuts." Political unfastening unwinds time to a previous territorial order; it is the goal of secessionists. Tearing, by contrast, involves a new or fresh cut, a rip, a gash, a slash; only with remarkable luck will it resemble an unfastening. A political partition therefore is a fresh border cut through at least one community's national homeland, creating at least two separate political units under different sovereigns or authorities.

The formal justification of a political partition is that it will regulate, that is, reduce or resolve, a national, ethnic or communal conflict. Opponents protest the freshness, the novelty, the brutality, and the artificiality of dividing a "national" homeland. In India and Ireland they used medical metaphors: operation, dissection, amputation, dismemberment and vivisection. Their protests took the organic unity of the national territory for granted. Premodern dynasties, by contrast, treated lands as real estate; in feudal and patrimonial regimes, "partition" had no political meaning outside of estate law. The "Partitions of Poland" in 1772, 1793 and 1795 among the Romanovs, Hohenzollerns and Habsburgs changed terminological history, generated the pejorative associations of partition, and foretold the legitimacy of nationalist presumptions: each nation has a homeland in which it is entitled to govern itself. It also foretold the illegitimacy of imperialist acquisition and territorial conquest. Against the norm

A Companion to Border Studies, First Edition. Edited by Thomas M. Wilson and Hastings Donnan.

of respect for "territorial integrity" proposals to partition are now judged wrong, and unlawful. (Particular nationalities, of course, may not regard the integrity of existing states as respectful of their national homelands.) The diffusion of democratic and nationalist understandings of self-determination means that the treatment of political partition as illegitimate "tearing" has become standard. Even those who propose partition defend it as "political triage." Triage is the allocation of treatment to patients to maximize survivors: amputation is individual-level triage, the cutting off of rotten limbs that might otherwise kill the patient. In political partitions, the proponents hope that the rump and the amputated limb will do better without each other. Proponents and opponents accept that a "fresh cut" is involved; the proponents hope for surgical precision, the opponents deny this is possible.

Partition, on this account, involves the truncation of at least one prior unit, even if it involves the extension of others (the extension of prior states should be called "annexation" when there is no consent across the entities being unified). Three examples of partitions as "fresh cuts" after World War I were the partition of Ireland in 1920; the partition of Hungary in 1920 under the Treaty of Trianon that did not respect its borders within the old empire; and the Treaty of Lausanne (1923) that partitioned Kurdistan, a newer entity foreseen by the Treaty of Sèvres (1920), between the novel entities of (British mandate) Iraq and (Kemalist) Turkey. After World War II, the most famous partitions have been those of India and Palestine. India's partition created a novel border, separating India from two entities, West and East Pakistan. The new lines did not restore old Mughal jurisdictions, just as the United Nations' proposals to partition Palestine did not conform to Ottoman or British Mandate administrative boundaries. The partition of Cyprus in 1974 was executed by the Turkish army and created a novel political border. These examples all illustrate "fresh cuts."

"Partitions" and "secessions" are often conflated. It is, however, both historically and analytically useful to distinguish them. For example, Ireland was partitioned by the British government in 1920, but in subsequent negotiations Ireland was permitted to secede from the United Kingdom, and what became Northern Ireland was permitted to secede from the Irish Free State. The reverse sequence is also possible. A recognized province or region may try to secede, and after the secession is underway a partition of part of a national homeland may occur. South Sudan's current secession may be followed by the partition of Abyei. Employing these distinctions, Kurdish nationalists are unable to secede from Turkey, or Syria or Iran or Iraq, before they establish a Kurdistan unit. There is now a Kurdistan Region in Iraq and a Kurdistan Province in Iran, which make secession possible, but the establishment of a Kurdistan Region in Turkey or Syria would have to occur before a secession could be even entertained. Therefore only a putative "equal with a recognized territory" secedes; by contrast, an "unequal without a recognized territory" struggles for liberation. Secessionists have territories; liberationists, by contrast, must establish theirs. They may, however, base such claims on earlier historic jurisdictions, in which case their movement will resemble a secession. This distinction between secessionists and liberationists implies no bias, and conforms to much political language, but what if the liberationists take territory in which others' nationals are resident; does that involve a partition? Subjectively this will be experienced as an annexationist partition by those nationals who are living in what they credibly regard as their national territory, within formally established boundaries.

Not all border adjustments therefore are "political partitions," other than in the literal sense that new political parts are created. A partition involves a border adjustment, because there must be a fresh, novel border, but a secession involves a border transformation, that is, the conversion of the previous internal border into a sovereign demarcation. On the understanding advocated here, the breakup of an empire or state (of a confederation, or federation, or union under a common crown) around its existing internal jurisdictions may involve more than one secession, but it does not constitute a partition, unless there is at least one fresh cut.

Partition should be distinguished both from secession and from the recognition of a secession by a political center. This distinction is partly a matter of agency. Empires or states execute partitions. Secession, by contrast, is an action of regions, or provinces, or member states of a federation or union state that may, reluctantly, be accepted by a political center (states only have a presumptive right of secession within confederations). By contrast, partition is something states do, that they can execute on a seceding region, against a national liberation movement, or during "downsizing" (O'Leary et al. 2001). Downsizing is executed by a political center. If that leaves prior provincial borders untouched, there is no partition; it is either decolonization (if there is an organized transfer of authority to a previously unrecognized entity), or dereliction (if there is not).

TYPES OF PARTITION

Partitions are intended to regulate or resolve national, ethnic or communal conflicts. They may be distinguished by whether they partition national or multinational polities; whether they are external or internal; by the agents promoting, supporting and implementing them; and by the political status of the partitioned entities.

National versus multinational partitions

National partitions divide relatively homogeneous national homelands, for instance, the partitions of Germany, Korea and Vietnam at the onset of the Cold War. More debatable examples include the partition of Mongolia, Kurdistan and Armenia – here prior unity is contested. Another is the division of China and Taiwan, debatable because of the sharp cultural differences between the natives of historic Formosa and the settlers from the losers of the Chinese civil war. National partitions are generally caused by civil wars accompanied by large-scale interstate wars (or cold wars or foreign interventions) that stabilize the lines of control. These partitions produce "schizophrenic" entities which claim to be the true embodiment of the nation, and which seek its reunification in their image. In Germany, the capitalist liberal-democratic West eventually prevailed; in Vietnam, the communist north prevailed, the reverse of what seems likely to occur in Korea. National partitions are initially characterized by mutual nonrecognition by the respective regimes, though this may give way to rapprochement and coexistence. Full democratization in the parts of the divided nation usually leads to reunification movements to reverse national partitions.

Multinational partitions divide ethnically, religiously, communally or nationally heterogeneous polities (Henderson and Lebow 1974). These can lead to more nationally homogeneous entities being created, but the deliberate breakup of national or ethnic units within an empire, federation, or a union state may be a national partition for each nationality that has its homeland divided. When the maintenance of heterogeneity within units is the political goal of border designers, as in the drawing of the boundaries of Soviet republics, and the jurisdictions beneath them, and as has been true of the military redesigns of Nigeria's federation, we should code such cases as national partitions: the goal was to partition as many nations as possible. By contrast, redesignings of federations to form internal political borders that correspond with ethnonational homelands or linguistic units are "restorative" architectures, especially when executed with consensus. They should not be coded as national partitions.

Internal versus external partitions

Internal partitions are driven by one of three strategic goals: control, integration or autonomy. Control involves the deliberate organization of one or more ethnonational group, and the disorganization and domination of others. Gerrymandering and provincial fragmentation deliberately dilute the local political concentration of the dominated group(s). Such internal partitions are widespread around the world. Internal partition for integration, by contrast, carves out heterogeneous units of government and representation with the intention, through "mixing," of diminishing conflicts between national, ethnic or religious communities. Lastly, an internal partition may be organized to promote the autonomy of a particular group that has no previously recognized jurisdiction. Such internal partitions need lead to no change in the existing external sovereign border of the state (empire or federation or union state) in question. External partitions, by contrast, necessarily involve both the modification of prior homeland jurisdictions, and the transformation of the status of the existing sovereign border. The partition of Hungary is a good example. So are the partitions of India and Cyprus.

Inside versus outside agents

The agents of partition are "outsiders" or "insiders." Outsiders include conquerors (imperialists, interventionists and leagues or alliances engaged in temporary occupations) and perhaps international organizations. Sovereign insiders include central governments and their local collaborators. Partitions may occur through interactions between outsiders and insiders. Outsiders often want nations divided for military reasons. Where national partitions flow from internal civil wars, insiders would fight their civil war to the finish until reunification occurred, or peacefully negotiate their reunification, that is, all insiders, at least initially, regard the partition as temporary. So, unless there is a military stalemate, without outsiders' actions such partitions will not endure. By contrast, the partitionists of plurinational, pluri-ethnic, plurilingual and pluricommunal entities include both outsiders and insiders. The outsiders believe that partition will eliminate (or at least reduce) ethnonational or other identity-based political differences; and they will be supported by at least some insiders who argue the same case. For them, partitions are proposed as long-run resolutions of conflict.

Political status of partitions

We may also distinguish the political status of the partitioned entities, both of their territories and their peoples. In external partitions, the territories may be empires or states that have lost wars. In internal partitions, they may be the provinces of union states or federations, entities with equal legal status to other provinces. Within empires, they may be colonies (held under direct or indirect rule), and of unequal status to provinces in the imperial core. The peoples in partitioned territories may be citizens or colonial subjects (including migrant workers). They may be nomads or hunter-gatherers, who are not recognized as having any national consciousness, as with the subjects of many of the colonial partitions of Africa.

Periodization

Some distinguish partitions that occurred during decolonization (Ireland, India and Palestine); that were the product of the Cold War (Germany, Korea, Vietnam, China and Taiwan); that were the product of a decisive neighborhood power (Turkey in Cyprus, and, I would add, in Kurdistan); and that took place in more recent times as the byproduct of democratization processes in the multinational states of the former USSR, the former Czechoslovakia, the former Yugoslavia, and Ethiopia (Schaeffer 1999). The distinction between decolonizing partitions and Cold War partitions is coterminous with my distinction between multinational and national partitions. The partition of Cyprus partly flowed from its decolonization and the treaties that accompanied it, and cannot be separated from the multinational cases. The breakup of communist federations, occasioned by multiple secessions, should not, however, be treated as partitions, even though some attempts at partition accompanied these secessions, notably in Bosnia-Herzegovina, and more durably in the Armenian cutting of a land corridor to Nagorno-Karabakh. The democratization of former multinational communist states had striking similarities with the post-World War II decolonizations.

Results and prospects

This definitional discussion and classification has an important implication. In the later twentieth century, if we leave aside the temporary partitions during major wars, there were far more decolonizations with colonial borders left intact, and far more secessions, both peaceful and violent, than there were external partitions. If my proposed coding is accepted, this has decisive implications for evaluating past and future trends. Executed partitions are, of course, much fewer than the number of proposed partitions.

Since the end of World War II we have had small numbers of enduring partitions, including Azerbaijan/Nagorno-Karabakh, Cyprus, Palestine and India, although there is an argument for recognizing the Indian case as involving three distinct partitions, of Punjab, Bengal and Kashmir. The former Yugoslav state of Bosnia-Herzegovina is debatable. Its external borders, within which it seceded from Yugoslavia, were restored intact when the Dayton Agreement was made in 1995, but internally one of the two entities recognized, namely Republika Srpska, had been created by expulsions and partition, and in consequence so was its "partner," the Federation of Bosnia-Herzegovina. However we resolve these cases, we are left with a very small total number – though as we go to press the Russians accuse the Americans of having partitioned Serbia, and the Americans accuse the Russians of having partitioned Georgia.

The small number of external partitions since World War II may reflect two features of the postwar international order: taboos on territorial change by conquest, and on partition by decolonizing powers, after the great bloodbaths between 1947 and 1949. Great powers have generally upheld colonially established borders in Africa and Asia, and accepted that conquest and prolonged occupation is now illegal. It is far easier to have a secession, uncontested or otherwise, recognized (for example, in Croatia, Slovakia, Bosnia-Herzegovina, Macedonia, and the successor states of the USSR) than it is to have a partition recognized (for example, the Turkish Republic of Northern Cyprus (TRNC), and Armenia's occupation of Azeri territory). Even Kosovo's secession from Serbia has more recognition than the TRNC. External (as opposed to internal) partitions have become taboo. One of the functions of this chapter is to maintain that they should stay that way.

EXPLAINING PARTITION

Most explanations of partitions are indistinguishable from justifications, that is, they explain the motives of the partitionists as the results of their ethical and practical beliefs, and these justifications are examined below. I suggest that the key explanation of why these justifications exist is the pressures that flow from democratization. The latter entails defining the people, the most intractable problem in democratic theory and practice. Externally proposed and imposed partitions of national and of multinational units occur where there is no agreement on who should constitute "the people," though that is not the end of the story.

The great powers

The world's borders have been shaped by the great powers. The British had the greatest territorial empire in human history. Irish, Indian and Palestinian nationalists are tempted to think that partitions are peculiarly British: British policy-makers inclined toward "two nations" and "two irreconcilable religions" arguments in Ireland, India and Palestine; and they had a prior history of "divide and rule" strategies. When one removes "rule" from the formula, "divide" remains, and that is the charge: imperialists prepared partition by their modes of rule. The British supported and were supported by one minority (Ulster Unionists, Zionist Jews, Indian Muslims and Turkish Cypriots) against the emergent national majority in each colonial entity. The precedent set in Ireland in 1920, and perhaps by some of the frontier adjustments of the League of Nations, encouraged British imperial elites to think of partition as a viable strategy in Palestine and India.

Alas, however, one cannot solely hold British imperialists culpable for partitionist enthusiasm; other empires were "internally" partitionist when they seized colonies or merged territories, notably the Soviets. Partitions have also been advocated in regions that were never inside the British Empire: in the Balkans (for example, in Bosnia and Kosovo); in the Caucasus (for example, Chechnya); in Africa (for example, Rwanda and Burundi); and in regions which have left the British Empire (for example, postcolonial Iraq, and Afghanistan). But, significantly, partitions in these regions have not been (fully) executed, recognized, or (in some cases) even attempted.

Cyprus does not neatly fit the hypothesis of British imperial culpability. Its partition occurred after decolonization. Palestine also does not fully fit the hypothesis. The Foreign and Colonial Offices were divided over the merits of partition, and it was the United Nations (UN), including the United States and the USSR, and Abdullah of Transjordan, rather than the British, who provided the final external impetus for partition. In Ireland, the demand for the exclusion of (at least parts of) Ulster from home rule and Irish independence came from unionists in both Britain and Ireland, so it was a metropolitan as well as a colonial question. Partition of Ireland was not a Liberal or a Labour enthusiasm; Unionists drove it. Labour's leaders were not keen on the partition of Ireland (Ramsay MacDonald), of Palestine (Ernest Bevin), or of India (Clement Attlee, Stafford Cripps). A generic British political disposition to partition cannot be generated from these histories, and the British did not partition all their other multi-ethnic or their bicommunal colonial territories, such as Sri Lanka, Sudan, and Malaysia. By then they had learned that partitions do not work, at least not as intended.

Yet, other decolonizing empires, France, the Netherlands, Spain, Portugal and the USSR, did not partition their colonial territories on their departures, so there is merit to the idea of British distinctiveness. Proposals were made to partition Algeria, to keep a French enclave, but were rejected. Protecting territorial integrity and promoting linguistic assimilation within their colonial units led the French to be faithful to their Jacobin heritage. The Dutch, the Spaniards and the Portuguese were too enfeebled on exit from their colonies to implement partitions. Both Spain and Portugal were so weak that Morocco and Indonesia, respectively, conquered "Spanish Sahara" and "East Timor" – the former has yet to be reversed, the latter has been liberated after Indonesia's democratization. Remarkably, the Russian Federation resisted the calls of Alexander Solzhenitsyn and others to partition Kazakhstan, despite the proximity of Russian and Russian-speaking settlers to the Russian core. So far, it has not contemplated partition in response to the contested secession of Chechnya. Whether this reflects a republican, anticolonial or Soviet heritage warrants scrutiny. The United States, aside from its support for the formation of Israel, has not promoted partitions to resolve ethnic conflicts in its exercise of global hegemony after 1945. US policy advocates of partitioning Bosnia, Kosovo, Afghanistan and Iraq who sound like their British predecessors are, it must be said, rarities.

The role of nationalists and their opponents amid democratization

One reason why there may have been a higher incidence of partition under or after British rule is that some meaningful democratic government was granted within the empire. Ethnonational mobilization in Ireland occurred against a background of the widening of the franchise. Four-fifths of Ireland's voters insisted upon home rule for four decades from the 1880s, but the descendants of colonial settlers, mostly concentrated in Ulster, opposed them, with the help of the unreformed House of Lords. The issue polarized Irish and British politics, being the principal cleavage between the Liberals and the newly named Unionists (Conservatives and Liberal Unionists). The refusal of autonomy to Ireland eventually made a violent and democratic secessionist bid certain. Its materialization forced the British to downsize, but the presence of Unionists in Great Britain ensured support for Ulster Unionist resistance. In India, nationalist and communal mobilization occurred against a widening of the franchise. The Congress Party and the Muslim League were beneficiaries of increasing representative and responsible government at provincial level. In Palestine, Jewish settlers were internally democratically organized. In Cyprus, democratic mobilization occurred shortly before decolonization, and competitive pressures among Greek Cypriot politicians made it less likely that the 1960 accommodation with Turkish Cypriots would be maintained. The hypothesis is that democratization encouraged party formation around existing national, ethnic or communal cleavages, thereby making the conciliation of competing demands more difficult, and the formation of "a common demos" problematic. Partition came onto the policy agenda amid emergent democratization and rapid ethnonational mobilizations.

Though this hypothesis may explain why partition reached the policy agenda, it does not explain why it was chosen or implemented. Blaming ruthless and ambitious political entrepreneurs is currently a favored theme of historians and political scientists. Applications of this style of thought may be found in many accounts in which partition is seen as the byproduct of a multilayered bargaining game over power and resources between the propartition minority, the antipartition majority and imperial or other third parties. The minority leaders who sought partition in Ireland, Palestine, India and Cyprus are fascinating specimens: Edward Carson and James Craig, Chaim Weizmann and David Ben-Gurion, Muhammad Ali Jinnah, and Rauf Denktash. None began as advocates. Carson, the Dublin unionist, accepted home rule for Northern Ireland and Irish independence with deep reluctance; indeed, he regarded it as a failure. Craig, by contrast, thought a six-county Northern Ireland would be a new impregnable colonial Pale from which to resist Irish nationalism. Both men were ruthless in advocating the abandonment of their co-unionists in counties Monaghan, Cavan and Donegal, the rest of the ancient province of Ulster. A secure majority was more important than securing as many unionists as possible. Mohammed Ali Jinnah, a Bombay Muslim, did not become an exponent of partition or of the two-nation thesis until his sixties. He had been an early, prominent and successful Congressman, and an advocate of secular politics, which he remained. His transformation remains debated. Among the favored suggestions are resentment at loss of salience during Gandhi's ascendancy; the unwinding of the Lucknow pact on separate electorates; opportunism after the electoral failure of the Muslim League in 1937; and the persuasiveness of Iqbal's arguments on two nations and the definition of Pakistan. Jinnah's past persuaded the Congress Party and British officials that he was not a serious exponent of Pakistan, but was just bargaining on behalf of his own and Muslim interests. They saw him as a communal manipulator. They called his bluff. They found themselves in error, though like Carson and Craig, he eventually recommended abandoning his supporters elsewhere in the non-Muslim majority provinces. Weizmann and Ben-Gurion were prominent early Zionists, and definers of the prospective boundaries of "Eretz Israel." They became early "partitionists" (of mandate Palestine) because they thought it better to have a state than not, and were willing to be ruthless in establishing such a state, whence Ben-Gurion's interest in "transfers."

Hardline leaders, solidly endorsed by their most militant and insecure followers, themselves of settler colonial origin, or regarding themselves as of formerly dominant and superior origin, are all parts of the story in Ireland, Palestine, India and Cyprus, but why did such leaders succeed? In Ireland, India and Cyprus, but less so in Palestine, revisionist historiography blames the respective nationalist leaders of the majority communities for placing other priorities ahead of national unity, or for failing to demonstrate inclusive nation-building. Sinn Féin's leaders (Eamon de Valera, Michael Collins and Arthur Griffith) are held responsible for prioritizing sovereignty ahead of the integrity of the national territory, and collectively and individually criticized for mishandling the negotiations with Lloyd George's coalition government and not conciliating unionists. They should have, as they had planned, made Ulster rather than the Crown the break-issue in the negotiations. Congress's high command is similarly held culpable by some historians. Nehru's underestimation of communalism, Patel's pandering to Hindu versions of it, and Gandhi's pervasively Hindu discourses are taken to task, to debunk Congress's secular self-representation. Congress's leaders placed the attainment of independence and a strong central government ahead of accommodating the identities, interests and ideas represented in the Muslim League, which it underestimated. Its failure to ensure that the Congress-run provinces accommodated the League after 1937 is much emphasized – it undermined Muslim support for an all-India state. In Cyprus, Archbishop Makarios is held culpable for seeking to unwind the generous settlement reached with Turkish Cypriots, though it is recognized that he risked being outflanked by ultra- and pro-enosis nationalists (as confirmed in the coup that toppled him). (Little revisionist literature, by contrast, criticizes Palestinian leaders for insufficiently accommodating the interests of Zionists.)

These arguments are reminders of the flaws of the respective nationalist leaders and movements, but go too far in emphasizing their freedom of choice. The leaders had constituencies. Irish and Indian independence had been long sought and blocked by British imperialists. Irish, Indian and Cypriot nationalism were all formally civic, and not devoid of initiatives to compromise with their respective minorities. The first two showed willingness to compromise in key negotiations over future institutions, on a provincial parliament for Ulster within Ireland, on a loose federation for India, and the Greek Cypriots agreed generous consociational terms for Turkish Cypriots in 1960.

The respective elites certainly mattered, but what, we might ask, of their publics? What responsibilities for partitions lie with mass public sentiments and activities?

There is a view that partition is driven by irreconcilable collective identity differences, emanating from long-established hatreds (or recently established hatreds), inflamed by religious differences. Its corollary is that democratization, decolonization and the prospect of a new political order, after imperial or dictatorial rule, bring such passions to the fore. It will not do simply to dismiss these theses. Cosmopolitans in our times insist that our identities are always flexible, multiple, open, fluid, unpredictable, and not driven by inherited traditions, and tend to deny that ethnonational conflicts are ever rooted in ancient hatreds or recent history. This is not the place for a general treatment of these facile arguments, but we can say that it is necessary, for serious ethnonational conflict to occur, that politicians, paramilitaries and others make claims about historic maltreatment of their peoples and warn of future insecurities, but also it is essential that these claims have some resonance, some credibility, with the targeted publics if they are to have results. Ethnonational grievances and religious communalism had prior histories in Ireland and India, long before democratization. Zionism, secular or otherwise, was a response to Jewish collective grievances, mostly at the hands of European rulers, magnified exponentially by the Holocaust. Cypriots were divided by language, religion and political identification. It would be foolish to deny histories of international, interethnic and cross-religious cooperation within places that subsequently were partitioned, but it makes no sense to deny that collective identities and sentiments, and their expressions in hostile and stereotypical forms, provided fertile grounds for political mobilizations and counter-mobilizations. Collective identities do not, however, whatever view we take on their rigidity or longevity, suffice to explain partitions, except, perhaps, in accounting for the motivations of the partitionist.

THE POLITICS OF PARTITION

Partition, ultimately, is a political decision. In the cases discussed it was taken by leaders who believed in irreconcilable differences between local parties, and who determined a final settlement (in conditions of democratization and/or decolonization) rather than allow the local agents to be decisive. They implemented such partitions, during or after wars, when downsizing or decolonizing. Perhaps, in future, they may do so after humanitarian wars of intervention.

This thesis caps the explanatory story. Partition needs partitionist agents, as well as collaborators. The agents need to be appropriately motivated. The aftermath of World Wars I and II weakened Britain's power in Ireland in the first case, and in India and Palestine in the second. The ascendancy of the US and the USSR ranged the doctrines of national self-determination against the maintenance of empire abroad, and made the denial of autonomy at home less viable. In the post–World War II cases, the British quit, with a speedily managed partition in one case, in the other by handing over the decision to the United Nations. For the first and the last time in its history (to date), the UN proposed a partition, the details of which were later rendered irrelevant by a war, the consequences of which still haunt the region.

The Cyprus case inspires a final thought in explaining partitions in the twentieth century. Partition ceased to be an internationally approved instrument of sovereign, or great, powers; it ceased to be as thinkable or condonable as it once was. This has been so since the United Nations formulated new codes and practices. Had the UN been handed the Palestine mandate in 1960, after it had expanded, it is likely that it would have recommended the formation of a binational state, rather than partition (i.e., it would have reversed the rankings of its majority and minority reports in 1947). It has become taboo for external powers to redraw lines on the map as they see fit, just as it is no longer acceptable for some imperial people to rule others. Neither the European Union nor the US could bring themselves to play the role of formal partitionists in Bosnia. When there is nominal equality between states and peoples, to propose partition is to propose that it be executed by paternalistic partitionists, which requires an imperial hegemon. None now present themselves as such, and the most likely hegemon, the US, has resisted calls for it to act as a partitionist in Bosnia, Kosovo, and in Iraq.

JUSTIFICATIONS OF PARTITION

When partition has been invoked the most powerful arguments used may be labeled respectively "historicist," "last resort," "net benefit," "better tomorrow," and "realist rigor."

Historicists assume that history is evolving in a given direction, and conclude we should give it a nudge. They insist that once conflicts pass a certain threshold that they will end in partition, and they may detect such tendencies in residential, educational and employment segregation, in the formation of nationalist, ethnic or communal parties, in short in what W.H. Auden's poem on "Partition" satirizes as "peoples fanatically at odds,/ With their different diets and incompatible gods" (Auden 1976). Historicism shapes policy because it is seen as realistic: partition is inevitable, facts have been established "on the ground," it should be speeded up to reduce the pain. Advocates of the partition of Bosnia maintained that the sole question was whether it would be organized or left to the methods of the ethnic cleansers. There is, however, no confirmed social science law that *all* segregation – voluntary or forced – leads inevitably to the breakup of states. Not only has no one identified clear thresholds of violence (absolute or proportional to population) beyond which partition (or separation more broadly) becomes inevitable, but many recent conflict-settlements show that there can be peace without separation.

The *last resort* argument acknowledges that alternative strategies exist to manage or resolve national, ethnic or communal conflicts, such as federalism, consociation, arbitration or integration, and that these alternatives should be attempted before partition is considered. But if these options fail, so the argument goes, partition should be chosen to avoid genocide or large-scale ethnic expulsions. Exponents of this argument often invoke the "security dilemma." In conditions of emergent anarchy, that is, when an empire or a regime is collapsing, the relations among ethnic groups becomes akin to that of individuals in a Hobbesian state of nature. One distrustful community will seek to enhance its security, which will enhance the insecurity of the others, creating a vicious and escalating cycle. Ethnic groups with strong and durable identities will be mobilized for war, and attack ethnic islands of the other community, or protect their own by expelling others. Partition is justified, in these conditions, because it ends the imperatives to cleanse and rescue, and renders war unnecessary to achieve mutual security. In Auden's poem, the partitionist lawyer Radcliffe is told, "It's too late/ For mutual reconciliation or rational debate/ The only solution now lies in partition." The logic, the modeling and the poetic satire are neat, but critics suspect the underlying psychology and sociology.

The *net benefit* argument need not presume the existence of a security dilemma, or justify partition only when absolutely necessary to prevent genocide or large-scale expulsions. It suggests instead that partition should be chosen when, on balance, it offers a better prospect of conflict reduction, that is, it is a desirable preventive strategy. This argument was maintained in the last years of British imperial rule by the leading politicians of minorities who opposed independence within existing colonial borders. Partition was justified to prevent a loss of freedom – they did not maintain that genocide and ethnic expulsions were going to be carried out by Irish, Indian or Palestinian nationalists. Some consider partition an appropriate policy choice simply where there are ethnically intermixed populations, because they are capable of sustained pogroms, massacres, expulsions and genocide. The argument, of course, licenses too many partitions: after all, of which groups could it be said that they are incapable of genocide?

In the *better tomorrow* argument, all partitionists maintain that after the deed is done there will be a reduction in violence and conflict recurrence. New more homogenized polities will have better prospects of stable democratization, of political development, and of better relations. After the trauma is over, the former partners will conduct themselves better, because their interests will not interfere so intimately with one another's identity, pride and emotions. This argument rests on key and questionable counterfactual assumptions, namely, that without partition there will be significantly more conflict and conflict recurrence; and that more heterogeneous polities have poorer prospects of democratization, political development and intergroup relations.

The tough-minded maintain in the *realist rigor* argument that any difficulties with partition flow from irresolution – a thoroughgoing revision of borders, which fully separates the relevant antagonistic communities, is what is required. Good fences make good neighbors; bad fences provoke disputes. Policy-makers must devise borders – and provide incentives for controlled population movements – to create sufficient homogeneity, so that the incentives for national, ethnic, religious and communal violence are radically reduced. Another and better cut will be advocated to rectify the surgery if it was botched the first time.

These five standard arguments for partition are political and moral. They are not simple apologias, though they may provide cover for more contemptible motives. The arguments are not obviously racist, sectarian or civilizationist. They present partitionism in its best light. These five arguments are only partially testable. One accepts historicist philosophies or approaches, or one does not. The leap from demographic trends to assumptions of future political behavior by propartitionists is not scientific; the same trends may be compatible with a range of political relationships – from genocide to federal or consociational coexistence. The "realistic rigor" thesis is not testable, because confronted by the evidence of catastrophe partitionists will claim that the tragedies lie in the imperfection of the attempted project not the idea itself. Though there is now an interesting literature which tests partitionist claims in statistical studies, it is marred by deep disagreement on the coding of partitions. Partitionists implicitly predict either a linear or an exponential relationship between the degree of national and ethnic heterogeneity of a place and the security dilemmas that provoke violence (which can be shown to be false). Ultimately their arguments suggest it is foolish to insist on maintaining unviable multinational polities.

The modalities

Principled partitionists come in two general types – proceduralists and paternalists. *Proceduralists* favor justice and agreement, while paternalists favor imposition in others' interests – they put order before justice. Proceduralists advocate consultation with the "affected parties," and try to establish rules to which reasonable partitions should conform. They see roles for commissions, and particularly judges and technical experts. The British Empire set up boundary commissions in twentieth-century Ireland, Palestine and India. The UN attempted to be a proceduralist in Palestine in 1947.

Honest proceduralists reject proposals that do not meet fairness and feasibility requirements. Arend Lijphart (1984) has specified the requirements of a fair partition: when it is negotiated by all the affected groups rather than imposed; when it involves a fair division of land and resources; and when it results in homogeneous, or at least substantially less plural, independent states. The major difficulty with this reasonable conception is the sheer unlikelihood of the first requirement: nonimposition. The affected parties – politicians and their publics – are not likely to agree unanimously, and even if representative politicians do concur, it is unlikely that the adversely affected people will agree, even if offered significant compensation. Partitions involving the movement of people or of their sovereign territory just do not proceed with technical agreement and political consensus.

Lijphart's other criteria offer good benchmarks against which to evaluate the fairness of partitions of binational or multinational polities. The Radcliffe "Award" in Bengal in 1947 is unusual because it almost perfectly met the second and third criteria. West Bengal, an area of 28,000 square miles, was to contain a population estimated at 21.19 million people, of whom 29 percent were Muslims. East Bengal, to become East Pakistan, an area of 49,000 square miles, contained a population of 39.11 million, of which 29.1 percent were Hindus. West Bengal was to get 36.6 percent of the land to accommodate some 35.1 percent of the Bengal population, while East Bengal was to get 63.6 percent of the land to accommodate 64.8 percent of the population. The ratio of majority to minority populations was almost identical, and the resulting entities more homogeneous than their predecessor, partitioning a polity with a Muslim:Hindu ratio of 56:44 into two with 70:30 majority:minority ratios. We might equally conclude, however, that Radcliffe created two large Northern Irelands out of Bengal, and few regard the bloody Indian partition as a success story.

Others have argued that rules should govern "transfers." Borders should be drawn to leave as few people as possible in the "wrong" state; each individual may emigrate to the "right" state; and each state should be entitled to evict members of the other group. But why should an equal number of "wrongly" placed people be regarded as a fair outcome, as opposed to an equal ratio of "wrongly" to "rightly" placed people? Surely fairness should include proportionality, not just absolute numbers? Such transfer rules, moreover, not only license ethnic expulsions, but also may incentivize them.

Paternalists by contrast to proceduralists assume that the local communities are incapable of agreement, except perhaps after protracted wars. They propose that a sufficiently powerful outsider should determine a durable partition, and reduce conflict credibly – and quickly. Addressing security imperatives is more important than meeting participation requirements or considerations that might flow from abstract social justice. "Better rough justice than none" is the outlook.

THE COUNTERCLAIMS OF ANTIPARTITIONISTS

Nationalists reject the rupturing of their national territories; multinationalists reject the historicist assumptions of homogenizers, and their negative assessments of the prospects for multigroup coexistence. They share common appraisals of how partitions are perverse, of how they jeopardize existing relationships, and of the impossibility of achieving fair partitions. Their arguments may be headlined as follows.

The rupturing of national unity   This is, say the critics, a violation of the right to territorial integrity of the partitioned entity. In the twentieth century, partitions were rejected by most of the affected majority nationalists whose national homelands were freshly cut, and they were rejected as undemocratic: imposed against the expressed preferences of the relevant majorities in their national territories. They complain that partition was proposed in the interests of privileged minorities, and was especially brutal in its impact on those who became new "border communities." The Sikhs of the Punjab or the Irish nationalists of south Armagh, Tyrone, Fermanagh, Derry city and Newry were those who suffered.

Advocacy of binationalism or multinationalism   The democratic pluralist case is that plurinational arrangements must be properly exhausted before partition is considered. If there were two nations in Ireland, India, Palestine and Cyprus, or three in Bosnia Herzegovina, no automatic case for partition follows. The undesirability, infeasibility or insecurity of binational, federal, consociational or confederal arrangements must be demonstrated, not assumed. In the three British imperial cases, most of the relevant minorities – Ulster unionists, the Muslim League, and Zionists – appeared unwilling to propose or experiment with such formulae. Their veto of alternative formulae, backed by force, was rendered more effective by the declarations of the imperial power that they would not coerce the relevant minorities. That partition was "a last resort," or a regrettable choice "when all else had failed," therefore usually rings hollow.

The impossibility of just partition   Antipartitionists argue that just partitions demand the wisdom of Solomon, which by definition is rare. International procedures, including World Court jurisprudence, have addressed some border disputes between states. Typically, however, these arise from ambiguities in historic treaties or legislative documents, or they involve maritime jurisdictions, or are occasioned by natural geographical changes in terrain and river beds. Legal procedures are not, however, appropriate for what is at stake in political partitions. From 1945 until 2009 only two disputes where homelands were arguably at stake, both involving marginal islands, were settled by the International Court of Justice, one being the Minquiers and Ecrehos Islands located between the English-speaking Channel Islands and French Normandy. It remains to be seen whether the recent Permanent Court of Arbitration at The Hague has successfully determined the borders of Abyei, which are at issue between Sudan and South Sudan.

King Solomon did not partition the disputed baby, but adopted a procedure, the threat of partition, to establish its true mother. No such procedure, however, is likely to work well amid mass ethnonationalist politics. The credible threat of partition encourages preemptive action, ethnic expulsions, to establish "facts on the ground." These repercussions are more likely than the disputing parties coming to their senses. Partitionists get the causality wrong: it is partition which generates a security dilemma. It is they who occasion the "security dilemma," not the mere presence of heterogeneous populations.

Antipartitionists observe that boundary commissions usually give "pivotality" to the relevant big power in that the big power has the decisive vote. The Irish Boundary Commission of 1924–1925 and the 1947 Radcliffe Commissions in Punjab and Bengal had British appointees in the chair. In Auden's words, Radcliffe was told "We can give you four judges, two Moslem and two Hindu/ To consult with, but the final decision must rest with you." The key difficulty for such chairs is what we may call Solomon's agenda, namely

1   Which should be the units around which new boundaries should be drawn?
2   Should there be subunit opt-outs? If unit A opts to be with one state, but B, a concentrated minority within A, wants to go with another, may it opt out?
3   How should units' preferences be determined? If there is agreement on the units of determination, then how should the new boundary respect popular preferences? Through local plebiscites, or through determining people's presumed preferences through their ascriptive identities as recorded in census data (that may be unreliable)? If plebiscites, what rule should be adopted for determining whether a given unit goes to one jurisdiction or another: a simple majority, an absolute majority of registered voters, or a weighted majority? If working from census data, who should count: adults, or adults and children?
4   Should local popular preferences be considered just one criterion to be balanced among others? Should contiguity, preserving a cultural heartland, retaining a unit within an economic, geographical hinterland or infrastructure, or ensuring militarily secure borders be balanced against popular preferences?
5   If such other factors are to be considered in designing new borders, should local popular preferences be subordinated to these other considerations, and, if so, which ones – and who should make that determination?

6   Should there be constitutional amendments to ratify the commission's proposals or referendums, and should there be provisions to enable their subsequent revision?

It is not surprising that Radcliffe, who drew the partition of Bengal and the Punjab, refused to be interviewed on his work for the rest of his life: "Return he would not/ Afraid, as he told his Club, that he might get shot." Radcliffe's commission worked fast, and it mattered; its resolutions were implemented. The commission chaired by Richard Feetham in 1924 did not work in a hurry, and eventually made no difference to the partition line in Ireland. But Feetham's minimalist judgment of his terms of reference decisively shaped the commission's outcome. This case, of a failed commission, demonstrates the procedural conundrums attached to boundary commissions, and the unpredictable consequences of giving judges vague terms of reference. It is difficult to imagine impartiality in the appointment and management of a boundary commission – an empire or regional power has its own interests, and their officials will take great care over appointments to such bodies.

The likelihood of disorder and violence   Antipartitionists maintain that partitions encourage ethnic expulsions; trigger partially chaotic breakdowns in order, leading to flight, opportunist killing, rapes, and looting; produce more violence than that which preceded them; have domino effects; contribute to postpartition wars, and insecurities; and set precedents that lead to demands for repartitions. Their case is that partitions are perverse: they achieve the exact opposite of their goals. In raw numbers of dead and forcibly displaced, the critics are correct across the cases of India, Palestine, Ireland and Cyprus. The partition of India was accompanied by a death toll variously credibly estimated at between 200,000 and 2 million. Involuntary and expelled cross-border refugees and displaced persons may have approached 15 million. The partition of Palestine and the war that accompanied Israel's declaration of independence led to the deaths of approximately 6,000 Israeli Jews, and over 10,000 Arabs, the expulsion and flight of over 750,000 Palestinians, and, as a by-product, over half a million Jews fled or were expelled from surrounding Arab states. In the Turkish invasion and partition of Cyprus, 6,000 Greek Cypriots were killed and 2,000 reported missing, and some 1,500 Turks and Turkish Cypriots killed. After the partition more than 10,000 Greek Cypriots were pressurized into leaving Northern Cyprus, on top of the nearly 160,000 who had fled before the Turkish army. The partition of Ireland was accompanied by the least violence amid twentieth-century partitions, but the violence was nevertheless much higher than the death toll before the partition. Moreover, thousands of Catholics were expelled from their jobs and their homes in Belfast and fled south; and thousands of Protestants emigrated from independent Ireland. At bottom, partitionist claims are counterfactual rather than empirical: without partition the conflict will be worse; partition was not the problem per se, but rather the particular partition was defective. Partitions are especially perverse when they have domino effects – triggering postpartition wars. The Arab-Israeli wars of 1956, 1967 and 1973, and the Israeli-Lebanese wars, show that the partition of Palestine did not end conflict. India and Pakistan have fought three wars, in 1948, 1965 and 1971.

The receding goal of homogenization   Critics maintain that partitions do not produce more homogeneous states. Postpartition India and Pakistan are vast, populous and multi-ethnic, and remained multireligious; and West Pakistan experienced a fresh infusion of linguistically differentiated refugees. Postpartition Israel was left with a significant Palestinian Arab minority, and soon had waves of new Jewish refugees of diverse ethnic formation. Northern Ireland was left with a unionist and cultural Protestant/nationalist and cultural Catholic ratio of 67:33, which has since shifted to 60:40, and may move past 55:45 toward parity. Pakistan, however, is certainly proportionally more Islamic than India, even though India had, and still has, the largest minority Muslim population in the world. In Ireland, ethnicity and religion were fused in many people's identities, but the Irish Free State was more Catholic than prepartition Ireland, and Northern Ireland was more Protestant than historic Ulster. Israel was more Jewish, and the West Bank and Gaza more Muslim and Christian, than prepartition Palestine. The units of postpartition Cyprus are very ethnically, linguistically and religiously homogenized by comparison with pre-1974 Cyprus. So the case literature here is indecisive.

Critics of partition are more effective when they say that partition *alone* is unlikely to generate the desired homogenization. The rigorous realists rely on a tacit assumption: the necessity of expulsions. They must pursue "transfers," and are driven to condone or organize expulsions, while postpartition states may pursue policies that encourage potentially or actively disloyal minorities to emigrate, and encourage inward immigration of the "right" people. Partitions without comprehensive expulsions generate two kinds of orphaned minorities: former prospective majorities, and formerly dominant minorities, who may both become part of irredentist movements, or campaign for a further partition.

Damage to successor states   Antipartitionists maintain that partitions generate new security crises of an interstate form, but also cause significant economic disruption, and not just because of communal conflict and warfare, and sudden flows of refugees. They disturb established monetary and exchange networks, increase transactions costs, enhance the likelihood of protectionism, and provide incentives for smuggling and other border-related criminality. They have led to the depreciation of significant capital investments in transport, as roads, railways and canals, and ports and airports, have their original functions terminated or damaged, and to losses that may flow from failures to cooperate in agriculture, water management, natural resource extraction, and energy production and distribution. The new postpartition entities retain common functional and infrastructural interests flowing from their shared pasts, so they often end up, ironically, considering postpartition cross-border functional cooperation.

Of the cases considered here, Northern Ireland was not a success story before 1998. Postpartition Pakistan is acknowledged as a developmental disaster. The story of postpartition Palestine is known to the world. The unrecognized Turkish Republic of Northern Cyprus has an unenviable reputation. There is a pattern here: one entity (Ireland, India, Israel and Greek Cyprus) has done better than the other. Partitionist triage has certainly not been equally good for all.

On the failure to make a clean or elegant cut Partitionists' maps bleed, as may be seen in the shape of West Bengal, or the meandering border of Northern Ireland, or those planned for Quebec or Bosnia. Partition may worsen the "compactness" of the postpartition entities by contrast with their precursors. "Compactness" is the physical solidity of a state – once widely believed to have implications for its military security, it still affects popular assumptions about the right shape of a state, however much academicians reject the thesis of "natural boundaries."

The partitionist and antipartitionist arguments just considered are universal; they recur in response to, or in the aftermath of any proposed or actual partition. The arguments also figure in any rounded historical explanations of why partitions occur: they must have been found compelling for at least one powerful agent, though they may not be sufficient to explain why they occur.

CONCLUSION

Antipartitionists, the foregoing evaluation suggests, have better arguments, judged by realistic, political and moral criteria. When partition threatens, the appropriate slogan should not be John Lennon's "Give Peace a Chance," or Edward Luttwak's "Give War a Chance," but rather "Give power-sharing a chance." Partitions have not generated better security environments. Most have been biased toward privileged or dominant minorities – pushing conflict downstream. Partition processes and postpartition arrangements have been worse than those predicted by supporters of partition, for at least one successor unit. Prudence therefore mandates opposing partition as a tool of international public policy-making, and placing the burden of proof on its advocates.

The arguments surveyed here are not intended to hold sway against the merits of peacefully negotiated secessions within recognized boundaries. There are good and bad secessions, but, by contrast, it is hard to find a good twentieth-century partition. Of course, it cannot be known in advance that there will never be any cases where partition truly is a better policy option than the alternatives, but the standard for making that argument should pass an extremely high threshold, namely that partition is demonstrably the best way to prevent genocide, or its recurrence.

NOTE

This chapter summarizes, synthesizes and clarifies arguments in O'Leary 2007 and 2011.

REFERENCES

Auden, W.H. 1976. Partition. In *Collected Poems*, ed. E. Mendelson. New York: Random House.

Henderson, Gregory and Lebow, Richard Ned. 1974. Conclusions. In G. Henderson, R.N. Lebow and J.G. Stoessinger, eds,

Divided Nations in a Divided World, pp. 433–456. New York: D. McKay.

Lijphart, Arend. 1984. Time politics of accommodation: reflections – fifteen years later. *Acta Politica* 19 (1): 9–18.

O'Leary, Brendan. 2007. Analyzing partition: definition, classification and explanation. *Political Geography* 26 (8): 886–908.

O'Leary, Brendan. 2011. Debating partition: evaluating the standard justifications. In K. Cordell and S. Wolff, eds, *The Routledge Handbook of Ethnic Conflict*, pp. 140–157. London: Routledge.

O'Leary, Brendan, Lustick, Ian S. and Callaghy, Thomas, eds. 2001. *Right-Sizing the State: The Politics of Moving Borders.* Oxford: Oxford University Press.

Schaeffer, Robert K. 1999. *Severed States: Dilemmas of Democracy in a Divided World.* New York: Rowman & Littlefield.

CHAPTER **3**

Culture Theory and the US–Mexico Border

Josiah McC. Heyman

Border cultures are important both to border specialists and to social analysis in general, the latter because border cultures have been held to challenge unitary one-state-one-territory/one-society-one-culture conceptualizations, predominant until recently (a point especially made by Rosaldo 1989). The United States–Mexico borderlands have particularly been the setting of key ideas and debates over border cultures, although Donnan and Wilson (1999) have offered a wider-ranging synthesis, and in recent years studies of other borders have clearly surpassed the US–Mexico border in creativity and perceptiveness (examples and references can be found throughout this book). Nevertheless, the fundamental positions have been staked in this region, and it is through the phenomena of this region that I develop my reanalysis of the question of the distinctive characteristics of border cultures. The main debate has occurred between theorists celebrating border cultural hybridity (e.g., Anzaldúa 1987; García Canclini 1995; Rosaldo 1989) and an important respondent, Pablo Vila (2000, 2003), emphasizing cultural and identity separation, distinction, and polarization. The pioneering border scholar Oscar Martínez (1994) also emphasizes transnationalism and hybridity, using material from this border, though more on the basis of descriptive generalizations than at the high level of theory of a Rosaldo or a García Canclini.

In this chapter, I argue that both hybridity/resistance to state boundaries and polarization/embracing of state boundaries are emergent features of deep sociohistorical processes. Both cultural differentiation and polarization are contingent outcomes that need to be explained, and are likely to co-occur at borders, rather than being ontological natures of border cultures as such, which would require an absolute debate over which characterization is correct. Because they are emergent states of being, this requires a historical structural approach to borders. Nor are these cultural stances the distinct possessions of well-defined social groups. Within the border setting, some populations are carriers of specific processes, but often the same people

---

A Companion to Border Studies, First Edition. Edited by Thomas M. Wilson and Hastings Donnan.

are affected by both tendencies and manifest both cultural styles at different times and in different relationships.[1] I aim to show how a sociocultural process analysis works by using the rich materials of the US–Mexico border.[2]

A few words about comparative implications are needed. Because I use literature and materials specific to the US–Mexico border, the surface content of my analysis cannot be extended in a precise way to other borders. Yet I respect the critique made by scholars of other borders of the tendency of US–Mexico scholars to be oblivious to the importance of other borders, and comparative border studies more generally. My contributions to border studies are, I hope, as follows. The first is the emphasis on generative social processes and institutions as shaping specific cultural patterns. My work at this border points other scholars to ask what key generative processes are involved at other borders. The second concerns the specific processes I identify, including border polarizing processes, border crossing and blending processes, and combined and uneven relations. Their particular manifestations and relative weight will differ among borders, but it is useful to envision all of them potentially being useful rubrics in the analysis of a given border.

Finally, my third contribution is a historical structural approach. We expect borders to differ in this approach, because each has a specific history, though with some relevant comparisons linking them. But more important is the conceptualization that cultures are historically produced by various social relations, saturated with power and struggle. The conceptualization is unified, even as the specific manifestations differ. Border scholars can speak one language, including vocabularies of polarization, inequality, and hybridity, without needing to make highly similar statements about one given border. What I offer then, in my case study, is an exemplary method for thinking across borders.

The Border Culture Debate and Beyond

The core idea of "border culture" (as a theoretical position) is that there is a distinctive nonstate or even antistate cultural formation at borders. This classically was articulated in the work of Renato Rosaldo (1989), Nestor García Canclini (1995), and Gloria Anzaldúa (1987). Rosaldo critiques the identification of culture with definitively bounded units, such as nations, which he terms "monumentalism." Monumentalist approaches ignore internal complexity and interconnection, and treat border-crossing people and cultural traits as marginal and deviant. Rosaldo revalues nonmonumentalist phenomena as central to the study of culture. García Canclini offers a similar analysis, focusing on "hybridities," or mixtures of seemingly disparate cultural elements. Anzaldúa envisions border culture as emerging from challenges by subordinated and often voiceless subject positions to dominant cultural frameworks and their valued subject positions: Mexican-origin people in the United States challenging Anglo-American definition of US culture, indigenous people challenging Western colonizers, women challenging the dominant male framework, and gays and lesbians challenging normative heterosexuality. Rather than maintaining these dichotomies (calling for reversing them, for example), she values a mixed, constantly crossing ("mestiza") position between them.

Vila (2003) subjects these authors to a powerful critique. The border culture literature assumes that borders, as opposed to national interiors, have a distinctively hybridized culture. The idea seems to be that national interiors have unitary cultures and identities but that where they meet, cultures and identities inherently blend and combine. Vila points out that we cannot assume that this process is automatic, we cannot assume it occurs in the same way on both sides of the boundary, and we cannot assume that a hybridized border culture or identity is the most common or most highly valued feature of the borderlands. He emphasizes the occurrence of differentiation and polarization at borders, especially in identities. While Vila recognizes hybridity and resistance to nationalism and states at borders, he stresses the importance of the drawing of distinctions through the use of national identities at borders.

Vila's work on narrative identities at the US–Mexico border is empirically and analytically impressive. Yet it still calls for further analysis. Let us take just one example. Established Mexican-Americans (or Chicanos) see themselves as separated from the poverty and corruption of contemporary Mexico, but also distinguished from Anglo-Americans[3] (or Whites) by their possession of romanticized past Mexican traditions (the time feature of this narrative also separates them from recent Mexican immigrants). They stake out this position within a context framed by dominant, largely Anglo-American discursive stigmas toward Mexico and Mexicans. In the larger work, Vila characterizes specific clusters of narrative identities, but ones that constantly refer to the wider network of social relationships. What are these key relationships? The key symbols, ideologies, institutions, and power relations call out for historical structural work to clarify their emergence, reproduction, and content.

Or we can turn to the fascinating typologies of borderlanders provided by Martínez (1994), largely on the basis of culture content but mixing in identities also. He clusters his typologies by nation, Mexicans and Northamericans, and then into two ethnoracial groups in the United States, Mexican Americans and Anglo Americans. Within each set, he identifies two basic types: national borderlanders (oriented to the interior culture) and transnational borderlanders (oriented to border crossing, cultural and physical). There are various subtypes within each cluster: commuters, consumers, newcomers, and so on. Each is characterized by directions of influence. Looking at one of his types (Martínez 1994:70), Mexican commuters to the US side, we see in his diagram and textual description strong influence arrows ("shaping and maintaining the person's lifestyle or culture") on the Mexican side for education, social interaction, employment/income, consumerism, core culture, and popular culture, and "fundamental" influence arrows on the US side for employment/income and consumerism. There are "strong link or exposure" arrows for social interaction and popular culture, and "superficial" ones for education and core culture (all terms in quotation marks from Martínez).

His typological characterization calls out for further structural and historical contextualization. He generalizes from Mexican-side residents who commute, with or without US immigration authorization, to work on the US side, with a smaller subset who commute to purchase goods in the United States that are retailed in Mexico. Both of those activities, and the sorts of cultural sets that emerge within them, are key economic processes in the borderlands, and more abstractly, they are class relations encoded in race, nationality, and so forth. The many strong arrows emanating from the Mexican side in the commuter diagram likewise speak to the wider set of socialization and enculturation institutions in Mexico, most notably education organized by the nation-state. Each of Martínez's borderlander diagrams, then, represents a set of surface cultural manifestations emerging from generative processes and relations that merit further study. It is to such an investigation that we now turn.

A BASIC TYPOLOGY

Here I offer a typology of three culture-forming processes. They are simplistic, both useful and flawed in the way of all ideal types. They are, most of all, pointers to thinking, rather than ontologically unified categories of phenomena.[4]

First, some processes explicitly reinforce borders. They make social interactions and cultural content different (or more different), especially in ways that can broadly be delineated by state territories. They also undergird powerful polarizations of identities. An obvious example is the buildup of border enforcement since 1994 (with deeper roots), which Joseph Nevins (2002) has analyzed as an enduring process of territorial state formation. A less overt, but telling example is the nationalistic education pervading public schools in each country, Mexico and the United States, affecting both culture content (e.g., language) and identity in ways that reinforce cultural boundaries (Rippberger and Staudt 2002).

Other processes undercut such boundaries, however. Border defying or hybridizing processes cut through both nations, but they are more common in the setting of geographic proximity and extensive interpersonal relations at the border. Elites, for example, of the two sides conduct valuable business deals across apparent national-cultural boundaries, meet each other socially, and cultivate bilingual and bicultural skills needed for such settings. The poor of the two sides also cut across boundaries, partly because of the processes of migration (working-class Mexicans coming to the United States) but also because of structural parallels in their lives on both sides, as illustrated by comparable informal housing development in *colonias* (US) and *colonias populares* (Mexico) (Ward 1999).

Finally, processes of combined and uneven development (Smith 1984) pervade the border (Heyman 1994, 2004, 2007). Combined and uneven development is a situation where differentiated and unequal social components are in a relationship of exchange, usually unbalanced. This is neither separation nor blending; it involves both connection, and sometimes but not always mutual recognition and sharing of some cultural elements, but also differentiation and perpetuation of inequalities and distinctions. A characteristic US–Mexico border example is the maquiladoras, export-oriented processing and assembly factories in Mexico, that under the orchestration of transnational corporations join prosperous consumers in the United States and Canada with poor workers in Mexico (from a vast literature, a superior introduction to the political economy of these factories is Kopinak 1996). A whole series of social-cultural roles in both nations involve conducting this unequal exchange. Combined and uneven development challenges the simple dichotomy at the core of the border hybridity/polarization debate; it involves both flows and connections (cultural as well as economic) while maintaining and even exacerbating divisions and distinctions.

The Historical Construction of "Mexico" and the "United States"

The US–Mexico border was set in place by historical processes with enduring effects. Obviously, the actual boundary was historically set by the Mexican-American War, the Treaty of Guadalupe Hidalgo (in 1848), and the Gadsden Purchase (in 1853). There is little that is geographically inherent in the boundary; much of it is straight lines across open land, and even the Río Grande (US usage) / Río Bravo (Mexican usage) is in most locations trivial as a barrier or separating factor. But more importantly, the border as a distinction between state-territorialized social-cultural spaces took place over long periods of time, in dynamic, complex, and still quite incomplete ways.

Many borders in the world split closely related, if not identical, social and cultural groups. In turn, the elements of close social and cultural resemblance and enduring relations tend to operate as subversive factors acting against the monumentalism of the newly bounded nation-states. The US–Mexico border has such elements. Native Americans had both countries, and their boundary, imposed on them, and some groups still crisscross the border (e.g., numerous California tribes and the Arizona-Sonora Tohono O'odham). There were a number of Mexican settlement areas (e.g., San Antonio, South Texas, the Paso del Norte area, New Mexico/southern Colorado, the Santa Cruz river corridor, and much of California) in areas accessioned by the United States. The model of arbitrary borders leading to antimonumentalist cultural formations applies to these populations, though in historically specific and complex ways.

However, this is insufficient for understanding the contemporary border. Holding off, for the moment, on important later historical processes, we need to emphasize that in some ways the border between Mexican and Northamerican cultural formations is deep and profound, not arbitrary and artificial (wherever it finally was delineated, geographically). Here I am not talking about essences; all cultures are constructed. But I *am* pointing to the borderlands as a colliding ground of two major sociocultural formations. Both are postcolonial societies, forged in the capitalist world economy and the imperialism of Europe against the rest of the world.

The core formation of Mexico took place in the central highlands, based on the unequal power relations and cultural syntheses of indigenous and Spanish elements, which was then carried northward to the frontier regions where the modern border is now located. Its basis was the early modern imperialist Castilian rule (cultural as much as political) seizing control at the top over hierarchical indigenous Mesoamerican societies, especially the Aztec empire. The core formation of the United States took place in the slavery and indentured servitude-based British settler colonies of the east coast of the United States, synthesizing African and European cultural elements. These were carried westward in the US expansion. Now, such cultural formations are not simple and unitary (both cultural complexes were based on unequal relations among differentiated components), nor do they have a simple, transhistorical essence over 500 years. Their transformations and encounters in the borderlands also reshaped them; while basically each evolved separately, once they met, they became mutually constitutive. But naive hybrid accounts of US–Mexico border culture are often too casual about the profound historical distinctiveness of these two monumental cultural formations. Mexico, even at its border, is indeed strikingly different from the United States, and vice versa.[5]

For example, Mexico from nearly the beginning has been marked by a strong emphasis on corporatism, organizing society through well-marked, vertically ranked communal segments with specific activities, roles, and expressions. This history extends from the colonial governance of Indian communities and Spanish guilds, through the intensive use of corporatism by post-Revolutionary (1920–2000) authoritarian Mexican governments (it has declined, however, with the imposition of neo-liberalism since 1982). Mexican corporatism is not just a matter of governance; it deeply shapes everyday social relations and culture (Wolf 1959). The US social-political system has, from its colonial beginnings, emphasized "possessive individualism" (Macpherson 1962), again with clear cultural effects. It is also a profoundly racialized, post-slavery society. Of course, no unequal social-political system is devoid of corporatist features, including the United States, and likewise possessive individualism is often found in Mexican life. But any account of cultural encounters at this border, whether hybrids or contrasts, must begin with the recognition that each side of the boundary embodies its own distinctive historical and current social-cultural formation, though with important penetrations between them.

In addition to the deep history and the imposition of the boundary line in war, a key set of historical formation processes took place starting with the capitalist and nation-state development of borderlands, beginning in the 1850s and accelerating from the 1880s forward. During this period, all three processes occurred, but most importantly, the pattern of combined and uneven development between the US southwest and northern Mexico was set in place, mediated by border exchange points (which become border cities, of course) (among many works, see González Herrera 2008; Heyman 1991; Mora-Torres 2001; Tinker Salas 1997).

Starting immediately after 1848, the legal system of the United States was deployed to expropriate land, water, other rights and resources, and political power from the Mexican-origin population in favor of the Anglo-Americans. These same patterns of expropriation took place in late nineteenth-century Mexico, where both Mexican and US elites participated in this process (Mora-Torres 2001; Tinker Salas 1997). Modern capitalist culture was imposed, though in different ways and with complexly diverse effects and responses, spanning the border in both nations. This was encoded in a discourse of racial and cultural superiority versus inferiority that was quite similar in both societies. Meanwhile, Mexican migrant laborers moved back and forth with no meaningful inspection or barriers before 1917, and facing only weak and easily bypassed limitations before 1929. Then, gradually across the rest of the twentieth century, "Mexicans" were construed as a specific kind of outsider migrant.[6] In tandem, the border was culturally and ideologically reworked as a territorial expression of "control" over such subordinate laborers (Nevins 2002; Ngai 2004). There was an experiential and cultural unity before 1929 that has not been possible since (Heyman 1991: 119–120; Vélez-Ibáñez 1996).

After the interregnum of the Great Depression, the long but ultimately massive development of the US border enforcement apparatus took off (1940 to the present), which differentiated the United States and Mexico more clearly and rigidly. In parallel, the consolidation of the postrevolutionary Mexican state (e.g., in schools) saw the deep penetration of national culture and identity-shaping institutions on the Mexican side (Joseph and Nugent 1994). A similar growth of "everyday state formation," though longer, deeper, and more racially divided, took place in the United States. One feature of US state formation was the Mexican-origin civil rights movement from the 1910s onward, which ironically differentiated (if incompletely) the previously border-spanning Mexicano population, by demanding inclusion in the US national cultural framework (see Johnson 2003 on this history and Ochoa 2004 on its current manifestations).

To understand how this history shapes border culture in the present, it is illustrative to consider a brief typology of three historical inheritances. There is, first, the cultural lineage descended from preborder northern Mexican frontier people. It has hybridized with subsequent cultures, but it is less a postborder hybrid as such than it is a subordinated alternative culture, especially in the United States. It is essentially a variant of central Mexican culture (brought north in the process of frontier expansion), quantitatively very small in the contemporary borderlands. Second, there are modern (post-1880) hybrids, mixtures (and creative outgrowths) of two preexisting cultural formations, that is, the cultures of post-1880 Mexican immigrants to the United States and their descendants. Similar are the enduring cultural effects of the United States inside Mexico, including its northern border cities, brought by post-1880 capitalist expansion. Finally, there are polarization formations, in which Mexican and "United Statesian" identities and cultures are mutually constituted as opposites precisely by their interaction, examples being US tropes of superiority over Mexico ("all poverty is Mexican," as Vila (2000) found). The historical productive forces include US economic penetration into Mexico and internal domination over working-class Mexican migrants, and Mexican nationalism as a reaction back against US imperialism.

The border culture debate involves claims to both cultural and identity separations between the two sides, and patterns that either simply do not fit a bounded national-cultural model or that creatively hybridize elements from the two sides. These both do occur. They occur because a specific history has assembled the key parts, contents, and relations. The power of this historical construction renders uninteresting various statements of abstract "border culture" as a state of being, an inherent in-betweenness. History, rather, shapes and arranges major society/culture generating institutions fundamental to the present, as we will see in the next section.

THE PRODUCTION OF CULTURES AND IDENTITIES IN THE US-MEXICAN BORDERLANDS

Nation-creating/reinforcing processes

As mentioned above, government-controlled schools, the vast majority of educational institutions in both Mexico and the United States, powerfully nationalize identity and cultural content (Rippberger and Staudt 2002). The relationship between schools and identity outcomes is complex and processual, interacting with other contextual factors, such as families and peer groups. And there are many young people whose education is binational, divided into periods in each country (because of migration, cross-border educational commuting, or binational families). We unfortunately do not have good research on how binational shuttling affects cultural and identity formations. But broadly, once the two nation-states became consolidated on each side of the border, government-controlled education became an important generative force for identity and cultural content division at the border.

Central government employment also promotes nationalization of identity and content (but see comments below). The importance of central government employment in borderlands has rarely been emphasized, yet borders are major loci of state bureaucracies. My study of US Immigration and Naturalization Service (now Homeland Security) officers of Mexican ancestry found that employment with that border control organization was a strong force both drawing on and producing/reinforcing US citizen identities (Heyman 2002). Culturally hybrid content (e.g., extensive use of Spanish and/or Spanglish among US officials or with the public) coexists with polarized narrative identities (anti-Mexican, pro-US). There is likely some difference between Mexico and the United States in this regard, because many of the central state agencies of the United States aim at excluding or controlling outsiders (Mexicans), and thus have a polarizing structural role, while many central state agencies of Mexico aim at controlling insiders (again, Mexicans). Little is known about the latter case.

Central state agencies do not just shape their own employees. In both countries, they generate propaganda, often in conjunction with education. El Paso has Border Patrol academies and Young Federal Law Enforcement Explorers programs for teenagers, for example. My university (University of Texas at El Paso) has military, intelligence, and homeland security career-oriented majors for advanced students. Military and police recruitment target working-class Latinos in the United States, not just by direct recruiting activities, but by creating a cultural climate of patriotic fervor. And government jobs that are decently paid, have excellent health and other benefits, and are stable, are "glorified" (in the words of one of my informants) in the marginalized US border economy (Heyman 2002). (Much less is known about Mexico.) It is hardly surprising that there is such identification with the central state on the US side of the border.

Key ideologies bound each nation as separate from the other, and to a lesser extent span them. Ideologies do not simply determine narrative identities located in specific social fields, but rather enter into complex interactions with them, as Vila indicates (2005: 230–258). Nevertheless, accounts of important national and transnational ideologies are needed to understand fully border identities. Because they affect the value given to specific cultural elements, they also affect indirectly culture content through differential enculturation and usage.

Mexico, for example, has had political projects and related ideologies of modernization and nationhood since the mid-nineteenth century. These frameworks involve a complicated, two-sided attitude toward the United States, with shifting emphases at different times. On the one hand, the United States is viewed (realistically) as an overbearing and sometimes directly threatening power. Nationalist ideologies thus promote identity and culture content polarization (e.g., Spanish language purism). On the other hand, the United States is admired as a model of modernity, favoring some aspects of positive identification with the colossus of the north, as well as extensive culture borrowing (e.g., Spanglish). One sees this duality quite clearly in the ambivalent *fronterizo* narratives Vila documents (2000:51–80).

The United States has long had a racial-nationalist sense of superiority to Mexico, characterized as traditional, backward, corrupt, exotic, and so on. This has been expressed both externally, as negative tropes about the country of Mexico, and internally, as negative tropes about Mexican immigrants (González 2004). Both dimensions of this discriminatory ideology come together at the border, for example in the central trope of "all poverty is Mexican" uncovered by Vila. Responses to this stigma emerge in his material in interesting ways: for instance, as a motive for Mexican-origin people in the United States to identify with the US nation-state and to disparage Mexico, except for a romantic Mexican past (Vila 2000: 111–124). There are also stances that resist these discriminatory ideologies, revaluing immigrants in the United States and workers in both countries on the basis of cross-border human rights and social justice ideologies. Such cross-border counter-ideologies are quantitatively rare and often hybridize in contradictory ways with dominant frames (e.g., pro-immigration movements with an emphasis on US citizenship) (Dunn 2009).

The media (television, radio, the internet, and print) are important institutions of enculturation and identity formation in contemporary societies. Unfortunately, with respect to the questions asked here, they are poorly studied in this region. Thinking in a loose observational way about the mass media in my own locality, El Paso, USA, and Ciudad Juárez, Mexico, the national division is very striking. There are Spanish-language television and radio stations in both countries, but they are heavily weighted to one home country or another in terms of news, events, and topical references, rather than being evenhandedly border crossing. They do cover material from the other side of the border, but in notably reduced fashions. Cultural crossing, such as use of Spanglish (linguistically dense interweaving of the two languages) can be heard in US-side radio, but is not common, and the content is still US oriented. The US English language media are overwhelmingly (and infuriatingly) US oriented, with a tendency to neglect Mexico except in highly visible, negative stories. However, media are readily accessed across the border, such as Mexican stations listened to by immigrants in the United States, so that border crossing is easy to perform as an individual or household choice. Still, the media seem to be fairly nationalized.

Finally, it bears repeating that Mexico and the United States are often quite different at the everyday, experiential level, for reasons discussed in the history section above. One can certainly find examples of both similarity and contrast when crossing the border. But border people are basically correct in their impression that they occupy two very different spaces, culturally, socially, economically, and politically, even as they cross them frequently, even daily (see the important critical response of Alegría Olazábal 2009 to Herzog 1999 on urban form differentiation). At the level of experienced lifeworlds, there is as much basis for drawing national contrasts at this border as there is for imagining third, nonnational or postborder spaces.

Many of these nationalizing processes, it remains to be said, are driven by the long historical institutionalization of the two territorial nation-states and their constitutive effects on society and culture. But not all are; differentiating and polarizing processes emerge from a number of sources (e.g., the "all poverty is Mexican" ideology can be attributed to the US state only in limited ways, and has deep roots in US economy and society).

Border-crossing processes

Economic activities and other social and cultural relations broadly promote border crossing. Of course, many economic activities are entirely bounded by the national territory, even in border cities, but US–Mexico border cities historically have emerged from and currently still substantially rest on economic transactions that cross borders, both cultural and legal-political (see Ganster and Lorey 2008, and for more theorized (critical political economy) analyses, see Fernandez 1977 and Heyman 1994, 2004). The processes include both border-eroding ones, discussed here, and the more ambiguous combined and uneven relations addressed in the next section.

Corporations, business people, and other managers of substantial wealth (money, real estate, etc.) often cross the border as part of their combined economic activities and way of life. Investments by transnational corporations in Mexican maquiladoras are discussed below; here I focus on wealthy Mexicans operating in the United States and their US counterparts. Wealthy Mexicans have long sheltered capital in the United States, in dollars, from risks such as the devaluation of the Mexican peso. They purchase real estate, such as second homes, and other assets, on the US side, not just as investments, but also as alternatives to a possibly risky Mexico (for instance, currently many prosperous Mexicans are buying homes in El Paso or moving into properties previously held in that city, as a response to the widespread violence and criminality in Chihuahua state; often they already have dual citizenship). Finally, they shop for consumer goods of various kinds (vehicles, consumer electronics, etc.) on the US side of the border.

These transactions require a basic knowledge of the United States (e.g., commercial geography) on the part of the Mexican elite, and often much greater cultural sophistication. They also support a substantial bilingual, bicultural workforce in businesses on the US side of the border. Most US-border banks, for example, have staff with the linguistic and cultural skills to do business with prosperous Mexican customers. Comparable – though not mirror image identical – comments can be made about Mexican-side businesses that serve prosperous (and some not so prosperous) customers from the United States.

Another culturally generative set of economic transactions involves cross-border imports and exports. They vary considerably in content and scale of trade. Medium to large import-export businesses and related trades, such as customs brokers and trucking firms, are quite important. Their biculturality has been well documented by Robert Alvarez (2005) for the fruit and vegetable sector. Traders of small consumer goods (clothes, appliances, consumer electronics, etc.), who range from microscopic to quite substantial in their volume and revenue, are also culturally and socially as well as economically important (Gauthier 2007, 2010; Heyman 1997; Staudt 1998).[7]

Employment also sustains cultural border crossing. Many people – unfortunately not counted, however – daily cross the international boundary to work. An even larger number, mostly in the United States, cross linguistic and cultural borders to work, because of the inclusion of the Mexican-origin population in the US workforce (especially relevant here is the inclusion of people enculturated in Mexico in US workplaces). As yet unpublished sociolinguistic research in El Paso by Amado Alarcón and Josiah Heyman delineates a complex set of segmentations – both cultural and economic – and brokerage across the divisions, of both formal and informal, upper and lower register English and Spanish. These processes give rise both to hybrids (e.g., Spanglish) and polarization (e.g., linguistic tensions between bilingual Mexican-Americans and monolingual Mexican immigrants).

Both migration and everyday mobility help create hybrids.[8] Much of the "hybrid border culture" literature is really about migration and migrants, and especially about the children and grandchildren of migrants in the new society.[9] Arguably border culture covers the wider situation of the cultural effects of migration between distant points (e.g., between the interior of Mexico and the interior of the United States), but this topic transcends this chapter (for a start, see Suárez-Orozco and Suárez-Orozco 2001). But such effects occur also in the immediate borderlands setting, where it interweaves with daily cross-border movement.

Mexican migrants living in El Paso (drawing on my ethnography) often have tight relationships with relatives living nearby on the Mexican side; these nearby bonds provide personal satisfactions that make up for living near the border, a region in the US characterized by competitive and poorly paid labor markets. People also marry or have other close personal relationships across the border. Many workers commute from Mexico to the United States because of the wage differential and job opportunities; they also choose to commute for social-personal reasons – they want to maintain residence in Mexico (family, lifestyle, etc.) while being employed north of the border.[10] Cross-border labor commuters sometimes emerge from cross-border personal relations, as a person lives with a partner and children on one side and works on the other. Other cross-border forms also emerge, such as postdivorce families with one partner in each country and children moving or visiting back and forth between them.

In all these instances, there is a fertile ground for the development of binational, bicultural mixes, as seen in case studies in Martínez (1994). The ability to interact across the border, including commuting and constant visiting, may produce and maintain hybrid cultural content in a way that would be less frequent in the national interiors of either country. Linguistically, border proximity to Mexico – not just physical proximity but direct, daily interactions – reduces or reverses Spanish language loss among second and deeper generation migrants (Mora et al. 2005). Border interactions also support a relatively small but distinctive set of Anglo-Americans who gain Mexican cultural and linguistic skills. However, this simple generalization about proximity leading to hybridity needs to be carefully examined. Some unskilled labor, such as construction work, takes relatively little cross-cultural skill on the part of the worker, but does require either a culture broker (e.g., a contractor), or cross-cultural negotiations between employer and worker (e.g., an employer with some command of Spanish and knowledge of this labor force). The cultural content of such interchanges may be quite limited.

Finally, classes often face similar structural situations across borders, resulting in shared cultural responses. For example, economic uncertainty disproportionately affects people in Mexico and Mexican-origin people in the United States alike. Carlos

Vélez-Ibáñez (2010) has documented the use of rotating credit associations (usually called *tandas*) in parallel in both countries. A few literally span the border, but more common is that the Mexican cultural template for *tandas* is used in parallel contexts in both countries. It is a border-crossing form of culture, in both the sense that cultural materials spread through migration and that a shared structural situation characterizes both sides of the border.

COMBINED AND UNEVEN DEVELOPMENT AND CULTURE

Combined and uneven relations have mainly been analyzed in terms of economics and material exchanges. A telling example, as delineated previously, are the economic arrangements that make the maquiladoras lucrative to transnational corporations. But no economics can operate without social relations and cultural coding, and combined and uneven relations exist as much at the level of border culture as border economics (Heyman 2010).

In a relational perspective, many connections to the other side of the border (literally and culturally) are indirect – that is, effects of various structural arrangements – rather than being experienced immediately by a given individual. Hence, instead of direct cultural polarizing or blending, we encounter a chain of intersocial, intercultural connections. Important segments on each end are divided and separated from each other, even as they are closely related. For example, maquiladora workers are undeniably part of a US-dominated capitalist economic system, projected geographically into Mexico. Culturally, their work discipline is shaped by current transnational corporate practices, inflected by specific US, East Asian, Mexican, etc., managerial traditions, and also by specific production processes and local social relations within Mexico (Peña 1997). But such workers may well only deal with Mexican supervisors. Their lives outside of work may entirely be contained within Mexican political and social structures. They may not have a permit to cross into the United States and may never go there. The "border" structure may indeed be hybrid, but this does not necessarily apply to all individual positions within it.

Some positions, however, can mediate, translate and negotiate such relations, and are thus more likely to be occupied by individuals with hybrid backgrounds and skills. Melissa Wright (2006: 93–121) offers an exemplary case study of a female maquiladora supervisor who controlled and motivated her female workforce using distinctly Mexican, blue collar, and gendered idioms and relationships, achieving high levels of productivity and quality, while at the same time connecting this productivity to the goals of male, white collar Mexican and North American corporate management. Wright focuses (for good reason) on how men in management devalued this performance, but for my purposes it is sufficient to note that a direct form of hybridization was necessarily carried out at some point in the relational web, but that other positions in the relational web[11] thus did *not* need to cross borders, nationally, culturally, of class, and of gender. I suggest that, structurally, all border processes have something of this form, with points of translation between differentiated and (usually) unequal positions (see Heyman 1994, 2010).

A variety of labor transactions can be understood as combined economic and cultural interchanges in a context of border-based inequalities. Howard Campbell

(2005) delineated a characteristic border cultural situation in which an Anglo-American farm-owning family and a Mexican-American farmworker family had an enduring patron–client relationship. The families converged to some extent in terms of learning cultural content (e.g., becoming bilingual) but remained culturally and socially sharply distinguished from each other. In other words, culture enabled interchange, but one that reproduced the distinction and the inequality between each end point, though with some convergence.

Another important domain of combined and uneven relations at the border, with profound cultural and material effects, is the differentiated and contrastive stereotypical meanings of Mexico for the United States, and the United States for Mexico. In the face of more complex reality, Mexicans think of the United States as modern, wealthy, efficient, and futuristic, but also cold and inhuman. Northamericans think of Mexico as sensuous, tropical, exotic, and traditional, but also corrupt and immoral. Not only are these discourses defined as contrasts with each other, but they also help constitute apparent border-crossing practices – shopping, leisure, tourism, even socializing of various sorts – that both promote narrowly framed cultural interchanges but also reproduce divisive distinctions.

This brings us to reflect on a crucial point. Culture is not a bounded set of traits (though such traits are learned and used culturally). Rather, it is a set of publicly exchanged meanings (Geertz 1973) deployed in social relational processes (Wolf 1982: 385–391). This is true of all cultural situations, but is particularly heightened at borders (Heyman 1994). One of the most serious flaws in the border culture debate is that it conceptualizes culture as the singular character of a culture bearer (as in Martínez's 1994 work). But culture is often best described as emerging out of relationships between differentiated actors (see Heyman 2001, 2010). The great culture theorist Anthony F.C. Wallace terms the former view the "replication of uniformity" and the latter the "organization of diversity" (1961: 26–29).

Thus, to understand border culture requires that we also understand the complex patterns of interrelated inequality in the borderlands. Obviously, Mexico is on average significantly poorer than the United States, a disparity that is particularly salient at the border (and even though the US side is poor by comparison to the rest of the nation, and the Mexican side richer). But this is not enough. Both nations are complex, race and class stratified societies, so that a vast web of unequal exchanges – cultural as well as economic – takes place between variously situated actors, such as working-class young Mexican-Americans waiting on wealthy Mexican shoppers in US border cities, tensely playing out cultural exchanges, jabs, and responses of language, social status behavior (egalitarian versus hierarchical), nationalism, and so forth. Seen in this perspective, border hybrids are an important phenomenon, but do not exhaust all border experiences and positions. Rather, the overall gestalts of relations, and codes of communication and behavior entailed in them, are deserving of attention in border studies.

CONCLUSION

The first wave of border cultural theory provided us with important, enduring insights, in particular the critique of assumptions about timeless, essential, and unitary cultures, associated with bounded societies. The subsequent reification of their vision of border culture and the apparently endless repetition of a naive reading of such works is highly frustrating, however. Vila's (2003) critique of that literature was important (also see Heyman 1994). To make progress in border studies beyond these critical replies requires attention to wider causative processes.

This contextualization has three themes, each of which should be useful for border studies. First, the particular formations and the overall patterning need to be understood as historical constructions. This helps us escape debates over ungrounded assertions about the essence of border cultures. History is often relegated to being background; in a constructionist view, it is crucial to understanding the character of the present. Second, key institutions and power processes affect the cultural content and identity formations of individuals and intimate social groups involved in them, although this influence is not simple or narrowly determinative. Some of these are reasonably well studied, but many of them are surprisingly little examined. Border studies requires considerably more documentation and analysis of these major structures – not only in the economic and political senses, which is how they are usually (if at all) considered, but also as involving specific sorts of cultural performances. Finally, border cultures of various sorts need to be considered as positions in differentiated and unequal webs of relationships. Border cultures are not free-floating discourses, or traits of specific social groups, but rather are public codes and meanings that emerge and operate in interactive formations, in which apparent opposites (e.g., hybrids and nationalisms) are sometimes processually connected. The formations as wholes, as much as the content of particular positions, merit attention.

This work has focused on a theoretical literature grounded in the US–Mexico border, and it has relied on empirical examples from that site. Its lessons are, however, portable – as ways of thinking, rather than as literal descriptions of how all borders are or should be. Three abstract processes – border reinforcing, border crossing, and combined and uneven relationality – generate emergent cultural phenomena. A laundry list of specific culture-producing domains is worth considering as manifesting these general processes. The domains include states, including border law enforcement, government employment, and educational systems; the media of various sorts; and major ideologies, especially national and ethnic ones. They also include mobility and migration; labor; trade of various items and at various scales; corporations and managerial/technical organizations; and household economies and social arrangements of both rich and poor. And in these activities, it is important to attend to exchanges among those unequal in resources and power. In this view, culture is produced, used (practiced), interchanged, reproduced, and transformed, not as a separate domain but as an integral dimension of social, political, and economic process.

NOTES

1   The relationship between structural contexts and individual culture and identity is complex. There is room for individual or small group deviation, change, and creativity. Culture has its own dynamics, and cannot be simply reduced to social structure and process.

Nevertheless, it is a basic assumption of the social sciences that people learn their individual cultural and social frameworks within wider structural contexts – multiple and often
contradictory contexts, including families, peers, media, schools, work experiences, legal
identities, and so forth – and thus that such contexts matter to understanding both individuals and wider cultural phenomena.

2   An important distinction is worth noting. Cultural content – the various traits of people's
learned meanings and behaviors – differs from the narrower domain of cognized identities
(Vila 2003: 308). Much of the force of Vila's critique of the naive border culture literature comes from insisting on that distinction. For example, people may speak the
hybrid "Spanglish" blend of English and Castilian when they contrast their identities as
Mexican or as American. Both culture content and identities are affected by historical
structural processes, though not always the same ones. In other words, both need further
analysis.

3   Anglo-American is a common regional term for people of European or Mediterranean
ancestry who are not Mexican (above all), African-American, Asian-American, or Native
American.

4   I would entertain an argument, however, that border-reinforcing processes do have some
unity caused by the formation and institutionalization of the nation-state. Capitalist processes and householding, on the other hand, sprawl more incoherently across all three
types that I discuss in the text (e.g., capital sometimes undermines borders by mobilizing
investment, property rights, labor, consumption, etc., across boundaries, but also sometimes reinforces borders through the reproduction of distinctions within combined and
uneven exchanges).

5   This is a way in which the present case differs from many other world borders.

6   They were treated not just as racial subordinates, but also as noncitizens, outsiders to
the national community of the United States, which had not mattered much in the
earlier era.

7   For a comparable Brazilian/Paraguayan/Chinese case that specifically theorizes such
traders as an alternative "globalization" to corporate and elite globalization, in social and
cultural as well as economic senses, see Ribeiro 2009.

8   Migration identifies changes that are relatively long-term and substantial in distance,
though not necessarily permanent, while mobility covers movement more generally,
including shorter distances and more constant changes, such as the commuting mentioned in the text.

9   Vila suggests this indirectly, when he notes that it is a Chicano-oriented literature, and
tends to neglect Mexico (2003: 307).

10   Such workers fit into a variety of occupations, from educated professionals to home
cleaners and construction workers, and have a variety of legal statuses when crossing
the international boundary, from US citizens to people working without authorization, after crossing on a Border Crossing Card (this card, provided to some but not
all Mexican northern border residents, allows entry to the US border zone for up to
30 days, but not for work or residence; it is supposed to be used for shopping, visiting,
etc.).

11   US home corporate and technical staff, Mexican low-level technical staff, immediate
supervisors, and workers often rely on brokers to cross linguistic and cultural boundaries.
Positions most commonly held by brokers (and thus carriers of cultural hybridity) include
US and Mexican factory-level management and office personnel, and key border region
technical staff. Factory set-up/turn-key operators and industrial park developers also often
are brokers.

REFERENCES

Alegría Olazábal, Tito. 2009. *Metrópolis transfronteriza. Revisión de la hipótesis y evidencias de Tijuana, México y San Diego, Estados Unidos.* Mexico City: Miguel Angel Porrúa.

Alvarez, Jr, Robert R. 2005. *Mangos, Chiles, and Truckers: The Business of Transnationalism.* Minneapolis: University of Minnesota Press.

Anzaldúa, Gloria. 1987. *Borderlands: The New Mestiza = La Frontera.* San Francisco: Spinsters/Aunt Lute.

Campbell, Howard. 2005. A tale of two families: the mutual construction of Anglo and Mexican ethnicities along the US–Mexico border. *Bulletin of Latin American Research* 24: 23–43.

Donnan, Hastings and Wilson, Thomas M. 1999. *Borders: Frontiers of Identity, Nation and State.* Oxford: Berg.

Dunn, Timothy. 2009. *Blockading the Border and Human Rights: The El Paso Operation That Remade Immigration Enforcement.* Austin: University of Texas Press.

Fernández, Raul A. 1977. *The United States–Mexico Border: A Politico-Economic Profile.* Notre Dame: University of Notre Dame Press.

Ganster, Paul and Lorey, David E. 2008. *The US-Mexican Border into the Twenty-First Century.* Lanham: Rowman & Littlefield.

García Canclini, Néstor. 1995. *Hybrid Cultures: Strategies for Entering and Leaving Modernity.* Minneapolis: University of Minnesota Press.

Gauthier, Mélissa. 2007. Fayuca hormiga: the cross-border trade of used clothing between the United States and Mexico. In Emmanuel Brunet-Jailly, ed., *Borderlands: Comparing Border Security in North America and Europe*, pp. 95–116. Ottawa: University of Ottawa Press.

Gauthier, Mélissa. 2010. Researching the border's economic underworld: the "fayuca hormiga" in the US–Mexico borderlands. In Hastings Donnan and Thomas M. Wilson, eds, *Borderlands: Ethnographic Approaches to Security, Power, and Identity*, pp. 21–34. Lanham: University Press of America.

Geertz, Clifford. 1973. Thick description: toward an interpretive theory of culture. In *The Interpretation of Cultures*, pp. 3–30. New York: Basic Books.

González, Gilbert G. 2004. *Culture of Empire: American Writers, Mexico, and Mexican Immigrants, 1880–1930.* Austin: University of Texas Press.

González Herrera, Carlos. 2008. *La frontera que vino del norte.* Mexico City: Taurus and El Colegio de Chihuahua.

Herzog, Lawrence A. 1999. *From Aztec to High Tech: Architecture and Landscape across the Mexico–United States Border.* Baltimore: Johns Hopkins University Press.

Heyman, Josiah McC. 1991. *Life and Labor on the Border: Working People of Northeastern Sonora, Mexico 1886–1986.* Tucson: University of Arizona Press.

Heyman, Josiah McC. 1994. The Mexico–United States border in anthropology: a critique and reformulation. *Journal of Political Ecology* 1: 43–65.

Heyman, Josiah McC. 1997. imports and standards of justice on the Mexico–United States border. In Benjamin S. Orlove, ed., *The Allure of the Foreign: Postcolonial Goods in Latin America*, pp. 151–184. Ann Arbor: University of Michigan Press.

Heyman, Josiah McC. 2001. On US–Mexico border culture. *Journal of the West* 40 (2): 50–59.

Heyman, Josiah McC. 2002. US immigration officers of Mexican ancestry as Mexican Americans, citizens, and immigration police. *Current Anthropology* 43: 479–507.

Heyman, Josiah McC. 2004. Ports of entry as nodes in the world system. *Identities: Global Studies in Culture and Power* 11: 303–327.

Heyman, Josiah McC. 2007. Environmental issues at the US–Mexico border and the unequal territorialization of value. In Alf Hornborg, J.R. McNeill and Joan Martinez-Alier, eds,.*Rethinking Environmental History: World-System History and Global Environmental Change*, pp. 327–344. Walnut Creek: AltaMira Press.

Heyman, Josiah McC. 2010. US–Mexico border cultures and the challenge of asymmetrical interpenetration. In Hastings Donnan and Thomas M. Wilson, eds, *Borderlands: Ethnographic Approaches to Security, Power, and Identity*, pp. 21–34. Lanham: University Press of America.

Johnson, Benjamin H. 2003. *Revolution in Texas: How a Forgotten Rebellion and Its Bloody Suppression Turned Mexicans into Americans*. New Haven: Yale University Press.

Joseph, Gilbert M. and Nugent, Daniel, eds. 1994. *Everyday Forms of State Formation: Revolution and the Negotiation of Rule in Modern Mexico*. Durham: Duke University Press.

Kopinak, Kathryn. 1996. *Desert Capitalism: Maquiladoras in North America's Western Industrial Corridor*. Tucson: University of Arizona Press.

Martínez, Oscar J. 1994. *Border People: Life and Society in the US–Mexico Borderlands*. Tucson: University of Arizona Press.

Macpherson, C.B. 1962. *The Political Theory of Possessive Individualism: Hobbes to Locke*. Oxford: Clarendon Press.

Mora, Marie T., Villa, Daniel J. and Dávila, Alberto. 2005. Language maintenance among the children of immigrants: a comparison of border states with other regions of the US. *Southwest Journal of Linguistics* 24: 127–144.

Mora-Torres, Juan. 2001. *The Making of the Mexican Border: The State, Capitalism, and Society in Nuevo León, 1848–1910*. Austin: University of Texas Press.

Nevins, Joseph. 2002. *Operation Gatekeeper: The Rise of the "Illegal Alien" and the Making of the US–Mexico Boundary*. New York: Routledge.

Ngai, Mae M. 2004. *Impossible Subjects: Illegal Aliens and the Making of Modern America*. Princeton: Princeton University Press.

Ochoa, Gilda L. 2004. *Becoming Neighbors in a Mexican American Community: Power, Conflict, and Solidarity*. Austin: University of Texas Press.

Peña, Devon Gerardo. 1997. *The Terror of the Machine: Technology, Work, Gender, and Ecology on the US–Mexico Border*. Austin: Center for Mexican American Studies, University of Texas at Austin.

Ribeiro, Gustavo. 2009. Non-hegemonic globalizations: alter-native transnational processes and agents. *Anthropological Theory* 9: 297–329.

Rippberger, Susan and Staudt, Kathleen. 2002. *Pledging Allegiance: Learning Nationalism at the El Paso–Juárez Border*. New York: Routledge/Falmer.

Rosaldo, Renato. 1989. *Culture and Truth: The Remaking of Social Analysis*. Boston: Beacon.

Smith, Neil. 1984. *Uneven Development: Nature, Capital, and the Production of Space*. Oxford: Blackwell.

Staudt, Kathleen. 1998. *Free Trade? Informal Economies at the US–Mexican Border*. Philadelphia: Temple University Press.

Suárez-Orozco, Carola and Suárez-Orozco, Marcelo M. 2001. *Children of Immigration*. Cambridge: Harvard University Press.

Tinker Salas, Miguel. 1997. *In the Shadow of the Eagles: Sonora and the Transformation of the Border during the Porfiriato*. Berkeley: University of California Press.

Vélez-Ibáñez, Carlos G. 1996. *Border Visions: Mexican Cultures of the Southwest United States*. Tucson: University of Arizona Press.

Vélez-Ibañez, Carlos G. 2010. *An Impossible Living in a Transborder World: Culture, Confianza, and Economy of Mexican-Origin Populations*. Tucson: University of Arizona Press.

Vila, Pablo. 2000. *Crossing Borders, Reinforcing Borders: Social Categories, Metaphors, and Narrative Identities on the US–Mexico Frontier*. Austin: University of Texas Press.

Vila, Pablo. 2003. Conclusion: the limits of American border theory. In Pablo Vila, ed., *Ethnography at the Border*, pp. 306–341. Minneapolis: University of Minnesota Press.

Vila, Pablo. 2005. *Border Identifications: Narratives of Religion, Gender, and Class on the US–Mexico Border*. Austin: University of Texas Press.

Wallace, Anthony F.C. 1961. *Culture and Personality*. New York: Random House.

Ward, Peter M. 1999. *Colonias and Public Policy in Texas and Mexico: Urbanization by Stealth*. Austin: University of Texas Press.

Wolf, Eric R. 1959. *Sons of the Shaking Earth*. Chicago: University of Chicago Press.

Wolf, Eric R. 1982. *Europe and the People without History*. Berkeley: University of California Press.

Wright, Melissa W. 2006. *Disposable Women and Other Myths of Global Capitalism*. New York: Routledge.

CHAPTER **4**

The African Union Border Programme in European Comparative Perspective

Anthony I. Asiwaju

Regional integration demands the effective devaluation of the barrier functions and effects of the boundaries between participating sovereign states. The elimination of the border as barrier and its promotion as a bridge constitutes the acid test of the sincerity of purpose of national states engaged in a regional integration project. Manifestations of "closed borders," including the unrelenting exercise of restrictive controls, suggest the absence of a sense of commitment and a lack of seriousness of intention on the part of the participating state actors.

In Europe, beginning with the Western European initiatives in the immediate aftermath of World War II, the spectacular regional integration success story has derived from an ever-increasing lowering of borders as barriers between the world's oldest nation-states which had, hitherto, a history of recurrent and devastating territorial and border conflicts and wars. The inauguration of the European Union was based on the theory and practice of the concept of a "Europe without frontiers." This concept was enshrined in the Maastricht Treaty, the Schengen Agreements of 1992–1993, and the evolving European constitution which was milestoned in the 1997 Amsterdam Treaty and recently amended by the Treaty of Lisbon of 2007, on the European Union and the Treaty Establishing the European Community.

The result of these developments, in the elimination of restrictive controls on the internal frontiers of the European Union and the pooling of policy in respect of policing, immigration and the administration of criminal justice, has been a growing European regional constituency and a consciousness that tends to transcend national boundaries and identities. Of particular significance for the European regional integration process has been the lobbying influence, if not power, exercised by the directly affected local populations in the diverse border areas which has been organized

A Companion to Border Studies, First Edition. Edited by Thomas M. Wilson and Hastings Donnan.
© 2012 Blackwell Publishing Ltd. Published 2012 by Blackwell Publishing Ltd.

through the highly proactive Association of European Border Regions (AEBR), with headquarters in Bonn, Germany, and an influential operating office close to the European Parliament in Strasbourg, France. The pivotal role of the AEBR and, indeed, the wider organized civil society has ensured the evolution of the European Union as an organ not only of the democratically committed states and governments but also, and even more importantly, the people themselves.

In Africa, as indeed in other regions of the developing world, on the other hand, regional integration experiments have not met with similar success, despite demonstrable similarities in the basic structures and functions of state territories and boundaries. In the particular case of Africa, the record of failure has been remarkably dismal. While the desire has remained strong, the actual performance has been disappointing. The events have long been an affair of governments rather than of the people; and the chances of success are constantly put to flight by contra-indications of negative nationalism and the attendant actual and potential boundary and territorial disputes and conflicts within and, more manifestly, between many territorially adjacent African states. Of particular importance in this record of failure has been that pro-integration decisions, usually taken in the context of summits of heads of states and governments, are not reflected in the behavior of the law and border-enforcement agencies of the individual national authorities.

The recently inaugurated African Union Border Programme (AUBP) is aimed at changing the trend in Africa in the general direction of mirroring the more desirable developments in the European Union. Based on a solemn Declaration of the historic Conference of Ministers in Charge of Border Issues held in Addis Ababa, Ethiopia, on June 7, 2007 and a unanimous endorsement by the Executive Council of the African Union in its 11th Ordinary Session held in Accra, Ghana, on June 26–29 of the same year, the AUBP is a fourfold policy instrument targeted on a simultaneous pursuit of (1) accelerated demarcation of the international boundaries between member states; (2) cross-border cooperation focusing on a regional approach to the planning and development of "cross-border areas" or "Afregios" ("African regions"), equivalents of the more familiar "European regions" or "Euregios" in the European integration process; (3) capacity-building with particular reference to relevant knowledge infrastructural innovations and specialized training and research programs in support of cross-border cooperation initiatives and wider regional integration orientations; and, finally (4) relevant resource mobilization within and outside Africa. The strategies for implementation embrace roles for local, national, regional, and continental levels of execution, based on a strict adherence to the principle of subsidiarity.

Clearly the most comprehensive policy instrument ever designed at continental level on the issue of Africa's borders, which were notoriously inherited in most instances from European colonial powers, the AUBP has resulted from a long historical process that dates back to the accidental origination of the modern African state territories and boundaries in the European "scramble" and subsequent imperialist partition of the continent at the turn of the nineteenth century.

This chapter, which focuses on the African Union Border Programme in the context of a comparison with the European historical experience, is organized into five distinct but interrelated sections. The first offers a brief discussion of the conceptual challenges posed by issues of comparison with special reference to the question of comparability between Europe and Africa in the matter of state territories and boundaries. The second provides a sketch of the history of the border factor in the European regional integration process. The third is a critique of the history in Africa with special reference to border policy-making and policy implementation in the era of the defunct Organisation of African Unity (OAU) from 1963 to 2002. The fourth, on the ongoing African Union (AU) phase, is a more detailed description of the recently launched Border Programme. The essay concludes with a critical reflection on the Euro-African historical comparison and the logic for linkages and networkings of organized research and training programs and institutions.

AFRICA AND EUROPE COMPARED

Comparisons evoke controversy.[1] With particular reference to Africa and Europe, objections are encountered on both sides: national and racial pride gives rise to opposing emotions. Whatever the reservations about comparisons between Africa and Europe, however, it is reasonable to consider the political boundaries and related borderlands in the one continent essentially as extensions and a replica of those in the other. In Europe, as in Africa, most borderlands represent areas of distinct official languages, national histories and cultures as well as divergent economic systems, mutually opposed legal traditions and parallel administrative practices.

This is not surprising since the boundaries, which spawned the borderlands of Africa in the first instance, were creations of rival European imperialists who drew and, for a long time, managed them on the model of the boundaries of their own respective metropolitan countries. As has been discussed in several scholarly works, the boundaries of modern Africa are so much the result of European impositions that all the legal instruments for dealing with them have remained exactly the same "treaties," "agreements," "protocols," and "notes" as were established between the erstwhile European colonial powers.

The rulers of independent African states, territorial successors of the former European colonies, have maintained the status quo. Not only were the legal instruments inherited; the institutions, personnel and the procedures have either remained the same or were derived from the methods which Europeans used in dealing with boundary problems. Little wonder, then, that border relations in Africa have continued to feature the same kinds of mutual jealousies, conflicts and tensions that characterized such relations in the Europe of the nation-state. Structurally, the borders of Africa pose as many obstacles to international cooperation and regional integration as their European equivalents did.

African and Africanist scholars are quick to lament that Africa was badly partitioned. They point out that boundaries of modern African states are artificial, often arbitrarily drawn with little or no regard for preexisting socioeconomic patterns and networks; that the boundaries have erratically split unified culture areas and hopelessly disintegrated coherent natural planning regions and ecosystems; that a great deal of Africa's contemporary economic problems have stemmed from the fact of territorial division into such a large number of competitive, rather than complementary, national economies; and, finally, that many of the continent's current political problems have originated from the "arbitrary nature of the colonial boundaries [which, among other things] results in . . . artificially juxtaposing incompatible or antagonistic groups" (Balandier 1966: 44).

However, the crucial point that is often missed is that, in all these matters, the boundaries of national states in Africa are not substantially different in nature from the European ones. Far more than Africa – the second largest continent in the world, divided into 54 national states – Europe, territorially less extensive than West Africa, has been structured into 35 or so sovereign states, including such ministates as the Vatican City, Andorra, Liechtenstein, and Luxembourg, not to count enclaves such as Llivia, a Spanish settlement across the Franco-Spanish border in France, completely surrounded by French villages.

The point has been elaborately made elsewhere that Africa was not the only or even the first continent to be partitioned (Asiwaju 1985: 223); that Africans were not the first or the only partitioned peoples; that, indeed, the European partition of Africa in the last quarter of the nineteenth century was essentially an extension of a process by which the same powers who partitioned Africa had partitioned and were continuing to partition their own continent and peoples among themselves; and, finally, that the phenomenon of artificially partitioned ethnic groups, or what Myron Weiner (1985) has called "transborder peoples," is not just a feature of boundaries and borderlands in Africa but also a feature of Europe and the wider nation-state world created by Europe.

One major limitation in arguments that seek to emphasize the uniqueness of the European experience vis-à-vis the rest of the world is that they are often made without the benefit of empirical data derived from in-depth case histories. Take, for example, Prescott's influential opinion that "there are more important differences in respect of the boundary evolution between Europe and the rest of the world than there are between any other two continents" (1987: 175). Each of Prescott's arguments has been strongly contradicted or, at least, seriously questioned by findings of case studies.

The first of such arguments, for instance, is that "boundary evolution in Europe was entirely an indigenous process . . . [whereas] in the other continents . . . the indigenous process of boundary evolution was overlain and generally halted by [European] colonial activities" (Prescott 1987: 175). A major problem with this argument is that it leaves unanswered the fundamental question of what it is to be "indigenous." Except when a subjective racial perspective is adopted or the reference is to an imaginary Europe that is socially an undifferentiated mass, it is difficult to see any significant difference between, on the one hand, the position of the Catalans, "an ethnic group, neither French nor Spanish" (Sahlins 1989: 22), split into two by the Franco-Spanish border drawn through their homeland in the Cerdanya valley of the eastern Pyrenees; and, on the other hand, the Yoruba, also an ethnic group, neither English nor French, split into two by the Anglo-French colonial (now international) boundary between British Nigeria and French Dahomey (now Republic of Benin) drawn through the homelands of specific subgroups in Western Yorubaland (Asiwaju 1976).

Available evidence leaves one in no doubt of the extremely close similarity between Catalan and Western Yoruba perceptions and modes of response to the intersovereignty borders drawn and maintained across the respective ethnic home-lands, the Catalonian stretching further south and north of the Franco-Spanish border, just like the specific Yoruba subgroups in Western Yorubaland in the wider context of the culture area that stretches much further east and west of the Nigeria–Dahomey colonial border. For Catalans and the Western Yoruba, the border between France and Spain in the European case, and that between British Nigeria and French Dahomey in the African case, could not be considered as indigenous.

European national states were as much territorial as their colonial possessions in Africa and elsewhere. Both in Europe and Africa, as the Catalan and Western Yoruba case histories can be effectively used to demonstrate, partitioned and locally impacted communities initially viewed the intersovereignty boundaries in their backyards as impositions from outside. Politically, socially and economically, the boundaries of modern national states, in Europe first and then in Africa and elsewhere, were known to have intruded into and strongly impacted on local community life. In the Cerdanya and Western Yorubaland, as indeed in other specific partitioned ethnic homelands, acceptance or rejection of the boundary was dictated, as is to be expected, by the extent to which the boundary policy in operation coincided or failed to coincide with the interest of the respective local communities or even individuals. Both the Catalan and Yoruba case studies featured very interesting episodes of armed revolts and, more typically, protest migrations against unpopular policy measures in operation from time to time on one or the other side of the borders (Asiwaju 1976: chs 5 and 6; Sahlins 1989: ch. 3).

With regard to the problem of national identity faced by politically partitioned peoples, the argument for comparability of African and European experiences has been remarkably reinforced by the findings of yet another fascinating case study, that by William Miles (1994), focusing on the Hausa astride the Nigeria–Niger boundary. Not only has the Hausa study complemented the Yoruba case study by its specific focus on the problematic of national identity in a borderland, it has shared more or less the same basic concerns with our European case, that of the Catalans across the Franco-Spanish border. By reason of the divergent socialization processes put in place on the different sides of the borders, the elites are drawn in opposite directions in their sense of national identity in spite of a common prepartition history and indigenous culture.

At home or overseas, European powers are known to have adopted basically the same methods and procedures to acquire and possess territories for the state. While the time-frame might be substantially different, taking centuries in Western Europe and only a few decades to accomplish in Africa, the processes are exactly the same everywhere. Both in Europe and Africa, for example, boundary evolutions passed through basically the same three phases of allocation, delimitation and demarcation. In Alsace-Lorraine, as in the Cerdanya and Western Yorubaland, European statesmen, politicians and diplomats employed the same combinations of "conquest, trickery and cession" (Prescott 1987: 175) to acquire territory and achieve the allocation, delimitation and demarcation of the boundaries. A reader of the Catalan case study who is familiar with African parallels would be entertained by stories of identical diplomatic maneuvers between representatives of metropolitan states engaged in territorial acquisition both in Europe and overseas.

Especially intriguing is the way in which incidents of "blatant and unscrupulous manipulations of facts" (Sahlins 1989: 47) by one party in diplomatic negotiations vis-à-vis the other, in Europe, remind one of the same type of "maneuver" in Africa in the era of the European scramble and partition. Take the issue of the widespread incidence of falsified protectorate treaties produced by German officials to prove or strengthen their case against rival British or French claims in West, Central and East Africa. Most of such treaties were believed to have been forged or invented in ways similar to the "many reasons" that Marco, one of the officials on the French side of the negotiation for the 1659–1660 Treaty of the Pyrenees, had to invent simply to make the Spanish side "uncomfortable" (Sahlins 1989: 47).

In the Cerdanya, as in Western Yorubaland and similar African localities that have been subjected to focused research, the negotiations at the allocation and delimitation stages of boundary evolution were undertaken exclusively by high-up state function-aries with little or no reference to the interests and views of the local people. Thus what has been written with respect to the Franco-Spanish boundary in the Cerdanya could very well have been written about other similarly partitioned localities in Africa or elsewhere: namely, that at the end of the allocation and delimitation exercises, what the two sides of the negotiations settled for was "a boundary that was not a natural frontier . . . [but an artificial boundary] which ran counter to any conceivable history of the Cerdanya" (Sahlins 1989: 53).

At these stages – of allocation, dominated by heads of state signing treaties, and of delimitation, dominated usually by the foreign ministers – certainty about geo-graphical positions did not count for much. Cardinal Mazarin, the French foreign minister and key figure in the negotiations of the Treaty of the Pyrenees, was already three weeks into the discussions at the Isle of Pheasants before consulting a map (Sahlins 1989: 39), and when, in the Accord of May 13, 1660, the Spanish conceded "thirty-three villages together with their jurisdictions," it was not known what and where these villages were,[2] or more importantly, what the actual limits were of their jurisdiction (Sahlins 1989: 48–50). This uncertainty eventually gave rise to familiar controversy when technical experts appointed by the two governments to carry out the actual demarcation finally met to undertake the practical counting, leading to the French acquiring "effectively more than fifty villages" instead of the 33 stipulated in the delimitation accord (Sahlins 1989: 49).

Thus, contrary to another patently faulty argument that boundary evolution in Europe, unlike in other continents, was rendered much simpler because of a more complete geographical knowledge (Prescott 1987: 176), the same kind of problems of uncertainty of knowledge about the limits of preexisting jurisdictional sovereignties were encountered in respect to traditional African states as was the case with villages, counties, cantons and bailiwicks, to mention just a few examples of the jurisdictional units of pre–nation-state Europe. Indeed, so elusive did the limits of jurisdic-tional authorities prove that the transition from jurisdictional to territorial sovereignty and boundaries took centuries to attain in Europe: in the particular case of the Cer-danya, this was not fully achieved until 1868. At this final phase of boundary evolu-tion, that of demarcation, whether in Europe or Africa, the ultimate alignments were more significantly influenced by grass-roots level realities than ever entered into considerations at the earlier phases of allocation and delimitation.

If, then, there are more similarities than differences in the history, structure and functions of state territories and boundaries in Europe and Africa, lessons of experience in the one continent must not be lost on those engaged in the scholarly study and policy analysis of the problems in the other continent.

The history of modern Europe, as homeland of the nation-state and its border problematics, confronts Africa with one of only two choices: the path of war and human tragedy, which constituted the emphasis in the era from the Treaty of Westphalia in 1648 to the end of World War II, on the one hand; and, on the other, the option of peaceful cooperation characterized by commitment to regional integration and transborder cooperation of the period since 1945. While in the one era, that of nationalism, the basic concern was for sovereignty and boundary maintenance, in the other period, of internationalism and regionalism, the dedication has been to a simplification of the border. As Lord Curzon (1907) indicated, the choice is between boundaries as factors of war and death and boundaries as factors of peace and life.

The choice for Africa cannot be the war and death side of the border equation. The lessons in European experience are not to be sought in Europe's pre-1945 history, characterized by negative nationalism, international conflicts and extremely destructive territorial wars. Nor should the tragic events that led to the disintegration of Yugoslavia be regarded as the likely outcome for Africa's mostly multi-ethnic ex-colonial states. What must be of great attraction for Africa is Europe as the region of the most evolved history of political boundaries, and the alternative provided by the practical and fruitful experience of the post-1945 era. This period has witnessed phenomenal achievements not just in matters of regional integration, but also and even more significantly in the elimination of borders as barriers and precipitants of conflicts, and their systematic entrenchment as catalysts for international cooperation and sustainable development.

THE BORDER FOCUS IN THE EUROPEAN INTEGRATION PROCESS

Africa cannot achieve regional integration without having directly to confront the question of the obstructionist and conflict-generating boundaries between the national states seeking to integrate. There has to be a concerted effort to convert those boundaries from their prevailing traditional postures as ramparts into new roles and functions as bridges of active cooperation between territorially adjacent states, consistent with a serious commitment to a wider regional integration agenda. In this regard, Africa's search for relevant lessons in the post-1945 European historical experience must not be limited to studies and analyses of the workings of the European Economic Community (EEC) and its better known establishments in Brussels; the search must be purposively extended to focus particularly on the extremely crucial complementary role of the Council of Europe in Strasbourg, including such of its pivotal institutions as the European Conference of Ministers Responsible for Regional Planning and, more critically, the Conference of Local and Regional Authorities of Europe, which, together, have distinguished themselves in pioneering and nurturing the institutionalization of a distinctly cooperative border policy regime for postwar Europe.[3]

There is no doubt about the tremendous contribution of the European Economic Community and its better resourced institutions in Brussels to the entrenchment of the new transborder cooperation policy regime in Europe of the Union. This is especially so with regard to the issue of a special development focus on the border areas. Consider, for example, the benchmark execution of the Single European Act of 1986 and the emphasis placed on the primacy of "regions" as basic units of planning and development. The border areas have been exceptionally privileged by that policy instrument. Apart from being the heart of the "transregional" category, so explicitly defined in the Act as "regions in different States, especially those on both sides of borders between member States," the European border areas also benefited directly from the disbursement of a special European Regional Development Fund, which finances a five-yearly program to support interregional development between peripheral border areas. This program, known by the acronym INTERREG, was launched in 1990 to accelerate infrastructural improvement of the European "cross-border areas," in borderlands similar to those at the meeting of Scotland and England, "the Border Country" described by George Frazer (1986: 37). As we shall see below, the concept of *pays frontières* or "cross-border areas" caught the fancy of the most influential African integrationist of our time, Alpha Oumar Konare, who, successively as president of Mali, chairman of the Economic Community of West African States (ECOWAS) and, latterly, chairperson of the African Union Commission, has introduced it to all three interconnected policy-making arenas.

But substantial as the EEC's contributions have been, it is very important to recognize that the initiation and nurturing of the more challenging political aspect of the formulation of the new territorial and border policy for postwar Europe were achievements, primarily, of the Council of Europe. It was founded in 1949 and headquartered in Strasbourg, the highly strategic and historic French border town on the Rhine, on the boundary with Germany, a town which also eventually became the seat of the European Parliament. Together with such subinstitutions as the European Conference of Ministers Responsible for Regional Planning, and more especially, the Conference of Local and Regional Authorities of Europe, the Council of Europe provided the institutional framework for all the vital processes that preceded and have since followed the adoption in 1984 of the truly historic European Outline Convention on Transfrontier Cooperation between Territorial Communities or Authorities.[4]

The Convention is, perhaps, the most significant policy instrument ever adopted by any regional body anywhere in the world, targeted on a determination to convert international boundaries and borderlands from classical nation-state postures as barriers into more regional-integration friendly and conflict preventative roles and functions as bridges of cooperation between integrating states. The preparatory series of European Symposia on Transborder Cooperation in 1972 and 1975, the drafting of the Convention up to and including its opening to signature in Madrid in 1980, plus the flurry of meetings and conferences to ensure implementation after it came into force in August 1984 were all activities that took place and are still taking place within the framework of the Council of Europe.[5] The Council of Europe provided the political space for the vital contributions made by civil society organizations, notably the Association of the European Border Regions and the European academic community. The European Outline Convention provides and remains the inspirational model for Africa, including ongoing processes on the effective implementation of the African Union Border Programme.

AFRICAN BORDER POLICY AND THE ORGANISATION OF AFRICAN UNITY (OAU), 1963–2002

When, in the aftermath of the tragic World War II, European states were beginning to give serious thought to putting an end to the era of recurrent international conflicts and border wars and putting in place an alternative program of preventative regional integration and transfrontier cooperation, Africa was entering the new phase of decolonization or liberation and the attainment of political independence by the erstwhile European colonial territories.

The independence gained by modern African states was achieved in every case within the framework of the boundaries arranged in the context of the rivalries between the European powers and their notorious "scramble" for African territories at the turn of the nineteenth century. Ill-defined and hardly completely and satisfactorily demarcated, for the most part, African boundaries were fraught with enormous risks for conflict and tension within and, more particularly, between several territorially adjacent states. Rival interests in cross-border natural and strategic resources are unlikely to have helped matters.

Nevertheless, considerations of continental peace and jealous defense of newly won sovereignties dictated the maintenance of the inherited boundaries in preference to the alternative boundary redrawing that was and is still being advocated by some. It is against this background that one must seek to understand the policy of boundary maintenance initiated and vigorously sustained in the era of the defunct OAU from its inception in 1963 to its disbandment and replacement by the African Union in 2002. The OAU policy was anchored in the specific provisions in Articles II (1c) and II (3) of the foundation Charter and the Resolution of the very first session of the Assembly of Heads of State and Government, held in Cairo from July 17 to 21, 1964.

Thus, contrary to the opinion that the OAU did nothing about Africa's problematic borders (Soyinka 1994), the border factor was indeed at the forefront of the Organisation's policy agenda. However, as if to repeat and reorchestrate the opposite effect of the Berlin Treaty of February 26, 1885, which, instead of mitigating European powers' territorial rivalry in Africa, merely accelerated the pace of the scramble and the partition, the OAU Charter of 1963 and the 1964 Cairo Resolution were not notable for stemming the tide of boundary disputes and conflicts in the continent. The proposal made by Nigeria to the 37th Session of the OAU Council of Ministers in Nairobi in 1981, for the establishment of an OAU Boundary Commission that would function as the continental body's own specialized border problem-solving agency, indicated the gravity and topicality of border-referenced conflicts in the region. The fact that the 1981 proposal was revived as an item on the 1991 OAU

Summit agenda at Abuja illustrates the extent to which Africa's border problems have remained sensitive, if not degenerating into a running sore, mostly because of inadequate care.

The number of actual border wars and threats of war is legion. To the long list of cases of conflict arising from territorial claims made by specific states over their proximate neighbors may be added the equally numerous examples of civil wars incidental to secession attempts within borders of a good number of the member states. Accordingly, Africa became the theater of the most devastating wars that have plagued the world since 1945. The causes of these conflicts vary as widely as the specific cases themselves. However, with particular reference to the international dimension in focus, a great many of the occurrences have involved the problems of the generally indeterminate character of the borders, and rival national interests in transborder economic and strategic resources. Whatever the causes, the border wars and threats of war have continued to compromise the prospects of peace and stability and proved completely detrimental to the cause of regional integration and the orderly economic planning and development of the continent and its constituent subregions.

If, in the twenty-first century, Africa is to leave behind the era of recurrent and destructive border conflicts and be launched into a new millennium of durable peace and accelerated development of the type that has been witnessed in the post-1945 European Community, policy-makers and executors in the continent must be made to embrace a radicalized reconceptualization of the role of shared international boundaries. In the place of the familiar but essentially obsolete sovereignty-insistent assumptions and perspectives which have tended to perpetuate the vision of shared borders more as factors of conflict than of cooperation between states, emphasis must now be placed on the functions of borders as bridges rather than barriers between contiguous national states.

The "war" and "death" factors in a border equation, as noted earlier, must be deliberately and systematically discarded in favor of the "peace" and "life" alternatives. Transborder natural and human resources, traditional precipitants of conflicts and wars, must now be systematically explored and promoted for their potential as factors of opportunity for positive international interaction. The recently inaugurated African Union Border Programme is the response to this quest for a more appropriate border policy regime.

THE AFRICAN UNION BORDER PROGRAMME

The African Union Border Programme (AUBP) marks the climax of the long process of the evolution of comprehensive border problem-solving policy-making at continental level.[6] As already mentioned, it is based on a formal Declaration of the first ever Conference of African Ministers in Charge of Border Issues held in Addis Ababa in 2007 and the firm endorsement by the African Union Executive Council made in Accra in the same year.

Since African countries attained political independence, their borders, drawn in a context of rivalries between European imperialist powers and their late nineteenth-century scramble for territories in Africa, have been a recurrent source of conflict both within and, particularly, between the discrete sovereign states. Most of the borders are poorly defined and not adequately demarcated. The location of strategic and natural resources in cross-border areas has posed additional challenges. The AUBP has been designed to respond comprehensively to these and related challenges.

The Programme is based on the conviction that, while the intersovereignty boundaries may be maintained to preserve the identity of each individual state, the achievement of greater unity and solidarity among modern African states and peoples requires the reduction of the burden of the borders separating them. The member states of the African Union are correctly persuaded that by transcending the borders as barriers and promoting them as bridges linking the states with one another, Africa can significantly deepen the ongoing regional integration process and, by so doing, strengthen continental unity and promote regional peace, security, stability and sustainable development.

The AUBP is implemented interactively at national, regional, and continental levels. As clearly indicated in the Ministerial Declaration, the responsibility at each of these levels is defined on the basis of the principle of subsidiarity, wherein decisions are made at the political levels presumed to be the most appropriate ones for successful outcomes, and at levels of decision-making closest to those people most directly affected. With regard to border delimitation and demarcation, for example, primary responsibility lies with the sovereign decision of states. They must take the necessary steps to facilitate the process of delimitation and demarcation, including maritime boundaries, where such an exercise has not yet been undertaken. The Regional Economic Communities (RECs) and the African Union are to assist the states in mobilizing the necessary resources and expertise, including facilitating exchange of experience and promoting inexpensive but effective border delimitation and demarcation practices. The AU Commission should conduct a comprehensive inventory of the state of African boundaries and coordinate the efforts of the RECs. The Commission should also launch a large-scale initiative aimed at sensitizing the international community to the need to mobilize the required resources and other related support, including ensuring that the former colonial powers grant free access to all the information in their possession regarding delimitation and demarcation of the African borders.

Concerning cross-border cooperation, similarly multiple-level roles have been stipulated and prescribed for the various stakeholders, including, in this case, the local territorial authorities and communities at subnational level. Thus, the local stakeholders should be the direct initiators of cross-border cooperation under the auspices of the states. The states should, with the assistance of the AU, facilitate the expression of local initiatives and mandate the RECs to implement regional support programs for cross-border cooperation.

The RECs and AU, following the example of the Council of Europe with respect to the achievement of the 1984 European Convention on Transfrontier Cooperation between Local and Territorial Authorities or Communities and the European Economic Community with regard to the creation of regional development funds, should provide the legal frameworks necessary for the development of cross-border cooperation and establish regional and continental funds for financing such cooperation. The AU should take necessary steps to ensure the inclusion of cross-border cooperation in all major international initiatives launched for the continent. It should also coordinate and facilitate the exchange of information and good practice between the RECs.

As regards capacity-building, the AU Commission is to carry out an inventory of African institutions that offer training in this domain; explore avenues for collaboration with relevant training centers outside Africa, especially the European Union; and, on the basis of the aforementioned exercise, design a capacity-building program in the area of border management, including cross-border cooperation and wider regional integration orientations.

The planning of the AUBP implementation strategy was the subject of a special international seminar held in Djibouti on December 1–2, 2007. The seminar was well attended by representatives of Africa's Development Partners in Europe, North America and Asia, as well as of the United Nations and its relevant organs. Apart from mobilizing for funding and technical support, an important outcome of the active interest taken in the AUBP by foreign national and international organizations and institutions is the demonstration of a commonality of interests based on the global replication of the African experience of the phenomena of international boundaries and borderlands.

Of particular importance here, and of special relevance to this essay, is the exceptionally active participation of Europeans and European organizations, notably representatives and high-ranking officials of the European Commission and the policy-influential Association of European Border Regions:[7] they not only attended but made powerful contributions, both at the Djibouti Seminar and in the other AUBP foundation events, including the crucial preceding Meetings of Experts in Bamako in March and Addis Ababa in June 2007.

European encouragement has since continued into the ongoing critical phase of program implementation, not only in terms of weighty contributions to discussions at each of the five regional sensitization workshops in 2008 and 2009 in Kampala for East Africa, Algeria for North Africa, Ouagadougou for West Africa, Libreville for Central Africa, Windhoek for Southern Africa, and more recently, at the Second Conference of Ministers in Charge of Border Issues in Addis Ababa in March 2010. The only source of funding for the actual implementation of the AUBP, so far, is also European, a grant-in-aid of the German foreign ministry, administered through a specially created African Commission desk of the German Technical Cooperation Agency (GTZ) in Addis Ababa.

To date, the implementation process has followed the three broad operational areas of the AUBP objectives, and in proportion to the relatively limited funding obtained from the GTZ. In respect of border demarcation, which constituted the top priority, the specific projects undertaken are the completion of the Mali–Burkina Faso border as delineated in the preceding judgment of the International Court of Justice, and Mozambique's borders with its neighbors. Also closely related to issues of border delimitation and demarcation were the international Symposium on Rivers and Lakes Boundaries, held in Maputo, Mozambique, in December 2008, and the African Regional Conference on Maritime Boundaries held in Accra in December 2009, all funded from the GTZ grant-in-aid.

The capacity-building component of the AUBP implementation schedule has absorbed the bulk of the GTZ support fund, surpassed only by the allocation to the border delimitation and demarcation, and the concentration has been on creating and reinforcing the requisite capacity of the African Union Commission itself. A very significant achievement in this regard is the establishment of the AUBP Unit, a specific office with personnel and equipment, within the framework of the Conflicts Management Division of the Department of Peace and Security, which had exercised the responsibility of coordinating the Programme. One critical component of the AUBP Unit is the Border Data Base, an extremely useful Geographic Information System, relevant to the success of the Programme's implementation. The Unit has also provided the framework for coordinating two important book projects – one titled *From Barriers to Bridges: The African Union Border Programme* (in press), aimed at providing readers with relevant information on the historical evolution and milestone policy instruments relating to the Programme; and the other, published in March 2010 in Addis Ababa, on *Boundary Delimitation and Demarcation: An African Union Border Programme Practical Handbook*.

Outside Addis Ababa, a fraction of the allocation from the GTZ fund for 2008 was made available to the African Regional Institute that operates to promote training and research for African cross-border and regional integration initiatives, located at Imeko, Ogun State, Nigeria. This relatively modest budgetary allocation enabled the institute not only to improve the infrastructural facilities but also to organize two major training programs. The first was a Train-the-Trainers Programme on International Boundaries and Borderlands Studies in August and September 2008, which involved a participating class of 27 mid-career academics drawn from 13 selected Nigerian universities, to sensitize them to relevant research and teaching interests. The second was a one-week pilot Executive Border Security Training Programme held in December 2008, which enlisted the participation of senior supervising personnel of police and border-enforcement agencies, drawn from both sides of the Nigeria–Benin border in Ogun State.

THE CHALLENGES OF COMPARATIVE HISTORICIZATION

The point of this essay is that the lead being provided by Europe and Europeans to support the AUBP should be seen as deeply rooted in the comparability of the modern state territorial structures and boundaries in both Europe and Africa, those in the latter being evidently the extensions of those in the former. In metropolitan Europe, as in Africa, where the modern state is an implantation of erstwhile imperialist Europe, international boundaries and borderlands are known to pose a paradox.

Raimondo Strassoldo has explained the "ambiguities": "[Borders] divide and unite, bind the interior and link it with the exterior; [they] are barriers and junctions, walls and doors, organs of defence and attack. Frontier areas [borderlands] can be managed so as to maximize either of such functions. They can be militarized as bulwarks against neighbours, or made into areas of peaceful interchange" (1989: 393).

It is the fact of these "ambiguities" that had obviously impelled Lord Curzon in 1907 to observe, as we noted earlier, that "frontiers [i.e., borders] are, indeed, the razor's edge on which hang suspended the modern issues of war or peace, or of life or death to nations." As we have noted, these "ambiguities" suggest that the range of policy choices open to decision-makers about border management is limited to only two options, no matter how well delineated and demarcated the borders may be: conflict or cooperation; or, to return to Lord Curzon, "war or peace . . . death or life."

The Berlin West African Conference of November 15, 1884 through February 26, 1885 marked for Africa the inception of the modern state system based on the exportation of the classical nation-state of pre-1945 Europe, with a demand for a precise and, characteristically, artificial and often arbitrary territorial framework. While the founding fathers of the Organisation of African Unity were well aware of the problems of peace and stability posed by the colonially inherited state territories and boundaries, the policy of retention that they initially wisely decided on and sustained always stood in need of a supplementary instrument for a systematic conversion from an inherited role of boundaries as barriers to more positive roles as bridges between the member states.

However, the primary concern for sovereignty and a preoccupation with the total liberation of the continent from all traits of European colonialism, including the apartheid regime in South Africa, did not leave room for the next-level policy review to bring about a systematic conversion of the continent's colonially inherited borders from being barriers and conflict generators into becoming bridges, conflict preventers and facilitators of a special development focus. In spite of relevant scholarly research, publications and advocacy, mainstream African policy-making continued throughout the years of the OAU to ignore the demonstrable potential of the continent's international boundaries for cooperation, peace and security building and sustainable development.[8]

Indications for the more desirable policy turnaround began to show in the dying hours of the Organisation and its eventual replacement by the African Union. Witness, for example, the adoption of the Memorandum of Understanding on Security, Stability, Development and Cooperation in Africa (CSSDCA) by the Assembly of Heads of State and Government, held in Durban, South Africa, in July 2002; and, more importantly, the provisions of the Constitutive Act of the African Union. Although its Article 4b lists among the principles of the Union respect for borders that exist on attaining independence, the Act also stipulates that the Union's objectives include achieving greater unity and solidarity among African peoples, accelerating the political and socioeconomic integration of the continent and promoting peace, security and stability. In all these respects, the African Union Border Programme adopted in June 2007 is, to date, the climax and most inclusive policy instrument. Although the contents are distinctively African, there is no doubt about the historical impact and stamp of the European Union on the format of both the African Union Commission and even the African Union Border Programme.

This essay certainly bears all the features of the standard disadvantages of comparative historical methodology.[9] As listed by Jorgen Kocka, these include overdependence on secondary literature, because the linguistic skills required for cross-cultural comparisons at the level of primary and archival sources exceed the abilities of most historians; taking cases out of their ordinary spatial and temporal locations and contexts; isolating otherwise interconnected events to permit their being meaningfully compared, an approach that runs foul of mainstream disciplinary doctrine; and, finally, the absence, generally, of causal interactions between the two or more social phenomena focused on (Kocka 2003: 39–40, cited in Lindenfeld 2003–4: 122–123).

However, and as Kocka himself has admitted, these disadvantages of "far-flung, decontextualized comparisons" (Kocka 2003: 40) are outweighed by the benefits, including "a more enhanced heuristic value; more easily demonstrated relevance to 'a global age'; and, above all, the bridging of the gaps often created by commonplace engagements with overspecialization. While not overlooking the contextual distinctiveness of each region, modern state territories and boundaries in Africa and other regions of former European colonization are too similar to those of the erstwhile metropolitan countries for any meaningful historicization of the former to ignore a comparison with the other. Africa's search for "best practices" in the management of boundary problems can ill-afford to lose sight of the lessons in the historical experience of Europe.

NOTES

1   The content of this section draws on Asiwaju 2003.
2   Compare this observation with the more popular one made by Lord Salisbury, the well-known British prime minister, in an after-dinner speech delivered in London on the occasion of the signing of the Anglo-French Convention of 1890 that delimited the Nigeria–Niger border: "We have been engaged in drawing lines upon maps where no white man's foot ever trod; we have been giving away mountains and rivers and lakes to each other, only hindered by the small impediment that we never knew exactly where the mountains and rivers and lakes were . . ." (cited in Anene 1970: 3).
3   For a more extensive discussion of the comparatively more significant historical role played by the Council of Europe as the "best practice" for Africa, see Asiwaju 1984.
4   The full texts of this and related legal instruments are contained in Ricq 1992.
5   The reports on the Symposia of 1972, 1975 and 1984 are fully cited in Nugent and Asiwaju 1996.
6   A handbook on the AUBP is currently in press. The book is intended to be an authoritative source of information and a guide for the on-going implementation process.
7   For up-to-date information on the AEBR and its operation, see *Practical Guide to Cross-Border Cooperation* (AEBR 2000), a compendium widely distributed at the Meeting of Experts for the AUBP in Bamako and Addis Ababa.
8   Much of my academic and policy research career and public life has been devoted to this cause, as is discussed in the essays in Akinyeye 2009. See also Asiwaju 1984.
9   For a more detailed discussion of the comparative methodological challenges and their application to African studies, see Asiwaju (2003–2004b), particularly the essays by Asiwaju (2003–2004a) and Manning (2003–2004). Although an anachronism, this special issue of

the journal *Afrika Zamani* is based on the presentations for the Specialized Theme One (African History in Comparative Perspective: New Approaches) at the 20th Congress of the Comité International des Sciences Historiques (International Committee of Historical Sciences) in Sydney in 2005.

REFERENCES

AEBR (Association of European Border Regions). 2000. *Practical Guide to Cross-Border Cooperation.* 3rd edn. European Commission.

Akinyeye, A.O., ed. 2009. *That They May Be One: African Boundaries and Regional Integration: Essays in Honour of Professor Anthony Ijaola Asiwaju.* Imeko: African Regional Institute.

Anene, J.C. 1970. *The International Boundaries of Nigeria, 1885–1960: The Framework of an Emergent African Nation.* London: Longman.

Asiwaju, A.I. 1976. *Western Yorubaland under European Rule, 1889–1945: A Comparative Analysis of French and British Colonialism.* London: Longman.

Asiwaju. A.I. 1984. *Artificial Boundaries.* Professorial Inaugural Lectures Series. Lagos: University of Lagos Press.

Asiwaju, A.I., ed. 1985. *Partitioned Africans: Ethnic Relations across Africa's International Boundaries, 1884–1984.* New York: St Martin's Press.

Asiwaju, A.I. 2003. *Boundaries and African Integration: Essays in Comparative History and Policy Analysis.* Lagos: PANAF.

Asiwaju, A.I. 2003–2004a. African history in comparative perspective. In *Comparative African History: Prospects and Challenges, special issue of Afrika Zamani: A Journal of African History* 11 and 12: 1–17.

Asiwaju, A.I., ed. 2003–2004b. *Comparative African History: Prospects and Challenges. Special issue of Afrika Zamani: A Journal of African History* (CODESRIA for the Association of African Historians, Dakar) 11 and 12.

AUBP (African Union Border Programme). 2010. *Boundary Delimitation and Demarcation: An African Union Border Programme Practical Handbook.* Addis Ababa: AUBP.

AUBP (African Union Border Programme). In press. *From Barriers to Bridges: The African Union Border Programme.* Addis Ababa: AUBP.

Balandier, G. 1966. The colonial situation: a theoretical approach. In I. Wallenstein, ed., *Social Change: The Colonial Situation.* New York: Wiley.

Curzon, Lord. 1907. *Frontiers.* Romanes Lectures Series. Oxford: Oxford University Press.

Frazer, G.M. 1986. *The Steel Bonnets: The Story of the Anglo-Scottish Border Reivers.* London: Harvill.

Kocka, J. 2003, Comparison and beyond. *History and Theory* 42: 39–44.

Lindenfeld, D. 2003–2004. The Taiping and the Aladura: a comparative study of charismatically based Christian movements. In A.I. Asiwaju, ed., *Comparative African History: Prospects and Challenges, special issue of Afrika Zamani: A Journal of African History* 11 and 12: 119–135.

Manning, P. 2003–2004. Commentary: a comparison of comparisons. In A.I. Asiwaju, ed., *Comparative African History: Prospects and Challenges, special issue of Afrika Zamani: A Journal of African History* 11 and 12: 182–190.

Miles, W.F.S. 1994. *Hausaland Divided: Colonialism and Independence in Nigeria and Niger.* Ithaca: Cornell University Press.

Nugent, P. and Asiwaju, A.I., eds. 1996. *African Boundaries: Barriers, Conduits and Opportunities.* London: Frances Pinter.

Prescott, J.R.V. 1987. *Political Frontiers and Boundaries.* London: Allen Unwin.

Ricq, C. 1992. *Handbook on Transfrontier Cooperation in Europe*. Strasbourg: Council of Europe.

Sahlins, P. 1989. *Boundaries: The Making of France and Spain in the Pyrenees*. Berkeley: University of California Press.

Soyinka, W. 1994. Bloodsoaked quilt of Africa. *Guardian*, May 17, 1994.

Strassoldo, R. 1989. Border studies: the state of the art in Europe. In A.I. Asiwaju and P.O. Adeniyi, eds, *Borderlands in Africa: A Multidisciplinary and Comparative Focus on Nigeria and West Africa*. Lagos: University of Lagos Press.

Weiner, M. 1985. Transborder peoples. In W. Connor, ed., *Mexican Americans in Comparative Perspective*. Washington, DC: Urban Institute.

CHAPTER 5

European Politics of Borders, Border Symbolism and Cross-Border Cooperation

James Wesley Scott

The issue of state borders, their functions, symbolism and changing significance presently looms larger than at any time during the last decades. The commonplace of global debordering, supported by optimistic notions of globalization and a new post–Cold War world order, has arguably succumbed to the reality of increasing complexity and instability in the world system. Even within an ostensibly borderless European Union (EU), national borders are again seen as central to the organization of political community and the protection of group interests. Clear symptoms of rebordering tendencies within various nation-states in the EU can be recognized in discussion on neonationalism, protectionism and illegal migrants crossing the EU's external borders – leading even to suggestions, as in the case of the Greek-Turkish border, of constructing formidable barrier fences.

These concerns are partly reflected by the contemporary state of the art in border studies; state borders are commonly understood as multifaceted social institutions rather than solely as formal political markers of sovereignty. In this view, borders help condition how societies and individuals shape their identities (Kolossov 2005; Meinhof 2002; Paasi 2001). At the same time, borders themselves can be seen as products of the social and political negotiation of space; they frame social and political action and are constructed through institutional and discursive practices at different levels and by different actors (Popescu 2008; van Houtum 2002). As Albert et al. argue, borders can be conceived as "social structures that are constantly and communicatively reproduced" (2008: 21). Borders are reproduced, for example, in situations of conflict where historical memories are mobilized to support territorial claims, to address past injustices, or to strengthen group identity, often by perpetuating negative stereotypes of the "other" (Papadakis 2005). However, through new

---

A Companion to Border Studies, First Edition. Edited by Thomas M. Wilson and Hastings Donnan.

institutional and discursive practices, contested borders can also be transformed into symbols of cooperation and of common historical heritage (Laine and Demidov 2011).

While the above considerations are of more general societal importance, they are of specific relevance to Europe and the political, social and cultural evolution of the European Union. The European Union has in large part been a project of transcending national borders and their logics of division. In the process, the EU has reterritorialized and reshaped nation-states through its policies and political institutions and through promoting a sense of supranational political community. At the same time, the EU is searching for a sense of political community based on (geo)political, social and cultural identity. For these reasons, the EU represents a particularly salient example of how the functions, significance and symbolism of state borders have shifted. While imperfect, the experiment of creating supranational sovereignty within Europe has not been attempted elsewhere and thus serves as a laboratory of political, social, economic and cultural modes of "bordering."

The notion of bordering that will be developed here suggests that borders are not only semipermanent, formal institutions but are also processes that cannot be finalized. At its most basic, the process of bordering can be defined as the everyday construction of borders, for example through political discourses and institutions, media representations, school textbooks, stereotypes and everyday forms of transnationalism. There are (at least) two broad and often overlapping ways in which bordering can be understood: one *pragmatic* (deriving generalizable knowledge from practices of border transcendence and confirmation), and the other *critical* (theorizing and questioning the conditions that give rise to border-generating categories). These bordering perspectives come together, among other ways, in the present geopolitical climate where, in stark contrast to the 1990s when discourses of "debordering" Europe enjoyed substantial currency, the EU's external borders have become formidable barriers symbolizing civilizational difference between East and West.

This essay consists of three parts. In the first I will relate the state of the art of border studies to processes of European integration and enlargement. The second part will address the concept of bordering, both in more general terms as well as with regard to the "politics of borders" that have been an integral part of the European Union's project of integration, enlargement and regional cooperation (e.g., as embodied by the European Neighbourhood Policy). The third section will then focus on cross-border cooperation as an expression of bordering within Europe and hence as border-transcending and/or border-confirming projects. These reflect the changing political significance and symbolism of borders in Europe but also raise questions as to the consequences of restrictive bordering practices, both for the EU and its regional neighbors.

EUROPEAN INTEGRATION AND THE STUDY OF BORDERS

Borders, whether de facto, de jure or popularly imagined, have had a powerful influence on the constitution of "Europe." Throughout Europe's long history, empires, kingdoms and (nation-)states have sought to manifest their power and unify heterogeneous groups of subjects by the symbolic and spatial bordering of territory. Collective representations of borders have been constructed through various means, including limes, fortifications, monuments and maps. These representations of space continue to influence popular imagination and political discourse; together with various other factors, they give sustenance to notions of a shared European history but also serve as powerful markers of national and local identity. This is particularly visible in the post–Cold War context of European interstate relations. With the collapse of ideological borders and geopolitical categories of European space based on bloc confrontation, historical and cultural notions have reemerged as important elements of regional identity and are captured by the renewal of concepts such as "Norden," "Central Europe," the "Balkans," and so on. Not surprisingly, the study of borders has rapidly developed within the context of European integration and its post-1989 enlargements.[1]

The suspension of hostile, dividing state borders and the negative impacts they have had on interstate relations is perhaps a uniquely European achievement. For this reason, the European Union's political identity – and indeed its raison d'être – are closely intertwined with the symbolism of transcending and transforming national borders in the interests of integration and peaceful coexistence. For example, cross-border cooperation, supported by the EU since the mid-1980s, has become a "trademark" of integration and Europeanization and is now firmly established in many border regions within the EU and in numerous neighboring countries. Furthermore, and in contrast to other international cooperation contexts such as North America, the European Union has actively promoted local and regional cross-border interaction through its regional development and structural aid programs.

Processes of EU integration and enlargement have affected how borders and boundaries have been perceived, both in the academy and in everyday life. Similarly, momentous transformations in the constitution of Europe's territorial states during the twentieth century have been inseparable from paradigmatic shifts in the perceptions of the political function and socio-spatial significance of its borders (Scott 2011a). Multifaceted changes in social life associated, for example, with globalization, postsocialist transition and sociocultural transformation have elicited reexaminations of received notions of state–society relations, citizenship and, as a result, state borders. The emergence of a European political community has itself shattered many certainties that have enshrined the nation-state as a locus of territorial identity. Nation-states have evolved into "states" with political actors exercising more limited sovereignty in terms of territorial governance, and have been robbed of the exceptionalist myths that were reified by Ratzel's 1903 and Maull's 1925 investigations into the "organic" relationships between cultures (Völker), territories (Boden), and the state (Staat) (Ratzel 1903; Maull 1925).

One of the major conceptual shifts in border studies thus lies in acknowledging that state borders are complex political institutions transecting social spaces not only in administrative but also in cultural, economic and functional terms (Donnan and Wilson 1999; Kramsch 2010; Liikanen 2011). Central to this perspective are multiple interpretations of border significance, border-related elements of identity formation, sociocultural and experiential bases for border-defining processes, power relations in society and geopolitical orders, as well as critical analyses of geopolitical discourses.

Border studies have also been amenable to the cultural turn in the humanities and social sciences (see Schimanski and Wolfe 2010). This is evidenced by a questioning of the essence and the assumed immutability of national identities as well as by challenges to the notion that nation-states might be – out of some civilizational necessity – a permanent feature of the world system.

One important characteristic of contemporary border studies is its frequent ethical nature. This is evident in the European context where the political concept of "open borders" has been decoded as a partial policy of exclusion that emphasizes border management and that has submitted state boundaries within Europe to general policing and security policies (Bigo and Guild 2005; van Houtum and Boedeltje 2009). By the same token, officially promoted "European" shifts in political/territorial identity and understandings of state borders often sit uncomfortably with identities that operate socially and culturally (and thus also politically) at the local level (Tamminen 2004). This dichotomy can be (and has been) expressed, if somewhat schematically, by simultaneous processes of "debordering" and "rebordering." What this simplified dichotomy implies is that sovereignty and borders have been de-emphasized within the process of EU integration and consolidation of political community. At the same time, borders as expressed by visa regimes, citizenship, residence rights and the physical control of the EU's external frontiers give evidence of the creation of new categories of cultural/geographical distinction and thus of new contested and partly dividing borders (Pickering 2011). It is also necessary to interpret political, social and cultural framings of state borders as competing projects. While the softening of borders is often seen as a fundamental precondition for greater democracy, many critics consider, on the contrary, that national borders are the natural frame for political community. In this sense, the symbolisms of "open," "permeable," or "closed" borders are an elementary part of the discussion on the future of national (e.g., European) democracies (see Jönsson et al. 2000).

THE BORDERING PERSPECTIVE

Border concepts have evolved around specific aspects of societal transformation that problematize relationships between the state, state territoriality, citizenship, identity and cross-border interaction (these have often been referred to, and sometimes confusingly, in terms of "postnational," "postcommunist," "postcolonial," and "postmodern" perspectives). The central conceptual shift lies in an understanding of borders as something inherently social and cultural rather than exclusively political (Kramsch and Brambila 2007; Scott and van Houtum 2009). Viewed from a contemporary perspective, a major research task lies in understanding borders through comparative frameworks that express their multilevel complexity – from the geopolitical to the level of social practices at and across borders. On this view borders can, for example, be studied in terms of local coping strategies, the development of cross-border cultural, economic and personal networks and their use as "place-making" instruments.

This complexity is captured by the concept of "bordering" in which borders are constantly made through ideology, symbols, cultural mediation, discourses, political institutions, attitudes and everyday forms of border transcending and border confirming. Put in somewhat different terms, bordering can be understood as the production and reproduction of boundaries in response to shifting relations between nation, state, territory and identities (Scott and van Houtum 2009). Through the concept of bordering, the somewhat abstract level of conceptual change can be brought to bear on actual "on the ground" situations. In this reading, bordering is, by nature, a multilevel process that takes place, for example, at the level of high politics, manifested by physical borders and visa regimes, as well as in media debates over national identity, legal and illegal immigration and language rights (see van Houtum and van Naerssen 2002; Newman 2006; Linde-Laursen 2011). Another important and closely related element in bordering is the embedding of social understandings of borders within everyday border crossings associated with gender, family sexuality and cultural expression.

The production and reproduction of borders affect, among others, processes of cross-border interaction, social and cultural relations, ethnic minority rights and everyday life in border regions themselves. Furthermore, as territorial markers of citizenship and "belonging," borders define access to national welfare systems, making it often very difficult for many migrant workers and persons sanctioned for "unauthorized mobility" to receive benefits or proper legal protections (see Pickering 2011). Similarly, borders can also be seen through the prism of gendered practices of migration in which women who seek to cross state borders "illegally" for economic, family or other reasons are subject to specific forms of criminalization and discrimination. Similarly, as Benhabib and Resnik (2009) show, female border-crossers face a set of specific challenges and dangers (such as sex-trafficking) that challenge traditional links between citizenship, social rights and cultural belonging. Borders can also be interpreted in terms of "ethnosexual frontiers," as "the territories that lie at the intersections of racial, ethnic, or national boundaries . . . sites where ethnicity is sexualized, and sexuality is racialized, ethnicized, and nationalized" (Nagel 2003: 14). As Nyman (2009) has shown in the case of literary treatments of immigrant romance and marriage, borders can be used as strategies of "hybridization," contesting traditional, middle-class (and often nationally oriented) notions of marriage as cultural assimilation.

The bordering perspective provides a powerful link between and among processes of social and political transformation, conceptual change and local experience. It is therefore also a theoretical and empirical tool with which to understand the deeper significance of borders in different political and cultural contexts. Important historical processes in this regard include nation-building, postcolonial experiences, cross-border and transnational conceptualizations of citizenship and identity, postsocialist transformation and post–Cold War geopolitics. In addition, all of these processes have profound political, economic and sociocultural consequences: not least because they reflect tensions in state–society relations, for instance, in challenges to the state's monopoly of power, the emergence of supranational political institutions, processes of economic and political integration, processes of Europeanization and reconfiguration of state borders.

Table 5.1 provides a schematic overview of ways in which the notion of bordering has been employed in European border research based on specific political, social and

Table 5.1 Categories of bordering

Bordering categories	Examples of bordering dimensions
Discursive (political and social framings)	– ways in which commonality/difference between groups is framed and referenced in cultural, ethnic, geographic and historical terms; – ways in which strategies, threats/common concerns, cooperation are framed through the use of border concepts
Practical (material and substantive areas)	cultural, pragmatic avenues of cross-border interaction and conflict amelioration; economic agendas of cooperation; political agendas; lifeworld strategies
Perceptual (group/individual/ place-based interpretations of borders)	group specific, locally specific conceptions of borders in terms of identity, community and belonging, everyday needs and strategies, everyday experiences
Representational (cultural, media generated images)	Literary and artistic works that reference borders in terms of – resistance and challenges to the exclusionary nature of borders; – transformation of border symbolisms; – expressions of identity and alienation related to borders

cultural perspectives. The concept of bordering is a way of understanding borders rather than a grand theory. As the table indicates, however, the concept points the way to an interdisciplinary and critical dialogue that breaks down communicative barriers between different schools of border research and thus different framings of borders. Thus, geopolitical discourses that create or confirm categories of cultural difference are not privileged over popular forms of identity politics or media representations of "otherness" – indeed, in this view they are often closely related. Furthermore, and as implied above, the bordering perspective in European border studies can be related to phases of EU integration, enlargement and postenlargement, as well as the political rationales and discourses they have brought forth. This includes, furthermore, understanding European borders as symbolic representations of different degrees of cultural affinity, familiarity and "otherness."

Arguably, the process of "Europeanization" – which involves a gradual diffusion of supranational and potentially "postnational" understandings of citizenship, territoriality, identity and governance – is closely related to changing concepts of borders, both within the EU and beyond the EU's own borders (Scott and Liikanen 2010). A central aspect of this process is the definition of rules, norms and practices that recast national spaces as integral elements of an international political community (O'Dwyer 2006); from this derive the objectives and values that create a common set of discourses in which various political and social issues can be negotiated. However, as Harmsen and Wilson (2000) indicate, Europeanization is a multidimensional process of change rather than mere policy convergence; it suggests cultural hybridization, social modernization as well as the adaptation of national political thinking to local, regional and supranational perspectives. One principal characteristic of Europeanization is the transcendence of strictly national orientations in public policy, development policies and identity. Indeed, the construction of the European Union is in large part an attempt to create a coherent political, social and economic space within a clearly defined multinational community (the EU 27). Borders play an important role in the representation of European nation-states and the EU itself, as well as in the representation of the EU's relations to its neighbors. Cross-border cooperation (CBC) at the interstate, regional and local levels is seen to provide ideational foundations for a networked Europe through symbolic representations of European space and its future development perspectives. As Anderson et al. (2003) have shown, CBC is not only a political but also a social and cultural arena; it has provided a framework within which new regional ideas and a reevaluation of national histories have been promoted (see below).

Nevertheless, this "postnational" debordering of the European Union that CBC often implies is at the same time problematic. The political identity of an integrated community of states such as the EU begs the question of the geopolitical significance and ultimate geographic location of the EU's external borders. Similarly, it also implies processes of bordering through which the political, social and cultural foundations of EU membership are defined. Thus, if cross-border cooperation within the EU can be understood as an exercise in the symbolic dismantling of borders and the consolidation of political community, the external projection of the EU – as a political, cultural, economic and social space – involves an emphasis of the EU's outer border, both in terms of border policies and symbolisms.

This is not only an academic question. With the inauguration of the European Neighbourhood Policy in 2004, the EU has envisaged new comprehensive cooperation agendas that cut across political, economic and cultural dividing lines and, in effect, involve the partial transfer of internal (community) practices beyond the EU's own borders (Scott 2011b). The EU's emerging geopolitics can be understood in terms of an internal consolidation of political community (in yet another sense of the term "Europeanization") and the development of regional partnerships with neighboring states (that is, as a "New Neighbourhood"). Both of these processes can be understood as examples of bordering in which geopolitical discourses and practices can be related to regional development issues. On the one hand, these bordering practices establish rules, objectives and discourses that promote common political agendas and a sense of community. On the other hand, they create a strategic distinction between "us" and "them" that serves to orient international cooperation. Various aspects of EU-Europeanization as well of the EU's relations within neighboring states are quite revealing in this context and will be briefly discussed below. The picture that emerges is one of contradictory bordering practices in which a considerable gap exists between geopolitical vision and its translation into action.

As this EU policy instrument evolves, tensions due to simultaneous dynamics of inclusion and exclusion are very much in evidence. The idea of a European Neighbourhood is telling in itself: here, a sense of inclusion and belonging to a working political community is implied despite the fact that direct membership is not an immediate or probable option for several states that consider themselves very close to the EU (Smith 2005). Therefore, and as Dimitrovova (2008), van Houtum and Boedeltje (2009) and others contend, bordering is taking place in the form of the creation of distinctions between groups of people according to varying degrees of "Europeanness" (e.g., EU-European, non-EU-European, close neighbor, distant neighbor). This is a logic informed by security and control concerns, a logic very much associated with state-centered politics of interest. Furthermore, while the EU expresses a desire to avoid new political divisions, new visa regimes and other restrictions of cross-border interaction threaten to exacerbate development gaps between the EU-27 and non-EU states.

INTERPRETING CROSS-BORDER COOPERATION THROUGH A BORDERING PERSPECTIVE

In the previous sections I have alluded to the multifaceted social character of borders as well as to the ambiguities of the European Union's bordering practices. Discussion will now focus on a specific issue – that of cross-border cooperation at the EU's internal and external borders. Cross-border relations in Central and Eastern Europe have changed dramatically during the last two decades. With the last vestiges of the "Iron Curtain" removed, both between East and West as well as within the former Soviet bloc itself, citizens, communities and regions have chosen to open new avenues of communication with their neighbors across state borders. Furthermore, in those contexts where states have (re)gained their independence and new borders have emerged,[2] Euroregions, cross-border city partnerships and similar cooperation vehicles have also come into being (Scott 2006). These attempts at cooperation with the EU and at the EU's external border aim at managing issues that transcend the confines of individual communities – issues that include social affairs, economic development, minority rights, cross-border employment and trade, the environment, and so on. Cross-border cooperation also involves attempts to exploit borderlands situations, using borders as a resource for economic and cultural exchange as well as for building political coalitions for regional development purposes (Popescu 2008).

Referring back to the general categories suggested above, cross-border cooperation reflects the multilayered and multifaceted nature of bordering processes. The EU has played a crucial role in supporting local and regional cross-border cooperation as these are seen to be important aspects of interstate integration and a mechanism for deepening relations with non-EU neighbors. However, cross-border cooperation has not only been based on top-down projects of framing borders and their wider European significance, but also on everyday political, social and cultural practices of border negotiation (Anderson et al. 2003). So-called Euroregions were pioneered and developed as locally based cooperation initiatives in Dutch-German border regions as early as the 1960s (Scott 2000). The officially publicized goal of these organizations has been to promote binational initiatives that address specific economic, environmental, social and institutional problems affecting their respective regions. At the same time, Euroregions have been exploited as vehicles for cultural communication across borders and as a means to diminish resentment and mutually "deconstruct" negative stereotypes.

Euroregions have also played an important role in channeling European regional development aid into border regions. In order to structure their long-term operations and, at the same time, satisfy new European requirements for regional development assistance, Euroregions periodically define transboundary development concepts (TDCs) that identify objectives of cross-border cooperation and define possible courses of action. TDCs build the basis for concrete projects, proposals for which can then be submitted to the EU, national governments or other funding sources for support. The success of the Euroregion concept is undeniable. These associations are now a ubiquitous feature along the EU's external borders as well in many non-EU European contexts (Bojar 2008; Perkmann 2002; Popescu 2006). The EU structural initiative INTERREG, now in its fourth programming phase (2007–2013), has supported numerous transboundary and transnational cooperation projects between regions. Financed out of the EU's structural funds, INTERREG has disbursed well over €10 billion, making it the community's largest structural initiative. In addition, programs targeted for Central and Eastern Europe and the former Soviet Union, most prominently PHARE (Pologne, Hongrie Aide à la Reconstruction Économique), TACIS (Technical Assistance for the Commonwealth of Independent States) and more recently the European Neighbourhood Policy Instrument, have provided supplemental funds for cross-border projects in regions on the EU's external boundaries.

At another, more symbolic level, Euroregions can be understood as a spatial metaphor in the sense that they evoke a sense of transnational community, developed in free association and contributing to wider European integration. Cross-border cooperation has thus been promoted by the EU on the assumption that national and local identities can be complemented (perhaps partly transcended) and goals of codevelopment realized within a broader – a European – vision of community. As such, borders have been used as explicit symbols of European integration, political community, shared values, and hence identity, by very different actors (Lepik 2009; Perkmann 2005; Popescu 2008). Consequently, the Euroregion concept has proved a powerful tool with which to transport European values and objectives.

Nevertheless, the normative political language of integration often contrasts with local realities where cross-border cooperation (CBC) reflects competing territorial logics at the EU, national, regional and local levels and conflicting attitudes toward more open borders (Popescu 2008). As a result, cross-border cooperation is not uncontested. A resurgence of nationalism and retreat into national cultures have taken place in several EU member states and have, for example, affected local cooperation between Germany and Poland and Hungary and Slovakia.[3] Conflicts between "Europeanizing" and "renationalizing" conceptions of borders can in fact be interpreted in terms of identity politics serving specific groups within border regions.

The EU has supported the establishment of Euroregions and other organizations that facilitate interregional networking but often attempts to impose its own particular agendas on local actors (Nielsen et al. 2009). Furthermore, national governments, particularly those of new members and neighboring states (such as Russia, Ukraine and Moldova), often view such border transcending exercises with skepticism and try to co-opt or regulate cross-border cooperation in ways that serve national interests (Popescu 2006). Frequently, popular attitudes toward cross-border cooperation are a rather unpredictable variable. For example, Meinhof (2002) has demonstrated how borders influence collective memories in border regions that have undergone signifi- cant political changes. As Meinhof and her fellow researchers have indicated, the trauma of Cold War separation and fortification of borders continues to affect the action spaces and perceptions of the "other side" – as in Austrian-Hungarian border regions – years after the fall of state socialism and despite active policies of European enlargement and integration.

The case of the German-Polish border region

The German-Polish border after 1989 is an excellent example of the multilayered nature of bordering and border representations in the contemporary European context. Through the use of symbolisms of the border as a unifying element between neighbors, the German-Polish relationship has been recast in a wider European context of overcoming the "scars of history."[4] Because of the legacy of Nazi aggres- sion and past conflict, the German-Polish relationship is a special one. Political cooperation, and most certainly cross-border cooperation, have been closely inter- twined with rapprochement and a desire to develop a culture of mutual goodwill. At the same time, the common border has become a backdrop for the orchestration of a new post–Cold War European order, one based on democratic values and with a clear mission of social transformation (Krätke et al. 1997; Scott 2007). As a result, much has been invested in the symbolism of binational cooperation as a response to historical traditions of conflict and prejudice (Bielawska and Wojciechowski 2008).

Despite some hesitation on the part of more conservative groups, political dis- courses at the highest levels of the German and Polish governments have thus pro- moted a conversion of negative border images of closure, separation and aggression into a site of affirmation of a new European future (as borders of cooperation). Aca- demic debates have mirrored these political and cultural reinterpretations of the German-Polish border with a view to transcending the historical legacy of national particularism and conflict (Bürkner 2002). Implicit in these debates has been a criti- cism of both Polish and German populist temptations to renationalize debate on territory and borders and to counter historical perspectives that might call into ques- tion the legitimacy of the post-1945 German-Polish border (Matthiesen and Bürkner 2001). This has been accompanied by literary and other cultural representations of the border as a "bridge" in which journalists, poets, writers and artists have partici- pated. One example of this is the "Slubfurt" artists' initiative located in the "twin cities" of Frankfurt (Oder) and Słubice and which aims to bring local societies closer together.[5] A similar example is that of architects and art historians who have attempted to "denationalize" the history of the border region by revealing its complex multi- ethnic past.

Meanwhile, the popular media have echoed tensions between official "borderless euphoria" and rejectionism in the local populace, particularly on the German side (Kotula 1994; Bürkner 2009). Local press coverage of day-to-day relations between Poles and Germans makes quite clear that European orientations of the local populace are much stronger on the Polish side and that German border cities have struggled to exploit positively the benefits of open borders (Lenz et al. 2009). These have brought out tensions between political, intellectual, business-oriented and cultural initiatives to de-emphasize confrontational difference and fears of the citizenry of insecurity, a loss of identity and decreasing social well-being (Armbruster and Meinhof 2004). Within this context, German-Polish Euroregions have promoted a cross-border platform for political dialogue and regional development that has struggled to gain more popular acceptance.

Bordering, cross-border cooperation and the Finnish-Russian case

The Finnish-Russian border, and thus the borderland, is an emblematic case of political change in post–Cold War Europe and an example where the reassessment of common historical experiences and relationships is serving to develop a new sense of cross-border "neighborliness" (Belokurova 2010). Of rather recent creation after Finnish independence in 1917, this border has been shaped as a consequence of wars, several territorial shifts and decades of closure. The EU-Russian relationship since 1991 has thus been one of cautious, perhaps uneasy, interaction; driven by pragmatism and the recognition of interdependence but yet informed by historical (mis) apprehensions. As a result, the Finnish-Russian border has remained in many ways a hard, separating border, albeit definitely more permeable since the elimination of Soviet-era travel restrictions. Within this environment, the bordering perspective allows for a highly complex interpretation of emerging cross-border cooperation in the Russian-Finnish borderlands.

Directly after the collapse of the Soviet Union, nostalgia, curiosity and the search for new opportunities generated new cross-border flows of people. Within this context of (re)discovering the "other side," an often ambiguous politics of memory has emerged in which war memorials, lost territories, borders, battlegrounds, sites of conflict, abandoned homes, settlements and so on have served to construct national identities but also to bridge cultural differences and transcend historical animosities. In this way, wartime experiences, expulsions and annexations are mixed with more positive historical associations with Czarist Russia in which Finland enjoyed a "pre-national" autonomy. Of particular salience to this discussion of bordering is the region of Karelia which straddles the common border. In terms of its historical development, Karelia can be understood as a zone of transition, politico-religious division and, most recently, of a Finnish-Russian rapprochement and reevaluation of common experience. The case of Karelia also reminds us that borderlands are often rich in historical memory and the nationally symbolic. In the past, Karelia has referred to an indeterminate territorial but very symbolic space that has in more recent times been charged with meaning for the formation of Finnish national identity (Härynen 2008). In a way similar to Shields's (1991) notion of liminal spaces, Häyrynen (2004) has described Karelia as a periphery within the Finnish national landscape imagery but also as a place of powerful nostalgic significance. Similarly, Böök (2004) describes the significance of Karelia (particularly the areas ceded to the Soviet Union after the war) as a past "heartland" of Finnish Orthodoxy and the mythical last reserve of the "original Finnish" *Kalevala* culture.

Politically, economically and culturally motivated cross-border cooperation (partly supported by the EU) is one aspect of this process. Contacts between universities have intensified, and representatives of local and regional governments have developed working relationships. The Euroregion Karelia, established in 2000, has been marketed as a pilot project for the creation of joint administrative structures between EU member states and Russian regional authorities (Shliamin 2001). From the Finnish perspective, the institutional forms adopted with Russian counterparts are seen as exporting "border know-how," generating a model or at least a set of experiences that can help elaborate cooperation policies at the EU's shifting external borders (Cronberg 2000; Eskelinen 2000). Thus, at one level, we can understand the Finnish-Russian borderlands as a product of "place-making" in the intentional sense of regional identity politics capitalizing on border locations, cross-border cooperation and a historical notion of cross-border region (the region of Karelia). At another level, these borderlands are characterized by more subtle processes of intercultural dialogue in which history and landscape and townscape symbolism are used in order to create narratives of cross-border "regionness." Finally, the borderlands can be understood as a state of mind in which local and regional identities reflect life on borders, and where changes in the political, functional and symbolic meanings of historical landscapes have had deep impacts on local communities and consciousness (Isachenko 2004, 2009). While the Karelian landscape has changed, intercultural dialogue (as a result of nostalgic tourism and greater general interaction) has now contributed to a shared notion of Karelia, with different discourses of region possible; post-Soviet images are now cognizant of the political reality and the multicultural nature of Karelia (Niukko 2009). For example, as Izotov (2011) illustrates, former Soviet border garrison towns have now become important tourist destinations, transforming both local identities and the perception of tourists from Finland, other parts of Russia and elsewhere.

It is important to emphasize, furthermore, that broader political and geopolitical contexts are at work here. Finnish-Russian cross-border interaction is strongly influenced both by Russia's postsocialist modernization project, the changing nature of Finnish-Russian relations and the increasing role of the EU as agenda-setter of regional cooperation. Karelia is a positive case of a mutual rediscovery and exploitation of historical commonalities, common landscapes and regional traditions, but it is not immune to the vicissitudes of security policies, strict border and visa regimes as well as the shifting fortunes of EU–Russia relations.

CONCLUSION

What is the practical utility of the bordering perspective? Bordering – used as an interpretive concept – brings out in rather sharp contours confrontations, for example, between politics of national historical memory and "postnational" identity politics that are played out in everyday life and virtually everywhere within Europe. This perspective also allows us to understand borders in ways that question, for example, nationalist or hegemonic interpretations of history, the geopolitical traditions of nation-states and the European Union's manipulation of border symbolisms in order to further its community-building agendas. As this discussion has suggested, the

European Union's project of supporting cross-border cooperation is as much about transcending borders as it is about confirming their community-building and stabilizing significance. In more recent years this has contributed to a trend of exclusion and closure that threatens to undermine the more progressive and idealist aspects of European integration.

Within this context, borders can be read in terms of (1) a politics of identity (who is *in*, who is *out*), (2) a geographical definition of difference (defining who is a neighbor, a partner, a friend or rival), and (3) a politics of interests (in which issues of economic self-interest, political stability and security play a prominent role).

Given this critical and contextualizing outlook, border studies can provide substantial contributions to conflict resolution, cross-border cooperation, intercultural understanding, cultural policy and other areas where borders have ambivalent or negative impacts on society. Despite its historical achievements in overcoming borders of animosity and confrontation, the European Union has no reason to be smug on this issue. As the historian Jürgen Kocka writes: "borders have to be drawn in the interests of identity, but they should be composed in such a way that Europe can continue to practise that which has always been its special strength: being open to the world, absorbing from others and assuming foreign elements. Difference and entanglement belong together" (2007: 48).

NOTES

1   See, for example, Paasi 1999; Berg and van Houtum 2003; Scott 2006.
2   Such as the Baltic States, Ukraine, Moldova, Russia and the Balkans.
3   See Bürkner 2006. In its edition of October 20, 2009, the Hungarian daily *Népszabadság* ("Nem jött létre a 'régiók Európája," reporter: István Tanács) lamented a lack of true cross-border cooperation with neighboring states, citing national particularisms and limited European vision.
4   Robert Schuman's pronouncement that national borders in Europe represented scars of history ("Les cicatrices de l'histoire") has become an evocative political discourse in the processes of European integration and enlargement.
5   For a wide array of German-Polish cultural initiatives, see the website of the Büro Kopernikus (www.buero-kopernikus.org).

REFERENCES

Albert, Mathias, Diez, Thomas and Stetter, Stephan. 2008. The transformative power of integration: conceptualizing border conflicts. In Thomas Diez, Matthias Albert and Stephan Stetter, eds, *The European Union and Border Conflicts: The Power of Integration and Association*, pp. 13–32. Cambridge: Cambridge University Press.

Anderson, James, O'Dowd, Liam and Wilson, Thomas M. 2003. Culture, cooperation and borders. In James Anderson, Liam O'Dowd and Thomas M. Wilson, eds, *Culture and Cooperation in Europe's Borderlands*, pp. 13–29. Amsterdam: Rodopi.

Armbruster, Heidi and Meinhof, Ulrike H. 2004. Memories of home? Narratives of readjustment on the German/Polish and former German/German borders. In Joanna Thornborrow and Jennifer Coates, eds, *The Sociolinguistics of Narrative*, pp. 41–65. Amsterdam: John Benjamins.

Belokurova, Elena. 2010. Civil society discourses in Russia: The influence of the European Union and the role of EU–Russia cooperation. *Journal of European Integration* 32 (5): 457–474.

Benhabib, S. and Resnik, J., eds. 2009. *Migrations and Mobilities: Citizenship, Borders, and Gender.* New York: New York University Press.

Berg, Eiki and van Houtum, Henk, eds. 2003. *Mapping Borders between Territories: Discourses and Practices.* Aldershot: Ashgate.

Bielawska, Agnieszka and Wojciechowski, Krzysztof. 2008. *Europäischer Anspruch und Regionale Aspekte. Grenzüberschreitende Universitäre Zusammenarbeit in der Deutsch-Polnischen Grenzregion Angesichts der Zukünftigen Herausforderungen in Europa.* Berlin: Logos.

Bigo, Didier and Guild, Elspeth, eds. 2005. *Controlling Frontiers: Free Movement into and within Europe.* Aldershot: Ashgate.

Bojar, Ewa. 2008. Euroregions in Poland. *Tijdschrift voor Economische en Sociale Geografie* 87 (5): 442–447.

Böök, Netta. 2004. Border Karelia through rose-coloured glasses? Gazes upon a ceded territory. *Fennia* 182 (1): 33–45.

Bürkner, Hans-Joachim. 2002. Border milieux, transboundary communication and local conflict dynamics in German-Polish border towns: the case of Guben and Gubin. *Die Erde* 133: 339–351.

Bürkner, Hans-Joachim. 2006. Regional development in times of economic crisis and population loss: the case of Germany's eastern border regionalism. In James Wesley Scott, ed., *EU Enlargement, Region-Building and Shifting Borders of Inclusion and Exclusion*, pp. 207–215. Aldershot: Ashgate.

Bürkner, Hans-Joachim. 2009. Der lokale Staat als Akteur im Feld kreativer Nischenökonomien. In Bastian Lange, Ares Kalandides, Birgit Stöber and Inga Well-mann, eds, *Governance der Kreativwirtschaft. Diagnosen und Handlungsoptionen*, pp. 247–259. Bielefeld: Transcript Verlag.

Cronberg, Tarja. 2000. Euroregions in the making: the case of Euroregio Karelia. In Pirkkolisa Ahponen and Pirjo Jukarainen, eds, *Tearing Down the Curtain, Opening the Gates: Northern Boundaries in Change*, pp. 170–183. Jyväskylä, Finland: University of Jyväskylä.

Dimitrovova, Bohdana. 2008. The re-making of Europe's borders through the European neighbourhood policy. *Journal of Borderlands Studies* 23 (1): 53–68.

Donnan, Hastings and Wilson, Thomas M. 1999. *Borders: Frontiers of Identity, Nation and State.* Oxford: Berg.

Eskelinen, Heikki. 2000. Co-operation across the line of exclusion: the 1990s experience at the Finnish-Russian border. *European Research in Regional Science* 10: 137–150.

Harmsen, Robert and Wilson, Thomas M. 2000. Introduction. In Robert Harmsen and Thomas M. Wilson, eds, *Europeanization: Institutions, Identities and Citizenship*, pp. 13–26. Amsterdam: Rodopi.

Häyrynen, Maunu. 2004. A periphery lost: the representation of Karelia in Finnish national landscape imagery. *Fennia* 182 (1): 23–32.

Häyrynen, Maunu. 2008. A kaleidoscopic nation: the Finnish national landscape imagery. In M. Jones and K.R. Olwig, eds, *Nordic Landscapes: Region and Belonging on the Northern Edge of Europe*, pp. 483–510. Minneapolis: University of Minnesota Press.

Isachenko, Gregory A. 2004. The landscape of the Karelian Isthmus and its imagery since 1944. *Fennia* 182 (1): 47–59.

Isachenko, Gregory A. 2009. Cultural landscape dynamics of transboundary areas: a case study of the Karelian Isthmus. *Journal of Borderlands Studies* 24 (2): 78–91.

Izotov, Alexander. 2011. Repositioning a border town: Sortavala. In Heikki Eskelinen, Ilkka Liikanen and James W. Scott, eds, *The EU–Russia Borderland.* London: Routledge.

Jönsson, Christer, Tägil, Sven and Törnqvist, Gunnar. 2000. *Organizing European Space.* London: Sage.

Kocka, Jürgen. 2007. The mapping of Europe's borders: past. present and future. In Hans-Åke Persson and Bo Strath, eds, *Reflections of Europe: Defining a Political Order in Time and Space*, pp. 37–48. Brussels: Peter Lang.

Kolossov, Vladimir. 2005. Border studies: changing perspectives and theoretical approaches. *Geopolitics* 10: 606–632.

Kotula, Andrzej. 1994. Die deutsch-polnische Grenze in der polnischen Presse. *Transodra* 4–5: 38–40.

Kramsch, Olivier. 2010. Camuspace: Towards a geneaology of Europe's de-colonial frontier. In Chiara Brambilla and Bruno Riccio, eds, *Transnational Migrations, Cosmopolitanism and Dis-located Borders*, pp. 87–118. Rimini: Guaraldi.

Kramsch, Olivier and Brambilla, Chiara. 2007. Transboundary Europe through a West African looking glass: cross-border integration, "colonial difference" and the chance for "border thinking." *Comparativ*, 17 (4): 95–115.

Kratke, Stefan, Heeg, Susanne and Stein, Rolf. 1997. *Regionen im Umbruch. Probleme der Regionalentwicklung an den Grenzen zwischen "Ost" und "West."* Frankfurt: Campus.

Laine, Jussi and Demidov, Andrei. 2011. Civil society organisations as drivers of cross-border interaction: on whose terms, for which purpose? In Heikki Eskelinen, Ilkka Liikanen and James W. Scott, eds, *The EU–Russia Borderland.* London: Routledge.

Lenz, Sebastian, Herfert, Günter and Bergfeld, Annedore. 2009. The German-Polish border region from a German perspective – quo vadis? In Wendelin Strubelt, ed., *Guiding Principles for Spatial Development in Germany: German Annual of Spatial Research and Policy*, pp. 51–66. Berlin: Springer.

Lepik, Katri-Liis. 2009. Euroregions as mechanisms for strengthening cross-border cooperation in the Baltic Sea region. *Trames* 13 (3): 265–282.

Liikanen, Ilkka. 2011. Origins of the eastern border as the grand controversy of Finnish national history writing. In Tibor Frank and Frank Hadler, eds, *Disputed Territories and Shared Pasts: Overlapping National Histories in Modern Europe*, pp 177–199. London: Palgrave Macmillan.

Linde-Laursen, Anders. 2010. *Bordering. Identity Processes between the National and Personal.* Aldershot: Ashgate.

Matthiesen, Ulf and Bürkner, Hans-Joachim. 2001. Antagonistic structures in border areas: local milieux and local politics in the Polish-German twin city Gubin/Guben. *GeoJournal* 54: 43–50.

Maull, Otto. 1925. *Politische Geographie.* Berlin: Gebrüder Borntraeger.

Meinhof, Ulrike H., ed. 2002. *Living (with) Borders: Identity Discourses on East–West Borders in Europe.* Aldershot: Ashgate.

Nagel, Joane. 2003. *Race, Ethnicity, and Sexuality: Intimate Intersections, Forbidden Frontiers.* Oxford: Oxford University Press.

Newman, David. 2006. Borders and bordering: towards an interdisciplinary dialogue. *European Journal of Social Theory* 9 (2): 171–186.

Nielsen, Kristian, Berg, Eiki and Roll, Gulnara. 2009. Undiscovered avenues? Estonian civil society organisations as agents of Europeanisation. *Trames* 13 (3): 248–264.

Niukko, Kirsi. 2009. The concept of landscape among Karelian migrants in Finland. *Journal of Borderlands Studies* 24 (2): 62–77.

Nyman, Jopi. 2009. From black Britain to the Caribbean: the return of the (im)migrant in Caryl Phillips's "A State of Independence." In Jopi Nyman, ed., *Home, Identity, and Mobility in Contemporary Diasporic Fiction*, pp. 37–56. Amsterdam: Rodopi.

O'Dwyer, Conor. 2006. Reforming regional governance in East Central Europe: Europeanization or domestic politics as usual? *East European Politics and Societies* 20 (2): 219–253.

Paasi, Anssi. 1999. Boundaries as social practice and discourse: The Finnish-Russian border. *Regional Studies* 33 (7): 669–680.

Paasi, Anssi. 2001. "A borderless world": Is it only rhetoric or will boundaries disappear in the globalizing world? In Paul Reuber and Günter Wolkersdorfer, eds, *Politische Geographie. Handlungsorientierte Ansätze und Critical Geopolitics*, pp. 133–145. Heidelberg: Heidelberger Geographische Arbeiten.

Papadakis, Yiannis. 2005. *Echoes from the Dead Zone: Across the Cyprus Divide*. London: I.B. Tauris.

Perkmann, Markus. 2002. Euroregions: institutional entrepreneurship in the European Union. In Markus Perkmann and Ngai-Ling Sum, eds, *Globalization, Regionalization and Cross-Border Regions*, pp. 103–124. Basingtoke: Palgrave Macmillan.

Perkmann, Markus. 2005. Cross-border co-operation as policy entrepreneurship: explaining the variable success of European cross-border regions. CSGR Working Paper 166/05, University of Warwick.

Pickering, Sharon. 2011. *Women, Borders, and Violence: Current Issues in Asylum, Forced Migration, and Trafficking*. Berlin: Springer.

Popescu, Gabriel. 2006. Geopolitics of scale and cross-border cooperation in Eastern Europe: the case of the Romanian-Ukrainian -Moldovan borderlands. In James Wesley Scott, ed., *EU Enlargement, Region Building and Sifting Borders of Inclusion and Exclusion*, pp. 35–51. Aldershot: Ashgate.

Popescu, Gabriel. 2008. The conflicting logics of crossborder reterritorialization: geopolitics of Euroregions in Eastern Europe. *Political Geography* 27 (4): 418–438.

Ratzel, Friedrich. 1903. *Politische Geographie: Oder Die Geographie der Staaten, des Verkehres und des Krieges*. Munich: Oldenbourg.

Schimanski, Johan and Wolfe, Stephen. 2010. Cultural production and negotiation of borders: introduction to the dossier. *Journal of Borderlands Studies* 25 (1): 39–49.

Scott, James. 2000. Transboundary cooperation on Germany's borders: strategic regionalism through multilevel governance.

Journal of Borderlands Studies 15 (1): 143–167.

Scott, James, ed. 2006. *EU Enlargement, Region-building and Shifting Borders of Inclusion and Exclusion*. Aldershot: Ashgate.

Scott, James. 2007. Cross-border regionalization in an enlarging EU: Hungarian-Austrian and German-Polish cases. In Harlan Koff, ed., *Deceiving (Dis)appearances: Analyzing Current Developments in European and North American Border Regions*, pp. 37–58. Bern: Peter Lang.

Scott, James. 2011a. Borders, border studies and EU enlargement. In Doris Wastl-Water, ed., *Ashgate Research Companion to Border Studies*, pp. 123–142. Aldershot: Ashgate.

Scott, James. 2011b. Reflections on EU geopolitics: consolidation, neighbourhood and civil society in the reordering of European space. *Geopolitics* 16 (1): 146–175.

Scott, James and van Houtum, Henk. 2009. Reflections on EU territoriality and the "bordering" of Europe. *Political Geography* 28 (5): 271–273.

Scott, James and Liikanen, Ilkka. 2010. Civil society and the "neighbourhood": Europeanization through cross-border cooperation? *Journal of European Integration* 32 (5): 423–438.

Shields, Rob. 1991. *Places on the Margin: Alternative Geographies of Modernity*. London: Routledge.

Shliamin, V.A. 2001. Euregio Karelia – new challenges and new opportunities. *Bulletin of the TACIS Project: Euregio Karelia as a Tool of Civil Society* 1. At http://www.gov.karelia.ru/News/2001/0518_01a_e.html#05 (accessed Mar. 19, 2010).

Smith, Karen. 2005. The outsiders: the European neighbourhood policy. *International Affairs* 81 (4): 757–773.

Tamminen, Tanja. 2004. Cross-border cooperation in the southern balkans: local, national or European identity politics? *Southeast European and Black Sea Studies* 4 (3): 399–418.

van Houtum, Henk. 2002. Borders of comfort, spatial economic bordering processes in the European Union. *Regional and Federal Studies* 12 (4): 37–58.

van Houtum, Henk and Boedeltje, Freerk. 2009. Europe's shame: death at the borders of the EU. *Antipode* 41 (2): 226–230.

van Houtum, Henk and van Naerssen, Thomas. 2002. Bordering, ordering, and othering. *Journal of Economic and Social Geography* 93 (2): 125–136.

CHAPTER **6**

Securing Borders in Europe and North America

Emmanuel Brunet-Jailly

Since 9/11, security issues have been at the forefront of border policy developments both in Europe and North America. The European Union (EU) member states and the North American states (Canada, Mexico and the United States) have, however, responded in a fundamentally different fashion. The European experience within the EU is largely influenced by its regional policy, with its tradition of local level and intergovernmental networks and policy-making practices, but also by a need to secure both internal and international borders in a manner coherent with preexisting policies of partnership and cooperation. The resulting international border security policies engage bordering states on issues of economic development and security matters, while internal security is increasingly the responsibility of large networks of territorial and functional governments[1] and organizations concerned with shared security across all 27 member states. In North America, Canada and Mexico have been subjected to alignment pressures from the United States. Border security perspectives are primarily informed by the US administration's understanding of criminal and immigration issues on its southern border, that, in turn, is subject to considerable demographic and market pressures. This, then, leads to attempts to unify policy answers to vast and regionally varied borderlands.

This chapter explores these varied and nuanced issues by comparing border security policies in the European Union and the North American Free Trade Agreement (NAFTA) areas. Understanding border security policies sheds light on the nature of states. Social scientists generally agree that "dense economic, cultural, or political human activities . . . straddling a borderland result in increasing porosity" and that only "cooperation, collaboration and the co-production of security goals can alleviate porosity" (Andreas and Biersteker 2003: 3; Brunet-Jailly 2007: ix–x). This, however, is a rather counterintuitive idea from the perspective of state policies. Indeed, in the modern era the Westphalian logic that boundaries are internationally recognized markers legitimizing power over a demarcated territory remains prevalent, and raises

A Companion to Border Studies, First Edition. Edited by Thomas M. Wilson and Hastings Donnan.
© 2012 Blackwell Publishing Ltd. Published 2012 by Blackwell Publishing Ltd.

questions about the very nature of those necessary coproduced border security policies.

The early literature on borders underscored their function as buffer zones: good borders were not settled by humans and were possibly desert-like (Semple 1911; Holdich 1916; Lyde 1915). More recently, there has been renewed interest in West-phalian fences and walls (Chaire Raoul-Dandurand 2011) and also in the much less visible policies of territorial partnerships where core–periphery hierarchies of territo-ries develop in multiple rings of concentric circles. For example, Zielonka (2006) suggests that legal, economic, security and cultural policies in the European Union are likely to overlap. For Zielonka, Europe is an empire in the making, a "neo-medieval" world where the boundaries between constituent regions are fuzzy. By contrast, Andreas and Biersteker suggest that post–9/11 border policies in North America are "politically successful policy failures: They succeeded in terms of their symbolic and image effects while failing in terms of their deterrent effects" (2003: 3). Hence, comparing the European Union and North America opens a discussion on the nature of their security policies, their border policies and the very nature of the state and state relations in the making, and raises questions about their funda-mental assumptions in this new security era.

In this chapter, a range of examples drawn from the literature and from current affairs in Europe and North America illustrate these security and border issues. The main argument is that today security at the border, and border policies in general, do not focus solely on screening threats and illegal immigrants but instead address a wide range of social, economic and security issues in borderland regions, and that cooperation and partnership may not always lead to the most cost-effective policies. This chapter also examines data which point to a critique of the assumptions found in the primarily Westphalian North American border security model, a model that may not be as successful as that which has developed in the neo-medieval EU of cooperation around concentric circles of friends.

I begin by discussing conceptual definitions of security, borders and borderlands and relate them to the European Union and its member states and to North America, with a particular focus on the borders of Canada, Mexico and the US. The next section discusses Schengen and asks what can be learned from this experiment in borderland security that is now almost 25 years old. The third part of the chapter compares the security assumptions and policy choices in North America with those in Europe and explores the differences between them. Finally, I review current Euro-pean and North American policy assumptions.

CONCEPTUAL ISSUES

The traditional or "narrow" debate about security studies focused on the enduring primacy of military security (Gray 1994a, 1994b; Buzan et al. 1998). In this view, security studies were concerned with military conflict (Ayoob 1995). "Political actors" were central, and "states as actors" were at the core. Security, viewed this way, is "the study of the threat, use and control of military force" (Walt 1991). In contrast, the "wider" debate about security points to sources of threat that are not military, indicating that "threats" should be conceptualized in economic (Buzan 1991; Luciani 1989), environmental and human terms (Deudney 1990). According to Buzan et al. (1998: 2), in the immediate post–Cold War period security studies focused on military and nuclear issues; from this perspective, security was about "anything that concerns the prevention of superpower nuclear war." But once the Berlin Wall fell, the entire strategic community had to rethink its analyses. No longer was security about the East–West confrontation but instead about globalization and its economic, environmental and human consequences.

In other words, contemporary security analysts view security issues from varied perspectives. In the military domain, security is about the state (and, in general, military security studies are about military affairs), but this is obviously an incomplete view because in contemporary democracies state defense is only one function of the state. The military perform many functions that have nothing to do with security (for example, they also deliver humanitarian aid and engage in emergency actions). In the political domain, security is about sovereignty. It takes the form of a state "ideology." States and international organizations such as the United Nations and the European Union can be threatened by "rule changes"; in most cases these take the form of new international agreements and treaties that change the nature of existing agreements. For instance, because of disagreements between Canadians over the Kyoto standards and Canada's inability to influence the Kyoto negotiations, the Canadian oil industries felt threatened by the Kyoto Agreement on carbon dioxide reduction. Indeed, the Agreement largely redefined international standards (rules) of accepted pollution levels, which caused tensions throughout Canada, and particularly between the province of Alberta and the federal government. The current federal government, in line with the position of the province of Alberta, therefore refuses to sign the Kyoto Agreement and actively lobbies in the US and across the world to change its terms (McKitrick and Essex 2002). In the economic domain, security is about the sustainability of entire economies, where not just corporations but whole economic sectors may be at stake (for example, the 2008–2011 banking sector meltdown and government support in the US and Europe). In the social domain, threats emerge from contentious collective identities, nations and national ideologies and regional and religious or ethnic groups that may subvert or militate against states. Finally, in the environmental domain threats may be very broadly understood, as, for instance, when population survival is faced with epidemics (as in Mad Cow and influenza pandemics).

In summary, security was traditionally conceived as monosectoral and focused on the military, but renewed contemporary approaches are now multisectoral. This suggests the importance of thinking clearly about the balance between sectors, types of threats, actors and elements, which together have important implications for security policies. Security policies are more complex because issues identified as security threats are also more diverse; they are plural and multifaceted in nature. Border security policies struggle with these new complex dimensions of security. Indeed, this new complexity is reflected in various uneven ways in state border and borderland policy and affects neighborly and international relations. This increased complexity in security matters also has consequences for definitions of borders and borderlands.

THE EUROPEAN UNION'S SCHENGEN AGREEMENT

Since antiquity there have been borders – lines, zones, strips of land - which separate and divide other zones of confrontation and passage. Borders and borderlands established an authority, which at the dawn of the Middle Ages was basically about providing security and controlling territory. In the aftermath of the Peace of Westphalia (1648), the international recognition of boundaries further strengthened state-building. Today, however, as Balibar and his colleagues (2002) suggest, borders "vacillate": borders need not coincide with the boundary line itself but are instead everywhere and multiple. Clearly, internationally recognized boundary lines still function as the Roman limites once did. They mark the end of one "sovereignty" and the beginning of another. They are where obligations and currencies change, where tolls are paid and where customs inspections are carried out. But scholars and policy observers are also witness to new and government-designed norms that are internalized by citizen-subjects. These norms result in renewed production of referents of collective and individual identity, where rights are internalized with the help of technological markers that replace language, ethnicity and religion. Ideal borders are invisible at the boundary line. The contemporary borders are biometric borders, markers and gates at the departure points of people and goods, and are in addition to other internal controls and zones of transit. Population flows are held up before exit or entry and migrating populations negotiate individually their right of border crossing. In this context, however, the trade of goods and services, and the environmental threats that cross borders, are often able to resist control and cannot be stopped at the boundary, as illustrated by Chernobyl, Mad Cow disease, the AIDS virus, or images on CNN.

Thus, conceptually, boundaries are no longer only the location and markers of superimposed sets of state functions resulting from the exercise of sovereignty; for example, military, tax and administrative powers and cultural, economic or environmental policies. Borders are vacillating because they are no longer easily localizable. They may be internalized and they may result from technological markers or from social and economic factors that pledge legal rights. Border locations often vary because they are coupled with policy and territorial functions. De facto, borders are actually at "home" where the goods, services or individuals prepare their journey.

Understandings of security in international relations have undergone significant transformation since the fall of the Berlin Wall. Discussions over concepts have gone from referring to unitary phenomena to referring to multilayered, complex and multifaceted phenomena. As illustrated below, this newly discovered complexity is not reflected in the same way in Europe, particularly the Europe of the Schengen Agreement, which looks at the security of its borders as a complex of socioeconomic and environmental issues where policing, control, security, surveillance and partnership with neighboring countries have to work together. In North America, by contrast, issues of national sovereignty and varied policy goals interfered until very recently with some of the broad pan-American policy goals which Canada, Mexico and the United States could share. Clearly, for border scholars and policy-makers these changing understandings of what security is about have had an impact on border security policies, as I examine next in the context of Europe.

The European approach to border security is multifaceted and complex. On the one hand, important aspects of European Union security policies include pan-European programs that collect and distribute security and strategic information across networks of security agencies at all levels of government and among public-private partnerships, most of which are set by EU framework laws and coordinated by the European Commission and its agencies. These are generally referred to as "Schengen" policies. But, on the other hand, the European Union has also invested billions of euros in third countries neighboring the 27 members of the EU to secure and pacify its immediate peripheral region. As shown below, the so-called "Neighbourhood Policies" are clearly conceived as linking security with other policy issues, yet in practice they only loosely link in this way, which results in great flexibility of implementation.

In the EU, security discussions did not start until the 1970s, when a number of large EU countries faced the terrorist activities of homegrown ideological, regionalist or nationalist extremist organizations. While by then most EU member states had taken individual measures to prevent terrorism of either domestic or foreign origin, they nonetheless initiated intergovernmental cooperation on these issues in 1975 as part of what was called the Trevi Group. In a step-by-step approach, EU member states agreed progressively to implement perimeter security measures. The realization that terrorism was at an international scale, which could only be addressed with a pan-European strategy, became prominent.[2]

In December 1996 Schengen brought together under the heading of "Freedom, Security and Justice" several preexisting initiatives and many new ones that were considered fundamental to EU security. An "ad hoc immigration group" had originally drafted a convention on immigration and external borders in 1989. But the Schengen Agreement went further by moving forward on the control and surveillance of external borders. In Schengen, "strengthening and protecting" was understood as a "compensatory measure" for the elimination of internal borders (European Parliament 2011). Initiatives include, for instance, Europole, which collects and analyzes information on international terrorism; Eurojust, which helps coordinate investigations and procedures (assistance, coordination, extradition) and places "joint investigation teams" across Europe; and AGIS, which helps with cooperation among national, regional and local police forces, judiciaries and other professionals to fight crime, as well as to offer pan-European training programs. The EU also harmonized definitions of legal offenses, rules of competence and rules for arrest warrants, and set up networks of expertise among law enforcement and intelligence communities across Europe. It is interesting to note that the European Commission funding commitment to this framework is limited to about €540 million per year, which stands at 0.5 percent of the annual budget of the EU.

Following up on Schengen, the European Council meeting in Laeken in December 2001 adopted a European Commission suggestion that an EU agency manage external borders, including surveillance, analysis of risks, personnel and equipment, and that a European Border Police and a European Border Council be established. Shortly after Laeken, in June 2002, the European Border Council approved a broad policy framework on the "management of external borders," including agreements on joint legislation and operation, including training, repatriation, treatment of aliens and cooperation with third countries. It also approved the creation of ARGO, a program that promotes cooperation between national administrations to encourage uniform application of EU law, transparency and efficiency, and, in 2005, the creation of an EU Agency for the Management of Operational Cooperation at the External Borders. This new agency is called FRONTEX (Frontières Extérieures).[3] It is in charge of 42,672 kilometers of sea borders and 8,826 kilometers of land borders around the Schengen countries. FRONTEX was intended to be an effective barrier to cross-border crime. Its mandate included risk analysis, information gathering, research and development, operational cooperation between member states, training to set common preparation standards for Europe's 400,000 border guards, management of units of 700 staff with capability for rapid crisis response, and coordination of member states in joint operations. The budget of FRONTEX stands at €87 million, a fraction of the cost of US Homeland Security, which stood at $56 billion in 2010.

What is commonly referred to as "Schengen" today originally focused only on internal borders, but by the 1995 European Council in Madrid, member states had agreed that terrorism should be seen as a threat not only to democracy but also to the broad exercise of human rights and economic and social development across Europe, a pan-European public good, needing Europe-wide protection. The 1998 Vienna Action Plan and the Amsterdam Treaty of 1999 further enhanced cooperation and implementation of what is now commonly referred to as the "Area of Freedom, Security and Justice."

The Tampere Council of 1999 completed these initiatives and at the Laeken meeting in 2001, European Council member states agreed:

> Better management of the Union's external border control will help in the fight against terrorism, illegal immigration networks and the traffic in human beings. The European Council asks Council and Commission to work out arrangements for cooperation between services responsible for external border control and to examine the conditions in which a mechanism or common services to control borders could be created. (European Council 2001: 12, para. 42)

By 2001, all these policies, also commonly referred to as "Schengen," applied to Norway, Iceland, Sweden, Denmark and Finland. By 2002, the Council and European Parliament had approved the integrated management of external borders of EU members, although the UK and Ireland had only agreed to parts of "Schengen." The Seville European Council of June 2002 approved the Action Plan on the Management of External Common Borders, which implemented common legislation, services and joint operations between national border control services, and went as far as implementing new training, repatriation, treatment of illegal aliens and cooperation with third countries.

Control and surveillance are the two key policy objectives of Schengen. Control encompasses all activities regarding permission to "enter or to leave the common area of freedom of movement" that is, the EU. It concerns people, vehicles and their possessions. Surveillance involves all activities and operations of prevention of people circumventing official border crossings in order to evade checks when entering or leaving the European Union. These two principles organize the uniform and systematic implementation of border security policies on the external borders. Their implementation requires proper documentation, which varies greatly depending on the origin of the person, vehicle or goods considered. These are recorded with biometric trace in a centralized information system. In 2001, the Schengen Information System (SIS 1) was modernized, using the latest information, to form SIS 2, which allowed more information to be stored and retrieved from a greater number of participating countries, and within these countries allowed access to a greater number of organizations.

Surveillance is primarily the responsibility of EU national authorities within the EU framework that organizes cooperation among member states. The assistance of the European Commission, however, is delivered through the ARGO action program for administrative cooperation in the fields of external borders, visas, asylum and immigration. The ARGO program funds up to 60 percent of the costs of all approved national projects, and its activities are coordinated by a committee made up of officials of the EU and member states. In 2005, as noted above, the Commission launched the European Agency for the Management of Operational Cooperation on External Borders. In 2006, the systematic implementation of biometrics was introduced.

In 2003, the European Commission started implementing bilateral agreements with all countries on the eastern and southern borders of the Union. EU security was further developed with the launch of the European Neighbourhood Policy (ENP) in 2004. The ENP offers broad-based policies that are meant to foster a ring of good neighbors around the EU. The stated goal is to secure Europe in a better world: "Even in an era of globalization, geography is still important. It is in the European interest that countries on our borders are well governed. Neighbours who are engaged in violent conflict, weak states where organized crime flourishes, dysfunctional societies or exploding population growth on its borders, all pose problems for Europe" (Council of the European Union 2009: 35). The Commission also declared: "Our task is to promote a ring of well governed countries to the East of the European Union and on the borders of the Mediterranean with whom we can enjoy close cooperative relations," and suggested that "the European Union's interests require a continued engagement . . . through more effective economic, security, and cultural cooperation" (Solana 2003: 7, 8). The Commission made clear that issues of peace and security had to be linked with those of human rights: "There cannot be sustainable development without peace and security, and without development and poverty eradication there will be no sustainable peace. Threats to public health, particularly pandemics, further undermine development. Human rights are a fundamental part of the equation" (Council of the European Union 2009: 20).

These multifaceted goals of the ENP were reasserted in the constitutional Lisbon Treaty, which further committed the EU to the "development of a special relationship with neighbouring countries aiming to establish an area of prosperity and good neighbourliness, founded on the values of the Union and characterized by close and peaceful relations based on cooperation" (European Union 2010).

Today, 14 out of 19 neighbors of the European Union which are in the Mediterranean and to the east – that is, Armenia, Azerbaijan, Belarus, Egypt, Georgia, Israel, Jordan, Lebanon, Moldova, Morocco, Palestinian Territory, Tunisia, Ukraine and Russia – are signatories and beneficiaries of agreements of good neighborly relations. Algeria, Kazakhstan, Libya, Mauritania and Syria are still negotiating. Morocco provides a good example of what is expected from a signatory to these "good neighbors" policies. Morocco is engaged in political dialogue with the EU regarding human rights issues, democratization, the establishment of a Moroccan/EU Parliament Commission, assistance for local elections, business and trade relations, including import-export issues, support for the creation of a Moroccan Development Bank, information exchange on legal and illegal migration, the Morocco–Spain contention over Ceuta, drug trafficking, membership in the European Convention on cybercrime, and European Council cooperation in the training of judges. The European Investment Bank lent €654 million to Morocco to implement these policies and initiatives from a total of €8.4 billion for all 14 countries in the ENP.

In summary, EU policies have centralized information and programs to increase the collection and redistribution of security information on a wide range of issues through pan-EU networks of public and private agencies that are trained to comply with pan-European certification standards and procedures. These are networks of states and state security organizations that are willingly engaged in developing common security standards and procedures. What is notable is the EU capacity to develop common policies across a large number of states, regions and security- and border-related organizations. EU policies also bridge security with many other policy areas, including democratic values and institutions, human rights, environmental and economic development and social issues. Indeed, the result is policies specifically conceived and negotiated with a ring of friendly neighboring countries, but also, de facto, a maze of policies where boundaries are fuzzy and where border security policies are not always as clearly visible as they used to be. The following section details how different the North American approach is to security matters and to North American borders and borderlands.

THE CANADA–UNITED STATES PERIMETER

Canada and the United States are each other's number one trading partner and they represent the world's largest two-way trading partnership (Brunet-Jailly 2000). They trade more goods and services between themselves than Japan and Mexico together trade with the United States. Their two-way trade has increased by 1,400 percent since the late 1970s. Nearly 70 percent of all Canadian exports go to the US, and US exports to Canada account for 22 percent of its total exports. This has had a significant impact on jobs in the US, where well over 8 million jobs depend on the Canada–US trade.[4] This long-standing economic interdependence has led political analysts of Canadian-American relations to point to Canadians' ongoing fear that too much economic integration might lead to continental integration. Kim Nossal, for instance, described the debate between those he called "economic nationalists" and "integrationists," thus equating economic independence with sovereignty

(Nossal 1985; see also Brunet-Jailly 2011b). Nossal also suggested that economic integration is not safe for Canadians, because it is very plausible that economic integration may lead to political integration.

This notion has had tremendous influence on the security debate. While much has been written that has equated the Canada–US relationship to a "security community," which is, according to prominent observers such as Adler and Barnett (1998), "a trans-national region comprised of sovereign states whose people maintain dependable expectations of peaceful changes," there is agreement in the scholarly community that Canada and the United States are more than a security community. As traditionally defined by Deutsch (1957), both countries share a tradition of day-to-day cooperation and have developed an "intimate" knowledge of each other that is apparent in the current tradition of quiet diplomacy and low-level functional solutions (Kitchen 2002). Prominent public intellectual and former leader of the Liberal Party in Canada Michael Ignatieff (2003) noted that Canada was so comfortable in this relationship that it asserted its views better today than in the past. Indeed, Canadian leaders think the increased policy parallelism (Brunet-Jailly 2011b) observable across Canada–US borderland regions facilitates relations and trade (Brunet-Jailly et al. 2006).

Prior to 2001 and 9/11, Canada and the US shared the longest "undefended" border in the world. While the Canadian government had taken care of staff and infrastructures reasonably well, the US, by contrast, had focused its efforts on its southern border, because of increased illegal immigration and trafficking there, intense interactions across the border resulting from the expanding maquiladoras borderland economy and increased trade within the NAFTA area. The events of 9/11 changed all this dramatically.

Until 2001 the US had implemented "light" border policies, particularly on the Canada–US boundary line. The 9/11 Commission in the United States identified a number of problems with existing border policies, including low level funding of agencies, interagency competition and a lack of communication among key agencies. Both Canada and Mexico also reviewed their security policies. All three countries passed new legislation, for instance, in the US the Patriot Act and the National Homeland Security Strategy in 2002; in Canada the Antiterrorism Act and Immigration and Refugee Protection Act, and the National Security Policy in 2004. From the beginning, scholars such as Pastor (2001) had offered "European" ideas, and Manley, Aspe and Weld (2005) were lead scholars on the idea of a North American Community. But the view that quickly imposed itself in the US and then in Canada and Mexico was that to provide secure borders it would be necessary to "push US borders out" (Flynn 2003) beyond the US territorial boundary. Both Canada and Mexico shifted their own policies to follow this view. This is now consistent with the exportation of preclearance units and the signature of preclearance agreements with major trading partners around the world, so that people and goods are screened prior to reaching the US–Canada boundary. Also, security is now understood as focusing on terrorism prevention, that is, within the conceptual realm of security studies this is a new, narrower definition of security. It led to policy ideas that borders should be "smart," that border/boundary line policies needed a radical shift, including much greater resources and technology to screen people and goods prior to their arrival in North America. These initiatives were conceived as primarily top-down, with the respective governments implementing new norms and policies down to the border. New government departments were formed: the Department of Homeland Security (DHS) in the US and the Department of Public Safety and Emergency Preparedness in Canada, and it was assumed the two would develop close relations to secure their countries.

As early as 2001, starting with a well-staffed and well-equipped border infrastructure, the Canadian government committed $1.2 billion for intelligence, $1.6 billion for policing, and $1 billion for screening and possibly detention and treatment of refugee claims. It also developed new passports using fraud-resistant material and biometric technologies. The Royal Canadian Mounted Police (RCMP) were the "spine" of efforts at each level of government, in line with the suggestion of RCMP High Commissioner Giuliano Zaccardelli that all levels of government and related agencies had to work together to combat crime efficiently (Zaccardelli 2002, 2003). In contrast, the United States was faced with fragmented, understaffed and under-resourced agencies, and as a result, ill-equipped borders. In 2000, there were fewer than 1,000 staff on the US side of the Canadian border, which at the time reflected the perception of that border as safe. At the same time, there were about 10,000 staff on the US side of the Mexican border; since then, US staff numbers have increased threefold at both borders.

As part of the US response to terrorist threat after 9/11 the Bush administration initiated the regrouping and recentralization both of major border policy agencies and of border security itself. In March 2003 the DHS resulted from the merger of several agencies, which involved well over 40,000 staff. Also, since the creation of the DHS its annual budget has grown significantly, from $2 billion in 2001 to $56 billion in 2010; this illustrates the prioritization of security in the United States. Today, as a response to past criticism that US border policies and procedures were fragmented due to the multitude of agencies involved, all US border services are unified under one line of command. The "one face at the border" goal originally set by the White House is being achieved. Customs and Border Protection (CBP) officers graduate from the same school (based with the Federal Law Enforcement Training Center), where they train to become part of specialized airport inspection, antiterrorism and passenger analysis units.

Canada, the United States and Mexico signed agreements to enhance further their security and protect their trade relations. The first such agreement was the Smart Border Declaration, which focused on implementing secure borders to trade flows. It was followed by the Western Hemisphere Travel Initiative (WHTI) in 2004, a US initiative which is primarily known for unilaterally requiring and implementing passports for border crossing in North America. WHTI is a provision of the Intelligence Reform and Terrorism Prevention Act of 2004 that requires all travelers from Canada and Mexico to present a passport or another form of secure documentation in order to enter the United States. It was supposed to start on January 1, 2007 for air travelers, and a year later for land or sea crossings. WHTI was so controversial that implementation was postponed to June 2009. This was something nearly revolutionary, and particularly between Canada and the US, where crossing had always taken place with limited documentation such as a credit card or a driver's license. In the meantime "enhanced" drivers' licenses (i.e., with a passport level of security) were being introduced for land crossing for residents of British Columbia, Washington, Ontario and Michigan (Insurance Corporation of British Columbia 2009). These "enhanced drivers' licenses" are being issued in the provinces of British Columbia, Manitoba, Ontario and Quebec, and in the states of Michigan, New York, Vermont and Washington. Although comprehensive travel data for 2010–2011 is not yet available, anecdotally, single-day trips by US residents to Canada appear to be the most adversely affected by the new regulations (*Bangor Daily News* 2010; *Funworld Magazine* 2010). In March 2005, the first meeting of the Security and Prosperity Partnership of North America took place in Crawford, Texas to discuss a long list of security policies such as border improvements and joint port security exercises. Most of those items had already been part of the Canada–US 32-point Action Plan of the Smart Border Agreement (SBA). The leaders of all three countries met again in Cancun in March 2006, in Montebello in August 2007, and in New Orleans in April 2008, and finally in Guadalajara in 2009.

The SBA is particularly important because it set up the partnership on security for Canada and the US, including control of trade and immigration flows and drug, firearms and illegal immigrant trafficking prevention in the regions surrounding major ports of entry.[5] It was announced to the public on December 12, 2001, when Governor Tom Ridge, then US Director of the newly established DHS, joined John Manley, then Canadian Minister of Foreign Affairs, in Ottawa. At the press conference that followed the ceremony of signing the agreement, both commented on the importance of securing trade. Manley stated that "keeping the flow of people and goods moving efficiently across the Canada–US border" was the priority, while Ridge (2001) remarked that "there is no trade-off between our people's security and a trade friendly border. We need both, for in fact they reinforce each other."

The SBA, however, has not led to the creation of a new North American organization of cooperation similar to that found in the European Union. Instead, it has led to the development of networks of officials to work out the implementation of policies that are narrowly focused on specific modes of transportation of goods and through which intelligence is progressively shared, albeit with difficulties. In the area of information sharing the two countries are still far behind the European Union's FRONTEX information system; indeed, both Canada and the US have police and intelligence information databases but cooperation is hampered by the number of agencies, the diversity of laws and rules regulating their use, and by the diversity of standards used to collect or retrieve available information.[6] However, there are also very successful instances of cooperation.

The Canadian-American Transit Container Targeting Program, which became the model for the pan-US Container Security Initiative, is a good example of Canada–US collaboration. This program has Canada Customs and Revenue officers posted in Newark and Seattle, and American CBP officers working in Halifax, Montreal and Vancouver to prescreen containers in transit to an American or Canadian destination (CBP 2008a, 2008b). Massive investments in new scanning technologies, particularly large-scale X-ray imaging systems, have increased the capacity of ports of entry to check seaport containers as well as trains and trucks crossing land border gates. Thus, while in 2001 only 7.6 percent of containers were inspected, this percentage rose to 12.1 in 2003: specifically, 9 percent versus 22.6 percent of train containers, 2 percent versus 5.2 percent of sea containers, and 10.3 percent versus 15.1 percent of truck containers (Bonner 2003). Interestingly, the program is still developing common security standards to identify, prescreen, and label containers when secured. Agents work side by side but cannot act in each other's country, where they only work in an advisory capacity. Behind issues of sovereignty protection, there are discussions relating security norms to competitiveness, where operators' concerns are always about their possible loss of business. Trains are also inspected. The Vehicle and Cargo Inspection System is in place on seven rail crossings on the US side and one on the Canadian side.

Similarly, the Free and Secure Trade (FAST) program certifies specific Canadian and US firms that are then able to apply for security preclearance. FAST enforces key criteria on transportation firms (trucking corporations primarily) and drivers. These gain the right to cross the border without stopping. They slow down so that a transponder can transmit their information directly to the border gate officials. FAST is supposed to free resources so officials can then focus on non-precleared goods and individuals. The agencies involved are the US Customs and Border Protection, Customs-Trade Partnership against Terrorism, the Border Security Agency, and the Partner in Protection program. However, since 2003, CBP has only approved 6,900 businesses and 90,000 truckers, which is a minority of the firms that trade across the border.

The creation of FAST lanes has in turn led to the development of new infrastructure. A case in point is the construction of lanes at Windsor-Detroit, where about 50 percent of all Canada–US trade crosses the border. The new Detroit River International Crossing (DRIC) was agreed upon, despite much local opposition, in 2009. In the end, funding support came from the Canadian government to the government of Michigan in the amount of $550 million. All in all, the cost of the new border gates and bridge rose to $5.6 billion. However, one problem was access to the FAST lanes; hence the construction of the DRIC south of the Ambassador Bridge. The DRIC proposal is supported by the Canadian government, which believes it should not be privately held (Jang 2010; Shea 2010). Similar programs exist for individuals who cross the border frequently by boat, car or plane and want to expedite their crossings: the NEXUS program targets preapproved individuals. The program provides these individuals with a "smart card," which basically certifies their status as "precleared" individuals. Today, the six busiest border gateways, at Blaine (British Columbia, Canada/Washington, US), Buffalo (New York, US) and Windsor-Detroit (Ontario, Canada/Michigan, US) offer such expedited crossings. Policy-makers justify the development of NEXUS by explaining how it allows skilled workers to cross seamlessly, while at the same time limiting disruption at the border gate. In 2010, 265,000 people were recipients of these cards and were able to use them at 16 land border crossings, 8 airports and 33 marine/harbor crossings. NEXUS cards have passport-level security but face continuous problems; a 2007 jointly commissioned study was able to demonstrate the benefits associated with the card but also raised a number of unresolved legal, institutional issues regarding land ownership and enforcement powers, including the right to carry firearms. A report in 2008 of the US Government Accountability Office, *Secure Border Initiative* (US GAO 2008), also illustrated disagreements over arrest authority, fingerprinting practices and the right to withdraw US entry applications at the preclearance office.

The Security and Prosperity Partnership of North America process stopped with the meeting of Guadalajara in 2009; yet the new Obama Administration reaffirmed its commitment to continue past efforts on North American cooperation, and to meeting with neighboring leaders but under a different approach than that framework. One aspect of the new framework was announced in early 2011 when Prime Minister Harper and President Obama met to launch two new initiatives, which do not include Mexico. The first is regulatory cooperation that will take the form of a US/Canada Regulatory Cooperation Council. The second is a joint declaration on US/Canada, "Beyond the border: a shared vision for perimeter security and economic competitiveness," that lists principles and objectives for future actions.[7] Together, these have been called the Washington Declaration.

It is too early to judge whether this declaration is a game-changing event, or to tell what is at stake. Indeed, the usage of the word "perimeter" is revealing of changes, but of what scale? Is it the development of a North American Union similar to the European Union, where member states relinquish sovereignty and establish institutions of cooperation? Or will it be more in line with a tradition of interest and policy parallelism? Also left unanswered is whether, given that the perimeter is a broad action plan to prepare an agreement on Canada–US security, it was an inevitable policy response to current security and border conditions.

These two initiatives, and in particular the one on the border security perimeter, are typically part of the Canada–US form of integration, deemed policy parallelism, in an area where Canada and the US already share a long history (Brunet-Jailly 2011a). Current border practices are in harmony with the history of bilateral cooperation in the areas of trade, free trade, energy, water management and military cooperation. Few of these involve Mexico and none of these agreements have led to any institutional development similar to that found in the EU. What Canada and the US have in common is a rather long history of collaboration: note the reciprocity treaty of 1854,[8] the agreements on water issues in 1902 and 1909, the 1965 Autopact, the Free Trade Agreement of 1989 and NAFTA in 1994. Provinces and states (and even communities) that straddle the border have signed agreements in diverse policy areas. Also, in the areas of defense and security alone, more than 2,500 agreements link Canada and the United States, but little institutional development has resulted from them. The Permanent Joint Board on Defence, which was established in 1940, and the 1957 North American Defence Agreement (NORAD), are good examples. NORAD in particular seems to have become the foundation of the Washington Declaration of February 2011, which actually excludes Mexico from most policy discussions concerning Canada and US perimeter strategy.

Although these agreements represent a long and well-established tradition of close cooperation between the two federal administrations and bureaucracies and their agencies and other lower-level governments in various areas of public policy, these agreements have never led to any international institutional developments. Primarily, they have established functional linkages of cooperation and have relied on the shared values of expertise and efficiency. The Smart Border Declaration of December 12, 2001 focused on cooperation in four areas of policy: information sharing, customs, immigration, and security. In contrast, the Security and Prosperity Partnership summits were not successful, resulting in years of stalled negotiations on economic and security rules and regulations conducted by officials of Canada, Mexico and the United States. They did not differentiate between northern and southern border issues, and did not tackle internal inefficiencies or conflicts between US Border Patrol and US Forest Services, Immigration and Customs Enforcement, and the Drug Enforcement Administration, and furthermore, underestimated Canadian efforts to secure the US border, including cases of close cooperation contributing to US security (US GAO 2008, 2010; Sands 2011).

Hence, while clearly unsuccessful in the US security perimeter idea, the Bush administration was able to implement very successful programs with Canada, including the Container Security Initiative. Also, the Integrated Border Enforcement Teams (IBETs) and the Integrated Maritime Enforcement Teams have been very successfully implemented as joint networked forces of the US and Canada security agencies. The Terrorist Watch List is also integrated to serve better the needs of immigration officials. Airline and cruise liners also provide Advanced Passenger Information and programs to allow trusted travelers and shippers to cross the border faster. These programs are coordinated with a new regional all-service command, US Northern Command, which coordinates US involvement in NORAD.

In conclusion, the recent Washington Declaration was in many ways inescapable and is very different from the EU Schengen Agreement. It is unlike the Schengen perimeter agreement because Schengen required member states to apply strict checks on people entering and exiting the area; this has subjected all members to common rules, including border controls, surveillance and conditions of permission for entry (including visas), all of which have been codified in the Schengen Border Code and are coordinated by FRONTEX. These activities have been further coordinated by the Schengen entry-exit SIS information system and were fully incorporated into mainstream European Union law with the Amsterdam Treaty of 1997. In essence, the Washington Declaration brings Canada–US relations back to traditional bilateral relations. Canadian and US officials were possibly frustrated with the lack of progress of the Security and Prosperity Partnership, with the increasing complexity of a process that was possibly more inclusive but did not make much headway and amalgamated two very different contexts, that of Canada and that of Mexico. There seems now also to be a return to less transparency and both business and civil society organizations complain that access is difficult. In the end, the goals of the Washington Declaration are very different from the Schengen Agreement. It differentiates the northern and southern borders' policy perspectives, a Canadian goal since 2001. It brings cooperation on entry-exit within reach. It is substantially more expensive, at $56 billion in 2010. It is notable that it is not likely to lead to the creation of a coordinating agency similar to FRONTEX, but instead may lead simply to more policy parallelism.

In short, in North America border security policies are typical of the specific and functionally focused approaches found in all agreements between Canada and the United States since the beginning of the last century, where function does not spill over into overlapping policy arenas. These are state policies that are steeped in sovereignty issues and where the fundamental principles established by Westphalia are not in question. Security policies are visible and target specific functions necessary to trade. They are focused on specific aspects of security; these are not the broad-principled framework policies unifying information systems or understandings of security from a multisector perspective found in Schengen and the Neighbourhood Policy, which are much less visible. On the contrary, Canada–US agreements are focused on tackling security matters from the narrower perspective of potential terrorist threats, with security not being broadly understood as potentially multisectoral but as primarily associated with criminal activities. These are policies that need political visibility but whose effectiveness is continuously in question. The Washington Declaration will not change these fundamental assumptions even if it is premised on the creation and implementation of a secured perimeter around Canada and the US.

CONCLUSION

Comparing border security policies in the European Schengen and NAFTA arenas provides us with two very different perspectives on what security in borders and borderlands is all about. Schengen illustrates a fundamentally different administrative, organizational, political and cultural system at play. Nevertheless, Schengen yields some important ideas that may inform current discussions of the Washington Declaration on a Canada–US perimeter project, as well as discussions of academics and policy-makers on securing borders and borderlands.

Europeans premise Schengen on complex and multifaceted understandings of security in borders and borderlands, whereas in North America security emerges from Westphalian assumptions of inalterable sovereign boundaries, where security is about terrorist and criminal activities, and borders are functional boundary lines. Because European member states implement policies coherent with their understanding of a principle of regional solidarity and the protection of the common good, they are able to design policies that share cost and concentrate funding efficiently in neighboring borderlands in matters of security, development and cooperation. North Americans, by contrast, are bound to focus their policy efforts on visible policies serving and securing trade. These are inherently much less multisectoral and assume boundaries are inalterable. For the European Union international relations are about cooperation and partnership, whereas in North America they are about upholding one's power and security unilaterally. In the European Union strong institutions allow for the working out of complex policies shared by very diverse but unified polities, whereas in North America, a narrow policy focus remains an issue of contention.

However, because of the new perimeter the Canada–US boundary may vanish, while policy alignment and increased parallelisms in security policy, along with altered alignments between local, provincial officials and the respective federal governments, will be the focus of policy-makers. Security and boundary concerns and common policy may move away from the Canada–US boundary line to the large inflows of goods and people entering the northern, southern or Atlantic and Pacific North American regions, which in turn will lead to renewed continental imperatives.

Indeed, because security is multifaceted, security policies will have to become multifaceted and multisectoral as well. This includes multi-tier level partnerships, as currently developed with the IBET or the enhanced driver's license initiatives. At the same time, strengthening the Canada–US boundary line may become much less important than focusing on points of entry and the exiting of goods and services, and on individuals, in a process of preclearance expansion where the borderlands of North America will reach the shores of states around the world with which trade is intense (EU member states, China and Japan, for instance). As a result of these new focuses, the land border cutting across the Canada–US borderlands should soften, but sea borders around Canada and the US should harden. This may include renewed relations with partners of the south (Mexico) and of the north (Russia, Finland, Sweden, Norway, Iceland and Denmark). Also, the need for greater concentration and formalization of security information will increase. The standardization of diffusion of security information across specialized and trained networked organizations will also increase; hence, the plausible development of policy parallelisms and coordinating mechanisms not unlike those in place for the management of NORAD. In short, North American border security policies are bound to remain profoundly different in nature – Westphalian in principle, focused and bounded; yet they may also one day reach the shores of the EU.

NOTES

1   See Marks and Hooghe (2001), who suggest that vertical and horizontal modes of governance link two types of organization: (1) general purpose government, and (2) task-specific organizations, which I call here a functional or a unifunctional organization.
2   The European Community created the Trevi Group during the European Council Summit in Rome, December 1–2, 1975 (Bunyan 1993).
3   FRONTEX is an independent EU body responsible for coordinating operational cooperation between member states for border security. The activities of FRONTEX are intelligence driven. See www.frontex.europa.eu/ (accessed Feb. 14, 2011).
4   See http://www.canadainternational.gc.ca/washington/bilateral_relations_bilaterales/commercial_relations_commerciales.aspx?lang=eng (accessed Feb. 14, 2011).
5   The Smart Border Declaration included 30 different items of cooperation: http://www.cephas-library.com/nwo_smart_border_action_plan.html (accessed May 2011).
6   North American information systems are fragmented into many different databases and agencies. In Canada, the Canadian Police Information Centre, the Field Operational Support System and the Intelligence Management System are among those mechanisms. In the US, the National Crime Information Center (NCIC), an agency of the Federal Bureau of Investigation, has collected information since the 1960s, but with no one standard. Since 2003 the FBI has not been required to provide up-to-date information on NCIC anymore. Another system is the Immigration and Customs Enforcement System. The diversity of these systems and of the laws and rules that regulate their functioning all reduce their efficiency when compared to second generation FRONTEX.
7   See Joint Statement by President Obama and Prime Minister Harper of Canada on Regulatory Cooperation, at http://www.whitehoU.S.e.gov/the-press-office/2011/02/04/joint-statement-president-obama-and-prime-minister-harper-canada-regul-0 (accessed Feb. 25, 2011). The joint declaration on the US–Canadian border is at http://www.whitehoU.S.e.gov/the-press-office/2011/02/04/declaration-president-obama-and-prime-minister-harper-canada-beyond-bord (accessed Nov. 2011).
8   Reciprocity was the first free trade agreement for nonmanufactured goods.

REFERENCES

Adler, Emmanuel and Barnett, Michael. 1998. *Security Communities*. Cambridge: Cambridge University Press.

Andreas, Peter and Biersteker, Thomas. 2003. *The Rebordering of North America: Integration and Exclusion in a New Security Context*. New York: Routledge.

Ayoob, Mohammed. 1995. *The Third World Security Predicament: State-Making, Regional Conflict and the International System*. Boulder: Lynne Rienner.

Balibar, Étienne, Laclau, Ernesto, Mouffe, Chantal and Jones, Christine. 2002. *Politics and the Other Scene*. London: Verso.

Bangor Daily News. 2010. US tourists staying away from Canada. Apr. 6.

Bonner, Robert. 2003. Remarks at the Border Patrol Change of Command Ceremony. Mar. 3. At http://www.cbp.gov/xp/cgov/newsroom/speeches_statements/archives/2003/mar032003.xml (accessed Dec. 2011).

Bunyan, Tony. 1993. Trevi, Europol and the European state. In *Statewatching the New Europe*. At http://www.statewatch.org/news/handbook-trevi.pdf (accessed May 2011).

Brunet-Jailly, Emmanuel. 2000. Globalization, integration and cross-border relations in the metropolitan area of Detroit (USA) and Windsor (Canada). *International Journal of Economic Development* 2 (3): 379–401.

Brunet-Jailly, Emmanuel. 2007. *Borderlands*. Ottawa: University of Ottawa Press.

Brunet-Jailly, Emmanuel. 2011a. The Canada–US perimeter. In *Canada–Europe Transatlantic Dialogue*, Policy Brief, Ottawa, June, pp. 1–4.

Brunet-Jailly, Emmanuel. 2011b. The emergence of cross-border regions and Canadian-United States relations. In M. Amen, Noah J. Toly, Patricia L. McCarney and Klaus Segbers, eds, *Cities and Global Governance*, pp. 69–91. Farnham: Ashgate.

Brunet-Jailly, Emmanuel, Clarke, Susan E. and Nijnatten, Debora Van. 2006. An Emerging North American Model of Cross-Border Regional Cooperation – Leader Survey on US–Canada Cross Border Regions: The Results in Perspective. Working Papers Series 008. Ottawa: Government of Canada, Policy Research Initiative.

Buzan, Barry. 1991. *People, States and Fear: The National Security Problem in International Relations*. Rev. 2nd edn. Chapel Hill: University of North Carolina Press. First publ. 1983.

Buzan, Barry, Weaver, Ole, and Wilde, Jaap de. 1998. *Security: A New Framework for Analysis*. Boulder: Lynne Rienner.

CBP (US Customs and Border Protection). 2008a. Customs-trade partnership against terrorism: a year in review. Jan. 31. At http://www.cbp.gov/xp/cgov/newsroom/news_releases/archives/2008_news_releases/jan_2008/01312008.xml (accessed Nov. 2011).

CBP (US Customs and Border Protection). 2008b. Free and Secure Trade factsheet. At http://www.customs.gov/linkhandler/cgov/newsroom/fact_sheets/travel/fast/fast_fact.ctt/fast_fact.pdf (accessed Nov. 2011).

Chaire Raoul-Dandurand. 2011. Conference on Fences, Walls and Borders: State of Insecurity? Chaire Raoul-Dandurand en Études Stratégiques et Diplomatiques. At www.dandurand.uqam.ca/ (accessed Nov. 2011).

Council of the European Union. 2009. *European Security Strategy: A Secure Europe in a Better World*. Brussels: European Communities. At http://www.consilium.europa.eu/uedocs/cms_data/librairie/PDF/QC7809568ENC.pdf (accessed June 20, 2011).

Deudney, Daniel. 1990. The case against linking environmental degradation and national security. *Millennium: Journal of International Studies* 19: 461–476.

Deutsch, Karl. 1957. *Political Community and the North Atlantic Area*. Princeton: Princeton University Press.

European Council. 2001. Presidency conclusions: European Council meeting in Laeken, 14 and 15 December 2001. At http://ec.europa.eu/governance/impact/background/docs/laeken_concl_en.pdf (accessed May 2011).

European Parliament. 2011. *Management of External Borders*. Fact Sheet. At http://www.europarl.europa.eu/ftu/pdf/en/FTU_4.12.4.pdf (accessed Dec. 2011).

European Union. 2010. Lisbon Treaty. *Official Journal of the European Union C83*, 30.03.2010 See http://bookshop.europa.eu/is-bin/INTERSHOP.enfinity/WFS/EU-Bookshop-Site/en_GB/-/EUR/ViewPublication-Start?PublicationKey=FXAC10083 (accessed June 19, 2011).

Flynn, Stephen. 2003. A false conundrum: continental integration vs. border security. In Peter Andreas and Thomas Biersteker, eds, *The Rebordering of North America: Integration and Exclusion in a New Security Context*, pp. 110–127. New York: Routledge.

Funworld Magazine. 2010. Rules of the road. April At http://www.iaapa.org/industry/funworld/2010/apr/features/RuleRoad/index.asp (accessed Nov. 2011).

Gray, Colin S. 1994a. Global security and economic well being: a strategic perspective. *Political Studies* 42 (1): 25–39.

Gray, Colin S. 1994b. *Villains, Victims and Sheriffs; Strategic Studies and Security for an Inter-war Period*. Hull: University of Hull Press.

Holdich, Thomas H. 1916. *Political Frontiers and Boundary Making*. London: Macmillan.

Ignatieff, Michael. 2003. Canada in the age of terror – multilateralism meets a moment of truth. *Policy Options* (Feb.).

Insurance Corporation of British Columbia. 2009. *Your Guide to British Columbia's Enhanced Driver's Licence Program*. At http://www.icbc.com/driver-licensing/getting-licensed/edl (accessed June 18, 2011).

Jang, Brent. 2010. Ottawa's $550 million loan offer for new bridge launches war of words in Michigan. *Globe and Mail*, Apr. 29. At http://www.theglobeandmail.com/report-on-business/ottawas-550-million-loan-offer-for-new-bridge-launches-war-of-words-in-michigan/article1551117/ (accessed Nov. 2011).

Kitchen, Veronica. 2002. Canadian-American border security after September 11th. Working Paper, Department of Political Science, Brown University.

Luciani, Giacomo. 1989. The economic content of security. *Journal of Public Policy*. 8 (2): 151–173.

Lyde, Lionel W. 1915. *Some Frontiers of Tomorrow: An Aspiration for Europe*. London: A & C Black.

Manley, John, Aspe, Pedro and Weld, William. 2005. *Building a North American Community*. New York: Council of Foreign Relations.

Marks, Gary and Hooghe, Liesbet. 2001. *Multi-level Governance and European Integration*. Boulder: Rowman & Littlefield.

McKitrick, Ross and Essex, Christopher. 2002. Why Canada should not ratify Kyoto. *Kitchener Waterloo Record*. At http://www.uoguelph.ca/~rmckitri/research/kwrec.pdf (accessed June 21, 2011).

Nossal, Kim. 1985. Economic nationalism and continental integration. In Denis Stairs and Gilbert Winham, eds, *The Politics of Canada's Economic Relationship with the United States*. Toronto: University of Toronto Press.

Pastor, Robert. 2001. *Toward a North American Community: Lessons from the Old World to the New*. Washington DC: Institute for International Economics.

Ridge, Tom. 2001. September 11, 2001: attack on America. Press Conference, Ottawa, 9:30 a.m., Dec. 12. At http://avalon.law.yale.edu/sept11/ridge_012.asp (accessed July 2011).

Sands, Christopher. 2011. *The Canada Gambit: Will It Revive North America?* Washington, DC: Hudson Institute. At http://www.hudson.org/files/publications/Canada%20Gambit%20Web.pdf (accessed Mar. 2011).

Semple, Ellen Churchill. 1911. *Influences in Geographic Environment*. New York: Holt.

Shea, Bill. 2010. Bridge Q&A: your DRIC questions (mostly) answered. Apr. 30. At http://www.crainsdetroit.com/article /20100430/STAFFBLOG03/304309988 (accessed Nov. 2011).

Solana, Javier. 2003. *A Secure Europe in a Better World.* Talk of the EU High Representative for the Common Foreign and Security Policy at European Council, Thessaloniki, June 20. At http://www.consilium. europa.eu/uedocs/cms_data/docs/ pressdata/en/reports/76255.pdf (accessed June 20, 2011).

US GAO (US Government Accountability Office). 2008. *Secure Border Initiative: Observations on Deployment Challenges.* Testimony before the Committee on Homeland Security, House of Representatives, GAO–08–1141T. At www.gao.gov/ new.items/d081141t.pdf (accessed Feb. 2011).

US GAO (US Government Accountability Office). 2010. *Border Security: Enhanced DHS Oversight and Assessment of Interagency Coordination Is Needed for the Northern Border.* Report to Congressional Requesters, GAO-11-97. At http://www. gao.gov/new.items/d1197.pdf (accessed Feb. 2011).

Walt, Stephen. 1991. The renaissance of security studies. *International Studies Quarterly* 35 (2): 211–239.

Zaccardelli, Giuliano. 2002. The challenges of policing in the new global environment. Speech, Rideau Club luncheon, Nov. 19.

Zaccardelli, Giuliano. 2003. Intelligence, security and integration of law enforcement. Conference of Canadian Association for Security and Intelligence Studies on the New Intelligence Order: Knowledge for Security and International Relations, Ottawa, Sept. 26–28. (Author's notes.)

Zielonka, Jan. 2006. *Europe as Empire: The Nature of the Enlarged European Union.* Oxford: Oxford University Press.

CHAPTER 7

Border Regimes, the Circulation of Violence and the Neo-authoritarian Turn

John Borneman

Much has changed in the border regimes of Europe and the Middle East since I began research in Germany in 1982, and in Lebanon and Syria in 1999. Germany is no longer divided into two peoples; many of the borders within Europe, between East and West and North and South, have been radically revised if not dissolved in stunningly peaceful revolutions beginning in November 1989. Lebanon, however, is still divided by sects in borders more culturally and religiously distinct than territorially discrete; its internal borders in the minds of its residents are more tribal than ideological, as in Germany, and because of this Lebanese resist the current changes wrought by larger pan-Arab forces stirring revolt throughout the Middle East, with revolutions already displacing leaders, and perhaps political forms, in Tunisia and Egypt. Yet, even in Lebanon, there has been radical change, when the Israeli Defense Forces unilaterally withdrew in June 2000, after an 18-year occupation, and Syria withdrew its so-called "presence" and troops, including military "checkpoints" throughout the country, in April 2005. And in the middle of these events, not to be neglected for its impact on European and Middle Eastern border regimes, was the attack on the World Trade Center in New York City, 9/11 in 2001, which seemed to crystallize in the Western mind a vision of radical alterity in "political Islam" brewing for centuries, leading to two wars and the stationing of European and American troops in two Muslim countries, Afghanistan and Iraq.

In this essay I wish to move from experiences in my two ethnographic sites to begin to think through these changes and their theoretical and practical import for the understanding of border regimes – the regulation of freedom, security, exchange, and violence – since the Victory of Capitalism. It was that victory, of capitalism, that was certainly not the cause but the condition of possibility for the radical changes in

---

A Companion to Border Studies, First Edition. Edited by Thomas M. Wilson and Hastings Donnan.

cultural, territorial, and economic borders in these two disparate yet linked geographical landscapes that I have witnessed in the brief period of 30 years of research. I had read my Marx before I began study, and, raised in the capitalist West, I had been skeptical of his prediction that the logic of capitalism was to do away with all borders between nations and to create a world market, and that the innovative and productive potential of capitalism as a form of exchange would lead to its concentration in the hands of a few and exploitation and immiseration of the vast majority of others.

In my experience of the Cold War, national borders remained strong, and class inequality remained in check, allowing for the creation of a vast consumer-oriented middle class in different parts of the world. Despite the "arms race" with its threat of Mutually Assured Destruction, security and equality were the aspirations and the experience of large populations, at least in the First and Second Worlds.

The fall of the Berlin Wall, in November 1989, opened the way for a change in that regime: suddenly capital began to move quickly and more freely (it had been largely restricted to geographical zones of exchange) not only between East and West Europe (the so-called First and Second Worlds that had been organized against each other into hostile fronts); and there was a radical expansion of exchange between the First (global North) and the Third World (global South). Since that opening, capitalism can claim a victory in the extended free movement of goods, but political liberalism must acknowledge a defeat in the free movement of people. Indeed, two new seemingly unrelated walls, unimaginable in 1989, have since been constructed outside Europe: the Israeli "West Bank barrier," whose construction began in 2003, ostensibly to protect civilians against "Palestinian terrorism," and the United States "border fence" with Mexico, whose construction began in 2007, ostensibly to protect against "illegal movement" coming from Mexico. These new border-walls, rather than the opening of the Berlin Wall, may be more accurate harbingers of our collective futures.

During the Cold War, the liberal, capitalist West had always used the rhetoric of unfreedom to criticize the authoritarian, socialist East, and to this criticism the East had no adequate response. The Soviet Union and its satellite states did claim, plausibly, that socialism needed the protection of territorial boundaries to prevent capital from taking over. Since socialist states heavily subsidized many subsistence goods and "necessities," to allow the free movement of goods from the West would, they said, have caused a collapse of their own systems of production – which did, in fact, occur after the removal of these economic borders. Admittedly, socialist rulers used this economic argument at the level of the system to declare all forms of political critique the products of enemy propaganda, creating large groups of internal "dissidents" whose dissatisfactions, in point of fact, stemmed not from lack of exchange opportunities but lack of political freedoms, including freedom of speech, association and travel (Borneman 1998).

Today these system arguments seem quaint, at best, as current divisions are nowhere structured by the tension between Communist and Capitalist ideologies or systems. Rather, all tensions play out within capitalism, and in the pairing of very similar capitalist principles of economic organization with different political forms. Thus the West posits Chinese "wildcat" capitalism and political authoritarianism as the only competitive systemic alternative to its own market capitalism and liberal-democratic political form, or it posits as the unreal alternative the specter of capitalism and Islamic theocratic form. However, neither communism nor any other collectivist movement poses a threat, real or imagined, to capitalism as an economic form. Criticisms of the principles of capitalism – profit for profit's sake and the right to contract "freely" one's own labor – are rarely voiced any longer in any political domain. Indeed, this lack of debate and uncritical acceptance of capitalism, even after the near collapse of the world economic system in 2008, suggests a new "captive mind" unwilling or unable to imagine alternatives, what the Polish poet and Nobel Prize winner Czesław Miłosz so perspicaciously criticized in 1953, during the time of Stalin (Miłosz 1981). Miłosz argued that the socialist intelligentsia overidentified with a Communist system that promised freedom but in fact increasingly limited freedoms while claiming it was doing the opposite. Ironically, the Capitalist victory has led to an internalization of the very cognitive form of political acquiescence and self-delusion that contributed to communism's collapse.

What are the major threats to today's border regimes? Since we all – including al Qaeda – operate only within capitalism, these threats must also come from within. We might identify two: first, the circulation of violence which accompanies the accelerated exchanges and movements of people and goods that contemporary capitalism demands; second, the generalization of the model of the corporation with limited liability in which today certain principles of property and ownership are not only not sufficiently checked by political authority, but are able to replace political authority, as its very rationale and precondition. This rationale, in its extreme, legitimates refusing to hold anyone, including corporations, responsible for the production of carbon dioxide and other human-produced pollutants that would seem to threaten global environmental catastrophe. To be sure, borders are being constructed around other kinds of threats also, some seemingly external, but in what follows I will limit my discussion to the circulation of violence and the corporation with limited liability.

EXTERNAL BORDERS AND INTERNAL LINES

In her stellar work on borders, Mary Douglas points to the relation between external boundaries – thresholds, doorways, crossroads – and the human body and its orifices. Bodily entrances and exits are used to symbolize the external boundaries of social structure, and in ritual the external boundaries of the social are then mapped onto the individual body. Moreover, she argues, there is danger "pressing on external boundaries . . . from transgressing the internal lines . . . [and] in the margins" (1966: 122). I want to take up these external boundaries in their most literal sense, as national borders, and relate them to "internal lines," which Douglas equates with the ambiguity and precariousness internal to group morality.

In the modern world system, group moralities are rarely any longer indigenously reproduced "internal lines" (that is, emotional-cognitive schemas of an isolable culture in the head) but increasingly inflected by inter-national relations, that is, by internalized external powers, or, as Taussig (1993) has shown for Latin American-US relations, the mimetic identification with external, colonizing powers. Both external borders and internal lines function as filters to define and regulate what belongs inside and outside the individual or group. Several disciplines have contributed greatly to understanding such filters: psychoanalysis for what is kept outside and allowed inside the mind, sociology for the filter between groups, international relations for the borders between states and nations. Anthropology traverses these specializations, attentive to the interrelations of intra- and inter-psychic, personal, group, and national borders.

External borders and internal lines often operate at cross-purposes. Let me offer several examples. Internal moral distinctions can enforce an external border (as in the use of anti-Muslim stereotypes by Greeks to enforce a physical border with Turkey), or create a radical extremity of something that was previously within the social body (as in the attempt to annihilate the Jews of Europe by placing them outside the social). Internal distinctions can stabilize tense relations between forms of difference (as in contemporary German-French differences, which are deployed as complementary and used to invert centuries of hostility), or destabilize those relations by preventing exchanges or delaying reciprocities (as with Cold War boundaries between Poles and Germans). A border in the mind may prevent some information from entering, thwarting the learning essential to change or survive, or, inversely, it may inadequately defend the self and let too much information in, overwhelming the emotional capacity to understand what is inside and outside in the first place.

The possible configurations of play and power between internal and external borders are infinite. Here, I want to focus on how (external) territorial borders physically quite distant from a center, from that which they are supposed to protect, become internal objects, mental representations to which one is attached. Through this attachment to the extremity, as Sahlins (1989) demonstrated in his classic study of French-Spanish border histories, and as Borneman (1991, 1992) did for the two Berlins during the Cold War, personal or group conflicts that are external to and outside oneself, that occur at some distant physical border, can become perceived as internal.

Therefore, having a border far removed from one's own center is no guarantee of peace and stability at home, as skirmishes at the border often have lasting effects on the center. This was the case for the United States and the Soviet Union during the Cold War, which as centers often fought proxy wars in geographically distant zones. The Berlin Wall and the borders between East and West Germany and East and West Europe performed these symbolic functions for the two centers. With the collapse of these Cold War boundaries within Europe, which of course never completely disappear as structuring devices, the borders within Europe no longer function to structure the borders of the US and Russia. World ideologies and world political-territorial-economic blocs have become unmoored.

Since 1990, Europe, instead of being the border zone for the border regimes of others, has now moved its own borders elsewhere, in fact outside instead of inside of Europe, and they revolve primarily around the Atlantic and the Mediterranean, its ocean on the west and sea on the south. To the west is the United States and the negotiation of relations with the American version of turbo-capitalism and political missionary work (Borneman 2003); to the south is the Middle East and the borders regulating the movement of people entering Europe, especially the Arabs in former colonies from Morocco to Syria; to the east, most significant are relations with Israel, whose demarcations around the West Bank and Gaza – to contain the Palestinians – and borders with Lebanon and Egypt, structure Europe's relations to its ghosts.

Europe is also involved through its relations with the US and the Middle East in the impossible attempt to construct borders around Afghanistan (impossible without curtailing European consumption of Afghan opium), and the even more tragic attempt to refigure Iraq (only increasing its internal schisms and integrating it more tightly with Iran). The border, or the new wall, between the United States and Mexico performs a similar function for the US, of creating the idea of an outside at a considerable distance from the center, while at the same time remaining permeable for the export of America's violent weapons to Mexico and the intermittent import of Mexico's needed illegal laborers and its narcotics to the US. All of these borders borrow from and exchange with each other tactics, technologies, and rationales.

Let me return, briefly, to this issue of borders with the past, and the meaning of the borders of Israel for non-Israelis. People generally attach much affect to the Israeli border regime, irrespective of where they come from. For Europeans and Americans, the borders of Israel are unusually charged with what Douglas called internal lines, and they mean much more than their strategic location alone would seem to warrant, as they are quite distant territorially from these two centers. They mean so much in part because of the integral role Europe played in both creating the need for a Jewish homeland outside Europe and then creating it in Palestine (Morris 2001).

The Israeli border regime is a very complex system that tightly regulates immigration of Jews from the entire world, and itinerant laborers, nearly all of whom come from underdeveloped countries, half illegal, and emigration primarily to Europe and the US, along with internal controls, including apartheid-like roads, illegal settlements, displaced person camps, the prison of Gaza, and vibrant and marginal cities (cf. Weizman 2007; Segal et al. 2003). The regime is surrounded by Arabs, with whom it also regulates relations, or the intended nonrelations more characteristic of the current state of affairs. The emotions these various borders, walls, and flows evoke cannot be easily cognized or rationalized. American scholars, along with journalists and others who write about Israel, have contributed greatly to keeping the emotional pitch high and the actual conversations muted, inserting themselves as oversized, finger-waving superegos in discussions Europeans have with themselves about their past and present relations with Israel. Germans, especially, given their singular role in the European Holocaust, are subject to collective discipline about the frames in which they can legitimately speak and think about Israel.

There is much evidence of success in influencing the "internal lines" of Germans, and it includes German wariness and fear in approaching Israel critically, at least in public. Evidence of internalization if not masochism is that the very first thing many Germans do when they arrive in Israel is to visit Yad Vashem, whose official task is "to perpetuate the legacy of the Holocaust to future generations." Certainly these visits should be seen first and foremost as an act of repentance, but however much the affect attached to responsibility for the Holocaust may represent historical justice generally, a reckoning with truth and history, it is sadistic to insist that the Germans have inherited a direct, unending generational transmission of responsibility for historical crimes, especially when this responsibility does not also acknowledge the contemporary reality of Palestinians within the narrative of Jewish victimization and emancipation.

Individual Germans or Americans or Israelis often sincerely believe they have a responsibility to the memory of the Holocaust. However, to the degree that Holocaust memory is not translated into heightened sensitivity and understanding about human suffering and its causes both generally and in other contexts and places, it leads merely to *Betroffenheit*, a repetitive sentiment that easily becomes self-pity. Such sentiment has the effect of monopolizing *Entrüstung* (indignation) for one community alone. In sum, the German relation to the contemporary Israeli state and society is usually directly inferred from the historical relations of Germans to Jews, a relationship overdetermined by ghosts from the past that are internal to the creation of external boundaries. Academics, by focusing almost exclusively on the issue of Germans and Jewish historical relations, play no small part in producing the affect that comes out of this proposition, which, in turn, obscures the fact that European borders are in fact being constructed in the Middle East.

CIRCULATING VIOLENCE

Borders are about security, and external borders are especially about security from violence, the building of barriers, material and immaterial, to arrest the flow of threats. Violence circulates, and security measures follow the circulation of violence as it is displaced. The route between various border regimes is circuitous, and often carries us to unexpected mental and physical places, such as, for example, German affect regarding Jews and, by extension, the relation between the Israeli border regime and new European borders. We can follow one such circuit of displacement by beginning outside of Europe, with the French term Levant, a term with a long history and many references. Geographically it refers to the meeting point of western Asia, the eastern Mediterranean, and northern Africa, and during the period of the Crusades became synonymous with the Holy Land. Today it refers to the particular ecosystem that includes the states of Lebanon, Syria, Jordan, Israel, and the Palestinian territory. Each territorial-political unit has a particular border regime, and they are all related to Europe, today mediated centrally through Israel. European troops, including German, are stationed along the Israeli-Lebanese border, which is where I encountered them, guarding the Lebanese coast, not from Israelis, of course, toward whom they are not to point guns, but to hinder the movement of Arabs and Muslims generally.

On Israeli maps the Palestinian territory, to the south of Lebanon, is usually lightly demarcated, and appears to have an independent integrity which in reality it does not. Maps from 1946 to the present show the remarkable transformation of Palestinian villages and cities into Israeli territory, and the reduction of land called Palestinian into small, discontinuous parcels.[1] The "West Bank barrier," mentioned earlier, whose construction began in 2003, walls in the largest single parcel of Palestinian territory near the center of Israel, with Israeli settlements inside this parcel. And then there is Gaza, which can only be described as a very large prison, that borders Egypt to the south.

Being very familiar with the Berlin Wall, and its rationalizations and criticisms, I see both the Israeli wall and the new, only partially constructed, American fence which has been built to regulate the flow with Mexico, as anachronistic. By comparison, the no-longer-existing Berlin Wall appears visually innocent, even playful, certainly less deadly. I would like to begin, then, with the security of Israel question, and trace the circulation of violence from one of its most recent eruptions, in the Israeli-Hezbollah War of 2006, which resulted in the stationing of European troops on the south Lebanese border with Israel.[2]

Claiming to be responding to a raid on July 12 by Hezbollah forces into Israel in which they abducted two Israeli soldiers and killed three others, and to a failed rescue mission in which five more soldiers were killed, Israel launched massive airstrikes and artillery fire on Lebanese civilian infrastructure, an air and naval blockade, and a ground invasion of southern Lebanon. The war lasted for 34 days, from July 12 to August 14, in the summer of 2006, and pitted Hezbollah (Party of God) paramilitary forces against the state of Israel. During the fighting, 159 Israelis were killed, most of whom were soldiers but including 41 civilians hit by some 4,000 Katyusha rockets and mortars indiscriminately lobbed by Hezbollah forces from Lebanon into northern Israel; another 997 were injured (75 "seriously" and 115 "moderately"), and approximately 300,000 Israeli civilians were temporarily displaced.

On the other side, 1,191 Lebanese were killed, nearly all civilians, with an estimated third of the fatalities being children under 12, the overall number including 43 Lebanese soldiers and police, 74 Hezbollah and 17 Amal combatants; some 4,490 Lebanese were wounded, and approximately 900,000 were displaced. Israeli attacks obliterated a few villages and sections of Beirut and Tyre, set some forests in the north afire, caused an estimated $280 million in agricultural damage, and in targeting power stations and oil refineries unleashed an oil slick in the eastern Mediterranean whose cost in environmental damage is estimated at $64 million. There was also the July 25 airstrike on a United Nations peacekeeping post in Khiyam, leaving four UNIFIL observers dead.

Perhaps the most controversial of these attacks was the artillery units' use of white phosphorous shells (which cause painful and often lethal burns), and the dropping by the air force, indiscriminately in civilian areas, of at least 1,800 cluster bombs containing 1.2 million cluster bomblets around the south of Lebanon. Now, to consider this war as a series of justified security measures (with regrettable collateral damage) to put an end to violence, as did Israel and the supportive American George W. Bush administration in its public statements, as well as some European governments and many scholars, is one way to look at the conflict. Another is to see this Israeli-Hezbollah War as circulating violence, more specifically a series of reciprocal, though disproportionate war crimes that countries like Israel and nonstate militias like Hezbollah inside Lebanon can engage in with legal impunity.

In early December 2006, at a large conference on legal anthropology at Yale University, I gave a talk on this war and the implications for international law of the lack of prosecution for war crimes. Eleven months later one participant described to me her perception of the audience reaction as "icy silence." The discussant and two quite renowned feminist lawyers on my panel were obviously outraged, if not embarrassed, and overtly avoided engagement with me. Shortly after, I visited Bint Jbail, a formerly beautiful, relatively prosperous, predominantly Sunni village in southern Lebanon, where I took photos of war damage. I have since published this material in a Canadian journal of international law (Borneman 2007).

Lebanon is a porous, weak state but with strong sectarian identifications. Syria has the same sectarian divisions but a large Sunni majority (85 percent), and, by contrast with Lebanon, is an authoritarian police state, much like the former East Germany. Where these two secular states, Lebanon and Syria, unite, if at all – despite the difficult relations between the two, including suspected Syrian assassinations of independent figures in Lebanon – is around a pan-Arabism based on an identification both with the victims in Bint Jbail and also with Palestinian suffering under Israeli occupation. In both countries the Palestinian issue is a daily item in print and on television. There are televisions on street corners in Aleppo, where I spent a year in 2004–2005, that play the entire day to passersby live pictures of Israeli violence against Palestinians and American violence against Iraqis, just pictures with no commentary. Only to the Israeli state, however, are individuals in Jbail identifying with Hezbollah the same as individuals in Gaza identifying with Hamas, which in turn brings about a counter-transferential identification that unites Arabs against Jews. Among themselves, as Arabs, the internal lines are as great as the external boundaries.

And here is where the circuit of violence moves from the space of the Levant backward in time to Europe. In the whole world, only in the Levant does European neocolonialism continue: settler movements, victor's justice, action with impunity from legal prosecution. From North Africa to the Arab Gulf States, this history of European colonial occupation is still very much alive as memory. Castles from the Crusades can still be found in Syria. Above all, though, this memory is alive territorially only in Palestine and Iraq. The Palestinian resistance draws its moral legitimacy from the same source Jewish Zionists drew from: European emancipation and state-building movements, along with former independence struggles from Europe. Before 2002, Hezbollah resistance to Israeli occupation of south Lebanon also drew from this same source.[3] It is through this lens of present occupations that most Arabs see the West, giving motivation to the more radical forms of resistance to it.

Although continuous with the resistance to colonial domination, this pan-Arabism is not necessarily anti-European or anti-American – too many Arabs live in Detroit, Paris, and London. After the Israeli withdrawal from South Lebanon in 2002, I met an amazing number of people from Detroit in the small, Hezbollah-friendly southern towns of Nabatiyah and Naqurah. But Europe and the United States are the guarantors of Israeli neocolonialism, and through this connection the violence in the Levant circles back in time and forward in space to Europe, where the new border regime intends to keep out precisely these people and this violence.

CORPORATE LIMITED LIABILITY IN THE NEW EUROPEAN BORDER REGIME

Among the mechanisms of internal policing of this new European border regime, perhaps the most underestimated has been the expansion of the notion of the limited liability corporation. Here I shall restrict myself to the legal form common in Germany and Central Europe, the GmbH: Gesellschaft mit beschränkter Haftung. In my experience of Europe over the last 40 years, I have hardly noticed this mechanism, despite radical material and ideological changes. If there has been an effect to the expansion of corporations, then, it has been insidious, unannounced by a movement or spokespersons, working with and through the present political form, which itself has changed little. The postsocialist transformation of authoritarian, planned economy into more democratic market-oriented states has not produced any novelties in the understanding of the political, or the organization and practices of the state. The one exception would be the Balkans, where the very mutability of the form of state and people makes it the exception or limit case within Europe to European order.

In short, despite the end of Cold War division, which entailed the unification of Germany, the strengthening and expansion of the EU into the East, and the indeterminacy of the Balkans, the territorial map of European states has changed little. What has changed are the demographics of the people: there are more elderly and more immigrants. Turks and North Africans and people from the Levant, along with select other groups, began arriving as temporary laborers in groups in the 1970s. Many have stayed, and they have dramatically changed the public face of most European countries. In some countries, foreign-born citizens number more than one-fourth. Along with this demographic change, which has meant more movement between European and non-European states, the European Union took over some of the powers of national governments – for example, in currency control, legislation, and science policies. Both changes signify new regimes of sovereignty at borders: new instances controlling the movement of objects and people through space. Territorial sovereignty and peoplehood were the two principles founding the modern, post-Westphalian European order, subsequently exported to the entire world. They are now severely challenged as modes of regulating internal and external borders, specifically the circulation of violence that operates through manipulation of border regimes.

Here is where the notion of the company with limited liability becomes significant as a mode of traversing people and space, of organizing relations between states as well as the relations of states to citizens and noncitizens, and as a mechanism for policing capital. One convincing explanation of why socialist Eastern Europe could not compete with capitalist Western Europe economically is the lack of transnational corporations in the East that could move freely between states and destroy the older national or even prenational structures of socioeconomic and political organization. After the opening of the Wall, I witnessed how these corporations, under the guise of "privatization" driven by the Treuhandanstalt, moved en masse into East Germany and took advantage of the new property regime to assume control over the essential sectors of food distribution, housing maintenance/renovation, manufacturing, and industrial production.

The notion of "limited liability" for corporations is much older, of course, and has different histories in English common law and the continental European civil law traditions, and then again there are differences in the German-dominated Central European civil law and the French-influenced sphere to the west. Regardless of the origin and sphere in which the concept has developed, it has been essential to creating the wealth that we associate with the European economy since the late nineteenth century, including the wealth that made possible the modern social-welfare state. In Germany, the laws regulating this form were adopted in 1892, and it has since become the most common corporate form there, if not in Europe as a whole. Its function was to raise large amounts of capital by selling shares to investors, who became partners in the corporation but were not personally liable for the company's debts.

Today, however, the limited liability company, as concept and institution, appears to be in direct conflict with and undermining the social-welfare state. While the extension of individual notions of personhood to corporations has been most advanced in the United States, in Europe, too, a parallel extension of the concept of limited liability to corporations has increasingly been used to evade communal or national responsibilities that in the past were assumed to follow from ownership of property. Such a concept normalizes hedonistic conceptions of social relations over any notion of shared sacrifice in the many spheres of life outside a narrowly conceived "economy," and facilitates the transformation of the individual from producer to consumer.[4] These transformations have been so naturalized, in practice and theory, that only ethnographic comparison of "the West" with other world culture-regions, such as New Guinea or Central Africa, might alert us to question how consumerist ideology and the model of the limited liability corporation organize relations between persons and things.[5]

It is important to ask how corporations with limited liability are refiguring territoriality within Europe – concepts of relations of people to each other, to land and property, and to the state itself. Such corporate refiguring is going on beneath the radar, so to speak, of most academic projects. For example, three of the most expansive and scholarly recent books about modern European history that engage extensively with economic processes – Charles Maier's *Dissolution* (1997), Niall Ferguson's *The Cash Nexus* (2001), and Tony Judt's *Postwar* (2005) – contain no entry for corporations in their lengthy indexes.

Ethnographically, it is impossible to miss this economic tsunami, for people everywhere in Europe are reacting to and commenting on its effects without being able to identify the causes. "Euro-pessimism" is one word used to gloss the reaction. Another, in German, is *meckern* – constant complaining. While some analysts might want to claim Europeans have always stressed the negative, or Germans have always found fault when possible, this current complaint is, I think, a reaction to a quite specific historical situation.

People are grumbling because life is becoming part of a neo-authoritarian laboratory, and because the EU is increasingly reduced to facilitating the creation of Europe as a free trade zone especially friendly to limited liability legal entities and to the "consumer." Current European capitalism no longer needs producers or democracy or, at the civil level, reciprocity, forms of politeness, or hospitality. The administrative integration of Europe proceeds like a juggernaut along market lines – with uniformization in production, pricing, policing, pensions, as well as in consuming, though, as always, class differentiated in experience. Before 9/11 and the legislation of new surveillance regimes, some scholars cast the new security arrangements as progressive. In the hopeful words of Mary Kaldor, the "extension of the rule of law and civil society across borders [is] . . . a continuous process of enlargement" (2000: 58). This extension and enlargement has been perversely in sync with the shift to neo-authoritarianism. The project is a hierarchical, centralizing one, but also a "rationalization" in the name of "evergrowing interconnectedness," with little acknowledgment of the ideals of European identification with human rights, multiculturalism, and tolerance and diversity, all of which Kaldor lists (2000: 60). Among European peoples, there is little popular understanding or agreement about the motivations or visions of the future other than orientation to a general consumer capitalism and security from an outside – Muslims, Arabs, the Israeli-Palestinian conflict, the American way – that is already internal to Europe.

From today's perspective, the 1990s were in fact a heyday and perhaps the endpoint for European political integration, which resulted in 2004 in the enlargement of the EU from 15 to 25 states, and the addition of 72 million individual East-Central European members. At the time, this incorporation into the EU was represented as a model of harmony between nation-states working for the common good, with a single foreign minister to represent all member countries to the exterior. Simultaneously, however, many of the social benefits achieved since World War II were rolled back, and forms of local welfare and sociality destabilized. To be sure, the effects of these policies were uneven, and I know of no large-scale study of the distribution of effects. But a visit to any of the small towns of East Germany, which have been renovated with heavy subsidies from West Germany, reveals a very sad landscape of social disintegration, resulting largely from the youth and brain drain to the West: ghost towns, empty apartments and houses with newly repaired sidewalks and a few lovingly renovated facades; and high unemployment and low productivity of those who do work, despite the widespread use of government-subsidized worker training programs (*Arbeitsbeschaffungsmaßnahmen*). Many of the corporations that moved in for quick profits and cheaper, skilled labor after 1990 subsequently left for greener fields. Yet, those people left behind, primarily the very young, very old, and the unskilled, have also become part of the enlarged EU, integrated into its political structure and market, with political representation, stable pensions, consumption of exchangeable goods priced in precious euros, and security from a threatening outside.

Worries about the dismantling of the welfare society, visible everywhere, are often displaced into longstanding concerns about the loss of national sovereignty, specifically with regard to immigration and the free movement of labor promoted by the Brussels-based bureaucracy of the EU. Along with the transfer of factories to new member states, and competition for corporations and their investment capital from countries with lower tax regimes, immigrants from the East have indeed, as widely feared, flooded into Western Europe, though not equally to every country. This population movement has reinforced the ideology of limited or even no liability at the individual level. To be sure, this new labor force kept wages down, making consumer goods cheaper than they would otherwise have been, but also it has squeezed the lower middle classes who, with less income relative to more expensive goods, can no longer afford the same level of services. The cheap labor in the West has also initially contributed greatly to general economic growth and productivity, much as cheap labor of *Vertriebene* (refugees from the eastern territories) did following World War II.

This movement of Europeans within Europe (omitting here the large movement of non-Europeans) has had not only negative but also serendipitous effects. A Greek friend of mine who lives in Berlin explained to me that, as younger Greeks no longer want to work on farms, a large number of Poles have taken the farms over, especially on the islands. As they brought needed skills and did not come in search of welfare, these Poles were welcomed and integrated into local life, much as many Albanians have been welcomed in the cities. It helps that the migrants learn the language and respect local customs. This story is not generalizable to wider European processes of integration, however. Africans and Arabs have an entirely different set of collective experiences, and perhaps this first group of first-generation postsocialist Poles are particularly industrious among East European immigrants, and this first generation of Albanian immigrants unusually assimilable.

What can be concluded, nonetheless, is that the immigrant "flood" from the East was the result of matching the needs of Western European countries for immigrants to fill shortages in skilled and unskilled labor and to support pension benefits for an ageing population unable to contribute to these benefits themselves. With the economic crisis in 2008, many of the educated, skilled, industrious laborers from the East lost their employment, and are now returning to their former socialist states, hoping that the faster growing economies there can reabsorb them. By contrast, there are the migrants from North Africa and Turkey, mostly Muslim and Arab, ranging from doctors to unskilled construction workers, who are perceived to threaten internal cohesion, or whatever is left of that expectation, within most of Europe. The entrance of Turkey into the EU is particularly controversial, and not only in France, which has the continent's largest Muslim population, but also in Germany, where recent studies suggest a generational divide among Turkish residents about the terms and merits of cultural integration.

EU governments, never adept at managing immigration, have been unable to agree on a common European policy (Peebles 1997; Dell'Olio 2005). Instead, each member state has enacted its own immigration curbs, giving the appearance of an uncoordinated Fortress Europe, and a protectionist sentiment further reinforced by the rejection of the proposed treaty establishing a constitution for Europe in French and Dutch referendums in 2004, effectively ending the ratification process (for an early analysis of the fortress concept, cf. Stolcke 1995). Past history suggests immigration slows if integration is successful, but that is unlikely to be predictive of the present. Even if integration is by some metric successful, there appears to be an enduring structural difference between the economies of Europe and those of the global south (with the exception of some with oil wealth), which will continue to generate a push factor in migration.

The project of Europe, then, has devolved into an authoritarian or administrative capitalism, in part driven by the linked ideological concepts of "limited liability" and "consumerism." This project has many paradoxes, including that the greatest opposition to immigration and EU expansion comes from the countries that profit most from its expansion and from European subsidies – Britain and France, for example. Ultimately, these well-fed countries stay on board precisely because the EU has become what Sloterdijk (2005) calls "a brainless system of transnational bank transfers to spoiled countries where national culture still dominates [and the] domain of

freedom [is] being eroded bit by bit." In sum, this new border regime, notwithstanding its multiple intents, contradictions, cracks, and serendipitous effects, tends both,
on the one hand, to reorient the symbolic order within Europe, redefining the relation of people to each other and to the state to accommodate the notion of limited
liability, and, on the other, to produce a new notion of security that protects the
politico-economic powers benefiting most from extensions of the concept of corporate personhood and conflation of the citizen with the consumer.

SECURITY

Finally, I want to return to the question of external security and the circulation of
violence, and to what I have written elsewhere as neo-authoritarian responses to the
twin threats of America and Islam (Borneman 2003, 2011). These threats are not to
territorial but to identificatory, ideological borders, to the security of a life course
(what anthropologists in the past often called a "way of life"). In 2003, I argued that
in the emerging post–Cold War form of triangulation structuring identifications
in and between the US and Europe, both physical and spectral elements of the Middle
East had replaced communism as the mediating Third. This new topos "Middle East," I wrote, was "now actively internal to both European and US development,
to their self-definitions and visions of the future" (Borneman 2003: 487). While I
still agree with this statement, the conclusion I drew – that "Europe's advanced secu-
larization of Christianity allows for a more consistent and more thinkable model of
Jewish and Muslim integration" – was way too optimistic. Instead, it appears to me
now that the current European position to perceived externalities is an inward-turned
passive-aggressiveness: some development aid and contribution to peacekeeping
forces outside Europe, but, above all, no relations with others that might deflate the
illusion of a life course that unfolds in a consumer paradise.

Europeans did in fact engage in some hand-wringing during the Israeli attack on
Lebanon in 2006 described above. But ultimately they were unwilling to sacrifice
anything that might shake their subservient relation to US militarism in the Middle
East, or to take the initiative to redraw the international order they have exported
– modeled on independent, sovereign, homogeneous nation-states – or to challenge
Israeli neocolonial policies with actual consequences, despite the fact that the bel-
ligerents in this conflict are already internal to Europe, bringing the violence there
within the European polity.

In order to save European liberalism from several kinds of tempting neo-
authoritarian turns (e.g., state, party, sentiment, media dictatorial), Sloterdijk (2005)
argues that there must be a new alliance between democracy and asceticism, "a
voluntary acceptance of competitive disadvantages."[6] But there is little evidence
that European consumers are willing to yield some of their prosperity, not as the
benefits of their welfare societies are being rolled back, at least not on any mass-
movement scale.

This takes me to a final issue, of what exactly this new border regime is keeping
out and allowing in. European political borders were originally and principally
conceived as a way to divide up the earth, to organize colonial adventures among

European countries, and to export Europe's political model. As scholars such as Anderson (1983), Balibar (2004), and Zolberg (1983) have long argued, this entailed exporting everywhere a notion of a people that itself created violent internal tensions, persecutions, and mass migrations. While Europeans have subjectively interiorized this idea of the border, resulting in a prosperous and relatively peaceful order among themselves, other parts of the world, including parts of Europe such as the Balkans, have not.[7] This idea of the border, however inadequate to account for the current state of affairs, or as orientation for the future, nonetheless has its uses, and that is, to underwrite a repressive mechanism that keeps certain realities – such as relations of circulating violence with the Balkans, Afghanistan, or Palestine, or relations evading collective responsibility resulting from the dominance of the consumer and limited liability corporations – at a distance.

NOTES

This paper was initially presented at a conference on Making Europe/Making Europeans: The Ethnographic and the Everyday, April 10–11, 2008, Center for European Studies, University of Texas, Austin. I thank the organizers, Werner Krauß and Ben Carrington, as well as the other paper presenters, for comments.

1   Ostensibly to protect Israeli citizens from Palestinian attacks, the state has constructed a labyrinthine system of roads, especially around settlements in the West Bank, with differential access. The Israeli High Court of Justice initially approved such constructions on Palestinian land with the argument that they would enable Palestinian movement. David Kretzmar, an emeritus professor of international law at Hebrew University of Jerusalem, recently accused Israel's High Court of Justice of "judicial hypocrisy" in its approval of one such road, Route 443. Initially rationalized as for the "local population," i.e., Palestinian use, it is now restricted to Israeli citizens alone. The court subsequently ruled this reversal of intent acceptable, for reasons of military security, and proposed as solution the construction of separate roads (a system of apartheid), i.e., a second one for Palestinians. See Kretzmar 2008. Recent studies by Israelis themselves have revealed that the settlements were always intended as permanent ways to shrink Palestinian and expand Jewish presence and control of land, in which all parts of Israeli society were involved (see Gorenberg 2007; Zertal and Eldar 2007).

2   The following facts are based on these reports: UN Human Rights Council 2006; UN News Centre 2006; Amnesty International 2006a, 2006b; *Daily Star* 2006; Erlich 2006.

3   The fact that these independence struggles have not been able to reproduce Europe's liberal democracies outside of Europe is another point, which deserves attention I cannot give here. One line of inquiry would be to explain how the rage against oppression of Palestinians is a displacement of one's own ineffectuality in establishing democratic sovereignty in one's own country. Of course, the culpability for this ineffectuality, especially the inability to depose the autocratic regimes throughout the Middle East, has much to do with the essential support – politically and in terms of payments for oil – provided by Western governments.

4   Corporate limited liability builds on and is a further development of the ideology of individualism, taking the corporate entity to be of a higher order, supplanting the individual and often the nation in law as a superior transnational legal unit. Louis Dumont was the first anthropologist to explicate what he called "the individualist revolution . . . a displace-

ment of the main value stress from society as a whole (holism) to the human individual taken as embodiment of humanity at large (individualism)" (1970: 32–33). Dumont posits this revolution as necessary in order to create the nation form, as "at once a collection of individuals and a collective individual."

5 Seen from this historical context, what does European integration, unification, whatever we want to call it, mean for the expansion of democracy? There are two common framings of the citizenship issue, one that argues the linking of citizenship to nationality makes it difficult to create any pan-European sense of citizenship, which might be possible if citizenship were tied instead to residence. Hence, despite the integration of new European states into the old EU – European enlargement – there has been no integrative mechanisms at the supranational level, as each individual is ultimately still dependent on his or her individual member state. That is, citizenship – rights and identity–is still inferred from nationality and neither dependent on any particular experience as a citizen, nor "experienced in the context of the EU" (Dell'Olio 2005: 10). The second framing has to do with the conflict between inclusion and security needs. The widespread expectation of Europeanization by those outside Europe (including the former communist bloc members recently integrated) is frustrated both by a perception of all immigrants as non-European, regardless of what they do, and by perceived security needs that tend to reinforce the exclusion of all strangers. In short, the inclusion argument gets constantly trumped by the exclusionary needs of security (cf. DeBardeleben 2005). These framings are on the surface correct, but they take for granted the notions of "corporate personhood" and "consumerism," which structure both the "integrative mechanisms" and "expectations of Europeanization".

6 Sloterdijk (2005) writes that the postliberal turn in the world generally is taking many authoritarian forms, including "China's 'party dictatorial' mode, the Soviet Union's 'state dictatorial' mode, the USA's 'sentiment dictatorial' mode and finally the 'media dictatorial' mode of Berlusconi's Italy."

7 Since the break-up of Yugoslavia, European reaction to the refiguring of the Balkans generally, as well as the ongoing indetermination of Kosovo, suggests an impasse in European integration of "the West," in particular in determining what is inside and outside of Europe. The Balkans was considered an "out of area" (as the political scientists call it) region that nonetheless required European intervention to prevent crimes against humanity (which had already taken place), all with American help and/or leadership. The use of European means (e.g., military by using the NATO alliance, political by insisting on state form with relations to the EU) to do anything other than freeze the conflict calls into question these means not only as a universal form but also as an index of Europe itself.

REFERENCES

Amnesty International. 2006a. Israel/ Lebanon: Hizbullah's attacks on northern Israel. Sept. 13. At http://www.amnesty.org/en/library/info/MDE02/025/2006/en (accessed Nov. 2011).

Amnesty International. 2006b. Lebanon: deliberate destruction or "collateral damage"? Israeli attacks on civilian infrastructure. Aug. 22. At http://www.amnesty.org/en/library/info/MDE18/007/2006 (accessed Nov. 2011).

Anderson, Benedict. 1983. *Imagined Communities: Reflections on the Origin and Spread of Nationalism.* London: Verso.

Balibar, Étienne. 2004. *We, the People of Europe? Reflections on Transnational Citizenship,* trans. J. Swenson. Princeton: Princeton University Press.

Borneman, John. 1991. *After the Wall: East Meets West in the New Berlin*. New York: Basic Books.

Borneman, John. 1992. *Belonging in the Two Berlins: Kin, State, Nation*. Cambridge: Cambridge University Press

Borneman, John. 1998. *Subversions of International Order: Studies in the Political Anthropology of Culture*. Albany: State University of New York Press.

Borneman, John. 2003. Is the United States Europe's other? *American Ethnologist* 30 (4): 487–507.

Borneman, John. 2007. The state of war crimes following the Israeli-Hezbollah war. *Windsor Yearbook of Access to Justice* 25 (2): 274–289.

Borneman, John. 2011. *Political Crime and the Memory of Loss*. Bloomingdale: Indiana University Press.

Daily Star (Lebanon). 2006. Timeline of the July War 2006. Nov. 10.

DeBardeleben, Joan, ed. 2005. *Soft or Hard Borders: Managing the Divide in an Enlarged Europe*. Farnham: Ashgate.

Dell'Olio, Fiorella. 2005. *The Europeanization of Citizenship: Between the Ideology of Nationality, Immigration, and European Identity*. Farnham: Ashgate.

Douglas, Mary. 1966. *Purity and Danger: An Analysis of the Concepts of Pollution and Taboo*. New York: Ark.

Dumont, Louis. 1970. Religion, politics, and society in the individualistic universe. In *Proceedings of the Royal Anthropological Institute of Great Britain and Ireland*, pp. 31–41.

Erlich, Reuven. 2006. Hezbollah's Use of Lebanese Civilians as Human Shields. Intelligence and Terrorism Information Center at the Center for Special Studies. Dec. 4. At http://www.ajcongress.org/site/Page Server?pagename=secret2 (accessed Nov. 2011).

Ferguson, Niall. 2001. *The Cash Nexus: Money and Power in the Modern World, 1700–2000*. New York: Basic Books.

Gorenberg, Gershom. 2007. *The Accidental Empire: Israel and the Birth of the Set-tlemetns, 1967–1977*. New York: Henry Holt.

Judt, Tony. 2005. *Postwar: A History of Europe since 1945*. New York: Penguin Books.

Kaldor, Mary. 2000. Europe at the millennium. *Politics* 20 (2): 55–62.

Kretzmar, David. 2008. Tyranny in tar. Jan. 31. At www.haaretz.com (accessed Mar. 1, 2008)

Maier, Charles S. 1997. *Dissolution: The Crisis of Communism and the End of East Germany*. Princeton: Princeton University Press.

Miłosz, Czesław. 1981. *The Captive Mind*. New York: Vintage. First publ. 1953.

Morris, Benny. 2001. *Righteous Victims: A History of the Zionist-Arab Conflicts, 1881–1999*. New York: Knopf.

Peebles, Gustav. 1997. "A very Eden of the innate rights of man"? A Marxist look at the European Union treaties and case law. *Law and Social Inquiry* 22 (581): 581–616.

Sahlins, Peter. 1989. *Boundaries: The Making of France and Spain in the Pyrenees*. Berkeley: University of California Press.

Segal, Rafi, Tartakover, David, Weizman, Eyal and Labudovic, Milutin, eds. 2003. *A Civilian Occupation: The Politics of Israeli Architecture*. London: Verso.

Sloterdijk, Peter. 2005. The end of democracy? Philosopher Peter Sloterdijk talks with Marius Meller about Europe's crisis and authoritarian capitalism. *Der Tagesspiegel*, June 24.

Stolcke, Verena. 1995. Talking culture. new boundaries, new rhetorics of exclusion in Europe. *Current Anthropology* 36: 1–24.

Taussig, Michael. 1993. *Mimesis and Alterity: A Particular History of the Senses*. New York: Routledge.

UN Human Rights Council. 2006. Report of the Commission of Inquiry on Lebanon. UN HRC, 3d. Sess., UN Doc. A/HRC/3/2.

UN News Centre. 2006. Lebanon: UN deminers hurt as agricultural damage from conflict hits $280 million. Nov. 27. At http://www.un.org/apps/news/story.

asp?NewsID=20728&Cr=&Cr1= (accessed Nov. 2011).

Weizman, Eyal. 2007. *Hollow Land*. London: Verso.

Zertal, Idith and Eldar, Akiva. 2007. *Lords of the Land: The War over Israel's Settlements in the Occupied Territories, 1967–2007*. New York: Nation Books.

Zolberg, Aristide. 1983. The formation of new states as a refugee-generating process. *Annals* 467 (May): 24–38.

PART II   States, Nations and Empires

CHAPTER **8**

Borders in the New Imperialism

James Anderson

In today's "new imperialism" state borders are becoming more complex, variable and differentiated in their permeabilities. Some borders are being weakened while others are strengthened. There are increasing differentiations in the ease or difficulty encountered by people and processes when crossing the border, and contradictory demands for tightening border security and freeing cross-border movements. Despite the alleged "decline of the nation state," a "borderless world" is clearly remote from present reality: a relatively unified global capitalist market continues to coexist with a diversity of many bordered states, over 190 sovereign entities at the last count. This contradiction might be enduring, but it does beg the question as to whether a "borderless world" is at least theoretically possible. With recent globalization, and particularly since 9/11, borders are perhaps more contradictory or paradoxical and more indicative of wider global transformations than ever before.

Increasingly seen as a bulwark against a diverse mix of threats, including drug smugglers, sex traffickers and political terrorists, but also migrant workers, state borders are now more porous for another diverse mix of forces encompassing trade and capital flows, cultural diffusions and information, and political "interventions." Borders which in the past were theoretically "sovereign," though never in practice sacrosanct, are no longer sacrosanct in theory either as great powers develop ideological justifications for military and humanitarian intervention in the internal affairs of other states. Largely economic involvement continues to be the main form of the new – or rather no longer so new – imperialism in its "neocolonial" or "informal" empires, where politically "independent" countries are in varying degrees dominated by more powerful ones and capital based in them. This has been the situation since the demise of Europe's traditional overseas empires after World War II, and since World War I in the case of the United States. However, the transcendence of state borders by capitalist production is ultimately dependent on armed force, and not least the United States's worldwide archipelago of military bases. Furthermore,

A Companion to Border Studies, First Edition. Edited by Thomas M. Wilson and Hastings Donnan.
© 2012 Blackwell Publishing Ltd. Published 2012 by Blackwell Publishing Ltd.

it seems that the historical tendency toward "nonterritorial" or "informal" empire is being at least partly reversed with a return to more direct, territorial control in the occupations of Iraq and Afghanistan (what some mean by "new imperialism"). Paradoxically, that may reflect not so much the still unrivaled military power of the United States as its declining hegemony. This decline, combined with economic crises, brings further turmoil and pressure on borders.

If borders are now indicative of these geopolitical and geo-economic transformations, borders themselves need to be understood and theorized in terms of them. Hence this chapter takes a historical and structural approach to contemporary borders. It focuses mainly on the "big picture" but seeks to develop a conceptual framework which can integrate macro with micro levels of analysis, linking political economy and subjective identity, for instance. It seeks to contextualize more familiar themes of borders research such as the creation of particular borders, their relations to ethnicity and nationalism, or the new "security" technologies of borderland surveillance. The chapter benefits substantially from, but also questions, some leading Marxist understandings, particularly from Harvey (2001, 2003) and Wood (1995). Hopefully it counters the fashionable "instant histories" of "new this" and "post-that" which often fail to identify what is genuinely new or possible in the foreseeable future.

The general nature and roles of state borders in capitalism are established (albeit schematically) in terms of three historical transitions: to capitalist production, to nationalism and national states, and to "informal" empires operating through them. In a contradictory world, where there is a more or less single integrated global economy but many national states, and where states claim sovereign equality and independence but willingly host foreign direct investment and other economic interdependencies, borders are pivotal. To put flesh on the bones of this argument, and signal the importance of shorter-term contexts – for things can change fast in today's crisis-prone capitalism – the chapter briefly explores the nature of borders through two contemporary prisms: first, the recent upsurge of migrant labor as a "spatial fix" for capitalist crisis; and secondly, the limitations of indirect control across borders, particularly in the context of global turbulence and declining US hegemony.[1]

THREE HISTORICAL TRANSITIONS AND STATE TERRITORIALITY

The pivotal nature of state borders in the world capitalist system, along with such related geopolitical phenomena as economic globalization and national democracy, territorial sovereignty and border conflicts, are best approached in terms of three related but historically and geographically uneven transitions. Qualifications and elaborations can come later, but contemporary state territoriality is basically the product of the transitions from precapitalist to capitalist production, and from prenational politics to nationalism and its expression in national states and popular democracy. These two transitions both enabled and necessitated the third transition from the old, traditional imperialism of "formal," territorial empires to the new

imperialism of "informal" ones which operate through and across supposedly independent, national states – now the wider geopolitical context of state territoriality.[2]

Territoriality can be defined as the uses of bordered geographical space to control,
classify and communicate (Sack 1986: 21–34), specifying what belongs to or can
move in and out of particular spaces of territories. It is about drawing or redrawing
lines around things, policing the lines or changing in situ their social meanings,
porosity or impermeability. It is socially ubiquitous for all sorts of purposes but two
of its leading expressions – state territoriality and private property – are central to the
transitions.[3]

The transitions to capitalism and to nationalism were long and complicated,
involving over four centuries of complex changes which in some respects and in some
areas have not yet been completed, and some may never be. Furthermore, the transitions built on earlier changes such as state centralization in early modern kingdoms
and absolutist regimes, while capitalist production and nationalist sentiment existed
in embryo in some places. However, the important point here is not the often con-
voluted history of the transitions per se, but their formative roles in shaping the
"end-results" of contemporary territoriality. And so it is possible to abstract from
the complexities of long time-span and great unevenness to concentrate on the
general territorial implications of nationalism and capitalist production as they were
progressively generalized and eventually globalized following the French Revolution
and the Industrial Revolution in Britain.[4]

The generalization of capitalist production brought to fruition a partial though
contested separation of the realms of "politics" and "economics." This is unique to
capitalism and has profound though largely hidden effects on territoriality, in keeping
with capitalism's nontransparent form of exploitation where underlying processes
generally require exposure through theory. As will be explained in more detail, the
partial separation enables surplus to be extracted from labor, including labor in
foreign lands, by what appear "purely economic" means. This smoothes over the
contradictions between on the one hand economic interdependencies and globalization, and on the other hand nationalism's ideal of independent "self-determination"
and political claims to "absolute" sovereignty within state borders. Through facilitating the exploitation of foreign labor in independent states, the separation made possible the third transition from "formal" to "informal" empires.

At the same time the transition to nationalism, though not a simple opposition to
the old imperialism (see Anderson and O'Dowd 2007), eventually resulted in the
breakup of formal empires into national states, as democratic self-determination
became a global aspiration if not a global reality. In a sense, what nationalism required
capitalism made possible – the transition to informal empires across national states –
though this transition was complicated and elongated by the traditional empires themselves incorporating both nationalism and capitalism, before eventually being undone
by them. The collapse of Europe's last overseas empire, Portugal's, only came in the
1970s, and Russia's USSR empire only broke up in the 1990s, with a further spate of
border creations. And so the apparently contradictory world of a global economy but
many bordered states can be approached by looking in turn at the transitions to capitalism, informal empire and nationalism, and then at contemporary migrant labor
which brings together borders, class exploitation and national identity.

"Politics/Economics" in Capitalism

In precapitalist societies extracting surplus from labor necessitated direct political control, and as Rosenberg (1994) has shown, Europe's overseas empires initially combined slave labor with territorial possession. The Spanish operated mines in Spanish-held territories, Dutch plantations were in Dutch colonies, British in British, and so forth. The long transition to present-day foreign direct investment (FDI) and economic globalization across independent states crucially depended on capitalism's partial separation or contradictory unity of "politics" and "economics."

This separation arises within the capitalist mode of production and rests on the way in which economic surpluses are extracted from the direct producers (Wood 1995). In precapitalist modes of production, economic surpluses had typically been extracted from the producers (e.g., slaves, serfs) by *extra*-economic means: the direct use of physical force and/or political and ideological, including religious, "persuasion," in for example slave-owning and feudal societies or ones ruled by priestly castes. In sharp contrast, surpluses in capitalism are generally extracted from the "free" labor of the producers (workers) through the economic operations of the "free market": employee and employer enter freely into an economic contract, and the "politics" of physical enforcement are apparently absent from the "economics" of the production process and market exchange.

However, the "politics/economics" separation is only partial. In reality, or despite appearances, "politics" and physical threat or force are still used but indirectly rather than directly. They have not been rendered unnecessary or dispensed with, but they are displaced to the realm of the national state, which acts as the enforcer of property rights and the "rule of law," without which "economic" production and the so-called "free" market could not operate. Ultimately force is needed to exclude workers from ownership or use of the means of production (e.g., land, machinery, raw materials) on their own behalf, so they have no viable option but to sell their labor power to employers who do own means of production. But the "politics" of force is less direct or transparent (than in slavery or feudalism, for example) because it is displaced from the "economic" sphere of production and exchange to the "political" sphere of the state.

This abstract formulation cuts through the complexities to highlight what is the capitalist precondition for three things: the historical switch from formal to informal empire; the coexistence of economic globalization and national state sovereignty as "opposite sides of the same coin"; and the relatively harmonious combination of one global economy but many bordered states. The complexities are of course important and throw further light on borders. The separation is contested as well as partial, and in practice varies greatly in extent from the extremes of separation in "depoliticized" economic laissez-faire to a substantial closure of the separation in the state capitalism of state-owned enterprises. Furthermore the "politics/economics" separation can usefully be recast as a "presence/absence of democracy" (Anderson 2001): present (at least in principle) in the "political" realm within state borders (and connecting with nationalism, which constitutes it as *national* democracy), but largely absent both from the "economic" realm of production and the market, and from the transnational sphere beyond and across borders. Thus democracy typically stops at the state border and at the gates of the workplace. It hinges on borders and territoriality, though borders themselves are caught up in the paradox of democracy's undemocratic origins, and generally are undemocratic and decided by force (Anderson 2010). Decisions about what to produce, where to invest and so forth, are almost invariably taken in the "economic," that is, "nonpolitical" and nondemocratic realm. Production, as in FDI, more easily straddles borders because it is beyond democratic control, and because democracy is also excluded from the transnational sphere beyond the border.[5]

The "politics/economics" separation is a precondition for the nexus of global economy, national states and informal empires. Although partial and contested, it usually finds strong material expression in discrete "political" and "economic" institutions and a "division of labor" between politicians and business people. Of course the modern state is always much more than the physical enforcer of laws which protect property and the market – the role overemphasized in Wood's (1995) clear but abstract formulation: states also regulate national economies, can include state capitalist production, and have a key role in welfare provision (as we shall see in conflicts about migrant labor). Nevertheless, organizing and monopolizing "bodies of armed men" and maintaining "law and order" remain core tasks for the state: these are separated from engagement in production and here the state can in principle operate in the interests of all capital within state borders, whether indigenous or foreign-owned.

On the political side, the partial separation from "economics" is a precondition for the state's claim to national sovereignty and self-determination. This claim to independence applies only to the "political" realm, and it has plausibility only because the "economics" are excluded from consideration: the claim would be undermined if FDI and economic interdependencies were considered. Simultaneously, there are converse effects on the economic side: it is because of partial separation from the sphere of "politics" that the undemocratic nature of production is widely accepted, as "economic" rather than "political" and hence outside the generally accepted realm of sovereignty and democracy. By extension globalization is underpinned to the (large) extent it involves "economics" (and culture or "*not* politics") and hence avoids breaching sacred sovereignty.

FROM FORMAL TO INFORMAL EMPIRES

Capitalism's separation of "politics/economics" and its transformation in how surplus is extracted from labor made possible the transition to informal empires operating through politically independent national states. The "laws of the market" could increasingly be enforced by independent states for foreign-owned as well as for indigenous capital. Exploiting foreign labor no longer required direct political control through the incorporation of territories in formal empires. Cross-border exploitation could now be on the basis of a "purely" economic contract between foreign employer and indigenous employee, free of *extra*-economic compulsion and on the same basis as indigenous employer–employee relations. The "foreignness" of the exploiter is effectively "depoliticized"; foreign capital has the same state-protected rights as indigenous capital in principle if not always in practice. Far from rejecting FDI as "foreign interference," "sovereign" states can fall over themselves trying to attract it. For while sovereignty is "political," investment in economic production is merely, well, "economic."[6]

Capitalism's historical development and global spread meant "economic" power increased relative to "political" power (Wood 2003); and as surplus generally came to be extracted from free labor by economic means, there was a decreasing need for direct political control in formal empires. Broadly speaking, the development of the partial separation was roughly matched by the sequence of types of labor employed – from slave or serf, to indentured, to free (Anderson 2001) – and by the spread of informal empire. In the nineteenth century the British Empire initiated a partial switch to this new form of imperialism in some of the independent national states of Latin America; since World War I the US empire has been almost entirely informal (Smith 2003); and by the 1960s informal empires (strongly encouraged by the US) had become the global norm with the European decolonizations and the globalization of nationalism.

A global economy but many states?

From this perspective one can begin to see how the partial separation facilitates the relatively harmonious functioning of a global market economy, informal empires in the plural and many bordered states. However, now that there is a relatively integrated global economy, are the latter, all 190 of them, really functional anachronisms, and like the vestigial appendix, no longer necessary in political economy terms? Perhaps inertia and the contradictory nature of borders, at once "barriers and bridges, symbols and resources" (O'Dowd 2003) serve to keep them going as relatively harmless leftovers from precapitalist times? Or perhaps they now follow a quite different logic of nationalism and identity politics, but in the longer term with the "decline of the nation state," are they destined to wither away in a "borderless world" (Omhae 1999)? Is this theoretically possible?

The argument so far about the rootedness of the world system's "political" as well as "economic" aspects in the capitalist mode of production suggests that a "borderless world" is not theoretically possible while capitalism lasts. This would relegate it to neoliberal fantasy, and make the left-wing demand for "open borders" without immigration controls (e.g., Hayter 2000) decidedly revolutionary. If "a global economy but many states" constitute a single, albeit contradictory, world system, and not two logically separate ones which are ontologically juxtaposed (as in the conventional disciplinary separation of political science and economics), then borders will last as long as capitalism does. However, some circumstantial evidence suggests otherwise. Many present-day borders do indeed predate capitalism, at least in terms of their locations, and states come in all shapes and sizes because of "historical accident" it seems, rather than any capitalist logic.

Harvey lends support when he associates the state with a territorial logic, conceptualizing "capitalist imperialism" as a "dialectical relation" or "contradictory fusion" of two distinct "logics of power," one "capitalist," the other "territorial" (2003: 26–36, 183, 204). His territorial logic involves states and empires, with imperialism "distinctly political" and "actors whose power is based in command of a territory" and the capacity to mobilize for political, economic and military ends. His "capitalist logic" involves processes of capital accumulation, imperialism as political-economy, and actors whose "command over and use of capital takes primacy." His two different sorts of actors and agencies – politicians and capitalists and their respective institutions – are similar to the institutionalized "division of labor" which, as was argued above, follows from the partial "politics/economics" separation. However, Harvey wants to insist that the "motivations and interests" of his two sorts of actors are very different: capitalists want to "accumulate more capital," politicians or state managers want to "sustain or augment the power of their own state vis-à-vis other states." The two logics are "distinctive and in no way reducible to each other, though they are tightly interwoven . . . [They] may be construed as internal relations of each other," but can sometimes be in "outright contradiction," as when a costly state war harms a vulnerable economy.

Harvey draws interesting contrasts between the fluidity of capitalists competing in "continuous space" as firms move location, merge or go out of business, and the spatial fixity of politicians competing in the "territorialized space" of states within relatively fixed borders. While state territories set the stage for capital accumulation, he (unlike Wood 1995) fully recognizes that the state is also a powerful economic actor; and he rightly insists on a dialectical recognition of contradictions in capital–state interrelations, avoiding a deterministic or functionalist approach. Nevertheless, a conceptualization based on Wood (1995) which roots the multiple states system as well as the global economy in the capitalist mode of production is better in my opinion.[7]

To counterpose a "territorial" to a "capitalist" logic implies that the former is *non*capitalist (perhaps even "precapitalist," though Harvey does not say so). But it could well be that the main motivations of state managers and strategies are indeed "capitalist," given the capitalist nature of "the state in capitalist society" (Miliband 1969). It is significant that Harvey (2003: 27) got the "two logics" from Arrighi (1994), who did not use them to differentiate "the motivations and interests" of state personnel from those of capitalist businesspeople. On the contrary, for Arrighi, they were alternative or complementary "modes of rule" *both* of which were used by *state* managers. States and rulers were following a "territorial logic" when they saw power in terms of the "extent and populousness of their domains," and capital was only a means or by-product of territorial expansion. But, conversely, state managers follow a "capitalist logic" when they identify power with capital and "consider territorial acquisitions as a means and a by-product of the accumulation of capital" (Arrighi 1994: 33–36). Ironically, Arrighi who is dealing transhistorically with world hegemony since the sixteenth century when production was precapitalist and territory was the main source of wealth, allows for an inherent capitalist logic within the state and politics, whereas Harvey, whose focus is contemporary, sees only a territorial logic.

In fact, Arrighi's formulation of a "capitalist logic" followed by "capitalist rulers" seems entirely appropriate where contemporary states are concerned with territorial matters: for them territory is "a means and a by-product of the accumulation of capital," rather than involving a different logic of territory for its own sake. States now follow a "capitalist logic," and borders, whether or not in the same locations since precapitalist times, have like states been transformed by capitalism.

However, the "capitalist logic" clearly does not determine the size and number of national states – there is nothing in capitalism that says there should be 190 sovereign entities, or twice or half that number. But the outcomes have hardly been completely random or "accidental" either,[8] and capitalism does set some general parameters which are perhaps best seen as "necessary but not sufficient" causes. The multiplicity of states (and informal empires) is consistent with capitalism's dynamic of competition between many capitals, their uneven development across space, the inherently limited spatial scope of many of their production and distribution processes, and the continued centrality of the "home territory" as a market even for many large multinational corporations. The multiplicity of states fits with particular capitals relying on territorially based states for support in their competition with other capitals in other territories; and for the social control and reproduction of labor, including regulation of migrant labor through border controls and nationalist ideologies. The implausibility of the alternative single world state or empire is well displayed in Hardt and Negri's (2001) influential but geographically challenged *Empire* in the singular, a "Marxist" version of "borderless world" and equally fantastical. They seem to have taken the partial truth of capitalists cooperating in the informal empires of the single global economy and turned it into a grotesque parody by "forgetting" some things: as in *Animal Farm* some capitalists and some states are "more equal" than others, with the still hegemonic US the biggest pig in the pen; capitalists compete against each other as well as cooperating; and competition in a geographically uneven system susceptible to covert or overt protectionism constitutes powerful pressures for separate state territories.[9] Single empire implies the end of borders but actually some borders are being strengthened; and it implies the end of interimperialist rivalries but actually they are intensifying along with the difficulties of hegemonic control.

The fact that investment and production straddle borders relatively easily means that capitalism's parameters are permissive, not economically deterministic. One of their key outcomes – and clearest evidence that for states the capitalist logic has now trumped the territorial – has been the historic switch from territorial or formal empires to informal ones. This is what genuinely put the "new" into the new imperialism. Capitalism's parameters allow states of "all shapes and sizes" to flourish, and border-crossing capital to work in and through them large and small. So the interim conclusion is that capitalist political economy both allows and encourages a multiplicity of states: a "single state, borderless world" is neither needed nor theoretically possible in capitalism. However, to substantiate this one needs to look beyond political economy, and particularly to culture, ideology and the transition to nationalism, to see that the actual configuration, number and size of states depend on subjective identities, political struggles and historical contingencies.

NATIONALISM AND NATIONAL STATES

If capitalism perpetuates "many states," the political struggles of nationalism and imperialism decide which ones. The outcomes are contingent, shaped by particular prenational starting points, and liable to revision in ethnonational conflicts. The earlier configurations conditioned which ethnic and regional population groups came together or diverged to constitute the separate "nations" which claimed sovereign rights to national self-determination, cornerstone of nationalist doctrine since the French Revolution. A fuller historical account, beyond the scope of this chapter, would trace how nation-building created *national* states and in some cases failed to create them, by transforming and reterritorializing traditional empires and kingdoms.

But in general the territorial units created by nationalisms were both smaller and larger than prenational foci of identity, where people had identified with bigger entities such as Christendom, the Holy Roman Empire or the multi-ethnic Habsburg Empire in Europe, or, usually more strongly, with smaller entities such as their parish, city or region. Nationalism, in welding the latter into national states, effectively continued the centralizing work of earlier kingdoms and absolutisms. And the creation of more centralized and ideologically stronger states was greatly aided by the increased material infrastructural power of the state thanks to capitalist production.

While nationalism required self-rule, simplistically counterposing imperialism and nationalism as implacable opposites forgets that imperial powers (such as France and Britain) developed state nationalisms at the core of traditional empires; that they spread nationalist aspirations among subordinated populations; and that some subordinate nationalisms allied with imperial powers (Anderson and O'Dowd 2007). It was only in the second half of the twentieth century that national states finally replaced traditional formal empires and became the present global norm (Mann 1993). Informal empires are now the easier, cheaper option in an era when nationalism and democratic ideals (if not practice) mean populations are easily mobilized to oppose "foreign rule." States may be undemocratic but their populations have democratic aspirations to exercise national sovereignty, and these quickly translate into rejecting the rule of foreign occupiers. Unlike the "economics" of FDI, this is transparently "political" and "foreign interference," and clearly contrary to the global norms of national identity and self-determination.

The current links between national identity and the political economy of borders are seen most clearly in migrant labor; and the limits of cross-border control through informal empire are revealed in declining US hegemony. These two prisms[10] signal the importance of short-term changes within capitalism, and global turbulence as the contemporary context.

Migrant Labor and Cross-Border Fixes for Crises

Low-paid migrant labor has surged dramatically in advanced economies in recent decades. In one estimate (Sum et al. 2002), over 13.5 million workers entered the United States in the 1990s, around 9 million of them were "undocumented," and in absolute numbers labor immigration was higher than during the classic era of US immigration a century earlier. Empirically, migrant labor exemplifies the contradictory nature of borders as physical barriers and markers of national identity that cheapen labor and weaken it politically. Migrant labor is arguably an alternative "cross-border fix" for capitalist crisis where labor is imported to "core" economies rather than capital being exported to "peripheries."

Migrant labor and the "third freedom" of borders

Broadly reversing the differentials up to the nineteenth century, capital, goods and information now generally cross borders relatively freely, while in comparison labor is less mobile and more or less caged materially and ideologically by national borders. With the general imposition of passports and anti-immigration laws, it is now people and especially workers whose mobility is reduced. According to Torpey (2000: 4–20), modern states have expropriated and monopolized people's legitimate "means of movement" across borders, as they monopolized the legitimate "means of violence" (Weber) and as capitalists monopolized the "means of production" (Marx). People were deprived of free movement and are deemed "guilty" until they prove their innocence with a passport.[11]

Borders as barriers to labor movement are criticized as a major contradiction of neoliberalism's "free movement" of factors of production (Amin 1996), but the reality is actually more contradictory than mobile capital/immobile labor. Labor actually migrates in large numbers; borders are "bridges" as well as "barriers" and they cheapen labor while appearing to keep it out. As ideological markers of non-belonging they serve to deprive migrants of various cultural and political capacities and rights; they foster divisions between workers on migrant/indigenous lines; and workers in general are weakened as a political force when nationalistic and chauvinist factions scapegoat migrants. For capitalists there is less contradiction: they are indeed deprived of needed labor in some circumstances, but in general they gain from cheap migrant workers and from labor being divided as a political force.

Migrant labor is central to the politics of border "securitization," a place of smoke and mirrors with both more and less than meets the eye. The migrant workers are often lumped in (purposely?) with various "threatening undesirables" such as drug smugglers and terrorists, but migrant labor is an "economic" factor of production as well as a "political factor" – you cannot have one without the other, though political capacities can be denied or reduced. The contradictory unity of "politics/economics" is embodied in the migrant worker, often valued as economically essential but politically rejected. It is noteworthy, for instance, that much hostility toward migrant workers questions them "exploiting" state welfare services or "undermining" national culture, rather than questioning economic issues of wages or competition for jobs (jobs indigenous workers often avoid as poorly paid, dirty and/or dangerous). That can change in an economic downturn when demand for labor falls relative to supply, and migration flows dry up or go into reverse – underlining the importance of short-term contexts. But in contradictory fashion that is when anti-immigration chauvinism generally peaks and even then it is often expressed in political rather than economic terms. In reality, migrant workers generally make much lower than average use of welfare services (partly because of their generally younger age profile), but as Harris (1995) points out, the "welfare state contract" that labor achieved (at least in Western Europe) cemented the popular identification of indigenous labor with the national state, and migrants were not party to the original contract and nor do they belong to the nation.

So ideologically as well as materially borders constitute a "third freedom" which renders the free labor of capitalism less than fully free. Marxists refer ironically to labor's "double freedom" – labor free of *extra*-economic compulsions but also "freed" of access to the means of production and independent livelihood. But this applies to the capitalist mode of production in the abstract, whereas in more concrete reality there is a "third freedom" for cross-border migrant labor: freed of national belonging and political rights or sometimes even a legal existence (for the "undocumented"). Here borders deliver additional *extra*-economic means of extracting surplus from not-so-free labor. Spatially there are further pressures in the ongoing shift from surveillance and exclusion at the state borderline to more zonal, empire-like systems of control. On the external side they depend on neighboring states and the state's own "advance outposts" beyond its borderline, while on the internal side there is more systematic targeting of suspected migrants who have managed to cross the border. It all adds to the superexploitation of migrants – *The New Helots* (Cohen 1987), *The New Untouchables* (Harris 1995).

On the US-Mexican border – as grotesque a gulf as any between core and periphery – massive steel fences coexist with a huge and growing Latino labor force in the US, which suggests that border fortifications were more for internal US political consumption than for stopping its economic supplies of cheap labor. Andreas (2000) sees border policing as *Border Games* – "a ritualized spectator sport," "performative and audience-directed" to reassure. In the 1990s cross-border integration in the North American Free Trade Agreement called forth massively increased border "security" to reaffirm symbolically the territorial sovereignty of the US. "[B]oth a border-less economy and a barricaded border" were constructed, because "opening the border to legal economic flows" required making it appear closed to illegal ones (Andreas 2000: x, 115, 138–143). As in "Fortress Europe" (Armstrong and Anderson 2007), there were narratives of borders "under siege" which implied a "golden age" when borders were "secure." Similarly Coleman (2005) paints a compelling picture of a "security/economy nexus" (akin to the contradictory unity of "politics/economics") which produced a tangled and inconsistent "Gordian knot" in the US–Mexico borderlands as more "security" met more liberalized cross-border economics in "gated globalization." The ratio of "security" to "economy" varies (e.g., higher at external European Union borders, lower at internal ones), but the contradictions are generally sharpest at what Andreas and Snyder (2000) call the "rich–poor divides of globalization" or *The Wall around the West* which separates cores from peripheries. They have a complex geography as capitalism's "reserve army of labor" is now effectively globalized, but the stark reality of huge income differentials (over tenfold for the poorest countries, up to fourfold even within Europe) helps to cut through the complexities and explain the fixes.

A theory of spatial fixes

Imperialism has long involved exporting "metropolitan" or core capital for investment in cheap-labor enterprises in the colonies or peripheries. As a "spatial fix" for capitalist crisis, Harvey (2001) traces it back to Hegel and Marx who rejected Adam Smith's theory that the "hidden hand" of the market could deliver "social harmony." Instead surplus capital had to be exported to the still largely noncapitalist periphery as a necessary if short-term answer to capitalist crises in the core. Later, the turn of the nineteenth century saw the actual heyday of capital export in the classic era of imperialism and "free trade" open borders – an earlier era of globalization – when ideas about this spatial fix were developed in vigorous debates by such theorists as J.A. Hobson, Lenin and Rosa Luxemburg.

Harvey (writing originally in 1981) suggested that the "fix" of capital export to peripheries alternated historically with the "fix" of economic autarky and relatively closed borders, as in interwar "protectionism" (Harvey 2001). However, neither alternative has really applied in the present era of globalization. There is little sign of autarky; and capital investment and export have largely stayed *within* the core and avoided most of the peripheries, for these not only lack adequate skill levels for modern capitalism but are often too politically unstable or unreliable for secure investment. But there is another alternative: importing plentiful supplies of cheap labor from the periphery into the core – a new fix in the family?

The fixes are for crises of capital overaccumulation or overproduction where capitalism is a contradictory victim of its own success. The problem then for capitalists is finding further profitable outlets in which to invest the profits being generated. Overaccumulation results in a tendency for the rate of profit to fall (less profit for the same amount invested), markets become saturated and opportunities for profitable investment decrease, and this generates countertendencies to stave off crisis. The solutions are generally partial and end up creating further problems, but they succeed for a time, and they include exporting surplus capital to peripheral areas of cheap labor ("Fix 1"), and now importing the cheap labor into the core ("Fix 2"). Reversing the usual stereotypes, mobile labor now combines with immobile capital and new markets are created in the core, particularly in personal services and construction, which along with agribusiness are the less mobile sectors where migrant labor is mainly concentrated (Anderson and Shuttleworth 2004).

However, this Fix 2 solution contains its own undoing – absorbing surplus capital through economic expansion within the core results in piling up yet more surplus capital. Exporting it as a Fix 1 solution is one obvious alternative, except that increasing global turbulence means that most of the peripheries remain risky and investors will probably continue to discriminate selectively against most of them. These risky areas may indeed continue as Fix 2 suppliers of cheap migrant labor, while the fewer favored peripheries (e.g., parts of China, Brazil and India) receive Fix 1 capital. So rather than switching historically as alternatives, both fixes may work at the same time but switch spatially for different territories, or even operate in tandem across the same time-space. There is some evidence for this in European Union enlargement (see Anderson and Shuttleworth 2007). In the 1990s Eastern Europe (with its "mafia capitalism") was generally too risky for Western investors, but countries like Poland supplied Western Europe with large quantities of migrant labor. Then political incorporation of East European countries into European Union membership greatly reduced the risks and capital exports flowed eastwards; though, with their migrants still employed in the West, Fix 1 and Fix 2 were now operating simultaneously across the same territories.[12]

GLOBAL TURBULENCE AND DECLINING HEGEMONY

The global conditions of uneven development and instability which gave rise to Fix 2 – and provide circumstantial evidence for it – are also the context of recent border transformations. Major features that bring added pressures on borders include the recurrent crises of capitalism since the ending of the postwar boom in the 1970s; an underlying decline, though with marked fluctuations, in the general rate of profitability; the end of the Cold War and arguably the last of the great territorial empires, the USSR and its satellites; but also the beginnings of decline in hegemonic control by the remaining superpower, the United States (Smith 2003). This latter is partly because of the relative economic decline of the US itself, but also because of the growing difficulties of exercising hegemony in a turbulent world of many states – the Achilles' heel of indirect control in informal empires.

The context can be summed up as "imploding globalization" (Hoogvelt 1997) and "ostracising imperialism" (Mann 2001) – two sides of the same coin which are manifested in the widening of rich–poor, core–periphery divides. Mann notes a long-running retreat of capital investment from large areas of the periphery or "global South," with international investment and trade becoming proportionally more concentrated within the "North" or core. Whereas "North-to-South" investment had comprised about 50 percent of the world total between 1850 and 1950 (which included the heyday of Fix 1 in a world still dominated by formal empires), since 1950 this share has declined to about 10 percent (so now around 90 percent of investment takes place *within* the core, and most FDI is *between* core countries). Of the South's decreased share, China alone was absorbing over half (Mann 2001: 54, 55, 72).

It seems that as formal empires gave way to informal ones and to politically independent and hence economically riskier national states, capital became more confined to the core, with capital export becoming more risk-averse and selective. "[A]fter being the main exporter of capital for thirty years," the 1980s saw the "emergence of the United States as the major recipient of direct foreign investment in the world" (Sassen 1988: 3). Increased global turbulence since the 2008 banking collapse is arguably making it even riskier to exploit the South's now massive "reserve army of labor" in situ; and the lack of legal investment sometimes encourages reliance on criminal economies like drug production, which further add to the risk and to the narratives of "siege" at borders.

Achilles' heel of informal empire

Hegemonic control, which helps secure FDI, works best as persuasion when independent states can believe that what is in the hegemon's interest is also in their own interests (as Western and many other states have mostly believed of the US, though with increasing reservations). It works well when states play by the rules of liberalism (e.g., as desired/imposed by the neoliberal "Washington Consensus"), and markets operate without "political interference." Or, more precisely, can be forced to play by these liberal rules, for it may not be in the states' interests to do so and many are far from "naturally" liberal. This is where the problems start, and particularly if the hegemon's powers of persuasion are beginning to decline. States may flout the rules; in practice they sometimes break their own rules to discriminate against foreign-owned capital; or on principle they favor more state control, in a worst case scenario "nationalizing" foreign assets. So investments in the peripheries rely on variably *un*reliable states with their own divergent and conflicting interests. The partial separation of "politics/economics" is not much defense against a state which actively contests the separation, whether through principled nationalization or unprincipled corruption.

Stronger measures are needed, including economic sanctions or, failing that, the threat of military force. But even this threat may not be sufficient to force recalcitrant governments to "play by the rules" and enforce them "fairly." Military attacks (e.g., air strikes) are sometimes the next option – and to be credible, threats of force do occasionally have to be carried out – or invasion becomes necessary as the last resort. In this context it was not the Iraq invasion per se, but rather full-scale invasion as almost the "first resort," followed by a prolonged US occupation, that was the aberration. Furthermore, the resulting costly mess of a colonial-style territorial regime in Iraq (as with the US in Vietnam, and the Russians, and then the US and allies, in Afghanistan) graphically demonstrates why informal rather than formal empire is the better option in an age of nationalism (Anderson 2003). But, if global hegemonic control continues to weaken, or global turbulence were to further increase, perhaps because of growing ecological problems, there could well be a strengthening of borders,[13] even a return to autarkic tendencies (as in Harvey's interwar alternation to "protectionism" from "Fix 1"). There could be a partial reversal of the transition to informal empire, with military occupation again becoming less of an aberration. However, informal empires, despite their weaknesses, will remain the norm so long as indirect control through nominally independent states (perhaps with more direct intervention behind the scenes) can be made to work.[14]

In the nineteenth century the British sent gunboats from their empire outposts, today the US tries to keep control by sending its aircraft carriers or planes from its worldwide "archipelago" of military bases in independent countries. Physical force has been displaced from territorial space to network space and hence is mostly "hidden" (analogous in some ways to the displacement of force from the "economic" point of production to the "political" state). But the military bases are mostly located within the territory of other national states and in some cases are subject to host-state laws or specific restrictions; and furthermore US economic leverage has declined as it is increasingly rivaled economically (e.g., by the European Union and China) and dependent on the US dollar being the global reserve currency. Despite its unprecedented and unrivaled military spending and superiority, the US faces the problem that the indirect control of informal empire can often amount to *less* control.

CONCLUSION

It has been argued that borders not only divide up the world into national states, they are pivotal to capitalism. Their position rests on capitalism's contradictory unity or partial and contested separation of "politics/economics." This allows the coexistence of a global economy but many states, and together these elements constitute a single, albeit contradictory, political-economic system. On the one hand, the separation enables cross-border *economic* ownership and FDI, economic interdependencies and globalization largely unimpeded by political claims to national independence. On the other hand, it simultaneously enables states to make plausible claims of *political* independence and national sovereignty, because economic production is largely excluded from considerations of national and democratic accountability.

This system was seen to result from three broad historical transitions: to capitalism, to nationalism, and (putting those two together) to informal empires – a new imperialism where economic and political power is transmitted through the market and indirectly through politically independent national states. But while structural features of capitalism provide the broad context for understanding contemporary borders, the narrower focus on cross-border fixes and on declining hegemony showed the importance of shorter time-frames, especially when situations can change rapidly in conditions of crisis.

The focus on migrant labor showed in more detail how borders operate in material and symbolic terms, and the importance of linking structural political economy with issues of identity and democracy to give a more rounded perspective on borders. The "contradictory unity" of "politics/economics" is embodied in the migrant worker, and it was argued that borders provide *extra*-economic means of controlling labor and constitute its "third freedom." Despite the contradictions (and because their adverse effects are mainly borne by labor and weaker capitals), territorial states bring positive advantages for capital. They provide support for spatially rooted capitals in competition with other capitals elsewhere, and they control labor by corralling it within the territorial and ideological borders of nationalism. In regulating what is now a globalized "reserve army of labor," borders are important instruments of class control, not about to be surrendered lightly whatever neoliberal ideologues might suggest.

While capitalism continues, a "borderless world" is neither possible in theory nor necessary in practice. Nor is a secular weakening of state borders inevitable, as seems to be implied if not already determined by globalization and an apparently unidirectional "decline of the nation state." Rather than positing a new epoch on the relatively meager and disputed evidence of a mere three or four decades – after three or more centuries of continuing national state formation – it might be better to think of contemporary change in more modest, less epoch-making terms, such as the partial separation of "politics/economics": the nature and degree of separation is always contested and reversible, in principle and sometimes in practice, as was dramatically demonstrated in the recent banking crisis.[15] Contradictory pressures for more "open" or weaker borders and for stronger ones with greater border security will likely continue, oscillating one way or the other depending on economic and political circumstances; and it is easy to imagine situations such as economic cum eco-crisis where borders might be substantially strengthened. Far from being harmless leftovers from precapitalist times, or anachronisms due to wither away, state borders are integral to global capitalism, its contradictions and problems.

NOTES

1   Space here is limited but some of these ideas are elaborated in Centre for International Borders Research electronic working papers in 2001, 2004 and 2005 (www.qub.ac.uk/cibr) and elsewhere (see the references below), some in collaboration with Ian Shuttleworth, and some with Liam O'Dowd, to whom I offer my thanks; and thanks also go to Tom Wilson and Hastings Donnan for their editorial work.

2   This three-part scheme in providing a general historical understanding of state territoriality helps in analyzing border conflicts, state–city relations and ethnonationally divided cities. It is developed here as part of the ESRC-funded research project Conflict in Cities and the Contested State: Belfast, Jerusalem and Other Divided Cities (ESRC RES-060-25-0015). See www.conflictincities.org (accessed Nov. 2011)

3   Uses of territoriality also range from the nursery to the workplace to ceremonial occasions (to control children, or workers, or to communicate social or symbolic importance); and with respect to state borders we need to consider not only its strengths but also its weaknesses as a blunt instrument (see Anderson 2010).

4   It was only with the Industrial Revolution that production processes in general began to come under the direct control of capitalists ("industrialists"); earlier, "merchant" capitalists made profits by trading in goods that had already been produced in noncapitalist modes (e.g., slavery, serfdom).

5   The territorial delimitations, confinements or exclusions of democracy relate mainly to state sovereignty and to private property as leading forms of territoriality. For further elaboration, see Anderson 2010.

6   However, FDI's "downside" of foreign direct *dis*investment and redundancies sometimes provokes political protest on nationalistic or chauvinist grounds.

7   Harvey wants to avoid an economic determinism where political outcomes are somehow read off from the "objective interests of capital." But to avoid that mistake, it is not necessary to counterpose a "territorial" to a "capitalist" logic. Capitalism is more than capable of generating its own contradictions; it involves the competition of many capitals; and their various agents have no "papal infallibility" in deciding what will further their own competing interests, never mind divining the "objective interests" of capital in general. For more elaboration, see Anderson 2005.

8   See, for example, Tilly (1992) on the role of capital, in different combinations with military force, in producing distinct patterns of European state formation.

9   See Anderson 2005, and for a variety of critical views, Balakrishnan 2003.

10   Here migrant labor and contemporary problems of hegemonic control are treated briefly to illustrate border features. For fuller treatment in their own right, see Anderson 2003, 2005.

11   Echoing the process of separating "politics" from "economics," the long transition from feudalism to capitalism involved a transition from private (employer) to state control over the movement of labor. Precapitalist territorial rulers had been more concerned about keeping people in rather than keeping them out; most controls were of movement within

state territories; and it was only in the late nineteenth century that states began to assert relatively effective control of cross-border movement into national labor markets (Torpey 2000: 8, 18–20, 93).

12   EU expansion can also be seen as creating the larger "home territory" which Arrighi (1994) has shown historically to be progressively necessary for exercising hegemonic control. Similarly, China's colonial expansion to its west and Tibet. Such expansions clearly involve territorial strategies reminiscent of traditional empires. Nevertheless, for contemporary rulers territory is a means to a capitalist end rather than an end in itself. All the conceivable hegemonic challengers have large home territories. Compared to the US, the EU has about half the area but over twice as many people; Russia about half the people but nearly twice the area; and China is very similar to the US in area but has about four times the number of people.

13   Resource depletion could result in eco-crisis and resource wars, with borders being strengthened as more powerful states and capitals adopt a "beggar my neighbor" approach to survival (Anderson 2006).

14   It is partly because of historical continuities and the present realities of continuing inter-imperial rivalry – US, Russia, the EU, China, Japan – that both the terms "empire" and "hegemony" are used, rather than choosing the latter concept over the former, or "hegemony without a hegemon," as was advocated by Agnew (2005: 12–36), though he makes good points about confusions in how the terms are used.

15   The most neoliberal states of "Anglo-Saxon capitalism" reversed from "laissez-faire" to massive economic intervention in 2008, though they have again reverted to type (until the next time?). There have been threats to reverse the EU Schengen policy of open or passport-free internal borders (e.g., *Guardian*, Apr. 27, 2011). More generally, epochal globalization has been seriously disputed (e.g., by Hirst and Thompson 1996); as has the "decline of state power" – strong states, particularly in East Asia, have often facilitated changes identified as "globalization" (Weiss 1998).

REFERENCES

Agnew, John A. 2005. *Hegemony: The New Shape of Global Power*. Philadelphia: Temple University Press.

Amin, Samir. 1996. The challenge of globalization. *Review of International Political Economy* 3 (2): 216–259.

Anderson, James. 2001. Theorizing State Borders: "Politics/Economics" and Democracy in Capitalism. CIBR (Centre for International Borders Research) Working Papers in Border Studies, No. 1, WP 01-1, Queen's University Belfast, at www.qub.ac.uk/cibr (accessed Nov. 2011).

Anderson, James. 2003. American hegemony after 11 September: allies, rivals and contradictions. *Geopolitics* 8 (3): 35–60.

Anderson, James. 2005. Borders, Fixes and Empires: Territoriality in the New Imperialism. CIBR Working Papers in Border Studies, No. 15, WP 05-3, Queen's University Belfast, at www.qub.ac.uk/cibr (accessed Nov. 2011).

Anderson, James. 2006. Afterword: Only sustain . . . the environment, "anti-globalization" and the runaway bicycle. In Josée Johnston, Michael Gismondi and James Goodman, eds, *Nature's Revenge: Reclaiming Sustainability in an Age of Corporate Globalization*, pp. 245–273. Peterborough, ON: Broadview Press.

Anderson, James. 2010. Democracy, Territoriality and Ethno-National Conflict. Divided Cities/Contested States Working Paper No. 18. At www.conflictincities.org (accessed Nov. 2011)

Anderson, James and O'Dowd, Liam. 2007. Imperialism and nationalism: the Home Rule struggle and border creation in Ireland,

1885–1925. *Political Geography* 26 (8): 934–950.

Anderson, James and Shuttleworth, Ian. 2004. A new spatial fix for capitalist crisis? Immigrant labour, state borders and ostracising imperialism. In Kees van der Pijl, Libby Assassi and Duncan Wigan, eds, *Contextualising Global Regulation: Managing Crisis after the Imperial Turn.* Basingstoke: Palgrave.

Anderson, James and Shuttleworth, Ian. 2007. Fixing capitalism and Europe's peripheries: West European imperialism. In Warwick Armstrong and James Anderson, eds, *Geopolitics of European Union Enlargement: The Fortress Empire,* pp. 125–141. London: Routledge.

Andreas, Peter. 2000. *Border Games: Policing the US–Mexico Divide.* Ithaca: Cornell University Press.

Andreas, Peter and Snyder, Timothy, eds. 2000. *The Wall around the West: State Borders and Immigration Controls in North America and Europe.* Lanham: Rowman & Littlefield.

Armstrong, Warwick and Anderson, James, eds. 2007. *Geopolitics of European Union Enlargement: The Fortress Empire.* London: Routledge.

Arrighi, Giovanni. 1994. *The Long Twentieth Century: Money, Power, and the Origins of Our Times.* London: Verso.

Balakrishnan, Gopal. 2003. *Debating Empire.* London: Verso.

Cohen, Robin. 1987. *The New Helots: Migrants in the International Division of Labour.* Aldershot: Avebury.

Coleman, Mathew. 2005. US statecraft and the US–Mexico border as security/economy nexus. *Political Geography* 24 (2): 185–209.

Hardt, Michael and Negri, Antonio. 2001. *Empire.* Cambridge: Harvard University Press.

Harris, Nigel. 1995. *The New Untouchables: Immigration and the New World Worker.* Harmondsworth: Penguin.

Harvey, David. 2001. The spatial fix: Hegel, Von Thunen and Marx. In David Harvey, *Spaces of Capital: Towards a Critical Geography,* pp. 284–311. Edinburgh: Edinburgh University Press. First publ. 1981.

Harvey, David. 2003. *The New Imperialism,* Oxford: Oxford University Press.

Hayter, Teresa. 2000. *Open Borders: The Case against Immigration Controls.* London: Pluto Press.

Hirst, Paul and Thompson, Graham. 1996. *Globalization in Question.* Cambridge: Polity.

Hoogvelt, Ankie. 1997. *Globalisation and the Postcolonial World: The New Political Economy of Development.* Basingstoke: Macmillan.

Mann, Michael. 1993. Nation-states in Europe and other continents: diversifying, developing, not dying. *Daedalus* 122 (3): 115–140.

Mann, Michael. 2001. Globalization and September 11. *New Left Review* 12 (Nov.–Dec.): 51–72.

Miliband, Ralph. 1969. *The State in Capitalist Society,* London: Weidenfeld & Nicolson.

O'Dowd, Liam. 2003. The changing significance of European borders. In James Anderson, Liam O'Dowd and Thomas M. Wilson, eds, *New Borders for a Changing Europe: Cross-Border Cooperation and Governance,* pp. 13–36. London: Frank Cass.

Omhae, Ken'ichi. 1999. *The Borderless World: Power and Strategy in the Interlinked Economy.* New York: HarperCollins.

Rosenberg, Justin. 1994. *The Empire of Civil Society.* London: Verso.

Sack, Robert. 1986. *Human Territoriality: Its History and Theory.* Cambridge: Cambridge University Press.

Sassen, Saskia. 1988. *The Mobility of Labor and Capital: A Study in International Investment and Labor Flow.* Cambridge: Cambridge University Press.

Smith, Neil. 2003. *American Empire: Roosevelt's Geographer and the Prelude to Globalization.* Berkeley: University of California Press.

Sum, Andrew, Fogg, Neeta and Harrington, Paul et al. 2002. Immigrant Workers and the Great American Job Machine: The Contribution of New Foreign Immigration to National and Regional Labor Force Growth in the 1990s. Prepared for the National Business Roundtable, Washington, DC.

Tilly, Charles. 1992. *Coercion, Capital, and European States, AD 990–1992.* Oxford: Blackwell.

Torpey, John. 2000. *The Invention of the Passport: Surveillance, Citizenship and the State.* Cambridge: Cambridge University Press.

Weiss, Linda. 1998. *The Myth of the Powerless State.* Ithaca: Cornell University Press.

Wood, Ellen Meiksins. 1995. The separation of the "economic" and the "political" in capitalism. In E.M. Wood, *Democracy against Capitalism: Renewing Historical Materialism,* pp. 19–48. Cambridge: Cambridge University Press. First publ. 1981.

Wood, Ellen Meiksins. 2003. *Empire of Capital.* London: Verso.

CHAPTER 9

Contested States, Frontiers and Cities

Liam O'Dowd

The politics of borders are central to the contemporary interstate order. They coalesce around a number of recurring themes: the global mobility of capital and information, securitization, immigration, crime, and the rights of powerful states or the "international community" to intervene in the "internal affairs" of some states and the latter's attempts to resist such interventions. In border studies, the complex and changing relationship of states to economic, political and cultural forms of globalization finds expression in discussions of deterritorialization and reterritorialization, debordering and rebordering, deregulation and reregulation. The privileging of national state borders pervades this literature. Ongoing debates coalesce around the changing meaning and significance of state borders and the fate of territorial sovereignty (O'Dowd 2010; Brown 2010). The related unsettling and reconfiguration of state borders means, in a sense, that all states and their borders may be seen as contested.

However, while such wider changes to borders form the context for this chapter, the term "contested state" is used here in a more specific sense to refer to states where the main political dynamic involves the (re)location of the territorial borders of the state, or indeed the very existence of the state itself. The central issue here is the claim of ethnonational groups to exclusive national homelands in what is shared territory. Such claims typically involve organized violence and coercion, either on the part of the "nation" seeking its own state or on the part of the state seeking to consolidate its own "nation."

Competing claims to national homelands are part of the lengthy and ongoing business of state- and nation-building.[1] I suggest that this "unfinished business" is best illuminated, conceptually and empirically, by focusing on frontier zones and

A Companion to Border Studies, First Edition. Edited by Thomas M. Wilson and Hastings Donnan.
© 2012 Blackwell Publishing Ltd. Published 2012 by Blackwell Publishing Ltd.

cities. Both are critical sites of ethnonational conflict. Such conflict is most visibly crystallized in cities in frontier zones (or "frontier cities") that have continued to be resistant to projects of nationalist homogenization (Kotek 1999). Contemporary examples of violently disputed frontier cities include Belfast, Jerusalem, Nicosia, Beirut, Mostar, Sarajevo and Kirkuk (Boal 1994; Bollens 2007; Calame and Charlesworth 2009). They are emblematic of many things that inform the scholarship of borders and states: wider conflicts at the historical edge of empire, linked interimperial rivalry, imperial retreat or collapse, or competition between opposed ethnonationalist movements for control over disputed territory.

The central argument of this chapter is that contested national state borders cannot be analyzed adequately without reference to two other territorial entities – empires and cities. The rise of the national state as the hegemonic polity globally has been accompanied by the decline in the perceived significance of empires. Additionally, many erstwhile imperial cities have been nationalized. No major contemporary state subscribes to an imperial mission similar to those embraced by the great nineteenth-century empires (Beissenger 2005). The conventional wisdom in both politics and social science is that the era of national states has decisively supplanted the age of empires. The major national states have distanced themselves from their imperial past and are most unlikely to represent any of their policies as imperial. Cities, on the other hand, have also been nationalized, that is, they are portrayed as integral and representative parts of bounded national territory. Many cities have been transformed in the process from centers of imperial power and control into centers of national power.

The argument advanced below, however, is that imperial frontiers and cities continue to provide indispensable vantage points from which to understand better the ethnonational border conflicts that have more than tripled the number of states in the last 60 years. Recognizing the role of empires and cities in shaping the contemporary interstate order is not just a question of illuminating the historical origins of contested state borders, it is also to acknowledge the continued significance of cities and imperial practices in a world of national states.

For mainstream Euro-American border studies and social science generally, empires and their frontiers seem to belong to the past.[2] As Kotek argues: "Since the advent of nation-states, homogenization, whether civic or ethnic, cannot be stopped. One after the other, frontier zones become frontier lines ('boundaries')" (1999: 232). Colas spells out a persuasive ideal-type distinction between the territoriality of empires and that of national states:

> Whereas empires thrive on fluctuating frontiers, national states can only survive within tightly demarcated borders; where empires rule diverse peoples through separate jurisdictions, sovereign states claim to unify populations culturally under a single overarching national jurisdiction; while empires mainly seek to control peoples, national states aim to control territories. (2007: 62)

In practice, however, the legacy of empires and their frontier zones and cities lives on beneath the mosaic of national states. While there are substantive differences between imperial polities and national states, as indicated in ideal-type distinctions,

there is much more actual overlap between empires and national states than is recognized in the border studies literature. As Mann (2007b) and Tilly (1992) demonstrate, imperial and national states have a common origin in the many wars of the
European continent. The states of Western Europe began as mini-empires although
they developed nations at their core through homogenization and assimilation processes to a greater extent than the multinational empires in the eastern part of the
continent. But all the bigger European states have been more imperial than national
throughout most of their history (Mann 2007b: 56–57).

The historical structure of empires and their network of urban centers have provided a framework for the proliferation of national states in Europe and beyond, as
well as for the ethnonational border conflicts that have characterized state- and
nation-building. Cities as garrisons and as trading, religious and cultural centers have
been central to the expansion of both archaic and modern empires (Tilly 1992).
Urban civilization was particularly strong in medieval and early modern Europe, but
by the early nineteenth century the Europe of cities and city states had been overcome
by an urbanizing Europe of the states (Le Galès and Therborn 2009). In the new
order of national states, the city was clearly subordinated to the state. It was at the
state level, rather than that of the city, that the bulk of economic, political and military
power was institutionalized. Until recently, this has contributed to a downplaying of
the role of the city in contemporary state formation and in disputes over state borders.
Therefore, a focus on frontiers and cities provides an important corrective to ahistorical analysis in border studies (O'Dowd 2010) which obscures the historical evolution
of the contemporary interstate order and the organized violence inherent in all state
borders.[3]

The first part of this chapter outlines the implications of seeing ethnonational
border conflicts through the prism of frontier zones and cities. The second part
develops these implications through reflections on a macro-frontier zone which
stretches from Eastern Europe through the Balkans to the Middle East. This has been
a zone of contending empires: Ottoman, Austro-Hungarian, Russian and German,
as well as a site of periodic interventions by Western imperial powers broadly promoting their own interests through helping to create and sustain a framework of national
states.[4] Despite its great internal diversities, since 1945 this region has been constituted as a frontier zone by the dominant bloc of states (notably the United States,
Britain, France, the European Union, and the USSR until the 1980s). It has proved
to be a volatile and problematical zone for creating national states emerging in the
wake of catastrophic wars and the defeat, retreat and collapse of various empires. The
final section briefly draws together some conclusions about the nature of contemporary frontier zones as arenas of contested state- and nation-building and the growing
importance of their cities as sites of border conflicts.

ETHNONATIONAL BORDER CONFLICTS THROUGH THE PRISM OF FRONTIERS AND CITIES

National states, empires and cities: analytical distinctions

The nation-state ideal not only involves the Weberian notion of monopolizing the
means of violence, it also includes the standardizing of political and administrative

governance and the pursuit of policies of cultural homogenization within a clearly bordered territory. Exclusive national homelands are based on the ideal of "one people, one culture, governed by one sovereign power" (Kotek 1999: 227). In principle, the power of an established national state should be as strong at its territorial limits as it is at its core (typically its capital city). Similarly, cities are unambiguously part of the national territory while the capital city in particular represents the central national "place" – the seat of political and symbolic power.

The ideal-type imperial state, in contrast, is much less committed to centralization, standardization of governance and cultural homogenization. Its geographical limits are seldom clearly defined boundaries but rather are frontier zones of mixed jurisdictions and multicultural populations; here imperial rule is often indirect, involving the co-optation and privileging of certain groups and the creation of outposts of imperial control in the form of colonial settlements, garrisons, castles, trading centers, or cities which may combine many of these functions. Imperial cities both at the core of empires and in imperial frontier zones may be more culturally diverse than their immediate hinterlands, reflecting long-distance trade networks and the presence of settlers and colonial administrations. Whereas national states aspire to territorial fixity based on the ideology of self-determination and a unique homeland, imperial states embrace territorial expansionism as a matter of principle. When this is not justified merely in terms of naked material interest and racial superiority, it is legitimized in terms of a universalistic "civilizing mission" often linked to spreading more advanced forms of religion, technology, and forms of governance.

Imperial frontier zones typically marked a declining power gradient from the imperial center to the periphery. Unlike "peripheries," however, "frontiers" imply confrontation with other powers. At times they encompass areas characterized by interimperial overlap and conflict. In the eighteenth and nineteenth centuries, for example, the conflict between the major European powers transformed overseas colonies into frontier zones in the Americas, Africa and Asia. Frontier zones manifest themselves in different ways at different times. They may be neocolonial frontiers, buffer zones or marches between richer and poorer states, or the kind of frontier which echoes the old Roman limes where the frontier functions as an edge that demarcates two worlds.[5]

The volatility of national borders

The ideological commitment of national states to border fixity contrasts with their actual proliferation globally since the mid-twentieth century. The great European empires arbitrarily divided the world among themselves on the basis of their capacity for coercion. While national states are predicated on the right of groups to self-determination, there are no agreed international criteria of eligibility for national statehood, nor a consensus on the number of national states that should exist. This enhances the prospects that war and coercion characteristic of imperial expansion will continue to determine the creation, maintenance and elimination of national borders. In practice, the number of national states (and by extension, capital cities) continues to increase dramatically. For example, the original 51 member states of the United Nations in 1945 have now expanded to 192. While there has been a steady growth of member states since 1945, two periods were particularly significant. Between 1956

and 1966 decolonization created 32 new African states, and with the collapse of the
Soviet bloc, 15 new states emerged between 1991 and 1993.[6] These accelerated
bursts of state formation took place in frontier zones characterized by imperial competition, retreat or collapse.

The borders being created, undermined or defended in the process of state and
nation formation mark the "caging" of multidimensional economic, political/
administrative, cultural or military infrastructural power (Mann 1993). Conflicts over
such borders are by definition totalizing and ethnonational. Neither frontier zones
nor cities lend themselves easily to such "total" borders, as they are typically characterized by complex specialized and often overlapping borders between diverse jurisdictions and cultural groups. This helps to make them key targets, or arenas of
mobilization, for the protagonists of ethnonational conflict. Cities located in historic
frontier zones frequently crystallize such conflict; they can serve, on the one hand,
as outposts of distant (imperial) powers, and on the other hand as putative power
centers for newly emergent national states. For example, Belfast and Jerusalem, historical objects of competing national claims, are located in historic frontier zones,
respectively on the edge of empire and where empires competed and overlapped. The
same applies to other divided cities such as Mostar, Sarajevo, Nicosia, Beirut and
Kirkuk (e.g., see Kotek 1999 for a discussion of the precarious status of "frontier-
cities" in a world increasingly shaped by processes of nationalist homogenization).

Rethinking contested national borders

Failure to acknowledge the importance of frontier zones and cities for ethnonational
border conflicts has facilitated an excessively sharp distinction between imperialism
and nationalism and between the age of empires and the uncertain beginnings of the
era of the national state.[7] This suggests that there is no overlap between imperial and
national states and that national states are necessarily anti-imperial. In this narrative,
imperialism and globalization are antithetical to the structures of the contemporary
interstate order. But ignoring the continuities between imperial and national states
risks confusing the ideal type of the Western sovereign state with the reality of actual
states. No state was ever able to wield total sovereignty within clearly demarcated
territorial borders; and likewise, few, if any, states succeeded in making state and
nation fully congruent.[8]

Certainly, the *ideal* of the Western-style sovereign nation-state remains both a
powerful global ideology and the hegemonic discourse about state borders. It is
hegemonic because it is the discursive currency that links the 192 states in the global
interstate order and allows interstate communication and mutual recognition. It also
implies a form of nominal equality rooted in the right to self-determination. Within
the territorial borders of existing states, the nation-state ideal also promises democratization, the rule of law, and a more reciprocal relationship between rulers and ruled
where taxation (and in some cases, military service) entitles the ruled to accountable
representation, security and citizenship rights. In other words, unlike empires, national
states have a powerful popular or democratic appeal – and clearly demarcated territorial borders of national states are a necessary, if not sufficient, condition for representative democracy and accountable government.

The ideal of the sovereign nation-state is also based on a loose institutional template to which all states subscribe, which allows for some kind of accountable government in various types of deliberative assembly, justice system, bureaucracy, taxation system and policing and military institutions. In theory, at least, this template allows for mutually supportive, institutionalized communication between national states in international and transnational agencies. It also conveys an ideal that existing states have mutual respect for each other's territorial borders, while subscribing to principles of noninterventionism and a clear distinction between external and internal affairs.

While the interstate order supports a degree of fixity or inertia in existing state borders, it does not prevent the nation-state ideal being used to justify ongoing border conflicts and wars. It provides a ready-made ideological goal for stateless nations that are mobilizing for a state of their own, and a *casus belli* for existing states wishing to quash or forestall such secessions.

Borders and the imperial aspects of contemporary national states

However powerful the ideological appeal of the sovereign nation-state is, it obscures the role of power and coercion in shaping and maintaining the contemporary interstate order. The strength of states and the significance of their territorial borders depend on the degree of "infrastructural power" that they wield. The 192 states currently recognized by the United Nations may be nominally equal but they encompass states that are hugely unequal in terms of their power, size and the degree of effective sovereignty they can wield within their borders.[9] This inequality stems partly from their imperial past and partly from contemporary power inequalities between national states. Contrary to the national state ideal, the most powerful states continue to abrogate to themselves the right to intervene militarily and otherwise into the internal affairs of other states to protect their interests. Not only was this evident in the two world wars, but also in what passes for peacetime. The US, Britain and France and their allies have frequently invoked the support of the "international community" for direct military intervention in other states in "old" frontier zones such as the Middle East, the Balkans and North Africa. Similarly, large states like Russia, India and China periodically intervene within their areas of influence or in their and others' frontier zones, but are able to preclude similar intervention in their own domestic affairs. In other words, the distinction between external and internal affairs is contingent on the highly variable power of states to maintain it.

Certainly, no major contemporary national state incorporates territorial expansionism as a central principle of state policy in the manner of the nineteenth-century empires. However, in the willingness to intervene economically, militarily and politically in the affairs of weaker states, a state may pursue highly specific imperialistic policies which largely ignore national democratic accountability. At times, the US and the European Union (EU) appear to embrace a form of twenty-first century "civilizing mission" on behalf of the "international community" that claims to link democratization, the "rule of law," the spread of neoliberal capitalism and the "war on terror." In other words, the dominant states assume periodic responsibility for maintaining the existing interstate order and for minimizing the potentially disruptive capacities of volatile frontier zones.

As Mann (2007a) observes, those strong states most deeply embedded in the core of the global economy are those whose institutional structure is most dense and that have the greatest capacity to promote nationalist solidarity and to shape taxation, incomes, consumption, health, education and the family life of their citizens.[10] In other words, their infrastructural power (economic, political/administrative, cultural and military) and hence their degree of "boundedness" is strong. This "boundedness" means that they are "pacified zones"; they are able to render unthinkable the direct intervention of other states in their internal affairs while managing to "forget officially" their own origins in protracted war, violence and periodic ethnic cleansing.[11] The states with most infrastructural power are best placed to regulate cross-border relationships and interstate relationships for their own advantage, particularly in regard to the rules of the global economy and the infrastructure for capital accumulation and alliances with other strong states to increase their control of internal and cross-border movement of people. Constellations of the most powerful economies (e.g., the EU, the North American Free Trade Area, the G8 and G20 countries[12]) and military alliances (such as NATO) are mechanisms for regulating the global economy and facilitating intervention in troublesome frontier zones in order to defend geopolitical interests and preclude far-reaching disruption within the global interstate order. The effective sovereignty of states varies widely, therefore, over time and space, as does the capacity and desire of the powerful states to intervene in regions well beyond their borders.[13] Mann (2007a) has pointed to an "ostracizing imperialism" which excludes or marginalizes a third of the states recognized by the United Nations from the world economy. Many of these ostracized states are in Africa, for example, where localized ethnic, national, religious or tribal conflicts may be left to fester in areas deemed to be marginal to economic and political interests of the dominant states. Neo-imperial interventions in twenty-first century frontier zones work through the medium of state- and nation-building rather than through the direct control, colonial settlement and occupation of land. The "problem" of controlling frontier zones has been redefined as one of "rogue," "failed," "weak" or "fragile" states. Such accounts, which American and Eurocentric social science has helped shape, are a comment on the contemporary interventionist agenda of the US and its allies in the Balkans, the Middle East, Afghanistan, Iraq and North Africa (see, for example, Hesselbein 2008; Mair 2008; Beall et al. 2011). The ideal stable bounded, democratic national state, however, remains a rather remote ideal in regions characterized by economic underdevelopment and internecine conflict, and heavily influenced by the economic, strategic and security interests of the US and its allies.

The geopolitical and geo-economic significance of frontier zones varies greatly, both historically and geographically, in ways that influence the likelihood of great power intervention and exacerbate ethnonational conflicts. Core–frontier relationships are variable and complex and seldom characterized by overall coherence or rationality. Strong states may intervene militarily in frontier zones, overtly or covertly, or they may arm proxy or client states and even attempt periodic occupations as in Iraq and Afghanistan. Economically, intervention may encompass selective capital investment in manufacturing capacity, extracting raw materials and energy supplies or ensuring the supply of primary commodities, and seeking to promote Western forms of civil society through international nongovernmental organizations.

Core state interventions frequently intersect with, and often fuel, organized violence between competing state- and nation-building projects on the frontier, and serve to reactivate older antagonisms rooted in imperial legacies and religious divisions. The global interstate order is further threatened when the "externalized" violence threatens to be imported back into the core. This importation of frontier conflicts back into the pacified core did not begin with the so-called war on terrorism, that is, with the relationship between Tora Bora and New York. While the relative peace of nineteenth-century imperial Europe coexisted with ongoing interimperial wars in the colonial frontiers, by the twentieth century the interimperial rivalries, ethnic cleansing and racism were to be reimported into Europe in two devastating world wars. Peace in Europe after World War II coincided with the peasant insurgencies and wars of decolonization. Korea, Vietnam, Afghanistan, the Middle East, the Balkans and parts of Africa and the Caucasus remained zones of intervention for the dominant neo-imperial states, notably the US and its leading allies and Russia.

Of course, frontier zones are never merely passive or inert objects of "great power" intervention. Frontiers can spawn alternatives to the dominant geopolitical order reflecting long-term shifts in the locus of global economic and political power. For example, the US, now the dominant global superpower, emerged from the western frontier of European imperial and colonial expansion. More recently, powerful states such as Brazil, Russia, India and China have emerged to form part of an increasingly "multipolar" geopolitical order. Along with other large states such as Iran, Turkey and Indonesia, these states are multinational and confront ethnic, national and religious conflicts in their own frontier zones based on demands for separation or varying degrees of political autonomy.[14] As Beissenger (2005) notes, these states are increasingly subject to being labeled as empires by their dissident minorities.

At present, however, the US and the EU remain the dominant definers of cores, peripheries and frontiers. While the leading Western states externally intervene in global frontier zones, they are simultaneously developing more stringent border securitization policies aimed at selectively regulating the cross-border flows of immigrants, goods, diseases, and criminal and terrorist activities. Here, for example, enhanced regulation along the US-Mexican border and the external border of the EU are (often contradictory) attempts to make a clearer demarcation between core national states and troublesome frontier zones. The historical specter of interimperial wars, and the related arbitrary and coercive demarcation of borders, continues to haunt the US–Mexico and EU borderlands.

A focus on frontiers and cities facilitates the recognition that the gestation of the contemporary state order and the vast inequalities in power which brought it into being long predate the hegemony of the nation-state ideal. Frontier zones mark the declining power of states (both imperial and national) at their peripheries, while they are also a reminder that dominant states always seek to structure core–frontier relationships to their advantage. Cities in frontier zones continue to be key sites of transition in the relationship between imperial and national states, where the changing relationships between imperial states and emerging national states are encapsulated and expressed.

From imperial to national cities

Until recently, much of the vast literature that has developed around the proliferation of ethnonational conflicts in the second half of the twentieth century has paid little attention to the role of cities in such conflicts. Similarly, border studies have tended to focus on cities at the borders of existing states, rather than on those in more broadly conceived frontier zones. Yet, cities have encapsulated the imperfect and incomplete transitions from a world of empires to the world of national states. Not only were they centers of imperial authority, administration and culture, they were also key sites of state- and nation-building. Their roles in frontier zones were particularly contradictory. On the one hand, cities (especially local capitals) were often more culturally diverse than their immediate hinterlands as a result of their role as nodes in the political, administrative and trading networks of empire. On the other hand, they were targets of ethnonational movements that wanted them to be more representative of their surrounding rural populations. Cities in frontier zones, therefore, are often political fulcrums, balanced between new state- and nation-building projects and the defense of imperial or neo-imperial influences.

In one sense linking frontiers and cities is somewhat counterintuitive in that cities are typically seen as physical and geographical centers of power, while frontiers indicate degrees of distance or remoteness from the centers of power. Mumford, in developing a transhistorical concept of the city, sees it as concentrating physical and cultural power: "By means of its storage facilities (buildings, vaults, archives, monuments, tablets, books) the city became capable of transmitting a complex culture from generation to generation" (1961: 648). This form of power was variously linked to economic, political/administrative and military power in ancient and modern empires and city states. The great nineteenth-century empires were to an extent constituted by a skeletal network of interlinked cities. Core cities such as London, Paris, Madrid and Berlin served as the hubs of rimless wheels linking them to cities on the imperial frontier. Frontier cities such as Belfast, Danzig, Trieste and Jerusalem intensified ethnonational conflict with the retreat of empire and the rise of nationalist movements (Boal 1994; Hepburn 2004; Bialasiewicz and Minca 2010). They became sites for a more aggressive and centralizing form of imperial nationalism, which in turn provoked counternationalisms seeking to claim them for independent national states.

Since World War I, in particular, imperial frontier zones and their cities have proved to be volatile arenas for ethnonational conflicts and contested forms of state- and nation-building. Here, in contrast to the more established, powerful and pacified states, the coercive or arbitrary origins of state borders have proved more difficult to "consign to the past."[15] Frontier zones are reminders of the efficacy of organized violence, not least that wielded by the victors of major wars in the *progressive* "unmixing" of populations on ethnic, national and religious grounds (as, for example, in east and southeast Europe). Where mixed populations continue to exist, they reflect the legacies of competing empires and the existence of obstacles in the path of ethnonationalist mobilization and projects of cultural homogenization.

Anti-imperial forms of state- and nation-building were often rendered difficult by the legacy of differential incorporation of different groups into decaying or retreating imperial or colonial structures. Viewed from the standpoint of the "modern national state," whether in capitalist or state socialist guise, frontier zones in the overseas colonies, eastern and southeastern Europe and the Middle East appeared as assemblages of "bits and pieces" where older polities and forms of social organization (ethnic, tribal and nomadic groups, religious polities and forms of familial organization) survived and coexisted.

The growing urbanization of the world's population has stimulated a renewed and broader interest in city–state relationships (e.g., Taylor 2007; Therborn 2011) and, more particularly, in the role of cities in the formation and breakup of states (Beall et al. 2011). One strand in the literature associated with the global cities perspective underlines the extent to which cities have become disembedded from their respective states as they become nodes in a globalized capitalist economy (see, e.g., Taylor 2007). In this perspective, cities are conceived as engines of economic development and innovation and as "spaces of cross-border flows." By implication this view of cities removes them from the territorialist parameters of ethnonational conflicts, making them more amenable to diluting or avoiding the zero-sum nature of such conflicts. Yet, as Therborn (2011) points out, cities are also "spaces of places," encompassing an increasing proportion of the world's population. In this guise, cities are part of the national territory or homeland for which they provide an integrating function, economically, demographically and symbolically. Moreover, ethnonational conflict over state borders may coexist, and interact, with a great variety of other forms of conflicts in urban space, ranging from micro-level forms of coercion and criminality (see World Bank 2010) to geopolitical conflicts that use cities as "battlespaces" (Graham 2010).

Cities absorb, therefore, much of the impact of national, regional and internationally fueled conflict (Beall 2007: 13). As places or reservoirs of deep-rooted conflict, coercion, insecurity and inequality (O'Dowd and Komarova 2011), they pose a challenge to states' capacity to monopolize the means of violence. Hence new forms of surveillance, gated communities and more repressive policing are illustrative of states' attempts to reimpose order on growing urban areas. Cities appear as sources and targets of crime and terrorism, as victims of wars organized by states, or by those contesting the borders or the very existence of the state (Graham 2006; Savitch 2008; Beall and Fox 2009).

The dual representation of cities as engines of global capital accumulation and as threats to social order also links cities to questions of ethnonational border conflict. For example, in summarizing the research program on Cities in Fragile States at the London School of Economics, Beall, Goodfellow and Rodgers emphasize how cities manifest themselves not only as crucibles of state-making but also as primary sites of state erosion (2011: 3; see also Beall and Fox 2009). Similarly, Davis and Libertun de Duren (2011) represent cities as key sites where the sovereignty and even the existence of states are being contested. However, these cities also manifest the uneven impact of imperialistic policies of intervention or neglect.

Viewed in this light, cities may constitute frontier zones in their own right, where the struggle over the state is most concentrated. Nowhere is this struggle more intense than in capital cities, as they are of particular economic, political and symbolic significance in contested national states (Therborn 2006; Landau-Wells 2008).

REFLECTIONS ON CHANGING FRONTIER ZONES, CITIES AND ETHNONATIONAL CONFLICTS

The preceding section of this chapter pointed to the importance of understanding ethnonational border conflicts through the prism of imperial frontier zones and cities. This section seeks to illustrate the argument by reference to east-central Europe and the Middle East. Viewed from conventional contemporary perspectives, this vast geographical area stretching from the Baltic to the Arabian Sea is more notable for its internal divisions than for any underlying shared historical legacy. One such division seems particularly important – between east-central Europe on the one hand, and the Balkans and Middle East on the other. In the former, in the wake of the collapse of the Soviet bloc, there has been a consolidation of democratic national states with agreed borders under the aegis of the eastward enlargement of the EU. In the Balkans and the Middle East, state- and nation-building remains a coercive and often violent process. The rise of radical Islamist politics challenges Western geopolitical agendas of establishing an interstate order approximating that established in Europe.

Yet, a broad historical perspective helps to highlight the connections that bridge this apparent gulf between Europe and the Middle East. The historic importance of urban Jewish populations in Eastern Europe, anti-Semitism, the Zionist project, and above all the Holocaust are directly connected to the creation of the state of Israel and the dispossession of the Palestinians. The eruption of the Balkan conflicts in the 1990s was a reminder of how the Balkans in general served as a historical bridge between Europe and the Middle East, and of the role of the Ottoman Empire in the formation of southeastern Europe.[16] Moreover, the success in establishing stable and democratic national borders in Eastern Europe was facilitated by organized violence. Two world wars, genocide, massive ethnic cleansing and population displacement were the midwives of "successful" national state formation in Eastern Europe. From this perspective, conflicts in Cyprus, the Balkans and the Middle East are merely a continuation of a long historical process dating from the early twentieth century.

In the context of this chapter, the wider region from the Baltic to the Arabian Sea has served for at least 150 years as a vast geopolitical frontier zone vis-à-vis imperial Europe and more recently the US. This region has been characterized by prolonged, if episodic, conflicts over state borders made manifest in the changing relationships between empires, cities and ethnonational movements.

From empires to national states in Eastern Europe

From the mid-nineteenth century to the end of World War I, east-central Europe (including the Balkans) and the Middle East were arenas of ongoing contestation, between the retreating Russian, Austro-Hungarian and Ottoman empires. World War I finally confirmed their collapse and the victory of Western imperial states built around national cores and based on an industrial capitalist economy. The eastern empires, unlike their western counterparts in the US, United Kingdom, France and

Germany (up to 1918), were slowly modernizing, loosely integrated, decentralized formations presiding over cities and territories that were culturally diverse and multi-ethnic. As Therborn notes (2006: 190–191), east-central Europe from Helsinki to Ottoman Istanbul was the most multicultural and multi-ethnic part of the European continent, held together by a network of Habsburg and Ottoman cities. These cities typically differed legally, economically and culturally from the surrounding countryside and often had different ethnic and linguistic characteristics than their hinterlands.

In analyzing the changing role and ethnic composition of capitals in the frontier zones of eastern and southeastern Europe, Therborn also notes that 150 years ago, of 15 current capitals in the region from Sofia to Helsinki and from Prague to Kiev, only three, Ljubljana, Warsaw and Zagreb, had an ethnocultural majority of their current nations (2006: 191).[17] Interimperial wars, immigration to industrial centers and the spread of democratic nationalism changed the ethnic composition of nine of these future national capitals before 1914. But the unmixing of populations in what amounts to the cultural homogenization of state populations and their (capital) cities was a direct result of the region becoming a major battlefield of the two world wars. The Holocaust and the forced displacement of German minorities and other forms of ethnic cleansing were to shape city–state relations, largely transforming multi-ethnic polities into their culturally homogeneous nationalist successors.

The defeat of the Nazis was followed by the dominance of the USSR over its Eastern European satellites. The Soviet empire presided over a group of dependent national states where cities were clearly subordinate to centralized state administrations. After 1989, the collapse of this system led to the mass impoverishment and economic marginalization of the former state-socialist countries. Foreign investment and tourists then flowed selectively to several of the national capitals, including Prague, Warsaw, Budapest and Bratislava. Rediscovering their presocialist European heritage, they became outposts of Western neoliberalism and relative prosperity. This differentiated these cities once again from their hinterlands, albeit now on socioeconomic rather than on ethnic grounds.

The violent disintegration of Yugoslavia, however, meant the collapse of the remaining multicultural and multinational state in the region and the attempted completion of the long-term processes of the various forms of ethnic cleansing and population displacement. The mixed ethnonational and religious populations in Yugoslavia, a legacy of the Ottoman and Habsburg empires, had survived the two world wars, and were now violently fragmented into a number of new more homogeneous, if still polarized, states. Formerly mixed and pluralistic cities such as Sarajevo, Mostar and Skopje became sharply divided on ethnonational grounds, reflecting the new polarized jurisdictions in which they were located.

Contested states and cities within Ottoman lands

Historically, the Ottoman Empire had spanned southeast Europe and the Middle East through a grid of interconnected, multicultural cities. These were eventually to become the capitals and major cities of Balkan national states. They have a culturally diverse and often cosmopolitan history forged in the nineteenth-century conflicts between the Ottoman, Russian and Habsburg empires and by older, overlapping cultural zones colored by Orthodox and Latin Christianity and Islam. Bucharest, Belgrade, Thessaloniki, Sarajevo, Skopje and Sofia had varying relationships to Ottoman Istanbul in the nineteenth century. Wars and ethnonationalist movements and the extensive interference of Western imperial states combined, however, to undermine urban cosmopolitanism and cultural diversity, as well as intercity networks. With the emergence of a Turkish national state, and waves of national state formation in the Balkans, the multicultural characteristics of southeast Europe became attenuated.[18] More culturally homogenized, and sometimes polarized, cities were now incorporated into national states that were relatively weak and often contested from within and without. The Yugoslavian wars mark a further stage in what has been a long-term process of contested state and nation formation.[19]

Ottoman lands outside Europe were even less amenable to the homogenizing thrust of ethnonational movements. As Vucinich (1962) observes, at any one time the Ottoman Empire involved vast congeries of discrete cultural and societal elements which shifted and related much like the particles in a kaleidoscope. Beyond Europe the wide regional differences in Arab countries were cross-cut by divisions between Sunni and Shia, pastoralists and agriculturalists, sedentary and nomadic communities, and a variety of Christian sects including Greeks, Serbians, Bulgarians, Maronites, Coptics and Armenians.

After World War I, the imperial victors, the UK and France, played a decisive role in carving up the Middle East into states, a process complicated by the Zionist project in Palestine and by the consequences of the Holocaust, notably in Eastern Europe. Since 1948 the wars, colonizations, population displacement and ethnic cleansings associated with the establishment of the Israeli settler state have provided the focus for ongoing ethnonational and geopolitical conflict in the region as a whole. It also marks the critical imperial interventions of the US and the larger Western European states in supporting, if not controlling, Israeli state-building. While this support would appear to contradict the geopolitical aim of stabilizing a troublesome frontier zone, it nevertheless fits with a long Western tradition of violent state-building

As recent geopolitical developments have shown, the actual states of the Middle East, that is, Saudi Arabia, Lebanon, Syria, Iran, Iraq and the Gulf States, fall far short of the Western ideal of the democratic national state. The contradictions and conflicts are crystallized most clearly in the capital cities of the region – in Jerusalem above all, but also in Beirut and Baghdad. It is in these cities that interaction is most contentious between the legacies of imperialism, the imperatives of contemporary state- and nation-building, and the role of radical Islamist movements. Jerusalem serves as the iconic representation or distillation of all these conflicts. The subject of multiple claims by the imperial powers of the nineteenth century, its holy places are claimed by three monotheistic religions, while more immediately, it remains the highly contested and putative capital of two national homelands (Dumper 2008; Pullan and Gwiazda 2008). Its built environment and social organization demonstrate how cities themselves can become frontiers (Pullan 2011), and how they can become critical interfaces between wider frontier zones and the most powerful states in the world system.

Frontier cities

Like their predecessors, cities (particularly capitals) in today's frontier zones are caught between the forces integrating them into a transnational political, economic and cultural order dominated by the core states, and those in their national hinterland. As such they are Janus-faced. On the one hand, they are sites of interaction among corporate elites and representatives of other states, international organizations and transnational civil society. On the other hand, they act as magnets for migrants from the countryside and as putative sites of national integration. To Western states, they may be outposts of civilization, sites of modernization, pluralism and cultural diversity, but to unassimilated and exploited groups within their state territories they may be threats to long-established ethnic, tribal and religious polities. This is a recipe for ethnonational conflict over the city, fueled not only by internecine conflicts within frontier zones but also by the selective, arbitrary and often violent interventions by powerful states trying to shape the relations between core and peripheral states in the world system.

Cities, however, are never merely creatures of empires, national states, corporate capitalism and spaces of flows in a globalized world. They are also durable settlements characterized by built environments and particular forms of sociability that are not reducible to any one phase in the history of capitalist development or state formation. They may be fundamentally affected by these phases and their sedimented legacies but they retain forms of territoriality linked to enforced and close cohabitation, to the dynamics of their demography, and to interdependence and frequent functional border crossings that distinguish them from more extensive territorial units. History, memory and contested myths of origin look different from an urban as opposed to a national state perspective. Cities may be seen as resilient transhistorical centers of civilizational or cultural heritage which in some senses have survived the rise and fall of successive imperial states.[20]

The interventionist policies of the dominant states remain key factors conditioning urban ethnonational conflicts. As the world's population has become more urbanized, and the economic and cultural significance of cities has grown, they have become both the targets and the means of intensified violent conflict. Cities, and particularly capital cities, have come to serve as proxies for their respective states, especially in frontier zones. A functioning capital is a necessary, if not sufficient, condition for a functioning state. The state's capacity to control the capital city militarily, even if it does not wield effective sovereignty in the rest of the state's territory, is a sine qua non for the recognition of the state to be institutionalized within the interstate order (see Landau-Wells 2008). Here cities become ensnared in new ways in ethnonational conflicts over the state.[21] Moreover, the enhanced significance of cities as centers of population, economic dynamism and cultural symbolism for the protagonists of ethnonational conflict make them both targets and sites of asymmetric wars that are integral to the relationship between the stronger states and the weaker constellation of states in frontier zones.

CONCLUSION

A number of implications for contemporary border studies may be derived from the above discussion. The first points to the importance of historical analysis. Mainstream border studies have a tendency to emphasize spatial rather than temporal analysis. They rather take for granted that imperialism and the "age of empires" can be consigned to the past, while they concentrate on the current "era of the national state" and its future prospects. While there are very important analytical and ideological distinctions between imperialism and nationalism, I have argued here that they are much more closely interwoven in practice, not least in the disputed frontier zones of the interstate order.

Secondly, the focus on frontiers and cities is a reminder of the dangers of reading history backwards from the standpoint of contemporary national states and their borders. This is a particular danger in a period when the number of national states is proliferating and many are threatened by intrastate ethnonational conflicts. Frontier zones are "workshops" of state and nation formation that are best understood over long periods and at multiple scales ranging from the geopolitical, to the national and the urban.

Thirdly, border studies, even when case study oriented, tend to be based on theorizing what is happening to *the* state and its borders. Given the great variability in the size, provenance and structural power of existing states, the empirical basis for this theorizing is unclear and ethnocentrism is an ever-present danger. A focus on frontiers and cities suggests the merit of assuming the global interstate order as the underlying unit of analysis rather than any one state. This allows for a more dynamic and differentiated view of state borders. Bringing cities into the framework of border studies also underlines the importance of historical analysis, and the changing role of cities in the formation and disintegration of imperial and national states.

Finally, the perspective adopted in this chapter underlines the role of violence, wars and ethnic cleansing in the history of national state formation. The relatively homogenized states and cities of east-central Europe, which are the outcome of organized violence on a catastrophic scale, are currently stable, democratic members of the EU and the general interstate order. One of the outstanding political and moral questions that might suffuse border studies is whether similar forms of organized violence in the Balkans and the Middle East (often imperial in form) are a necessary or inevitable means to a similar outcome, that is, successful state-building in the Middle East. Or alternatively, do the particular legacies of interimperial conflict and the long history of the Ottoman Empire, its cities and social organization render the implantation of European-style interstate order impossible in the Middle East. These legacies are manifest, for example, in the US arming of client states, in the American military bases that dot the Middle East, in the spreading Israel settlements in the West Bank, in Hamas-controlled Gaza, in Hezbollah's "state within a state" in southern Lebanon and in the rise of transnational Islamic radicalism. The violence of unsettled borders in this frontier zone and others also casts a long shadow on the violence congealed in the stable and legitimate national borders of the "West."

NOTES

This chapter contributes to a collaborative research project, Conflict in Cities and the Contested State: Everyday Life and the Prospects for Conflict Transformation in Belfast, Jerusalem and other Divided Cities (2007–2012) ESRC Grant Number: RES-060-25-0015. I wish particularly to thank one of my colleagues on this project, James Anderson, as well as the two editors of this volume for their comments on this chapter.

1   Of course, projects of state- and nation-building are not confined to states that are currently characterized by ethnonational conflict. They characterize all states but are not unilinear in nature. In practice, they may either strengthen or weaken the claim of a state or a nation on its people and vice versa. They may either preempt or weaken ethnonational movements aimed at altering the boundaries of the state, or alternatively, they may sow the seeds for future ethnonational conflicts.

2   There has been a revival recently in the historical and social scientific study of imperialism which questions the sharp distinctions between the "age of empire" and the "era of the national state" and which has the potential to highlight the role of frontier zones and cities in ongoing state formation (see Anderson and O'Dowd 2007 and O'Dowd 2010).

3   Reflecting the European experience, Malcolm Anderson (1996: 37) notes that the great majority of the world's frontiers were established by force and intimidation, but in the long term they are considered sustainable because *ex post facto*, they rest on self-determination and consent. This assessment seems less applicable, however, to frontier regions comprising weak and often repressive states prone to violent challenge from within and without.

4   This process was intimately linked to the two world wars and their outcomes, as well as to the recent collapse of the Soviet empire.

5   See the discussion by Walters (2004) of the merits of archaic terms such as marches and limes to describe the operation of contemporary frontier zones. He adds to these terms that of colonial frontiers and what he terms "networked non-borders" between strong, prosperous states.

6   Serbia and Montenegro joined the United Nations in 2000 and 2006 respectively, while Kosovo also emerged as a separate jurisdiction, if not as a UN member (www.un.org/en/members/, accessed June 28, 2011).

7   There is remarkable disagreement over when the era of the national state actually began. It is variously traced to the French Revolution, the radical nationalisms of early nineteenth-century Europe, the national independence movements of Latin America, interwar Europe and post–World War II (O'Dowd 2010: 1044). Meanwhile, of course, many globalization theorists have been busy writing obituaries for the nation-state.

8   Throughout this chapter I have used the term "national state" in preference to "nation-state." The former refers to states that legitimate themselves by claiming to represent a specific nation. The latter suggests that a congruence between nation and state has been achieved – an outcome rarely, if ever, achieved in the contemporary global order.

9   Howland and White (2008: 16) suggest that sovereignty is the nomenclature with which states are described, institutionalized and interrogated, but they argue that the actual quality of sovereignty is never really the determinant of the recognition of states or of a state's success or failure. While this may be the case at the level of international relations, states characterized by weak infrastructural power are ill-equipped to cope with ethnonational challenges to their borders.

10 Mann (2007b) is probably right to argue that today's strong states are generally more cohesive and monocultural than they were in their classic imperial form a century ago.

11   For example, Ernest Renan noted that what binds a nation together is the collective ability to forget the conquests, massacres and enslavements that brought a people together with a desire to live together and perpetuate a shared heritage (see Howland and White 2008: 11–12).

12   The G8 countries include France, Germany, Italy, Japan, UK, US, Canada and Russia. The G20 group includes the G8 countries plus Argentina, Australia, Brazil, China, India, Indonesia, Mexico, Saudi Arabia, South Africa, Republic of Korea, Turkey and the EU.

13   The debate about the rise and potential demise of *the* national state is somewhat misplaced insofar as it is based on the experience of the stronger and more prosperous core states rather than the majority of contemporary national states. Rather than measure the significance of state borders in terms of some putative (and highly dubious) unilinear decline in state sovereignty, a more adequate point of departure might be to recognize the great variability in the size, infrastructural power and cohesiveness of states within the wider interstate order (O'Dowd 2010). In other words, the factors are pointers to how "bounded" states are.

14   Such demands are not confined to areas outside the core of the global capitalist economy. In Northern Ireland, and in the Basque Country and Catalonia, the UK and Spain respectively continue to be subject to ethnonational and regional demands for separation or greater autonomy.

15   The case of Ireland, and Northern Ireland in particular, is a reminder that frontier zones can persist close to the heartland of empire. From the 1960s onward, the Northern Ireland conflict was a reminder of the violence and coercion involved in the formation of the UK and Irish states.

16   Twentieth-century history also emphasized the role of the Mediterranean as a barrier rather than as a bridge between Europe and the Middle East, in contrast to its role as a center of political, economic and cultural activity since the time of the Roman Empire. See Segal et al. (2011) for a discussion of the potential of the Mediterranean as the basis of a unifying political narrative that might challenge the multiple geopolitical divisions that currently characterize the region.

17   Helsinki was Swedish-speaking, Sofia was Muslim and Jewish more than Bulgarian, Bucharest, largely Greek. Others, such as Reval/Tallinn and Buda, were mainly German; today's Bratislava was German and Hungarian, and Wilna/Vilna/Vilnius was above all Jewish.

18   The exchange of Turkish and Greek populations in 1923 was a further example of the "unmixing" of populations. The case of Thessaloniki epitomized the process. Its centuries-long history as an important multicultural, polyglot city ended with it becoming overwhelmingly Greek in the 1920s (Hepburn 2004: 23–25). This process of segregation was taken a stage further with the partition of Cyprus and its capital Nicosia in the 1970s.

19   Herscher (2005) has argued that it was the destruction of Yugoslavian cities seen as frontier outposts of European heritage and civilization that prompted most EU engagement with the Croatian and Bosnian conflicts. He argues that Dubrovnik, Vukovar and Sarajevo were perceived as European because of their cultural heritage. On the other hand, he suggests that the EU was less enthusiastic about treating the populations of their hinterlands as potential EU citizens.

20   For example, Mumford notes that it is consoling that cities have "repeatedly outlived the military empires that seemingly destroyed them forever. Damascus, Baghdad, Jerusalem, Athens still stand alive on the sites they originally occupied, though little more than fragments of their ancient foundations remain" (1961: 69).

21   Sassen (2010: 33) has argued that while national states have responded historically by militarizing conflict, cities have tended to triage conflict through commerce and civic

activity. This characteristic of cities would seem to be heavily constrained, however, with respect to ethnonational conflicts over state borders.

REFERENCES

Anderson, James and O'Dowd, Liam. 2007. Imperialism and nationalism: the Home Rule struggle and border creation in Ireland, 1885–1925, *Political Geography* 26 (8): 934–950.

Anderson, Malcolm. 1996. *Frontiers: Territory and State Formation in the Modern World*. Cambridge: Polity.

Beall, Jo. 2007. Cities, Terrorism and Urban Wars of the Twenty-First Century. Crisis States Working Papers Series 2, Paper No. 9, London School of Economics.

Beall, Jo and Fox, Sean. 2009. *Cities and Development*. London: Routledge.

Beall, Jo, Goodfellow, Tom and Rodgers, Dennis. 2011. Cities, Conflict and State Fragility. Crisis States Working Papers Series 2, Paper No. 85, London School of Economics.

Beissenger, Mark R. 2005. Rethinking empire in the wake of Soviet collapse. In Zoltan Barany and Robert G. Moser, eds, *Ethnic Politics after Communism*, pp. 14–45. Ithaca: Cornell University Press.

Bialasiewicz, Luiza and Minca, Claudio. 2010. The "border within": inhabiting the border in Trieste. *Environment and Planning D: Society and Space* 20 (6): 1084–1105.

Boal, Fred W. 1994. Encapsulation: urban dimensions of national conflict. In Seamus Dunn, ed., *Managing Divided Cities*, pp. 30–40. London: Keele University Press.

Bollens, Scott A. 2007. *Cities, Nationalism and Democratization*. London: Routledge.

Brown, Wendy. 2010. *Walled States, Waning Sovereignty*. New York: Zone Books.

Calame, Jon and Charlesworth, Esther. 2009. *Divided Cities: Belfast, Beirut, Jerusalem, Mostar and Nicosia*. Philadelphia: University of Pennsylvania Press.

Colas, Alejandro. 2007. *Empire*. Cambridge: Polity.

Davis, Diane E. and Libertun de Duren, Nora, eds. 2011. *Cities and Sovereignty*. Bloomington: University of Indiana Press.

Dumper, Mick. 2008. The Multiple Borders of Jerusalem: Policy Implications for the Future of the City. Divided Cities/Contested States Working Paper No. 4. At http://www.conflictincities.org/workingpapers.html (accessed Nov. 2011).

Graham, Stephen. 2006. Cities and the "War on Terror." *International Journal of Urban and Regional Research* 30 (2): 255–276.

Graham, Stephen. 2010. *Cities under Siege: The New Military Urbanism*. London: Verso.

Hepburn, Anthony C. 2004. *Contested Cities in the Modern West*. Basingstoke: Palgrave.

Herscher, Andrew. 2005. Urban formations of difference: borders and cities in post-1989 Europe. *European Review* 13 (2): 251–260.

Hesselbein, Gabi. 2008. The slippery road: the imperative for state formation. *Harvard International Review* (Winter): 46–50.

Howland, Douglas and White, Luise. 2008. Introduction: sovereignty and the study of states. In Douglas Howland and Luise White, eds, *The State of Sovereignty: Territories, Laws and Populations*, pp. 1–18. Bloomington: University of Indiana Press.

Kotek, Joël. 1999. Divided cities in the European cultural context. *Progress in Planning* 52: 227–237.

Landau-Wells, Marika. 2008. Capital Cities in Civil Wars: The Locational Dimension of Sovereign Authority. Crisis States Occasional Paper 6, London School of Economics.

Le Galès, Patrick and Therborn, Göran. 2009. Cities in Europe: From City-States to State Cities, and into Union and Globalization. Working Papers, Villes et Territoires, 2009/4, Sciences Po, Paris. At http://

blogs.sciences-po.fr/recherche-villes (accessed Nov. 2011).

Mair, Stefan. 2008. A new approach: the need to focus on failing states. Harvard International Review (Winter): 52–55.

Mann, Michael. 1993. *The Sources of Social Power*, vol. 2. Cambridge: Cambridge University Press.

Mann, Michael. 2007a. The age of nation-states is just beginning. Plenary paper presented to Beyond the Nation conference, Queen's University Belfast, Sept. 12; available from the author, Department of Sociology, University of California, Los Angeles.

Mann, Michael. 2007b. Predation and production in European imperialism. In Sinisa Malesevic and Mark Haugaard, eds, *Ernest Gellner and Contemporary Social Thought*, pp. 50–74. Cambridge: Cambridge University Press.

Mumford, Lewis. 1961. *The City in History*. London: Penguin Books.

O'Dowd, Liam. 2010. From a "borderless world" to a "world of borders": bringing history back in. *Environment and Planning D: Society and Space* 20 (6): 1031–1050.

O'Dowd, Liam and Komarova, Milena. 2011. Contesting territorial fixity? a case study of urban regeneration in Belfast. *Urban Studies* 48 (10): 2013–2029.

Pullan, Wendy. 2011. Frontier urbanism: the periphery at the centre of contested cities. *Journal of Architecture* 16 (1): 15–35.

Pullan, Wendy and Gwiazda, Max. 2008. Jerusalem's "City of David," the Politicisation of Urban Heritage. Divided Cities/Contested States Working Paper No. 6. At www.conflictincities.org/workingpapers.html (accessed Nov. 2011).

Sassen, Saskia. 2010. When the city itself becomes a technology of war. *Theory, Culture and Society* 27 (6): 33–50.

Savitch, Harvey. 2008. *Cities in a Time of Terror: Space, Territory and Local Resilience*. New York: M.E. Sharpe.

Segal, Rafi, Cohen, Yonatan and Mayer, Matan. 2011. Seabound cities and the Mediterranean ports. July 19. At www.opendemocracy.net (accessed July 21, 2011).

Taylor, Peter J. 2007. Problematizing city-state relations: towards a geohistorical understanding of contemporary globalization. *Transactions of the Institute of British Geographers ns* 32: 133–150.

Therborn, Göran. 2006. Capitals and nations: Eastern Europe in the Twentieth Century. In Anne Haila, ed., *Forward Look in Urban Science*. Strasbourg: European Science Foundation.

Therborn, Göran. 2011. End of a paradigm: the current crisis and the idea of stateless cities. *Environment and Planning A*, 43: 272–285.

Tilly, Charles. 1992. *Coercion, Capital and European States AD 990–1992*. Oxford: Blackwell.

Vucinich, Wayne S. 1962. The nature of Balkan society under Ottoman rule. *Slavic Review* 21 (4): 597–616.

Walters, William. 2004. The frontiers of the EU: a geostrategic perspective. *Geopolitics* 9 (3): 674–698.

World Bank. 2010. *Violence and the City: Understanding and Supporting Community Responses to Urban Violence*. Washington, DC: World Bank Social Development Department, Conflict, Crime and Violence Team.

CHAPTER **10** The State, Hegemony and the Historical British-US Border

Allan K. McDougall
and Lisa Philips

In recent years, the study of borderlands has extended insight into entrepreneurial and identity dynamics emerging from life on the edges of states. Rooted in geographic, economic and social patterns, life and activities in the borderland are assessed within the context of the potential contrast, or limit, provided by the very presence of the border; likewise, borders are marked by the configuration of neighboring social, economic and political characteristics. Such studies have opened significant insights into the challenges and opportunities arising from the intersection of contrasting domains but they often presume, or remain focused on, the contemporary functional or social assumptions, demoting or ignoring the essential limits of negotiation surrounding the border itself. On the one hand, this has sometimes led to the false assumption that the fundamental essence of a border may be subject to negotiation rather than being subject only to minor modification or reinterpretation. On the other hand, many of these studies do provide interesting insights into the relationship between wide-ranging and local changes such as global capital flow, borderland forms of entrepreneurial potential, migration and national security, or the innovation available in identity formation.

This chapter assumes a different tack, presenting a counter-construction to those who focus on life in the borderlands – where the geopolitical border is often taken as given – in order to promote further dialogue over the role and fundamental character of state borders. It will attend first to the essential character of a state border and then will focus on the impact of the imposition of the border in two regions in the British-United States borderlands in North America. In this way, we will focus on the instrumental use of the border – as it was imposed – by those who used its potential to assert control over life and resources in those nascent borderlands. Thus,

A Companion to Border Studies, First Edition. Edited by Thomas M. Wilson and Hastings Donnan.

instead of addressing the characteristics surrounding a border within the borderlands, we will focus on the instrumental potential of a border to realize the agenda of those ascendant within the borderland to impose their will across the emerging borderland communities. In this way, we will address the potential of the border in the context of the social and political dynamics that emerged through the imposition of the border in two regions of the British-US borderland.

THE STATE AND SOVEREIGNTY

The essential definition of a state is that it holds the ultimate power to regulate affairs within its territory (for a thorough review of these points see Stone 1966: ch. 13). A state can enter agreements with other states through treaty, but that treaty must be accepted by the sovereign authority in each state. The border between states is defined first through negotiations between the states directly involved, and then through its acceptance by other states. Only states can participate in treaties, and borders represent the geographic limit of their jurisdiction. This special characteristic makes the state unique, as participation in the treaty process is limited to members of this "statist club." At the same time, the state is not inert, since those who control the constitutionally defined decision centers of the state have agendas. The parties with the authority to negotiate those agendas with other states are plenipotentiaries. Interested parties at the regional or international level can advocate change or attempt to capture entrepreneurial opportunities provided by contrasting economic or social conditions in the borderlands, but only plenipotentiaries can negotiate changes in the border itself. We make this distinction in order to strip away some of the entrenched and collateral issues that often surround the study of borders. We do not dismiss border politics, but we do wish to set the counterfoil to such assumptions, which must, after a certain point, be addressed. For example, despite recent emphasis on globalization, commercial corporations are not states. Likewise, transnational and international nongovernmental organizations are not states. These entities may play a significant role in the form of linkages and interests that swirl across the globe, and they may lobby at national and international forums, but they are not members of the statist club whose members alone make treaties and translate agreements or disagreements into performatives.[1] No matter how popular an agenda may be, it still must pass through the treaty process to be formally realized.

THE BORDERLANDS

This chapter focuses on two regions along the British colonial/United States border in North America, the Old Northwest and the Pacific Northwest (also known as the Oregon Country or the Columbia District), where sovereign authority was shared by two states for an extended period of time. Based on empirical evidence from the experiences of residents in the two regions, we address the following questions: What was the impact of the imposition of this border? What impact did the struggle for

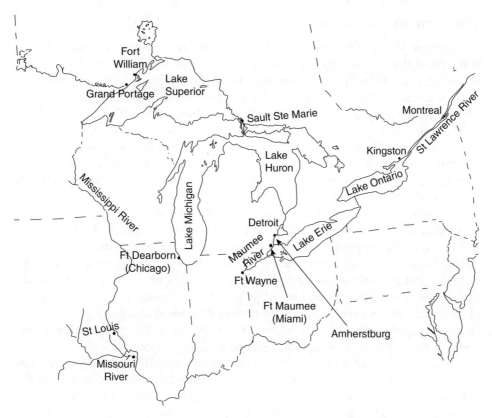

Figure 10.1 The Northwest Territory circa 1790
Source: Serge A. Sauer Map Library at the University of Western Ontario.

the legitimation of sovereign right have on identities in the two regions? What devices were used to consolidate legal potential for the ascendant faction? What happened to those who were not recognized by the new sovereign authority once control of the region was clarified? What impact did translocal influences have on the form of the resulting social order?

The first borderland considered in this chapter was known historically as the "Northwest" and later as the "Old Northwest." The region is bounded on the south by the Ohio River and on the east by Pennsylvania; it stretches north of Lake Erie to upper Lake Huron and west past the southern portions of Lake Michigan to the northern reaches of the Mississippi River (see Figure 10.1). Just prior to the imposition of the border in this area, Aboriginal peoples led the fight against encroaching settlement from the 13 colonies. Their military victories included the Pontiac uprising and the successful resistance to American military advances into their lands during the 1780s and early 1790s (see Sugden 2000 for an excellent review of the Native Confederacy).

The sovereign construction

Through the Treaty of Paris in 1783, the United States and Britain imposed a border that divided the Old Northwest. That division, which was drawn down the center of the Great Lakes waterway, was confirmed in the Jay Treaty of 1794. Despite these treaties, control of the borderland region remained under contention for quite some time. Although formally under the control of the United States, the British held part of the region hostage pending the settlement of United Empire Loyalists' claims against the United States for losses incurred during the Revolutionary War. Throughout this early period in the imposition of the border, neither state consulted the Native American inhabitants, even though First Nations retained the military capacity to defend their own homelands.

Throughout the eighteenth century, Detroit was the central place for the region. Controlled initially by the French, its hinterland at times included Lake Michigan and its limits were contested on the southwest by the Spanish at the confluence of the Illinois and Mississippi rivers and by English colonists from Pennsylvania through Pittsburg and from Kentucky along the Ohio River. From 1700 to 1760, the fur trade in the area flourished (see Innis 1956 for an excellent and much broader review of the Great Lakes fur trade). As the fur trading community developed in the region, farms were established to provide grain and food for the fort with the consent of the French colonial governors in Québec. French settlement remained contained, unlike the colonial settlers from the eastern seaboard, who were attempting to move westward across the Ohio River. The more pervasive American style of settlement posed a threat to the First Nations in the Detroit hinterland; such settler incursions led to a number of uprisings in which the French sided with the Natives.

With the defeat of France in the Seven Years' War and the Treaty of Paris of 1763, the British replaced the French at Detroit. The transfer coincided with the end of Pontiac's Rebellion and the Royal Proclamation of 1763, which pledged to have the British Crown enter treaties with indigenous communities prior to opening land for settlement. As part of the process of transferring control of the Old Northwest, the British Northern Superintendent of Indian Affairs, Sir William Johnson, signed a Treaty of Peace and Friendship with the Huron in 1764 (National Archives of Canada (NAC) R2162847E, Six Nations' Superintendency records). This treaty provided for the continuation of the limited settler occupation that had been enjoyed by the French on the Detroit River and Lake St Clair, and the right to peaceful passage for the British through Lake Erie to Detroit. Councils with the Algonquian and Iroquoian nations at Niagara, near Detroit and Oswego, recognized the British presence throughout the region (NAC RG10, Indian Affairs). Members of the British Indian Department maintained contact with the local tribes and, after the American War of Independence, participated with them in wars against American encroachments from the colonies.

Economic and social patterns

In the early years under both French and British control, Detroit was a shipping and trading center rivaled only by Sault Ste Marie, which linked Montreal to the Upper

Great Lakes and from thence to the west. Settlement beyond Detroit was not encouraged as treaties had not been signed with local communities and settlers were detrimental to the fur trade. All regional forts answered to the commander at Detroit. During this period, the local commercial class had ties of credit and supply to Montreal and from there to Europe. Their wealth depended on the sale of trade goods and the value they could receive for furs in Asian or European markets. There was some competition along the Ohio River from traders bringing their supplies overland from the American colonies, most typically from Virginia, as well as from the Spanish at St Louis on the Mississippi. The rivalry between the French and Spanish on the lower Mississippi minimized the advantage of the river for trade into the Old Northwest and its potential as a trading route was never fully realized. The flow of goods through Detroit was sustained even when the fur trade dwindled, as goods remained cheaper when shipped along well-established trade routes in the Detroit hinterland (Farrell 1968).[2] In fact, British wool shipped through Detroit remained cheaper than wool imported up the Mississippi as far west as the confluence of the Illinois and Mississippi rivers (Innis 1956: 185). Through the 1780s, the St Lawrence route was ascendant. The British governors assumed control of shipping on the Great Lakes in 1780, banning private vessels from Lake Erie, and were able to control trade to Detroit despite increasing American interest (see Haldimand to Lord George Germain, NAC, Q XV11 Pt 1, pp. 1428).

The imposition of the border

Although Detroit was not directly involved in the American War of Independence, it was the base for the British military throughout the Northwest. The popularly recognized regional position of Detroit was illustrated by petitions to Britain from a number of Pennsylvania loyalists who requested land at Detroit so that they could continue to live under the British Crown following the War of Independence. However, the Treaty of Paris of 1783 had placed the border at the center of the Detroit River, locating Detroit within the sovereign territory of the United States. North of the newly defined border, the pressure from settlers to move into British-controlled territory led to the negotiation of treaties with local First Nations communities so that the colonial authorities could make land available for settlement. By the fall of 1790, the north shore of Lake Erie in Upper Canada had been ceded by the First Nations, effectively opening all of the eastern shore of the Detroit River for settlement, with the exception of two reserves held by the Huron Nation. By 1793, all the available land had been occupied by settlers, many of whom were former military personnel who had been guaranteed land in return for their military service to the British Empire.

South of Lake Erie, settler pressure led to increased tension with Aboriginal communities resulting in the reemergence of the Northwest Confederacy. Through the 1780s, George Rogers Clark, Josiah Harmer, Brigadier General Charles Scott, Colonel James Wilkinson and Governor Arthur St Clair led military campaigns against Native communities in the region, but the Northwest Confederacy repeatedly defeated these military incursions into their territory. Then, in 1794, General Anthony Wayne was ordered to seize the region for the United States. He organized a unit of 2,000 regular soldiers and with the support of 1,000 mounted militia from Kentucky[3] won a battle over the Confederacy at the battle of Fallen Timbers. His triumph coincided with the conclusion of negotiations over the Jay Treaty between Britain and the United States that confirmed the border set in 1783.

The function of Detroit changed with the signing of the Jay Treaty and the presence of General Wayne's forces in the region to protect settler communities (Farrell 1968: 304). After the border was imposed, both the British (Canadian) and American governments undertook to negotiate further treaties with local Native communities to open the region to settlers. Uncertainty in the region over the future of Detroit, which had long been in French and then British hands, led to a freewheeling economy. The fur resources of the region were pillaged by local traders in anticipation of their loss of the region to the Americans. The demand for furs exceeded the capacity of the region and it never recovered. Merchants and some Indian agents such as John Askin became major land speculators. After Wayne's military had established itself in the region and as the Americans prepared to enter a treaty with the tribes of the Northwest Confederacy, speculators bought unceded Indian land and then attempted to have their deals entrenched in the Treaty of Greenville, which opened land in Ohio for settlement. The speculators were well organized and persistent. Eventually one of their group was jailed for attempting to bribe members of the Senate during the ratification process. To his credit, the US Commissioner, General Wayne, refused to include such personal deeds in the treaty.

A profile of John Askin provides an illustration of an individual who accommodated to the shifting economy. An independent trader in Detroit from 1780 through 1798, Askin undertook new ventures when the fur trade declined. He operated a general store and provided a blacksmith service, but his debts mounted as the fur trade declined through the 1780s and 1790s. When the price of land rose in the early 1790s, Askin became a land speculator. In 1798, he wrote to a friend from Montreal saying that, if his creditors in Montreal had not agreed to purchase 40 lots from him in return for his debts, he would have been ruined (Farrell 1968: 150–180).

As the American presence was becoming paramount, many early merchants in Detroit lobbied for a town on the British side of the Detroit River. In 1795, the British allocated 19 lots beside their new fort, Fort Malden, for those who wished to move to the British side of the river. In May and June 1796, stores were moved from Forts Miami and Detroit to the new fort; in July, the British forces evacuated Detroit, and two days later, Detroit was occupied by the Americans. Many members of the (Indian or First Nations) Confederacy who had fought against the Americans for decades feared to live in the United States. Most moved to the British side of the Detroit River, staying as close to their old communities as they could. In Upper Canada, they were able to retain their contacts with the (British) Indian Department and they continued to work with Indian Agents Alexander McKee and Matthew Elliot, who had also been forced to move from what had become the American side of the border. The military commander at Fort Malden, on the other hand, complained to Lord Dorchester, the Governor General of the Canadian colonies, that many members of the Confederacy were living around the fort with no food and with nothing to do. Lord Dorchester responded that they should be offered land along the shores of Lake Huron, a response that was possible only because the external boundary of the colony had now been established. The only problem was that the land he promised had not yet been ceded to the Crown by the First Nations in the area.

Six weeks after Detroit had been turned over to the Americans, Alexander McKee, the British Deputy Superintendent General of Indian Affairs, addressed a Council of Chippewa and Ottawa Chiefs at Chenail Ecarte, just north of Lake St Clair on the east side of the St Clair River. When chiefs of the Northwest Confederacy expressed their concern at not being consulted over the border, McKee explained that the Crown had "taken the greatest care to the rights and independence of all the Indian nations who by the last Treaty with America [the Jay Treaty] are to be perfectly free and unmolested in their trade and hunting grounds and to pass and repass freely and undisturbed to trade with whom they please" (NAC, RG10 v.9, pp. 91678). McKee outlined that the Crown wished to purchase a block of land on the north side of the Chenail Ecarte for those First Nations from the Northwest who wanted land under the British Crown. However, McKee's promises were not recognized by the British military, which was preoccupied with the adequacy of land grants for retired soldiers and sailors, as set out in the Royal Proclamation (1763).[4] When the border was defined, Native American people were demoted in the bureaucratic politics of empire and the agenda of the Indian Department was eclipsed.

The American Treaty of Greenville in 1795 was followed by treaties in 1807 and 1817, which opened the land around Detroit, along the United States side of the St Clair River, and around the eastern end of Lake Erie for settlement. On the British side of the river, the treaties of 1790, 1822 and 1827 opened that region for settlement (Canada 1891). Both governments worked quickly to consolidate and populate their sides of the border, but in the process the old hunting lands vanished. Traders, in good entrepreneurial fashion, switched their focus to the provision of staples and equipment for the new settlers. Another activity that Detroit dominated in the regional economy was shipping. Detroit's docks were used to build ships for the Upper Great Lakes and, by the turn of the eighteenth century, ferry services were established to haul lumber from sites along the river and to send provisions to local communities on both sides of the river. The traditional lifestyle and economy of the Native American communities became nonviable as settler homesteads spread first along the waterways and then inland by the 1810s. Natives sold lumber from their reserves and continued to hunt and fish for their own subsistence. The rapid settlement of southern Michigan between 1817 and 1828 led Aboriginal people from that area to cross the St Clair River to hunt in the more sparsely occupied lands on the British side. This contributed to the drain on resources in that region for the local First Nations communities. In this way, efforts by the states to settle their territory accelerated the demise of the hunting grounds – critical to the welfare of the First Nations – on both sides of the border.

The hinterland of Detroit continued to change through the late 1790s. With American settlers moving north from Kentucky and east from Pittsburg, transportation from the American colonies was improved. As road and canal access increased, the backward economic linkages, which crossed the newly imposed border, from Detroit to Montreal were challenged. Land companies formed by entrepreneurs in states ranging from Virginia to Kentucky demanded supplies and maintained supply lines linking their state to the new settlements. These incursions undercut the old trade routes that had been centered on Detroit. These new activities and new alliances shifted the balance of economic power toward the south.

The border also had a political impact on the emerging settler communities on either side. In Canada, the "family compact," or ruling elite in the colony, fostered a hatred for Americans and promoted the region near Lake Erie as a place to settle "reliable" retired military personnel. On the American side, the Kentucky partisans, personified by Henry Clay, championed a form of manifest destiny and the removal of British colonies in America, placing the blame on the British for the Indian Wars. Such political constructions were fueled by memories of the struggles between the settlers and Indians.

The imposition of the border in 1796 marked the conclusion of a long period of contested sovereignty in the Old Northwest. The border both confined the aspirations of the nationalist and promoted the presence of the "other." This was so despite the interdependence of settlers at the border and parallel but separate policy initiatives occurring within each jurisdiction in the borderlands.

One of the most far-reaching effects of the imposition of the border was that it set limits of jurisdiction for the states. Once those bounds were set, colonial administrators in the Canadas and public officials – and land company owners – in the United States undertook to develop their resources, as they perceived them, within their own jurisdiction. The public agenda shifted to the building of roads, opening of land for settlers through treaties, and the building of trade based on the needs of settlers. With the change to development, the entrepreneurial traders became shopkeepers, land speculators and service providers. Detroit became a regional center now supplied by resources from the eastern colonies, which provided construction goods and materials for its hinterland, a hinterland smaller than that of the fur trade and now limited by similar centers that had emerged in eastern Ohio, in Kentucky, and in Chicago and St Louis to the west.

In Upper Canada, events were similar. Treaties were signed, First Nations were increasingly limited to their reserves, and settlement was encouraged so that the colony might become wealthy through the harnessing of its resources. The border defined both the limit of the internal and the threat of the external. Entrepreneurs became land speculators, shopkeepers and politicians oriented to colonial politics and the potential of patronage through the acquisition of land or jobs. The jealousy of the colonial elite to retain control over settlement and land relegated the population on the border to the margins of the colonial economy. Their centralized control and exercise of patronage in Upper Canada differed from the more freewheeling economy in Detroit and was a major factor in the failure of the settlements on the Canadian side of the Detroit River to rival those on the US side.

THE PACIFIC NORTHWEST: THE SOVEREIGN CONSTRUCTION

The second borderland we examine in this chapter is in the Pacific Northwest (see Figure 10.2). Its boundaries were set by the statist club following extensive jockeying

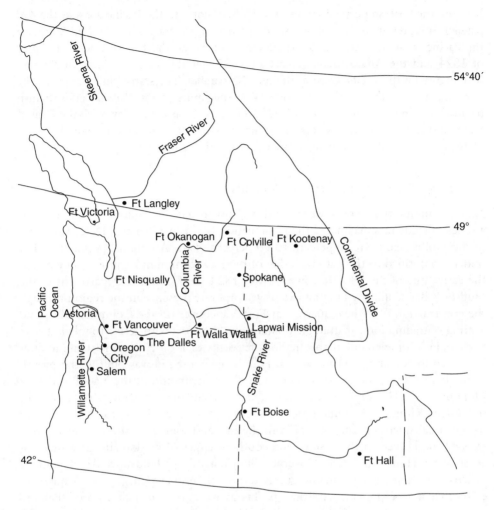

Figure 10.2   Oregon Country, Columbia District, 1818–1846
Source: Oregon Historical Society.

for position by the states, as they attempted to have their claims recognized by their peers. At the most basic level following the war of 1812, the Treaty of Ghent (1814) set sovereign entitlements between England and the United States. Joint commissions appointed by both states were to resolve boundary disputes. The Convention of 1818 set the 49° parallel as the boundary between Rupert's Land and the Louisiana Territory to the Rocky Mountains. During the discussions, the Americans proposed extending the border along the 49° parallel to the Pacific coast. The British countered, suggesting that the border be set along the Columbia River. Eventually the two sides agreed not to choose a border. Rather, they would defer the decision and allow joint occupation of the region for 10 years, since the Nootka Convention had provided the statist precedent of equal access to the British and Spanish in 1790, and the Americans had inherited Spanish rights to the coast in 1819 through the Adams-Onis, or Transcontinental Treaty. The Adams-Onis Treaty extended the border between the Spanish possessions and the United States to the Pacific coast at the 42° parallel. It represented the first statist acceptance of presence of the United States on the Pacific coast. Less than a decade later, two treaties, the Russo-American Treaty of 1824 and the Anglo-Russia Treaty of 1825, set the southern limit of Russian sovereignty on the Pacific coast at the 54° 40′ parallel. The statist club was gradually clarifying title to the northwest coast. With the limits of the Russian and Spanish territories defined, the coast between 42° and 54° 40′ was left in play, with the United States and England as contestants. Joint jurisdiction was subsequently extended until 1846, when a border was finally drawn dividing the contested area.

Life in the Pacific Northwest borderlands

Native communities were powerful and well organized throughout the region, but a series of epidemics decimated their population between 1775 and 1832. Estimates of their toll range from 70 percent to 90 percent of the Aboriginal population. Fur traders conformed to the pattern of life of the local communities just as they had in the early years of the Old Northwest. After 1824 the Columbia Department of the Hudson's Bay Company built an extensive corporate presence in the region through the construction of its headquarters at Fort Vancouver on the Columbia River and a string of trading forts at strategic points along the coast with access to inland trade. Such points complemented the trading networks of local Aboriginal communities interested in acquiring outside wares. Fort Langley (1827) was built at the mouth of the Fraser River, then Fort Simpson (1830) at the mouth of the Nass River, Fort McLoughlin (1833) on Millbank Sound, and Fort Stikina (1840) near the mouth of the Stikina River. At the same time, in an attempt to make the region less attractive to potential American competitors from the east and southeast, the Company over-trapped the beaver on the eastern and southern edges of its domain. At a meeting at Spokane House in 1824, Governor Simpson of the Hudson's Bay Company ordered this approach in unambiguous terms: "If properly managed no question exists that it would yield handsome profits as we have convincing proof that the country is a rich preserve of Beaver and which for political reasons we should endeavor to destroy as fast as possible" (Ross 1913: 367; and cf. Binns 1967). The strategy was designed to protect the Department from competition, but the destruction of the beaver population led to retaliation from the Snake people, who depended on it for food. The region became turbulent with American and Hudson's Bay Company trappers competing, while the Snake people stole the trappers' horses and supplies and harassed them as they could.

As settlers began to arrive from the east in the mid-1830s, John McLoughlin, the Chief Factor of the Hudson Bay Company's Columbia Department, directed them south of the Columbia River. Many settled in the Willamette Valley, a rich agricultural area where many former members of the fur trade had taken up residence. Once settlers were established, their excess produce was bought and resold by the Company in the broader market. In 1833, the Company established a farm at Fort Nisqually in southern Puget Sound. In 1836, the Company joined with farmers in the Willamette Valley, to create the Willamette Cattle Company, which purchased cattle in California and brought them to the valley to build local livestock herds. The Columbia Department bankrolled the operation in return for calves that would later be incorporated into its herds. The next year, farming was extended to the Cowlitz valley and a water-powered sawmill was built near Fort Vancouver. At the same time, the Columbia Department developed the capacity to sell produce internationally. In 1832, the Hudson's Bay Company appointed a broker to represent its interests in Hawai'i. It became one of five brokerage houses on the islands; American companies operated the other four. Through its offices, the Company sold Columbia River salmon, flour, surplus farm produce, and lumber. In return it bought coffee, sugar, molasses, rice, and oriental and European ware (Bancroft 1884: 522–523).

The imposition of state structures and the presence of missionaries spurred on by an evangelical revival in the eastern United States were two primary translocal influences that transformed life in Oregon. The arguments of the plenipotentiaries of Britain and the United States provide insight into the translocal impact of the statist club on life in the Pacific Northwest. At the same time, their justifications for their claims illustrate the distance of the plenipotentiaries from events on the west coast, the importance of national perceptions, and the significance of politics linked to distant state capitals rather than regional political realities. At the same time, the arguments offer a window into the vision of the future held by persons with pretensions to ownership over the territory but with little direct knowledge of it. The arguments evolved from the first agreement to allow joint occupancy in 1818, through interim negotiations that lasted from 1825 to 1827, to negotiations and posturing before the final settlement in 1846. Many arguments describing the future for the Northwest were surprisingly prescient. None addressed the practices of existing communities along the coast; instead they focused on strategic economic and demographic incursions into the area.

How did the two states construct their claims to sovereignty? First, the United States argued that by the Treaty of Florida of 1819, or the Adams-Onis Treaty, and the Convention with Russia in 1824, it had acquired Spanish and Russian rights to the Pacific coast north of the 42° parallel and south of 54° 40'. It then invoked the purchase of the Louisiana Territory from France, which included the watershed of the Mississippi, as defined in a treaty with Spain in 1763. Next, the United States invoked British practice of setting the boundaries for its original colonies from the Atlantic to the Pacific Oceans in its charters to its colonies on the eastern seaboard between 1580 and 1732. Therefore it followed that, since the United States purchased Louisiana, its borders should be extended west – following British practice – to the Pacific coast. The Americans then invoked a convention under the Treaty of Utrecht (1713) that set the boundary between the Louisiana Territory and Hudson's Bay Company land at the 49° parallel. Therefore the 49° parallel should be the border to the Pacific.

Such arguments of sovereign contiguity were invoked to support the United States's claim in various forms but, by 1828, a new political force was emerging, which asserted that it was American destiny to expand to the Pacific. When manifest destiny was linked to the legal case in the 1840s, the issue was launched into the national political arena.

The British countered that on October 20, 1790, Britain and Spain signed the Nootka Convention that acknowledged the right of both to fish, trade and settle on the Pacific coast north of already established Spanish settlements. This treaty meant that, even though the United States signed the Adams-Onis Treaty with Spain in 1819 that gave it Spain's rights north of the 42° parallel, Britain retained equal rights through its earlier treaty with Spain. That equality made joint occupancy possible under the Convention of 1818, since it reflected the equality in rights set in the Nootka agreement. The British then recounted the discoveries and claims of Drake, Cook, Vancouver and especially Lt Meares of the Royal Navy. The United States countered with Grey's claims to the discovery of the mouth of the Columbia River, and then invoked Lewis and Clark and their travels down the river in 1805, and finally reminded the British again that the United States had also inherited all the rights of discovery of the Spanish explorers through the Adams-Onis Treaty.

By the second round of negotiations in the 1820s, the British were claiming occupancy of the Columbia District through the presence of the Hudson's Bay Company. In 1821, the British government passed an Act giving the Company the capacity to enforce the laws of the colony of Upper Canada. The law, in part, resulted from violence at the Selkirk settlement on the Red River near the present Manitoba–North Dakota border, where the rival Northwest and Hudson Bay Companies had had a confrontation. In the negotiations over the border, the existence of this statute was brought into play. The United States argued that it was a sovereign assertion in an area of joint occupancy and countered that the United States wanted the right to establish military posts in the region, since that was their way of protecting their settlers. Britain countered that the Act was designed to apply to British subjects and not to citizens of the United States. The United States's counterproposal offered an interesting insight into the contrasting views of the two negotiating teams on the form of public order they assumed:

> The establishment of a distinct Territorial Government on the west of the Stony Mountains would be objected to, as an attempt to exercise exclusive sovereignty. I observed that, although the Northwest Company might, from its being incorporated, from the habits of the men they employed, and from having a monopoly with respect to trade, as far as British subjects were concerned, carry on a species of government, without the assistance of that of Great Britain. It was otherwise with us. Our population there would consist of several independent companies and individuals. We had always been in the habit, in our most remote settlements, of carrying laws, courts, and justices of the peace with us. There was an absolute necessity, on our part to have some species of government. Without it, the kind of sovereignty, or rather jurisdiction, which it was intended to admit, could not be exercised on our part. (Bancroft 1884: 30)

By the third round of negotiations in the 1840s, this argument had lost its strength. American settlements had grown rapidly in the 1830s and the discourse changed markedly as a result. In 1828, Thomas Hart Benton, an American Senator representing Missouri, assumed that westward expansion was the American destiny. The British claim to joint occupancy and Hudson's Bay Company presence were challenged in the following terms: the British only claimed joint jurisdiction over the whole territory while the United States claimed exclusive or sovereign jurisdiction over the southern half. Over time the United States would win; it was its destiny.

The sovereignty tangle ended with reference to national symbols:

> [Britain] could not acquiesce in acts on the part of the United States, which would give sanction to their claim of absolute and exclusive sovereignty, and calculated also to produce collisions having a national character. Occasional disturbances between the traders of the two countries might be overlooked; but any question connected with the flag of either power would be of a serious nature, and might commit them in a most inconvenient and dangerous manner. (Bancroft 1884: 35)

The United States countered, shifting the ground to the Hudson's Bay Company presence. The United States contended "that the British Charters, extending in most cases, from the Atlantic to the South Seas, must be considered as cessions of the sovereign to certain degrees, to the exclusion only of his other subjects, and as of no validity against the subjects of other States" (Bancroft 1884: 63–64). The United States's position then linked that entitlement to citizenship. An American assertion of sovereignty would exclude others, especially employees of the Hudson's Bay Company, its traders, and others affiliated with it. Grants of land to settlers were used to encourage American immigration, and settlers required state protection, including a military presence. The British countered that equal access and joint control were enough. Their position lacked the simplicity of the American assertion of a single sovereign authority and was not able to be heard in the statist framework.[5]

The missionaries

The presence of missionaries, spurred on by an evangelical revival in the eastern United States, was the second translocal influence that transformed life in the region. In 1831, four Nez Perce or Flathead men arrived in St Louis in search of "The Book of Heaven." They stated that Iroquois, who had traveled west with the fur trade, had introduced their community to it (*New World Encyclopedia* 2011). In New York in 1832, the *Christian Advocate and Journal* published an emotional account of their search. It became a clarion call to the already zealous missionary societies on the eastern seaboard. Jason Lee volunteered to the Mission Society of the Methodist Episcopal Church and was commissioned to minister to the Flatheads. He arrived in the west in 1834, and after a discussion with McLoughlin, he decided to establish his mission in the Willamette Valley. In 1836, the Society sent 13 more men and women to expand his post. In 1838, Lee returned east to seek more funds and recruits, but this time he also wanted to encourage "good Protestant" settlers to move west. The justification for establishing Oregon as an American territory added a new dimension to his message. The Oregon Petition of that year delivered by Lee in Washington DC argued that reputable settlers would not migrate to a "lawless land." Lee's call raised $100,000 and 50 volunteers, including 32 adults and 18 children. The Great Reinforcement sailed west on the *Lausanne* from New York in 1839.

The American missionaries linked political development to civilization and Christianity. Many of the Great Reinforcement, reflecting the advertising in the east urging westward expansion, shared a deep-seated dislike of England and its local manifestation in the Hudson's Bay Company (Morrison 1999: 377–382). They also hated Catholicism, which further lowered their estimation of McLoughlin when he converted in 1842. They campaigned for the institution of a system of American laws and defense to maintain order in society. They invoked images of manifest destiny to bolster the legitimacy of their claims. Interfaith tension was imported to the region with the denominational divide. The Roman Catholics remained the church for the French, mixed communities and Christian natives. The Protestant missionaries associated with Lee's mission focused increasingly on the emerging settler community.

In 1842, Elijah White led 114 Americans across the Oregon Trail urged on by the promise of free land and the messianic On to Oregon movement. Their presence and number added a new dimension to the drive for earlier settlers to organize. If the new settlers had been promised land, what protection was available to established settlers to ensure that they could retain theirs? There could be no deeds unless they were registered with a public authority. The problem added a sense of unity and urgency to the formation of a government. The American settlers were divided and, over the winter, debated the options of creating an independent state following the lead of Texas or working to join the American union, at watering holes such as the Pioneer Lyceum and Literary Club at Willamette Falls or the Oregon Lyceum. At the same time many members of the Lee mission were rabidly against the Hudson's Bay Company. They rejected any system that would guarantee the right of the Company or its employees to hold property. Under the guise of establishing a bounty on wolves, the settlers met in early 1843 and struck a committee to define a settler government. In May, the committee reported to a gathering of settlers at Champoeg located in the French Prairies. The residents defeated the committee's recommendations but then voted to continue to work toward the creation of a provisional government. That resolution was passed by a vote of 52 to 50. Two members of the French community, F.X. Mathieu and Etienne Lucier, voted with the Americans. Mathieu, who had supported Papineau in a nationalist rebellion in Québec in 1837, had had enough of the British after his experiences, and he convinced Lucier of the need to support an American state.

Nine settlers then were elected to create a Code of Laws and report back to the residents at a meeting in July. On July 5, 1843 a legal code, including a lengthy section on property rights, based on that of Iowa was accepted. By its provisions, Lee's mission was to receive a township and each resident, including each individual missionary, was to receive 640 acres. That fall, 875 new residents arrived, having traveled across the Oregon Trail. They were unimpressed with the land laws proposed by the provisional government. By their sheer numbers, they dominated the election for the new legislature and introduced a more inclusive system. Newcomers' rights to register claims were made similar to the requirements of earlier residents and the Hudson's Bay Company would be included if it paid taxes to the provisional government. They also removed the requirement for an oath of allegiance that had precluded British citizens from participating. Jessie Applegate, who was part of the new contingent, presented the proposal to McLoughlin, who accepted it. The agreement strengthened the provisional government at a moment when war between Britain and the United States over the territory seemed likely.

The implementation of the border in 1846 left the provisional government defined by the American settlers as the universal government in American territory. British and American subjects were now subject to its policy, although the Oregon Treaty extended property rights to British settlers if they already lawfully held land, which meant that they had to have paid taxes to the provisional government. Inside the Hudson's Bay Company, McLoughlin was eased out for his pro-American generosity and his campaign against the Company's Governor Simpson. Peter Skene Ogden remained at Fort Vancouver to wind down the Company operations on the Columbia. James Douglas, who had been McLoughlin's second in command and who later became the second Lieutenant Governor of the British colonies north of the border, undertook to relocate the enterprise to Victoria and to adjust its operations to the geographic constraints imposed by the border (Johansen and Gates 1967: 193–194).

CONCLUSION

The imposition of the border in both cases made it possible to apply the governing practices of each state to their respective portion of each region. As a first step, once the border was defined, the statist system transformed life by enabling a legal system to be applied universally across the land and by authorizing public officials to use public force to implement the decisions reached by those authorized to govern by state-determined procedures.

In both the Old Northwest and Oregon Country, the trappings of the state were used to entrench the dominant faction. At the same time the border permitted those in power on either side to construct those on the other side as alien and as a threat. The struggle to entrench control through governing structures had a significant, but somewhat different, impact on settlement and status in each region. Those governing were able to enforce exclusionary categories of persons and potential citizens. North of the border, affiliation with the British military and acceptability to the colonial elite were crucial. South of the border, Native Americans were disenfranchised and limited to reservations, since they were not allowed to hold property under emerging laws. In Oregon, the settler-dominated legislature defined who was included and who was excluded from governance. A telling example in Oregon was the prohibition of African-American settlers and the early denial of the vote and citizenship to Native Americans. North of the border, former officers of the Hudson Bay Company remained in control until they were gradually submerged by British military officers and legal immigrants.

North of the Great Lakes in the Old Northwest, the Family Compact – a distant elite – curried favor with local politicians through patronage, and in reaction a border identity was nurtured on the British side of the Detroit River region for settlers marginalized by the agenda of the (American) colonial elite. South of the lakes, the actions of British Indian agents, who supported First Nations' raids against Americans, provoked long-standing anti-British feelings in Kentucky and Ohio.

Arguments legitimating the state were founded on the translocal beliefs of the ruling group, invoking, among other symbols, the British Empire or the War of Independence. What devices were used to consolidate legal potential for the ascendant faction? North of the Great Lakes, the dominant faction was defined by its links to the empire. In Oregon, it was based on sheer numbers of settlers in a democratically structured system. Once in office, their worldview provided the context for policy initiatives, which included the exclusion of others. Those marginalized by the new elite suddenly had to negotiate their individual status from outside the system.

Translocal sources that were linked to the broader statist domain bolstered the emerging elites. The Family Compact in Upper Canada and new social leaders in British Columbia invoked the British Empire and polite society. In Oregon, the missionaries were bolstered by messianic Protestant fervor linked to the Great Reawakening along the eastern seaboard. In all cases, translocal forces were ascendant and became entrenched in manifestations of collective regional identity. For example, the accession list of the Oregon Historical Society defined artifacts added to their collection through references to events in the War of Independence or to the history of settler/donor ownership. Artifacts from the region had no such description. Similarly, north of the border, services for, and favors from, imperial authorities provided social and political legitimation. Over time these practices and affiliations set the thresholds of history. Collective history became the history of the dominant (for a more complete analysis of this phenomenon see McDougall 2010).

REVISITING THE BORDERLAND CENTURIES LATER

Life in the borderland remains complex. The proximity of differences opens potential for residents but it also sets limits. The multifaceted character of the impact of the border on life in the borderlands in the two regions studied is reflected in the complexity of the impact today. One recent story from the southern Great Lakes illustrates the point. As increasingly free trade in the 1980s through the 1990s was seen as improving the flow of goods across the Detroit and St Clair Rivers, thus furthering economic integration, the legal implementation of universal health insurance in Canada (Canada Health Act of 1984) meant that since Americans were not covered by the Canadian medicare system, they could no longer travel to a Canadian city to have a child. This long-used device for achieving dual citizenship in the border region, one that offered a special coherence to the borderland community, thus fell into disuse and the border population was further divided. The interpretation of the impact of the free trade agreement and the Canada Health Act on border communities depends on the orientation of the analyst. To the economist, the changes reflected economic integration and globalization. To the local resident, social policy increased the separation within the borderland community.

The border is fundamental to – and as complex as – the policy mix and political manipulation of each center and periphery. Its influence extends from the nature of governance, to the character of the ascendant elite, to their construction of legitimation and to their construction of their history. It also sets physical limits and opportunities. The challenge is to combine the material analyses and social analyses in recognition of the complexity that characterizes life in the borderland.

NOTES

The authors wish to thank the Social Science and Humanities Research Council of Canada (SSHRC) for the funding of grants that made the research for this chapter possible. The authors and publisher gratefully acknowledge the permission granted to reproduce the copyright material in this chapter.

1 The use of performatives in speech act theory captures both the necessary preconditions and the efficacy of making the stipulations of a treaty into fact.
2 In 1785, Detroit sent 3,000 bales valued at £30,000 to Montreal, while Michilimackinac sent 5,000 valued at £75,000. Just a few years later in 1789, Detroit sent only 1,900 bales to Montreal. The value of the furs from Detroit also fell as beaver had been overhunted and less valuable muskrat and raccoon furs were being harvested instead (Farrell 1968).
3 Between 1786 and 1791, most of the American military units involved were based in Kentucky.
4 The military were to receive land grants along the Rivière La Tranche and from the 1790 McKee Treaty, while the First Nations were to have the land from this purchase of 1796.
5 It was at the time that Simpson was reigning in McLoughlin, closing forts and planning to move the Columbia Department to Vancouver Island.

REFERENCES

Bancroft, Hubert Howe. 1884. *History of the Northwest Coast*, vol. 27. San Francisco: A.L. Bancroft.

Binns, Archie. 1967. *Peter Skene Ogden: Fur Trader*. Portland: Binfords & Mort.

Canada. 1891. *Indian Treaties and Surrenders from 1680 to 1890*, vol. 1. Ottawa: Queen's Printer.

Farrell, David R. 1968. Detroit 1783–1796: the last stages of the British fur trade in the Old Northwest. PhD diss., History Department, University of Western Ontario.

Innis, Harald A. 1956. *The Fur Trade in Canada: An Introduction to Canadian Economic History*. Rev. edn. Toronto: University of Toronto Press.

Johansen, Dorothy O. and Gates, Charles M. 1967. *Empire of the Columbia*. 2nd edn. New York: Harper & Row.

McDougall, Allan K. 2010. Migrating people and constructions: truth, untruth and consequences. Paper presented at the Association of Borderlands Studies, Reno, Apr. 14–17.

Morrison, Dorothy Nafus. 1999. *Outpost: John McLoughlin and the Far Northwest*. Portland: Oregon Historical Society Press.

New World Encyclopedia. 2011. Confederated Salish and Kootenai tribes of the Flathead Nation. At http://www.newworldencyclopedia.org/entry/Confederated_Salish_and_Kootenai_Tribes_of_the_Flathead_Nation?oldid=948631 (accessed Mar. 27, 2011).

Ross, Alexander. 1913. Journal of Alexander Ross – Snake Country Expedition, 1824. Editorial notes by T.C. Elliott. *Oregon Historical Quarterly* (14) 4:366–388.

Stone, Julius. 1966. *Social Dimensions of Law and Justice*. London: Stevens.

Sugden, John. 2000. *Blue Jacket: Warrior of the Shawnees*. Lincoln: University of Nebraska Press.

CHAPTER **11** # Nations, Nationalism and "Borderization" in the Southern Cone

Alejandro Grimson

This chapter will analyze the historical transformations of the border process in the Southern Cone. After a brief sketch of the colonial period, the analysis will cover the fraught and intense border processes that accompanied the state- and nation-building period in the region. It then discusses the transition from a militaristic, geopolitical conception of borders as the potential cause or objective of war to what is now an ongoing process of regional integration in the Mercosur bloc. On the one hand, to understand borders in the Southern Cone it is necessary to analyze the convergence of the political and cultural histories of these borders, as well as the intellectual history of border studies. On the other hand, it is necessary to distinguish identity borders from cultural ones.

A glance at the modern political map of the Southern Cone, or even of Latin America, leads to a deceptively simple question: How could a region where there were only two colonial powers end up producing so many countries, and so many political borders? To answer these questions I will look into the formation of these borders through the use of the concept of "borderization" (Grimson 2003a). This term refers to the historical process in which the many elements making up a border are shaped by the interaction of central powers with border populations. It also highlights how, from a sociocultural perspective, the border is never a fixed "fact", but always remains unfinished and unstable. The border is an object that is constantly being contested and, as the historical outcome of human action, it is something that can be – and is – restructured and resignified over time.

From this perspective, all political borders have four constitutive elements that are influenced by the action of social groups. These are the demarcation line itself and the territories it divides; the population settled on either side of it; the succession of

A Companion to Border Studies, First Edition. Edited by Thomas M. Wilson and Hastings Donnan.
© 2012 Blackwell Publishing Ltd. Published 2012 by Blackwell Publishing Ltd.

different sociocultural regimes in the border area; and, finally, the different meanings the border acquires. A border is much more than a juridical division of territory and goes beyond a simple description of the demographic structure and ethnic composition of the population on either side of it. A border is characterized by regimes of material and symbolic movement across it, and a great variety of economic, political, social, and cultural relations. The joint effect of these elements (territory, population and material and symbolic movement regimes), as well as other sociohistorical relations, is what creates the meanings that the border comes to acquire for social actors. And any of the elements can become the basis for dispute between states and border populations. Put another way, territorial disputes have counterparts in such things as trade wars, media disputes and diverse conflicts concerning identity. All these disputes are ultimately about the border, which is itself shaped by them.

The borderization process in Latin America, considered in the longue durée, can be divided into stages, including of course the period prior to the establishment of national states. In Latin America, it is evident that borders (territorial, economic and symbolic) did not spring fully formed out of the nation-building process. The genesis of Latin American borders lay in the colonial period. Indeed, between the collapse of the colonial regimes (first and second decades of the nineteenth century) and the beginning of centrally directed nation-building processes (during the last third of the nineteenth century), the borders that were created in some regions carried a commercial, political and identificatory significance linked to a strong sense of localism and provincial patriotism.

The borderization process of the colonial period is characterized by a dynamic of expansion. Repeated clashes between Spanish and Portuguese explorers resulted in a series of treaties that sought to trace out the territorial limits between the two empires. The colonization of the "New World" was therefore accompanied by a proliferation of border situations. These were caused by the expansion of Spanish, Portuguese and other European colonists into territories inhabited by native populations. This movement, which continued into the twentieth century, meant that in almost all American countries the idea of "border" became linked to the experience of coming into contact with indigenous populations.

Political borders were also being constructed during this period. The first juridical border was completely imaginary, or at least conjectural, as it divided unknown territories. The 1494 Treaty of Tordesillas between Spain and Portugal established a line: westward the land would be Spanish, while the east was reserved for Portugal. Nationalist geographers and historians in Argentina have dwelt endlessly on how the ultimate political borders of the region constitute "violations" of the treaty. They seem to believe that their objections to the very existence of Brazil can somehow bring back to life Pope Alexander VI, who went so far as to grant Spain all lands west of Europe as long as "these were not the domain of a Christian prince" (the Treaty of Tordesillas/Tratado de Tordesillas 1494).

The first decades of the seventeenth century saw the emergence of a new kind of border situation, very different from the one that had been "resolved" by the line drawn at Tordesillas. This came about when the Spanish and Portuguese, setting forth from different centers of settlement, started expanding into the interior. The Portuguese *bandeirantes*, for example, set out from the Atlantic coast for the western interior, seeking gold, silver and slave labor for the coffee and sugar plantations near the coast. This border situation produced peculiar alliances, such as the arrangement reached among the Guaraní Indians, the Jesuits and the Spanish Crown to resist Portuguese encroachment. The Jesuit missions became a military buffer against the Portuguese advance. The Viceroy of Perú authorized the Guaraní in the Jesuit *reducciones* to acquire firearms, with which they were often able to fend off *bandeirante* incursions. As a reward for bolstering the frontier, the Guaraní were exempted from forced labor under the *encomienda* system and obtained a number of tax exemptions (Stern 1992: 60).

All this changed in 1750, when the Spanish Crown agreed to redraw the border (leaving seven Jesuit villages within Portuguese territory) in exchange for Portugal ceding its settlements in modern-day Uruguay, thus allowing the Spanish, now in control of both sides of the River Plate, to combat smuggling more effectively. No sooner had Spain and Portugal begun to draw the new lines than the indigenous population proclaimed itself in defiance of them (Aubert 1991; Cárcano 1972). The Guaraní refused to make the population transfers required by the treaty and began open resistance in 1754, exploiting their possession of firearms. Spanish and Portuguese troops combined to crush this resistance during the Guaraní War. While it has not been proven that the Jesuits actively encouraged the resistance of the Guaraní, they do not seem to have done much to stop it. Thus, this war is an instance where border actors came to fight the two metropolitan centers to which they were nominally subject, resisting a redrawing of borders that ignored over a hundred years of historical experience (Quarleri 2009).

By the end of the eighteenth century, the difficulties of combating smuggling in violations of the colonial trade regime led the Spanish Crown to create the Viceroyalty of the River Plate, the only colonial institution that gave any centrality to the city of Buenos Aires, a determining factor in the political role it would play after independence. When the Hispano-American independence processes began at the start of the nineteenth century, there were thus three Viceroyalties in South America. The existence of these three centers of political authority was a necessary condition for the subsequent divisions between former Spanish colonies, but it did not prove to be sufficient, since no fewer than nine (rather than three) countries came into being south of Panama. In the twentieth century, Argentine nationalist historians saw every country created out of the former Viceroyalty of the River Plate as a territorial loss, especially Paraguay and Uruguay. However, the fact remains that when the Spanish Bourbon regime collapsed after the French invasion of 1808, power in the colonies devolved upon the larger cities (Chiaramonte 1997), none of which was able to construct a political regime spanning the territory of the former Viceroyalty.

The struggle for liberation left a number of independent states that lacked any founding principle of nationality. Local loyalties were linked only to a general identity as inhabitants of America (Chiaramonte 1997), in a process that extended from the wars of independence to the long and bitter civil wars that followed. This process continued up to the War of the Triple Alliance (1864–1870), in which Argentina, Brazil and Uruguay combined against Paraguay (whose male population would be almost wiped out over the course of the conflict).

The consolidation of nation-states marked the territorial stage of borderization in the Southern Cone, with treaties and outright wars occurring down to the late nineteenth century, and in some cases even into the twentieth, as shown by the Chaco War between Bolivia and Paraguay in the 1930s or the border tensions between Argentina and Chile in the 1980s. Once political frontiers dividing states become legally established, there were no longer overt disputes over border territories. This did not end the borderization process but merely transformed it. To take one example, it is a matter of record that, up to the mid-1980s, Argentina, Brazil and Chile all considered it a possibility that they might invade or be invaded by one of their neighbors. Secondly, there were strategic plans and projects, not always exclusively military in nature, by means of which states sought to exercise politico-cultural influence over neighboring populations.

The foremost feature, then, of the borderization process for most of the twentieth century has been the shift from a struggle over border territories to one over border populations. The prerequisite for such a struggle is the "nationalizing" of border spaces. This became especially important after 1930, when state policies moved away from the control of geographical space and became focused on securing the allegiance of the population on both sides of the border. This was the time when several Southern Cone countries embarked on a policy of "peopling the frontier" by creating state enterprises, building schools and stationing Army garrisons. This policy –termed "the living frontier" in Brazil – sought to further the national interest by increasing the active presence of the state in border areas. The contemporary strategic balance, however, would determine whether the objective of the state was one of development or of deliberate underdevelopment. In areas thought to be highly vulnerable to cross-border attack, it was thought best not to develop infrastructure that could be exploited by an invading force.

As previously stated, this stage of borderization came to a close in the mid-1980s, with the onset of one of the longest sustained democratization processes to date in the Southern Cone. States (especially Argentina, Chile and Brazil) left behind the obsession with wars and threats of war, turning gradually to projects for regional "integration." These projects were characterized by a discourse proclaiming the disappearance of interstate borders. This has only been realized, in part, in the area of interstate trade. In any case, however much "the end of borders" was proclaimed by commercial agreements such as Mercosur – signed in 1991 and coming into effect in 1995 – or by the general rhetoric of globalization, the borderization process during this time was once more only transformed, not ended.

One reason why claims of vanishing borders cannot be accepted uncritically is that there is no necessary reason why the integration process could not be halted or even reversed. In the same way that the struggle for influence over border populations always had the potential to generate territorial conflicts, states continue to pursue their own interests, and this may modify their approach to border populations, distancing them from the current integration discourse. But changes have occurred. Today states are focused not on territory or populations but rather on cross-border trade. Interstate struggle can therefore manifest itself in strategies to maximize a state's exporting capacity while limiting that of its neighbors. This can affect not only cross-border movements, but also the sense in which the border is viewed.

While in the past it was assumed that once borders were established, they could only be modified by armed conflict, today most states in the region have decided that the costs of war would be excessive and the benefits dubious. However, the final location of territorial borders perpetuates in international law what was the result of the specific balance of power that existed when these borders were drawn. Local, national or international factors may well change the real balance of power over time. States modify their border policies either on their own initiative or because of pressures from border populations, thus changing the characteristics and the meanings of their borders. These transformations – and the tensions arising from the different functions and meanings of the border – are still ongoing. Thus, a longue durée analysis of the borderization process in the Southern Cone shows how the focus has gone from territory to population and now to transborder flows. There has been a general shift from territory to movement, from sovereignty to the regulation of cross-border traffic.

THE THREE PHASES OF INTERSTATE BORDER THEORY

From the late nineteenth through most of the twentieth century, state agents and officials, sometimes entire regiments, went to border regions to survey and trace them out, to occupy and defend them. Maps were drawn and redrawn, with those made in one country often contradicting those made in others. Treaties were signed, often piecemeal in their provisions, when not directly in conflict with those made with other countries. Each political center saw its border periphery as an area of risk, as virgin land vulnerable to violation, infiltration or invasion by neighbors perceived as enemies. Militaristic fantasies left a strong mark on states' understanding of their borders, and the political geography of the period reveals how these actors understood the nature of international relations in the region. This kind of nationalism, hegemonic for many decades of the last century, had an important result: it associated the ideas of nation and sovereignty with a paranoid fear of foreign invasion and regional disintegration, and of authoritarianism and militarism as the only possible means of preventing them. The horrifying outcomes that resulted from these imaginings have also meant that many people in these societies came largely to reject the very idea of nation and sovereignty, seeing them as linked to absurd, self-serving nation-state rivalries as well as to authoritarianism and dictatorship.

For most of the twentieth century, the social sciences in Latin America maintained close links with the nation-building process. At one extreme, some variants of the established school of political geography sought to give systematic expression to the problems the state faced in establishing a sense of nation and in its disputes with neighboring countries (Rey Balmaceda 1979). However, work began to appear in the 1970s that explored individual experiences and collective imaginaries in ways that challenged the idea that political and cultural borders necessarily coincided. Against this commonsense notion that states tried to establish, the new research on borders revealed the existence of many channels of exchange, as well as shared codes and languages, which reflected the existence of a shared sociohistorical identity on both sides of the border. This approach is now being complemented by studies that have shown the material and symbolic effects that resulted from the setting of fixed delimitations between nations, as well as from the cultural devices used to bolster them and the political consequences that followed. The subjective identity of those living in border areas could hardly be immune to the processes of nation-building and the nationalistic politics that accompanied them.

About 20 years ago, the social sciences began to question the study of the "national" territories that were assumed to exist in the state's imaginary, and took the imaginary itself as the object of study (Anderson 1990; Chatterjee 1993). States tend to believe that what they possess is inherently theirs. The analytical distance that social science is able to achieve allows researchers to interrogate this "natural" understanding of the spaces of the sovereign state. While once the prevailing discourse had been geopolitical, with its imperative to unite the nation with "its" territory, now the dominant approach of deconstructive historicism stresses the artificiality of this discourse and of the deliberate strategies used to shape individuals' ideas about the border. A result of this new theoretical approach was the weakening of the idea that national borders had a real existence that was inevitably significant in dividing populations. Scholars dealt almost exclusively in terms of porosity and contingency. Once sociological discourse had been detached from the priorities of the nation-state, they came to argue that, in effect, the state had barely existed even within its own boundaries, and that each and every identity not recognized by the state had waged a heroic resistance against the onslaught of schools, the mass media, the Army and the attempts of the state to register each person by issuing ID documentation. Juridical borders now became denatured , while social identities, especially ethnic ones, became essentialized.

The local people who inhabited border regions were now at the center of academic research. Formerly treated in the geopolitical discourse either as patriots (their normative obligation) or as insufficiently patriotic (because of "cultural contamination" from their neighbors), they now became something like crusaders in scholarly accounts that stressed interculturality. Often those who lived along borders were seen as possessing a kind of essential multiplicity, thus becoming key actors in a postnational era. A certain kind of (de)constructivism saw in the Southern Cone the root of all evil in the state – imagining and implementing an artificial homogeneity onto its territory – and idealized border populations as "noble savages" who had best been able to resist it.

From studies of the Mexico–US border came the idea of a legal boundary that divided a people, who had, nevertheless, retained a transhistorical authenticity. At this point a key feature of the geopolitical narrative was given a kind of new life in ethnographic studies. The "homogeneous community," questioned if not denied at the level of nation-states, now reappears and is imputed to tribes, ethnicities or other social groups. The community still possessed a territory, implying physical borders. And it still had culture, implying symbolic borders.

For a long time militarism had made it impossible to study borders from a critical perspective, since this could endanger "national security." However, antimilitaristic approaches often encouraged a kind of populism that idealized "integration from below," placing great emphasis on the study of the ways in which borders strengthened "trans" relations and undermined established identities and autocratic sovereignties. Certain anthropological studies were not immune to this populism. Yet the fact remains that this kind of wishful thinking is an epistemological limitation: the scholar has forced herself to show that the border was what she wanted it to be. When one reads works where every border dweller is a border crosser, expressions of a sort of Latin American poetry, what comes to mind is the caution made to even the greatest anthropologists: "This is too good to be true." One is even tempted to question whether this new paradigm is as positive as its proponents believe.

Two Essentialisms: Fraternity and Hybridism

Much contemporary research on borders in the Southern Cone arose out of a theoretical and political challenge to what had become the mainstream of identity and cultural studies. It had become almost a commonplace to stress the multiplicity of identities and their fragmentary nature, while neglecting power relations in general and the role of the state in particular. This was unfortunate because borders are a particularly fruitful field in which to analyze power relations in a sociocultural sense, since the interests, actions and identifications of local actors interact and may conflict with the plans and policies of national states. State crises, as one can see in many border regions, manifest themselves as crises of social welfare, but the systems of control and repression (of small-scale smuggling and transborder migration) often become reinforced. This is why the state retains a dominant role as arbiter of control, violence, order and organization, even for those whose identity is being changed by transnational, global trends. Yet it remains de rigueur to underestimate the role that the state still plays in the daily life of its own and of foreign citizens. In several countries in the Southern Cone, nation-states prepared for potential war scenarios by creating an infrastructure that would allow them to intervene overwhelmingly in the daily lives of those who lived along their borders (Vidal 2000).

The risk of underestimating the role of the state is that one can fall into believing in an essential brotherhood or in an essential hybridity among all border dwellers. These twin essentialisms are now the standard assumption among scholars and politicians dealing with the borders of Mercosur countries (Grimson and Vila 2004). Each essentialism has its origin in metaphors of "union," "fraternity," and "crossing." Thus, one frequently hears about the "brotherhood of neighboring peoples" in the Southern Cone (Recondo 1997). These metaphors, and others such as the statement one often sees in scholarly publications that "borders exist only on maps," have one point in common: they tend to obscure the social and cultural conflicts that often characterize political borders, even those that separate an ethnically homogeneous group. Ignoring conflict as a key dimension of "cultural contact," this perspective makes it impossible to perceive the power asymmetries among social groups and between states, as well as a growing exclusionary dynamic in some border areas.

As previously mentioned, an important strand of the research on Latin American borders has been characterized by the image of an "integration from below," where the sense of brotherhood among border populations defeats the bellicose discourse of states. In other regions of the world, scholars have also tended to analyze border populations as a "community," minimizing the role of the state, nation and even the borders themselves (Wilson and Donnan 1998: 6). The political and theoretical effort to deconstruct national identifications has often led to an excessive emphasis on the "nonexistence" of borders for those who live near them. In the case of the Mercosur countries, the image becomes frozen in a time before the construction of states, as though the long and intense intervention on the part of the state had had no effect on local populations. This is a Romantic as well as an essentialist view, and it has systematically obscured the cognitive, political, and cultural significance of the state and the nation for those who live in border areas.

In the Southern Cone, the very fact that local border discourse is full of statements about a "shared culture" and the absence of cross-border conflict should make any ethnographer doubt the "truth" of such claims (at least those who remember that identity discourses can have strategic and manipulative dimensions to them). Perhaps the strangest paradox created by this discourse in the Southern Cone is that it joins an idea of "false consciousness" to the kind of populism that has had such a great effect in the region over the past 50 years. The nation is an example of "false consciousness," but the scholar's response is not to undertake a critical study of its role, but rather to argue that it never really existed because of the resilience and autonomy of "the people." Scholars then must deal with a tendency toward cultural and identificatory totalization that makes it difficult to understand the relevance of alliances, interest formation, and conflict to contemporary political struggles. Border areas represent liminal spaces where both transnational identity and intergroup conflict occur.

Anthropological and ethnographic studies of Southern Cone borders carried out over the past years (such as those by Vidal 2000; Escolar 2007; Baeza 2009; Karasik 2000; Gordillo and Leguizamón 2002, and many others) are part of what could be termed a third theoretical approach against essentialism and postmodernism. Its objective is not to influence what happens on the border or to extract ethnocentric lessons about our own identity imaginaries. The goal is simply to understand the borders, those who live on each side of them and the actors who interact with them. Through the use of deep narratives and analysis, these studies seek to understand the multiple points of view that comprise, at each historical moment, the political and cultural configuration of the frontier.

This ethnographic approach leads to an appreciation of the differences and particularities of each case, riven as all are by different processes of provincialization, migration, and relations with the state and with indigenous populations. The result is to return heterogeneity to our understanding of border populations, where the concept of "outsider" can apply not only to a person living on the other side of the border, but also reflect and legitimize inequalities on one's own side of the border. As Baeza has shown, on border zones "the social groups that may call themselves founders, pioneers, patriots, settlers or 'born-and-raised' create a representation of their time as natives that is independent of any objective notion of time" (2009: 255). In other words, the idea of "length of settlement" becomes a political artifice to legitimize sociological inequalities the origins of which lie elsewhere. Such studies also show in detail what has shaped the social experience of each group. Those who dwell on the frontier are active agents in their own history but in circumstances not of their own choosing. These circumstances are the result not only of the actions of the state, but also of other local agents, since these studies do not presuppose – and indeed do not find – any homogeneity of feelings, meanings or identities among border populations as a whole.

An area that is especially important at the local, national and even global level is the so-called "Triple Frontier" joining and separating Brazil, Paraguay and Argentina (see Figure 11.1), bounded by two rivers, the Paraná and the Iguazú. Besides featuring one of the most popular tourist destinations in the region – the Iguazú Falls – it also has the largest hydropower station in the world, the Itaipú joint venture between Paraguay and Brazil. The relatively small Argentine town of Puerto Iguazú is joined by a bridge to the Brazilian Foz de Iguazú, which is linked, by the "Bridge of Friendship," to Ciudad del Este in Paraguay.

It is this latter city and its role as a gateway to Brazil that has made the "Triple Frontier" a place of global concern, after the mass media and various government agencies depicted it as an area exploited by drug traffickers and terrorists (Montenegro and Giménez Béliveau 2006; Giménez Béliveau and Montenegro, 2010). The US State Department included this border area as a battlefront in its "war on global terrorism" (Ferradás 2010). The settlement in this region of people of Arab origin (especially Lebanese), as well as Chinese and Koreans, and the fact that Ciudad del Este is an entrepôt for the flow of Chinese goods to Argentine and Brazilian markets (Rabossi 2009; Pinheiro-Machado 2008) suffice to give the region great transnational salience. This includes a wide network of *paseiros* and *sacoleiros* involved in small-scale smuggling (Rabossi 2009), as well as significant cross-border migration, such as the one that created the so-called "brasiguayos" (Sprandel 2000; Amorim Salim 1996). Focusing on this region, Ferradás (2004) analyzed tensions between globalization and nation-states. Her research shows how early concerns with security that were primarily focused on the territorial integrity of nation-states have been replaced with security concerns of a more global nature, and how environmental concerns are increasingly becoming conflated with other current forms of securitization such as terrorism and narcotraffic, with devastating effects on poor people (Ferradás 2004, 2010).

Anthropological research into such border areas resulted in the recognition of two important facts. One is that border regions are spaces not only of crossing and dialogue but also of conflict and increasing inequality. Second, it is impossible to ignore at a conceptual level what Barth (1976) has already shown: crossing a border does not necessarily imply its disappearance. In the same way that a link can be conflictual as well as harmonious, communication between groups can serve the purpose of distinction and separation as much as those of union. Nobody, after all, feels the need to distinguish themselves as different from faraway groups. "The others" are generally neighbors: groups that are at our geographical or symbolic border.

The historical process by which each border was traced out and the constant social process of bargaining and conflict meant that the interaction of state and people was often unique in each different border area. Several works (Gordillo 2000; Escolar 2007; Karasik 2000; Vidal 2000; Grimson 2002) treated the anthropological study of border areas as simultaneously a study of the everyday life of both the state and the people and the relations between them. These studies revealed that the

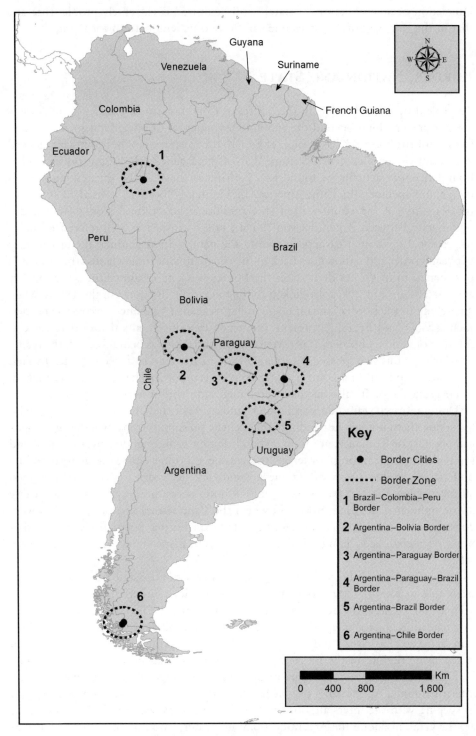

Figure 11.1 Border zones of the Southern Cone, 2011
Source: Drawn by Adrián Iulita, IDAES–UNSAM.

interaction between "nation," "state," and "culture" is extremely problematic and that in the vast majority of cases one can find no general pattern for them.

BORDER, NATION AND STATE

The kaleidoscope of borders in the Southern Cone presents a puzzle. Is this variety a result of something beyond the action of asymmetries of power and social inequality? In Bolivia, "border" has always referred to the frustration of becoming landlocked as a result of the nineteenth century War of the Pacific, although at present other boundaries may actually be found in a parliament that has the greatest number of indigenous members in Latin America. In Uruguay, "border" is used to reference the founding of the country itself (the traditional geopolitical story of creating a buffer-state between Argentina and Brazil), but it can just as well reference one of the regional divisions that appears within the nation. In Argentina, the articulation between border and nation goes back to the occupation of Indian lands (the "desert") in order to form the modern state: the border was one of agriculture, the military and citizenship. But it was also linked to the militaristic discourse of the 1970s, when "marching to the border" meant taking up arms against "enemies" across the border, such as Chile and Brazil. At present, one reads announcements that declare the dissolution of national borders as the Mercosur regional bloc is being formed, the reality of which, in this first phase, is verifiable only in the area of foreign trade. In fact, daily social and cultural control along Argentina's borders has been strengthened, challenging the political objective of free migration within Mercosur countries.

Doing research on borders and understanding what they mean to the people who live along them implies suspending ethnocentric presuppositions, whether geopolitical, populist or Romantic in origin. When bringing to light and analyzing social and symbolic conflicts among border groups and neighboring cities, the goal should be understood as one of providing the groundwork necessary for constructing solid alliances, given the fact that a community of interests is more aspiration than reality at the moment. The long process in which the Latin American national states were constructed has had social and cultural effects on border populations, effects that must be recognized, along with the many practical meanings of nationality they reflect.

In the Southern Cone, systematic action on the part of the state has, in some cases, been able to modify indigenous groups' own identity categories. Different groups, such as the Tobas and Wichís, who live along the middle Pilcomayo use the river as a demarcation line for categorizing indigenous communities according to the opposition between "up river" and "down river." But the growing presence of national states in the region, in the form of military personnel, has brought about a change in indigenous perception: there are cases in which some groups have begun to define intertribal limits on the basis of which side of the river they reside – a demarcation in keeping with the interstate border (Gordillo and Leguizamón 2002). Then there are the Guaranís along the Argentine-Bolivian border, who do not perceive demarcation as an insuperable obstacle and whose villages maintain close cross-border ties.

The Guaranís who live in Bolivia, however, use the word *mbaporenda*, "the place where there is work," to refer to Argentina. And for the Guaranís who live in Argentina, their counterparts on the other side of the river are *ñandetararëta*, "our family," the place of origin of their ancestors (Hirsch 2000). These native categories appear to allude to a bond but also to the very real existence of national states. Both the place where ancestors are from and the place where work is found are located *on the other side* of the political border. In this case, state and nation have been incorporated into native categories and practices in a different way than was the case for the Tobas and the Wichís.

It is clear that in heterogeneous Latin America the relationship between national and ethnic identification varies according to the indigenous population in question and its relationship with the national state. But the incorporation of categories deriving from the nation is visible even in areas where state presence is relatively weak: in the Amazon, for example, the Tükuna have incorporated the Brazilian, Peruvian and Colombian nationalities as part of their local identification patterns (López 2001).

Cities with no indigenous population to speak of represent a very different case. Here national definitions prevail: interests and feelings are defined in national terms (see Karasik 2000; Grimson 2003a). These areas have strong systems of commercial, political and cultural interchange. In this sense, borders can be more or less permeable. But these social relations do not necessarily affect identity classifications and self-proclaimed national affiliations. The determining factor is, instead, the existence of a border along which a social system of interchange grows up between groups which consider themselves different from one other. In other words, from both a practical and an analytical point of view, border localities have a system but no single social organization. This is why, at critical junctures in a nation's history, "common sense" among ordinary people can lead to nationalistic rhetoric and behavior (see Grimson 2003a).

In Latin America it would be false to claim that "the border, this product of a juridical act of delimitation, produces cultural differences in the same way that the border itself is a product of that difference" (Bourdieu 1980: 66). The border produces cultural differences *to a much greater degree* than these differences produce it. There are innumerable populated areas where differences are the exclusive product of the border and all that it implies: school systems; military units; means of communication; the condition of being affected by a "national" economy and political system when there is a territory where there is an economic crisis or political repression on one side but not on the other; and where the potential or real border is perceived as a tool for improving living conditions, which makes it worthwhile for local sectors to sustain.

It is almost impossible to find a border in Latin America that coincides with a pre-Columbian cultural difference. This circumstance is as remarkable as it is misleading: there are those who still believe that this lack of coincidence between cultural distinctions and territorial limits is the case today. But the drawing of borders has changed the framework within which indigenous populations think and act, to say nothing of the people who have come to colonize the borders between countries. This is why we now have a kind of border – as territorial institution of states that believe themselves nations, of institutions and of social forces that stake out cultural claims – that is the "bottom line" for diacritical production, rather than the result of any prior cultural objectivity. Borders arise from the interests of and the balance of power between social groups and armies, which are the starting point for the distinctions that will then be created and reproduced. However, an error as misleading as it is common in much of the scholarly literature is to assume that because borders are artificial, because they are constructed or created, they are somehow less powerful.

In the course of long-term historical process, some borders, which in the beginning really "only existed on the map," became a reality through the action of the state and, in some cases, through that of local populations which acted in order to mark out territory for new political and cultural distinctions. While some borders have never existed outside of a map (a paradigmatic example being the Tordesillas partition of the New World), others have become real. An enormous amount of territory has become borderized as a result of the daily life of the people who live there, as well as because of the worldview and practices of all inhabitants and citizens of the border territory. One general result of the research carried out in the Southern Cone is the general empirical confirmation, which counteracts certain universalizing hypotheses with an exaggerated emphasis on culture in the literature, that borders continue to be barriers to trade, migration and identities. This has been the case throughout history, and the characteristics and meanings of these barriers are being recreated today by the "regional integration" discourse and policies that have arisen within the framework of global dynamics.

IDENTITY BORDERS AND BORDERS OF MEANING

In the historical ethnography I carried out on the border between Argentina and Brazil (Grimson 2001), I showed that one of the problems with the concept of border is its polysemous character. The word "border" refers at one and the same time to very different processes and categories: a line appearing on a map, a concrete landmark or river, what separates legal systems and sovereignties, and the limit between identities and cultures. I showed the relevance of distinguishing between the kinds of limits demarcated by a border: these can be juridical-political, institutional (which appear when customs, immigration officials or security forces intervene), and economic (demarcating productive systems and also determining what a product will cost and how much tax must be paid on it). Borders obviously fulfill the general function of determining sovereignty (which establishes territories with different law enforcement agencies and citizenship rights), and acting as a dividing line between regimes of identity and meaning.

These distinctions challenge the term border as used in cultural analysis, which has become exceedingly imprecise. This has resulted, in particular, in a confusion between identity borders and cultural ones. I define identity borders as those that are related to the categories used to classify individuals or groups. On the border between Argentina and Brazil, where there are no significant indigenous groups, national categories are the most relevant for distinguishing "us" from "them." The local relevance of the national definition is such that it also serves to define the person and establish different types of people. This provides empirical evidence on which to base the importance of the border for the local population.

Other elements appear to support the opposite argument. It is often said that along Latin American borders political exile is commonly associated with the crossing of borders, as are cross-border marriages and shared cultural practices. My study analyzed each one of these three elements and showed that they constitute ethnocentric presuppositions that ignore the concrete meanings ascribed by the local population. First, until 30 years ago, a strong tradition of political exile did exist. However, an analysis of exile relationships shows that these political and humanitarian relations did not escape the cultural structure of the image of national superiority–inferiority. These transborder relations were interrupted by systematic cross-border repression and by the effect of growing nationalization processes. At present, local politics in border areas is more national than it was 50 years ago. In spite of the existence of numerous forums where politicians from Argentina and Brazil meet and sign cooperative accords, current relations between the two countries in the borderlands are much less intense and salient than five decades ago.

Second, the assumptions about interborder marriages are easily disputed. A quantitative analysis of the percentage of Argentine-Brazilian marriages, out of the total number of marriages in different periods during the twentieth century, clearly shows that mixed marriages have become increasingly rare. In the early 1900s almost 10 percent of all marriages were "mixed," while in the 1990s it was less than 1 percent. Given that these figures come from two cities joined by a bridge, any anthropologist would be quick to conclude that nationality has become a preferential category when selecting a mate in the course of the twentieth century. If, as I have shown, people do not want to marry neighbors of a different nationality, then a person's national identification is clearly very relevant to them.

The above case refers concretely to the concept of identity borders. Such borders are clearest and have been studied the most in the context of urban groups. When studying any two ethnic groups, an analysis of their political and matrimonial relations will establish the degree of permeability or lack of permeability of symbolic borders. A classic assumption in migration research was that successive generations of migrants would be less endogamous than their predecessors, both literally and metaphorically. This is what determined whether migrants were considered more or less "integrated" into their destination society. In stark contrast, the Argentine-Brazilian border is characterized by the opposite tendency. Over the course of the last century, more, rather than fewer, identity borders have been built up by local groups.

The third typical statement in the Southern Cone about border areas is that "the same culture" is found on both sides, a "border culture" or, at least, a culture that shares certain characteristic behavior and rituals. In the section of the Argentine-Brazilian border that I studied, one could certainly find Afro-Brazilian religions, Carnival celebrations, and *gaucho* rituals carried out on both sides. From a superficial point of view, it might seem that transborder cultural practices exist.

However, these practices have different meanings depending on whether they take place in Argentina or Brazil (see Grimson 2003a). Since the meaning of Carnival, Afro-Brazilian religions and gaucho rituals is very different depending on the side of the border you are on, any claim of shared border culture is misleading. Afro-Brazilian religions occupy a salient, public position in Uruguayana (Brazil), while they are considered subaltern and looked down upon in Paso de los Libres (Argentina). The gaucho culture, with its distinctive style of dress and special dishes and rituals, is the official culture in the state of Rio Grande do Sul in Brazil. It is the pride of its inhabitants, who are known as "gaúchos" if they were born there, regardless of whether they are light-skinned and blonde or of African descent. But on the Corrientes side of the border in Argentina, the gauchos are discriminated against for being from the poorest and least educated sector of society.

In a region like Rio Grande do Sul, where the most important celebrations are the gaucho ones and where cultural reference points are remarkably different from those considered "typically Brazilian," the way Carnival is celebrated provides an opportunity to affirm that, in spite of all the differences, the gaúchos belong to the Brazilian nation. By contrast, in Paso de los Libres, the Carnival celebration is what distinguishes its inhabitants from the rest of the Argentine nation and brings them close to Brazil, although they insist that their way of celebrating is specifically local and all their own.

The idea that the same culture exists on both sides of the border is stated also, in some circumstances, by border inhabitants themselves. However, what is interesting is that prototypical examples of "transborder culture" differ according to which side of the border you are on. In other words, an analysis of the arguments made by border dwellers to affirm that the border "doesn't exist" in a cultural sense – an affirmation that is heard when they try to distinguish themselves from people who live in the main cities of the two countries – point to the presence of borders of meaning, or rather borders of signification. Each city shapes symbolic references in its own way in order to construct its own identity.

The purpose of these examples is to demonstrate the existence of a subtle border that is difficult to perceive and to analyze. It is the limit that separates and brings into contact two fields of national interlocution, two specific forms of diversity (Segato 1998). It is a border between meanings and between systems for articulating meaning. The difficulties in perceiving and conceptualizing this border are what usually lead to the term "transborder cultures" being used, since there are practices and beliefs that are shared by people living on both sides of a common border.

The nation remains the main mode of identification in this area. It is the framework within which historical experience has been shaped over time. State policies, economic and political experiences, cultural transmission and many other elements are viewed differently depending on which side of the river you are on. In fact, and more important, they have been perceived, given meaning and visualized in different ways historically, thus instituting different ways of imagining, thinking and acting that have been articulated according to the dynamics obtaining in each country. It is because of this that the nation has become a condition for the production of meaning, a historical space out of which a dialogue between identities and practices has been built up and has grown in importance from the late nineteenth century to the present day. This is why transborder relations and cultural elements have become a key area where symbolic borders are produced and reproduced, both on the level of personal and group identifications and on that of the meaning of their practices.

Is it at all possible, then, to postulate some type of local cultural system that takes the form of a border culture? The expression "border culture" is somewhat superficial at best, and becomes downright misleading when it claims the existence of homogeneous patterns of belief, as well as a common discourse and common practices and identifications on both sides of the demarcation line. But it is true that multiple differences acquire meaning within the system of interactions instituted by the border itself. In Paso de los Libres and Uruguayana the differences, especially the mechanisms for identity distinctions, are a product of the institution of the political border that has resulted from borderization processes.

It is in this context that "cultural contact" has emerged. The concept of "cultural contact," as used by Cardoso de Oliveira (1976), refers to the way in which the links between groups that relate to each other on the basis of distinctive identifications operate. These relations can be symmetrical, asymmetrical or directly hierarchical; they can also be based on a system of domination and submission, as is the case in areas of interethnic friction (Cardoso de Oliveira 1976: 37–38). A cultural contact situation implies the development of a system of identity contrasts, oppositions and manipulations that arise out of these links. These groups relate to each other and engage in different kinds of disputes, all of which tend to generate common patterns and a shared logic for marking differences among themselves.

What are, then, the characteristics of the contact culture found in Paso de los Libres and Uruguayana? There is, as noted above, a transborder circulation of certain symbolic goods such as beliefs and practices linked to Carnival, gaucho life and Afro-Brazilian religions. However, given the border context, these shared elements form part of different systems, and consequently, their meanings differ according to the side of the border one is on. Cultural practices are affected by hybridization processes. Hybridizations, however, are limited and, above all, not significant when analyzing the processes of identity manipulation that occur in interborder disputes. Similar ways of living, imagining and acting found in Paso de los Libres and Uruguayana are linked to a particular geographic and sociocultural border location. This spatial dimension is crucial for understanding how local residents construct their identifications and sense of belonging. These constructions differ greatly from one city to the other, since the inhabitants find their particular destiny necessarily linked to the future of their respective nations.

Although these national identifications are evidently different (as Brazilians and Argentines), nationality is a key factor for interpersonal relations in both places. On both sides of the demarcation line, the border constitutes a decisive element for defining the conceptions, practices and meanings constructed by the people living there. The nation does not always occupy a central position in all political border situations. National identifications can be comparatively more diffuse (Escolar 2000), combine in complex ways with ethnic identifications (López 2001), or imply segregation through migratory processes and fragmented actors (Vila 2000). The culture of contact in Paso de los Libres and Uruguayana, the ways of speaking, bonds, matrimonial preferences and sociopolitical conflicts are all affected by national identifications.

REGIONAL INTEGRATION AND NATIONALISM

The start of the twenty-first century saw great changes in Southern Cone countries. Neoliberalism lost its status as the hegemonic economic and political paradigm, or at least as the only legitimate discourse. Countries such as Uruguay and Brazil elected center-left governments, which began to implement welfare and redistributive policies. Bolivia elected its first-ever indigenous president: the greatest cultural, social, and political change experienced by any one country in the region for a long time. In Chile, two consecutive Socialist governments, the second led by a woman president, were more tentative in implementing welfare policies, and recently the "modern" neoliberal approach appears to have regained its supremacy. In Argentina, after the financial catastrophe of 2002, the neoliberal consensus was utterly broken, and a recovery marked by rapid, export-led growth was accompanied by the implementation of some redistributive policies. Paraguay, Ecuador, and Venezuela all had presidents who believed in the strengthening of regional ties.

These conditions created the most propitious environment seen for a long time – perhaps ever – for regional integration to move forward. And there have been many significant achievements in this regard. For example, the creation of the Union of South American States brought all countries south of Panama into a multilateral institution where political as well as economic subjects could be discussed. The non-economic aspects of the Mercosur project were deepened, especially as regards laws and regulations concerning the free movement of people within the bloc. In Argentina, for example, a law was passed giving every person, including those without legal documentation as citizens or residents, the right of full access to education and public health, and accelerated the regularization of the status of hitherto illegal immigrants.

Nevertheless, the borderization process did not finish. It is changing. The process was not free of nationalistic outbursts or of complex situations in border areas. Nationalism itself now had a different focus. Rather than being concerned with the possibility of aggression by or against neighboring states, it is now centered on defending a country's sovereignty against breaches by international organizations and First World countries intent on extending a neoliberal agenda into the region. The influence of the United States began to wane in a region that now sought closer ties with China, Russia, India and other countries. In this case, globalization has allowed sovereign spaces to be strengthened, rather than weakened, as the traditional discourse would have it.

At a regional level, there have been tensions marked by nationalistic rhetoric and policies. The upheaval in Bolivia that brought Evo Morales to power also resulted in the nationalization of oil and gas, which affected not only First World multinationals but also Brazilian investors. While Morales defended the recovery of these spaces of economic life using a discourse of the natural right of the Bolivian state over its resources, in Brazil some sectors of the opposition accused Ignacio Lula da Silva (the first working-class president in the country's history) of allowing himself to be humiliated by an "Indian," thus revealing how colonial categories still survive in present-day South America. This working-class president, however, was one of the most level-headed players in this crisis, and the one who tried hardest to find a multilateral, regional solution. His policies should not be seen as a retreat of Brazilian nationalism, but rather as its reinterpretation into a more complex and sophisticated national project.

This increasingly successful regional integration was marred, however, by one of the bitterest bilateral disputes, which oddly enough occurred between countries that have historically had close, friendly relations, Argentina and Uruguay. The Uruguayan government authorized the construction of a cellulose plant on its side of the Uruguay River. The residents of the Argentine city of Gualeyguachú, on the Argentine bank of the river, protested that the effluent from this plant (owned by a Finnish-based corporation) would contaminate the river, and that the Uruguayan government had violated treaty obligations in not consulting its Argentine counterpart before authorizing the plant.

The conflict has carried on for years, with the mobilization of a broad-based social movement in Gualeyguachú that feared that its way of life and tourist-based economy were being threatened by environmental degradation. Argentines, after essaying sporadic blockings of the bridge joining Gualeyguaychú with the Uruguayan city of Salto, finally announced an indefinite interdiction of all traffic. The Argentine president arrived at Gualeyguachú to lead a popular protest against the plant, while the foreign minister went as far as to say that Argentina was ready to implement any and all countermeasures "short of the invasion of Uruguay." The smaller nation of Uruguay saw the whole affair as an example of Argentine arrogance and the result was a clash of hostile nationalisms. Several initiatives by intellectuals on both sides of the river to establish a forum where negotiation and dialogue could be conducted in a spirit of cooperation came to grief as the conflict escalated beyond the control of any one of its participants. The progress that had been made in regional integration was of no assistance during the crisis, since the Argentine government ignored regional institutions and appealed to the International Tribunal at The Hague. While in 2011 there are some indications that a bilateral treaty might lead to joint control over the pollution from this cellulose plant, this episode has changed many perceptions in both countries, leaving a bitter taste. The lesson may be that unless regional integration efforts proceed at a faster pace, if similar conflicts break out the countries involved will appeal not to those regional institutions created and strengthened in the past decades in Latin America, but rather to the more established forums of Europe.

In the midst of regional integration, nationalism and border people are not a thing of the past. Militaristic meanings may be better approached in their historical roles, but today, with new meanings and social actors, new forms of borderization and nationalization are ongoing in the Southern Cone.

REFERENCES

Amorim Salim, Celso. 1996. A questão dos Brasiguaios e o Mercosul. In Neide Patarra, *Migrações internacionais. Herança XX, agenda XXI.* São Paulo: United Nations Population Fund.

Anderson, Benedict. 1990, *Imagined Communities*, London: Verso.

Aubert, Maxime. 1991. Jesuitas indios y fronteras coloniales en los siglos XVII y

XVIII. Folia Histórica del Nordeste (Instituto de Investigaciones Geohistóricas, Resistencia) 10.

Baeza, Brígida. 2009. *Fronteras e identidades en Patagonia Central (1885–2007)*. Buenos Aires: Protohistoria.

Barth, Fredrik. 1976. Introducción. In *Los grupos étnicos y sus fronteras*, pp. 9–49. Mexico City: Fondo de Cultura Económica.

Bourdieu, Pierre. 1980. L' identité et la représentation. Eléments pour une réflexion critique sur l'idée de région. *Actes de la Recherche en Sciences Sociales* (35): 63–72.

Cárcano, Miguel. 1972. *La política internacional en la historia argentina*. Buenos Aires: Eudeba.

Cardoso de Oliveira, Roberto. 1976. *Identidade, etnia e estrutura social*. São Paulo: Pioneira.

Chatterjee, Partha. 1993. *Nation and Its Fragments*. Princeton: Princeton University Press.

Chiaramonte, José Carlos. 1997. *Ciudades, provincias, estados. Orígenes de la Nación Argentina*. Buenos Aires: Ariel.

Escolar, Diego. 2000. Identidades emergentes en la frontera argentino-chilena. In A. Grimson, ed., *Fronteras, naciones e identidades*. Buenos Aires: CICCUS-La Crujía.

Escolar, Diego. 2007. *Los dones étnicos de la nación*. Buenos Aires: Prometeo.

Ferradás, Carmen. 2004. Environment, security, and terrorism in the trinational frontier of the Southern Cone. *Identities* 11: 417–442.

Ferradás, Carmen. 2010. Researching the triple frontier of the Southern Cone: security and ethnography. In Hastings Donnan and Thomas M. Wilson, eds, *Borderlands*. Lanham: University Press of America.

Giménez Béliveau, Verónica and Montenegro, Silvia, eds. 2010. *La triple frontera. Dinámicas culturales y procesos transnacionales*. Buenos Aires: Espacio.

Gordillo, Gastón. 2000. Canales para un río indómito. Frontera, estado y utopías aborígenes en el noroeste de Formosa. In A. Grimson, ed., *Fronteras, naciones e identidades*. Buenos Aires: CICCUS-La Crujía.

Gordillo, Gastón and Leguizamón, Juan Martín. 2002. *El río y la frontera. Aborígenes, obras públicas, y Mercosur en el Pilcomayo*. Buenos Aires: Biblos.

Grimson, Alejandro. 2001. Fronteras, migraciones y Mercosur. Crisis de las utopías integracionistas. Apuntes de Investigación (Buenos Aires) (7).

Grimson, Alejandro. 2002. Hygiene wars on the Mercosur border. *Identities: Global Studies in Culture and Power* 9: 151–172.

Grimson, Alejandro. 2003a. *La nación en sus límites. Contrabandistas y exiliados en la frontera Argentina–Brasil*. Barcelona: Gedisa.

Grimson, Alejandro. 2003b. La nación después del (de) constructivismo. *Nueva Sociedad* (184): 33–45.

Grimson, Alejandro and Vila, Pablo. 2004. Forgotten border actors: the border reinforcers. A comparison between the US–Mexico and South American borders. *Journal of Political Ecology* 9: 69–87.

Hirsch, Silvia. 2000. Misión, región y nación entre los guaraníes de la Argentina. In A. Grimson, ed., *Fronteras, naciones e identidades*. Buenos Aires: CICCUS-La Crujía.

Karasik, Gabriela. 2000. Tras la genealogía del diablo. Discusiones sobre la nación y el estado en la frontera argentino-boliviana. In A. Grimson, ed., *Fronteras, naciones e identidades*. Buenos Aires: CICCUS-La Crujía.

López, Claudia. 2001. Ticunas brasileros, colombianos y peruanos. Etnicidad y nacionaldad en la región de fronteras del alto Amazonas/Solomões. PhD diss., Centro de Pesquisa e Pós-Graduação sobre as Américas, Universidade de Brasilia.

Montenegro, Silvia and Giménez Béliveau, Verónica. 2006. *La triple frontera. Globalización y construcción social del espacio*. Buenos Aires: Miño & Dávila.

Pinheiro-Machado, Rosana. 2008. China–Paraguai–Brasil. Uma rota para pensar a economia informal. *Revista Brasileira de Ciências Sociais* 23 (67): 117–133.

Quarleri, Lía. 2009. *Rebelión y guerra en las fronteras del Plata*. Buenos Aires: Fondo de Cultura Económica.

Rabossi, Fernando. 2009, *En las calles de Ciudad del Este*. Asunción: Universidad Católica.

Recondo, Gregorio, ed. 1997. *Mercosur. La dimensión cultural de la integración*. Buenos Aires: CICCUS.

Rey Balmaceda, Raúl. 1979. *Límites y fronteras de la Argentina*. Buenos Aires: Oikos.

Segato, Rita. 1998. Alteridades históricas/identidades políticas. Una crítica a las certezas del pluralismo global, Série Antropologia (Universidade de Brasília) (234).

Sprandel, Marcia. 2000. Brasiguayos. Una identidad de frontera y sus transformaciones. In A. Grimson, ed., *Fronteras, naciones e identidades*. Buenos Aires: CICCUS-La Crujía.

Stern, Steve, ed. 1992. *Resistencia, rebelión y conciencia campesina en los andes*. Lima: Instituto de Estudios Peruanos.

Vidal, Hernán. 2000. La frontera después del ajuste. In A. Grimson, ed., *Fronteras, naciones e identidades*. Buenos Aires: CICCUS-La Crujía.

Vila, Pablo. 2000. *Crossing Borders, Reinforcing Borders*. Austin: University of Texas Press.

Wilson, Thomas M. and Donnan, Hastings. 1998. Nation, state and identity at international borders. In Thomas M. Wilson and Hastings Donnan, eds, *Border Identities*. Cambridge: Cambridge University Press.

CHAPTER **12** # Debordering and Rebordering the United Kingdom

Cathal McCall

On the subject of the external frontier of the European Union (EU) Malcolm Anderson (with Eberhard Bort) concluded: "The European frontier is a subject worthy of a great debate. Unfortunately, such a debate will inevitably be a disorderly one and carry with it the risk of disintegration into highly specialized discussions" (Anderson with Bort 2001: 183). The same could be said for the United Kingdom (UK) border. The twenty-first century narrative of threat and insecurity, compounded by the inter-related concerns, prejudices and fears relating to the large-scale mobility of EU workers after enlargement of the EU in 2004 and illegal immigration in a period of severe economic instability, recession and rising unemployment, has reinvigorated interest in the UK border. The dynamism of the European integration project in the 1980s and 1990s engendered intense academic reflection on the processes of globalization, Europeanization and regionalization and their impact on debordering Europe, including the UK. However, the current thrust of the debate in academic, political and media circles is on rebordering states by recreating borders as security barriers to help prevent "international terrorism" and illegal immigration. In the UK, the state security rebordering process is symbolized by the erection of large signs declaring "The UK Border" in the international arrivals halls of British airports.

Contemporary globalization has been commonly understood to be a process that eases and speeds the movement of goods, services, capital and knowledge, with major implications for the configuration of modern state territorial borders. Global information flows, the global movement of capital, and global media and culture have serviced a debordering debate (Bauman 1998; Held 1995; Mlinar 1992; Stiglitz 2003; Weiss 1998). Within the EU, debordering is underpinned by the process of Europeanization eliciting nascent notions of supranational citizenship and identity, as well as more substantial forms of supranational governance and territoriality. However, the drama of the September 11, 2001 attacks in the United States had the effect of subordinating the debordering narrative to the extent that cross-border cooperation,

A Companion to Border Studies, First Edition. Edited by Thomas M. Wilson and Hastings Donnan.
© 2012 Blackwell Publishing Ltd. Published 2012 by Blackwell Publishing Ltd.

hitherto implicit in debordering, became more of a rebordering security initiative in political discourse (Andreas 2003; Walters 2006). The "dark side of globalization," embodied in the global proliferation of terrorism under the spurious umbrella of Islamic jihad, the neo-imperial response in Afghanistan and Iraq, and secondary concerns about illegal immigration and international crime, was encapsulated in a rebordering narrative (Kuus 2007; Newman 2006; Pickering and Weber 2011). "Dark globalization" has initiated a response from Western states in the form of individual and collective action on enhancing systems of border control and security, particularly to counter real and perceived threats emanating from Islamic fundamentalists, international criminals and illegal migrants.

Heeding Anderson's warning about the risks involved in entering into a great frontier (or border) debate, this chapter engages initially with the currently dominant rebordering state security narrative on borders, particularly the debate on "e-borders" in the UK and Ireland as recorded in Hansard[1] and Dáil Éireann Parliamentary Debates,[2] as well as in the British and Irish newspaper media. However, the subject of rebordering the UK through e-bordering and a developing border security regime requires contextualization in a wider debate. Consequently, rebordering is also examined from the perspective of intrastate regionalization and empowerment as embodied in the post-1998 UK devolution project. Longer-term debordering via the enduring process of Europeanization is an overarching theme that is considered throughout. It is argued that Europeanization (in the political science usage regarding the development of supranational institutions and policy-making), cross-border cooperation[3] and rebordering (regionalization) in the form of UK devolution continue to offer important counterpoints for border studies to the rebordering (state security) narrative. As such, the UK border represents a vibrant site for studying the impact of globalization, Europeanization and regionalization on debordering and rebordering, particularly in the contexts of institution-building and power relations.

SECURITY AND THE UK BORDER

A key point of departure for Vaughan-Williams in *Border Politics: The Limits of Sovereign Power* (2009) is Étienne Balibar's thesis that "borders . . . are no longer at the border" (Balibar 1998). In the UK border context, Vaughan-Williams details efforts made by the UK government, through the enactment of "offshore" bordering practices, to create an eclectic border zone around Britain that is not necessarily coterminous with the UK border itself. The creation of this border zone through offshore bordering practices represents a concerted effort to reborder and, thus, meet and defeat the threats posed by international terrorism, illegal immigration and crime. The raison d'être is that these threats should be neutralized at foreign source before they arrive at the UK border. Consequently, the UK border zone now extends territorially to the European continent, with UK border guards, armed with the white heat of border control technology (carbon dioxide probes, X-ray scanners, heartbeat sensors and heat detectors), stationed in Boulogne, Brussels, Calais, Coquelles, Dunkerque, Frethun, Lille and Paris. It is being reinforced by border intelligence agents such as Airline Liaison Officers, who advise foreign law enforcement agencies on the potential illegal movement of people deemed to be "illegitimate" or "undesirable" travelers (Vaughan-Williams 2009). No doubt, it is also top of the agenda of British intelligence agencies engaged in clandestine governance.

According to Waever, "security is a practice, a specific way of framing an issue. Security discourse is characterized by dramatizing an issue and giving it absolute priority" (1996: 103–132). The September 11, 2001 attacks in the United States, especially those on the Twin Towers in New York, dramatized the issue of Islamic fundamentalist threat in a very literal and visual way and effectively turned the page in the Western political discourse on borders. This shift was particularly stark in the EU context because, hitherto, the narrative of debordering through supranational institution-building, policy-making and cross-border cooperation was a central focus of border studies research (see, for example, Donnan and Wilson 1999; Perkmann 1999; Scott 1999; Anderson et al. 2003). Similarly, though somewhat less dramatically, the threat from illegal immigration regularly makes the headlines in the British media, particularly in the right-wing tabloid press. Calais, Sangatte and "the Jungle" have been portrayed as sites of perennial threat for Britain and "the British way of life." Of course, the wider issue of the post-2004 arrival of "legitimate" transient workers from central-eastern Europe is the prejudicial bedrock on which this narrative is based. The Channel Tunnel is a particular point of interest for those concerned with rebordering Britain to halt illegal immigration. Unlike a land border, the Channel Tunnel is a singular port of entry or "choke point" that all vehicles, goods and people have to pass through and, as such, presents a relatively straightforward site for the exercise of a security regime (Anderson with Bort 2001: 184).

Supported by a staff of 20,000 employees in the UK Border Agency, the UK border security regime represents a sophisticated and energetic response to perceived threats emanating from Overseas and is largely focused on "border portals" and "choke points" – airports, ports and the Channel Tunnel – as well as activities in an electronic/intelligence border zone with nodes that extend to the European continent and beyond (Vaughan-Williams 2010). However, on the face of it, there appears to be a yawning gap in this rebordering process in the shape of the UK's open land border with the Republic of Ireland – the Irish border.

THE IRISH BORDER: LEAVING THE BACK DOOR AJAR?

Estimates of the length of the Irish border vary from 350 kilometers to 450 kilometers, such is its meandering course through towns, townlands and even homes. After the creation of the EU Single Market in 1992 and the onset of the Irish peace process in 1994, the Irish border's customs posts and military checkpoints were abandoned, secondary roads were reopened and the Irish border region gradually became demilitarized through the dismantling of British Army mountain-top watchtowers and the closure of heavily fortified security bases (McCall 2011). The result is that the physical manifestation of the Irish border itself is hardly discernable save for a change in road markings. These road markings themselves may not serve well, except to locals, as indicators that the border has in fact been traversed, as shown for example when

Erasmus exchange students studying at Queen's University Belfast struggle to identify the Irish border upon crossing it on weekend jaunts to Dublin.

Debordering the Irish border region has involved deemphasizing state sovereignty and is embodied in Europeanization and the 1998 Good Friday Agreement[4] as well as the subsequent removal of the British security regime. Fundamentally, Europeanization has involved the creation and empowerment of international and supranational EU institutions. The EU remains the most developed international/supranational polity for concerted economic, legal, political and cultural action above the nation-state level, with important consequences for the notion of state sovereignty and the borders of member states (Sørensen 1999; Wallace 1999; Keating 2004). EU member states retain popular sovereignty. However, they have relinquished a measure of legal sovereignty to the European Court of Justice and the European Court of Human Rights. An emphasis on collective EU action has implications for political sovereignty, not least because the EU represents an extension of political space beyond the territorial borders of member states. The cultural sovereignty of the state is also under pressure from globalization and Europeanization, as well as from regionalization driven by substate regionalist and minority nationalist mobilization (Laffan et al. 2000).

Debordering Ireland was embedded by the creation of a cross-border, North/South infrastructure under the terms of the 1998 Agreement (McCall 2002). It consists of the North/South Ministerial Council, comprising ministers from the Republic of Ireland and Northern Ireland with sectoral responsibility for education, health, transport, agriculture, the environment and tourism who meet to progress cross-border cooperation in these areas. The North/South Ministerial Council is supported by a number of North/South Implementation Bodies which concentrate on the specifics of cross-border, all-island cooperation in the areas of food safety, minority languages, trade and business development, aquaculture and waterways, as well as EU programs. A cross-border limited company – Tourism Ireland – also functions as a de facto implementation body to promote the island as a tourist destination (Coakley et al. 2007).

British Army watchtowers, security force checkpoints and border fortifications were emblematic of the UK's Irish border security regime. This infrastructure of British security on the Irish border began to be decommissioned as the Irish peace process progressed. However, even during the height of the Northern Ireland "Troubles" (1969–1994), the Irish border region was a relatively "security force free" zone. Writing in 1983, Richard Rose, the celebrated political scientist and authority on Northern Ireland governance, could claim with some justification:

> in practical terms, the border between Northern Ireland and the Republic is virtually wide open; there is easy movement back and forth of people with business and friends on both sides of the border, including IRA [Irish Republican Army] units. The British Army and RUC [Royal Ulster Constabulary] maintain some patrols on the border, but these are not comprehensive and continuing, as for example, are patrols along the much longer border separating West and East Germany. (1983: 25)

The reason Rose gave for this apparent lapse in securing the UK's only land border was "no political will at Westminster" for fear of giving offense to the forces, political and violent, dedicated to its destruction (1983: 25–6). With "no political will at Westminster" to secure the Irish border at the height of the Troubles, the idea of such an undertaking in "postconflict"[5] Ireland would be unthinkable. Thus, in August 2009, a splinter IRA group could plant a large bomb outside Forkhill, County Armagh and run a concealed command wire across fields and over the border into County Louth. The bomb was not found by the UK security forces for a week after a telephone warning was given. Despite the find, the British government stated categorically that British troops would not be introduced to secure the border (*Irish Times*, Sept. 10, 2009).

THE BRITISH BORDER

To examine reasons for the absence of political will at Westminster in securing the Irish border, it is necessary to give consideration to the dynamics leading to the partition of Ireland (and the United Kingdom of Great Britain and Ireland), as well as the distinctive political culture that evolved (or rather devolved) in Northern Ireland after 1921. Anderson and O'Dowd, who have detailed the imperial underpinnings of home rule and partition, argue that "the conflict over home rule and early partition proposals up to 1916 was essentially a conflict between different interpretations of how British imperialism should find expression in Ireland, and how the main factions . . . would share in the fruits of imperialism" (2005: 3). The border that was created resembled an "imperial frontier" imposed by an empire in retreat, though it eventually became a fully fledged state border through state-building in Sáorstat Éireann (Irish Free State) and the UK's retreat from imperial power to a national state. With the new Northern Ireland government also left largely to its own devices, Ireland, South and North, was now effectively left out of British politics and the reconfiguring *British* national state (Anderson and O'Dowd 2005: 13).

That reconfiguration remained incomplete. In Weberian terms, a secure territorial border is understood to be one of two defining attributes of the modern state (the other being a monopoly of violence controlled by the state) (Giddens 1987). However, "the Crown" describes the central political authority of the UK which is not delimited by territory. According to Rose, "the domain of the Crown has referred to less than the UK, or in days of Empire, much more. In effect, the Crown is a concept of infinite domain" (1983: 3). The Common Travel Area between Britain and Ireland may be understood as an imperial residue of the UK state and a symbol of Ireland's neo-colonial dependency on Britain.[6] Despite the formation of Sáorstat Éireann in 1921 and its exit from the Commonwealth in 1949, citizens of the "Free State" and then of the Republic had the legal right to enter Britain and avail themselves of the same rights as British citizens. Echoes of this imperial consciousness reverberated in Section 2 of the UK's 1949 Ireland Act: "Notwithstanding that the Republic of Ireland is not part of His Majesty's Dominions, the Republic of Ireland is not a foreign country for the purposes of any law in force in any part of the UK."[7]

The post-2001 effort to secure Britain's borders in an "e-border" regime potentially challenged the Common Travel Area between Britain and Ireland. It also threatened to exclude Northern Ireland, much to the annoyance of Ulster British unionist politicians speaking on behalf of the "British citizens of Northern Ireland."[8] The e-border system involves the electronic collection and analysis of passenger information for the purpose of a security check. The system includes a watch list of "undesirables" and generates an "alert" if such a person's information is entered in the system.[9] With the publication of the British government's Borders, Citizenship and Immigration Bill in January 2009 it became apparent that, upon enactment of the Bill, passengers traveling from the Republic of Ireland to Britain would have to show passports in order to be processed in the British e-borders system and gain entry into Britain (Travis 2009). This proposal had obvious deleterious consequences for the Common Travel Area. Moreover, unionist politicians in Northern Ireland were quick to spot the possibility of travelers departing from Northern Ireland to Britain receiving similar treatment, given the porous nature of the Irish border. For example, Jim Allister (leader of Traditional Unionist Voice) wrote to the then British Home Secretary, Jacqui Smith, as follows:

> It is reported that tighter passport controls between Ireland and the UK will mean anyone travelling between Ireland and Britain from 2009 will have to carry a passport, but that these controls will not apply to the Republic's border with Northern Ireland. If so, then how will the new controls be effective, since those present in the Republic of Ireland could simply enter through Northern Ireland, unless you anticipate the preposterous suggestion of imposing passport/control restrictions internally within the UK at the point where travellers enter GB [Great Britain]? (*Irish Times*, Oct. 24, 2009)

The possibility of the e-border proposal giving substance to a British border also excited Member of Parliament Sammy Wilson, Democratic Unionist Party (DUP), who claimed that the Bill would have "radically changed the United Kingdom's borders [creating a] tight border around Great Britain but would have left Northern Ireland exposed and isolated." (*Irish Times*, July 16, 2009). However, unionist leaders have not always demonstrated deference to the integrity of the UK border, at least where cattle are concerned. During the 2007 outbreak of "foot and mouth" disease in Britain, for example, the Rev. Ian Paisley, then DUP leader and Northern Ireland First Minister, was at pains to emphasize that there was "clear blue sea" between Great Britain and Northern Ireland (cited in Coakley and O'Dowd 2007: 877).

In the event, and in face of DUP opposition and amendments from the Conservative Party and the Liberal Democrats, the clause in the 2009 Borders, Citizenship and Immigration Bill on the requirement to show passports when traveling from the Republic of Ireland to Britain was removed and the Common Travel Area retained (*Guardian*, July 15, 2009). In practice, however, the Common Travel Area is severely compromised by the fact that passengers traveling from Britain to the Republic of Ireland are routinely asked for their passports, though there is no passport control for passengers traveling into Britain from the Republic. In addition, immigration checks on passengers arriving from Britain commenced in June 1997. In 2007, then Taoiseach Bertie Ahern told the Dáil: "After 11 September 2001 some of the major advantages of the common travel area were lost, as passports or photo identification became a requirement in most locations."[10]

Initiatives for securing the border of Britain, rather than that of the UK,[11] have historical precedent. After the fall of France in 1940 Irish travelers were required to carry passports or limited travel documents for "war-work" to gain entry to Britain. A full return to freedom of movement in a "common travel area" did not happen until 1952 (Meehan 2000: 26). In the security context a British border became a swift reality again under the 1974 Prevention of Terrorism (Temporary Provisions) Act in response to the IRA bombing of two public houses in Birmingham. The Act gave the British Home Secretary the power to prevent (male) individuals moving from Northern Ireland to Britain, and also to deport individuals from Britain to Northern Ireland:

> If the Secretary of State is satisfied that –
> (a) any person (whether in Great Britain or elsewhere) is concerned in the commission, preparation or instigation of acts of terrorism, or
> (b) any person is attempting or may attempt to enter Great Britain with a view to being concerned in the commission, preparation or instigation of acts of terrorism, the Secretary of State may make an order against that person prohibiting him from being in, or entering, Great Britain.[12]

Between 1974 and 1990, 6,932 people were detained under the Act.[13] In addition, special "domestic" security arrangements – for example, X-ray machines, random frisks and hand luggage searches – for inbound and outbound Belfast passengers had been a feature of British airports' "Belfast gate" long before they were applied across the board in the aftermath of the September 11, 2001 attacks in the US. This British border within the UK, combined with the permeability of the UK's land border with the Republic of Ireland and Westminster's willingness to allow Northern Ireland to secede unilaterally (unlike Scotland or Wales) in the event of a majority in Northern Ireland approving such a move, is problematic for the idea of a UK border that is coterminous with the UK state. These factors support Rose's claim that Great Britain is the de facto state and its borders are "fuzzy" (1983: 31–32).

A BRITISH ISLES BORDER OR THE SCHENGEN FRONTIER?

During the e-border controversy, the Right Honourable Lord Trimble of Lisnagarvey (David Trimble, former leader of the Ulster Unionist Party and former First Minister of Northern Ireland) suggested that a "Schengen-type" British Isles border would be preferable to a British security border and the possibility of a requirement for British citizens from Northern Ireland to produce proof of identity when traveling to other parts of the UK. On November 21, 2007 he asked the House of Lords:

> Would it not be much better to take the existing informal common travel area and put it on a formal basis analogous to the Schengen agreement that applies elsewhere in Europe? This would solve the problems that arise in practice and relieve the difficulties experienced by the Home Office, which seems to be intellectually challenged by the idea of a land frontier.[14]

Following Britain's e-border plans announced initially in the Bill, then Taoiseach Bertie Ahern stated: "the potential impact of the electronic border control on the travel of Irish citizens was discussed by the Government. We are considering a proposed Irish border information system." He went on to suggest that an Irish border system would be "similar in some ways to the British system."[15] The plans for the Irish system that transpired were similar in virtually every way to the British system. Air and sea passenger details would be forwarded by airlines and ferry companies to a new Irish Borders Operation Centre (I-Boc) and processed into a database with watch lists and alerts (*Irish Times*, Nov. 9, 2007). Obviously a high level of cooperation and information sharing between the two systems would, in effect, create a "Schengen-type" British Isles border, as suggested by Trimble. The idea of a common British Isles border security system was also given voice by the then British Home Office minister, Tony McNulty, though couched in language that was sensitive to the notion of sovereign statehood and a history of British-Irish conflict over it: "These things do need to be done in a very sensitive fashion, and in a fashion that respects the relationship between the two countries over the last 30 years." However, mutual interest determined the development of the "most effectively-protected borders that we can" (*Irish Times*, Nov. 2, 2007).

In terms of intelligence and state security it may be assumed that information sharing between relevant intelligence agencies in Britain and Ireland is highly developed. Meetings of the British-Irish Intergovernmental Conference[16] regularly note the "continuing excellent cooperation" between the Police Service of Northern Ireland and An Garda Siochána (the Irish Police), while giving little detail apart from information on relatively benign North/South police exchanges.[17] The premium on secrecy in state intelligence precludes academic examination beyond historical investigation of files released. As such, the relationship between MI5 and Garda intelligence/Special Branch units – in terms of cooperation, control and the operation of clandestine governance – is beyond the realm of this chapter.

In the Irish e-borders debate it may be argued that if the Westminster government was to enact a policy of e-bordering Britain and end the Common Travel Area then the island of Ireland would be best served joining the Schengen system. It may be further argued that the island of Ireland would be best served by such a move in any event because of the benefits to business and tourism that free movement – involving, for example, the avoidance of lengthy queues at passport control – in "Shengenland" would afford. Now encompassing 25 states, the Schengen system comprises a body of EU law that enables free movement for people within the Schengen zone and provides for security measures to protect the integrity of the zone's external frontier (Bigo and Guild 2005).[18]

Why does the Republic of Ireland not apply to join Schengen and avail itself of this opportunity? After all, EU Justice Commissioner Franco Frattini commented that "joining Schengen would be positive for Ireland" and that he would welcome an application (*Irish Times*, Dec. 21, 2007). As analyst Hugo Brady (Centre for European Reform) has suggested: "Following on from Ireland's decision to follow London and opt out of key parts of the EU Reform Treaty, it increasingly looks like Ireland is a small country latched to Britain like a koala on justice issues . . . By choosing Schengen, Ireland would gain independence and an equal place at the EU table"

(*Irish Times*, Nov. 13, 2007). However, the Republic of Ireland cannot join Schengen without Northern Ireland, because it would entail the erection of border posts along the Irish border to secure the new external frontier. This is not an option for the Irish government, not least because when it was configured as a political barrier between North and South the Irish border was the major ideological and practical focus for ethnonational conflict in Northern Ireland. It has been the debordering of the Irish border that has helped diffuse that conflict, not least through the creation of a transnational border cultural space in which Ulster British unionist and Irish nationalist ethnonational groups can address narratives of threat, insecurity, victim-hood, loss, betrayal and defeat, and begin to explore and accommodate their differences in the absence of threat (McCall and O'Dowd 2008; McCall 2011). As Elizabeth Meehan has commented: "to have agreed to lift controls on EU routes, while the British retained them, may have had a paradoxical result; the imposition of border formalities between north and south at the very time when both governments and Northern Irish politicians have agreed to minimize the effects of there being two jurisdictions on the one island" (2000: ix). Therefore, the only available option for the Irish government is to follow the UK's lead on e-borders given that joining the Schengen system is not a viable option for a UK government and Ulster British unionist politicians would not contemplate Northern Ireland entering Schengen with the Republic of Ireland in the absence of Britain. As Jim Nicholson, Member of the European Parliament (Ulster Unionist Party), asserted, "I certainly would not advocate this action. I think it could demean the Britishness of Northern Irish people and cause legal problems" (*Irish Times*, 13 Nov. 13, 2007).

THE IMAGINED UK BORDER

In a consideration of the UK social and political rebordering process one must delve deeper than the security aspect and consider historical, political and cultural factors that underpin perceptions of that border. State borders are forged in the national imagination through a history of war, political endeavor and cultural enterprise. Consequently, they are imagined as physical parameters of possession, protection and exclusion that can provoke emotions of love, hate and violence (Berezin 2003: 4). Totems such as "This Sceptred Isle" and the "White Cliffs of Dover" that pervade heroic, romantic and nationalist accounts of British history are most readily inculcated in the British communal imagination through retelling in popular cultural media, for example, in the 10-week BBC Radio 4 series *This Sceptred Isle*, the BBC's television comedy *Dad's Army* and its documentary series *Coast*.

All too often the imagined borders of the UK retreat to those of Britain – This Sceptred Isle – among the British political elite, the British media and the population of the island generally. Political psychologists have found that, in the British context, "allusions to the geographical boundaries of imagined community [the island] may be used as a substitute for reference to the common and distinctive character or "identity" of the population" (Abell et al. 2006: 223). At the political elite level, this was demonstrated by the then security minister Lord West of Spithead when he referred to people traveling from Northern Ireland "to the United Kingdom" during the e-borders debate in the House of Lords: "We know both anecdotally and from taking samples that there are people who either come through the Republic of Ireland, move into Northern Ireland and then come across to the United Kingdom or vice versa." This "slip" was pounced on by an indignant Lord Trimble who responded: "My Lords, does the Minister not realise that, when he spoke a moment ago of travelling from Northern Ireland to the United Kingdom, he demonstrated clearly his lack of understanding of the basic concept?"[19] This exchange provides some evidence to support Meehan's conclusion that "Great Britain being an island is still crucial to the outlooks of governments on the maintenance of frontier controls" (2000: 60). It is often forgotten by politicians in Britain that Northern Ireland is a part of the UK, much to the chagrin of Ulster British unionists.

Nationally, polling evidence suggests that a large majority of the "Great British public" do not imagine Northern Ireland as part of the UK. For example, in an Independent Communications and Marketing (ICM) opinion poll published in the *Guardian* newspaper on August 21, 2001, the question posed to a sample of British people in Britain was: "Do you think Northern Ireland should be part of the UK?" – 26 per cent responded that it should remain part of the UK, 41 per cent that it should be joined with the Republic of Ireland, and 33 per cent responded "don't know." The detached reality for Ulster British unionists is reinforced by a distinct political system in Northern Ireland – from governance to political parties – and was actually underlined in comments made by Member of Parliament Jeffrey Donaldson (DUP) published by the newspaper the following day. He maintained that such findings were irrelevant because "the constitutional and political reality [is that] under the principle of consent [unionists'] future will be determined *by the people of Northern Ireland themselves*" (*Guardian*, Aug. 22, 2001, emphasis added).

Edensor has argued that the nation is not just imagined through the printed page (as Anderson (1983) suggests), or indeed just through radio, television and cinema, it is also imagined through, among other things, "a plenitude of embodied habits and performances" (Edensor 2002: 7). In an increasingly secularized Europe, sport challenges religion as a habit and performance "site" through which the nation is imagined. MacClancy contends that sport "may be used to . . . define more sharply the already established boundaries of moral and political communities; to assist in the creating of new social identities; to give physical expression to certain social values and to act as a means of reflecting on those values; to serve as potentially contested space by opposing groups" (1996: 7). Gaelic games provide habits and performances with an Irish nationalist undertow that increasingly influences an imagined Irish national community, including a sizable proportion of it in Northern Ireland. Perhaps one measure of a British cultural border is the nonexistent coverage of Gaelic sports in the Monday sports section of British broadsheet newspapers, even after two teams from Northern Ireland – Armagh and Tyrone – met in the 2003 All-Ireland Gaelic Football final in front of 83,000 spectators.

REBORDERING AND REGIONALIZATION

While the British communal imagination remains fixed on the border of Britain, regionalization in the form of devolution for Scotland, Wales and Northern Ireland in 1998 presented a new challenge for that border through an internal rebordering process. The asymmetrical devolution of powers from the UK center to these peripheral regions served further to differentiate them from England. In the case of Scotland the extent of powers devolved is usually demonstrated by citing the shorter list of reserved powers, that is, those retained by Westminster. These reserved powers relate to UK constitutional issues; foreign affairs and defense; fiscal, economic and monetary policy; economic matters; some infrastructural arrangements; natural resources; Home Affairs; and the social rights associated with citizenship (Trench 2007a: 51–52). This enables the Scottish government to exercise power in key areas such as education, health, local government, the environment, agriculture and fisheries, public transport, languages, and policing and justice (Trench 2007a: 54). Of course, that rebordered power is complicated by the fact that the debordering process of European integration entailed wholesale EU regulation, particularly in the policy areas of transport, economic development, the environment and agriculture and fisheries. Moreover, the EU is a foreign policy area which is a reserved power of the UK center. So, while rebordering through devolution suggests that the state has relinquished some powers to devolved regions, many of these powers have been compromised by the debordering process of European integration. The ability of the regions to engage with the EU on these issues is restricted because UK places at the EU Council of Ministers table are reserved for UK ministers (Jeffery and Palmer 2007). Therefore, many of the powers devolved can be lost to the EU supranational level unless regional ministers are similarly represented in the EU Council of Ministers. In the absence of such representation, Westminster continues to provide the vital conduit to the EU for devolved administrations (Mitchell 1998: 78–80).

Despite this caveat, UK devolution has lead to a significant degree of differentiation for substantial segments of the UK population, for example, university students and the elderly. In 2000–2001, up-front tuition fees for Scottish students at Scottish universities were abolished. Instead, after graduation, Scottish students were required to pay a graduate endowment which financed a student hardship fund. However, that charge was also abolished in 2008. In 2002 a policy of free personal care for the elderly was introduced in Scotland. It covered the personal care costs incurred by elderly people living at home, as well as those living in nursing homes (Keating 2010: 209–222). Therefore, devolved power and regional autonomy may be limited, but devolved administrations have been able to formulate unique bordered policies (Trench 2007b: 12). Nevertheless, nationalists remain unsated. For example, in 2010 Alex Salmond (Scottish First Minister and Leader of the Scottish National Party) referred to the Scottish Parliament as a "pocket money parliament" and called for more powers.[20] Europeanization may also have offered encouragement to such stateless nations. Accession to the European Economic Community held out the promise of giving smaller states, like the Republic of Ireland, increased stature relative to larger and more powerful member states. Whether this inspired "stateless nations" like Scotland and Catalonia to make decisive demands for regional empowerment is a moot point. However, the fact that powerful German Länder had already made it to the EU Council of Ministers table, if only on matters directly related to their subnational region, could not have gone unnoticed (Wallace 1999: 511).

Scottish nationalists may also have been encouraged by the creation of the British-Irish Council (BIC) under the terms of the 1998 Good Friday Agreement because it presented another potential opportunity for further reconfiguring Britain's borders. The BIC comprises representatives from the two governments, the devolved bodies of Northern Ireland, Scotland and Wales, as well as three British Crown dependencies: the Isle of Man, Guernsey and Jersey. Vernon Bogdanor argued in 1999 that in postdevolution Britain, Scotland and Wales would have major representation on the BIC and might not have UK interests at the top of their respective agendas. Rather, the BIC would probably have the opposite effect and continue the process of loosening UK ties as Scotland and Wales sought to capitalize on any further leakage of power from Westminster into this debordering institution (Bogdanor 1999: 298). It was even suggested that, under the auspices of the BIC, Irish politicians and diplomats were fomenting separatist instincts in Scotland and Wales (Luckhurst 2001). While the first years of the BIC produced very modest advances, it did at least symbolize British Isles processes of debordering (Lynch and Hopkins 2001).

Distinctive histories, languages, religions and other cultural resources have been the wellspring of an ongoing social and political rebordering devolution process in Britain. This is not to say that the UK state is necessarily weakened by such a process. Rebordering through regionalization may add to "postdevolution blues" in the northeast of England. However, perceptions of a strengthening divide in economy, society and polity across the "Anglo-Scottish border" is qualified by the continued bridging provided by the UK state context (Pike 2002: 1079). The UK was not a unitary state before devolution. Rather, it has rested on multiple asymmetrical unions that have changed in response to circumstances. Thus far, response has been a key to survival. The longevity of state borders generally is dependent on their ability to reconfigure in response to pressures emanating from globalization, Europeanization and regionalization. For James Mitchell, "Dicey's concern that parliamentary sovereignty should be preserved and his insistence that this is of vital importance might actually serve to undermine the very state he strenuously defended" (2009: 222). "The harder they come, the harder they fall" may be a fitting soundtrack for borders constructed as rigid divides. Survival entails a flexibility that may require permeability, cross-border exchanges and the devolution of power to peripheries. An inability to accommodate change arising from the pressures of globalization and Europeanization contributed to the collapse of the Berlin Wall in 1989. In the UK context, a process of "ever looser union" may be a consequence of devolution (Mitchell 2009: 226) and, as such, lead to the survival of the UK and its borders rather than to the "breakup of Britain."

CONCLUSION

Political authority in the UK is derived from the Crown, and the domain of the Crown lacks definitive territorial precision (Rose 1983: 3). This determines that the UK border is a constantly shifting threshold depending on issues deemed to be important for the "national interest." Post-2001 threats to security have been the dominant border-related issue at Westminster and in the media. Consequently, the threshold of the UK border has shifted to portals on the European mainland and the machinations of UK border agents have moved onto a global stage. At the same time, the UK's only land border with the Republic of Ireland is open and unguarded.

The political debate on e-borders and the British government's Borders, Citizenship and Immigration Bill served as a reminder that Great Britain is imagined as the UK border by the British political elite. It is an imagined border that is disseminated in popular British media cultural practices and is reflected in the British public as evidenced in public opinion surveys. It was only when Ulster British unionists reminded Westminster of the fact that the UK includes Northern Ireland that the Bill was amended, the Common Travel Area retained, and the focus of the debate shifted to securing a British Isles border zone, albeit in cooperation with the Irish government.

Joining the wider Schengen free movement and security regime is not countenanced by UK political elites, the media and the British public. The reasons for this are similar to those cited for the UK being an "awkward partner" in the EU, namely, imperial and war history, an island geography informing perceptions of "the British people," and a British culture underpinned by strong notions of parliamentary sovereignty. Meanwhile, the Irish border dictates that the Irish government cannot join "Schengenland" without Northern Ireland and must therefore follow Britain's lead in securing a British Isles border zone.

Rokkan and Urwin (1983: 123) argue that territory is a neutral concept that only becomes significant politically when an interpretation and value is placed on it by people. The processes of globalization, Europeanization and regionalization challenge the territorial integrity of the British national state. Consequently, these processes also challenge the interpretation and value placed on territory by people and the territorial resource of communal identity itself. Debordering and rebordering are the responses of Westminster to these challenges, with the goal of ensuring the survival of the UK as a viable state entity and Britishness as a distinctive national identity.

NOTES

1 At http://www.publications.parliament.uk/pa/pahansard.htm (accessed Dec. 19, 2010).
2 At http://debates.oireachtas.ie/Main.aspx (accessed Dec. 19, 2010).
3 For multidisciplinary perspectives on Europeanization see Harmsen and Wilson 2000.
4 The 1998 Good Friday (Belfast) Agreement was the outcome of multiparty negotiations aimed at addressing the causes of the British-Irish/Northern Ireland conflict.
5 "Postconflict" describes the current stage in the conflict transformation process in Ireland where the use of political violence has largely ceased but political and cultural manifestations of conflict persist in Northern Ireland.
6 Elizabeth Meehan has pointed out that the Common Travel Area was referred to as "the common travel area" in policy documents before becoming the Common Travel Area when internationally recognized in the 1997 Treaty of Amsterdam (2000: 1).
7 At http://www.legislation.gov.uk/ukpga/Geo6/12-13-14/41 (accessed Apr. 4, 2011).
8 Northern Ireland is an ethnonationally divided society wherein unionist politicians, invariably drawn from the Ulster Protestant community, have the preservation of the United Kingdom of Great Britain and Northern Ireland as their overriding priority. They maintain

that the Union, rather than a united Ireland, is in the best interests of the British citizens of Northern Ireland, who are also drawn mainly from the Ulster Protestant community. Irish nationalist/republican politicians argue for a united Ireland and draw their support mainly from the Irish Catholic community.

9   At   http://www.ukba.homeoffice.gov.uk/sitecontent/newsarticles/2011/april/08-e-borders-captures-criminals (accessed Dec. 21, 2011).

10   In Dáil Debate, vol. 640, no. 2 (Oct. 24, 2007), at http://debates.oireachtas.ie (accessed Dec. 19, 2010).

11   Northern Ireland is a part of the UK state, that is, the United Kingdom of Great Britain and Northern Ireland.

12   Part II Exclusion Orders, 3:3, Prevention of Terrorism (Temporary Provisions) Act 1974. At http://cain.ulst.ac.uk/hmso/pta1974.htm (accessed Apr. 19, 2011).

13   See http://www.radstats.org.uk/no049/statewatch.pdf (accessed Apr. 19, 2011).

14   At http://www.publications.parliament.uk/pa/ld200708/ldhansrd/text/71121-0002.htm#07112167000249 (accessed Dec. 19, 2010).

15   In Dáil Debate, vol. 640, no. 2 (Oct. 24, 2007), at http://debates.oireachtas.ie (accessed Dec. 19, 2010).

16   The British-Irish Intergovernmental Conference is an East–West institution provided by the 1998 Good Friday Agreement "to promote bilateral co-operation at all levels on all matters of mutual interest within the competence of both Governments." At http://www.dfa.ie/home/index.aspx?id=26690 (accessed Mar. 22, 2011).

17   At http://foreignaffairs.gov.ie/home/index.aspx?id=25791 (accessed Dec. 20, 2010).

18   Of the 27 EU member states, the UK and Ireland opted out and Bulgaria, Cyprus and Romania have yet to implement Schengen. Non-EU member states that have opted into the Schengen Area include Iceland, Norway and Switzerland.

19   At http://www.publications.parliament.uk/pa/ld200708/ldhansrd/text/71121-0002.htm#07112167000249 (accessed Dec. 23, 2010).

20   At http://www.bbc.co.uk/news/uk-scotland-scotland-politics-15336007 (accessed Dec. 21, 2011).

REFERENCES

Abell, Jackie, Condor, Susan and Stevenson, Clifford. 2006. "We are an island": geographical imagery in accounts of citizenship, civil society and national identity in Scotland and England. *Political Psychology* 27 (2): 207–226.

Anderson, Benedict. 1983. *Imagined Communities: Reflections on the Origins and Spread of Nationalism*. London: Verso.

Anderson, James and O'Dowd, Liam. 2005. *Imperial Disintegration and the Creation of the Irish Border: Imperialism and Nationalism 1885–1925*. Dublin: Institute for British-Irish Studies.

Anderson, James, O'Dowd, Liam and Wilson, Thomas M., eds. 2003. *New Borders for a Changing Europe: Cross-Border Cooperation and Governance*. London: Frank Cass.

Anderson, Malcolm, with Bort, Eberhard. 2001. *The Frontiers of the European Union*. Basingstoke: Macmillan.

Andreas, Peter. 2003. Redrawing the line: borders and security in the twenty-first century. *International Security* 28 (2): 78–111.

Balibar, Étienne. 1998. The borders of Europe. In Pheng Cheah and Bruce Robbins, eds, *Cosmopolitics*, pp. 216–232. Minneapolis: University of Minnesota Press.

Bauman, Zygmunt. 1998. *Globalization: The Human Consequences*. Cambridge: Polity.

Berezin, Mabel. 2003. Territory, emotion and identity: spatial recalibration in a new Europe. In Mabel Berezin and Martin Schain, eds, *Europe without Borders: Remapping Territory, Citizenship, and Identity in a Transnational Age*, pp. 1–30. Baltimore: Johns Hopkins University Press.

Bigo, Didier and Guild, Elspeth, eds. 2005. *Controlling Frontiers: Free Movement Into and Within Europe*. London: Ashgate.

Bognanor, Vernon. 1999. *Devolution in the United Kingdom*. Oxford: Oxford University Press.

Coakley, John and O'Dowd, Liam. 2007. The transformation of the Irish border. *Political Geography* 26: 877–885.

Coakley, John, Ó Caoindealbháin, Brian and Wilson, Robin. 2007. Institutional cooperation: the North–South implementation bodies. In John Coakley and Liam O'Dowd, eds, *Crossing the Border: New Relationships between Northern Ireland and the Republic of Ireland*, pp. 31–60. Dublin: Irish Academic Press.

Donnan, Hastings and Wilson, Thomas M. 1999. *Borders: Frontiers of Identity, Nation and State*. Oxford: Berg.

Edensor, Tim. 2002. *National Identity, Popular Culture and Everyday Life*. Oxford: Berg.

Giddens, Anthony. 1987. *The Nation-State and Violence*. Berkeley: University of California Press.

Harmsen, Robert and Wilson, Thomas M., eds. 2000. *Europeanization: Institution, Identities and Citizenship*. Amsterdam: Rodopi.

Held, David. 1995. *Democracy and the Global Order: From the Modern State to Cosmopolitan Governance*. Cambridge: Polity.

Jeffery, Charlie and Palmer, Rosanne. 2007. The European Union, devolution and power. In Alan Trench, ed., *Devolution and Power in the United Kingdom*. Manchester: Manchester University Press.

Keating, Michael. 2004. European Integration and the Nationalities Question. *Politics & Society* 32 (3): 367–388.

Keating, Michael 2010. *The Government of Scotland: Public Policy Making after Devolution*. Edinburgh: Edinburgh University Press.

Kuus, Merje. 2007. *Geopolitics Reframed: Security and Identity in Europe's Eastern Enlargement*. New York: Palgrave Macmillan.

Laffan, Brigid, O'Donnell, Rory and Smith, Michael. 2000. *Europe's Experimental Union: Rethinking Integration*. London: Routledge.

Luckhurst, Tim. 2001. The wit of the Irish. *Spectator* 24: 20–22.

Lynch, Philip and Hopkins, Stephen. 2001. The British-Irish Council: progress frustrated. *Regional Studies* 35 (8): 753–758.

MacClancy, Jeremy. 1996. Sport, identity and ethnicity. In Jeremy MacClancy, ed., *Sport, Identity and Ethnicity*, pp. 1–20. Oxford: Berg.

McCall, Cathal. 2002. From barrier to bridge: reconfiguring the Irish border after the Belfast Good Friday Agreement. *Northern Ireland Legal Quarterly* 53 (4): 479–494.

McCall, Cathal. 2011. Culture and the Irish border: spaces for conflict transformation. *Cooperation and Conflict* 46 (2): 201–221.

McCall, Cathal and O'Dowd, Liam. 2008. Hanging flower baskets, blowing in the wind? Third sector groups, cross-border partnerships and the EU peace programmes in Ireland. *Nationalism and Ethnic Politics* 13 (4): 29–54.

Meehan, Elizabeth. 2000. *Free Movement between Ireland and the UK: From the "common travel area" to the Common Travel Area*. Dublin: Policy Institute.

Mitchell, James. 1998. What could a Scottish Parliament do? In Howard Elcock and Michael Keating, eds, *Remaking the Union: Devolution and British Politics in the 1990s*, pp. 68–83. London: Frank Cass.

Mitchell, James. 2009. *Devolution in the UK*. Manchester: Manchester University Press.

Mlinar, Zdravko. 1992. Individuation and globalization: the transformation of territorial social organization. In Zdravko Mlinar, ed., *Globalization and Territorial Identities*, pp. 15–34. Aldershot: Avebury.

Newman, David. 2006. Borders and bordering: towards an interdisciplinary dialogue. *European Journal of Social Theory* 9 (2): 171–186.

Perkmann, Markus. 1999. Building governance institutions across European borders. *Regional Studies* 33: 657–667.

Pickering, Sharon and Weber, Leanne. 2011. *Borders and Globalization: Deaths at the Global Frontier.* London: Palgrave Macmillan.

Pike, Andy. 2002. Post-devolution blues? Economic development in the Anglo-Scottish borders. *Regional Studies* 36 (9): 1067–1082.

Rokkan, Stein and Urwin, Derek. 1983. *Economy, Territory, Identity: Politics of West European Peripheries.* London: Sage.

Rose, Richard. 1983. *Is the United Kingdom a State?* Glasgow: Centre for the Study of Public Policy.

Scott, James. 1999. European and North American contexts for cross-border regionalism. *Regional Studies* 33 (7): 605–617.

Sørensen, Georg. 1999. Sovereignty: change and continuity in a fundamental institution. *Political Studies* 47: 590–604.

Stiglitz, Joseph E. 2003. *Globalization and Its Discontents.* New York: W.W. Norton.

Travis, Alan. 2009. UK-Irish travellers to face passport checks. Jan. 15. At http://www.guardian.co.uk/uk/2009/jan/15/uk-irish-republic-border-passports (accessed Dec. 20, 2010).

Trench, Alan. 2007a. The framework of devolution: the formal structure of devolved power. In Alan Trench, ed., *Devolution and Power in the United Kingdom,* pp. 48–85. Manchester: Manchester University Press.

Trench, Alan. 2007b. Introduction: territory, devolution and power in the United Kingdom. In Alan Trench, ed., *Devolution and Power in the United Kingdom,* pp. 1–23. Manchester: Manchester University Press.

Vaughan-Williams, Nick. 2009. *Border Politics: The Limits of Sovereign Power.* Edinburgh: Edinburgh University Press.

Vaughan-Williams, Nick. 2010. The UK Border security continuum: virtual biopolitics and the simulation of the sovereign ban. *Environment and Planning D: Society and Space* 28: 1071–1083.

Waever, Ole. 1996. European security identities. *Journal of Common Market Studies* 34 (1): 103–132.

Wallace, William. 1999. The sharing of sovereignty: the European paradox. *Political Studies* 67 (3): 503–521.

Walters, William. 2006. Border/control. *European Journal of Social Theory* 9 (2): 187–203.

Weiss, Linda. 1998. *The Myth of the Powerless State.* Cambridge: Polity.

13 "Swarming" at the Frontiers of France, 1870–1885

Olivier Thomas Kramsch

How is the revolutionary subject to be tensed and spaced out, centered and decentered, sober and drunk, German and French, at one and the same time?

(*Eagleton 1988: ix*)

A Blanquist look at the terrestrial globe: "I contemplate from on high the globe in its rondure,/ and I no longer seek there the shelter of a hut" . . . The poet has made his dwelling in space itself, one could say – or in the abyss.

(*Benjamin 1999: 352*)

Early in the morning of Saturday, March 18, 1871, a crowd of mostly women and children spontaneously left the relative safety of their crowded Parisian apartments and clambered up the hill of the Buttes de Montmartre. Their goal was to prevent the regular national army from seizing assembled rows of cannons to be transported later that day to the government-in-exile in Versailles. An eyewitness at the scene recounted:

> The women and children were swarming up the hill-side in a compact mass; the artillerymen tried in vain to fight their way through the crowd, but the waves of people engulfed everything, surging over the cannon-mounts, over the ammunition wagons, under the wheels, under the horses' feet, paralyzing the action of the riders who spurred on their mounts in vain . . . Like breakers, the first rows of the crowd came crashing on to the batteries, repeatedly flooding them with people . . . The women especially were crying out in fury: "Unharness the horses! Away with you! We want the cannons! We shall have the cannons!" . . . A National Guardsman who had managed to reach the scene of the action climbed on to a milestone and shouted: "Cut the traces!" The crowd let out a great cheer. The women closest to the cannons, to which they had been clinging for half an hour, took the knives that the men passed down to them from hand to hand. They cut through the harnesses. The same National Guardsman now shouted: "Open up the ranks! Spur on the horses! Let them through!" The maneuver was carried

---

A Companion to Border Studies, First Edition. Edited by Thomas M. Wilson and Hastings Donnan.
© 2012 Blackwell Publishing Ltd. Published 2012 by Blackwell Publishing Ltd.

out amid joyful laughter and cheering. The artillerymen . . . were soon won over to the side of the rebels. The cannons had been retaken. The cannons were in the hands of the people (D'Esboeufs, cited in Edwards 1973: 62–63).

The upward, disorderly movement of women and children along the craggy out-croppings of Montmartre's *buttes* in the spring of 1871 prefigured a global border for Europe, the unresolved legacy of which is its lived reality today. Although responding to a quite specific and localized disaster – the Prussian defeat of the French Second Empire at Sedan and the "dishonorable" peace treaty negotiated by the subsequent government of Adolphe Thiers – the experiment in Parisian Communard self-rule ushered in by the retaking of the cannon and its wartime antecedent pro-duced a watershed rupture in the transboundary politics of European nation-states. Within the *longue durée* of "historical capitalism" such a politics had traditionally expressed the sovereign state's capacity and responsibility to control movement across its borders (Wallerstein 1983). Accordingly, the historical role played by European nation-state borders has been to naturalize a division of labor rooted in the separation of an international economic realm on the one hand and a political arena of ostensibly sovereign states on the other. As such, borders are understood to act primarily as the expression of the territoriality of states, constituting the "end point" for any legiti-mately democratic politics (Paasi 1996; Newman and Paasi 1998; Newman 2006). The Prussian threat and the Paris Commune had the effect of temporarily scrambling and denaturalizing these spatial divisions, making their constitutive processes visible again, from the local shop floor outwards into national, "European" and wider impe-rial arenas. This shock and its aftermath set the stage in the last quarter of the nineteenth century for the projection of a double boundary of European rule: an internal "European" borderland clearly demarcating French from German territorial sovereignty following the traumatic loss of Alsace-Lorraine; and an external, French "civilizational" frontier rimming a vast colonial ante-theater: Tunisia, Indochina, Madagascar. Together, these two borderscapes worked to clarify and radiate aspects of European modernity domestically and throughout the world, while reinforcing national cultural differences with metropolitan rivals, primarily England, Germany, Belgium, Netherlands and Italy (Cooper and Stoler 1997).

With the aim of reestablishing order in the wake of France's military defeat and the subsequent anarchy of *Communardisme*, both acts of rebordering, in a dynamic interplay which would soon become a common feature of European metropolitan colonial governance, produced a new space. They also produced new thinking about space in which the ideal of a firmly bounded *Hexagon* free of social strife both inter-nally and with its surrounding neighbors would be complemented by a largely empty and passive *outre-mer*. This had the effect of pushing from view the global overde-termination of Europe's borders, obscuring the constitutive relations linking Europe's internal borders and external frontiers, shunting their multiple interdependencies "underground" and offstage, so as to reassert the purity of nationally centralized authority over internal province and external colony alike.

The spatial legacies of this purification, I argue, haunt the European integration project today, as well as the broader border studies literature which has been a key intellectual "traveling companion." Specifically regarding the latter, three issues in contemporary border studies scholarship may be drawn out for which this chapter constitutes a critical response. First, this contribution seeks to address the increasingly felt need for proper historicization within border studies. Rather than making the facile and timeless claim that "[w]e live in a world of lines and compartments" and that "the basic ordering of society requires categories and compartments, and that borders create order" (Newman 2006: 142; see also van Houtum and van Naerssen 2002), current border scholarship is calling for a revitalized historical lens for understanding the specific orderings brought about by the dense imbrication of nationstates, empires and borders, both in past configurations as well as in terms of their ongoing legacies (O'Dowd 2010). As Anderson and O'Dowd (2007) recall, rather than stand as the "nemesis of imperialism," in many cases imperialism and nationalism directly interacted in competition and in cooperation, and elements of both are embodied in the borders they created. In short, imperialism and nationalism have always been "mutually constitutive" (Anderson and O'Dowd 2007: 935; see also Kramsch 2002; Kramsch and Hooper 2004).

Secondly, a reminder of the historical entanglement of nationalism and imperialism is timely and welcome, as it problematizes assertions made only half a decade ago relating to borders and identities that "most of us retain strong ethnic or national affiliations and loyalties, be they territorial-focused or group affiliations" (Newman 2006: 147). This may be the case in some instances, but this can no longer be taken as a trans-spatial truth; indeed, the experience of empires shows us a complex dialectic between national metropolitan borders and imperial frontiers whose outcome cannot be reduced to the production of a single, national "affiliation" or "loyalty." As this essay shows, the imperial frontier played a transformative role in reshaping the substantive content of core metropolitan states, and actors located below the level of high statecraft played an important role in resetting the terms of engagement across the imperial divide separating national core and colonial periphery (B. Anderson 2005). This chapter thus develops the potential of the "swarm at Montmartre" so as to reconnect what has been sundered by the apparent irreconcilability of nationalizing metropolitan borderlands and their respective imperial frontiers, thereby granting a widened spatial perspective which dovetails with recent attempts to infuse a "cosmopolitan" and "global" dimension to the study of European borders (Rumford 2008; Rovisco 2010).

Finally, much has been made of the fact that 9/11 has reinforced the barrier effect of borders in many parts of the world. For some this has constituted a "paradigm change in the study of borders" (Newman 2006: 149), refocusing attention on the process through which borders can be more tightly controlled (see also Andreas 2003; Brunet-Jailly 2004; Nicol 2005). Border scholars inspired by Foucauldian governmentality approaches have also become fixated on the means by which borders have become the object as well as the agency of heightened surveillance and repression (Walters 2004; Amoore 2006; Salter 2010). What has been lost in these moves, I argue, is a sense that borders and frontiers can become sites not only of discipline and domination but also of political *possibility*.

This "possibility of the border" I explore through the ideas of "vision" and "hiddenness," each of which have their own conceptual genealogies. As Santos (2010) has argued recently, in pursuing the broader goal of tracing imperial boundary change and its political effects "from below," we may need to train greater attention on the epistemological as well as material fractures produced by the "abyssal lines" of an imperial modernity which carved the world into a territorial realm of colonial "reason" and colonized "unreason," producing lines of "visibility" and "invisibility" which continue to charge relations of inequality in the world-system at large. Crucially, this approach, rather than merely serving as a pretext to trace "historical variations in imperial meanings and methods" across various nationalizing contexts (Anderson and O'Dowd 2007: 937), would allow for an exploration of geohistorically specific conjunctures permitting a reenvisioning of boundaries and frontiers as part of wider, emancipatory political projects. In this view, borders, in addition to separating spatio-temporal fissures across the modern colonial divide (itself the product of colonialism's spurious teleologies), could then be linked to an epistemological space from which to open out onto "worlds of borders" (Khatibi 1983; Kramsch and Brambilla 2007; Robinson 2011).

In reenvisioning European metropolitan borders and imperial frontiers thusly, we may draw productively upon a stratagem of following French Communard "outcasts" into the penal tropics of the New Caledonian frontier, their numbers augmenting year by year as the decade of the 1870s lengthened. Contemporaneous debates within the French metropolitan core, both popular and of high statecraft, over the fate of the Communards located 6,000 kilometers away in the Pacific, helped to reshape the national imaginary of the French state in decisive ways. It did so first in an attempt to reestablish the moral foundations for France's regained bourgeois civility at home while projecting its "civilizing mission" overseas. Secondly, in debates over Communard "amnesty," it aided in delineating the contours of national citizenship within the emergent Third Republic. Exploring the impact of the frontier on the French national imagination thus allows for an important practical as well as theoretical depth to frontierspace which would otherwise be lacking in accounts which merely view the frontier as the outer membrane of state territoriality, as mere container of state sovereignty (M. Anderson 1996).

Furthermore, such a move provides a window on the relational dynamics between bordered metropolitan centers and peripheries which can focus analysis on contradictions and surprise reversals in colonial rule, revealing transversal solidarities between metropolitan core and imperial periphery that would otherwise remain under the radar of a reified, scalar and territorial understanding of the border as the "end of the state" or the "end of politics." On the contrary, the experience of the Paris Commune and French penal frontier at New Caledonia, both located within the tight historical window of 1871–1885, is the subject of an intense political process whose outcome is none other than the future shape and constitution of the French Republic.

COMMUNARD BARRICADE: STREETS AND LIVING ROOMS TURNED OUTSIDE/IN AND INSIDE/OUT

Un sentiment de fatigue d'etre Francais; le désir vague d'aller chercher une patrie, ou l'artiste ait sa penseé tranquille et non a tout moment troublé par les stupides agitations, par les convulsions betes d'une tourbe destructive.[1] (Goncourt, cited in Priollaud 1983: 38)

The explosive social space that inaugurated the Paris Commune's brief experiment in self-rule on March 18, 1871 was not entirely unprecedented. According to its protagonists, the term "Commune" itself hearkened self-consciously to the French Revolution, notably Year II (1793), a date invoked by the Communards in the face of Napoleon III's defeat at Sedan (Edwards 1973). But closer antecedents were also easily at hand. In Lyon, silk-workers had risen up in revolt in 1831, followed by further labor unrest again at Lyon and Paris in 1834. The Europe-wide insurrections of 1848 found their pride of place in Paris in June of that same year. But for some close observers such as Marx (1974: 155), the very existence of the Commune represented something entirely unforeseen, a true "invention of the unknown." Marx understood only too well that the historical capacity of the state to detach itself from civil society was achieved through an increasingly fine-meshed social division of labor. That the primary aim of the Commune was to abolish such compartmentalization in order to organize all aspects of social life freely "beyond the state" was seen by him to be one of the most original contributions of the Communard revolt to the nineteenth-century history of social struggle and emancipation.

The Commune, then, represented not just an uprising against Napoleon III's Second Empire but also against all forms of social regimentation. Indeed, the original concern of the Parisian Communards was less about gaining control over the means of production than about targeting those figures – the *curé*, the gendarme, the concierge – responsible for the social classification and policing of everyday life.[2] In the struggle to break down the barriers between social, political, cultural and economic categorization, two figures stand out: poet Arthur Rimbaud and social geographer Élisée Reclus.

For Rimbaud, critique of the bourgeois division of labor was intimately related to the dawning spatiality of European high imperialism. Against the expansive, metric and strategic space of imminent colonial exploration, Rimbaud counterposed a space marked by flight, affect and latent event (Steinmetz 2001). Through this gesture, Rimbaud is a European who "becomes African" at the threshold of Europe's civilizing mission. His goal was "devenir-bete," "devenir-negre":

Oui, j'ai les yeux fermés a votre lumière. Je suis une bete, un negre. Mais je puis etre sauvé. Vous etes de faux negres, vous maniaques, féroces, avares. Marchand, tu est negre; magistrate, tu es negre; general, tu es negre; empereur, vieille démangeaison, tu es negre . . . Le plus malin est de quitter ce continent, ou la folie rode.[3] (Rimbaud 1932: 87)

Rimbaud's immediate target would be those poets of the Parnassian School who attempted to impose an order on the anxious and turbulent world of rapid urbanization and industrialization. This they would attempt to do by reverting to a form of poetic "landscapism" in which space was proposed as a natural referent, devoid of conflict and history. Towards this stance Rimbaud would respond caustically that the Parnassians merely "describe what they see" (Derfler 1998: 89). For the young rebel-artist, such a poetics revealed an underlying elitism and racism. Concerned with the disorienting effects of modernity notwithstanding, Parnassians only succeeded in reproducing in their texts the boundary-reinforcing relations of a rapidly nationalizing identity which they mistook as paradigmatic sign of their times. As a "bastard," border-crossing figure of displacement and vagabondage, Rimbaud's reply to the dualistic social constructions of his day would be succinctly put: "Je est un autre" (1932: 90).

The "empty" landscapes of Parnassian poetry would find their analogue in the emergence of "university geography" in France, embodied by the central figure of Paul Vidal de la Blache. Enamored with the "science of objective space," de la Blache set himself the task after the French defeat of 1870 of crafting a "spatial history" that defined landscapes as natural physical referents located within an immemorial time drained of historicity (Vidal de la Blache 1917). Such a static spatial imaginary would be imposed both on the internal domestic *pays* of France as well as on its overseas colonial dominions, enclosing both within the amber of a timeless time in which any form of contestation or struggle was eviscerated. As with Rimbaud's reaction to the Parnassians, the rise of Vidalian geography in France was viewed as anathema to the anarchist geographer Elisée Reclus. Reclus's political life as well as professional geographical commitments were both deeply marked by his active participation in the Paris Commune (B. Anderson 2005). He was an active participant in the quarrel that led to the break between Marx and Bakunin in 1872, while defending anarcho-communist ideals in articles published in *Le Révolté* and *La Liberté*. Proposing that "geography is nothing but history in space," Reclus (1905–1908: 335) was the first to refer to the term "social geography" as a replacement for the Vidalian notion of "landscape." Attentive to the power geometries binding empires, states and peoples, across a range of work spanning decades, Reclus, in a direct challenge to Vidal de la Blache, came to view space as a deeply social product.

In confounding the natural boundaries between poetic Self and exteriorized Other, "social" and "landscape" geographies, Rimbaud and Reclus expressed late nineteenth-century forms of spatial thinking rooted in a perspective which aimed to dissolve the privileged notion of space as a natural and nonhistorical referent, one in which alterity was eliminated. These vibrant spatial imaginaries constituted real threats to those like the Parnassian Catulle Mendes, who, in his private journal *Les 73 journées de la Commune* (1871), objected to the kind of varied activity expressed by someone "who can make excellent boots like Napoléon Gaillard, or paintings as good as Gustave Courbet's" (1871: 166). Mendes was here concerned primarily with the *bel ouvrage*, and its imminent demise in a topsy-turvy world where boot-makers become painters and painters boot-makers.

But the genius of the Commune lay precisely in its ability to destabilize the idea of "proper métier" or "proper place" in favor of a permanent exchange between sites, places, streets and neighborhoods. Of paramount importance here, recognized by Henri Lefebvre's tribute in the next century, was the local *quartier*, whose autonomy and self-governing capacity was strengthened in the absence of central state authority. At the height of the Commune's resistance to the forces of reaction represented by the army of Adolphe Thiers, the street barricade became the most poignant architectural expression of the Communard experiment in displacement. In his *Mémoires*,

Gustave-Paul Cluseret, the Commune's first Delegate of War, explained that the barricade had to be built as quickly as possible, in contrast to the unique, well-situated and centralized civic monument whose power derived from its isolation and stability. Barricades, for Cluseret, were not meant to have a unique and "proper place," as they were produced through a *bricolage* of "overturned carriages, doors torn off their hinges, furniture thrown out of windows, cobblestones where these are available, beams, barrels, etc. (Cluseret 1887: 274–287).

As the Paris Commune's grand old man Auguste Blanqui made clear in his *Instructions pour une prise d'armes* of 1868 (Blanqui 2000a), the immediate function of the barricades was to prevent the free circulation of enemy troops throughout the city. Complementing the barricade's effects, Blanqui described a strategy involving the "lateral piercing of houses," in which Communard troops gutted adjoining rows of apartments in such a way that insurgents could move freely in all directions, along passageways and networks, rendering the enemy stationary and vulnerable. In this way, according to Blanquian strategy, unlike the experiences of 1830 and 1848, Communard combatants could remain "out of sight and out of reach of the enemy" (2000a: 109). Barricade fighting would take place "from the windows" of adjacent houses. Thus "out of sight," within urban neighborhood enclaves whose grand nineteenth-century facades enclosed laboratories of autonomous governance purposefully erected on the model of Fourierist phalansteries, a space of hiddenness is inaugurated in European modernity, whereby the Communard barricade-border, acting more than a device for military separation and defense, produced the outer membrane of self-created *border worlds* (Kramsch and Dimitrovova 2008).[4]

It is perhaps one of the more moving ironies of European history that the lineaments of such a worldly borderspace (*espace frontière-monde*) would itself have been secreted within the most constrained and confined space imaginable: an island prison located several kilometers off the shores of Britanny. On May 17, one day before the dramatic events on the hills of Montmartre, Blanqui was arrested and transported to Le Fort du Taureau. Forbidden from "seeing the ocean" that surrounded him, cut off from the revolutionary developments on the mainland, Blanqui sat down to the task of writing what we might call in hindsight a manual in political astrology. Originally penned as a reply to certain scientific theories of the contemporaneous astrologer Laplace, *l'Éternité par les astres* of 1871 (Blanqui 2000b) is a text of hallucinatory power, a redemptive meditation on space-time in which the failure of the experiment in Communard self-rule, subsequent state repression and imperial rebordering are anticipated and then deftly sublimated by way of reflection on the state of the universe and the movement of the stars. As the title of the book, eternity via the stars, suggests, *l'Éternité* addresses the nature of the universe as infinite and eternal space:

> The universe is infinite in time and space, eternal, without restrictions and indivisible . . . [L]et's admit for an instance the existence of [a] surface, that finds itself the limit of the world. This limit, shall it be solid-liquid, or gaseous? Whatever its nature, it immediately becomes the prolongation of what it contains or purports to contain. Let us assume that on this score there exists neither a solid, nor a liquid, nor gas, not even ether. Nothing but empty and black space. This space does not lack three dimensions, and would necessarily have as a limit what would be called continuation, another portion

of space of the same nature, and then after that, another, then again another, and so on, *indefinitely*. (Blanqui 2000b: 231–233, author's translation)

Here, in what Walter Benjamin (1999: 111, 352) would later affirm as Blanqui's attempt to "open new doors in his dungeon," to make "his dwelling in space itself," the old revolutionary would conjure the central themes of a frontier politics that reverberates into our day as with the flash of an "illumination": the limit of a "world" (*monde*) serving not only as a barrier but as a spatio-temporal hinge opening onto other "worlds"; the indeterminacy and ambiguity of all spatial demarcations, caught between an "infinite" universalism and the arbitrary particularity of all set lines; and, finally, in his long rumination on comets, the movement of "astral" material preventing the "stasis and glaciation" of the world, as bearing newness by way of their "inconsistency, and . . . vagabond habits" (Blanqui 2000b: 271). Of comets, Blanqui argued:

> Are they not rather captive supplicants, chained for centuries to the barriers of our atmosphere, and demanding in vain either liberty or hospitality? From its first to last ray [of light], the intertropical sun shows us these pale Bohemians, who pay so brutally for their indiscreet visitation to established society. Comets are veritable fantastic beings . . . Our world in particular is gorged with them, and yet, more than half escape from sight, even from the telescope. How many of these nomads have chosen residence among us? . . . One of these days, they will raise up their legs and will go join their numberless tribes in the imaginary spaces. (1871: 260–261, author's translation)

Blanqui's spatial syntax would be prescient, anticipating the defeat of the Communard experiment in worker self-rule,[5] the brutal reinscription of spatial divisions of labor within core European nation-states, matched by a tense standoff along the Rhineland border between France and the newly minted German state, and the deportation of Communard "vagabonds" – "pale Bohemians" all – to the penal colonies of Guyana and New Caledonia, where they were to be rehabilitated through hard labor. It is here, on Europe's proto-imperial overseas frontier, where the barricade logic of being "out of sight and out of reach" would reveal its truly "worldly" dimension.

For, in what we might productively describe as the "explosion" of the urban barricade-as-border out into global-imperial space, a secondary border zone for France is created, one that complements the firmly nationalizing internal borders of the French *Hexagon* with that of a fluid frontier located in the Pacific Ocean, some 6,000 kilometers from the French capital. As its internal logic would serve as a dress rehearsal for full-blown colonial expansion over the coming years in Tunisia, Indochina and Madagascar, the New Caledonian penal frontier would crystallize a contradictory space for France. In this arena, the goals of universal self-improvement and moral reform of Communard prisoners would clash with the extreme physical hardship of locally enforced labor, often carried out with local indigenous Kanak populations.

At stake in this frontier penal experiment would be the crafting of a renewed bourgeois-civil order for the French nation, as well as a complementarily reenergized overseas civilizing mission. As with the Parisian urban barricade, however, the spatial distance separating frontier penal colony from European metropole would produce its own space of "hiddenness" far removed from the socially regimented world of French metropolitan society, a quality which allowed for the (not unproblematical) re-negotiation of identities, particularly between French Communard and Kanak. Moreover, as the object of heated legislative debate in the French National Assembly over the decade of the 1870s–1880s in relation to the issue of amnesty and repatriation of political prisoners, the activities of the exiled ex-Communards and their metropolitan interlocutors actively succeeded in reshaping the Republican nature of the emergent Third Republic in ways that demonstrated the highly ambiguous political dimension of bordering practices within the European imperial theater.

THE MORAL REHABILITATION OF VAGABONDAGE ON THE NEW CALEDONIAN FRONTIER

> Is it really to troublemakers that we should confide the mission of communicating the lights of our civilization? (Faucher, cited in Bullard 2000: 138)

The Franco-German borderland, site of defeat for the Second Gallic Republic, would haunt the French imperial enterprise in the years to come. In the last quarter of the nineteenth century, political life in France would be riven to one degree or another by two opposing tendencies: the one set on the path of revenge against Germany, the other swept up in the civilizing mission of overseas colonial rule. Both geopolitical orientations embodied discrepant and partly overlapping bordering logics, as the former was tied to regaining and protecting lost territory and maintaining a "peaceful" export-orientated social division of labor, while the latter involved the establishment of a mobile frontier charged with the task of radiating France's universal values throughout the world. The ideal of a uniquely French "civilizational morality," however, would connect both internal and external borderlands in a complex web of interdependence.

The contrapuntal dynamic linking internal/external bordering tendencies found their initial expression not in the colonization of fresh territories but in the population of the existing French overseas penal archipelago. France, of course, had established penal colonies in the decades prior to the Third Republic of Jules Ferry, but on an institutional level they came into full maturity only with the arrival of thousands of ex-Communard prisoners on the extraterritorial islands of French Guyana, off the coast of Venezuela, and New Caledonia, in the Pacific Ocean. In particular, the deportation of 4,500 Communards to New Caledonia figured prominently in the Third Republic's moral regeneration of France. Already in the waning days of the Commune, the military actions of Thiers and his Versailles troops had been widely perceived as a "social cleaning" of Paris (Bullard 2000: 67). In preparing for the mass deportations to come, the governments of Thiers and Ferry designated the Communards as "savages," thus placing them outside both the legal and moral boundaries of civilized society. In this way, the Communard "savage within" would be seen as a primary threat to *la cité morale*, an element that had to be returned to a state of nature "beyond politics" (Bullard 2000: 73).

But in the context of the wider French civilizing mission, the deported Communards, considered "savages" in the metropole, were burdened with the paradoxical
task of "civilizing" the local indigenous population, the Kanak, on the New Caledonian islands of Nouméa and Isles des Pins. In order to do so, the Communard
prisoners would have themselves to undergo a moral regeneration, requiring not just
a change in political convictions and desires but a profound reorientation of the
soul in relation to good and evil (Bullard 2000: 93). This, it was hoped, would be
achieved by virtue of the overwhelming moral force of nature surrounding the penal
colony. Here, the influence of Vidalian "landscape" geography would be made
apparent, as it was believed that the natural physical contours of the environment,
reshaped through hard labor, would prove sufficient to rehabilitate Communard and
Kanak alike.

Through the enforced deportation of Communard prisoners half a world away
from the French metropole, hopes for the moral regeneration of French society, the
rehabilitation of internal "savagery" and the expansion of the French nation into
the southwest Pacific would be neatly bundled into a single overarching rationale.
Such an orientalizing of the tropical frontier would require a teleological collapsing
of "difference into space" (Gregory 1995). But it also signified a qualitatively
novel production of space, one marked not by a Benthamite order of surveillance,
vision and transparency characteristic of the metropole but by a redemptive "hiddenness" and partial invisibility located in lands as yet "unseen and unknown" by
Europeans.

The interplay between (en)lightened national metropolitan borderland and only
partially visible colonial frontier would generate a space of contradiction between
seemingly opposed principles – bourgeois/convict, political/common criminal,
liberty/reform, settled/deported, inside/outside, civilized/uncivilized. As a key
characteristic of the penal colony, partial invisibility would in turn spur the development of a border praxis which grasped these antinomies not as fixed and static entities
but as a ceaselessly mobile "swarming" whose terms could only be resolved by the
creative "coming into hiding" of Communard and Kanak alike (Bull 1999). The
contradictory rationality of French rule in New Caledonia would therefore be productive not only of a foundational paradox in the governance of modern interstate
borders but would generate the very resources for those oppositional strategies
seeking to transcend the bordered dualities it set in motion.

The ambiguities of this frontier modernity were plain enough to the Communard
déportés. Though banished from the territory of the *Hexagon*, ex-Communard prisoners were expected to assume all the obligations and burdens of French citizenship,
especially in the realm of employment. Toward this end the French government
provided prisoners with food, shelter and medical care, in addition to subsidized
concessionaires, either as land to be farmed, the right to practice a trade or profession
or run a shop. The ultimate goal would be to transform the prison population on
New Caledonia into self-governing communities on the basis of a pastoral ideal
(Bullard 2000). Through "work, civilization, and patriotism," ex-Communards were
thus offered the chance to regain their ties to a civil society from which they had
sundered themselves through revolutionary activities. Yet given that only a small
minority of Communards were condemned to enforced labor, the question arose

among penal administrators as to the best way to induce the Communards to colonize New Caledonia according to the agricultural model they had envisioned. As political prisoners, most *déportés* could only be "encouraged" to colonize; they could not be forced to do so. In a cunning ruse of space, d'Haussonville and his committee on deportation would come to pose on the French imperial frontier the same question that had vexed the Communards standing sentry at their Parisian barricades a few years earlier: "What is the basis of all society?" (cited in Bullard 2000: 129). For d'Haussonville the answer was self-evident: "[P]roperty and family: without property and without family, no civilization is possible" (Bullard 2000: 129).

Civilized domestication of the New Caledonian outback began in earnest when the National Assembly passed legislation granting wives a much greater right to property in the penal colony than they had been allowed under French common law. Under a system of specially devised land grants, the wives of ex-Communards were entitled to one-half the property rights of their husbands. By 1874 fifty-seven families had been reunited under the provisions of the new law, followed by 165 families the year after and 174 families by 1877 (Bullard 2000: 130). But the experiment in family-settler colonization proved short lived, as the agricultural ideal envisioned by penal administrators grated sharply against the harsh realities of penal life. Indeed, the French government's original perception of the Isle of Pines as well as Grande Terre as extensive nature was grossly mistaken, as the presence of a large Kanak indigenous community would prove. The dense overcrowding of penal colony lands further belied the pastoral ideal, as did French fears of a landscape associated with wild savages and uncontrollable criminals (Bullock 2000: 138). The resulting gap between the ideal and practice of the French penal system on New Caledonia would prove the ultimate undoing of a "designed wildness" which could not bear the weight of the tension between the logic of humanitarian reform and retributive punishment on the islands (Bullard 2000: 138-39). The spectacular and much publicized escape of the journalist Henri Rochefort and companions on 19 March 1874, signaled the demise of the French colonial idyll and the reassertion of a much more repressive policy of penal discipline.

"CONFUSIONS" ON ISLES DES PINS, OR THE RIGHT TO GO NATIVE

[W]e are still savages ourselves. (Michel, cited in Maclellan 2006: 74)

Despite the attempts of penal administrators to enforce discipline on the islands in the wake of Rochefort's escape, the Communard *déportés* located on the Isles des Pins created the "stimulus of a little confusion" on the French penal colony (Soja 1996: 280). Part of this state of affairs was self-inflicted; the French penal system had already partially erased the boundaries separating "civilized" *colon* and Kanak "savage" by allowing the latter to hunt down and beat recalcitrant White prisoners, a move which represented a radical racial inversion of the natural social order on the islands (Bullard 2000: 230). The confusion soon deepened, however, as the Governor of New Caledonia complained that the Kanak could no longer distinguish between potentially untrustworthy former convicts and "*colon libres.*" This was troubling for the governor, who in a letter to the Ministry of the Marine on 15 October 1872 complained that unsupervised former convicts "lived in the middle of the indigenous people, adopted their mores, or at least took on those which were agreeable, polyg-amy for example." Such a mixing of populations threatened "civilized order" (cited in Bullard 2000: 138).

For a large segment of the convict population, this disorienting miscegenation was experienced as a fear of "becoming savage." In letters to his mother and sister in France, *déporté* Henri Messager wrote, unwittingly echoing Rimbaud, "[W]e're becoming Kanak here, what do you want? . . . All about one sees the reign of the most profound boredom, which every three or four days, at payday or when post-checks arrive, changes into an orgy" (Messager 1979: 320-21). Ironically, men such as Messager repudiated Lafargue's Communard ethos and embraced precisely that pastoral dream envisioned for them by the French penal administration.

But as the eight-month Kanak insurrection of 1878 gained ground, many Com-munards demonstrated a more ambivalent attitude towards the "civilizing mission" of the French state in New Caledonia. Drawing obvious parallels between the repres-sion of Paris in 1871 and the crushing of the Kanak rebellion of 1878, prisoners developed active sympathies with their indigenous neighbors. Communards Achille Balliere and Francois Jourde, for instance, visited Kanak homes, where they dined and played with their children. Moreover, men such as Balliere actively sought out Kanak women; at least two marriages between a Communard and a Kanak were proposed within the first year of deportation alone (Bullard 2000: 201). Such mixed Euro-Asian marriages belied the strict separation of European and Kanak on the islands; the "Kanak" included large numbers of children with partly European parent-age, just as many "whites" were frequently of mixed ancestry. Colonial *creolization* became more pronounced with the arrival in 1871 of exiled Kabyle prisoners who had fought against French imperial rule in Algeria. Settling in the Nessadiou valley near Bourail, most remained in New Caledonia, eventually integrating completely into the island's European community. At the Nessadiou pass there is still to be found a *cimetière arabe.*

But the ties between European and Kanak were more than familial. Contrary to those *déportés* who purportedly died or went mad with "nostalgia" for France, and taking advantage of that "distance" from the metropole from which other comrades suffered, Louise Michel directed a school for the Kanak and became such a trusted confidante that she offered moral support to several young Kanak as they took part in the 1878 uprising (Bullard 2000: 201). In her memoirs of this period she wrote "I wondered which of us was the superior being . . . the one who assimilates foreign knowledge through a thousand difficulties for the sake of his race, or the well-armed white who annihilates those who are less well armed" (Michel, cited in Maclellan 2006: 128).

Produced "in hiding," Michel's scientific humanism would stand in counterpoint to a racially-tinged humanitarian discourse emanating from the French metropole. Despite the realities of colonial hybridity on the French imperial frontier, the French World Exhibitions of 1867 and 1878 solidified the image of the Kanak as lazy, dis-trustful and cannibalistic "earth animals" (Kircher 1986). Such distorted images of the Kanak on view in the French *Hexagon* would generate a counter-discourse of tolerance and human rights, one which paradoxically required a dehumanization of the Kanak in order for them to receive the enlightened benefits of civilization. Thus, as the boundaries between French citizen and Kanak hardened in the colonial metropole, they paradoxically softened and blurred on the imperial frontier, producing anxieties in the core regarding the nature and direction of national priorities in the context of France's wider overseas engagements.

"No One Answers Because There Is Nothing to Answer": The Issue of Amnesty

Acts of boundary blurring, whether in the French metropole or colonial antipodes, could also be used for conservative purposes, as illustrated by the fact that the precise legal status of the deported Communards remained a contested issue until the very end of the nineteenth century. That ex-Communards were so easily lumped together by penal administrators within the category of common criminals indicated one aspect of the domestic effort to de-politicize the period of the Commune as an aberrant rupture devoid of social or economic foundations. By rendering the boundaries between political and common crimes indistinguishable, the French penal system thus prepared the ground for conflicts that would afflict the national imaginary at century's end, notably during the Dreyfus Affaire. Anti-colonial activists and Communard sympathizers throughout Europe, on the other hand, worked hard to maintain the conceptual distinctions between the two categories of prisoners. The Belgian and British Internationals, for instance, declared the Communards "political men," embraced the Commune itself as "worthy as a great achievement of humanity" and pronounced that its members deserved "the right to the sympathy and respect of all brave men" (cited in Bullard 2000: 78).

The controversy that raged over the status of the Communards located thousands of kilometers from the metropole took on its most acute form in legislative discussions concerning the granting of amnesty to the *déportés*. In this we can observe the role of France's overseas penal frontier in inflecting the nature and direction of French re-nationalizing tendencies in the final decades of the nineteenth century. And it is in the political rhetoric for and against Communard amnesty in as far-flung places as Guyana and New Caledonia that we may trace the glimmering of a contrary process of re-bordering in which not only different views of the proper French imperial subject are invoked but also the very terms of national reconciliation. In a pattern that would repeat itself into the next century, efforts to expand the frontiers of bourgeois civic virtue to include a greater number of the dispossessed would only serve to produce greater societal tensions and rifts, as the partiality, arbitrariness and essentially reactionary nature of instituted boundaries would become increasingly visible both to domestic as well as overseas publics.

On 13 September 1871, barely four months after the failed uprising, radical Republicans in the National Assembly presented a motion calling for the amnesty of ex-Communards. Written by Henri Brisson and signed by 48 members of the opposition, the motion was to include all "condemned or prosecuted for political crimes or lesser offenses, at Paris and in the provinces, during the past year" (Joughin 1955: 68). No action was taken on this and subsequently similar motions for months. Meanwhile, the National Assembly busied itself with quashing the last domestic traces of Communard radicalism: all revolutionary sites were placed under martial law; the International Workingman's Association (IWA) was outlawed; and an investigation was begun into the causes of the Commune (Joughin 1955). Regarding the latter, the findings of a thirty-man commission under Comte Daru targeted Socialism as the primary offender, along with universal suffrage, popular sovereignty, freedom of the press and public education.

Despite the vigorous response to the events of the Commune in France, threats to the conservative model of republican rule persisted just across France's internal borders. London and Switzerland would quickly become safe havens for ex-Communards, who would busy themselves in publishing pro-Communard tracts and newspapers, to be then smuggled across French lines (Anderson 2005). In London, the support of Bakunin's Jurassian Federation would prove crucial in this effort (Joughin 1955: 84–85). The broader Communard diaspora in Europe would also receive moral energy from fellow ex-Communard and geographer Elisée Reclus, exiled in Lugano. In his public statements Reclus refused to think of himself as separate from the totality of the condemned men of the Commune. Indeed, the deported Communards, "hidden" from public view half a world away, impressed themselves deeply on the conscience of the European Communard diaspora, while unsettling the virtuous pieties of the conservative members of the National Assembly.

In the Spring of 1874, the Jurassian Federation opened a permanent subscription for the men and women deported to New Caledonia. In this task, Reclus was charged with getting money to the deportees, and when no longer capable he entrusted a fellow ex-Communard to send funds through a friend in London (Joughin 1955: 86). In three years, 6,000 francs were collected from refugees in Belgium, Switzerland and the United States. The dreadful condition of the deportees strengthened the bonds between the European exiles and pushed them to political action. In September 1875, a group of Swiss exiles, hoping to reawaken the conscience of the French proletariat, published a collection of letters from the "living dead at Noumea" (Joughin 1955: 86). The preface, attributed to Reclus, revealed the horrendous conditions at New Caledonia and stated "we are proud that we – we ourselves – are as one with these men" (Reclus, cited in Joughin 1955: 87).

Within conservative Republican circles, such solidarity would be countered by the belief that only by dealing with each Communard individually would it be possible to consider leniency under the terms of a pardon. In such a way, they believed the Republican values of universal and legal due process would be upheld, and the political crime of the Commune treated as a criminal one, to be adjudicated on a case by case basis. It is only from this position, they concurred, that one might expect ex-Communards to return to France and become reintegrated into French society. Towards this end, in June 1871 a Commission on Pardons was established to enable the Chief of the Executive Power to pardon the Communards at New Caledonia. Legislation defending the right of the Commission to pardon Communards individually was also shored up by government policies aimed at reviewing appeals, pardons and the reduction of sentences (Joughin 1955: 88).

Sympathetic to the cause of amnesty, Victor Hugo, a delegate to the Paris Municipal Council, published a letter in which he characterized Paris as a city martyred for her patriotism. For her heroic resistance against the Prussians, she had received only insults, he declared. But in 1876, Paris was asking "nothing for herself, everything for the country" (Hugo, cited in Joughin 1955: 93). In calling for amnesty, Hugo invited the electors of the Senate to "Create . . . a Republic to be desired, a Republic without martial law, without muzzles, without exiles, without political prisons, without a military yoke, without a clerical yoke, a Republic of truth and liberty" (Hugo 1876: 13–15).

Partially as a result of Hugo's intervention, debate over the destiny of men deported half a world away would have a significant influence in shaping the political discourse over the type of desired French republic at "home." The pressures of the amnesty question would soon impinge on legislative elections to the Chamber in the mid-1870s. Émile Acollas, whom the Commune had named Professor of Law *in absentia* while he was living in Switzerland, campaigned actively for a blanket amnesty. But the precise terms of this national "conciliation," hinging as it did on divergent and conflicting views over the status of the men to be returned to *la metropole*, was not to be made any clearer despite the demise of the monarchist-orientated National Assembly and fresh electoral victories by more moderate Republican candidates. As long as the amnesty question festered unresolved, the possibilities of achieving any lasting reconciliation appeared remote.

As the transport vessel *La Loire*, packed with new deportees bound for New Caledonia, chugged out to sea in March 1876, the journalist Gabriel Deville, in an article entitled "Amnesty and the center-left," argued that no political progress would be forthcoming as long as the Communards – "whose only crime was to think differently from those who govern us, whose great wrong was not to have succeeded" (Deville, cited in Joughin 1955: 101) – continued in their suffering. For Deville, the men of the Commune did not need a pardon, as a distinction had to be made between "political crimes" and "common law crimes." Blurring them, he claimed, had made possible the space of New Caledonia as a location for the arbitrary application of French governmental power. For Deville everyone must be amnestied, since there was no such thing as a common law crime under the Commune's reign:

In his desire for a full amnesty, Deville was joined by George Clemenceau, Édouard Lockroy and Olivier Ordinaire. But Léon Gambetta, President of the Chamber of Deputies, fearing that an unconditional amnesty would plunge the country into a prolonged crisis, struck a tone whose ambivalence reaffirmed the internal borders of the Republic, claiming: "No sacrifice will be made either to prejudice or to fear; no sacrifice will be made to the detriment of law, order, and public peace" (Gambetta, cited in Joughin 1955: 106).

In the Senate Chamber on May 22, 1877, after hearing the praises of the Commission on Pardons and the President of the Republic, Victor Hugo stood up and in a profound silence read a lengthy prepared speech, in which he argued that an amnesty ought to be voted because of justice and pity, and because of reasons of state. When he was finished, no one rose to reply. A voice called out: "No one answers because there is nothing to answer" (Raspail 1876: 30).

"Swarming" Borders, "Swarming" Border Studies

Exiled to the French penal archipelago, political prisoners at the end of the nineteenth century were routinely prohibited from looking at the sea from the windows of their cold and stony cells. This seemingly trivial datum is significant, for through this injunction the all-seeing eye of the modern French state sought to deprive revolutionary men such as Blanqui (and later in the century, Albert Dreyfus, deported to Isle du Diable, French Guyana) *the possibility of hope*. But as Blanqui intuited from his Breton island outpost, the power of the state to impose its governmentalizing vision, both within the firmly bounded nationalizing metropole and on its multiple carceral frontiers, was limited, riven with contradictions, and ultimately self-defeating. This is so, he argued, due to the inherent indefiniteness (*l'indéfini*) of all frontiers and boundaries, defined by the "manifest impossibility of locating or of conceiving a limit to space" (Blanqui 2000b: 233).

We may forgive Blanqui's "astral excesses," but from France's loss of an internal territorial borderland to Prussia at Sedan, the failure of the "Communard barricade" to shore up a utopian political project "beyond the state," and the contradictory experience of Communard *déportés* in New Caledonia we may deduce the lineaments of a dialectic linking an internal European borderland and an external frontier whose ambiguous and contradictory logics continue to resonate in our day. For this double-border dynamic to become manifest, I have argued, we must depart from the current fixation of border studies on clearly defined state sovereignty and territoriality as the only relevant parameters for understanding how borders function and change. This requires undertaking an equally serious examination of the ways in which geohistorically constituted frontiers have produced recursive effects on the nationalizing spatial imaginaries of states, through processes of transboundary interaction that have often occurred "in hiding," at the very limits of state visibility.

This insight addresses not only some of the epistemological blindspots of state-centric social science, but opens up a space of postcolonial "swarming" within border studies, one which could help refocus historical attention on the tensions and reversals in European transboundary rule, holding its internal borders and external frontiers within the same analytical frame. As foreshadowed by the "swarm at Montmartre," such a frame was able to convey the way in which under the Third Republic a project was undertaken to "naturalize" the penal frontier so as to reestablish the metropolitan core as a firmly bounded space of moral regeneration and bourgeois civility, only to have this clean division of "Us/Them" founder against the realities of Communard/Kanak allegiance on the Isles des Pins.

In similar fashion, as observed in French parliamentary debates over the issue of "amnesty," attempts to lump Communard prisoners together with common criminals ran against a swarm of opposition – unseen, beyond the borders of the *Hexagon* – from internationalists bent on preserving the ideal of a French Republic in which one's political convictions remained exempt from judicial scrutiny. In so doing, the relational geographies linking metropolitan borderlands and imperial frontiers reveal transboundary solidarities and alliances – spaces of "border possibility" – that would otherwise have remained invisible within an exclusively territorial narrative of the border defined as the "end of the state" or the "end of politics." "Swarming" at the frontiers of France, we may therefore join Blanqui (2000b: 260–261) in positing future worlds of "swarming border studies," whose flaring "comets . . . raise up their legs and . . . go join their numberless tribes in the imaginary spaces."

NOTES

1   "A feeling of tiredness being French: the vague desire to go look for a home country, where the artist has his tranquility, and not at every moment disturbed by stupid agitations, by the idiotic convulsions of a destructive mob" (author's translation).
2   In the famous Communard debating clubs that sprang up like mushrooms throughout Paris during this time, discussion over the banning of night-time work for bakers would exemplify this "antidiscipline" (Edwards 1973).
3   "Yes, I have my eyes closed at your light. I am an animal, a Black. But I can be saved. You are false Blacks, you ferocious, greedy maniacs. Merchant, you are a Black; magistrate, you are a Black; general, you are a Black; emperor, you old itchy brute, you are a Black . . . The most clever thing to do is leave this continent where madness reigns" (author's translation).
4   Kristin Ross locates the "emergence of social space" in the late nineteenth century at that very moment when the French National Guard topples the imperial-age column established by Napoleon III at the Place Vendôme, May 20, 1871 (Ross 1988). With respect to the proto-geography of European bordering strategies and counterstrategies, I situate this inaugural moment instead in a much less spectacular but for that matter no less vital space: the inverted world of the barricade-*monde* (barricade-world).
5   In the months that followed, the Communard "swarm" would be dealt with harshly by the government of Thiers, as in the last weeks of the uprising an estimated 25,000–30,000 Parisians were executed in the streets of the capital. Delescluze, that "old hyena," was shot beside a barricade, while it was surmised that Commissioner of Public Safety Félix Pyatt succeeded in stowing himself away in one of the balloons that were seen in the sky the day Versailles troops entered Paris (Priollaud 1983).

REFERENCES

Amoore, Louise. 2006. Biometric borders: governing mobilities in the war on terror. *Political Geography* 25 (3): 336–351.

Anderson, Benedict. 2005. *Under Three Flags: Anarchism and the Anti-colonial Imagination*. London: Verso.

Anderson, James and O'Dowd, Liam. 2007. Imperialism and nationalism: the Home Rule struggle and border creation in Ireland, 1885–1925. *Political Geography* 26: 934–950.

Anderson, Malcolm. 1996. *Frontiers: Territory and State Formation in the Modern World*. Cambridge: Polity.

Andreas, Peter. 2003. Redrawing the line: border security in the 21st century. *International Security* 28 (2): 78–111.

Benjamin, Walter. 1999. *The Arcades Project*. Cambridge: Belknap Press.

Blanqui, Auguste. 2000a. *Instructions pour une prise d'armes*. In *Instructions pour une prise d'armes; L'éternité par les astres, hypothèse astronomique; et autres textes*. Paris: Sens & Tonka. First publ. 1868.

Blanqui, Auguste. 2000b. L'éternité par les astres, hypothèse astronomique. In *Instructions pour une prise d'armes; L'éternité par les astres, hypothèse astronomique; et autres textes*. Paris: Sens & Tonka. First publ. 1871.

Brunet-Jailly, Emmanuel. 2004. NAFTA, economic integration and the Canadian-American security regime in the post-September 11 era. *Journal of Borderland Studies* 19: 71–93.

Bull, Malcolm. 1999. *Seeing Things Hidden: Apocalypse, Vision and Totality*. London: Verso.

Bullard, Alice. 2000. *Exile to Paradise: Savagery and Civilization in Paris and the South Pacific, 1790–1900*. Stanford: Stanford University Press.

Cooper, Frederick and Stoler, Anne Laura. 1997. *Tensions of Empire: Colonial Cultures in a Bourgeois World*. Berkeley: University of California Press.

Cluseret, Gustave-Paul. 1887. *Mémoires du General Cluseret*, vol. 3. Paris: Jules Levy.

Derfler, Leslie. 1998. *Paul Lafargue and the Flowering of French Socialism, 1882–1911*. Cambridge: Harvard University Press.

Eagleton, Terry. 1988. Foreword. In *Kristin Ross, The Emergence of Social Space: Rimbaud and the Paris Commune*. Minneapolis: University of Minnesota Press.

Edwards, Stewart. 1973. *The Communards of Paris, 1871*. London: Thames & Hudson.

Gregory, Derek. 1995. Between the book and the lamp: imaginative geographies of Egypt, 1849–50, *Transactions of the Institute of British Geographers* 20 (1): 29–57.

Hugo, Victor. 1876. *Lettre de Victor Hugo, le délégué de Paris, aux délégués des 36,000 communes de France*. Paris.

Joughin, Jean T. 1955. *The Paris Commune in French Politics, 1871–1880: The History of the Amnesty of 1880*, vol. 1. Baltimore: Johns Hopkins Press.

Khatibi, Abdelkebir. 1983. *Maghreb pluriel*. Paris: Denoel.

Kircher, Ingrid A. 1986. *The Kanaks of New Caledonia*. London: Minority Rights Group.

Kramsch, Olivier. 2002. Re-imagining the scalar topologies of cross-border governance: eu(ro)regions in the post-colonial present. *Space and Polity* 6 (2): 169–196.

Kramsch, Olivier and Brambilla, Chiara. 2007. Transboundary Europe through a West African looking glass: cross-border integration, "colonial difference" and the chance for "border thinking." *Comparativ* 17 (4): 95–115.

Kramsch, Olivier and Dimitrovova, Bohdana. 2008. T.H. Marshall at the limit: hiding out in Maas-Rhein *euregio*. *Space and Polity* 12 (1): 31–46.

Kramsch, Olivier and Hooper, Barbara. 2004. *Cross-Border Governance in the European Union*. London: Routledge.

Maclellan, Nic. 2006. *Louise Michel*. Havana: Ocean Sur.

Marx, Karl. 1974. *Grundrisse der Kritik der politischen Ökonomie 1857/58*. Jena: Friedrich-Schiller-Universität.

Mendes, Catulle. 1871. *Les 73 journées de la Commune*. Paris: E. Lachaud.

Messager, Henri. 1979. *239 lettres d'un communard déporté: Ile d'Oléron, Ile de Ré, Ile des Pins*. Paris: Le Sycomore.

Newman, David. 2006. The lines that continue to separate us: borders in our "borderless" world. *Progress in Human Geography* 30 (2): 143–161.

Newman, David and Paasi, Anssi. 1998. Fences and neighbours in the postmodern world: boundary narratives in political geography. *Progress in Human Geography* 22 (2): 186–207.

Nicol, Heather. 2005. Resiliency or change? The contemporary Canada–US border. *Geopolitics* 10: 769–790.

O'Dowd, Liam. 2010. From a "borderless world" to a "world of borders": "bringing history back in." *Environment and Planning D: Society and Space* 28 (6): 1031–1050.

Paasi, Anssi. 1996. *Territories, Boundaries and Consciousness: The Changing Geographies of the Finnish-Russian Border*. Chichester: John Wiley & Sons, Ltd.

Priollaud, Nicole. 1983. *La France colonisatrice*. Paris: L. Levi/S. Messinger.

Raspail, F.X. 1876. *De la nécessité de l'amnistie*. Paris.

Reclus, Élisee. 1905–1908. *L'homme et la terre*. Paris: Librairie Universelle.

Rimbaud, Arthur. 1932. Mauvais sang. In *A Season in Hell*, pp. 234–241. London: Fortune Press.

Robinson, Jennifer. 2011. Cities in a world of cities: the comparative gesture. *International Journal of Urban and Regional Research* 35 (1): 1–23.

Ross, Kristin. 1988. *The Emergence of Social Space: Rimbaud and the Paris Commune.* Minneapolis: University of Minnesota Press.

Rovisco, Maria. 2010. Reframing Europe and the global: conceptualizing the border in cultural encounters. *Environment and Planning D: Society and Space* 28 (6): 1015–1030.

Rumford, Chris. 2008. *Cosmopolitan Spaces: Europe, Globalization, Theory.* London: Routledge.

Salter, Mark. 2010. *Mapping Transatlantic Security Relations: The EU, Canada and the War on Terror.* London: Routledge.

Santos, Boaventura de Sousa. 2010. Más allá del pensamiento abismal. De las líneas globales a una ecología de saberes. In Heriberto Cairo and Ramón Grosfoguel, eds, *Descolonizar la modernidad, descolonizar Europa. Un diálogo Europa–América Latina*, pp. 101–146. Madrid: IEPALA,

Soja, Edward W. 1996. The stimulus of a little confusion: a contemporary comparison of Amsterdam and Los Angeles. In *Thirdspace: Journeys to Los Angeles and Other Real-and-Imagined Places*, pp. 280–320. Oxford: Blackwell,

Steinmetz, Jean-Luc. 2001. *Arthur Rimbaud: Presence of an Enigma.* New York: Welcome Rain.

van Houtum, Henk and van Naerssen, Ton. 2002. Bordering, ordering and othering, *Tijdschrift voor Economische en Sociale Geografie* 93: 125–136.

Vidal de La Blache, Paul. 1917. *La France de l'Est (Lorraine-Alsace).* Paris: A. Colin.

Wallerstein, Immanuel. 1983. *Historical Capitalism.* London: Verso.

Walters, William. 2004. Secure borders, safe haven, domopolitics. *Citizenship Studies* 8 (3): 237–260.

14 Borders and Conflict Resolution

David Newman

The world's major conflicts and global flashpoints are no longer focused on territorial and border issues. Issues relating to the contested positioning of borders and the desire for territorial expansion are largely passé within the contemporary international scene, as the major conflicts now seem more focused on the rise of fundamentalism, global terrorism and, in some regions, the struggle for the control of dwindling natural resources, notably oil and water. Indeed, many of today's conflicts point to a world in which borders are crossed without difficulty, through the unhindered dissemination of global capital, ideas and ideologies, such that one of the traditional functions of a border – to act as a barrier preventing movement – is far less significant than in the past. This is true even in the post–9/11 era, when the physical construction and sealing of borders have reemerged in an attempt to prevent "alien" elements from moving beyond the state boundaries.

Given the contemporary technologies of travel, the cyber dissemination of ideas, and the sophisticated production of transit documents and visas, the renewed attempt at resealing borders has met with only limited success. That does not mean to say that territorial issues are completely redundant (Kahler and Walter 2006). State borders continue to delineate the extent of sovereignty, even if this is not as absolute as it was in the past. Borders continue to constitute the agents through which processes of inclusion and exclusion are practiced, through which citizenship and belonging are determined, and through which the state is able to undertake the mechanics of control within the territorial compartments over which it exercises de facto and de jure control (Newman 2004, 2006b). It is the dynamics of the bordering process, rather than the location of the physical border per se, that is of greater significance, at a variety of spatial levels ranging from local, through the state, and to the regional and global (Paasi 2003; van Houtum 2005). The border is, in its own right, part of the process through which ordering and control take place, rather than just the physical and static outcome of the political process.

A Companion to Border Studies, First Edition. Edited by Thomas M. Wilson and Hastings Donnan.
© 2012 Blackwell Publishing Ltd. Published 2012 by Blackwell Publishing Ltd.

There remain a relatively small number of locations where the traditional concern with the physical demarcation and delimitation of the border continues to be part of a process of reterritorialization and conflict resolution. The focus is on borders as an essential component of power relations both within and between countries (Newman 2003; Paasi 2009). In recent years, the establishment of new states in East Timor, Kosovo and Southern Sudan has necessitated the recognition of fixed territorial borders by the international community. In some cases, this has been no more than a process through which existing administrative borders have been transformed into state boundaries, while in some cases it has required political negotiations leading to bilateral agreements and the demarcation of new lines of territorial and physical separation. The emergence of these new states has in large part been the end process of conflict resolution, one in which states define the territorial extent of the entity over which they practice control, and indicate a clear countertheory to the notions of "borderless" and "post nation-state" worlds. Globalization processes may, indeed, have made many borders more porous and easier to cross (not just in their physical sense), but it has not brought about the end of a world in which the territorial compartments of states constitute the major component and building block of the global structure (Newman 2006a; Newman and Paasi 1998; Kolossov and O'Loughlin 1998; Paasi 2009).

DEMARCATING BORDERS IN CONFLICT ZONES

This chapter focuses on the Israel–West Bank border, but there have been other border demarcation hot spots elsewhere in the globe in recent years. For example, recent cases of boundary demarcation and conflict include Cyprus (Peristianis and Mavris 2011), the Balkans (Klemencic 2000; Meha and Selimi 2010), East Timor (Abuza 2010; Clad 2010) and the newly created state of South Sudan. In the Balkans, most of the border disputes arose with the demise of Yugoslavia, although some of them have been smoldering for a century, from the Balkan Wars and the end of World War I. Becoming independent states, the former Soviet Union provinces accepted the old administrative boundaries to avoid opening historical territorial claims, but they have not been immune to their revival. The former Yugoslav federal units have been obliged by the Badinter Arbitration Commission to keep the old administrative boundaries as one of the conditions for being internationally recognized as newly independent states. Despite that, negotiations over where to draw borders concretely reflect how these new states define their national interests. Border issues have increased tensions and often served as a fundamental stumbling block to wider regional cooperation in economics, security and ethnic relations.

There are well-known agreements and disagreements that have lasted for decades between Turkey and Greece over territorial waters, national airspace and continental shelves in the Aegean Sea. Some Turkish boundary disputes that date back to the time of the Ottoman Empire wait to be solved after the ongoing normalization of relations between the two countries. Romania still considers some parts of Moldova and Ukraine, including Bessarabia, to belong historically to its territories. However, most of the actual problems regarding border corrections and demarcations in the Balkans belong to the countries that emerged from the dissolution of Yugoslavia.

There, other regional border conflicts include Slovenia and Croatia, where the main issue for both countries is an area of around 20 square kilometers in the Slovenian Bay of Piran. Croatia insists the border should be drawn down the middle of the bay, while Slovenia wants the whole bay because it is the only direct access for its merchant ships to international waters. An old tavern on the small Bregana River, which borders both Slovenia and Croatia, has become more crowded by customers and people from the media than ever before in its 150-year history. The line of demarcation between the two countries after the dismemberment of Yugoslavia divided a small restaurant, Kalin, as well, so that one part belongs to Slovenia, and the other to Croatia. Not to confuse guests, who have their meal and drink in one country and pay the bill in another, the owner painted a fluorescent line along the floor to delineate his property. The line even goes over the billiard table, so that billiard balls illegally and regularly cross the frontier between two sovereign countries. From May 2004 on, this table became part of the border of the European Union at which the Croatian side was left out.

In Croatia and Bosnia and Herzegovina there is a similar problem to the Slovenia–Croatia dispute because of Bosnia's problems with Croatia regarding sea access. Slovenia has around 45 kilometers of Adriatic coastline and Bosnia and Herzegovina only around 22 kilometers, while Croatia is blessed with almost 2,000 islands and a coastline longer than 1,700 kilometers. Due to its claim on a few hundred square meters of rock in the Bay of Neum, Croatia's plan is to build a bridge over the tiny Bosnian seaside resort to connect its mainland with its southernmost enclave, including the famous tourist center of Dubrovnik. This is not acceptable to Bosnia, where the authorities and the public complain that such a design will disturb Bosnia's only access to the sea.

Croatia and Serbia are also in dispute over borders, where Croatia liberated – partly by force and partly by international mediation – territories that were under Serbian occupation during the early 1990s. Serbia, however, still refuses to return two small islands in the Danube, explaining that they are nearer to the Serbian side of the river. The Croatian maps also show their border as passing through some Serbian villages and fields. Serbia is also in dispute with Macedonia because Serbia denies the independence of Kosovo, thus failing to recognize the border between Kosovo and Macedonia, which was earlier part of the border between Serbia and Macedonia. Additionally, the authorities in Belgrade believe the self-proclaimed government in Pristina has given part of Serbia's territory to Macedonia. The border between Macedonia and the rest of the former Yugoslavia was demarcated in 2001. Although Skopje recognized Kosovo as independent, the two have been unable to solve the dispute over a border area where Albanians staged protests against the demarcation in 2001, when escalating conditions at the Tanusevci–Debalde border with Kosovo also prompted the Macedonian Army to prepare for war. There two villages, situated only 100 meters apart on opposite sides of a steep mountain, had been the focus for Albanian incursions into Macedonia. In October 2009, Kosovo and Macedonia ratified an agreement over the border between the two countries. The document resolves an eight-year dispute over the region, used by Albanian guerrillas in 2001 to launch attacks during Macedonia's rebel Albanian insurgency. The document was supported by 83 members of Kosovo's 120-seat parliament, and by 72 members of Macedonia's 120-seat parliament.

Kosovo Serbs blocked roads leading to two disputed border crossings with Serbia, as Pristina announced it would take control of the posts. These border clashes erupted when the Pristina government dispatched special police to take over the two posts to enforce a ban on imports from Serbia that was imposed in retaliation for an earlier Belgrade ban on goods from Kosovo. The Serbian ban was imposed in protest at Kosovo's 2008 declaration of independence from Belgrade, which Serbia, backed by Russia, has refused to recognize. The European Union's law-enforcing mission EULEX Kosovo assumed control of the two contested border crossings amidst escalating tensions in the volatile ethnic Serbian enclave in the north of the new republic. The control over the Jarinje and Brnjak crossings has continued to be a bone of contention, with the ethnic Serbs populating the northern corner of Kosovo refusing allegiance to the ethnic-Albanian dominated government in Pristina.

Finally, in the Balkans there is also the border dispute between Bosnia and Herzegovina and Serbia where there is a small territorial conflict that has remained unresolved from the time of Yugoslavia. The River Lim, a tributary of the Drina River, comes from Montenegro, runs through the northern part of Sanjak and enters Bosnia, but only for a few kilometers. Then it flows back to Serbia and then again to Bosnia at Rudo, leaving several small villages physically out of Serbia's territory.

Other border conflicts, outside of Europe, also offer parallels to what is happening in the Middle East. Among them is the most recent border challenge at the contentious new boundary between Sudan and Southern Sudan. Sudan's authorities managed to agree that the new border would be drawn along existing administrative boundaries, but many regions of this border remain disputed. The new atlas will acknowledge the disputed region of Abyei, where 1,000 Ethiopian troops, deployed by the United Nations Security Council, arrived in November 2011 in an attempt to keep a level of peace. But this atlas will not acknowledge the struggle in Sudan's Nuba mountains, close to the newly redrawn border, where many of the Nuba people still believe in the vision of a democratic and united Sudan propagated by the late Sudan People's Liberation Army (SPLA leader, John Garang).

THE GREEN LINE: THE EVOLUTION OF A BOUNDARY IN CONFLICT

Perhaps the most significant process of ongoing conflict, which contains both a major territorial component and failed attempts at conflict resolution, in the globe today is the case of Israel–Palestine (Falah and Newman 1995a; Newman 2002; Harker 2010; Long 2011). Unique to states in the contemporary world, only two of Israel's five potential land borders have the status of internationally recognized boundaries. The two borders, between Israel and Egypt, and Israel and Jordan, only achieved that status following the respective peace agreements between Israel and Egypt in 1979, and Israel and Jordan in 1995. Prior to that date, all of Israel's borders were, at the best, agreed armistice lines drawn up in the wake of Israel's War of Independence in 1948–1949, or imposed lines of administrative division following the Six Day War of 1967. The fact that the actual demarcation and location of the borders as part of the Peace Agreements were based on past boundary lines which existed prior to 1948 or 1967, as is to be expected of some of the future boundary demarcations (such as that between Israel and Lebanon, or Israel and Syria), does not change the fact that for as long as there is no formal agreement between neighboring states concerning the course of the line, they remain temporary and open to change or modification as part of future negotiations aimed at bringing about conflict resolution.

The history of boundary demarcation in this region is recent, dating from the final breakup of the Ottoman Empire in the second decade of the twentieth century and the division of the territory between the two Mandate Powers, France and Great Britain, by the League of Nations. The northern boundary of the British-administered territory (the southern boundary of the French territory) is almost identical to Israel's northern boundary with Lebanon, the line which was determined in the armistice talks in Rhodes in 1948–1949, and to which Israel withdrew in 1990 following its 18-year-long occupation of southern Lebanon. Israel's southern boundary with Egypt, formally agreed as part of the Israel–Egypt peace accords in 1979, is based on the southern boundary line of the British Mandate area, while Israel's eastern border with Jordan (not including the section bordering the West Bank) is the line drawn up by the British Mandate authorities in 1921, following the partition of historical Palestine and the creation of the new state of Trans-Jordan.

Israel's most famous border is, in effect, a nonexistent border in international terms. The Green Line, separating Israel from the West Bank, was drawn up as an armistice line immediately after the country's War of Independence in 1948–1949, following the Rhodes armistice talks which took place between Israel and Jordan. The Line largely reflected the position of the respective troops at the cessation of hostilities. It was delimited and fortified during the subsequent two years, and remained as the official line of separation between Israel and the West Bank (a territory administered by the state of Jordan up until the Six Day War in 1967, during which Israeli troops conquered the West Bank and extended their control as far as the Jordan River in the east). Since 1967, Israel has constituted the occupying power throughout the West Bank, such that the Green Line was relegated to the status of an internal administrative boundary between sovereign Israel and those territories under occupation and governed according to the Civil Administration of the Military Government (Newman 2009).

Despite successive Israeli governments pronouncing the demise of the Green Line and even removing it from all official maps and atlases, the Line continued to demarcate Israel from the Occupied Territories, if only because no Israeli government attempted to annex the newly acquired territories to the state of Israel (with the notable exception of East Jerusalem). As such, the laws appertaining to the civilian administration of the Palestinian population residing inside the West Bank (and Gaza Strip) were different from those inside Israel, while no citizenship rights were granted to the Palestinian residents of this region, who remain – until today – stateless for as long as there is no formal international recognition of an independent and sovereign Palestinian state in this region.

Following the first Intifada (popular Palestinian uprising), which took place in 1987 (20 years after the Six Day War), the Israeli government began to reimpose a boundary regime on the West Bank as a means of preventing the unchecked flow of Palestinians from the Occupied Territories into Israel, often as daily commuters to fill the menial jobs within the Israeli capitalist economy. Curfews and the closing down of the Occupied Territories took place regularly along or in close proximity to the Green Line almost by default, the major exceptions being in those areas where the construction of Jewish settlements had served to blur the clear distinctions between the two sides (Long 2006; Newman 1997). Over the next 20 years, the boundary was reinforced, largely due to a series of security concerns defined by the Israeli government and military authorities, culminating in the construction of what has become known as the Separation Barrier from 2004 onward.

This barrier, in part electrified fence, and in smaller part concrete wall (especially in urban areas), has redefined the Green Line according to new physical realities. The Separation Barrier is true to the course of the Green Line for approximately 70 percent of its length, deviating from the Line mostly in those areas where the government has desired to keep the Israeli settlements on the Israeli side of the line. Many of these demarcation deviations have been ruled as illegal by both the International Court of Justice and the Israeli Supreme Court and have, in some areas, had to be redrawn. In no case has the line deviated to the west, inside Israel, meaning that all such deviations have effectively annexed Palestinian land from the West Bank into Israel. It is this reality which has given rise to the idea of land exchanges as part of a permanent territorial solution to the conflict based on Two States, in which the Palestinian state will have no less land than was originally the case following the drawing up of the Green Line in 1949.

The physical construction of the Separation Barrier has meant that the border discourse inside Israel has been transformed from one based on an abstract notion of physical and territorial separation, at the best practiced on maps by cartographers and diplomats, to one which is concrete and tangible and based on the reality of a border which is encountered by both Israelis and Palestinians on a daily basis.

Many Israelis encounter the border as they drive through Jerusalem or along the Trans-Israel highway. The vast majority of Israeli citizens, who never travel into the West Bank either out of fear for their personal safety or because they are opposed to driving into what they perceive as illegally occupied territory, are now more fully aware of the specific point beyond which they should not cross. Five distinct border crossing points have been constructed along the course of the Separation Barrier, at which point travelers have to show their documents or be recognized as bona fide travelers to pass from one side to the other.

For their part, Palestinians encounter the barrier as a border which prevents freedom of movement and, to a large extent, cages them inside the West Bank territorial compartment. They require special permits to enter Israel (Israelis do not require any special documents to enter the West Bank) and cars with Palestinian license plates are not allowed beyond the border. Some Palestinians, caught between the Green Line to the west and the new courses of the Separation Barrier to the east, have become spatial hostages, with their physical movement – be it to places of employment, hospitals, schools or consumerism – limited to micro-territories trapped between the two borders, and whose status will have to be determined as part of a final process of territorial resolution of the conflict.

Palestinian claims to a sovereign territory of their own have increasingly focused around the calls for a return to "borders of 1967," namely the Green Line. For them, this is a minimalist demand as they no longer lay claim to the rest of Mandate Palestine (over 70 percent of the territory which now constitutes the state of Israel). For Israel, the calls for a return to the Green Line are perceived as being a maximalist demand, as though the Palestinians should be prepared to "compromise" over some parts of that territory, given the geographical and demographic changes which have taken place in the 45 years which have passed since the 1967 War, most notably the construction of Israeli settlements beyond the Green Line. It is this counterclaim to boundary demarcation which serves as the basis for understanding the political discourses surrounding the territorial arrangements and negotiations for a final resolution of the conflict.

CONFLICT RESOLUTION AND TERRITORIAL AND CARTOGRAPHIC IMAGINATIONS

Conflict resolution invariably breaks down over those issues which remain symbolic and zero sum to either or both of the two sides. Concrete and tangible issues, those which can be quantified, negotiated and exchanged (bartered for each other), can invariably be resolved. A piece of territory can be exchanged for a piece of territory, a settlement for a water source, and a strategic location for a given number of refugees. But that does not necessarily mean that all territorial issues are, by definition, quantifiable. When territory is discussed in terms of its religious and ancient rights, when borders are based on the versions described in the Bible, or when the city of Jerusalem is perceived as constituting the "eternal" capital of the Jewish people, the process of conflict resolution then gets bogged down in zero-sum arguments, about which neither side is prepared to make the necessary compromise or exchange that is required for an agreement to be reached. In the case of Israel–Palestine, there remain a significant number of territorial issues which remain symbolic, although these have diminished in recent years. Notwithstanding, since the signing of the Oslo Agreements in 1993 and 1995, there have been ongoing discussions and negotiations concerning the future demarcation of a border as part of a proposed Two State solution (Biger et al. 2006). This has taken place at a number of levels, largely within the context of the Track II meetings which provide important professional input for decision-makers and government leaders if, and when, Track I – namely, direct political negotiations between heads of states – take place. As negotiations continue, even when they become repetitive, the idea that all territorial issues can be transformed from the symbolic and unresolvable to the tangible and the solvable is part of an ongoing process of attrition through which such notions as territorial compromise and exchange become more acceptable, if only through a familiarization with the idea that everything has its alternative or its compensation.

The default position for border demarcation is the Green Line. From a Palestinian perspective, this is the border which existed prior to the events of the Six Day War in June 1967 and which would transform the armistice line of 1948–1949 into an internationally recognized boundary. It would also signify the Palestinian acceptance of the West Bank as constituting the territory of an independent Palestinian state, and their abandoning of claims to other parts of Israel which were also part of the prestate single Mandate territory of Palestine between the Jordan River and the Mediterranean Sea. From a Palestinian perspective, this is perceived as a significant concession, as it accepts only 27 percent of the Mandate Palestine territory as constituting their sovereign state.

From an Israeli perspective, a return to the Green Line is more problematic, owing to the settlement infrastructure which now exists within the West Bank, encompassing a network of small towns and communities consisting (as of 2011) of over 300,000 residents – not including the neighborhoods of East Jerusalem, which include a similar number of residents, but which Israel insists is not part of the Occupied Territories, owing to its unilateral annexation of the entire city and the redrawing of the municipal boundaries, and is not therefore, in their eyes, up for territorial exchange.

The alternative scenario to an automatic return to the Green Line is based on the argument that an Israeli government (even of a left-wing position) is unwilling, or unable, to remove forcefully over a quarter of a million settlers, a large percentage of whom have settled this area for ideological and religious reasons and are therefore unwilling to give up their homes in return for generous financial compensation and resettlement back inside Israel proper. The scenes which accompanied the forced removal of the 7,000 settlers of the Gaza region in the summer of 2005 are seen as a small prelude of what could be expected if a similar scenario occurred to the entire West Bank settler population, which could potentially lead to levels of violence between settlers and soldiers on a scale which the government is unable to manage. As such, Israeli governments are wary of their ability to commit to such a scenario and have constantly sought to legitimize part of their occupation policy by seeking alternative border demarcations which would enable a significant part of the settler population to remain in their homes and under Israeli sovereignty.

The initial proposals for the redrawing of boundaries to retain control of much of the settlement infrastructure in situ was assumed, by Israeli policy-makers, to mean that the extent in area of a Palestinian state would be smaller than that encompassed by the West Bank, a scenario which is of course unacceptable to even the most moderate of Palestinian negotiators. While the Israeli territorial perspective is based on a discourse which views only the West Bank as the source of the conflict and therefore a territory which can be further divided, the Palestinian territorial discourse is one which sees the entire prestate area of Palestine as the territory to be divided, and so the entire West Bank is a minimalist territorial demand on their part.

In the later stages of border discourse there has therefore been acceptance that even if the territorial shape of the West Bank undergoes change as a result of bilateral conflict resolution, the size of the Palestinian territory must remain the same, without further encroachments. Notions of territorial exchange and land swaps, ideas which would have seemed fictional to the average Israeli as recently as the period of the Oslo Agreements in the mid-1990s, have now become a central part of the discourse. This is based on the idea that if Israel were to demand the redrawing of the border in such a way as to annex anywhere up to 10 percent of the region to the state of Israel, the Palestinian state would have to be compensated by an equal amount of land along and around those parts of the Green Line which are unsettled on the Israeli side of the border.

Imaginative land swap alternatives have also included such ideas as compensating the Palestinian state with an area of land adjacent to the densely populated Gaza Strip region, which, in current thinking and despite the political rise to power of the Hamas movement in this region, is still perceived by most as constituting part and parcel of a Palestinian state consisting of two territories, connected by a land link and safe passage through the south of Israel. Professor Ben-Arieh, a geographer and past rector of the Hebrew University of Jerusalem, went as far as proposing a regional series of land swaps and territorial exchanges which would include both Israel and Egypt transferring land to the Gaza area in order to expand its land base and allow it some breathing space, Israel, Jordan and Egypt exchanging land in the Red Sea Elat-Aqaba regions, and the transfer of land in the West Bank to Israel. A territorial solution of this nature would, in the view of Ben-Arieh, add an important regional dimension to the nature of conflict resolution (Ben-Arieh 2005).

Regarding land swaps around the Green Line, two areas of potential exchange have been identified, with vastly different political and demographic significance for both Israel and a Palestinian state. The area south of the Green Line, south of Qirya Gat and bordering on the Be'er Sheva and Hebron Hills region, is an area which is largely unsettled inside Israel, although there have been attempts to bolster the Jewish presence in this region during the past two decades. This is also an area where the country's growing Bedouin population (roughly estimated to be around 200,000 at the beginning of 2011) is concentrated. Cross-border links between the Bedouin population of this region and the Palestinian residents of the southern parts of the West Bank exist, although this has become increasingly difficult with the construction of the physical Separation Barrier and the difficulty of crossing from one side to the other.

The second area of potential land swaps to have been identified is in the northern section of the West Bank. Unlike the relatively unsettled southern area, the northern region consists of a dense population of Arab-Palestinian citizens of the state of Israel, including such major towns as Um el Fahm and Tayibe, and numerous smaller townships and villages. Right-wing politicians within Israel, many of whom are still opposed to the principle of a Two State solution to the conflict, have stated their reluctant acceptance of such a solution if the land swaps were to include some of the Arab towns and villages inside Israel. In this way, they would even further reduce the percentage of Israel's Arab minority population (which is currently around 20 percent) and implement their own policy of "transfer" without actually having forcefully to evacuate a single resident. This is the position held by Israel's extreme right-wing foreign minister (as of 2010–2011), former Russian immigrant Avigdor Lieberman. This is seen by most negotiators, on both sides, as constituting an immoral position, not least because public surveys of the country's Arab residents show categorically that despite their support in principle of the establishment of a Palestinian state, they are unwilling to be part of that state and prefer to remain as citizens of a democratic state of Israel, however imperfect that situation may be at present. The notion that such imposed re-demarcations of borders took place in twentieth-century Europe, often without plebiscites, is an argument used by those who support the idea, but is unacceptable to the majority of decision-makers who understand that the world of 2011 cannot be managed or organized according to the dictates of a hundred years previously or in the period immediately following the end of World War I – in both Europe and the Middle East.

The land swap ideas do not deal with a critical issue concerning settlement, namely the fact that at least a third of the Israeli settlements (approximately 100,000) still remain on the "wrong" side of the line and, as such, would have to be evacuated by the Israeli government. Not only is this a large number, but it consists of the most ideologically oriented groups among the settler population, those who came out of a historic or religious belief that the land belongs to them, and not for economic incentives such as the cheap houses or free-of-interest mortgages which have been offered to Israeli residents by the right-wing governments as an incentive to get them to relocate beyond the Green Line, although most of these reside in close proximity to the Green Line, not in the interior regions of the West Bank. There is a geographic paradox here, in that many of the settlers who would be prepared to self-evacuate voluntarily if and when they were offered adequate economic compensation to purchase a house back inside Israel would not have to relocate because of border changes which would leave their settlements inside Israel. Those who would refuse to relocate under any circumstances, and would have to be forcefully evacuated by the government, with real fears of physical violence and fatalities, are mostly located in those areas which, under any form of territorial redrawing of the borders, would remain on the Palestinian side of the line. This is one of the major difficulties for any Israeli government in moving ahead with the implementation of a Two State solution.

Ironically, as the support of a Two State solution within the Israeli consensus became more apparent in the period of the new millennium, even being promoted by right-wing politicians such as prime ministers Ariel Sharon and Ehud Olmert, it became increasingly difficult to implement, owing to the changing political situation. While the alternative solution of a single binational Jewish Arab state, with equal rights for all, had previously been an ideological position held by small groups on the Israeli left and within larger sections of the Palestinian community, this now became a realistic alternative (other than that of continued Occupation) because of the changing realities on the ground and the inability of an Israel government to commit to withdrawal and settlement evacuation. Facts on the ground change daily, especially as settlement construction continues to take place at an accelerated pace (regardless of Israeli government pronouncements of a settlement freeze as a means of placating an increasingly frustrated United States administration). The number of settlers has almost doubled since the early days of the Oslo Agreements, while the pro-peace government (1992–1995) of assassinated Israeli Prime Minister Yitzhak Rabin was responsible for rapid settlement construction.

Public sentiment opposing a single binational state solution to the conflict (because this would essentially mean an end to the concept of a Jewish State of Israel) and an increasing awareness among pragmatists that a Two State solution is becoming more difficult to implement by the day, have also led to some new thinking "outside the box," at least as far as interim solutions to the conflict are concerned. This has resulted from the fear that the ongoing status quo only serves to strengthen the infrastructure of occupation and that it is essential to put something in place in order to ensure future movement toward more permanent conflict resolution, and also to show to the skeptics that the first stages of implementation will not bring about a renewal of the situation which followed Israel's unilateral withdrawal from the Gaza Strip and the firing of rockets into southern Israel from the Hamas-controlled territory.

SECURITIZATION DISCOURSES AND BORDER DEMARCATION

The demarcation of borders within the Israel–Arab context has traditionally focused on notions of security and defense in a country which perceives itself as being subject to constant threat from each of its neighbors, even those with which it has a peace agreement (Falah and Newman 1995b). The Israel–Egypt border negotiations were only finalized after agreement was reached concerning much of the Sinai peninsula as a demilitarized zone, controlled by an international peacekeeping force. The peace agreement with Jordan included clauses which forbid Jordan from allowing any form of foreign military intervention or presence of foreign troops in the country, which would be seen by Israel as a legitimate *casus belli*. The on-off discussions concerning an Israeli potential withdrawal from the Golan Heights as part of a future peace agreement with Syria focuses almost entirely around the security dimensions of this region and the perceived threat to the Israeli settlements in the Galilee region if the area were returned to Syrian control, with memories of the shelling which took place prior to the 1967 War.

The ongoing discussions concerning an eventual territorial withdrawal from the West Bank also have a strong security component, although this has become of lesser significance in recent years – with the major focus being on the issues discussed in the previous section of this chapter, namely the presence of Israeli settlements and the possibilities of land swaps and territorial exchanges along the course of the Green Line boundary. But the securitization discourse has emerged afresh as a result of the construction of the Separation Barrier between Israel and the West Bank, on the one hand, and the firing of rockets from the Gaza Strip (following Israeli withdrawal from this region), on the other.

The construction of the Separation Barrier was, first and foremost, a unilateral Israeli response to the worsening of its national security and the infiltration of suicide bombers from the West Bank and Gaza into Israel's main population centers. Although the security barrier has become transformed into an international border, with electrified fences, sophisticated surveillance technology and a limited number of crossing points (Alatout 2009), its initial rationale was, as far as the vast majority of Israelis were concerned, to prevent the movement of potential security risks (terrorism) from entering into Israel (Lagerquist 2004). It is for this reason that it enjoyed the support of most Israeli citizens, regardless of their positions along the right–left political spectrum, and that it was initially implemented by a right-wing prime minister, Ariel Sharon, who – at that time – was opposed to the idea of creating a political border between Israel and the West Bank. It continues to be opposed by the settler community, who now find themselves on the "wrong" side of the security barrier, which has rapidly become associated in the minds of most Israelis as a future political border between two independent states, within which the settlers will have no place. It has also transferred incidents of violence and terrorism from inside Israel proper to the settlements, as perpetrators of violence are no longer able to cross into Israel. For most Israelis, the construction of the separation fence has indeed resulted in a significant decrease in the incidents of violence and terror, and it is for this reason that they see a peace agreement as containing a clear commitment to boundary demarcation, and a closed, almost sealed, boundary between the two countries, at least in the first stages of implementation.

Prior to the 1990s, the return of the entire West Bank to Palestinian control was portrayed, mostly by right-wing politicians, as constituting a major security threat. It was common to show maps of the region with the missile radius from points along the Green Line border into the major Israeli cities and population centers. It was argued that the return of the area to the Palestinians would put almost the whole of Israel under threat of missile attack. This discourse has developed in two contrasting ways in the intervening period. On the one hand, following the first Gulf War in the early 1990s when, for the first time, long-range ballistic missiles from Iraq were fired into the heart of Israel, it was understood that the border played little significance in preventing such attacks from taking place, since the origin of the missiles was hundreds, even thousands, of kilometers distant. As weapon technology developed, so too would the long-range accuracy of such missiles and, as such, the precise location of the border would have little significance for this dimension of the securitization discourse. On the other hand, the return of the Gaza Strip to Palestinian control resulted in the firing of small-scale missiles from close range into the towns of southern Israel, such as Sderot, Ashqelon and even Be'er Sheva, causing damage to the civilian infrastructure which had not previously been experienced in Israel's wars.

This was repeated with the firing of missiles from southern Lebanon into the towns of northern Israel, reaching the major metropolitan center of Haifa and its oil refineries. In both cases, Israel undertook major reprisal actions in both Lebanon and the Gaza Strip, raising questions in the minds of many Israelis concerning the need to control (occupy) areas just beyond the border so as to prevent them from becoming transformed into missile launching sites, whether of the Iran-supported Hezbollah in the north, or Hamas-supported groups in the south. As such, the significance of the border vis-à-vis this aspect of securitization is an open question – while Israel's long-term strategy is to develop, in cooperation with the United States, a sophisticated "iron dome" policy, by which missiles can be detected and intercepted immediately after launching and before they hit any of their targets.

There has also been a major change in thinking concerning the security discourse of the country's eastern border. Following the June 1967 War, Israeli government policy until 1977 was governed by what became known as the "Allon Plan." This, prior to the mass settlement of the West Bank region, was aimed at returning large parts of the area to Jordanian control through the granting of autonomy to the Palestinian residents of the region, while at the same time maintaining direct Israeli control over the eastern border running along the Jordan Rift Valley. The autonomy area would be linked to Jordan through a territorial corridor running from the West

Bank town of Ramallah, north of Jerusalem, in a southeasterly direction to include the one Palestinian town in the Jordan Valley, Jericho. As such, Israel would not have to exercise direct control of the civilian population, while it would, according to security perceptions of that time, maintain control over what became known as its "defensive boundaries." This was part and parcel of Israeli political and security conceptions for over 30 years, but was brought into question following the first Gulf War and the firing of long-range ballistic missiles, and again following the signing of the peace agreement between Israel and Jordan in 1995. It was also increasingly understood by Israeli policy-makers that any attempt to reach a territorial solution to the conflict which would argue for the retention of the entire Jordan Valley by Israel would be automatically rejected by the Palestinians. Such a solution would mean that the Palestinian state would be denied huge areas of land, much of it – despite its difficult climatic conditions – available for development and even the settling of potential refugee return, as well as turning the new state into a virtual enclave, surrounded on all sides by Israel. Thus, the combination of these reasons – the changing security environment and the realization of political realities – has gradually removed the Jordan Valley defensible border concept from Israeli territorial thinking, although it was briefly raised anew by the post-2009 Netanyahu government.

TERRITORIAL ALTERNATIVES TO A TWO STATE SOLUTION

Much of the border discourse in this chapter could conveniently be described as being a "traditional" border discourse, focusing on such issues as the drawing of lines, the role of borders in enhancing physical security, and the relationship between borders and territorial sovereignty. It is the type of discourse which many border theorists have argued is no longer of relevance, either because almost all of the world's land boundaries have long been demarcated and there are only a few examples of territorial and political conflict in the contemporary world which arise out of "positional disputes," or because theories of globalization and postmodernity argue for a world in which territorial fixation and rigid compartmentalization is passé. In this latter view, borders are opening up and becoming increasingly porous, in a world of shared and hybrid political and social spaces (Kolossov 2005; Brunet-Jailly 2005; Newman 2011).

The Israel–Palestine case study is clearly a case where much of the traditional discourse is prominent. Israel is a country whose borders have not yet been determined, and which claims sovereignty and control over pieces of disputed territory where the security discourse remains a central part of the national psyche. Moreover, there are serious questions concerning the ability to implement a traditional solution of territorial separation and the delimitation of physical borders, given the rapidly changing political realities, not least the problems relating to settlement evacuation as they become strongly implanted as part of a new geographic and territorial reality – regardless of the morality or immorality of their construction in the first instance.

This situation has resulted in a new discourse which has begun to examine alternatives to a Two State solution, at least as part of an interim period of conflict resolution (Falah 1997, 2005). Such notions as temporary borders (Hasson et al.

2010), cross-citizenship (settlers remaining in the West Bank but retaining their Israeli citizenship, while Palestinian residents of Israel have the opportunity of choosing between Israeli or Palestinian citizenship), ethnocracy (Yiftachel 2006), and even a return to largely discarded notions of federalism and cantons (Elazar 1979) have provided fertile ground for political and territorial imaginations.

As far-fetched as some notions may appear at any specific political juncture, the Israel–Palestine case does prove that the withering effect of ideas, if pushed strongly enough within the public discourse, has a significant impact upon political thinking and the eventual acceptability of ideas which were deemed totally unacceptable just a few years previously. This is as true of the concept of a Palestinian state and a Two State solution (which were not even part of the Oslo Agreement terminology as recently as the mid-1990s) as it is of the idea of territorial exchange and land swaps (which would have been deemed a figment of the imagination less than a decade ago). The Israel–Palestine case study proves that territorial and political solutions, even if proposed 20 years previously and which might have given rise to conflict resolution then, cannot necessarily be adopted now when the political and geographical realities have changed the conditions on the ground. This has been a constant theme, and failure, of the conflict resolution process in this region, namely the willingness to adopt solutions which, if adopted at a previous time, could have been implemented successfully, if not without difficulties, but when they were eventually adopted proved to be almost impossible to implement.

The repeated failure of the so-called "windows of opportunity" which reopen every few years but invariably are sealed very quickly, each time with greater frustration and disappointment at the inability to realize the opportunities, is in great part due to the willingness to adopt solutions which are no longer compatible with contemporary realities. This has been a constant failure of both Israeli and Palestinian policy-makers, even at times – few and far between – when there has been a real desire on both sides to reach the first stages of conflict resolution, which would include the necessary territorial arrangements. Such arrangements, in turn, require the demarcation of borders and the delineation of clear spaces of sovereignty and control, although the most recent phases in the conflict would indicate that even this requires a structural reassessment, as this small piece of real estate, the source of the world's longest ongoing conflict of this nature, becomes intermeshed in a patchwork of micro-territories increasingly difficult to separate one from the other.

CONCLUSION

This chapter has focused on the complexities of conflict resolution and border demarcation in Israel-Palestine. But as can be seen from this case, as well as the many cases in the Balkans, the issues at stake concern cross-border ethnicity, where groups find themselves on the "wrong" side of the border. This is reflected in localized conflicts in micro-areas, often in towns and villages which are located on both sides of the border. In the case of Israel-Palestine, there is no clean-cut divide between Israeli and Palestinian citizens, while each group is opposed to forceful evacuation in attempts to create forms of ethnic homogeneity, as was a common occurrence a century ago, and even as recently as the division of Cyprus into homogeneous Turkish and Greek Cypriot areas following the Turkish invasion of 1974.

The redrawing of borders around ethnic groups may result in their forceful loss of the citizenship of one country and their adoption of an alternative citizenship without any actual physical movement or expulsion from villages and homes. This is almost as unacceptable as the forced ethnic cleansing of minority groups from one side of the border to the other, although where it is imposed from above by both governments, it is less of an infringement of the respective human rights than is the forced evacuation of refugees against their will by a single government.

In terms of the technical aspects of border demarcation, modern technologies such as GIS (geographic information system) and sophisticated computerized cartography enable negotiators to reach a resolution of meters, so that every house can be taken into account. Gone are the days when inaccurate maps, not widely known to the public at large, could be used as an excuse for the poor, or politically unequal, demarcation of the boundary. The data and information are available to all, much within the public domain, on memory sticks and laptop computers. Thus, politicians and diplomats have access to far more comprehensive data and cartographic knowledge than was the case even 50 years ago. This means that the ultimate decisions concerning the trade-offs involved with new border demarcations are even more political than in the past. In the case of the Balkans, of Sudan and of Israel-Palestine, the knowledge is available. It remains the responsibility of the politicians to show their desire for conflict resolution by drawing up borders which are equally satisfactory (or unsatisfactory) to the countries on both sides of the separation line.

At a wider level, it is clear that the borderless world which many of us were embracing 20 years ago has not arrived in many areas where ethnoterritorial conflict and attempts at conflict resolution are still the order of the day (Newman 2006a; Wastl-Walter 2011). Borderless worlds may work in some ways and for some people inside an expanded European Union, but the combination of securitization discourses following the events of 9/11, attempts to prevent the entry of "illegal" migrants from the poorer parts of the globe into the richer areas, and the residual conflicts, some of which have been outlined in this chapter, mean that the closing and sealing of borders is as much part of contemporary border discourse as is their opening and removal. We live in a world where parallel border dynamics are going on at one and the same time, in different locations, and even in the same location, with competition between economic lobbies pushing for more porous and flexible borders, and securitization and conflict lobbies calling for the reclosing and sealing of borders. This is a dynamic process which characterizes much of the global geopolitical change of the twenty-first century.

REFERENCES

Abuza, Z. 2010. Borderlands, terrorism, and insurgency in Southeast Asia. In James Clad, Sean M. McDonald and Bruce Vaughan, eds, *The Borderlands of South East Asia: Geopolitics, Terrorism and Globalization*, pp. 59–88. Washington, DC: National Defense University Press, Institute for National Strategic Studies.

Alatout, S. 2009. Walls as technologies: the double construction of geographies of peace and conflict in Israeli politics. *Annals of the Association of American Geographers* 99 (5): 956–968.

Ben-Arieh, Yehoshua. 2005. *Trilateral Land Exchange between Israel, the Palestinian Authority, and Egypt: A Solution for Advancing Peace between Israel and the PA*. Jerusalem: Truman Institute.

Biger, G., Newman, D. et al. 2006. A Framework for Demarcating a Border Between Israel and a Palestinian State: Parameters and Principles. Working Paper, Herzliya Conference, Jan. At http://www.herzliyaconference.org/_Uploads/2166Framework.pdf (accessed Nov. 2011).

Brunet-Jailly, E. 2005. Theorizing borders: an interdisciplinary perspective. *Geopolitics* 10 (4): 633–649.

Clad, J. 2010. Delineation and borders in Southeast Asia. In James Clad, Sean M McDonald and Bruce Vaughan, eds, *The Borderlands of South East Asia: Geopolitics, Terrorism and Globalization*, pp. 89–106. Washington, DC: National Defense University Press, Institute for National Strategic Studies.

Elazar, D. 1979. *Self Rule/Shared Rule: Federal Solutions to the Middle East Conflict*. Ramat Gan, Israel: Turtledove.

Falah, G. 1997. Re-envisioning current discourse: alternative territorial configurations for Palestinian statehood. *Canadian Geographer* 41: 307–330.

Falah, G. 2005. Geopolitics of "enclavisation" and the demise of a two-state solution to the Israeli-Palestinian conflict. *Third World Quarterly* 26 (8): 1341–1372

Falah, G. and Newman, D. 1995a. Small state behaviour: on the formation of a Palestinian state in the West Bank and Gaza Strip. *Canadian Geographer* 39 (3): 219–234.

Falah, G. and Newman, D. 1995b. The spatial manifestation of threat: Israelis and Palestinians seek a "good" border. *Political Geography Quarterly* 14: 689–706.

Harker, C. 2010. New geographies of Palestine/Palestinians. *Arab World Geographer* 13 (3–4): 199–216.

Hasson, S. et al. 2010. *Future Borders between Israel and the Palestinian Authority: Principles, Scenarios and Recommendations*. Jerusalem: Hebrew University of Jerusalem, Shasha Center for Strategic Studies. At http://public-policy.huji.ac.il/upload/english_21.2.pdf (accessed Nov. 2011).

Kahler, M. and Walter, B., eds. 2006. *Territoriality and Conflict in an Era of Globalization*. Cambridge: Cambridge University Press.

Klemencic, M. 2000. The border agreement between Croatia and Bosnia Herzegovina. *IBRU Boundary and Security Bulletin* 7 (4): 96–101.

Kolossov, V. 2005. Border studies and hanging theoretical perspectives. *Geopolitics* 10 (4): 606–632.

Kolossov, V. and O'Loughlin, J. 1998. New borders for new world orders: territorialities at the fin de siècle. *Geojournal* 3: 259–273.

Lagerquist, P. 2004. Fencing the last sky: excavating Palestine after Israel's "separation wall." *Journal of Palestine Studies* 33 (2): 5–35.

Long, J. 2006. Border anxiety in Palestine–Israel. *Antipode* 38 (1): 107–127.

Long, J. 2011. Geographies of Palestine–Israel. *Geography Compass* 5 (5): 262–274.

Meha, M. and Selimi, B. 2010. The Challenges of Border Demarcation Kosovo–Macedonia. Prepared for the 24th International Congress of the International Federation of Surveyors (FIG), Sydney, Apr. 11–16. At http://fig.net/pub/fig2010/papers/ts02a%5Cts02a_meha_4481.pdf (accessed Nov. 2011).

Newman, D. 1997. Creating the fences of territorial separation: the discourses of Israeli-Palestinian conflict resolution. *Geopolitics* 2: 1–35.

Newman, D. 2002. The geopolitics of peacemaking in Israel–Palestine. *Political Geography* 21: 629–646.

Newman, D. 2003. On borders and power: a theoretical framework. *Journal of Borderland Studies* 18 (1): 13–25.

Newman, D. 2004. Conflict at the interface: the impact of boundaries and borders on contemporary ethno-national conflict. In C. Flint, ed., *Geographies of War and Peace*. Oxford: Oxford University Press.

Newman, D. 2006a. The lines that continue to separate us: borders in our borderless world. *Progress in Human Geography* 30 (2): 1–19.

Newman, D. 2006b. The resilience of territorial conflict in an era of globalization. In M. Kahler and B. Walter, eds, *Territoriality and Conflict in an Era of Globalization*. Cambridge: Cambridge University Press.

Newman, D. 2009. The renaissance of a border which never died: the Green Line between Israel and the West Bank. In A. Diener and J. Hagen, eds, *Border Lines: History and Politics of Odd International Borders*. Lanham: Rowman & Littlefield.

Newman, D. 2011. Contemporary research agendas in borders studies: an overview. In D. Wastl-Water, ed., *The Ashgate Research Companion to Border Studies*. Farnham: Ashgate.

Newman, D. and Paasi, A. 1998. Fences and neighbours in the post-modern world: boundary narratives in political geography. *Progress in Human Geography* 22 (2): 186–207.

Paasi, A. 2003. Boundaries in a globalizing world. In Kay Anderson et al., eds, *Handbook of Cultural Geography*, pp. 462–472. London: Sage.

Paasi, A. 2009. Bounded spaces in a "borderless world"? Border studies, power, and the anatomy of the territory. *Journal of Power* 2 (2): 213–234.

Peristianis, N. and Mavris, J. 2011. The "green line" of Cyprus: a contested boundary in flux. In D. Wastl-Water, ed., *The Ashgate Research Companion to Border Studies*. Farnham: Ashgate.

van Houtum, H. 2005. The geopolitics of borders and boundaries. *Geopolitics* 10 (4): 672–679.

Wastl-Walter, Doris, ed. 2011. *The Ashgate Research Companion to Border Studies*. Farnham: Ashgate.

Yiftachel, O. 2006. *Ethnocracy: Land and Identity Politics in Israel/Palestine*. Philadelphia: University of Pennsylvania Press.

PART **III** Security, Order and Disorder

15 Chaos and Order along the (Former) Iron Curtain

Mathijs Pelkmans

On the central square of what was the Soviet-half of Sarpi – a village split into a Soviet-Georgian and a Turkish part in 1921 – there used to be a billboard depicting three men, with the accompanying text "The *entire* Soviet nation guards the border!" written in Russian.[1] The billboard was placed next to the border fence in the 1970s, but was removed shortly after the USSR collapsed in 1991. Several years later a new billboard was attached to the roof of the customs offices with the text "Welcome to Georgia" in English, Georgian and Turkish.

A literal reading of these border-marking texts evokes the familiar dichotomies: socialist protectionism versus capitalist laissez-faire; Soviet repression versus the freedom of democracy. Although there are indeed real differences between socialist and capitalist borders, the markers are equally telling for what they leave unsaid. By paying attention to the unsaid – by connecting the signs to their silences – the texts can serve as a starting point for a discussion that aims to elucidate the peculiarities of socialist borders.

When first shown a photograph of the Soviet billboard, I registered it as just another piece of rhetoric intended to scare off the "capitalists" across the border. But even though the capitalist enemy was a constant trope in Soviet discourse, this billboard suggested other things. First there was the text "The *entire* Soviet nation guards the border!" of which the word "entire" was italicized, drawing attention to the figures on the billboard: a boy with tie (a pioneer) and a middle-aged civilian standing next to a sturdy-looking soldier. If this raised the question of who the intended audience was, the fact that the text was in Russian (instead of Turkish) and that the billboard faced the village (rather than Turkey) provided an unambiguous answer. The message was meant to be read by Soviet citizens, reminding them of their duty to guard the border and indirectly also of the prohibition on crossing to the other side. Fences and walls are often erected to keep the unwanted out, but may just as well be built to keep people in. Socialist borders (here referring to borders

A Companion to Border Studies, First Edition. Edited by Thomas M. Wilson and Hastings Donnan.
© 2012 Blackwell Publishing Ltd. Published 2012 by Blackwell Publishing Ltd.

between socialist and capitalist countries) aimed to produce both effects simultaneously.[2] For example, in his study of the German–German border, Borneman (1998: 167) argues that official rhetoric about the need to protect socialist citizens from a fascist threat was used as a foil to conceal the fact that the more immediate function of the Iron Curtain was to prevent workers from leaving the country. It is clear that Soviet officials were certainly concerned about foreign attack or infiltration, especially in the pre-1940 period. The Sarpi billboard revealed the efforts of the Soviet leadership to engage the local population in sustaining the border, and thus that the Iron Curtain should not be seen unambiguously as an external imposition. A central question, indeed, is how and to what extent ordinary citizens were drawn into maintaining the border.

In contrast to the Soviet billboard, the new text "Welcome to Georgia" can only be read by travelers arriving from Turkey. Ironically, the trilingual display in English, Turkish, and Georgian makes the text difficult to understand.[3] While a contextualized reading of the Soviet billboard revealed some of the text's referents, here we seem to be dealing with an "empty signifier" (Laclau 1993). This "emptiness," reflected in the sheer universality of the invitation, inadvertently points at the darker sides of capitalist borders (because clearly, the welcoming is conditional and selective). In the case of Georgia the checkpoint turned into a "wild market" in the 1990s, an arena in which the price of each passage was individually defined. That is, here one could read the "welcome to . . ." as the seductive greeting of devouring officials who welcome the traveler to *their* terrain to "negotiate" the amount and means of payment. Different but equally dark dynamics unfold at the entrance of richer capitalist countries with more stable and impersonal state structures, where the checkpoint serves to separate desired from undesired (aspects of) movement; the welcoming a cynical sign reflecting the tension that while cheap labor is desired, the actual bodies in which this labor resides are not (Kearney 1998:125; see also Bornstein 2002: 16). In both the capitalist and socialist instances the "welcoming" is most telling for what it leaves unsaid.[4]

The Soviet and the post-Soviet border-marking texts respectively emphasize fixity and fluidity, but they *do* converge analytically. Boundaries are drawn to create order out of chaos (Douglas 1966), an act which is partly self-defeating because the lines are drawn on top of "reluctant" material, thereby creating new ambiguities, exceptions, and violations (cf. Strathern 1996). The Soviet border aspired to be an unambiguous dividing line between peoples, countries, and ideological systems, but lived experience in the borderlands resisted such categorization. The delimitation of the border created new "hybrids" for the very reason that people had lived their lives across what became two separate countries. In apparent contrast, the collapse of the USSR allowed for the (re)creation of transnational networks, but this "chaotic" new flux also triggered boundary-drawing activities. Even though benefiting economically from new transnational trading opportunities, the local population was at the forefront of activities aimed at taming the flow and (re)creating order.

Chaos and order hold each other in a tight embrace, something which is particularly evident along territorial boundaries. This essay aims to understand this interlocking of chaos and order by detailing the biography of the border between Turkey and (Soviet) Georgia, as one instance of the Iron Curtain that separated the socialist from the capitalist world. There are not many in-depth case studies of how social life unfolded along and in relation to the Iron Curtain, but instructive comparisons can be made between the case of Sarpi and the border village studied by Daphne Berdahl (1999) along the German Iron Curtain, as well as the town studied by Anssi Paasi (1996, 1999) on the Finnish–Russian border. All three cases look at communities that were divided by a virtually impermeable border, although the Soviet-Georgian border had a longer history of closure, dating back to the 1930s when those other borders did not yet exist. The cases also demonstrate an overwhelming proliferation of cross-border flux in the late 1980s and 1990s. The situation in Germany stands out from the other two, because the literal border disappeared with the unification of the two Germanies, whereas in the Finnish-Russian and the Georgian-Turkish cases the Iron Curtain was lifted but a more permeable national border remained. Therefore, although in all instances rapid changes occurred in the field of consumption and interpersonal relations, only in two of the cases did this lead to a proliferation of the activities that are so often associated with borders, such as smuggling and prostitution (see also Hann and Bellér-Hann 1998; Konstantinov 1996).

These cases reveal not only extreme oscillations between border impermeability and subsequent permeability, but also the complications that are involved in both the closure and the opening (or removal) of the border. As Berdahl suggests, in the borderlands "ambiguity creates clarity" (1999: 232), but the unstated reverse, namely that "clarity creates ambiguity," is an inherent part of the dynamic as well. This essay aims not merely to describe these tendencies, but to detail some of the mechanisms that spur the oscillations. The dramatic shifts between chaos and order that occurred in Sarpi make it a particularly useful vantage point for this purpose, not least because they illuminate the difficulty of achieving border closure, as well as the complications that ensued from its opening in the late 1980s.

CLOSING THE BORDER

Although nowadays the checkpoint in Sarpi is an important node in transnational movement between Turkey and the Caucasus, during most of the twentieth century the border was hermetically sealed. Apart from a handful of elderly villagers who completed the Herculean task of obtaining official permission to visit relatives in Turkey, no one from Sarpi had crossed the border between the late 1940s and the 1980s. During my research I tried to find out if alternative ways to move or at least to communicate across the divide had existed.[5] But my interlocutors dismissed the idea and several men even proudly stressed their own role in keeping the border watertight. The situation formed an ethnographic and analytic puzzle. Herzfeld, for example, talks about the ease with which "the most fiercely guarded borders can be penetrated" (2001: 138) and Driessen states that "no matter how clearly borders are marked on maps, how many border guards are appointed, how many fences are built, people will ignore borders whenever it suits them" (1996: 289). So what made this border different? If, as these authors rightly suggest, it is not merely an issue of fences and patrols, then why did it not "suit" inhabitants of Sarpi to ignore this border? In this section I focus on three factors. First, the Soviet regime did not depend on cross-border economic ties in the same way as capitalist states and thus did not see its fortification efforts undermined by pressures to turn a blind eye toward the influx of cheap labor. A second point is that the surveillance system was organized in such a manner that acts of resistance had the tendency to backfire and thus to further solidify the border regime. Third, even though this border was initially an "arbitrary divide" resented by villagers, the social dynamics generated by its existence meant that the border inadvertently became *their* border as well.

Like most boundaries that are drawn in far-away offices, this one arbitrarily cut across social and economic networks. Sarpi was located at the eastern end of an area inhabited by the Laz, who used to speak a language related to Georgian called Lazuri, and had converted to Islam in the sixteenth and seventeenth centuries. Seen from the bottom up the new border was, literally, a meaningless boundary, and even as a spatial construct it initially failed to divide. Although a barbed wire fence was constructed to mark the state boundary as early as 1921, it was still easy to cross. Most families owned land on the other side and they received permits with which they could cross the border to cultivate their fields. Cross-border marriages were common, the dead were still buried in the shared graveyard and elderly men attended the Friday prayers in the mosque on the Turkish side. Rather than acting as a divide, in the 1920s and 1930s the border often generated reasons to cross it. The central-ized distribution system which was introduced in the USSR resulted in numerous deficits, while cross-border price differences rose dramatically. Petty smuggling was widespread and the markets in the border region were well stocked with contraband.

This period of relative freedom of movement ended in 1937: the checkpoint dis-appeared and cross-border movement was banned. With the growing threat of war between the USSR and Turkey, new restrictions were introduced to halt cross-border communication. A night-time curfew was imposed and soldiers more frequently patrolled the fence and the village. The Soviet leadership's attitude toward the border and its population was ambivalent. On the one hand, the villagers were seen as a possible bridgehead for the USSR's expansionist ambitions. The secret service (NKVD) enlisted young men to carry out missions on Turkish soil. The village's visibility from across the border gave it a representative function: the "good Soviet life" in Sarpi should foster positive attitudes among the Laz living in Turkey. On the other hand, state representatives continued to be suspicious of villagers' loyalties. It was not just that all villagers had relatives in Turkey; they also came across as distinctly un-Georgian. Although classified as a Georgian subgroup, the Laz were Muslim, had Turkish-sounding names and spoke a different, even if related, language.

Inhabitants certainly did not passively accept the restrictions: they tested the limits of the border regime and tried to maintain contact with the other side. Women who had been born in Turkey (and had married into Soviet Sarpi) secretly kept their Turkish passports, anticipating that these might become useful again in the future. "Border-singing" was a means of communication for a few years after 1937. Informa-tion about deceased relatives, newborn children or weddings was woven into existing folk and funeral songs which were sung in Lazuri and were thus unintelligible to the border guards. But the practice triggered new regulations, with a military commander explicitly banning outdoor funerary wailing. Sarpians increasingly self-censored their behavior, as it became clear that many acts of resistance entangled them further into the webs of power spun by the state, making them more vulnerable to erratic and sometimes deadly decisions of the leadership. But these realizations often came too late.

The border was sealed through a series of tragic events. Since the mid-1930s individual villagers had been "disappearing," taken away by the NKVD (the predecessor of the KGB). Larger scale tragedies followed in the decades thereafter when three waves of deportations, aimed at cleansing and pacifying the border region, struck the village. The first to be deported (in 1944) were the eight Hemshin and Kurdish families who lived just outside the village proper, and whose seminomadic lifestyle was by definition suspect to a regime preoccupied with order and control. Five years later all women born on Turkish soil and still in possession of Turkish passports were deported to Siberia. In 1951 an additional 10 households from Sarpi were sent to Central Asia as "volunteers" to cultivate the steppes. In this last instance the deportees were probably suspected of having been involved in smuggling and other cross-border transgressions. But the reasons for deportation were never given and this obscurity was a key element by which the remaining population was pacified.[6] As in a perfect illustration of the panopticon, the sense of being observed was so penetrating precisely because the direction of the gazes remained unknown: the observer obscured from view (Foucault 1979: 207–208). In the words of a villager who had been a young man at the time: "all the neighbors were guilty, they simply betrayed each other, but nobody knows why."

In this atmosphere of distrust and fear the presentation of self was a precarious issue. Personal names, for example, changed in response to a combination of state pressure and local initiative. As part of a campaign of de-Turkification children were given Georgian-sounding names at school, while parents could no longer register their newborns with Turkish-sounding names. Although there was never a decree to alter surnames, most families changed them into ones that sounded more Georgian (for example, from Abduloghli to Abuladze). Interestingly, these new names were retrospectively seen as having induced changes in self-perception. Consider this statement of an elderly woman: "I am Muslim. But my grandchildren all have Georgian names. You see, everyone is Georgian in their passports, they eat pork, drink wine, and smoke cigarettes." Of course, a Georgian name does not turn people into wine-drinkers, but the centrality of names in presentations of self could not avoid having a palpable influence on ideas of selfhood among subsequent generations.

New border-surveillance technology was installed in the 1950s. Perhaps surprisingly, but understandably given existing hardships, this was seen as a positive development. One of my interlocutors put it succinctly when he remarked that after the new fences and alarm systems had been installed in 1956 "we were free in our village again." Villagers came to accept the border's permanence, avoided pointing to or staring at the other side, and cooperated in the maintenance of the border. School-children assisted soldiers in clearing twigs and leaves from the strip of land along the fences. Collective farm workers were often the first to detect "runners" from the Soviet hinterland in the border zone (*pogranichnaia zona*) – a strip of land several kilometers wide where movement was restricted.[7] The border had become a regrettable but accepted part of everyday life, especially for the new generation. Slightly exaggerating a commonly held opinion, one of my interlocutors said: "we were born here; we didn't even feel the presence of the border."[8]

At this point we may recall the centrally displayed text "The entire Soviet nation guards the border!" In one sense it referred to the practical tasks that villagers (had to) perform in border maintenance and defense. But the image and text on the billboard implicitly also referred to much harsher aspects of "united defense." Villagers defended or rather "fixed" the border through their actions. Sometimes these actions were intentional, as in the case of a man who prided himself on having caught three Russian "runners" or refugees in the border zone. At other times they were performed unwittingly, when attempts to beat the system ended up strengthening it instead. But it was also simply by muddling through, by shaping one's life within the given constraints, that patterns formed which followed, and gave substance to, the borderline.

Border impermeability is exceptional, and Donnan and Wilson are surely right when they point out that borders characteristically "unite as well as divide, and that their existence as barriers to movement can simultaneously create reasons to cross them" (1999: 87). The tremendous efforts needed to seal the Soviet border confirm this principle. Importantly, this sealing was not simply a top-down imposition. Rather, differently positioned ambiguities combined to reinforce the border regime. But even in this case one could point out significant imperfections: people still crossed the border in their imagination. Soviet Sarpians had not forgotten that across the border lived people just like them; there was still hope that bonds of kinship could be revived in the future. As Svašek (2002: 505) suggests when writing about expelled Sudeten Germans, it may be that "the experience of sudden loss" strengthens identification with the lost object, whether this is a lost homeland or lost relatives. Moreover, the stories brought back by the few Sarpians who received permission and traveled to the other side of the village via Moscow and Ankara continued to keep the discourse of one (unhappily divided) village alive. A sad irony of the border's biography is that imaginary and physical permeability were reversed in the 1990s.

OPENING THE BORDER

Negotiations between the USSR and Turkey about establishing a checkpoint in Sarpi were first held in the late 1970s. The final decision was endlessly deferred, such that when on the morning of August 31, 1988 it was announced that the border would be opened later that day, the news came as a complete surprise to the villagers. It was a local event of epic dimensions. Overwhelmed by their enthusiasm, the border guards allowed villagers from opposite sides to intermingle freely. In the years thereafter numerous family visits were made, a time remembered by one elderly lady as a "heavenly period." However, 10 years later this exuberance had not only subsided, the general opinion had reversed. Few went as far as the man who ended his tirade about the chaos (*bardak*) of the present by saying "I wished that they closed the border again" but negative attitudes were the norm.

It might be justified to say that the opening, precisely because it was so hopefully anticipated, was bound to be disappointing; after all, reality never lives up to the dream. Affirmation of this idea can be found in other cases, as in Svašek's (2002) documentation of the "odd feelings" that the expelled Sudeten Germans experienced when they visited their native homes and towns in the early 1990s. They displayed feelings of sadness, anger, but also relief when discovering that their "memories no longer corresponded with reality" (Svašek 2002: 511). Still, specific factors intensified the disillusionment, and in this section I focus on two of them. First, the border opening coincided with the post-Soviet economic and political crisis of the 1990s and thus became associated with it. Second, the opening was disappointing precisely because this "arbitrary divide" (which the border had been in 1921) turned out to be not so arbitrary anymore. While Sarpians had keenly anticipated that the border opening would enable them to reestablish kinship ties, it turned out that their long-awaited relatives had become strangers. Both factors triggered attempts to reestablish order. If the extraordinary aspect of the Soviet border was its physical closure, which was nevertheless transcended by people's imagination, the post-Soviet situation showed the reverse. Berdahl (1999: 166) noted a similar tendency when talking about "the wall in our heads" and quotes an informant who comments that Germans in East and West had been more united when the border had still been there. There and in Sarpi new physical permeability was accompanied with more stringent idea-tional division.

As early as 1988 it had become possible to obtain international passports and visit relatives in Turkey, but it was only after the USSR collapsed that cross-border move-ment surged, with an astonishing 800,000 people crossing the Sarpi checkpoint in 1992. Most travelers were "tourist traders" engaged in petty trade between Turkey and the Caucasus (Hann and Bellér-Hann 1992, 1998). While these tourist-traders made only modest profits, in Sarpi economic opportunities seemed unlimited. The village soon got the nickname "small Kuwait," because its residents were imagined to be sitting on a metaphorical oil-well – becoming millionaires without having to do much. They set up money exchange offices, sold food, drinks and cigarettes to travelers and engaged in various sorts of cross-border trade. The sums of money earned at the customs were even more fabulous, and well-placed officers were able to build luxurious villas at a time when the living standard of most citizens of Georgia sharply declined. The situation at the customs appeared chaotic, especially to first-time travelers who were confronted with all kind of "taxes" and extortion practices.[9] While chaotic in the sense that laws were differentially applied, below this fragmented legal template a coherent hierarchical system of predation formed which extended from customs officers up to the regional potentate, Aslan Abashidze. When these networks contracted and strengthened over the course of the 1990s and cross-border trade professionalized, only those with strong connections in the political arena were able to continue to profit from the open border.

If the border opening offered opportunities, it also introduced new inequalities between villagers. It is not that life in the Soviet Union had been egalitarian – the *kolkhoz* (collective farm) chairman had always earned more than a schoolteacher, who used to have higher status than a tractor driver – but new economic inequalities went far beyond what had existed before. While some families bought (relatively new) Mercedes Benz cars and expensively renovated their houses, other families were barely able to make ends meet. Moreover, the new lines of inequality upset previous indicators of status such as level of education. This sharp contrast with the pre-1990 "order" intensified the sense of chaos. Villagers commented that in Soviet times they had been able to leave their doors unlocked and stressed that everyone in Sarpi had known each other. The prison-like stillness of the border zone had produced a (not necessarily pleasant) sense of community which stood in sharp contrast to the frenzy and the differentiating dynamics of an open border situation.

The events of the late 1980s had enabled villagers to renew contacts with long-awaited relatives. Sarpians repeatedly told me that when the border opened they had overwhelmed their visiting relatives with a warm welcome, including large banquets and plentiful wine, and had sent them home loaded with gifts. But this is also where the trouble started. Rules of hospitality and ideas about reciprocity between kin had developed differently, with the effect that behavioral norms were repeatedly violated by both sides. For example, guests from Georgia felt insulted when served only "Turkish soup," while guests from Turkey felt uncomfortable when offered wine and vodka. The resulting tensions meant that the number of cross-border visits rapidly declined after the first years and that few long-term bonds were established.

In the perception of the Laz in Georgian Sarpi, relatives across the border not only had different lifestyles, but held radically different ideas about friendship, kinship, hospitality and trade. Turkish Laz purportedly had become more orthodox in their Islamic beliefs than all Laz had traditionally been; they had forgotten their language and history, and even their personalities had changed. Several of my interlocutors were adamant that "those people" were no longer Laz. One young woman remarked, "Pff, they have just become Turks, only the language remains, and even that is disappearing." The most difficult message in the reunion was that the people involved were not simply "others," but alienated versions of themselves, co-villagers who had always been visible in the distance. As I argued elsewhere, "whereas one expects – or at times at least accepts – deviant behavior from outsiders, it is harder to accept deviance from nearby relatives" (Pelkmans 2006: 86).

Not only the unexpected differences were problematic; the similarities were equally discomforting. The tensions that emerged through cross-border contacts generated a subsequent denial of resemblance. Denying inhabitants of the other side the status of Laz was one means to accomplish this. Similarities were not only unwanted because of the negative cross-border experiences, but also because they compromised the villagers' position within Georgia. Over the twentieth century they had not only shaped their lives within (Soviet) Georgian society, but had also started to identify with the Georgian nation. With the opening of the border Sarpians risked being associated with the population in Turkey, especially because of their religious affiliation. Although Islam had played only a minor role in public life since the 1930s, most villagers continued to see themselves as Muslim. This became problematic when in the 1990s Georgia was increasingly presented as a Christian nation. The tension surfaced when a new mosque was built on the coastline across the border in Turkey. It was visible from afar and was the first thing visitors would see on arrival in Sarpi. My interlocutors saw this new mosque as a "provocation," a hurtful one because it affected how inhabitants of Georgian Sarpi were perceived by their compatriots. In response – and in line with a process of conversion to Orthodox Christianity that started in the early 1990s – a group of young and middle-aged men made serious plans to construct a church on the Georgian part of the village (due to financial difficulties it was only in 2007 that a church was constructed near the coastline, clearly visible from the Turkish side).

Thus, the opening of the Georgian-Turkish border did not result in the kind of cultural intermingling that mainstream globalization theories predicted. Renewed contact proved disillusioning, similar to what happened in other locations along the Iron Curtain (Berdahl 1999; Svašek 2002; Mihaylova 2003). Indeed, the situation along the Georgian-Turkish border was reminiscent of Gupta and Ferguson's (1992) suggestion that "as actual places and localities become ever more blurred and indeterminate, *ideas* of culturally and ethnically distinct places become perhaps even more salient." While Gupta and Ferguson refrain from specifying the conditions and mechanisms that propel such ideational distinction, this case offers a few concrete indications. Differences mattered most when they were expected the least, and when social distances were shortest. Similarities were problematic because they made inhabitants of Sarpi "guilty by association." A process was set in motion whereby "minor" differences were expanded upon and "major" differences were set in stone.[10] While the two sides were physically drawn closer in the years after 1988, this softening of the physical divide was accompanied by a hardening of cultural boundaries.

MAKING IT STICK

The socialist borders separating East from West were exceptional borders in that they managed to accomplish almost perfect physical closure. This goes some way to explaining why socialist borders received relatively little academic attention. First, borders tend to get attention mainly when challenged, for example by cross-border movement. Second, impermeable borders did not fit the academic agendas that underlay the flourishing of border studies in the 1990s. Borders were interesting either because they provided insight into the complexities of connection or because they allowed for a critique of essentialisms (especially the modernist perspective that treated nations and states as coherent entities). Because socialist borders offered no obvious insight into the complexities of connection and seemed to affirm a modernist perspective, they were analytically inconvenient. This tendency has spilled over into the post–Cold War era such that even a volume with the "promising" title *Curtains of Iron and Gold* (Eskelinen et al. 1999) has strangely little to say about the material and social lives of the Iron Curtains.[11] Likewise, Green's *Notes from the Balkans*, which offers a rich account of the multilayered or fractal nature of the Greek borderlands with Albania, brushes the socialist period aside by saying only that "effectively, Albania, 'disappeared'" between the mid-1940s and 1990 (2005: 49). This is unfortunate, because closer scrutiny reveals the complexity of these seemingly straightforward and impervious borders. In this essay I have endeavored to show that closed borders are analytically interesting precisely because closure is so difficult to produce. It was not that the Soviet-Georgian border was never challenged but rather that top-down ambivalence and grassroots subversion interlocked in a way that solidified the border regime.

Fences and walls are constructed to deter or to channel movement: facing inward to prevent dissipation or outward to obstruct infiltration. The associated boundary-drawing activities are, as argued above, essential to thwart chaos and thus a precondition for meaningful action. But the issue is rather complex. The drawn boundaries may lack strength or depth, producing, as Mary Douglas wrote, (merely) a "*semblance of order*" (1966: 4).[12] This was evident in Sarpi, where the Iron Curtain initially corresponded very poorly with the far more messy reality on the ground. But although Douglas rightly stressed "semblance," it is important to point out that semblance does not necessarily mean superficiality. In fact, lines that are drawn arbitrarily may become "real" due to the structuring processes that are set in motion by the initial drawing. And when such processes intertwine with the interests and ideas of a population, they certainly may become worth defending. Thus, when villagers in Sarpi tried to remove the "superficial veneer" produced by an imposed Curtain that had prevented the continuation of family bonds, they discovered that there were no shared "deeper" layers – that is, the semblance *was* the substance.

If order can be deceptive, then this is also true of chaos; one could say that the removal of the grid (symbolized by the opening of the border) produced merely a "semblance of chaos." That is, the invocation of the notion of chaos does not preclude the simultaneous existence of an order that is successfully hidden from view, and may in fact refer to subterranean patterns and hierarchies that exist by virtue of their (partial) invisibility. The situation at the Sarpi checkpoint in the 1990s could be described along these lines. Things appeared to be "out of control," but beneath the visible surface, elements could be detected that pointed toward structured practices of extortion and accumulation. That is, the phenomena that were being referred to should not be interpreted as *pure* chaos (which anyway may prove indistinguishable from "pure order" [13]) but *experienced* chaos, which on the one hand denotes uncertainty, instability, and the difficulty of adjusting to a new situation (all of which produces a sense of turmoil), and on the other hand the displacement of "cultured orders," that is, the orders that are deemed essential for a "cultured" or "civilized" existence. I argue that it is this combination of uncertainty and perceived immorality that generates the urge to stop and solidify the flux.

The relatively ungraspable nature of this topic stems from the fact that while we seem to be talking about oscillations between two extreme points on a one-dimensional continuum – order and chaos – this is complicated by a concurrent process of foregrounding and backgrounding. As in the discussion of semblances above, the contrast between chaos and order is partly deceptive and dependent on the perspective and focus applied. However, it is not only a matter of perspective but also of dynamics. First, the act of categorizing and dividing produces hybrids because no boundary line perfectly follows already existing patterns of differentiation. As Strathern (1996: 522) argues (taking a cue from Latour 1993), "the more hybrids are suppressed – the more categorical divisions are made – the more they secretly breed." Thus, the establishment of the Soviet border triggered smuggling practices, it produced Muslim Georgians and it created Soviet citizens with Turkish passports. Second, and in contrast, the disorderly and limitless potential of human action and interaction needs to be reduced in order to guarantee a meaningful and manageable existence. State boundaries themselves are, of course, a prime example of this, and the need felt by inhabitants of Sarpi after the border opening to distinguish themselves from their

Turkish-speaking Muslim relatives on the other side illustrates the same principle. As Strathern demonstrates, the key issue is "how to control the flow" and "where to put limits" in the "limitless expanse" of social practice (1996: 519, 522): it is about "cutting the network," as she aptly titles her influential essay. Opposed sets of forces that transcend the blockage and that stop the flow are concurrently at work. Linking this back to the discussion above, one could say that chaos and order are unstable and relational categories that tend to invoke each other.

These statements about flows and blockages (or chaos and order) invoking each other are not fully satisfactory. I would argue that this is partly due to Strathern's lack of attention to time and the "sedimentary" effects of flows and blockages, which leads us to a discussion of the relation between stuff and boundaries (to use Barth's 1969 terms). In his work *Time Matters,* sociologist Abbott considers precisely this when suggesting that we "should not look for boundaries of things, but for things of boundaries" (2001: 261). His points of departure are the sites of difference or proto-boundaries that tend to be somewhat arbitrarily placed in what he calls "a soup of pre-existing actors and actions" (2001: 266). These proto-boundaries then initiate a process of structuration by which "thingness" is produced. In Abbott's words, "we should start with boundaries and investigate how people create entities by linking those boundaries into units" (2001: 261). Parallels with the history of the Georgian-Turkish border are obvious. The boundary drawn in 1921 did not initially represent a meaningful (or actual) divide, but its existence pushed people to organize their lives in response to it. It is important to point out that not *any* "arbitrary boundary" could have produced these effects: a powerful Soviet state had arranged its mechanisms of surveillance in such a way that villagers (inadvertently) reinforced them. The result was that categories such as Georgian nationality were eventually appropriated, thereby adding substance to the divide. Attention to the dynamics by which borders and stuff are co-constituted suggests that oscillations between chaos and order may be rather "sticky" events.

If "closure" is difficult (but not impossible) to achieve, "opening" is an equally complicated issue. Villagers had anticipated that they would reestablish meaningful contacts with their cross-border relatives if and when the border opened. But when this actually happened, these contacts upset cultural patterns that had formed within the closed border situation. And here we arrive at the paradox. Despite Soviet Sarpians' increasing identification with the Georgian nation and distancing from Islam, ambiguities had remained; but these Soviet-inspired attitudes became crucial ingredients for the renovation of imagined boundaries, long after the taboos surrounding the border itself had fallen. If the villagers of Soviet Sarpi had unwittingly and sometimes unwillingly been drawn into sustaining the border, those living in independent Georgia were ready to defend it, at least for a while. It is only to be expected that this will change with the passing of time.

NOTES

1   "Granitsu okhraniaiet *ves'* Sovetskii Narod."
2   In this chapter, the term "socialist border" refers explicitly to external borders of the socialist bloc, not to borders separating socialist countries or Soviet republics. While

external socialist borders became more permeable after 1989, borders between Soviet republics tended to move in the opposite direction, with previous internal movement becoming "internationalized," as Kanneff and Heintz (2006: 8) write. See also Megoran (this volume, chapter 27).

3   Respectively "Gürcistana Hoş Geldiniz" and "sakartvelo ketili iqos tkveni mobrdzaneba!"

4   One could also say that the "welcoming" is most telling for what it *makes invisible*, which is Coutin's (2005) argument when describing the ways in which the documentary regime along the US–Mexico border pushes many migrants into a vulnerable and marginal existence.

5   Research in Sarpi and the wider Georgian border region was conducted over 18 months between 1997 and 2001.

6   The Kurds and Hemshins never returned to Sarpi. The deportees of 1949 and 1951 who survived the often gruesome living conditions in exile returned between 1954 and 1956.

7   This reliance on self-policing was common practice along the Iron Curtain. Berdahl (1999: 51) mentions that a significant portion of adult men in Kella, a village located on the eastern side of the German Iron Curtain, were active as *Grenzhelfer* or *Volkspolizei-helfer*, in addition to an unknown number of individuals working as Stasi informants. Mihaylova (2003: 50–51) reports that similar assistance was provided by the Pomak border dwellers in Bulgaria along the border with Greece, and adds that some informants wryly commented that their name Pomak was derived from the Bulgarian verb *pomagam* which means "to help."

8   Paasi notes a similar attitude among the younger generation in both the Finnish and Russian parts of the town of Värtsilä, for whom "the boundary had been rather a neutral phenomenon, part of what was taken for granted in everyday life" (1999: 677).

9   See Pelkmans (in press) for an extensive discussion of these practices.

10 The adjectives major and minor are placed in quotation marks because the significance of difference is in the (changing) eye of the beholder.

11 Tellingly, Borneman's *Belonging in the Two Berlins* (1992), which is an early and excellent study of the dynamics of kinship, politics, and the nation in a divided city, hardly analyzes people's engagement with the Wall itself. To be fair, he does take up this issue in a later publication (Borneman 1998).

12 Mary Douglas argued that by demarcating and "exaggerating the difference between within and without . . . a semblance of order is created" (1966: 4). The word *semblance* underscores the frailty of the activity as well as the indispensability of disorder, because disorder "provides the materials of pattern" (1966: 94).

13 That "pure chaos" may be indistinguishable from "pure order" is beautifully (but unintentionally) shown by Nazpary when he starts his book *Post-Soviet Chaos* by quoting a Kazakh woman's description of the chaotic reality of Almaty in the early 1990s: "today people have become like savage animals. They behave according to the law of the jungle. Everybody who is strong hits, rapes, murders and robs everybody else who is weak" (2002: 1). A literal reading of this comment indicates perfect order because there is only one law – the law of the jungle – that defines all behavior.

REFERENCES

Abbott, Andrew. 2001. *Time Matters: On Theory and Method*. Chicago: University of Chicago Press.

Barth, Fredrik. 1969. Introduction. In Fredrick Barth, ed., *Ethnic Groups and Boundaries: The Social Organization of*

Culture Difference, pp. 9–38. Boston: Little, Brown.

Berdahl, Daphne. 1999. *Where the World Ended: Re-unification and Identity in the German Borderland*. Berkeley: University of California Press.

Borneman, John. 1992. *Belonging in the Two Berlins: Kin, State, Nation*. Cambridge: Cambridge University Press.

Borneman, John. 1998. Grenzregime (border regime): the Wall and its aftermath. In Thomas M. Wilson and Hastings Donnan, eds, *Border Identities: Nation and State at International Frontiers*, pp. 162–190. Cambridge: Cambridge University Press

Bornstein, Avram. 2002. *Crossing the Green Line between the West Bank and Israel*. Philadelphia: University of Pennsylvania Press.

Coutin, Susan. 2005. Being en route. *American Anthropologist* 107 (2): 195–206.

Douglas, Mary. 1966. *Purity and Danger: An Analysis of Concepts of Pollution and Taboo*. New York: Praeger.

Donnan, Hastings and Wilson, Thomas M. 1999. *Borders: Frontiers of Identity, Nation and State*. Oxford: Berg.

Driessen, Henk. 1996. What am I doing here? The anthropologist, the mole, and border ethnography. In W. Kokot and D. Dracklé, eds, *Ethnologie Europas. Grenzen, Konflikte, Identitäten*, pp. 287–298. Berlin: Dietrich Reimer.

Eskelinen, Heikki, Liikanen, Ilkka and Oksa, Jukka, eds. 1999. *Curtains of Iron and Gold: Reconstructing Borders and Scales of interaction*. Aldershot: Ashgate.

Foucault, Michel. 1979. *Discipline and Punish: The Birth of the Prison*. Harmondsworth: Penguin.

Green, Sarah. 2005. *Notes from the Balkans: Locating Marginality and Ambiguity on the Greek-Albanian Border*. Princeton: Princeton University Press.

Gupta, Akhil and Ferguson, James. 1992. Beyond "culture": space, identity, and the politics of difference. *Cultural Anthropology* 17 (1): 6–23.

Hann, Chris and Bellér-Hann, Ildikó. 1992. Samovars and sex on Turkey's Russian markets. *Anthropology Today* 8 (4): 3–6.

Hann, Chris and Bellér-Hann, Ildikó. 1998. Markets, morality and modernity in northeast Turkey. In Thomas M. Wilson and Hastings Donnan, eds, *Border Identities: Nation and State at International Frontiers*, pp. 237–262. Cambridge: Cambridge University Press.

Herzfeld, Michael. 2001. *Anthropology: Theoretical Practice in Culture and Society*. Oxford: Blackwell.

Kaneff, D. and Heintz, M. 2006. Introduction. Bessarabian borderlands: one region, two states, multiple ethnicities. *Anthropology of East Europe Review* 24 (1): 6–16.

Kearney, Michael. 1998. Transnationalism in California and Mexico at the end of empire. In Thomas Wilson and Hastings Donnan, eds, *Border Identities: Nation and State at International Frontiers*, pp. 117–141. Cambridge: Cambridge University Press.

Konstantinov, Yulian. 1996. Patterns of reinterpretation: trader-tourism in the Balkans (Bulgaria) as a picaresque metaphorical enactment of post-totalitarianism. *American Ethnologist* 23 (4): 762–782.

Laclau, Ernesto. 1993. Politics and the limits of modernity. In T. Docherty, ed., *Postmodernism: A Reader*. New York: Columbia University Press.

Latour, Bruno. 1993. *We Have Never Been Modern*. Cambridge: Harvard University Press.

Mihaylova, Dimitrina. 2003. Between a rock and a hard place: Pomak identities at the border between Bulgaria and Greece. *Focaal – European Journal of Anthropology* 41: 45–57.

Nazpary, Joma. 2002. *Post-Soviet Chaos: Violence and Dispossession in Kazakhstan*. London: Pluto Press.

Paasi, Anssi. 1996. *Territories, Boundaries and Consciousness: The Changing Geographies of the Finnish–Russian Border*. Chichester: John Wiley & Sons, Ltd.

Paasi, Anssi. 1999. Boundaries as social practice and discourse: the Finnish–Russian border. *Regional Studies* 37 (7): 669–680.

Pelkmans, Mathijs. 2006. *Defending the Border: Identity, Religion, and Modernity in the Republic of Georgia*. Ithaca: Cornell University Press.

Pelkmans, Mathijs. In press. Powerful documents: passports, passages, and dilemmas of identification on the Georgian-Turkish border. In Laura Bacas and William Kavanagh, eds, *Asymmetry and Proximity in Border Encounters*. Oxford: Berghahn Books.

Strathern, Marilyn. 1996. Cutting the network. *Journal of the Royal Anthropological Institute* 2: 517–35.

Svašek, Maruška. 2002. Narratives of "home" and "homeland": the symbolic construction and appropriation of the Sudeten German Heimat. *Identities: Global Studies in Culture and Power* 9: 495–518.

16 # Border Security as Late-Capitalist "Fix"

Brenda Chalfin

International border regimes are a principal technology of the global economy . . . critical to the expanding securitization of the nation-state and capital interests of elites.

(Cunningham 2009: 143)

In the first decades of the twenty-first century border zones across the United States and allied states worldwide bear the burden of an untrammeled quest for security driven by America's efforts to reassert hegemony post–9/11. Shaping the ordering and operation of land, maritime or aerial frontiers across the globe, US-led security imperatives cast a wide net as they seek to control normal as well as aberrant forms of mobility and stasis. Under this rubric, all persons, goods and communiqués moving across international border zones are subject to extensive scrutiny and implicit suspicion. Any vector of cross-border circulation that threatens or suggests a threat to individual or collective safety, however defined, may be apprehended, checked and, if necessary, destroyed by the agents of the state and international security apparatus.

These defining conditions of twenty-first century border security – of stopping and checking, suspicion, scrutiny, suspension, and the assertion of American might – appear to contrast sharply with the ideals of unfettered global flow defining the pre–9/11 imagination of a borderless world of free trade, transnational capital, corporate dominance and the accumulation of power and resources beyond the states of the North Atlantic core. How can these two moments – one of wealth creation, transnational circulation, multipolarity and the decline of state authority, the other of neo-imperialism, national defense, and the interruption of global interchange – be resolved?[1] Is the hardening of international boundaries under the US-led post–9/11 security regime a refutation of the promises of globalization and the supposed worldwide victory of capitalism and post–Cold War neoliberal ideals? Or, alternatively, is

A Companion to Border Studies, First Edition. Edited by Thomas M. Wilson and Hastings Donnan.
© 2012 Blackwell Publishing Ltd. Published 2012 by Blackwell Publishing Ltd.

the prevailing image of global integration itself distorted? One cannot discount the argument that the free flow of goods, information and financial investment characteristic of advanced capitalism has long been accompanied by a harsh edifice of control restricting a large portion of the world's population who seek geopolitical mobility in the pursuit of economic opportunity (Cunningham 2004).

Complicating both sets of claims, I address a different facet of this political economic puzzle. Rather than pose security as a challenge to the fundamentals of capitalist globalization or probe how the realities of global economic mobility are at odds with their ideological representation, I eschew the notion of a radical break (cf. Smith 2005). Instead I argue that twenty-first century border securitization is very much a late-capitalist formulation, partaking deeply of the mechanics and mores of pre–9/11 globalization. Just as established political alliances enabled the quick set-up of the post–9/11 security agenda, I demonstrate that both the security problem and solutions to it are artifacts of existing material conditions.

Despite a prevailing analytical preoccupation with the political valence of international frontiers (Anderson 1991; Prescott 1987), and the conventional treatment of security as the core of national defense, border security is as much economic as political in orientation, fundamentally shaped by material processes and logics. Whether in the age of mercantilism, industrialization or financialization, borders controls are bound up with the flow of commerce, labor and capital (Sassen 2006; Torpey 2000). Similarly, securitization, like other forms of militarization, is a fully economic endeavor, grounded in the deployment of resources, manpower and technology (Deger and Sen 1990; Lutz 2001; OECD 2004). The post–9/11 border security mandate is no exception.

Although it is widely accepted that the rebirth of the American security state and the broadcast of its objectives worldwide stems from the proximate political crisis of 9/11, this well-honed claim should not divert attention from the close connection between the global ascendance of the avowedly American border security agenda and a more generalized crisis of American and indeed, global economic restructuring. From the US perspective, the new millennium ushered in an economic sea change of notable proportion marked by America's waning grip on the conventional arbiters of capitalist growth (Harvey 2003). Reordering long-standing core–periphery relations, at this historical juncture not only were US-based exports and manufacturing falling behind, and with them the sustainability of the US labor market, but an older economic order based on tangible assets was being supplanted by the virtual economies of high-finance and information-based value, on which the US held a substantial but by no means exclusive grip (Robinson 2004).

With these conditions in mind, I contend that the conventions of twenty-first century border security, despite their purported political motivation, further the forms and functions, and fears and fantasies of late capitalism. While far from achieving their express political ends, these engagements nevertheless profoundly impact the political landscape, ultimately altering the distribution of political rights and recognition, the terms of political accountability and subjecthood, along with the very locus of government. Seen from this light, I maintain that the conventions of twenty-first century border security represent a distinctive "spatio-temporal fix" bridging the dilemmas and possibilities posed by the late-modern economy amidst the wider crisis of US hegemony and the territorially conceived state (Harvey 2001). A termed coined by David Harvey, the notion of "fix" is "a metaphor for a particular kind of solution to capitalist crises through temporal deferral and geographical expansion" (2003: 115) Apposite to the analysis of border controls, the term provides a useful shorthand for state-orchestrated responses to and through material conditions. As Harvey reminds us, and as will become clear below, any such fix is always partial, generating its own inequities and instabilities and setting the stage for further intervention and innovation.

In contrast to Harvey and like-minded scholars such as Smith (2005), who unpack the economic motives driving the US "War on Terror" (in Harvey's case, the oversight of Middle East oil reserves (2003: 21)), rather than focus on the economic *ends* of the US security agenda post–9/11, I hone in on the economic *means* of border securitization and their ensuing political ramifications.[2] In this regard, I investigate three sorts of political economic fix. One is the alliance of immigration reform and border security in the furthering of late-capitalist labor discipline. The second is the promotion of logics of mass consumption in the broadcasting of border surveillance. The third is employment of cutting-edge biometric technologies in the crafting of subjects accountable to a state security apparatus.

LABOR AND LATE CAPITALISM: THE IMMIGRATION-SECURITY FIX

Perhaps the most glaring economic determination of post–9/11 border security policy is the constitution of labor migration as a security concern. Officially and unofficially targeting the vast population of legal, illegal, semilegal, quasi-legal labor migrants within or seeking entry into American territory, the declaration of the "War on Terror" in the US coincided with the formulation of a variety of anti-immigrant and anti-immigration initiatives portrayed as integral to the national security agenda (see also Cunningham 2009). Whether formally credentialed, skilled or unskilled, this vast class of workers makes an essential contribution to small and large businesses alike and can be found across the US economy, from traditional growth poles such as agriculture and industry to newer ones such as construction, information technology and healthcare, alongside reproductive labor such as child and home care. Nevertheless, in a largely unquestioned fusion of the imperatives of national security with a generalized anxiety about threats posed by so-called foreign bodies and economies, this wide-ranging policy front adversely affects those construed as migrants and natives alike. Privileging capital over labor and substituting state investment in policing for social welfare, the result is a decline in working conditions and political standing for all.

The formation of the US Department of Homeland Security (DHS), one of the most decisive acts in the building of America's twenty-first century security platform, has played a key role in the actualization of this political economic agenda. Amalgamating nearly two dozen federal agencies, the founding of Homeland Security meant that the US Customs Service, originally in the Treasury Department, and the Immigration and Naturalization Service (INS, including the Border Patrol[3]), originally in the Department of Justice, were combined and rearranged to form three divisions. Characterized by distinct objectives though pursuing overlapping roles, this has fostered the duplication of efforts around punitive border enforcement. What may be construed as "integrative" immigration functions like naturalization are now the purview of the US Citizenship and Immigration Service (CIS). US Customs and Border Protection (CBP), combining the Border Patrol, INS inspectors and US Customs inspectors, is ostensibly dedicated to border control. Yet their border security agenda is closely shared with US Immigration and Customs Enforcement (ICE). Combining the forces of former INS investigators, US Customs investigators, the Federal Protective Service and the Federal Air Marshalls, ICE is detailed to immigration investigations, deportation and intelligence.

Compared to CIS's integrative functions, ICE is devoted to the reinforcement of sociopolitical and material distinctions, borders included. Tying the US CBP mission to its own, under Homeland Security, ICE is deputized to go after persons whom authorities on the border may have missed. Domesticating the operations of border agents, ICE has the authority to check documents as well as interrogate and apprehend suspects. Replicating the functions of border authorities, these arrangements also replicate the border's spatiality, as those suspected of flouting immigration requirements are subject to extended detention. Typically relegated to privately run holding centers, they rehearse the limbo of the border under incarceration-like conditions marked by the deprivation of care, contact and comfort (Liptak 2010; Bernstein 2010). Combined with the border security agenda in this way, immigration is turned into a threat in need of management by the strong arm of the state, and immigration enforcement transformed into a wide-ranging form of policing.

Advancing the interests of capital, the political economic implications of this sort of security fix are profound. Subject to the usual predations of management and further victimized by the excessive (and now, legitimate) authority of the security state, workers' vulnerability is heightened. Fostering a "race to the bottom" allowing little redress for labor in the face of management or the state, akin to the experiences of a globalized industrial working class under late capitalism (Collins 2003; Ong 2006), these arrangements enable the deterioration of wages and working conditions, affecting immigrant and nonimmigrant, legal and illegal workers alike (Preston 2009). At the same time, with local authorities voluntarily and involuntarily enrolled in this project in the name of national security (Rodriguez 2009), the rolling back of conventional social welfare supports characteristic of the global neoliberal turn is legitimated anew on the home front. Here, rather than the near total evacuation of the state services, as was predicted in the heyday of neoliberal globalization (Rose 1996), security functions are built up on the edges and interior of national territory by state authorities working in tandem with private capital.

CONSUMPTION, DATABASING AND THE POST–9/11 SECURITY-INDUSTRIAL "FIX"

It is not only late-capitalist labor conditions that are intensified under conditions of securitization. There are other facets of late-capitalist economies that play a driving role, defining the very terms of national security on the border and more generally. In this light, another critical "fix" linking the global capitalist milieu, state power and the burgeoning of border security in the twenty-first century is the "security-industrial complex": the technologies, firms, knowledge forms and skilled and unskilled labor involved in the production and pursuit of national security.[4] Founded on a host of self-evident as well as veiled connections and fostering a score of acknowledged as well as veiled outcomes, a key area of interchange between security and late-capitalist economic trends are the databasing technologies used by border authorities to track and apprehend suspicious travelers. Closely tied to familiar strategies of consumption and consumer research, their political fallout is wide-ranging and largely normalized.

In the US and the many other countries that conform to America's geopolitical platform, databasing technologies are highly prominent in the execution of the rubrics of post–9/11 border security. Cementing the link between border security and late capitalism, they are built upon and fully resemble the techniques of consumer research. Though consumer databases seek ultimately to entice, and security databases are used for purposes of suspension or arrest, they otherwise share an intriguing array of features. More than simply capturing information, both sorts of databases actively reorder it for purposes of modeling, tracking and prediction. Systematically compiling information about a huge population of actors, security and consumer databases likewise rely on the same sources of expertise in their design and application, including information technology giants such as IBM and Accenture. They are linked by a common investment in the surveillance of subject populations less in terms of overt or "visible" supervision, as Anthony Giddens puts it, than the indirect though comprehensive "use of information to coordinate social activities" (1991: 15).

Further allying the two, consumer and security databases strive to be panoptic on a temporal if not a spatial front via the collection of extensive retrospective and ongoing behavioral data. Each type of database is also reductive, breaking down a whole into notable parts to create a consumer or security profile. Geared to the identification of trends, they both seek to capture habitual action along with the triggers for unprecedented or innovative behavior. Hence, despite the tendency to use consumer research to manipulate or motivate behavior and security data to stifle it, the two technologies of knowledge management seek to shape and anticipate particular sorts of responses (Adey 2004: 1372). Turning personal features and behaviors into "types" to be managed by corporate and state bodies, each shares in what has been described by Giddens again as the "institutional reflexivity" of modern life: "which pries social relations free from the hold of specific locales, recombining them across wide time-space distances" (1991: 2).

Consumption and security databasing share more than formal similarities. Over time the latter has become thoroughly functionally dependent on the former. In this way, security rubrics undertake what might be called a "reflexive reworking of consumption," self-consciously applying consumer data to new ends in a manner that both affirms and reconsiders their founding logic. In the US, for instance, consumers' hotel and flight reservation information is routinely collected and reviewed by the DHS, where it is vetted by experts in the agency's National Targeting Center (Grossman 2009). Until challenged by the American Civil Liberties Union, at its inception

Homeland Security's "no fly list" similarly sought to utilize credit reports in the calculating of travelers' risk scores (Meckler 2005). The fusion of consumption and security is not restricted to the US. Also combining consumption and security data, a 2009 ruling in the UK mandates that international travelers submit their travel plans, including credit card information, to government authorities to be included in the database of the country's new "e-borders" program (Privacy International 2005).

Stabilizing what is otherwise mobile, this assemblage of personal data is both typological/ascriptive and discretionary/achieved in character. Once obtained by security agencies it is considered legal, evidentiary knowledge and serves as the foundation for ascertaining a subject's compliance or noncompliance with security standards. Compared to the chaotic assemblage of real life in real time, in order to assess compliance the information is logically ordered into modal portraits of individual persons, classes of persons, and wider populations. Giving rise to what Lyon calls "surveillant sorting" (2007: 124), outliers, considered the prime source of uncertainty and thus the purveyors of risk, are thereby distinguished from the norm and dealt with through the appropriate legal and extralegal means.

Compromising privacy even for those not considered security threats, the collection of personal consumption and lifestyle data regarding where, how and with whom one lives, works and travels augments the state's breadth of knowledge about persons, with powerful implications for political subjecthood. This is evident, for instance, in the now commonplace requisite screening of bodies and personal effects at airports around the world via organs such as the Transportation Security Administration. Reviving the scope of US imperium post–9/11, Transportation Security Administration (another element of the sprawling DHS) uses its close ties to the United Nations based International Civil Aviation Organization to institute shared protocols for the technologically assisted screening of passengers, baggage and air cargo in 100 countries around the world. On the surface geared to the search for dangerous items, these now international screening provisions in practice entail the routine revelation to the state and other members of the public of the status of individual travelers as consumers via the repeated public display and scrutiny of travelers' bodies, documents and personal effects. A situation intensified with the recent adoption of whole body imaging technologies at security check points, the display and temporary renunciation of items of personal consumption reduces travelers, stripped of shoes, possessions and select items of clothing, to a state of bare life (Agamben 1998), however brief, preemptory or socially redeeming in purpose.

The alliance of security and consumption is equally apparent in the fusion of securitized border sites and zones of consumption, with the two increasingly designed to resemble one another. Now that airports must function as sites of consumption due to the extended dwell time required by new security protocols, airport shopping is a highly lucrative investment, with "terminal shops found to earn double those on the high streets" (Adey 2004: 1375). And just as consumption functions have been imported into border spaces in the course of securitization, surveillance practices earlier considered border specific are being exported to ostensibly nonborder spaces of public consumption, demonstrated by the recent ramping up of security in New York's Times Square and the near ubiquitous presence of CCTV in public spaces in the UK (Morgan and Pritchard 2005). For more privileged consumers, securitization emerges as a lifestyle choice. A trend predating the post–9/11 security boom but growing out of the same forces and anxieties and augmented by it, residence in gated communities is considered a sign of socioeconomic success and a guarantor of socio-economic mobility (Lowe 2003). Under these circumstances securitization becomes a generalized practice marking the presence of mobile persons rather than territorial borders per se. Here we see what Cunningham calls the "internalization of the border" as "border regimes extend into the interior spaces of the nation, especially in terms of movement corridors . . . rendering public space a borderland" (2009: 147). Yet these developments also suggest the movement of the practices and logics of security into private domains of household and community.

Fundamentally enabled by border security rubrics relying on personal data and consumer profiling techniques, the stretching of the surveillance capacities of the state beyond the border proper is of significant import. Signaling the deepening striation of civilian political status in the world's leading states (Pallitto and Heyman 2008), while this trend reveals a modality of state power to which entire populations are subject, it is critical to recognize that different sectors of the public are subject to it in very different ways. It is no secret that the categories of person who are victims of excessive authority at the border are likely to find themselves subject to discrimination elsewhere, and vice versa. With border security rubrics found to be "calibrated white" (Wilson 2007: 208), this is evident in the US for instance in the post–9/11 mistreat-ment of persons of Muslim faith and/or Arab descent in both daily life and in the course of border crossing, and the ongoing crackdown on inadequately documented immigrants in border regions and more generally (Staeheli and Nagel 2008), whether in North America (Rosas 2006), the European Union (Balibar 2004), or other spaces of Anglo-European privilege such as Australia (Wilson 2007). Curbing rights, oppor-tunities, and often mobility, the reliance on ethnoreligious and racial profiling inher-ent in these modes of border security furthers stigmatization and induces a pervasive sense of insecurity for those at risk of discrimination, effectively extending the border, or the "borderland condition," into what Rosas (2006: 335) identifies as a permanent state of exception. Here, the same conditions promising inclusion via the lure of consumption provide new grounds for exclusion by way of security. A similar set of political dynamics is at work in other arenas of the post–9/11 security-industrial complex, as described below.

THE BIOMETRIC "FIX": THE SECURITY SURPLUS AND THE DEATH OF ACCOUNTABILITY

Holding much in common with databasing, biometry or biometrics is a likewise critical feature of the twenty-first century security-industrial complex. Closely aligned with the biotech and digital revolutions of the late twentieth century, the potentials of biometry have been brought to life anew in the age of securitization. Further revealing the interdependence of post–9/11 security initiatives and the dynamics of late capitalism, biometry is at once extensively employed in the pursuit of border security and an important growth pole of the twenty-first century economy.

Biometrics, as defined by experts in the field, "refers to the auto-identification (or verification) of an individual by using certain physiological or behavioral traits associated with the person" (Jain and Ross 2005). Treating the body as the ultimate identifier of a person, and thus the substantive link between a person and a proper versus suspicious act, through biometry the pursuit of border security has come to depend on a range of techniques of physical data capture. Just as the likeness of the typological sketch in nineteenth-century forensics was surpassed by the truth value of the fingerprint in the early twentieth century (Joseph 2001), current criteria of secure identification now home in on distinct and unalterable features of the body through techniques of digitized biometry. A phenomenon not at all restricted to border zones, these technologies reorder conventions of political accountability, reducing both the rights and the rendering of the political subject in the search for definitive proof of identity.

In its current computerized/digitized iteration, biometric security works through a four-step process, beginning with the acquisition of biometric data through a sensor, followed by the extraction of a digital feature set, the comparison of the feature set with a preestablished template, and finally, decision-making regarding either the identification of the source of the data or the verification that a claimed identity matches the biometrically determined one (Jain 2007). Located within a wide field of possibility, including numerous attempts at face and hand recognition via facial thermograms, ear shape, hand geometry and vascular palm maps, as well as gait tracking, heartbeat recognition, voice prints, written signatures and genetic data, among the most prominent biomarkers of border security are digital fingerprints and iris and retina scans, both amenable to quick, convenient and accurate data capture and rapid confirmation and comparison (Jain 2007).

Although the term biometrics has been in circulation for over a century (Molenberghs 2006: 5–6), biometric innovations used for purposes of border security have a much more recent vintage. Built upon the digital dot.com revolution of the 1980s and 1990s (Connell 2002), the latest revival of biometry is intimately allied with the core innovations of global capitalism rooted in space-time compression (Appadurai 2001; Sassen 2001), the cultivation of widely distanciated forms of sociality (Giddens 1991), and the creation of value around virtual knowledge. Sharing many features of other digital applications, twenty-first century biometrics depends on the quick manipulation of massive electronic datasets condensing an extensive range of information and computation onto a rapid relay micro-scale via integrated circuitry. Like other commercially successful developments of the digital age with intellectual capital at the fore, whether the internet, digital search engines, or file-sharing, biometry relies on the combined expertise of computer engineering and information science. Working across media, also similar to these applications, it is grounded in the ideal of seamless replication and perfect representation, putting a premium on the conversion of what is tangible and familiar into an alternative register of knowledge that may be easily transferred and transacted.

In addition to their roots in the digital economy, contemporary biometric applications are equally tied to the late twentieth-century takeoff of the field of biotechnology (Laver 2000). Coming into fruition through the overlap of the financial investments of "big pharma" in new health diagnostics and interventions (Petryna et al. 2006), sophisticated mathematical and computer-generated models of biological phenomena from academia, and a more general cultural outlook geared to risk assessment and the pursuit of bionormalcy by all (Rabinow and Rose 2006), biotechnology rose to prominence in the 1990s. An economic sector that is at once intensively knowledge based, fully applied, and dependent upon a combination of consumer choice and rarified expertise, it continues to occupy a leading edge of the new economy (Alpert 2004; *Business Week* 2003; Reaser 2002). By equally treating the human body as an anchor of knowledge, biometrics shares with biotechnology a focus on preemption. In both cases, detailed knowledge of the body serves as the basis for control (Rose and Novas 2005). While biotechnology uses the body to identify and correct or root out physiological pathologies, using a similar metaphor of infection to different ends, biometrics seeks out the embodied markers of social pathology, construed as being situated within an individual yet threatening society as a whole.

Further demonstrating the grounding of biometrics in the mainstream of global capitalism, the corporate structures of the three economic sectors exhibit homologous forms as well as outright linkages and interdependences. Just as the dot.com and biotech bubbles brought the notion of the start-up company into common parlance, today's biometric firms have followed the same course. Designing, marketing and manufacturing sensors and scanners, coding and encryption devices, surveillance cameras, biometric verification stations, virtual and physical access control packages, software, smartcards and microprocessors, all to dozens of different standards and specifications (indoor, outdoor, mobile, fixed, large scale, small scale, wireless, plugged in, real time and accelerated, and so on), the biometric industry is at once the offspring of top-ranking multinationals such as GE, IBM and Motorola (respectively numbers 5, 14 and 78 in the latest Fortune 500 ranking) and the seedbed for a host of smaller firms (*CNNMoney* 2009). All trawling for twenty-first century venture capital, many of them are linked in one way or another to university laboratories and research scientists (Grover 2005: 82). Holding names such as Morpho-Trak, Secugen, Iritrack, iQueue, Acuity, Net Nanny, Cogent, Validity, Sense Holdings, Cognitec, Identix, Viisage, AuthenTec, among others, their appellations reflect their intended mission of grasping ultimate bodily knowledge.

When digital biometry first came on the scene, applications were almost entirely commercial: geared to things like ATM usage and securing corporate data access (Adelson 2005). Following the events of 9/11, however, biometry made an unexpected (and some argue, premature) leap into the domain of government in the service of border security (findBIOMETRICS 2010). Geometrically enlarging the scale of operation and garnering a respectable share of the multibillion dollar budget of the DHS, the turn to biometric border security in the US infused the industry with substantial new capital and a renewed sense of purpose, along with new technical expectations and constraints. On the downside, DHS contracts, for instance, are often long in coming and marked by complicated accounting and contractual procedures. However, they can easily garner tens of millions a year to biometric service providers and are a lucrative source of publicity and a lure for private investors (Grover 2005: 82).

Attesting to the reach of biometric border security along with the vast span of US influence availed by these arrangements, US standards of biometric identification now bear upon the national identification practices the world over. This is evident in passport regimes. Laid out in the US Congress Enhanced Border Security and Visa Entry Reform Act of 2002, the US has devised and broadcast a new passport template requiring biometric identifiers – specifically, digital photographs allowing for facial mapping – for all travelers coming to the US under the auspices of the US Visa Waiver Program (DHS 2005). The program, with 36 participating countries, including most European Union members as well as Japan, Singapore, Australia and New Zealand, effectively forms an international benchmark, endorsed and monitored by the United Nations based International Civil Aviation Organization. Due to the widespread use, the growing interoperability of biometric technologies and their capacity to hold multiple types of biometric data along with homing devices such as radio-frequency ID tags, the potential for these technologies to provide definitive identification of individuals, establish their location and track their movement is immense. Deftly combining the technological possibilities of networking with the reach of international bodies and the might of US imperatives via a new sort of spatio-temporal fix, these protocols effectively lay the ground for an international surveillance regime transcending the geographic restrictions of nation-based border security.

Also shifting the political grounds of securitization, the stimulation of demand for border security applications has spurred both competition and research and development in the biometrics sector and incited the movement of biometric applications from the private sector to the public and back again (findBIOMETRICS 2010). Not only may government contracts provide the knowledge and funds to devise innovative private sector applications, but smaller scale private sector projects can serve as a testing ground for larger scale public ones. To chose a single example, this is the case with the San Francisco based Cogent, a biometric company specializing in fingerprint identification. In addition to working with the DHS on fingerprint capture for the purposes of border security, the firm holds contracts with the Los Angeles County Sheriff's Department, as well as a Bay Area company developing a fingerprint-based payment device. A notable result of these sorts of exchanges and interdependencies, not to mention the common mindset on which they are based, is the emergence of biometry as an increasingly generalized technology, with international borders a common but by no means unique location for their utilization.

Creating a wide-ranging "securityscape," to borrow a term from Hugh Gusterson (2004) built on the metaphorics of Appadurai (1990), this dynamic reveals the fanning out of biometric applications across multiple domains extending well beyond the border. Harking back to earlier commercial applications, biometry on the one hand is put to use for purposes of convenience, accommodating the flow of goods and people in the pursuit of leisure. A compelling case in point, Disney Resorts is a pioneer in the popularization of biometry, using digital fingerprint recognition to oversee access to its facilities worldwide. Likewise accommodating mass consumption, as described above, biometric applications are also being developed for the split-second online and in-store shopping in lieu of the more cumbersome conventions of cash or credit card payment. Beyond leisure and convenience, biometric identification and verification, on the other hand, also find a niche in contexts where the compromise of security would be physically risky or financially costly, such as power plants, research laboratories and health care settings in the case of the former, and banking transactions, personal identity data, and corporate network access in the case of the latter (Reeves 2008). Yet as biometric applications progress, the domains of convenience and safety are rapidly merging as biometrics becomes incorporated into everyday life far beyond the border. In addition to increasingly common workplace applications such as "smart" ID cards and access protocols, domestic applications are also on the rise, from biometric PCs, safes and door locks to flash drives secured with built-in thumbprint scanners (*Economist* 2006). The result is what might be called a "biometric surplus," marked by overlap, redundancy, and an excessive concern with truth-checking and confirmation. Generating an atmosphere of hypersecurity, as attested to in the following market report, it becomes difficult to sort out the conventional and the convenient from the necessary:

> With improvement in scan rates and new analytical software being introduced in the market, biometrics is no longer being marketed for the sole purpose of security, but rather as a tool to gather and assimilate information that would help in the management of an organization. As different types of security are being employed in a single building, system integrators have also ensured that the biometric systems are interoperable with other security systems to bring about a seamless operation. (Frost & Sullivan 2010)

Despite their increasingly quotidian nature, the social and political implications of these trends are in many ways profound. Not at all reserved for the border, they signal the melding of modalities of governing across the public and private sectors via common logics, technologies and contractual arrangements. A more general feature of late modernity, this blurring of boundaries is by no means unique to the security sector and is widely manifest in the privatization of essential state services and the emergence of corporately governed economic enclaves (Ong 2006; Ferguson 2006). However, in the broadcasting of biometric strategies of border security, there is a distinctive and in many ways troubling conflation in play. For one, biometric knowledge is presented as a fixed or immutable truth countering the uncertainties that mark the late modern condition. In this techno-political matrix, identity, reduced to biometry, is treated as anchored in the unique and unalterable features of the body (Amoore 2006). And security, in turn, is reduced to the definitive discernment of these biomarkers. Seeking to capture unique bodily traits both convertible into an algorithmic code and trackable due to their purported fixity, the body in the border security equation is doubly reduced from whole to piece, and piece to digitized datum (Lyon 2007: 124).

The problem here is twofold: first, security issues are mistaken for identity issues and vice versa, and second, a concern with the security of and from persons is conflated with national security. In this twist of twenty-first century essentialism, not only is the integrity of the person as a whole denied, but the preoccupation with the embodied self ignores the social networks and relations that make up the body politic (Fonio 2007). In this disembedding of the subject of security from a social matrix, we see a vivid illustration of what Rose calls the "death of the social," despite the claim of security policies to achieve collective ends of national protection (Rose 1996:

327). In its stead, a highly intimate apparatus of government contributes to the forging of a deeply individuated political subject.

The reliance on biometry for the purposes of border security reconfigures the received terms of governing in other ways, at once narrowing the realization of political rights and stepping up state demands for the accountability of its subjects. Namely, in the extraction of information via biometry, border security relies heavily on what Mark Salter, drawing on Michel Foucault, calls a "confessionary complex." As a "mechanism for the creation of the modern subject by a modern state," this confessionary amalgam relies on the biopolitical trio of "unconditional obedience, uninterrupted examination and exhaustive confession" (Salter 2006: 180; see also Foucault 1997: 81). For Salter, "It is not simply that the international population is managed, but that we come to manage ourselves through the confessionary complex" (2006: 180). Notably different from both the scenario of self-reporting and self-regulation sketched by Salter, and more direct forms of governance based on rote interviews or violence-tinged interrogation, in the development of techniques of biometric border security we find an impending situation of "confession without consent" or "auto-confession," as the body comes to testify for the subject without the person's full knowledge.

A startling demonstration of this claim, the latest biometric security developments are founded on the extraction of data entirely unknown and in many ways unknowable to the subject. Unlike fingerprints and iris scans, the referents of which are visibly known to their beholder, or even DNA, where genotype finds knowable expression in phenotype, these biometrics have no discernible manifestation to their holder. Some, for instance, such as "thermoscan Thermo-ID" are extrasensory, tracking "non-observable attributes of human uniqueness using non-observable patterns of infrared energy naturally emanating from within the human body" (Andresen et al 2005). Other biometric technologies focus on internal characteristics of the individual that are likewise neither immediately visible nor, for the sake of security, copyable. Stating that "individual humans are unique internally, just as they are unique externally," one recent biometric conference abstract recounts the advantages of this observation:

> Physical characteristics are visible or detectable from the exterior of the body. These external characteristics can be lifted, photographed, copied or recorded for unauthorized access to a biometric system. New biometric modalities have been developed which identify people based on their unique internal characteristics. For example, "Boneprints™" use acoustic fields to scan the unique bone density pattern of a thumb pressed on a small acoustic sensor. "Imp-PrintsTM" measure the electrical impedance patterns of a hand to identify or verify a person's identity. These internal biometric modalities rely on physical characteristics which are not visible or photographable, providing an added level of security. (Mortenson 2010: 1)

In the capture of such biometric security data, the body is made to speak at the same time as it is entirely disassociated from a knowing, self-conscious subject. Relegated to a sophisticated form of bare life similar but not identical to Agamben's (1998) unelaborated *zoe*, here the body is culturally specified but not subjectively realized. Because these types of biometric surveillance are both noninvasive and nondiscernible, there is no ground for challenge or recognition on the part of the subject. Made the purview of an expert technocratic domain, biometric knowledge at once becomes more intimate and more foreign. Compared to the sorts of "biosociality" emerging alongside the sharing and circulation of new knowledge about the body and disease that are considered a distinctive feature of biosciences today, here instead we see what can be considered a type of "bio-nonsociality" where datum is separated from the individual and the individual from the group (Rose and Novas 2004).

The political implications of the sharing of biometric data and techniques across social domains are manifold. As with any sort of identificatory data, there are fundamental privacy concerns. But the particular technological features of this late-modern "biomatrix," combined with the distinctive political climate surrounding their dissemination, bring a number of concerns to the fore. One is the networked or networkable structure of these knowledge forms derived from their shared digital and electronic form and the industry-wide push toward compatibility and interoperability, rendering *biometri apparati* a full-blown "identity infrastructure." The clincher here is not just that there is or will soon be an ever ramifying web on which identity data circulate. Rather, even more significantly, my point of concern is that the spread of biometrics as a security technology will render this web of knowledge a "critical infrastructure" upon which national and international safety and well-being is said to be premised.

Attuned to the risks and likelihood of such a trajectory, industry analysts point out that the post–9/11 spotlighting of biometry in the search for a governmental quick fix preceded thoughtful regulation (findBIOMETRICS 2010). This is more than a simple case of adoption preceding the formation of regulatory guidelines that will eventually and appropriately "catch up." Rather, given the distinctive character of biometry's means and ends, source and application, it is likely to fall into a regulatory gray area resistant to accountability. This is because biometry, on the one hand, holds much in common with other techno-political solutions to the security emerging under conditions of political emergency and delegated to low-level technocrats considered outside the law (Butler 2004). Equally resistant to political accountability, biometry, on the other hand, emerges out of a rarified domain of expert knowledge (see Mitchell 2002). In many ways extralegal, these underpinnings make biometric operations difficult to translate into terms transparent or accessible to the public. The result is a decidedly uneven dynamic in which subjects are increasingly accountable to a security apparatus, but that apparatus and the identities extracted by it are increasingly inscrutable to them.

CONCLUSION

Viewed through the lens of Harvey's notion of "spatio-temporal fix," the foregoing consideration of twenty-first century border security as an extension of late capitalism rather than antidote to it reveals the myriad paradoxes of the contemporary security apparatus. Answering to one set of political economic dilemmas, security solutions emerging in the wake of the events of 9/11 both inspire new political and economic possibilities and generate a host of contradictions and concerns.

These dynamics are boldly evident in the workings of the so-called "security-industrial complex." Not at all restricted to international boundaries, the technologies of border security are spread across a broad range of contexts. From office complexes and hospitals, to gated communities, amusement parks and shopping centers, as well as international frontiers, they include arenas of production and reproduction, work and leisure. The result is a broad-based "securityscape" woven through the defining domains of late-modern life. Often public in nature, these are arenas characterized by motion, social distance (whether spatio-temporal or status based), and abstract, machinic ideals regarding proper management. But, as the expanding use of biometrics makes clear, these same technologies also surface in the private domain of the household and in relation to personal property. At stake here are both new ways of marking intimacy as well as an externalization of the self-situating individual identities and behaviors within a virtual or distant public sphere. If indeed, as Cunningham (2009) and others (Euskirchen et al. 2007, 2009) suggest, there is an internalization of the border occurring with the late-capitalist revival of the security state, turning civil spaces into borderlands, also afoot is the crafting of the late-modern political subject via terms that are unique and deeply anchored yet nonintuitive. Under these conditions, a highly internalized and individuated biosociality becomes a substitute for civil or democratic conventions of political sociality. With the subject reduced to a difficult to discern and remotely experienced embodied identity, and the state authority dispersed among diverse agents and agencies, here we see a surprising sort of doubling or twinning between the source and object of security, what Agamben would refer to as the sovereign and *homo sacer*, mutually constitutive yet both ambiguous in their presence.[5]

Taken together, the multiple locations and applications of the rubrics of border security generate what can be seen as a surplus, or to borrow a term from Harvey, "over-accumulation" of security. Here, technologies of security, their application fully licensed in the post–9/11 quest to reassert sovereignty, become the object and agent of what Mbembe describes as "excessive expenditure" – a dynamic dually economic and political – on the part of the state (Hansen and Stepputat 2005: 27; Mbembe 2005). Characterized by overlap and redundancy, in such an environment it becomes hard to distinguish what security processes are in fact critical from the many made available and deemed necessary. In the resulting fusing of zones of security and zones of consumption, voluntary purchase and involuntary self-revelation, the boundary between the threatening and the normal breaks down, making it difficult to ascertain what sorts of rights and accountabilities should, can and do apply.

The political consequences of this sort of security surplus are multiple. Creating networked forms of power transcendent of individual states, they enable the formation of international border surveillance regimes, like those surrounding technologies such as the biometric passport or consumer/traveler databases. As demonstrated in the unabated fusion of immigration reform with security agendas, the stretching of security into all corners of public policy intensifies and links social exclusion across domains (public, private, national, international) as it shifts state investment from social programs to security. But because these arrangements are all built on excess, as is the case with the security-industrial complex assembled by the US DHS in the shadow of 9/11, dependent on partnerships, power-sharing and public-private contracts, this political edifice is also prone to governmental sprawl. Although inherently unstable, under such conditions the terms of access and regulatory oversight remain unclear, frustrating both reform and engagement. Though given concerted expression at international frontiers, the framing tenets of border security are thus both everywhere and virtually unlocatable.

NOTES

1   Hilary Cunningham probes the fading away of borders under global capitalism and their resurgence post–9/11. Raising a set of concerns similar to mine, she asks: "What are the territorially formed aspects of globalization?" (2009: 152).
2   While these political economic conjunctures might not be deliberately crafted, they are to some extent predictable, given their engagement of prevailing material forces.
3   See Peter Andreas (2000) for a discussion of the changing imperatives of the INS and Border Patrol.
4   For an earlier use of this term see Mills 2004.
5   This insight is suggested by the observations of Hansen and Stepputat 2005: 17.

REFERENCES

Adelson, Jay. 2005. From bailing wire to biometrics. *Security* 42 (3): 18.

Adey, Peter. 2004. Surveillance at the airport: surveilling mobility/mobilising surveillance. *Environment and Planning A* 36 (8): 1365–1380.

Agamben, Giorgio. 1998. *Homo Sacer: Sovereign Power and Bare Life*, trans. Daniel Heller-Roazen. Stanford: Stanford University Press.

Alpert, Bill. 2004. The fall outlook for biotech. *Barron's* 84 (38): T1.

Amoore, Louise. 2006. Biometric borders: governing mobilities in the war on terror. *Political Geography* 25 (3): 336–351.

Anderson, Benedict. 1991. *Imagined Communities: Reflections on the Origin and Spread of Nationalism*. London: Verso

Andreas, Peter. 2000. *Border Games: Policing the US–Mexico Divide*. Ithaca: Cornell University Press

Andresen, Bjorn, Fulop, Gabor F. and Norton, Paul R. 2005. Infrared Technology and Applications XXXI. Society of Photo-Optical Instrumentation Engineers (SPIE) Conference Series, vol. 5783.

Appadurai, Arjun. 1990. Disjuncture and difference in the global cultural economy. *Public Culture* (2) 2: 1–24.

Appadurai, Arjun, ed. 2001. *Globalization*. Durham: Duke University Press.

Balibar, Étienne. 2004. *We, the People of Europe? Reflections on Transnational Citizenship.* Princeton: Princeton University Press.

Bernstein, Nina. 2010. Jail protest by detainees is broken up. New York Times, Jan. 21, p. 37.

Business Week. 2003. The tech outlook. Some bright shafts that pierce the gloom: health and biomedical companies and artificial intelligence. Mar. 24, p. 153.

Butler, Judith. 2004. *Precarious Life: The Powers of Mourning and Violence*. London: Verso.

CNNMoney. 2009. Fortune 500: our annual ranking of America's largest corporations. At   http://money.cnn.com/magazines/fortune/fortune500/2009/full_list/201_300.html (accessed June 9, 2010).

Collins, Jane. 2003. *Threads: Gender, Labor, and Power in the Global Apparel Industry.* Chicago: University of Chicago Press

Connell, Judith. 2002. *The Role of Universities and Market Factors in the Location of Biotechnology Industrial Clusters.* Los Angeles: University of California.

Cunningham, Hilary. 2004. Nations rebound? Crossing borders in a gated globe. *Identities* 11 (3): 329–350.

Cunningham, Hilary. 2009. Mobilities and enclosures after Seattle: politicizing borders in a "borderless" world. *Dialectical Anthropology* 33 (2): 143–156.

Deger, Saadet and Sen, S. 1990. *Military Expenditure: The Political Economy of International Security.* Oxford: Oxford University Press.

DHS (Department of Homeland Security). 2005. DHS to require digital photos in passports for visa waiver travelers. Press Release, US Department of Homeland Security, June 15. At http://www.dhs.gov/xnews/releases/press_release_0691.shtm (accessed June 7, 2010).

Economist. 2006. Biometrics gets down to business. Nov. 30.

Euskirchen, Markus, Lebuhn, Henrik and Ray, Gene. 2007. From borderline to borderland. *Monthly Review: An Independent Socialist Magazine* 59 (6): 41–52. At http://monthlyreview.org/2007/11/01/from-borderline-to-borderland-the-changing-european-border-regime (accessed Nov. 2011).

Euskirchen, Markus, Lebuhn, Henrik and Ray, Gene. 2009. Big trouble in borderland: immigration rights and no-border struggles in Europe. Mute. At http://www.metamute.org/en/big_trouble_in_borderland_immigration_rights_and_no_border_struggles_in_europe (accessed Nov. 2011).

Ferguson, James. 2006. *Global Shadows: Africa in the Neoliberal World Order.* Durham: Duke University Press

findBIOMETRICS. 2010. findBiometrics year in review 2009. At http://www.findbiometrics.com/interviews/i/7676 (accessed June 1, 2010).

Fonio, Chiara. 2007. Surveillance and identity: towards a new anthropology of the person. Paper presented at the British Sociological Association conference, London, Apr. 12–14.

Foucault, Michel. 1997. *Ethics: Subjectivity and Truth,* ed. Paul Rabinow. New York: New Press.

Frost & Sullivan. 2010. Frost & Sullivan finds vast potential for biometrics industry in APAC. At http://www.frost.com/prod/servlet/press-release.pag?docid=194455857 (accessed Nov. 2011).

Giddens, Anthony. 1991. *Modernity and Self-Identity: Self and Society in the Late Modern Age.* Stanford: Stanford University Press.

Grossman, Wendy. 2009. Fasten your seatbelts: information security and the travel industry. InfoSecurity Magazine. At http://www.infosecurity-magazine.com/view/2347/fasten-your-seatbelts-information-security-and-the-travel-industry-/ (accessed June 2, 2010).

Grover, Ronald. 2005. Cogent: leaving its prints on the biometrics market. Business Week, June 6, p. 82. At http://www.businessweek.com/magazine/content/05_23/b3936416.htm (accessed Nov. 2011).

Gusterson, Hugh. 2004. *People of the Bomb: Portraits of America's Nuclear Complex.* Minneapolis: University of Minnesota Press.

Hansen, Thomas Blom and Stepputat, Finn. 2005. *Sovereign Bodies: Citizens, Migrants, and States in the Postcolonial World.* Princeton: Princeton University Press.

Harvey, David. 2001. *Spaces of Capital.* Edinburgh: Edinburgh University Press.

Harvey, David. 2003. *The New Imperialism.* Oxford: Oxford University Press.

Jain, Anil K. 2007. Technology: biometric recognition. *Nature* 449 (7158): 38–40.

Jain, Anil, and Ross, Arun. 2005. Biometrics. In *Encyclopedia of Cryptography and Security,* ed. Henk C.A. van Tilborg. New York: Springer.

Joseph, Anne. 2001. Anthropometry, the police expert, and the Deptford murders: the contested introduction of fingerprinting for the identification of criminals in late Victorian and Edwardian Britain. In J. Caplan and J. Torpey, eds, *Documenting Individual Identity: The Development of State Practices in the Modern World*, pp. 164–183. Princeton: Princeton University Press.

Laver, Ross. 2000. Biotech: the next big thing? *Maclean's* 113 (10): 41.

Liptak, Adam. 2010. Justices agree on detainee death case. New York Times, May 3, p. 20.

Lowe, Setha. 2003. *Behind the Gates: Life, Security, and the Pursuit of Happiness in Fortress America*. New York: Routledge.

Lyon, David. 2007. *Surveillance Studies: An Overview*. Cambridge: Polity.

Lutz, Catherine. 2001. *Homefront: A Military City and the American Twentieth Century*. Boston: Beacon Press.

Mbembe, Achille. 2005. Sovereignty as a form of expenditure. In Finn Stepputat and Thomas Blom Hansen, eds, *Sovereign Bodies: Citizens, Migrants, and States in the Postcolonial World*, pp. 148–166. Princeton: Princeton University Press.

Meckler, Laura. 2005. Security list for air travelers won't use commercial database. Wall Street Journal, Sept. 22. At http://online.wsj.com/article/SB112734156684447883.html?mod=todays_us_personal_journal (accessed Sept. 22, 2005).

Mills, Mark P. 2004. The security-industrial complex. *Forbes* 174 (11): 44.

Mitchell, Timothy. 2002. *Rule of Experts: Egypt, Techno-Politics, Modernity*. Berkeley: University of California Press.

Molenberghs, Geert. 2006. Biometry and biometrics. *Sensor Review* 26 (1): 5.

Morgan, Nigel and Pritchard, Annette. 2005. Security and social "sorting": traversing the surveillance–tourism dialectic. *Tourist Studies* 5 (2): 115–132.

Mortenson, Juliana. 2010. New biometric modalities using internal physical characteristics. Proceedings of SPIE, vol. 7667. At http://dx.doi.org/10.1117/12.847882 (accessed June 7, 2010).

OECD (Organisation for Economic Co-Operation and Development). 2004. *The Security Economy*. Paris: OECD.

Ong, Aihwa. 2006. *Neoliberalism as Exception: Mutations in Citizenship and Sovereignty*. Durham: Duke University Press.

Pallitto, R. and Heyman, J. 2008. Theorizing cross-border mobility: surveillance, security and identity. *Surveillance and Society* 5 (3): 315–333.

Petryna, Adriana, Lakoff, Andrew and Kleinman, Arthur. 2006. *Global Pharmaceuticals: Ethics, Markets, Practices*. Durham: Duke University Press.

Prescott, J.R.V. 1987. *Political Frontiers and Boundaries*. London: Allen & Unwin

Preston, Julia. 2009. Immigration crackdown with firings, not raids. New York Times, Sept. 29, p. 1.

Privacy International. 2005. UK introduces "e-borders" programme, proposing more surveillance and profiling of all. At http://www.privacyinternational.org/article.shtml?cmd[347]=x-347-260609 (accessed June 5, 2010).

Rabinow, Paul and Rose, Nikolas. 2006. Biopower today. *BioSocieties* 1 (2): 195–217.

Reaser, Azure. 2002. Jobs in biotechnology: applying old sciences to new discoveries. *Occupational Outlook Quarterly* 46 (3): 26.

Reeves, Alyson. 2008. Security matters: avoid being left behind in the identity stakes. Financial Times, June 23, p. 7.

Robinson, William I. 2004. *A Theory of Global Capitalism: Production, Class, and State in a Transnational World*. Baltimore: Johns Hopkins University Press.

Rodriguez, Robyn. 2009. Local politics of homeland security in New Jersey. Paper presented at the Professor and the Spy Conference, Newark, Feb. 12–13.

Rosas, Gilberto. 2006. The thickening borderlands: diffused exceptionality and "immigrant" social struggles during the "war on terror." *Cultural Dynamics* 18 (3): 335.

Rose, Nikolas. 1996. The death of the social? Re-figuring the territory of government. *Economy and Society* 25 (3): 327.

Rose, Nikolas and Novas, Carlos. 2005. Biological citizenship. In Aihwa Ong and Stephen Collier, eds, *Global Assemblages: Technology, Politics, and Ethics as Anthropological Problems*, pp. 439–463. Oxford: Blackwell.

Salter, Mark B. 2006. The global visa regime and the political technologies of the international self: borders, bodies, biopolitics. *Alternatives: Global, Local, Political* 31 (2): 167–189.

Sassen, Saskia. 2001. *The Global City: New York, London, Tokyo.* Princeton: Princeton University Press.

Sassen, Saskia. 2006. *Territory, Authority, Rights: From Medieval to Global Assemblages.* Princeton: Princeton University Press.

Smith, Neil. 2005. *The Endgame of Globalization.* New York: Routledge

Staeheli, Lynn A. and Nagel, Caroline R. 2008. Rethinking security: perspectives from Arab-American and British Arab activists. *Antipode* 40 (5): 780–801.

Torpey, John C. 2000. *The Invention of the Passport: Security, Citizenship and the State.* Cambridge: Cambridge University Press

Wilson, Dean. 2007. Australian biometrics and global surveillance. *International Criminal Justice Review* 17 (3): 208.

CHAPTER 17 Identity, the State and Borderline Disorder

Dan Rabinowitz

The modernist notion of political sovereignty hinges, among other things, on international and local recognition of state borders. Such recognition, which bears particular meanings for young, recently established states, is often associated with the ability to secure and control the home environment, to assert political coherence and to forge a sense of collective identity.

This chapter takes Israeli preoccupation with its borders as a case study for the sociocultural load associated with boundaries, stability and security. Sixty-three years after its establishment, which was immediately embraced by the international community, Israel is yet to have accepted borders. While their project is seen by others in the region, primarily the Palestinians, as a territorial, demographic and political transgression, Israelis perceive it as a modernist extension of a "cultured" Europe into an orientalized Arab space, justified by an ostensibly self-evident right of an ancient nation to return to its historic homeland and propped against blanket denial of a parallel right for Palestinians. Given the increasing contradictions inherent to such a position, and as Palestinians become increasingly effective in asserting their own rights, the Israeli quest for stable borders assumes dramatic dimensions. It is, in many ways, a desperate effort to consolidate Israeli time (Rabinowitz 2010).

Drawing on works by historians and social scientists, this chapter historicizes Israeli sensibilities toward boundaries by looking at the relevant state policies as well as at some of the discursive idioms deployed to normalize them. Analyzing the sociocultural and political meanings of this quest for stable boundaries is important for a better understanding of the past, present and future of Israeli-Palestinian relations (cf. Newman 2002). At the same time the theoretical and historical insights the chapter offers could inform comparisons with other instances whereby boundaries play significant roles in consolidating states, forging identities and harping on people's wish for a secure future.

A Companion to Border Studies, First Edition. Edited by Thomas M. Wilson and Hastings Donnan.

ISRAELI SECURITY IN THE 1950S: THE QUEST
FOR BORDERS AS CONTAINERS

The reality of Israel in the first decade after its 1948 inception can be described in terms of a failed border. To begin with, the 1,040-kilometer line that marked Israel's perimeter in the 1950s was provisional. The line was based on the positions held by Israeli troops in late summer 1948, a time when most military engagement with the Arab armies had subsided. Procedurally, the lines that separate Israel from Egypt, Lebanon, Syria and the West Bank (then under Jordanian rule) embodied the conclusion of four separate ceasefire agreements brokered by the United Nations in mid-1949. Known as "The Armistice Lines," these lines, which served as Israel's de facto limits until 1967, were never recognized as official borders by the international community, let alone the Arab world. They reflected an uneasy, provisional arrangement which, oblivious to the personal and human fate of Palestinians – the primary victims of the 1948 war – also left Egypt, Jordan, Syria and Lebanon bereft of stable borders along sectors of their perimeters adjacent to the Israeli front. My main concern here, however, is with the cultural load and political implications which the "borderline disorder" that emerged in 1948–1949, and became exacerbated in 1967, carried for Israel and Israelis.[1]

The procedural limbo surrounding Israel's state boundaries was not made easy by the frontier's topography. While some sections of the 1949 Armistice Lines followed landscape features providing limited demarcation, others – particularly the 360-kilometer frontier with the West Bank – made little topographic sense and were difficult to monitor. This was further complicated by the tenuous nature of Jordan's rule in the West Bank. Unable and probably unwilling to second the military force required to seal all segments of the line, the Hashemite Kingdom became a rather passive bystander in the Palestinian-Israeli battle for the frontier (Morris 1996).

In 1952 more than 16,000 clandestine entries of people into Israel were recorded, 11,000 of them from Jordan (Morris 1996) – an average of over 30 per night from Jordan alone. Virtually all entrants were Palestinian refugees who prior to 1948 had been inhabitants of villages and towns subsequently found on Israel's side of the Armistice Lines. Now residing in makeshift settings in the West Bank, these refugees were desperate to go back to their homes and property, to see it, rescue belongings and perhaps resettle. Israel's determination to halt this trickle before it turned into a flow and overwhelmed the Armistice Line was probably informed by an intuitive sense of what Frantz Fanon would later identify as the cardboard nature of colonial military power – a realization that garrisons are mere facades which, once revealed as vulnerable, become indefensible and crumble. The Israeli effort to withstand this putative pressure is reflected in the numbers of incoming Palestinians killed and injured by the Israeli Defense Force (IDF) and the police near the frontier: 19 dead in 1950, 48 in 1951, 42 and 44 respectively in the following two years, 33 in 1954, 26 in 1955 and 54 in 1956 (Morris 1996). Many more were injured.

According to Morris (1996), clandestine crossings into Israel by Palestinians in the early 1950s had three main forms. One, accounting for the vast majority of incidents, was the widespread movement of individuals seeking to collect personal belongings and agricultural crops from their old homes or just to inspect whether their villages and property were still intact.[2] Second, and less numerous, were politically motivated operations such as those sponsored by the Palestinian leader Haj Amin al-Husseini, who, after 1947, conducted his operations from Cairo and elsewhere outside the country. Designed to pressurize Israeli settlers into forsaking the frontier, operations sponsored by al-Husseini attempted to unsettle Israel's periphery, thus destabilizing the young state's political integrity. A third type of incursion across the Israeli line was instigated by the security forces of neighboring Arab states, particularly Egypt, embarked on a attempt to enhance military positions vis-à-vis Israel and to gain political capital within the Palestinian fold and in the Arab world at large.

Israeli preoccupation with the fragile border was widespread. It was reflected in regular newspaper and radio coverage of incursions, skirmishes and casualties near the border, in an ongoing debate in government and security circles about the border, its defense and future, and in various schemes to strengthen the frontier and better integrate it into Israel's geographic, political and sociocultural center. The backdrop for this intense preoccupation was an implicit idealized counterimage of the border as container, a concrete structure of defense which, if sufficiently robust, could shape a more favorable political reality. Israel, according to this logic, must consolidate defenses at the border in an effort to convince the Palestinians – peasant refugees immediately across the border and politicized urbanites in more metropolitan settings elsewhere alike – to relinquish hopes of undoing Israel.

A vivid illustration of this logic came in the famous speech made by Moshe Dayan, then Chief of General Staff of the Israeli Defense Force, on April 30, 1956 in Nahal Oz, a kibbutz established three years earlier a mile from the Armistice Line opposite Gaza. Dayan, who came to speak at the funeral of a member of the kibbutz ambushed and killed by armed men who crossed the line from Gaza[3] the day before, had this to say:

> Let us not blame the murderers today. How can we argue against their deep hatred of us? Eight years they sit in refugee camps in Gaza, watching us turn the lands and villages of their ancestors into our domain. . . . Across the border, which (in this section) is no more than a furrow, a sea of hatred overflows with passion for revenge, waiting for the moment when false serenity numbs our preparedness, luring us to heed malicious envoys of hypocrisy and lay down our arms. . . . Let us not recoil as we see the loathing that fills and fires up the lives of hundreds of thousands of Arabs sitting around us. We must not look away lest our hand is weakened. It is the fate of our generation, the choice of our lives. We must remain prepared and armed, strong and resilient, for if the sword slips out from our grasp our lives will be truncated.[4]

The speech, made at a time when Dayan was trying to convince the Israeli government to go for all-out war with Egypt, had publics on either side of the frontier as its potential audiences. Dayan's willingness to view the border – and the conflict generally – from the perspective of dispossessed and displaced Palestinians may have momentarily humanized the Palestinian angle.[5] At the same time, however, it urged Israelis to stay resilient and alert, making the border and the realities imagined on either side of it the discursive cornerstone of Dayan's military and political vision for decades. Its premise was that even if Israel gives up further territorial expansion, it must install around itself an iron wall of strength, and that only this resolve, if backed by efficient and effective action, can ever force the Palestinians and the Arab world at large to come to terms with Israel's existence (cf. Shlaim 2001). The link between viable borders, security and state durability, so central to much border scholarship in recent years, seems to have been intuitively present in Israeli security thinking in the 1950s.

THE LANGUAGE OF THE BORDER

The role of boundaries as physical, political and symbolic entities shaping Israeli identity in the 1950s was reflected also in discursive idioms. Informed by Israel's small scale and tangibly finite geography, and by the buffer zones and interstitial spaces that envelop it, the language became central to establishing and maintaining the theory and practice of upholding and safeguarding borders.

The standard Israeli term for the border in the immediate aftermath of the 1949 agreements was the technical idiom "The Armistice Lines" – *Kavey shvitat haneshek* in Hebrew. Invariably used in the plural form, the term invokes the UN-brokered lines agreed with Egypt, Jordan, Syria and Lebanon in 1949. Far from binding in terms of international law, the boundaries engendered by this line were held by Israelis as representative of something which indeed existed: a widespread international recognition of Israel. The contours of these boundaries, it should be noted, were favorable to Israel not only because of the recognition they connoted, but also because of the de facto inclusion within them of substantial territories specified by the UN Partition Plan of 1947[6] as segments of the Arab state – a detail countries which recognized Israel at the time tended to overlook.[7] Not surprisingly, this gap, which was fatally important for hundreds of thousands of displaced Palestinians, was conveniently dismissed from Israeli memory, another indication of the selective amnesia Israelis display vis-à-vis the consequences of 1948 for Palestinians.

Linguistically cumbersome and somewhat restrictive, the definitive "Armistice Lines" were later eclipsed by simpler terms. They reemerged decades later, when negotiators seeking accords between Israel and Egypt (over Taba in 1983–1984), Jordan (in 1994), the Palestinians (during the Oslo process of 1991–1994), the Lebanese Shiite Hezbollah (over the Shab'a farms in 2006–2007) and, on various occasions, Syria, looked for historic benchmarks that could help determine future borders.

A standard Hebrew term used by the media and the public to denote the boundary before 1967 was *hagvool* – "The Border" in definitive form. Often mutated to specify a particular frontier (i.e., The Egyptian Border, The Lebanese Border, and so on), it reflected a yearning for a state that serves as a cogent, stable and unshakeable "power container" (Tilly 1975; Mann 1993). Within this context, the country's territorial envelope is more than a simple administrative baseline. Embodying the idealized overlap between territorial integrity and ethnonational homogeneity, the durable partition implied by "The Border" connotes a path that promises stability, prosperity and an all-important international dignity of the kind the Palestinians currently (in 2011) seek as part of their quest for UN recognition of their new state.

This idealized depiction of rigid and impermeable boundaries was of course unrealistic. As already indicated, considerable segments of Israel's perimeter were indefensible, not least due to the unending drive on the part of Palestinian refugees to return to the homes and homeland from which they had been dispossessed not long before. One discursive tool deployed to obfuscate the yawning gap between the idealized iron wall and a reality in which it was consistently breached was to label those entering *mistanenin*. Originating from the root s'n'n ("to strain," as in filtering a substance through a sieve),[8] the term, which connotes attempts to block unwanted passage, surrenders a curious slip of meaning. When a sieve is put to work, the desirable substance is allowed to pass unhindered, while foul matter is trapped to be discarded. Describing clandestine entry into Israel as *histanenut* (literally "passing through a strainer") suggests the opposite. Those "infiltrating" become normalized, representing a purifying act not unlike an escape by soldiers from a prisoner of war camp, valorized by army codes and international conventions as an honorable duty. Freudian slip or not, the Hebrew adjective *mistanenin* is still embedded in the historic context of the 1950s, carrying the singularly negative connotation of dangerous aliens who maliciously transgress the national space, thus fundamentally threatening its integrity.

Another discursive device associated with the elusive border in the 1950s is the lexical terms developed to describe Israeli military incursions into the West Bank and the Gaza Strip. Framed by the Israeli leadership as responses to Palestinian "infiltration," these raids were labeled *Peulot Hatagmool*[9] – "The Retaliatory Actions." As in the case of *hamistanenin* ("the infiltrators"), the definitive and plural form, which connotes a particular historical juncture, is hardly ever applied in other contexts. Sometimes attached to the name of a village or a town in the West Bank or the Gaza Strip (e.g., the Kibya action, the Han-Yunis action, and so on), the generalized form of the definitive term ("The Retaliatory Actions") still indexes a particular historical period in which Israel's ability to defend itself became consolidated (Morris 1996).

Kemp's (1999, 2000) work on the border and its role in Israeli society in the 1950s provides an interesting sociological analysis of a syndrome that had previously been studied mainly by military historians (cf. Milstein 1985; Bar-On 1994, 1999; Golani 1994, 1998; Tal 1998). Kemp's preoccupation with the territorial languages that shaped Israeli discourse in the 1950s distinguishes between the political space of the state and the cultural space of the nation – two idioms embodied in divergent but complementary projects. The first, whose practical implications were primarily internal, was embodied in the effort to thicken and consolidate civilian presence at the frontier. The second, with obvious external implications, was the attempt to squash Palestinians' hopes of return through transgressive military actions across the line – the Retaliatory Actions just mentioned. Combined, the two were also geared to thwart demands that Israel should relinquish the comfortable Armistice Lines agreed in 1949 and withdraw to the considerably narrower perimeter designed for it in the UN Partition Plan of 1947.

The divergent nature of the two projects (settling the frontier and pushing out the boundary of military and policing actions) was mirrored in the agencies assigned to implement them: settlement of the periphery was taken up by the Jewish National

Fund, the Jewish Agency, the Ministry of Agriculture and "softer" army outfits,[10] while keeping Palestinians out was the domain of new crack army units. And the twin projects, Kemp demonstrates, produced divergent discourses. The one associated with retaliation, which seriously unsettled the ideology promoting a stable and impenetrable iron wall, was embodied in a spatializing discourse that turned trans- gressive actions into state rituals (Kemp 2000: 23). Personally promoted by Dayan, the crack units assigned with the Retaliatory Actions, and in particular the paratroop- ers' brigade, were deeply admired by Prime Minister and Minister of Defense David Ben-Gurion – a considerably older figure with no military background who was infatuated by the image of the new Israeli as fearless warrior.[11] Part of this mythology, Kemp shows, was attained through a discourse that mystified national space and exoticized the border (Kemp 2000: 24). This transgressive discourse, directed pri- marily at young members of the Israeli elite (the potential volunteers for the crack units), enabled them to find, within their army service, legitimate outlets for unful- filled desires to break through the confines of state borders – a compelling temptation at a time when Israelis had neither the financial means nor the logistical capacity to travel abroad.

The second border-related discourse, the one associated with control of the fron- tier through settlement, is analyzed by Kemp as "territorialist." The improbability of building a protective wall along the 1949 Armistice Lines soon gave way to an alter- native vision of a "live wall": young, idealistic volunteers who would willingly join state-sponsored institutional frameworks and relocate to pioneering frontier settle- ments (Kemp 2000: 20–23). The masses, however, failed to materialize, so a more workable plan was put in place: deploying new immigrant families, far less capable of resisting unfavorable placement, to settle the frontier. To help in this endeavor, a highly ideologized "territorial" language was invented to convince reluctant settlers that the frontier might be geographically peripheral but lay at the heart of the nation's patrimony. The border thus became not merely a component of planning the state but part and parcel of building the nation (Kemp 2000: 22).

One idiom that emerged in the 1950s to describe this settlement project was *Sfar*. Literally meaning an area or a place located near a border, *Sfar* is the standard Hebrew translation for a frontier zone.[12] Normally used as part of the combination *yishuvey sfar* (plural for frontier settlements), the idiom was often conflated with the notion of periphery. And while initially it tended to be used descriptively, it was soon insti- tutionalized as a key element of the Property Tax and Compensation Law (1961). Empowering the Minister of Finance to list particular communities as "Frontier Settlements," the law enables their inhabitants to claim state compensation for war damage.

The canonical standing of the *Sfar* was retrospectively consolidated in 1976, when Israel's postal service published a stamp commemorating the 1950s settlement of the frontier. Carrying the wording "Israel, Border Settlements" on its main part, the stamp's flap carries the biblical phrase "Thou hast set a bound that they may not pass over" (Psalms 104:9). The website of the Israel Philatelic Association, a voluntary organization closely connected to the state postage service, carries the following explanatory text about the 1976 stamp:

After the establishment of Israel as an independent state it transpired that its borders are long and vulnerable in many places. The Israeli frontier [*sfar*] became a severe problem that demanded immediate solutions. The first steps in this direction were made in the early 1950s. New towns were established in Upper Galilee by newly arrived immigrants . . . designed to fill the gaps along the northern border and to increase the Jewish population in this area. . . . These settlements were an ideational and practical continuation of [similar projects] established in the 1940s in the Eastern part of Upper Galilee. . . . Land for these settlements was prepared by the Jewish National Fund, while housing was the responsibility of the Jewish Agency and the Ministry of Housing. It is impossible to overlook the major contribution [these communities made] to the security of the sectors [of the borders] in which they were established. The security forces, and in particular units of the Border Guard [*Mishmar Hagvool*] received robust support [from frontier settlements] for actions carried out against infiltrators [*mistaneninm*] and terrorists [*mehablim*].[13]

1967: SHIFTING *THE BORDER*, MODIFYING PRACTICES, UPDATING DISCOURSE

The 1967 war, which ended with Israeli troops occupying the former frontier zones that hitherto had been beyond the 1949 Armistice Lines in Jordan (the West Bank), Egypt (the Sinai Peninsula and the Gaza Strip), and Syria (the Golan Heights), signaled the eclipse of the initial Israeli border regime and the demise of the old lines as Israel's de facto boundaries. The Israeli occupation of south Lebanon, which began in 1982 and lasted until 1999, brought about a similar suspension of the Armistice Line between Israel and Lebanon.[14]

Immediately after the 1967 war was over, Israel instated a military governorate over the Sinai, the Golan Heights, the West Bank and the Gaza Strip. Significantly, however, it has never moved formally to annex the territories under its control. The two exceptions to this were East Jerusalem, subsumed in Israel by virtue of the extension of the municipal borders of Jerusalem in the 1980s, and the Golan Heights, the legal status of which was altered when the Golan Law, which applies Israel's jurisdiction in the Golan, was passed by the Knesset in December 1981. Avoiding the use of the term "annexation," the Golan Law was modeled on a law passed in the Knesset weeks after the 1967 war. Essentially, the 1967 law authorized the government to apply Israeli jurisdiction to territorial segments now under its control provided they had been subsumed under the British Mandate over Palestine between 1917 and 1948. The status of the Golan Heights, a region that had not been under British Mandate in the past, did not change by the 1967 law, so in 1981 nationalist politicians were canvassing for a separate but similar law to bring it up to speed. Needless to say, the vast historical and political disparity between the 1967 and 1981 Acts makes all the difference here. Whereas the 1967 law was seen at the time as a temporary measure taken by a government wishing to facilitate administrative governability in newly acquired territories that were in jurisdiction limbo, the Golan Heights law, passed by a rightist coalition within weeks of Israel's historic consent to hand back the Sinai Peninsula to Egypt as part of a newly signed peace treaty, was seen by the Israeli opposition and by the international community as unilateral annexation. Condemned by the leftist opposition as well as by the international community, it was soon declared null and void by UN Security Council Resolution 497.

I bring the rather lengthy tale of the Golan as indication that the 1967 war did not merely spell a failure to clarify Israel's borders, it made an already complicated situation even more chaotic. The policy adopted by the Israeli government of keeping bridges over the Jordan River open for commerce and movement of people in and out of Jordan, and the decision to allow hundreds of thousands of Palestinians residing in the West Bank and in Gaza to commute to Israeli towns in search of work (Lewin-Epstein and Semionov 1987) further blurred the territorial boundaries of Israel. At the same time, Israel's administrative control of the judiciary, of land and water, electricity, transport, welfare and education in the occupied territories hampered Palestinian growth (Roy 1995), opened the way to large-scale expropriation of Palestinian land and encouraged a sweeping surge of Israeli settlement. Over a hundred settlements were built, currently inhabited by some 400,000 settlers – Israeli citizens who live in a region international law defines as occupied territory.[15]

The nebulous territorial reality engendered by the 1967 war quickly bred new terms and idioms to describe the substance, margins, boundaries, frontiers and outposts of the Israeli system of control, and the new technologies associated with their maintenance. The first worth mentioning here is the famous term "The Green Line" (*hakav vayarok*). Reflecting the pencil color used to delineate Israel's perimeter in the 1949 armistice agreements, the Green Line, which is technically identical in contour to the Armistice Lines mentioned above, emerged as a discursive tool only after 1967. The reason was that Israel's occupation of the Golan, the West Bank, the Gaza Strip and Sinai – territories which between them amount to four times the size of Israel within the 1949 Armistice Lines – needed some expression on official maps. Since none of the occupied territories were initially annexed, the Survey of Israel (SOI), an independent cartographic unit within the Ministry of Housing (which at the time was the only facility producing officially surveyed maps of Israel), had to distinguish between territories that had been subsumed within the 1949 Armistice Lines and parts appended in 1967. The SOI's solution was to separate the Israeli system of control from the main territories of Syria, Jordan and Egypt by a purple line.[16] It was the creation of this "Purple Line" that threw the 1949 Armistice Lines, now distinguishable by a green color, into discursive prominence.

Whereas the gap between the boundaries Israel might have had, had the UN Partition Plan of 1947 been implemented, and those it did have following its success in 1948 was easily erased from Israeli memory and international awareness, the gap between the Green Line and the post-1967 Purple Line was not as easily forgotten. Geographically ambiguous for most Israelis (Schnell 1994; Portugali 1993) and politically indeterminate, the Occupied Territories had to be circumscribed by more creative discursive means. A new battery of border terms had to be invented.

First, the old label for the physical entity delineating Israel's perimeter, *Hagvool* ("The Border"), gave way to a new term, at once more concrete and more ephemeral, denoting the outer limits of Israel's system of control – *geder hamaarekhet*. Literally meaning the "system's fence," the term refers to a buffer zone stretching along most of Israel's frontier with Syria, Jordan, Egypt and, as of the mid-1970s, Lebanon.

Consisting of an inner and an outer wire fence, with a powdery dirt road in between them on which tracks imprinted by nocturnal trespassers can be detected, it was patrolled at dusk and dawn by motorized crews. Moving between fortified bunkers dispersed along the line a few kilometers apart from one another, soldiers guarding the "system's fence" began employing new technologies of surveillance and detection. The dirt road, dubbed "obfuscation trail" (*shvil tishtoosh*), was refreshed nightly by a vehicle that dragged a wire mesh that smoothes over ("obfuscates") all tracks made the previous day, creating a clean slate for the nocturnal detection of intruders. Bedouin trackers, affiliated with a specialized IDF unit, began riding with the dusk and dawn patrols, to spot new marks and tracks, to make deductions about the identity, purpose and direction of trespassers and, when an opportunity presented itself, to lead the troops on hot pursuit after intruders as far inland as possible. New electronic means, installed into fence posts, deployed by vehicles at key locations every night or built into the bunkers, were hooked to new communication systems that alert the troops in real time. The bunkers, fully equipped to house and nourish a dozen or so foot soldiers for weeks at a time, which in earlier periods were called *mishlatim* ("control posts"), were renamed *Mootzavim* ("outposts") and later *maozim* ("strongholds"). Segments of the front, for example the one built and maintained by Israel along the Suez Canal between 1967 and 1973 – were now renamed "the line of strongholds." Ironically, the least durable line surrounding Israeli-held territory, located tens and sometimes hundreds of kilometers away from any Israeli population centers, was the one which, for a while, came closest to fulfilling the old ideal of a defensive iron wall.

Some elements of border defense installed at the outer limits of the territories occupied by Israel in 1967 were aided by the natural geography. The main frontier with Jordan, for example, ran along the Jordan River between the Sea of Galilee and the Dead Sea, and along the Arava valley to the head of the Gulf of Aqaba. In the Jordan valley there was a dual buffer zone that became useful for both the Jordanian and the Israeli armies: a chalky line of barren broken hills along the outer flanks of the river (called *ghor* in Arabic), and a thick vegetation cover immediately surrounding the river gorge itself (called *Zor* in Arabic). The Suez Canal provided a clear geographical separation between Israel and Egypt until 1979, while a line of extinct volcanic mounds crowning the eastern edge of the Golan Heights, and the massive Hermon ridge provide outstanding landmarks for important segments on the Syrian-Israeli frontier.

The new geographical reality, with Israel controlling so much territory, required a lexical revision of settlements too. For example, the term "frontier settlements" (*yishuvey sfar*), which prior to 1967 referred to communities located at a frontier that also had to be peripheral, now had to be eclipsed by a label that could subsume new settlements established near the edges of larger space controlled by Israel since 1967. To avoid ambiguity, all settlements located near an outer boundary – be it the Green Line or the Purple Line – were defined as "confrontation line settlements" (*yishuvey kav ha'imoot*).

Israeli governments of all political persuasions worked consistently over the years to bring about the gradual demise of the old Armistice Lines as de facto separation lines on the ground. "The Green Line" may have become a discursive reality, but in most parts it became a non-entity. In specific locations, such as some sections of Jerusalem which between 1948 and 1967 had distinct Jewish and Palestinian neighborhoods facing each other, it was maintained to some extent under a new term – "the stitch line" (*kav hatefer*). Later, when the security situation around the Israeli segments of Jerusalem deteriorated due to Palestinian suicide attacks, and Gaza under Hamas rule became a threat to towns and villages in the southwestern part of Israel, another appellation for the frontier zone emerged – the "envelope." The contour around Jerusalem on which the separation wall (see below) was built in 2005–2007 was labeled *otef Jerusalem* ("enveloping Jerusalem"), while the areas in the Negev that face rocket and mortar attacks from Gaza are called *Otef Aza* ("enveloping Gaza").

This array of terms and idioms for interstitial zones reflects a profoundly complicated geography of occupation, exacerbated further by the confused reality engendered by the Oslo agreements of the early 1990s. Israeli settlements and bypass roads designed exclusively for settlers dissect the Palestinian rural hinterland. And army camps, lookout towers, checkpoints, road blocks and temporary military positions create disruptive territorial patterns that Hanafi (2009) has labeled "spacio-cide."

The territorial reality created in 1967 remained fluid in spite of numerous political and military attempts to solidify it. A peace treaty signed between Israel and Egypt in 1978 had the Sinai Peninsula returned to Egypt, Israeli settlements in Sinai dismantled and an internationally recognized border between the two states agreed; Jordan relinquished its linkage with the West Bank in the late 1980s, and signed a separate peace agreement with Israel in 1994 that includes a mutually recognized international border in the Arava valley and along segments of the Jordan valley; the Oslo Accord brought considerable but fragmented segments of the West Bank under the control of the newly established Palestinian Authority, with a new zoning system distinguishing Palestinian towns (labeled Areas A) from Palestinian rural hinterlands (Areas B) and Israeli settlements and their environs (Areas C), each with their own measures of Israeli and/or Palestinian jurisdiction, thus creating further ambiguity. Commercial exchange across the boundary between Israel and the Palestinian Authority, with Israeli consumers seeking cheaper goods in Palestinian towns and villages and Palestinians seeking waged labor inside Israel, surges at times of relative calm and recedes when security on either side of the divide deteriorates. And all this takes place within an economic regime that, under the Paris agreement of 1994, has Israel, the West Bank and the Gaza Strip subsumed under a unified currency and customs area.[17]

In 2005, Israel withdrew from the Gaza Strip, dismantled the 11 settlements it had established there since 1967, handed the strip over to the Palestinian Authority but retained control of all terrestrial and marine outlets and the capacity to cut off electricity, fuel and other vital goods. A 2006 local electoral victory by Hamas in Gaza, followed by an executive takeover by Hamas of all administrative positions held by Fatah, had the Strip literally cut off from the West Bank. This left the 1.8 million Palestinians living in the Gaza Strip, many of them refugees who have been stuck in squalid camps since 1948, dependent on the UN for basic foodstuffs and on an elaborate system of tunnels under the Egyptian border for agricultural and industrial inputs, consumer goods and more. This situation was coming to an end in the summer of 2011, when Egypt finally allowed the border between the Gaza Strip and Sinai to be opened, thus breaking Israel's closure of the Strip. Meanwhile, the border separating Israel from Egypt in the Negev, which was mutually agreed in the peace treaty concluded between the two in 1978, remains impossible to seal. Crossed regularly by African asylum seekers seeking employment and a better life in Israel and by Bedouin smugglers, it too remains a far cry from the Israeli vision of a tightly controlled border.

The anomalous situation along large segments of Israel's frontier, and the ambiguous future status some of these segments have in a rapidly changing Middle East, highlight that 63 years since its inception, Israel's main territorial corpus is still highly anomalous, moving steadily away from the ideal of a stable wall that might provide security and peace. Yiftachel (2002) argues that the blurred space created by this series of anomalies feeds an Israeli illusion of normalcy at a tumultuous time. Efrat (2002) dubs Israel's boundary a "borderline disorder," while Benvenisti analyses the place of the West Bank in Israeli consciousness by saying:

> Although 35 years have passed[18] – almost twice the number of years of the existence of "small" Israel (from 1948–1967) – the occupied territories are still regarded in a static manner, as though time has stood still. At most, people mention demographic statistics on the number of settlers, which totals almost a quarter of a million or – on the other hand – on the growth of the Palestinian population. The revolutionary changes that have taken place in Israel/Palestine over the course of two generations have not brought similar changes in political outlooks, and the debate continues to rage as though the dilemmas remain as they were and all options are still open. (Benvenisti 2002: 35)

THE RISE AND FALL OF THE (NEW) GREEN LINE

Israel's self image as a modern reincarnation of an ancient local people claiming a self-explanatory right to an ancient homeland (Rabinowitz 2010: 498–499) imbues the yearning for coherent borders with more meaning than a simple craving for security or stability. It is a quest reflecting deep anxieties about acceptance and the destiny of "Israeli time." The modernist aspirations of the Israeli project engender an urge to dissociate Israel from a "traditional" and "primitive" East, personified in the highly stereotyped effigy of the ultimate Arab Other (Rabinowitz 2002). It is an urge that hinges on a relentless invention and maintenance of boundaries. Idealized somewhat self righteously as a legitimate measure adopted by a peace-loving nation against irrational Arab malice, Israel's boundaries became fertile testing grounds for exclusionary technologies. Demanding ethnic profiling, tight surveillance and stringent regulation of people's movement, and played out in arbitrary closures and itemized control of substances and objects, it has become an arena for intense regulation of a rigid partition (cf. Bornstein 2001).

This tendency became most poignant with the construction in the 1990s of the Gaza perimeter fence which separates the Strip from Israel and, since 2002, with the installation of the separation wall between Israel and the West Bank. The wall, which was built at a phenomenal cost roughly along the old 1949 Armistice Line, makes life a misery for tens of thousands of Palestinians without gaining real political or military advantages for Israel. Suicide bombings in Israeli towns may have subsided since 2005, but this is more sensibly attributable to a political determination on the part of the Palestinian Authority, propped up by military advice and financial assistance from the United States.

The fascination mainstream Israel has had with the wall should be considered in the light of Baumann and Gingrich (2004), who match notions of European grammars and genealogies of otherness, in which they see frontiers as loci where identities are asserted and contested. Fortress Europe's apprehensions vis-à-vis the imminent accession of Turkey to the European Union and mass immigration from Africa and Asia are a clear example of such dynamics (Rabinowitz 2003).

Significantly, the segment within Israeli society most preoccupied with unilateral separation has been the Zionist "left" (read: centrist moderates) as embodied in the historic Labor movement and, more recently, the Kadima Party established by Ariel Sharon as he departed from Likud in 2005. Firmly at the helm of the Zionist project since the 1920s, the middle class, predominantly Ashkenazi segment of Israel's population associated with Labor and later Kadima played a leading role in Israeli institutions before and after 1948. Consistently adherent to an ethos of a composite, uniform Israeli identity promoting an idealized cultural homogeneity unified behind a deserving elite (Shapira 1984), this hegemonic project mobilized and jealously guarded the state's external boundaries as loci of tension, complete with the discursive apparatus that gives impetus to this project as an effective means to obfuscate internal ethnic, socioeconomic and cultural tensions.

Shenhav's (2010) critique of mainstream Israeli dispositions toward borders focuses on the process by which the Green Line became mythologized to become a constitutive element of the social, cultural and political order of contemporary Israel. The Israeli "left," he indicates, views the 1967 war as a watershed event, fixing it as the cornerstone of a political memory that shapes an idealized political vision premised on two states. This while most Palestinians, including those advocating a two state solution, see the injustices inflicted on the Palestinians in 1948 – and their rectification – as the sine qua non for an acceptable future.

The nostalgic myth of the Green Line, according to Shenhav, informs a logic whereby withdrawal from the territories occupied in 1967 will help Israel regain its innocence and ethical integrity, thus exempting it from the painful need to come to terms with the moral and political consequences of 1948. This cultural myth has become particularly insidious when it has been harnessed, most successfully, to serve hegemonic economic interests, political institutions and cultural agendas.

Arbitrary, ahistorical and blind to community structures and kin realities, the assertion of the Green Line as a pivotal historical component condemns the pre-1948 struggle between Jews and Palestinians to oblivion. And the attempt, on the part of the nationalist and religious right's settlement project, to erase the Green Line helped the "left" further inflate the myth. This set the scene for the insistence of the "left," since the mid-1990s, that "separation" between Israelis on one side of the Green Line and Palestinians on the other could be a desirable and workable solution.

This resurrection of the Green Line frames the Israeli-Palestinian conflict as a simple duel between a composite pair of ostensibly clear-cut national movements – an oversimplification which obfuscates important inner divisions on either side, and which seems to bring Israeli views of the border, security and the state back to the 1950s.

CONCLUSION

On May 15, 2011, on the annual day of commemoration by Palestinians of "Nakba (disaster) Day" in reference to Israel's declaration of independence in 1948, a few hundred youngsters living in Syria committed a defiant act that inspired the Arab world and sent shock waves through Israel. Having arrived in buses from the Damascus area, they approached the border fence that separates Syria and the Israeli-occupied Golan Heights near the Druze village Majed al-Shams, braved the minefield built by Israel to deter intruders, ignored a handful of Israeli soldiers watching in bewilderment, forcibly removed the wire fence, walked across it, and made local and international headlines by spending a few hours in Majed al-Shams, before they voluntarily returned to the Syrian side of the frontier.

This intrusion into Israeli-controlled space took place at the foot of a hill situated on the Syrian side of the frontier, known as "Hill of Shouts." Situated only a short distance from the outlying houses of Majed al-Shams, the hill has been in use for decades now by Druze inhabitants of Majed al-Shams and other Druze villages in the Golan, whose contact with relatives in Syria was severed with the onset of the Israeli occupation in 1967, as locus for prearranged audio exchanges with kin across the border. Aided by loudspeakers, attendants shout across formal greetings, make family announcements and chant political slogans (mostly in support of the Syrian regime). Some encounters involve people who have never met in person and who may be denied a chance to do so for many years to come.

The massive daytime border crossing on Nakba Day 2011 was significant on a number of counts. To begin with, this time those men and women approaching the Hill of Shouts from the Syrian side were not Syrian Druze seeking contact with kinsfolk in the Golan but Palestinians, mostly residents of refugee camps inside Syria. Secondly, their defiance of the border was extremely loaded politically, being an explicit – and literal – first step in the direction of popular return to the Palestinian homeland lost in 1948. Their journey from the camps to the border was sanctioned and possibly encouraged by the Assad regime, which at the time was struggling to contain an unrelated tide of popular unrest – the Syrian version of the Arab Spring of 2011. But the flags, the signs and slogans they were carrying were nothing but Palestinian. In fact, while most of them, as noted above, returned to Syrian soil by evening, one ventured further into Israel. Holding no documentation other than his Syrian identity card, he hitched a ride with a group of Israeli and international peace activists who attended the event from the Israeli side, traveled with them to Jaffa – the town his family originated from before they were displaced in 1948 – established contact with an Israeli television journalist he had known from watching Israeli television, made a defiant statement on Israel's TV channel 10 that evening and surrendered to the police who escorted him across the Syrian border the following day.

The scene near Majed al-Shams was in many ways the Israeli nightmare of the 1950s reincarnated and enacted. The marching line of Palestinians, willing to defy death (a handful were in fact killed that day, although it is unclear how many); the failure of the border's "system fence" (the minefield proved too old and ineffective, and was crossed by hundreds without casualties, the wire fence took a half a dozen men working on it for less than 20 minutes before it gave way); the dilemma of the Israeli officers on site between indiscriminate shooting that would have caused a bloodbath and a sweeping condemnation of Israel abroad, and allowing a massive breech of a frontier Israel's security apparatus had been sealing off for over 60 years; the realization that the hundreds pushing through the fences – a parallel event took place on the same day in Lebanon, although without breaking the fence – could be the spearhead of millions of Palestinian refugees in camps in Syria, Jordan, Lebanon, Gaza and the West Bank, who might be ready to march, unarmed, toward their old homeland. All of these gripped Israeli media and public discourse for weeks, triggering an unprecedented, and uncharacteristic sense of fateful gloom.

Sovereignty, which in normal times tends to be taken for granted, becomes, at times of turmoil, a desperate necessity. Borders, their coherence, recognition and stability, the Israeli case suggests, play a major role in asserting an ability, however constructed and idealized, to assert political order and thus buttress a sense of identity and continuity.

Borders, and the policies and discourses that strive to have them function as viable containers for the state and its security, must be historicized and properly contextualized. Understanding the past, present and future of Israel's boundaries, which is the mirror image of the history and destiny of Palestine's prospective framework, is essential if a more nuanced analysis of the Israeli-Palestinian interface and its potentialities is to be attained (cf. Falah and Newman 1995). And since Israel-Palestine is by no means an isolated case whereby a territorial dispute, complete with long-standing tensions regarding boundaries, shapes identities and collective sensibilities about the meaning of time, the future and destiny, the lessons learnt in it can and should be applied elsewhere as well.

NOTES

Research for this essay was made possible through a Research Support Scheme grant from Central European University, Budapest, for which I am grateful. I also wish to thank the volume editors for their important input, encouragement and patience at various stages of preparing this essay for publication.

1   The psychotherapeutic term "borderline disorder" was first applied to the present context by Zvi Efrat, who used it in the title of a collection of short essays he edited on Israeli-Palestinian relations (Efrat 2002).
2   On some occasions such incursions also entailed the theft of livestock and farm equipment from Jewish settlers on the frontier.
3   According to Wikipedia, the party was later found to have been Egyptian army soldiers of Sudanese origins.
4   At http://tinyurl.com/3m845tb (in Hebrew, author's translation).

5   Dayan's 1956 speech was invoked by *Haaretz*'s Aluf Benn (2011b) a few days before the events of May 15, 2011, when a few hundred Palestinian refugees forcibly removed the border fence with Israel in the Golan Heights and entered Israel for a few hours (Benn 2011a). Benn suggested that the empathy with the Palestinian plight reflected in that speech, had it been articulated by an Israeli general today, would have provoked a jingoistic outcry from right-wing politicians now in power and emphatic calls to sack the general as a traitor.

6   The 1947 Partition Plan assigned approximately 11,000 square kilometers to the Jewish state. The Armistice Lines of 1949, in contrast, left Israel with a territory of 20,500 square kilometers.

7   The main acknowledgement on the part of countries friendly to Israel of its transgression in 1948 into parts beyond those designated to it in the UN Partition Plan of 1947 is their refusal, still in effect today, to place their embassies in Jerusalem – a territory the UN Partition Plan suggested should be under international jurisdiction and stewardship. Recognition of Jerusalem as the capital of Israel, however, is not withheld.

8   *Mistanenin* was usually translated into English as "infiltrators," as in the subtitle of Morris's (1996) book which refers to Arab "infiltration."

9   Sometimes also called *Peulot hagmool*.

10 The main one was the NAHAL, Hebrew acronym for Young Pioneering Youth, a newly established segment of the army where men and women conscripts volunteered to combine their regular military service with living in border kibbutzim, performing duties that included agricultural work and other civil tasks.

11 Ben-Gurion served as Prime Minister and Minister of Defense between 1948 and 1963, except for some short intervals: in December 1953 he withdrew from government altogether, returning in January 1955 as Minister of Defense under Prime Minister Moshe Sharet; in November 1955, he resumed the dual position of Prime Minister and Minister of Defense, which he held until his resignation in June 1963.

12 The word has an Arabic equivalent, *masfara*, denoting a periphery at the margin of a more metropolitan area. *Masfarat Yata*, for example, is the area near the town of Yata south of Hebron, inhabited by Bedouin families some of whom move seasonally between the town and the *masfara*.

13 Israel Philatelic Association, at http://www.israelphilately.org.il/articles/content/he/000032 (in Hebrew, author's translation).

14 Unlike the territories of the West Bank, the Golan Heights, the Gaza Strip and the Sinai occupied by Israel in 1967, where civilians were allowed to move relatively freely across the former lines that separate these parts from Israel, the occupation of south Lebanon did not undo the old boundary and the restrictions it imposed for civilians. Israeli civilians could not cross into south Lebanon, and it took a few years of occupation before Lebanese laborers were allowed to make tightly controlled daytime commuting trips to specific locations in northern Israel for work.

15 Settlement in an occupied territory by people other than the original inhabitants is illegal in international law.

16 The practice of including territories newly acquired into the Israeli system of control in official maps of Israel was not employed during the Israeli occupation of south Lebanon (1982 to 1999).

17 The Hamas takeover of Gaza, and the recent willingness of Egypt to open the Rafah pass and to connect the Gaza Strip with Egypt for commerce and supply have modified the physical reality of the Strip.

18 Since the 1967 war and Israel's usurpation of the West Bank.

REFERENCES

Bar-On, Mordechai. 1994. *Gates of Gaza: The Security and Foreign Policy of Israel, 1955–1957*, trans. Ruth Rossing. New York: St Martin's Press. First publ. in Hebrew in 1992.

Bar-On, Mordecai. 1999. [Small wars, big wars: further comments in the argument on Israel's security policy in the first decade.] *Katedra* 94: 115–154 (in Hebrew).

Baumann, Gerd and Gingrich, André, eds. 2004. *Grammars of Identity/Alterity: A Structural Approach*. Oxford: Berghahn.

Benn, Aluf. 2011a. The Arab Revolution is knocking at Israel's door. Haaretz, May 16. At http://www.haaretz.com/print-edition/news/the-arab-revolution-is-knocking-at-israel-s-door-1.361969 (accessed Dec. 2011).

Benn, Aluf. 2011b. Doomed to fight. Haaretz, May 9. At http://www.haaretz.com/weekend/week-s-end/doomed-to-fight-1.360698 (accessed Dec. 2011).

Benvenisti, Meron. 2002. The Green Line, 2002. In Zvi Efrat, ed., *Borderline Disorder*. Anthology for the Israeli pavilion, 8th International Architecture Exhibition, pp. 34–35. Venice Biennale.

Bornstein, Avram. 2001. *Crossing the Green Line: Between Palestine and Israel*. Philadelphia: University of Pennsylvania Press.

Efrat, Zvi, ed. 2002. *Borderline Disorder*. Anthology for the Israeli pavilion, 8th International Architecture Exhibition, Venice Biennale.

Falah, Ghazi and Newman, David. 1995. The spatial manifestation of threat: Israelis and Palestinians seek a "good" boundary. *Political Geography* 14: 689–706.

Golani, Moti, ed. 1994. *[Black Arrow: The Gaza Raid and Israel's Retaliation Policy in the 1950s.]* Tel Aviv: Maarakhot (in Hebrew).

Golani, Moti. 1998. *Israel in Search of War: The Sinai Campaign, 1955–1956*. Brighton: Sussex Academic Press.

Hanafi, Sari. 2009. Spacio-cide: colonial politics, invisibility and rezoning in Palestinian territory. *Contemporary Arab Affairs* 2 (1): 106–121.

Kemp, Adriana. 1999. [The mirror language of the border: territorial borders and the construction of a national minority in Israel.] *Sociologia Israelit [Israeli Sociology]* 2 (1): 319–349 (in Hebrew).

Kemp, Adriana. 2000. [The border as janus faced: space and national consciousness in Israel.] *Teoria U'vikoret [Theory and Criticism]* 16: 13–43 (in Hebrew).

Lewin-Epstein, Noah and Semionov, Moshe. 1987. *Hewers of Wood and Drawers of Water: Noncitizen Arabs in the Israeli Labor Market*. Ithaca: ILR Press.

Mann, Michael. 1993. *The Sources of Social Power*. Cambridge: Cambridge University Press.

Milstein, Uri. 1985. *[The History of the Paratroopers from the War of Independence to the Lebanon War]*, vol. 1. Tel Aviv: Shalgi (in Hebrew).

Morris, Benny. 1996. *Israel's Border Wars, 1949–1956: Arab Infiltration, Israeli Retaliation and the Countdown to the Suez War*. Oxford: Oxford University Press.

Newman, David. 2002. The geopolitics of peacemaking in Israel–Palestine. *Political Geography* 21: 629–646.

Portugali, Yuval. 1993. *Implicate Relations: Society and Space in the Israeli-Palestinian Conflict*. Dordrecht: Kluwer Academic.

Rabinowitz, Dan. 2002. Oriental othering and national identity: a review of early Israeli anthropological studies of Palestinians. *Identities: Global Studies in Culture and Power* 9: 305–325.

Rabinowitz, Dan. 2003. Borders and their discontents: Israel's Green Line, Arabness and unilateral separation. *European Studies* 19: 217–231.

Rabinowitz, Dan. 2010. The right to refuse: abject theory and the return of Palestinian refugees. *Critical Inquiry* (Winter): 495–516.

Roy, Sara. 1995. *The Gaza Strip: The Political Economy of De-development*. Washington, DC: Institute for Palestine Studies.

Schnell, Yitzhak. 1994. *[Identity Draws Geography.]* Raanana: Institute of Arab Israeli Studies (in Hebrew).

Shapira, Yonatan. 1984. *[Elite with No Successors: Generations of Leaders in Israeli Society.]* Tel Aviv: Sifriyat Poalim (in Hebrew).

Shenhav, Yehouda. 2010. *[The Time of the Green Line: A Jewish Political Essay.]* Tel Aviv: Am Oved (in Hebrew).

Shlaim, Avi. 2001. *The Iron Wall: Israel and the Arab World*. New York: Norton.

Tal, David. 1998. *[The Security Perception of Israel: Origins and Development 1949–1956.]* Be'er Sheva: Ben-Gurion University (in Hebrew).

Tilly, Charles. 1975. Reflections on the history of European state making. In C. Tilly, ed., *The Formation of National States in Western Europe*, pp. 601–638. Princeton: Princeton University Press.

Yiftachel, Oren. 2002. The illusion of the Israeli space. In Zvi Efrat, ed., *Borderline Disorder*. Anthology for the Israeli pavilion, 8th International Architecture Exhibition, Venice Biennale.

CHAPTER **18** African Boundaries and the New Capitalist Frontier

Timothy Raeymaekers

For some time now, students of cross-border economies in Africa have been engaged in a lively debate about the meaning of norms and rules underpinning such economic activities. On the one hand, a body of political science literature continues to address the ostensibly "criminal" nature of cross-border exchange, but in doing so refers to a rather monolithic understanding of (political) culture. Protagonists of this approach have been the French scholars Patrick Chabal and Pascal Daloz, who depict the state in such environments as "no more than a decor, a pseudo-Western facade masking the realities of deeply personalized political realities" (1999: 15–16; Allen 1999; Reno 1998, 2002; Reyntjens 2005).[1] On the other hand, a number of ethnographic and sociological studies have tried with varying degrees of success to root the social regulations underpinning everyday border practices in cross-border agency (Meagher 1990; Nugent and Asiwaju 1996; Flynn 1997; Chalfin 2001, 2010; Lentz 2003; Titeca 2006). If anything, this literature has brought to the fore a number of crucial questions regarding the configuration of states and markets in Africa worth discussing from a comparative perspective (see also Callaghy et al. 2001).

This theoretical gap in border studies has nevertheless become problematic for a number of reasons. Contrary to the idea of "felonious states" (Bayart et al. 1999), it has become increasingly evident that state administrations do not have a monopoly over cross-border regulations. A growing body of empirical evidence suggests that state practices and institutions are being *engulfed* by legal pluralism on the border, which by its very nature escapes straight state–society binaries (Roitman 2005; Raeymaekers 2009). However, this does not imply that such "informal" practices and institutions take place outside the law; on the contrary, participants in cross-border economies more often than not make use of the same legal texts and procedures employed in official channels (Abraham and Van Schendel 2005). Probably the most characteristic dimension of cross-border networks is that they tie formal and informal institutions together in a symbiotic relationship (Donnan and Wilson 1999: 44). This

---

A Companion to Border Studies, First Edition. Edited by Thomas M. Wilson and Hastings Donnan.
© 2012 Blackwell Publishing Ltd. Published 2012 by Blackwell Publishing Ltd.

is why culture is so fundamental to understanding the connection between territory, identity and power in such places.

In institutional(ist) vein, the reason for this formal-informal mixture would seem nonetheless to be straightforward. Borders are said to produce heterogeneous institutions characterized by the coexistence of starkly different political cultures and regulatory logics, but which continue to depend on the *idea* of the state for their proper existence (Lund 2006). Specifically with regard to borders, some authors have added that the logic of social action in this domain is driven by a number of micro-regulations that are to a different degree encapsulated by the state (Meagher 1990, 2003; Titeca and De Herdt 2010). However, the existence of "twilight" institutions does not provide much of an explanation of why such systems of transterritorial accumulation and regulation should systematically persist – or for that matter, dwindle[2] – in today's global capitalist order. Nor does it expose the originality of border systems in comparison with other forms of private vigilantism and street-level bureaucracy observed on the African continent as a whole (Blundo et al. 2006; Pratten and Sen 2006). Although certain social normativities and historical antecedents – like regional identities and precolonial trade routes – are usually invoked to claim some form of popular embeddedness of these economies, the core explanation given in institutional border accounts is often some kind of (political-economic) *necessity*: driven by economic marginalization and neglect, people in peripheral regions are forced to reproduce their own systems of self-regulation and social networks that become to lesser or greater degree entangled in predatory states (MacGaffey 1987, 1991; Meagher 2006; Titeca 2006, 2009). Ultimately, however, such analyses of institutional bricolage and tactical agency in African borderlands often leave one with the impression of a voluntaristic approach to social action devoid of *determinants* of political power (see also Cooper 2001; Cramer 2006).

To begin with, there remains the important consideration about the social foundations of economic rationality, or what Émile Durkheim would have called the regulation of economic contracts (Gudeman 2008: 2). Like any economic exchange, cross-border activity contains an intersubjective and a material dimension, which are dialectically connected. Although considered today as old-fashioned by many sociologists, the literature on the historical commodification of labor and economic value in Africa and beyond does point to the fact that what is often unproblematically depicted as rational economic behavior driven by utilitarian considerations in reality covers a wide range of transactions rife with tensions and conflict (Polanyi 1944; Mitchell 2002; Guyer 2004). The interesting question to ask in these cases, therefore, is not so much how tactical agents make use of economic opportunities and exchange, but in what particular ways cross-border markets are being reproduced as socially accepted institutions. At the same time, however, critics of the "formalist" approach to social anthropology sometimes too easily situate this dialectic between peoples and markets in terms of local-global processes of opposition and imposition (Forster and Koechlin 2011). One should clearly be aware of the particular places where capitalist development is occurring and literally *takes* (its) place (Ferguson and Gupta 2002). Because territorial borders seem to be exactly the kinds of places that privilege the observation of the *constitutive* character of transnational forces like transboundary market exchange and regulation (Callaghy et al. 2001: 7), the central question becomes how such forces become directly involved in the constitution of forms of order and authority in various social and political contexts. It is evident that this question necessitates a further reflection on the ways in which such emerging orders form and operate across multiple territories beyond the pursuit of economic rationality.

In my view, the persistent plurality of economic regulations in so many African border regions today is not exclusively related to tactical agency or global markets, but rather to a number of highly contemporary market conditions. Maybe paradoxically, it should be remembered that the emergence of informality as a social category originates first and foremost in state policy. With varying success, the dominant power strategy of postcolonial states and their colonial predecessors has been consciously to deprive peripheral populations of their revenue and social rights and define those as residual, that is, informal economies of survival (Nugent 2002; Roitman 2005). During the 1980s and early 1990s, the emergence of various "unruly" border regions across the continent in Central Africa, West Africa and the Horn were arguably the price ruling elites in the political center had to pay to mobilize resentment in the periphery against undesirable neighbors (Herbst 1990). The border between Zaire (later Democratic Republic of Congo (DRC)) and Uganda is only one example of a cross-border power complex that emerged as a result of regional economic interaction and which generated semi-autonomous rules and regulations (Prunier 1999; Vlassenroot and Raeymaekers 2004b). At the same time, the opaqueness of legal procedures and opportunities for extralegal accumulation in these border regions has ensured a steady diffusion of state authority over a wide range of political scales. Some interesting studies from North and Central Africa point at the utility of such borderlands for the redistribution of political legitimacy and economic wealth, a dialectic that has left the idea of a borderless Africa largely unpopular with many – both state and nonstate – border dwellers (Roitman 1998; Bennafla 1999).

Since the mid-1990s, the growing regionalization of economic accumulation schemes as a result of regionalized armed conflicts has nonetheless contributed to a number of fundamental transformations of state–market relations in Africa. Whereas extralegal forms of economic accumulation have been able to invert power relations at various scales of the political spectrum in countries like DRC, Liberia and Sierra Leone (Vlassenroot and Raeymaekers 2004a; Le Billon 2001; Reno 2002), the temporary – and forced – withdrawal of state authority over the cross-border economic domain has sometimes left regional private actors with a comparatively comfortable basis of power and legitimacy over central state authorities. Two particularly instructive – and remarkably similar – constellations of regional interests have been observed in this regard in North Kivu and West Nile (DRC and Uganda). Here, several business "tycoons" have used extralegal investments earned in the regional war economy in public works, partly also to ward off intrusive state regulations (Raeymaekers 2010; Titeca 2009). With some caution, therefore, one could argue that the growing pluralization of cross-border regulation in these regions indicates a growing encapsulation of the state by the market.

To bridge the apparently incommensurable gap between endogenous and exogenous factors in borderland development, this chapter will provide a geographical analysis of states and markets at the border – particularly using the concept of political scale (Cox 1998; Swyngedouw 1997). The concentration will be mainly on cross-border markets, which pose specific methodological challenges (Ellis and MacGaffey 1996). The chapter, which is based on extensive fieldwork in the border zone of Congo and Uganda,[3] will proceed in the following way. In the first section, I describe the "formalized informality" that regulates cross-border trade on the Congo–Uganda border and which connects some of the most booming centers of the global economy in East Asia to rural markets in East and Central Africa. Next, I disentangle how this everyday mode of regulation is capable of inverting power relations at various scales of the political spectrum. These observations will finally lead me toward a number of conclusions regarding the contribution of border studies to the analysis of the state in Africa and beyond.

PLURAL BOUNDARIES

Everyone who has had occasion to drive through the Kasindi–Mpondwe border post on a Friday morning will have been amazed by the fuzziness of its commercial markets. From sunrise onward long lines of market women and hauliers carrying food, fish and other products over the tiny barrier across the river Lubiriha dot this mixed "rurban" landscape (Trefon 2004). The location of the official border in the middle of the Virunga and Queen Elizabeth natural reserves has offered the possibility to carve out numerous smuggling routes between these two towns and the surrounding wastelands. Occasionally smugglers also use these routes to ship back petrol that has been officially exported to DRC from Uganda. The capital generated in this informal economy should not be underestimated. According to two studies carried out for the Uganda Bureau of Statistics (UBOS) in 2006/2007, for example, DRC figures second as Uganda's informal trade partner, with a total yearly trade of US$91.7 million and a trade surplus at US$ 70 million (UBOS 2007, 2008). It should be noted that these estimates only involve unrecorded trade at formal border crossings, so not for example the traffic of minerals and illegal goods that goes on across the lakes. The informal balance leans largely in favor of Uganda: while DRC informally exported US$11.2 million, Uganda exported US$80.5 million to DRC in 2006–2007. Congo informal exports mainly consist of agricultural products like bananas and beans, but also more specialized crops like vanilla, coffee and cacao. To the DRC, Uganda mainly exports industrial products like clothes, cars and bicycle parts (which are usually re-exports from the Far East), soft drinks, cigarettes, and other household products. In particular, Mpondwe figures as the second largest informal border station of Uganda, even before the important Malaba station on the Uganda–Kenya border. Trade has also grown steadily since the official ending of hostilities in the DRC, and despite the continuing problems along the border in Congo's North Kivu province and in the Ruwenzori Mountains. According to Congo customs authorities, the number of vehicles passing the border has grown from approximately 250 in 2003 to 450 in the first half of 2005 (Raeymaekers 2010). The UBOS study estimates the rise of informal Ugandan export levels from approximately 74 million in 2005 to 80.5 million in 2006 (UBOS 2007).

Although Ugandan authorities have become more alert to informal cross-border trade with the DRC in terms of internal consumption and lost tax benefits, they have largely neglected another, more systematic trade that has gone on for some years now with the complicity of the Ugandan and Congolese military. During the two Congo wars (1996–1997, 1998–2003), Ugandan army generals – with the tacit support of President Museveni – exported millions of US dollars worth of timber, gold and other valuable resources from the rebel strongholds they supported in Congo. Indirectly this illegal trade thus sustained an industrial transformation and export of these resources in Uganda (Reno 2000). The many industrial and timber factories situated today on the road from the border to Uganda's capital, Kampala, are living proof of the saying that war has been "good for business" (Fahey 2009). This is also confirmed by contemporary trade statistics: in 2007–2008, DRC continued to count as Uganda's main export destination of industrial products under unrecorded trade arrangements (UBOS 2007, 2008).

Following these observations, it becomes necessary to differentiate more accurately between different types of organizations and normative registers involved in this informal trade, which is sometimes too easily categorized as a united and discrete economic domain. This becomes evident when one considers the different legal categories implied in cross-border trade. Whereas minerals exported from territories not occupied by the government in DRC may be regarded as "illegal" internationally because of their conflict-generating revenue (see, for example, United Nations 2001), they still provide the basis for "legal" economic development and exports from Uganda. Most of these exports are also recorded in the DRC, as numerous studies indicate (Tegera 2001; Tegera and Johnson 2007). Similarly, the charcoal and counterfeit Chinese products that are openly sold on markets on the Congo–Uganda border increasingly infuriate international environmental bodies and firms that target these goods as illegal. In Congo and Uganda, these goods nonetheless continue to serve as necessary household assets tolerated by official authorities. The continuous conflicts over the legal status of these goods and market exchanges provide a good illustration of the fact that moral categories are never universally accepted but often hide fierce struggles over the *intelligibility* of socioeconomic action and its ramifications in political government.[4] That such struggles should not necessarily follow a clear state/nonstate divide becomes evident when one analyzes the practices and institutions underpinning them from an agency-oriented perspective. During market days on the Congolese side of the border, for example, it is not uncommon to meet public officials trying to make ends meet, openly smuggling coffee and other goods across the border. Border talk in Kasindi has it that the fanciest hotels and restaurants in the area have been built by customs officials reaping personal benefit from smuggling operations. As I have argued elsewhere (Raeymaekers 2009), it would be reductionist to conceptualize such practices either as pure corruption or antistate resistance, since everyday authority in the borderland is characterized by a continuous negotiation of regulatory authority that fragments state sovereignty along a range of distinct geopolitical scales. I try to explain below what this means in terms of scaled (or "nested") political orders.

CROSS-BORDER REGULATION

The system of relationships that regulates cross-border trade at the Congo–Uganda border can be depicted on three specific scales: (1) transcontinental, (2) regional, and (3) local. In the widest, transcontinental orbit, the trade is organized along a more or less stable commodity chain that connects Asian with East African markets. Goods are commonly imported by container from China or the Far East through big shipping companies like COSCO or CMA/CGM. To arrange such transport, Congolese traders spend months and years looking for the right business contacts on the Asian continent, sometimes leaving a representative behind to take care of daily administration (Raeymaekers 2007; Coloma 2010). Business transactions are usually concluded orally, without contracts and on the basis of trust. Asian and Congolese small businesses have much in common from this perspective, as they generally value trust more than contractual backing and the respect for legal requirements (Raeymaekers 2007).

Once the goods arrive in Africa (usually in one of East Africa's big ports like Mombasa), they are relabeled by private customs agencies as goods with a lower tax tariff (for example, electric generators become "bicycle parts," clothes become "rags," and so on). Although official Congolese customs authorities sometimes call these private customs agencies *laboratoires* or *agences pirates*, they are nevertheless recognized by the law in DRC. In a way they could be defined as legal agencies involved in partly illegal operations.

Once goods are declared in Mombasa, they follow their way to the station of Malaba, on the Kenya–Uganda border. There, another mystification attempt takes place by way of offloading and reloading containers onto trucks with canvas sheeting. Because these canvas trucks can carry one-and-a-half containers each, it becomes difficult for customs authorities to check original freight documents since goods get mixed together among different owners and destinations. This makes the official customs authorities increasingly dependent on the goodwill of private economic agents to declare their goods correctly, especially if one considers the lack of physical observation facilities and equipment to control goods passing the border. What often occurs as a result is that in return for a small fee (*matabishi*), Ugandan and Congolese customs agree to facilitate the crossing of goods and adapt the form according to the agents' declaration. On the Congolese side, a customs inspector then inspects this temporary declaration and sometimes does a virtual check "to avoid being completely arbitrary" (interview with customs agent, January 2008). However, goods are never inspected physically. Once the private agent agrees on the virtual check carried out by the customs inspector, duties are paid and the goods pass on to the provincial authorities, who demand a supplementary tax of a few hundred dollars to settle the final import declaration. The paper trail does not end there, however, as a plethora of state agents who depend on the border for their daily living (from the Congolese civil and military intelligence to hygiene and environmental services, national police and customs officers) still have to add their "informal" tax to this final declaration. Economic agents cannot refuse these taxes, since doing so would place them under the mercy of these same agents that moonlight during the darker hours as bandits on the main transport routes. Locally these moonlighting agents are referred to as *des personnes armées non autrement identifies* (unidentified armed persons), who systematically harass economic transports on the way to their final destination.

Notwithstanding the apparently "hybrid" nature of these border arrangements, the different levels of expertise involved in them suggest a structurally organized set of relationships. This becomes apparent through the role of economic intermediaries on the border, who often serve to spread the risk associated with dangerous cross-border enterprise. On market days, for example, the *passeurs* who live in Kasindi and Mpondwe earn their living by quickly unloading the big *poko poko* buses and freight lorries coming from Mabala and Kampala to haul its content over the border over the many smuggling routes. The work of these *passeurs* (or *trafiquants*) requires various skills, such as "passing covertly" (Swahili: *kofichika*), which basically means to avoid trouble with the Congolese services and Ugandan customs police ("Red Mamba") patrolling both sides of the border. To this end, *passeurs* often possess two identity cards – a Congolese and a Ugandan one – that are delivered for a price by immigration authorities. By far the most highly valued skill of these *trafiquants* is to have a "free hand," a term explained by smugglers as the ability to "bribe well" and without being forced to give more than one can afford. Businessmen usually use several autonomous *passeurs* to carry their goods across the border. Through this transborder traffic, therefore, transnational businessmen successfully avoid excessive border taxation. Smaller businessmen especially (who do not have access to the top-level administration) prefer this method to paying lump sums to the "central" state agencies, as these payments are much less predictable and are subject to violent imposition. One could argue that such cross-border traffic perpetuates the gendered construction of the border, since most of these *passeurs/trafiquants* working for (predominantly male) business people are either peasant women supplementing their agricultural income, or marginalized subjects like handicapped porters who are highly discriminated against in other sectors of the economy (see also Cheater 1998). Whatever freedom is gained in this creative enterprise should clearly always be weighed against the structural inequalities that give shape to such border opportunities in the first place.

Rather than dismissing the transboundary economic practices along the Congo–Uganda border as yet another example of Africa's "criminalized" economies (Chabal and Daloz 1999), a deeper social analysis of these activities reveals a logic that goes beyond classic state–society divisions common in mainstream political science literature on this region (Callaghy 1984; Schatzberg 1988; Reyntjens 2005). Such practices suggest an interesting interplay between place-based activities and socioeconomic flows that increasingly absorbs state institutions and regulations into their hegemonic realm. Through the gradual colonization of bureaucratic practice, this highly regulated cross-border market exchange even seems capable of imposing its normative order on state agencies and institutions, which consequently remain highly divided over their course of action. The result of these shifting power relationships is not a complete withdrawal of state institutions from the economic domain, but rather a differentiated engagement of economic actors with various scales of state and nonstate authority that remain intricately entwined.

In mainstream African border literature, this enhanced border agency is usually related to a number of sociocultural markers and institutions. Among these, ethnicity is central. For example, in Kasindi/Mpondwe, the common ancestry and language of the border's biggest populations (that is, Banande and Bakonzo) makes cross-border contact easier and less volatile (Mirembe 2005). The different regional soli-darities stemming from daily interaction at the border should not be underestimated, as they are increasingly formulated in opposition to official state policies. In particular, ethnic border solidarity seems to play a dominant role in discussions about state decentralization in Congo and Uganda, as it continues to serve as a bridge between different "traditional" authorities (like the Rwenzururu Kingdom), opposition politi-cal parties (like the Forum for Democratic Change in Uganda and various splinter groups in the DRC) and antigovernment militias such as the ADF-NALU that have continued to challenge Congolese and Ugandan state rule since the end of colonial-ism (Titeca 2006; Raeymaekers 2007).[5]

Beyond ethnicity, however, the reproduction of social order on the border seems to be animated increasingly by another, more global scale of interaction driven by transnational capitalist enterprise. In particular, the so-called "weak" social ties (Granovetter 1973) that are essential for maintaining fluidity and trustworthiness in cross-border transactions have gradually formed the foundation of a specific power-geometry (Massey 1992) that does not necessarily invert global-local relationships, but is nonetheless able to subvert existing webs of domination and subordination in a wider regional environment.

THE POLITICS OF SCALE

One concept that helps to explain the contingency of power relations on the border is that of geographical scale. Political geographers first introduced this concept to show how social relations of empowerment and disempowerment operate through and within socially constructed spaces (Swyngedouw 1997; Cox 1998). The concept of scale has been increasingly useful in demonstrating the contingent nature of power relations *between* rather than *within* geographical spaces, since it claims that there is no predefined pattern determining how political power should flow, for instance, from center to periphery or vice versa. In particular, the system of transboundary regulations in Kasindi/Mpondwe appears to have generated a number of important scalar effects that go beyond a simple imposition of global or national processes on local actors. Parallel to the concentric trade routes described earlier, it is evident that national centers of power have become increasingly dependent on this transboundary complex in terms of tax benefits and the containment of cross-border populations. Through a constant thwarting of the state's legal framework, participants in the border economy have been able gradually to reverse power relationships between central state administrations and various local agencies involved in cross-border regu-lation, including state customs, various revenue services and the national military that are all struggling to impose their authority on the border.

The fact that these regulations guiding economic action on the border are contingent on changing power relations at different geographical scales does not mean they are unregulated. Nor does it mean that these regulations take place outside the law; on the contrary, unofficial regulation follows exactly the same paper trail as official regulation, only it is guided by a different normative logic. From the commercial *laboratoires* in the major seaports to the customs inspectors and security agencies placed along the main transport routes, a trail of red tape confirms the various unrecorded revenue streams generated by this cross-border traffic. Participants refer to this system as *machicha yango*: (in Swahili) "that which belongs to me" – or in short: "my share." In sum, this system of revenue sharing is directly kept in place by state agents striving to secure a livelihood as well as private entrepreneurs' need for protection against random extortion. The unofficial evidence generated through this paper trail can be used to prove that all "informal" obligations between state and nonstate agents are met and and can be put to the test in case of violations.

Ultimately this specific interconnection of power and authority on the border recalls the concept of social hegemony developed by Antonio Gramsci (2007). This concept usually serves to explain the capacity of a dominant group (the "bourgeoisie") to impose its ideological vision on society so that people act to this group's advantage. Following critical geography, a more spatial definition of hegemony could be proposed here, which is the capacity of a distinct network of social actors at a particular spatial scale to impose its mode of regulation as the desired model of governance on the rest of society. According to Eric Swyngedouw (1997), the socio-spatial relationships that operate through such mechanisms produce a "nested" set of interpenetrating spatial scales that define the arena of struggle where conflicts are regulated and compromise is eventually reached.

Drawing on these notions of hegemony and scale, one could argue that the constant process of negotiation between state and nonstate, public and private actors and institutions has *itself* become productive of a political order that is capable of imposing its vision on society as a way of "making do" and ensuring cross-border reproduction. In contemporary Central Africa, this ideology of fending for oneself has a long history, from Désiré Mobutu's imposition of radical crisis measures during the 1970s and 1980s (Callaghy 1984) to the solidarity of despair observed in Congo's villages and cities (Trefon 2004, Vlassenroot and Raeymaekers 2004a). Rather than a transposed state order that still functions according to its own epistemological foundations (Roitman 1998, 2005), what we are witnessing at this Central African border is a changing logic of socioeconomic interaction that gradually absorbs the state's authority in its realm. The specific time-space configuration that continues to be reproduced through this set of socioeconomic interactions across a wide range of political and economic scales has found in this tiny border crossing a breeding ground for a substitute political order that may still look like a classic postcolonial nation-state, but really has become something quite different in institutional and organizational terms. On the surface, one might argue that this type of interaction between states and markets at the border is not so different from other instances of private vigilantism and street-level bureaucracy on the African continent. What makes this networked complex of power distinct, however, is the interdependent connection it maintains with global and (sub)regional economic markets, and which eventually guides its normative logic. This type of power configuration on one of Africa's busy borders confirms two things.

First, it shows how the line between public and private is always porous or characterized by a "semipermeable film," as in-depth anthropological research in the region convincingly demonstrates (Goffman 1961; Olivier de Sardan 2008; Geenen 2009). Particularly characteristic of the border is the sheer speed with which such public-private roles can be negotiated and sometimes even reversed. From an institutional perspective this makes sense, as border economies typically produce environments of rapidly shifting opportunities. In such environments, power becomes contextual and contingent upon moments of bodily negotiation (participants in the border economy refer to this as *la coop, match, la lutte*, and *punguza* – Swahili: to reduce, get one's share).

Second, it should be clear that the crossing of social boundaries divided by such semipermeable "twilight" zones (Lund 2006) is never free but requires the work of intermediaries who guide passengers between different lifeworlds. The role of such brokers is not only to erect barriers to participants' engagement with alternative options, but also to hold the system in place through particular incentives (such as gifts) and disincentives or sanctions (such as gossip, ostracism and even witchcraft; Wolf 1966; Migdal 1974). In the case of Mpondwe–Kasindi, a frequent strategy of participants in the border economy is the use of rumors (see also Jackson 2001). When new state bureaucrats are being inaugurated in Kasindi, their "renegade" colleagues immediately subject them to a stream of pressures and manipulations. Non-complying bureaucrats may even receive (death) threats if they do not refrain from meddling with the local business ethic. This shows once again the extent to which the network of agencies tied to cross-border trade is able to maintain an effective regime of violence that integrates, rather than imitates, dominant state authority. Whereas their actions are driven predominantly by "informal" rules and regulations, they are able to appear sufficiently official to continue imposing their regulations on translocal interests and linkages.

CONCLUSION

The daily experience of cross-border trade on the Uganda–Congo border shows quite clearly how state regulations, in this case of regional economic interaction, are dependent on the subjective understanding of authority and its ramifications by communities engaged in daily interaction and exchange. When social relations change, the norms underpinning their regulation also tend to change, and the specific configuration of "formal and informal practices" (Swyngedouw 1997: 147) underpinning action on the border absorbs an expanding network of public and private systems of rule. Because of the manifest presence of capitalist markets at territorial borders, it comes as no surprise that this network of regulations is fundamentally driven by liberal market values. Through the network of economic exchange that simultaneously exists at the local, regional and global levels, apparently subaltern subjects connected in one or another way to commercial markets – like petty businessmen, low-scale administrative personnel and cross-border smugglers – have gradually been able to redefine the terms of agreement subsumed in state laws that officially regulate national security, territoriality and socioeconomic exchange. The fact that these translocal networks of power in the borderland are increasingly able to enforce consent at different scales of the political spectrum not only shows how states and markets continue to depend on the "unpredictable and evolutionary dynamic" of everyday market exchange and community construction (Williams 2006: 216); it also confronts us with a number of important questions regarding the nature of state–society relations.

More specifically, the social order that I have argued is characteristic of the Congo–Uganda borderland has been able to force a gradual transposition of political power relations between transnational businessmen, subordinate administrative personnel and security forces tied to cross-border economic gains. This also constitutes the main reason why it is not useful to depict such transborder realities exclusively in terms of their illegality or criminality. On the one hand, it is evident that notions of legality and illegality are contested at the border. Because power there is contingent on access to privatized channels of wealth creation by public and private agents, economic regulations are characterized by a high degree of legal pluralism. On the other hand, this confirms the observation by legal anthropologists that the law should never be seen as a separate metaphysical domain detached from social action, but forms a dimension of social organization. Rather than focus on their "criminal" ramifications, therefore, future research on border economies should address the ways in which these different social organizations (like markets) transform and mold the hegemonic role of the state in matters of security, territoriality and cross-border economic exchange. The contingency of power relations on the Congo–Uganda border functions as an important warning in this regard, that the people and revenues crossing such spaces can easily destabilize and transform entire systems of government at both sides of the spatial spectrum.

NOTES

1   For an illuminating and sobering critique of this theoretical perspective, see Nugent 2010.
2   As in the case of the US–Canada border (Konrad and Nicol 2008).
3   Fieldwork for my doctoral dissertation was carried out in March–April 2003, January–February and October–December 2005, and September–October 2006. In the latter period, and again in January 2008, I undertook two shorter visits to the border town of Kasindi to explore cross-border interaction.
4   Such struggles can sometimes become extremely violent. In Virunga National Park, for example, an armed conflict between park wardens and militias whose finances depend on the continuing exploitation and trade in bushmeat and tropical timber has been waged for years. The argument used by these militias and their popular supporters in DRC is that they reclaim indigenous political space illegitimately taken from them as a result of colonial border-drawing. International environmental organizations nevertheless consider their occupation of the park illegal, because of environmental protection standards. Together with these organizations, the Congolese government is currently reimposing its authority over this region after years of conscious nonregulation and military warmongering.

5   The Allied Democratic Front (ADF), which partly grew out of the anticolonial Rwenzururu movement and partly out of Muslim opposition groups (among others, the National Army for the Liberation of Uganda, or NALU and the Tabligh i' Jamaat), took refuge in the locality of Mumbiri in the Rwenzori Mountains after a failed extermination attempt by the government of Milton Obote II (1980–1985). It was originally composed of combatants from Baganda, Banyoro, Batoro and Bakonzo from Uganda, and some allied fighters from DRC (mainly Banande from former rebel groups and rural militias). The ADF committed many atrocities in the late 1990s and consecutive government reactions against civilians resulted in tens of thousands of internally displaced people (IDPs), thus transforming this region into a hotspot of forced migration. A fight with the Congolese army in summer 2010 caused more than 60,000 IDPs.

REFERENCES

Abraham, I. and Van Schendel, W. 2005. *Illicit Flows and Criminal Things: States, Borders, and the Other Side of Globalization.* Bloomington: Indiana University Press.

Allen, C. 1999. Warfare, endemic violence and state collapse in Africa. *Review of African Political Economy* 26 (81): 367–384.

Bayart, J.F., Ellis, S. and Hibou, B. 1999. *The Criminalization of the State in Africa.* Oxford: James Currey.

Bennafla, K. 1999. La fin des territoires nationaux? État et commerce frontalier en Afrique centrale. *Politique Africaine* (73) (Mar.): 25–49.

Blundo, G., de Sardan, J.P-O., Arifari, N.B. and Alou, M.T. 2006. *Everyday Corruption and the State: Citizens and Public Officials in Africa.* London: Zed Books.

Callaghy, T.M. 1984. *The State–Society Struggle: Zaire in Comparative Perspective.* New York: Columbia University Press.

Callaghy, T., Kassimir, R. and Latham, R., eds. 2001. *Intervention and Transnationalism in Africa: Global-Local Networks of Power.* Cambridge: Cambridge University Press.

Chabal, P. and Daloz, J-P. 1999. *Africa Works: The Political Instrumentalization of Disorder.* Bloomington: Indiana University Press.

Chalfin, B. 2001. Border zone trade and the economic boundaries of the state in northeast Ghana. *Africa: Journal of the International African Institute* 71 (2): 202–224.

Chalfin, B. 2010. *Neoliberal Frontiers: An Ethnography of Sovereignty in West Africa.* Chicago: University of Chicago Press.

Cheater, A.P. 1998. Transcending the state? Gender and borderline constructions of citizenship in Zimbabwe. In T.M. Wilson and H. Donnan, eds, *Border Identities: Nation and State at International Frontiers.* Cambridge: Cambridge University Press.

Coloma, T. 2010. L'improbable saga des Africains en Chine. Monde Diplomatique, May.

Cooper, F. 2001. What is the concept of globalization good for? An African historian's perspective. *African Affairs* 100 (399): 189–213.

Cox, K.R. 1998. Spaces of dependence, spaces of engagement and the politics of scale, or: looking for local politics. *Political Geography* 17 (1): 1–23.

Cramer, C. 2006. *Civil War Is Not a Stupid Thing: Accounting for Violence in Developing Countries.* London: Hurst.

Donnan, H. and Wilson, T.M. 1999. *Borders: Frontiers of Identity, Nation and State.* Oxford: Berg.

Ellis, S. and MacGaffey, J. 1996. Research on sub-Saharan Africa's unrecorded international trade: some methodological and conceptual problems. *African Studies Review* 39 (2): 19–41.

Fahey, D. 2009. Explaining Uganda's involvement in the DR Congo 1996–2008. Paper prepared for International Studies Association conference, New York, Feb. 15.

Ferguson, J. and Gupta, A. 2002. Spatializing states: toward an ethnography of neoliberal governmentality. *American Ethnologist* 29 (4): 981–1002.

Flynn, D. 1997. "We are the border": identity, exchange, and the state along the Bénin–Nigeria border. *American Ethnologist* 24 (2): 311–330.

Forster, T. and Koechlin, L. 2011. The Politics of Governance: Power and Agency in the Formation of Political Order in Africa. Basel Papers on Political Transformations 1 (Jan.).

Geenen, K. 2009. The pursuit of pleasure in a war-weary town, Butembo, North-Kivu (DRC). Draft of diss., Institute for Anthropological Research in Africa, Leuven.

Goffman E. 1961. *Encounters*. Indianapolis: Bobbs-Merrill.

Gramsci, A. 2007. *Quaderni del carcere*. Turin: Einaudi.

Granovetter, M. 1973. The strength of weak ties. *American Journal of Sociology* 78 (6): 1360–1380.

Gudeman, S. 2008. *Economy's Tension: The Dialectics of Community and Market*. Oxford: Berghahn.

Guyer, J. 2004. *Marginal Gains: Monetary Transactions in Atlantic Africa*. Chicago: University of Chicago Press.

Herbst, J. 1990. War and the state in Africa. *International Security* 14 (4): 117–139.

Jackson, S. 2001. Nos richesses sont pillées. Economies de guerre et rumeurs de crime dans Les Kivus, République Démocratique du Congo. *Politique Africaine* (84) (Dec.): 117–135.

Konrad, V. and Nicol, H. 2008. *Beyond Walls: Re-inventing the Canada–United States Borderlands*. Aldershot: Ashgate.

Le Billon, P. 2001. The political ecology of war: natural resources and armed conflicts. *Political Geography* 20: 561–584

Lentz, C. 2003. "This is Ghanaian territory!" Land conflicts on a West African border. *American Ethnologist* 30 (2): 273–289.

Lund, C. 2006. Twilight institutions: public authority and local politics in Africa. *Development and Change* 37 (4): 685–705.

MacGaffey, J. 1987. *Entrepreneurs and Parasites: The Struggle for Indigenous Capitalism in Zaire*. Cambridge: Cambridge University Press.

MacGaffey, J. ed. 1991. *The Real Economy of Zaire: The Contribution of Smuggling and Other Unofficial Activities to National Wealth*. Philadelphia: University of Pennsylvania Press.

Massey, D. 1992. Politics and space/time. *New Left Review* (196): 65–84.

Meagher, K. 1990. The hidden economy: informal and parallel trade in Northwestern Uganda. *Review of African Political Economy* 17 (47): 64–83.

Meagher, K. 2003. A back door to globalisation? Structural adjustment, globalisation and transborder trade in West Africa. *Review of African Political Economy* 30 (95): 57–75.

Meagher, K. 2006. Social capital, social liabilities, and political capital: social networks and informal manufacturing in Nigeria. *African Affairs* 105 (421): 553–582.

Migdal, J.S. 1974. Why change? Toward a new theory of change among individuals in the process of modernization. *World Politics* 26 (2) (Jan.): 189–206.

Mirembe, O.K. 2005. Échanges transnationaux, réseaux informels et développement local. Une étude au Nord-est de la République démocratique de Congo. PhD diss., Université Catholique de Louvain.

Mitchell, T. 2002. *Rule of Experts: Egypt, Techno-Politics, Modernity*. Berkeley: University of California Press.

Nugent, P. 2002. *Smugglers, Secessionists and Loyal Citizens on the Ghana–Togo Frontier: The Lie of the Borderlands since 1914*. Oxford: James Currey.

Nugent, P. 2010. States and social contracts in Africa. *New Left Review* 63 (May–June).

Nugent, P. and Asiwaju, A.I., eds. 1996. *African Boundaries: Barriers, Conduits and Opportunities*. Edinburgh: Centre of African Studies.

Olivier de Sardan, J-P. 2008. *Researching the Practical Norms of Real Governance in Africa*. Discussion Paper, Africa Power and Politics. London: Overseas Development Institute.

Polanyi, L. 1944. *The Great Transformation: The Political and Economic Origins of Our Time*. Boston: Beacon Press.

Pratten, D. and Sen, A., eds. 2006. *Global Vigilantes: Anthropological Perspectives on Justice and Violence*. London: Hurst.

Prunier, G. 1999. L'Ouganda et les guerres congolaises. *Politique Africaine* (75) (Oct.): 43–59.

Raeymaekers, T. 2007. The power of protection: governance and transborder trade on the Congo-Ugandan frontier. PhD diss., University of Ghent.

Raeymaekers, T. 2009. The silent encroachment of the frontier: a politics of transborder trade in the Semliki valley (Congo–Uganda). *Political Geography* 28 (1): 55–65.

Raeymaekers, T. 2010. Protection for sale? War and the transformation of regulation on the Congo-Ugandan border. *Development and Change* 40 (4): 563–587.

Reno, W. 1998. *Warlord Politics and African States*. Boulder: Lynne Rienner.

Reno, W. 2000. *War, Debt and the Role of Pretending in Uganda's International Relations*. Occasional Paper. Copenhagen: University of Copenhagen, Centre of African Studies.

Reno, W. 2002. The politics of insurgency in collapsing states. *Development and Change* 33 (5): 837–858.

Reyntjens, F. 2005. The privatisation and criminalisation of public space in the geopolitics of the Great Lakes region. *Journal of Modern African Studies* 43 (4): 587–607.

Roitman, J. 1998. The garrison-entrepot. *Cahiers d'Études Africaines* 38 (2–4): 297–329.

Roitman, J. 2005. *Fiscal Disobedience: An Anthropology of Economic Regulation in Central Africa*. Princeton: Princeton University Press.

Schatzberg, M.G. 1988. *The Dialectics of Oppression in Zaire*. Bloomington: Indiana University Press.

Swyngedouw, E. 1997. Neither global nor local: "glocalization" and the politics of scale. In Cox, K., ed., *Spaces of Globalization: Reasserting the Power of the Local*. New York: Guilford Press.

Tegera A., ed. 2001. *The Coltan Phenomenon: How the Rare Mineral Has Changed the Life of the Population in War-Torn North Kivu Province in the East of the Democratic Republic of Congo*. Goma: Pole Institute.

Tegera, A. and Johnson, D. 2007. *Rules for Sale: Formal and Informal Crossborder Trade in DRC*. Goma: Pole Institute.

Titeca, K. 2006. Les OPEC boys en Ouganda, trafiquants de pétrole et acteurs politiques. *Politique Africaine* (103): 143–159.

Titeca, K. 2009. 'The "Masai" and "miraa": public authority, vigilance and criminality in a Ugandan border town. *Journal of Modern African Studies*, 47 (2): 291–317.

Titeca, K. and De Herdt, T. 2010. Regulation, cross border trade and practical norms in West Nile, Northwestern Uganda. *Africa* 80 (4) (Oct.).

Trefon, T. ed. 2004. *Reinventing Order in the Congo: How People Respond to State Failure in Kinshasa*. London: Zed Books.

UBOS (Uganda Bureau of Statistics). 2007. *The Informal Cross Border Trade Survey Report 2006*. Kampala: UBOS and Bank of Uganda.

UBOS (Uganda Bureau of Statistics). 2008. *The Informal Cross Border Trade Survey Report 2007*. Kampala: UBOS and Bank of Uganda.

United Nations. 2001. *Report of the Panel of Experts on Illegal Exploitation of Natural Resources and Other Forms of Wealth of the Democratic Republic of Congo*. Apr. 12. New York: United Nations Security Council.

Vlassenroot, K. and Raeymaekers, T. 2004a. *Conflict and Social Transformation in Eastern DR Congo*. Gent: Academia Press.

Vlassenroot, K. and Raeymaekers, T. 2004b. The politics of rebellion and intervention in Ituri: the emergence of a new political complex? *African Affairs* (103): 385–412.

Williams, J. 2006. *The Ethics of Territorial Borders: Drawing Lines in the Shifting Sand*. Basingstoke: Palgrave Macmillan.

Wolf, E. 1966. *Peasants*. Englewood Cliffs: Prentice Hall.

19 Bandits, Borderlands and Opium Wars in Afghanistan

Jonathan Goodhand

This chapter explores the linkages between the drugs economy, borderlands and "postconflict" state-building in Afghanistan. It does this through an analysis of Sheghnan, a remote district in the northeast province of Badakhshan, situated on the Afghan-Tajik border. It examines the historical development of the border through a number of different phases in its evolution; first, its prestate origins as an open border on the edges of contending empires; second, as a closed border, within a buffer state – a Cold War construct which divided Soviet and US spheres of influence; third, the prising open of the border after the collapse of the former Soviet Union and civil wars in Afghanistan and Tajikistan – in which the region reverted to its eighteenth-century status as an open frontier; and fourth, "postconflict" peace-building in Afghanistan and Tajikistan, in which the uneven attempts by both countries to "sharpen the edges" of the border have influenced institutions and economic practices within the borderland.

The chapter charts the opening and closing of the border; the movement of people, commodities and ideas across the border; the effects of changing political regimes; the role of resources and their effects on local governance; and the complex, multifaceted networks which span the border and are involved in the drugs trade. The drugs economy has been an important part of the story of borderland transformation in Sheghnan, and because of drugs, these borderlands are no longer marginal. The hinterland is a resource to be exploited by the center and, reversing prewar relationships, the latter is now dependent on economic activities in the former. Therefore, drugs have exerted a gravitational pull on the central state, by attracting state actors out to the borderlands. In contrast to conclusions reached in most mainstream policy debates, the drugs economy in Sheghnan has contributed to the

A Companion to Border Studies, First Edition. Edited by Thomas M. Wilson and Hastings Donnan.
© 2012 Blackwell Publishing Ltd. Published 2012 by Blackwell Publishing Ltd.

emergence of a measure of political order and has had significant developmental outcomes.

The chapter draws on Snyder's (2006) work on institutions of extraction to show how the bargaining processes between rulers at the center and private actors on the periphery have contributed to complex interdependencies between them, leading to the emergence of a new political equilibrium. However, I seek to nuance and extend upon Snyder's model, which tends to draw too sharp a distinction between state and nonstate actors, thus failing to capture the messy, hybrid nature of governance in Afghanistan (in 2010). Moreover, the model misses the important ways in which the existence of international and internal borders influence these bargaining processes. Rather than viewing the borderland as two separate regions on each side of the border, it is conceptualized here as a single spatial unit that straddles an international border (Baud and van Schendel 1997). Borderlands can be understood as frontiers or "spaces of transition," defined and shaped by proximity to the border, by differential developments on either side of the borderline and by the changing nature of the border itself (Newman 2006). As explored further below, the story of the Afghan-Tajik frontier's evolution into a "networked borderland" (Rumford 2006) has been simultaneously one of boundary making and boundary enforcement – including the changing porosity of the international border and emergence of new internal boundaries linked to competing politico-military formations – and the transcendence of boundaries with the emergence of a thriving transborder drug economy. Therefore, I will attempt to bring a borderland perspective to bear on Snyder's model. In doing so I draw upon an emerging borderlands literature which emphasizes their socially constructed nature, the practices and meanings attached to particular borders by the borderland populations themselves, and their dynamism as social and political constructs – borderlands are constantly subject to processes of rebordering and debordering, particularly in wartime (Passi 1996; Wilson and Donnan 1998; Anderson and O'Dowd 1999; Roitman 2005; van Schendel 2005; Newman 2006; Scott 2010).

Finally, this analysis of the frontier illuminates processes of state formation, state collapse and "postconflict" state-building. State formation is understood here to be a historical or immanent process, the largely unconscious outcome of conflicts, negotiations, compromises and trade-offs between competing politico-military elites and socioeconomic groups. State-building in contrast is understood to be a conscious, planned and often externally driven attempt to establish an apparatus of control. In this chapter, by studying immanent processes, I call into question the idea that state-building simply involves the gradual diffusion of power outward. A historical account of Sheghnan shows the decidedly nonlinear process of state formation, which has occurred in fits and starts – a process that might be described as one of "punctuated equilibrium" involving fragile power balances interspersed by periodic conflicts (Cramer and Goodhand 2003). The borderland is central to this story of Afghan state-building and state crisis. A focus on borderlands means taking seriously the "politics of place" (Stepputat 2001: 286) and examining the diffuse dynamics and localized projects that feed into and shape processes of state formation. Therefore, mainstream accounts of state-building that leave out the periphery "ignore a set of boundary conditions and exchanges which make the center what it is" (Scott 2010: 27).

WARS, STATES, BORDERLANDS AND ILLICIT FLOWS

In a study of brigandage and piracy from a world historical perspective, Gallant (1999) makes a convincing case for the role played by illegal networks of armed predators in facilitating the spread and global triumph of capitalism. Bandits were deeply insinuated in the process of state formation and state consolidation. As states expand they often leave peripheries poorly integrated into a central apparatus: "In these mountains and maritime fringes, weak state control can provide an opening for men of prowess – pirates, bandits, warlords or ethnic chiefs – to mediate between the centre and its margins" (McCoy 1999: 130). These men act as brokers between center and periphery, facilitating capitalist penetration of the countryside by increasing monetization, encouraging marketization and by providing a venue for upward economic mobility. Eric Wolf writes about the role of such brokers as follows:

> they stand guard over the crucial junctures or synapses of relationships which connect the local system to the larger whole. . . . [Brokers] must serve some of the interest groups operating on both the community and the national level. They cannot settle them, since by doing so they would abolish their own usefulness to others. They thus often act as buffers between groups, maintaining their tensions which provide the dynamic of their actions. (1956: 1075–1076)

Through a process of either co-opting or crushing rural outlaws in frontier regions, states experienced a "border effect" that strengthened their capacities. Put simply, "bandits helped make states and states made bandits" (Gallant 1999: 25). Many states today continue to be involved in the same processes of political and administrative pacification in their unruly borderlands, something that James Scott refers to as the "last great enclosure"(Scott 2010: 5). At a global level international peace operations may be driven by a similar impulse, to occupy and stabilize "ungoverned spaces" often located at the interstices of one or more "fragile states" (Duffield 2007). Contemporary state-builders may adopt similar tactics to their predecessors, for instance the Burmese drug lord Khun Sa played a catalytic role in state formation by forcing Rangoon to impose control over its frontiers (McCoy 1999: 158).[1] Similarly, Snyder (2006) convincingly argues that although opium initially fueled chaos in Burma by providing a key source of income to rebel armies, after 1990 it contributed to the consolidation of a stable military regime that ended the civil war and forcibly imposed political order. In the same vein, Volkov (2002) argues that "violent entrepreneurs" in early 1990s Russia responded to (and helped create) the demand for protection from nascent businesses at a time of widespread insecurity. Over time the means of coercion were centralized as a result of the struggles for survival and domination between violent entrepreneurs and the state.

War economies and shadow economies may therefore be seen as part of the long and brutal politics of sovereignty. Illegality and the state have been constant companions, and revenue from illicit flows, and their control, may actually strengthen the state. As Snyder (2006) notes, at one point in time lootable resources may be associated with state breakdown, but at another time with political order.[2] According to Snyder, the key is how institutions of extraction involving rulers and private actors develop around these resources. Four possible extraction regimes are posited – private, public, joint, or no extraction – each leading to different outcomes in terms of political (dis)order. If rulers are able to build institutions of joint extraction, lootable resources can produce political order by providing the revenues to govern. Rulers may deploy sticks – including coercion and legal instruments – to deny private actors independent access to resources, or carrots – including amnesties and tax breaks – to encourage them to share and invest their revenues. Patronage and corruption may also be part of the bargaining process, as Reno (2000) argues in his analysis of the political economy of weak states in Africa. Snyder's model is developed and extended below in order to examine the effects of the opium economy on political (dis)order in a border region of northeast Afghanistan.

SHEGHNAN: A BORDERLAND HISTORY

Sheghnan is a poor, mountainous district in northeast Afghanistan, situated on the border between Afghan Badakhshan and the oblast of Gorno-Badakhshan of Tajikistan. The border is defined by the Panj River,[3] which originates in the Pamir Mountains and flows westwards into the Amu Darya and eventually fills the Aral Sea. This drainage system has hosted trade for centuries between people living on both banks of the river, with primarily ethnic Tajiks living on the lowland western Panj and Ismailis along the highland eastern Panj. A number of Pashtuns, Uzbeks, Russians and Kuchis live among them.

Sheghnan has a predominantly Ismaili population of 33,000. Its traditionally agropastoral economy is subject to chronic food deficits due to land scarcity, the short growing season, geographical isolation,[4] and more recently three decades of war, leading to increased out-migration. By Afghan standards the population is highly educated, a legacy of the Soviet era investments in education and more recently the Aga Khan's involvement in this sector. Government salaries for teachers are vital to the local economy and roughly 800 Sheghnis work outside the district in other parts of Badakhshan province as government teachers.

For most of its history Sheghnan has constituted a marginal borderland in a wider region of open borders and trade routes. The logic of state consolidation and expansion was dictated by extracting resources and manpower (Scott 2010; Barfield 2004). Therefore the burdens of taxation fell on the "state spaces," and because resource-poor, mountainous regions could not be profitably administered or easily subdued, they remained largely autonomous.

Mountainous frontier zones also constituted places of refuge from the civilizational project of the valleys (Scott 2010). Flight, by self-governing peoples, was the state-breaking response to the state-building project of sedentarization, extraction and simplification (Scott 2010). The mountains become "spaces of avoidance" because "civilizations find it hard to climb hills" (Scott 2010). Even today Pashtun tribes that occupy the hills and deserts draw a sharp distinction between themselves who do not pay taxes (*nang*) and those Pashtuns who live under state control (*qalang*) (Barfield 2004: 267). As well as a means of escaping state taxation, the hills constitute a place of refuge from political or religious persecution. In Afghanistan, religious heterodoxy has tended, literally, to head for the hills, and the spatial pattern of settlement is characterized by Pashtun and Tajik occupation of the fertile lowlands and the Shiites (including Hazaras and Ismailis) occupying the marginal and high mountain areas.

Sheghnan's status as a marginal borderland changed as it was incorporated into the emerging Afghan state during the nineteenth century. The reign of Abdur Rahman Khan (1881–1901) was a defining moment as semi-autonomous regions were pacified through internal conquest, and open frontiers became internationally recognized and internally policed borders. An Anglo-Russian commission demarcated Afghanistan's northern and western borders with Central Asia, Iran and China between 1876 and 1896, and in 1893 the Durand line was drawn up demarcating the eastern limit of the Afghan administration. The British hoped that this would seal off their empire hermetically from the acquisitive interests of the Russians (Cullather 2002: 47). Through a combination of military campaigns,[5] alongside fiscal[6] and administrative reorganization,[7] Abdur Rahman centralized political and economic power in Kabul. While "nonstate spaces" like the northeast were to an extent successfully colonized, they remained weakly incorporated into, and marginal to the Mohamedzai Pashtun dominated state.[8]

Afghanistan's northern borders were hardened in the late 1920s and economic relations of the Soviet-dominated Central Asia were redirected and amplified toward Russia. Russian officers were appointed to police the border on the Soviet side and Pashtuns were relocated from southern Afghanistan to do the same on the Afghan side, following a rebellion in 1925 by the Sheghnis in response to King Ammanullah's policies on taxation and conscription. Sheghnan remained a neglected and semi-autarkic region for much of the twentieth century. This can be contrasted with the eastern borderlands, which were politically sensitive[9] and economically significant because of cross-border trade and the proximity of neighboring cities which catalyzed domestic revenues, investment and cultural exchange.

Although people and commodities could not cross the border, ideas and ideologies did, and during the Cold War period Sheghnan was influenced by wider political currents emanating from Kabul and beyond: "The majority of Ismaili elites maintained that only socialism could remedy their social and economic problems and they could see that their fellow Ismailis across the Oxus river in Gorno-Badakhshan and those in Sinkiang in China apparently enjoyed a more comfortable life under socialism" (Emadi 1997: 114).

The 1960s and 1970s saw the growing politicization of the Ismaili intelligentsia, who were attracted to Marxism as a result of the treatment of Ismailis by the Pashtun-dominated state and the visible improvements brought to Ismaili regions across the border.[10] Sheghnis joined either the Khalq pro-Soviet faction of the People's Democratic Party of Afghanistan (PDPA), or SAZA, a Maoist-oriented ethnonationalist party, which considered the national question (i.e., Pashtun supremacy) as being more important than the class question.

In 1978 the PDPA regime came to power after a coup (the Saur Revolution) and embarked on a radical reform program that provoked violent resistance in the countryside. A second coup followed in 1979, and with growing insurrection and a breakdown of social control the Soviets invaded later that year.

Sheghnan was not affected by the intense fighting experienced by many other regions during this period and many Sheghnis look back upon this time as a "golden age," largely because of the Soviet policy of elevating minorities. Sheghnis were promoted to high positions within the PDPA regime, with four becoming provincial governors, and many were trained as teachers or became high-level functionaries within the party apparatus. Many Ismailis studied in the Soviet republic of Tajikistan as well as institutions of higher education elsewhere in the Soviet Union. In 1987, President Najibullah's 1987 National Reconciliation government included both Khalqi and SAZA groups in the new cabinet. Therefore, during this period Sheghnis experienced improved material conditions and acquired a new political voice, with borderland elites becoming important brokers who were able to channel resources from the center to the periphery. The borderland population was no longer so marginal.

MUJAHIDEEN GOVERNMENT (1992–1996) AND TALIBAN RULE (1996–2001)

The fall of Najibullah's Soviet-backed regime in 1992 was followed by a mujahideen-led government in Kabul until the Taliban takeover of 1996. Mujahideen rule marked a new phase of the conflict in which it mutated from a Cold War conflict into a regionalized civil war. This transformed life in Sheghnan, with state breakdown occurring on both sides of the border and civil wars in Tajikistan and Afghanistan becoming part of a regionalized and extremely volatile conflict system connecting zones of instability in Kashmir, the tribal areas of Pakistan, Afghanistan, Tajikistan, the Ferghana valley and Chechnya (Goodhand 2004).

Therefore, what had been a closed, heavily policed border, and a construct of Cold War geopolitics, was now regularly transgressed by fighters, drug traffickers, traders, aid agencies and refugees. Afghans became increasingly embroiled in the politics of Tajikistan and were divided between those who supported the Islamic Revival Party and those backing the Moscow-based Dushanbe regime. At various times mujahideen from both sides of the border set up military bases in the other country.[11]

During this period the Sheghnis lost the privileged status they had enjoyed under the PDPA regime and once more became a marginal and increasingly threatened minority as a result of the penetration of the region by jihadi groups from both sides of the border. The borderland itself was now a strategic resource, first as an area of sanctuary for the Tajik mujahideen and second as a key node in the expanding drugs economy.

The growth in opium production in Badakhshan in the early to mid 1990s coincided with a number of structural shifts internationally and regionally (see Goodhand 2000), including the end of Cold War patronage, the collapse of the Soviet Union, the civil war in neighboring Tajikistan, the increasingly porous northern border, the growing monetization of the economy (Rubin 2000), and the end of Soviet wheat subsidies, which further impoverished the peasantry. Taken together these shifts created top-down and bottom-up incentives to cultivate and traffic opium. Because military entrepreneurs could no longer rely on external patronage, they had to draw increasingly on domestic economic activities as a source of revenue. Drugs, contraband smuggling, asset stripping, appropriation of state land, predation, tribute, taxation and tithes were some of the self-financing strategies employed by military entrepreneurs. The absence of many viable economic alternatives in Badakhshan, beyond the lapis and gemstone businesses, meant that control of the drugs trade was key to the successful mobilization of capital and coercion.

Between 1994 and 2000 there was a 43 percent increase in poppy production in Badakhshan (Thompson 2006: 170), and there are reports of traders from the leading poppy-growing provinces of Kandahar and Nangahar, in the south and east respectively, going to Badakhshan in the 1990s in order to encourage and disseminate poppy cultivation and processing. Opium was primarily cultivated in the districts Jurm, Argu and Kishum, and increasingly was refined in labs into morphine base and heroin within the province. Therefore, as the opium industry became more firmly established, upgrading occurred within the production chain.

Sheghnan became an important trafficking route and drugs were transported through the neighboring district of Baharak to Sheghnan, and from there to Khorag and on to Osh in Kyrgyzstan. According to the United Nations Office on Drugs and Crime (UNODC 2007), 18 percent of Afghanistan's heroin equivalent opiates are trafficked through Tajikistan,[12] and the principal crossing points are Ragh (Tangan); Shahri Buzurg; Sheghnan; and Ishkasham (see Figure 19.1). The relative importance of these different crossing points has fluctuated over time, reflecting changing governance arrangements and regulatory regimes on both sides of the border. In the 1990s, Sheghnan and Ishkasham were the principal routes, with opium going through Gorno-Badakhshan, Tajikistan and on to Osh in southern Kyrgyzstan.[13] Subsequently, the crossing points at Shahri Buzurg and Ragh have become more important because of the development of Afghan-Kulyabi trafficking networks and proximity to the Tajik capital Dushanbe.[14] After 1996, even though there was no Taliban presence in the province, opium produced in Taliban areas was trafficked through Northern Alliance opposition-controlled areas. Badakhshan's strategic position within the drug industry was heightened by the Taliban's ban on opium production in 2000. Demonstrating its footloose, flexible nature, cultivation migrated across the internal border between Taliban and Northern Alliance controlled territory. The ban precipitated a tenfold increase in prices. This, in addition to a long-standing drought, increased the incentives for farmers to switch to opium cultivation in Badakhshan.

The border therefore became a resource to be controlled and fought over, and Sheghnan became a "drug intensified borderland" (Gootenberg 2005), transforming political and economic dynamics in the district. During this period drugs smuggling in Sheghnan remained largely a cottage industry, shown by the interdiction of hundreds of small-time couriers who lacked the resources to bribe border officials. Therefore, at all levels, including cultivation, processing and trading, there were many actors involved and low barriers to entry into the drugs industry. Its organization was highly decentralized and extremely fluid, reflecting the political dynamics in Badakhshan at that time.

In the early 1990s Badakhshi Tajiks from the mujahideen moved into Sheghnan in order to gain a foothold at the border. Khalqi and SAZA factions in Shegh-

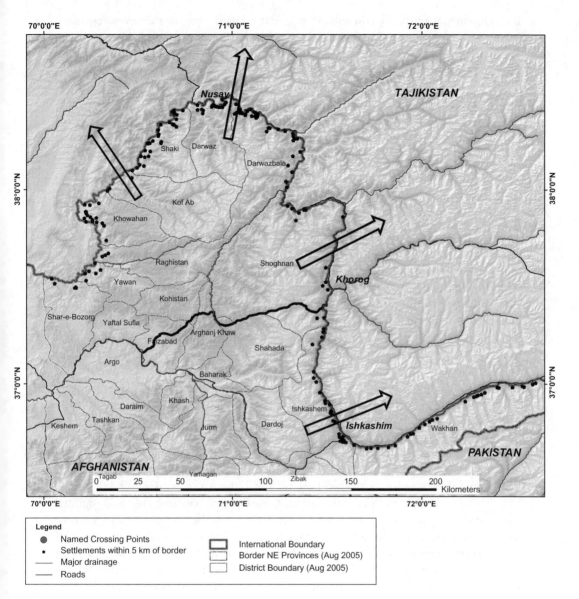

Figure 19.1 Badakhshan border crossings
Source: ALCIS, University of Reading.

nan attempted to leverage support from different mujahideen groups, while the latter
exploited these long-standing conflicts as a tool of governance. In 1996 this led to
large-scale fighting in which 180 Sheghnis and 200 Tajiks died. By the end of the
1990s, governance in Sheghnan was characterized by a complex mosaic of fiefdoms
in which mini-sovereigns fought one another for control of the border. This also
reflected the factionalization of the mujahideen more generally. Although at the time

Badakhshan was primarily controlled by Jamiat-e Islami (one of the seven resistance parties), this patrimonially based and unstable coalition was subdivided into the Rabbani and Massoud factions (Giustozzi and Orsini 2009). And at the local level there was a multitude of medium to small-scale commanders. In order to accommodate warlord interests, in 1992 Rabbani, the then President of Afghanistan, subdivided the 13 administrative divisions into 27 units. As a result, on the border there was a pluralization of regulatory authorities (Roitman 2005), leading to a regime of "private extraction" whereby private economic actors enjoyed exclusive, unregulated and untaxed control over the income generated by resources (Snyder 2006).

THE "POST-TALIBAN PERIOD" (2001–PRESENT)

The removal of the Taliban by the US-led coalition at the end of 2001 and the highly internationalized state-building effort that followed had a significant impact on local politics and the position of the Ismaili community. First, the "grand bargain" represented by the Bonn Agreement represented a significant power shift from southerners (the Pashtuns) to northerners (though Tajiks, particularly Panjshiris, were the main beneficiaries of Bonn).[15] Second, the new constitution explicitly recognized language rights and freedom of religious expression, giving Ismailis, a historically persecuted group, a certain level of confidence in the new dispensation. Third, the transition enabled a significant expansion of the Aga Khan support program in Afghanistan (this followed a meeting between the Aga Khan and President Karzai in 2002). Therefore to some extent the northeast experienced a peace dividend, unlike for instance the south of the country. Fourth, the security situation improved on both sides of the border; in both countries wars had ostensibly ended with peace settlements, and new "unity" governments were in power. With this transition came changed regulatory authorities on both sides of the border. As explored below, these transformations have exposed new tensions around how to "deal" with the border. While "peace" has opened up opportunities to strengthen cross-border economic links and regional integration,[16] it has also prompted a strong statist impulse to police and securitize the border in order to counter the threats posed by drugs, terrorism, and so forth.[17]

Post-Bonn political consolidation has occurred largely through what has been described as a process of "warlord democratization" (Rubin 2006). In other words, military strongmen have been co-opted into (rather than excluded from) the new political arrangements. This appears to have worked to some extent in the north, with Badakhshan experiencing an initial "security premium," manifest in the removal of check posts and the decline in internecine fighting between militias in the province. Regional strongmen who had built up a military and economic "strategic edge" during the war years have risen to prominence at the provincial level, entering the new administration as governors, district managers and so on, or becoming elected representatives as parliamentarians and provincial councilors. Most warlords regard the state as a desirable resource to gain access to and to control (Schetter et al. 2007: 149).

In parallel with the political transition, there has been a significant growth in the drug economy driven by a range of micro and macro factors. First, the Taliban's opium ban had the effect of a tenfold increase in prices, which for more wealthy farmers created strong incentives to allocate land to poppy. These factors were rein- forced by the end of a drought, which meant an increased availability of wheat and a freeing up of internal and external markets (Mansfield 2007). Second, the CIA's policy of providing several hundred million dollars to commanders, in order to buy their support in the "war on terror," had the effect of flooding the money market. The exchange rate of the dollar against Afghan currency was halved in two months. This rapid deflation created incentives to unload US dollars into other currencies or other profitable investments. Since the US offensive occurred during poppy planting season, dollars were quickly recycled into loans to farmers to finance the next spring's poppy crop. Third, coalition forces initially adopted a "laissez-faire" policy toward drugs, born out of the strong tension between counter-insurgency and counter- narcotics objectives. Counter-insurgency efforts require good local allies, and local warlords are unlikely to provide either support or intelligence to those who are destroying their businesses (Felbab-Brown 2005). Fourth, unlike previous phases of the conflict, when opium was essentially a licit commodity, its criminalization had the effect of keeping prices high because of the associated "risk premium" and forcing those involved in the opium industry to look for protection beyond the state – and there is no shortage in Afghanistan of nonstate specialists in violence. Conse- quently, military entrepreneurs have been able to generate political capital and revenue by providing protection to the peasantry and traffickers from state-led counter- narcotics efforts. Furthermore, disarmament, demobilization and reintegration (DDR) programs had the effect of pushing many mid- to low-level commanders into a closer relationship with the opium industry (Shaw 2006). Unlike the more senior regional strongmen, they did not have the option of a transition to politics.

The drug economy has been a central factor in the emergence of a new political equilibrium and power-sharing arrangements. Access to decision-making power over the political control of the border has become central to the workings of Sheghnan's political affairs. A stake in the border as a resource affords opportunities to profit from cross-border trade, including heroin, opium, gemstones, luxury cars and other consumer goods (Theuss and Gardizi nd: 13). Although opium cultivation dropped significantly in Badakhshan from 2006–2007, drug trafficking continued to be central to political and economic life in the province. In the 2010 parliamentary elections in Badakhshan the local control of routes and border crossings broadly corresponded with the map of political power within the province. Elections provided an opportu- nity to test and reformulate power balances and consolidate shares in the drug economy (Foschini 2010).

The logistics and supply chain mechanisms associated with cross-border trade have shifted from being a fragmented and dispersed cottage industry, whereby individual traffickers carried by night no more than 40 kilograms of heroin in rubber dinghies, to a far more orderly, regulated and consolidated system. Reflecting broader national trends, the drug industry has become more professionalized and vertically integrated. Dealers communicate with one another across the river via satellite phone or other forms of mobile communication. In order to operate, they are likely to need downcountry partners in Baharak and Faizabad, who may operate as hawala dealers (Theuss and Gardizi nd: 14).[18] These shifts in the drug economy at the border were summarized by a Sheghni teacher as follows: "in the last ten years the currency has changed from afghanis to dollars and opium has changed to heroin."[19]

It has been estimated that drugs produce an annual turnover of up to $40 million at the Sheghni border (Theuss and Gardizi nd). There is a three- to fourfold increase in prices as heroin crosses the border. Typically, consignments are exchanged for US dollars, luxury four-wheel drive vehicles,[20] bottles of vodka, other consumer goods or basic necessities such as flour. When traffickers cross the border, it is common for them to carry their own weapons, and gunfights between smugglers and border guards are reported to be common (Townsend 2006: 83). Domestic sales of Afghan opiates in Central Asia amount to no more than $30 million compared to the profit from their export to Russia and the rest of Europe, which is estimated at $2.2 billion (Fenopetov 2006: 7), though it should be noted that all figures on drugs must be treated with a certain level of caution (Mansfield 2006).

Drug dealers have adopted a number of strategies in order to secure a stake at the border. At the micro level, dealers may sell drugs to families who have an addict (there is an addiction rate of up to 30 percent in many villages) and/or to already impoverished families, thus leading to progressive indebtedness. Pressure is subsequently exerted by the creditor for the debt to be paid off through a distress sale of assets. The drug dealer may take advantage of this situation to marry the daughter of the family and use the wife's house as a base for drug trafficking. Drugs tend to be stockpiled in the villages rather than in the district bazaar and marriage can be a strategy for gaining a privileged position in the trafficking supply chain, thereby integrating the opium business into local social systems.

Therefore, at the micro level one can identify various forms of nonstate regulation, which is a point of continuity with earlier phases of the drugs trade. However, during the post-Bonn period, new state/nonstate hybrid regulatory authorities have emerged, mirroring closely Roitman's characterization of shadow networks in the Chad Basin: "the state is at the very heart of the proliferation of unregulated economic exchanges as well as the pluralization of regulatory authorities" (2005: 204). At the district level, the state apparatus has been co-opted, with politico-military entrepreneurs enrolling into key positions such as the *woliswol* (district) head, police chief, head of border security, and so on. These positions tend to be occupied by Tajiks, while Sheghnis occupy second-tier positions, including the deputy *woliswol*. They are therefore the junior partners in a principal–agent relation. Faizabad-based Tajik networks, through appointments from the provincial center, have begun to establish a structurally more permanent and predictable control over the political affairs of Sheghnan. This has enabled them to establish surveillance and to institutionalize more predictable forms of co-optation. While the state apparatus does not come close to a Weberian model, rulers are surprisingly effective at making things happen in the periphery through their state and nonstate networks – for example by deploying the threat of, or actually carrying out drug interdiction or eradication in order to discipline particular groups or individuals.

To be a player in the drugs industry and to retain a stake at the border one must have patrons at the national level. In particular, this means establishing relationships with power holders in the Ministry of Interior, particularly the police and border police. A police chief in a poppy-growing area reportedly needs to pay $100,000 to retain his job for a six-month period (when his salary is $60 per month) (Baldauf 2006). The Ministry of Interior has been described as a "shop for selling jobs" (Wilder 2007), confirming its reputation as one of the most corrupt ministries, just as the President's Office and the ministries of Finance and Commerce are also key players. Political entrepreneurs who want to be seen as "legitimate" have a remote control engagement with drugs trafficking at the border, and work through buffers lower down the chain. Therefore, borderland control occurs at different points within the political system and not necessarily at the territorial limits of the state. As Shaw notes, it is impossible to operate in the criminal "underworld" without patronage in the political "overworld" (2006: 198). The complex interrelationships between state and nonstate, legal and illegal, center and periphery which characterize the cross-border drugs trade are illustrated in the case study below of Aziz, a key broker on the Sheghnan border.

AZIZ, A BORDERLAND ENTREPRENEUR

Aziz is the key drug dealer in Sheghnan.[21] He is a Sunni Pashtun from Sarobi, in eastern Afghanistan, and before the war he went to military academy. He was a commander in the Soviet-backed Afghan national air force and become a leading Khalqi and a personal friend of Najibullah and other PDPA regime leaders. He took refuge in Pakistan in the mid-1980s, subsequently returned, and from the mid-1990s he established a foothold in the cross-border drugs trade.

Over time he has established relationships with a diverse network of provincial and national level actors. Interviewees said that he is well known in Jurm district of Badakhshan, where he buys opium in the bazaar, from where it is taken to Shiftan village for processing. He is also involved with trading precious stones, antiquities and commodities such as flour (see below) and his trading networks extend to India, Pakistan and Dubai. He has a house in Khair Khana, a wealthy neighborhood of Kabul. He has also forged strong links with players across the border. His primary business partner is an Ismaili Pamiri, who fought in the United Tajik Opposition and was involved with arms and drugs smuggling during the civil war, but who has moved increasingly into the gemstones business in recent years. This coworker has licit trading connections with Chinese commodity traders and is alleged to have high-level contacts with criminal networks in Tashkent, Osh, Almaty and Moscow.

At the time of my research in August 2006, Aziz had moved across the border and was living in Khorag, capital of Gorno-Badakhshan, Tajikistan, probably in an attempt to establish a foothold in the Central Asian trafficking networks higher up the value chain. More recently, he has married the daughter of his business partner from Khorag. He has also shifted increasingly into the gems business, side-stepping the Tajik government's restrictive regulations on gems trading by smuggling them across the border into Afghanistan.

Aziz's principal means of accumulation, at least initially, was through the drugs trade, and he was able to do this by gaining a strategic edge during the war years because of his diverse political contacts and access to the means of violence/protection. However, his actions have not been purely predatory and he appears to be conscious, particularly as an outsider, of the need to build local legitimacy. One indication of this may be his otherwise inexplicable actions in 2005, when he imported and flooded the local market with large quantities of low-cost flour at a time of severe food shortages. In doing so he undercut the local market and brought down flour prices. Theuss and Gardizi (nd) argue that these actions can only be understood as part of a conscious strategy by Aziz to build legitimacy and a support base among the peasantry. This indicates a recognition on his part that his strategic edge depends on the ability to mobilize political and social capital. A strategy that depends purely on access to the means of violence and predation and an exclusive focus on the drugs trade is high risk and unlikely to be sustainable in the long term.

In summary, Aziz has skillfully mobilized capital, coercion and legitimacy. His key strategies have included (adapted from Theuss and Gardizi nd):

• Building broad-based political networks on both sides of the border.
• Diversifying economic activities, including gemstones, antiquities, flour and fuel, as well as drugs. Thus a combination of licit and illicit commodities flow through the same networks.
• Forging relationships of vertical patronage with key high-level officials, particularly within the Ministry of Interior and the provincial administration.
• Establishing client relations with key district-level state actors.
• Deploying financial muscle by bribing officials and imposing informal taxes of low-level traffickers.
• Building legitimacy with societal groups/peasantry through displays of benevolence.

Aziz is perhaps the archetypal mid-level broker who in the Afghan context is crucial both to the drugs trade and systems of local governance. While his power is contingent on actors further up the political chain, he has the capacity to either make things happen or prevent things from happening on the periphery. Aziz and others like him are simultaneously the connective tissue and sources of friction between core and periphery.

INSTITUTIONS OF EXTRACTION AND POLITICAL NETWORKS

Following Snyder (2006), a joint extraction regime has emerged, whereby rulers and private actors must negotiate with one another in order to share the revenue generated by poppy-growing. Each can deploy a combination of sticks and carrots in order to deter the other from establishing a monopoly over the revenue streams from opium. State actors can use the threat of coercion through the deployment of the Afghan National Army, the police and border police. Like protection rackets they create a demand for protection – against threats from itself and from nonstate actors who are competitors in the drugs industry. They can also threaten a "no extraction" regime by deploying counter-narcotics instruments including eradication by the counter-narcotics police. The Ministry of Interior in effect operates as a shadow "Ministry of Opium" by controlling key positions in drug-producing and smuggling areas. Private actors cannot gain and maintain a foothold in the industry without securing patrons within the state at the district, provincial and central levels (Goodhand 2008).

However, state actors do not hold all the cards. Borderland elites still have militias in spite of DDR programs, which have been patchy, and this gives them considerable bargaining power. Furthermore, poppy as a diffuse, high-value, easily transportable and illegal commodity which is largely cultivated in borderland regions is a difficult commodity for state actors to monopolize, lending itself to joint or private extraction regimes. Finally, the porosity of the northern border and the footloose nature of the industry make it extremely difficult for rulers to establish monopoly control. Therefore, in effect, principals franchise out monopoly rights on the border to agents in return for a share of the profits.

The institutional arrangements around the border have not changed in gradual linear fashion but through a process of what was described earlier as "punctuated equilibrium." The shift from Cold War to civil war conflict involved a sudden rupture, followed by the emergence of new (though fragile) equilibrium. Violence – structural, symbolic and physical – has been central to border practices. It has been deployed as a tool of governance by Tajiks, who exploited intra-Sheghni divisions to establish control of the border. However, the nature of violence has changed in the post-Taliban period. In many areas it is now essentially about maintaining market share and securing contract compliance. Violence is bad for business and can be understood as a sign of market dysfunction. An increase in violence may be an indication that law enforcement is having a disruptive effect on drugs networks. As Volkov notes in the case of Russia, when wielders of force become owners of capital their ability to control their domain comes to depend on the logic and rules of economic activity, and "the more criminal groups strive to control the emerging markets, the more the markets control and transform these groups" (2002: 122). Violence is likely to be most intense in the "gray zones" where boundaries are disputed and networks become weaker.

The drugs trade involves multi-sited and heterogeneous cross-border networks, which tend to be far more eclectic than politico-military structures – from an ethnic, religious, political party or socioprofessional perspective. Although kinship is an important source of trust in a nonlegal business environment, market principles require that crime networks reach beyond these narrow means of securing and enforcing trust. These networks are successful because they establish weak ties, which cross political and ethnic cleavages. Drugs networks include the Sheghni elite of former military commanders aligned to PDPA factions at the local and provincial levels; Tajiks linked to Jamiat; Pashtun Ministry of Defense generals with a territorial overview; and on the Tajik side, government KGB and border control operations. These networks are geographically dispersed and operate at different levels/scales, connecting Khorag, Dushanbe (in Tajikistan), Bashur, Baharak, Faizabad and Kabul (in Afghanistan) and are underpinned by ties of kinship, or jihadi era socioprofessional (military) relationships. Therefore the opium trade, instead of being simply grafted onto preexisting networks, has played a constitutive role, acting as a binding agent, dissolving or reconfiguring intra- and intergroup boundaries and conflicts and creating complex interdependencies between groups. Rather than conceptualizing the opium industry as a single chain, or a pyramid structure, it may be more accurate to view it as a number of interconnected but constantly mutating networks. These networks are underpinned by distinct hierarchies of authority and power relations, linking production, consumption and exchange. And, as in other markets in Afghanistan, there tend to be low barriers to entry at the bottom end but more restrictions and forms of control further up the chain. Furthermore, these networks tend to be compartmentalized – no one has complete oversight and both enforcers and smugglers are only partially sighted.[22]

The drugs industry is therefore far from anarchic. It is underpinned by various forms of state and nonstate regulation, which involve the mobilization of capital, coercion and legitimacy, including indebtedness, addiction, bribes, gifts, violence, marriage and public displays of benevolence. The drugs industry also involves collaboration and collusion between state and nonstate actors, which have become increasingly formalized and even institutionalized in the post-Bonn period. This has happened to such an extent that it is arguable that today the removal of key actors within the system would have little effect on the overall functioning of the system – which makes a nonsense of arguments that the drugs industry can be countered by removing a few "bad apples."

International actors do not stand apart from these processes – they are part of the complex bargaining game. Links to international actors are deployed strategically by state and nonstate actors. For instance, the legitimacy and bargaining power of regional commander Nazar Mohammad is boosted by the fact that he provides his militia to the German Provisional Reconstruction Team in the provincial capital of Faizabad. Similarly, the threat of US airstrikes may be used by state officials in order to discipline unruly nonstate actors who become too autonomous or challenge the power base of their patrons.[23]

BORDERS AND BORDERLANDS

The international border, the internal boundaries and changing frontlines between different factions that emerged during the war years are central to the story of Sheghnan's emergence as a "networked borderland." Every time drugs move from one regulatory authority to another there is a premium to be paid, and it is clear that in this region states are not the only regulatory authorities. Nonstate actors, such as Aziz, may mimic the state, and in some respects (for example, by importing cheap flour), act in more statesmanlike ways than the state itself. This calls into question the simplified binary division that Thompson (1996), in her study of mercenaries and sovereigns, draws between illegitimate private violence and legitimate public violence. On the border, Aziz plays a critical "straddling" role by connecting different spaces and (state/nonstate) regulatory authorities.

Historical changes in the regulatory authorities along the Afghan-Tajik border have been crucial in shaping political and economic processes in Sheghnan. Although the intensity of flows of people, commodities and ideas back and forth across the border has varied at different historical moments, it is important to conceptualize the territory on both sides of the international border as a single territorial unit. For example, the drugs trade involves a triangular relationship between the district centers of Baharak and Bashur in Afghanistan and the provincial center of Khorag in Tajikistan. The intensity of interactions across the border may at certain times be greater than those between center and periphery in the same country. For central state actors and international state-builders, borderlands constitute ambivalent spaces which are sources both of wealth and insecurity. But as argued earlier, political and economic transformations on the margins play an important role in making the center what it is.

When there was an open border and decentralized political structures, cross-border drugs flowed across the border in the form of a "capillary action." With the consolidation of the drugs economy and increased controls at the border, there has been a funneling effect so that drugs consignments are larger and move through major crossing points – including the bridges built by the Aga Khan – where only those with the right connections can operate.

Therefore, these are translocal, multidimensional networks which span or transgress different regulatory spaces. They are underpinned by asymmetrical power relations and they connect different spaces and places with one another. The more militarized and tighter the border controls, the greater the incentives for transgression. Therefore attempts to securitize the border through increased policing, particularly on the Tajik side, have contributed to growing instances of Afghan drug dealers migrating across the border to Tajikistan in order to move up the value chain.

DRUGS AS A CATALYST FOR DEVELOPMENT AND STATE FORMATION?

Whereas in the prewar period the border regions suffered from a political economy of neglect – their sparse populations and limited resources made them unpromising sites for state formation – during the war years they became important strategic resources and sites of accumulation. The post-Bonn construction boom is largely funded by drug money, so economic activities in the hinterland are to a great extent responsible for the peace dividend experienced by the center. While much of the accumulated proceeds from the drug economy are invested outside the country, in drug producing and trafficking areas there are visible signs of inward investment and there has been a recycling of money into licit businesses. The opium economy has produced significant increases in rural wages and income and is an important source of credit for poor rural households. Opium profits fuel consumption of domestic products and support imports of high-value goods. Whereas other markets in Afghanistan are extremely fragmented, the drugs economy represents the nearest thing to a national market, involving multi-ethnic networks and a strong north–south integration. According to Byrd and Jonglez (2006) the opium economy has had a stabilizing effect on the currency by having a significant net positive impact on Afghanistan's balance of payments.[24] The IMF (2005) has warned that successful counter-narcotics efforts could adversely affect GDP growth, the balance of payments and government revenue.

To what extent are opium-fueled growth and the new independencies between center and periphery representative of immanent processes of development and state formation? Were the political and economic transformations wrought by the war and the drugs economy the motors for a process of primitive accumulation, in which the plunder of resources led to the transfer of surplus from peasants to bureaucrats and businessmen? Afghanistan has certainly experienced some major transformations during the war years, including a shift from subsistence agriculture to an export-based cash crop, the growing differentiation of the peasantry and a rapid accumulation of resources by political and military entrepreneurs. Perhaps the drug traffickers, businessmen and specialists in violence who prospered during this period represent an emergent capitalist class. Certainly, drugs networks are based on cross-cutting ties which transcend kinship relationships. And as Giustozzi (2007) notes, many of these actors have now invested too much in the "peace" for them to seek a return to war. What has emerged, at least in certain parts of Afghanistan, can be characterized as a "limited access order" (North et al. 2007). A dominant coalition creates cooperation and order by limiting access to valuable resources – in this case the revenue streams from the opium economy. The creation and distribution of rents therefore secures elite loyalty to the system, which in turn protects rents, limits violence and prevents disorder most of the time (North et al. 2007: 8). However, it is important to note that there continues to be a strong tension between the centrifugal economic forces of the opium trade and the centripetal political thrust of internationally supported state-building. Counter-narcotics policies may heighten these tensions and arguably undermine the emergent interdependencies between center and periphery. Eradication and interdiction policies frequently become a tool through which a narrow clique within the state can take out competitors, consolidate their hold over the drug economy and forge a more exclusive and illegitimate political settlement. In the south counter-narcotics policies, combined with foreign military intervention, undermined the legitimacy of the state and pushed the population into a closer relationship with the Taliban (Goodhand and Mansfield 2010). This reinforces the need to take seriously the politics of place and to examine the diffuse dynamics and localized processes that shape processes of state formation and crisis.

CONCLUSION

This chapter has traced the story of how Sheghnan has changed from being a marginal, neglected borderland into what might be characterized as a "central periphery." It has been argued that the borderland is not only reflective of power relations at the center, it is also constitutive of these power relations. The emergence and growth of the drug economy has been a crucial part of this story. This case study calls into question an influential policy narrative which associates lootable resources, such as drugs, with insurgency, warlordism and state collapse. In the Afghan case, however, the expansion of the drug economy has tended to parallel the emergence of the last two regimes with state-like ambitions – the Taliban (when poppy cultivation expanded from 10 to 23 provinces) and the Karzai government (when cultivation expanded from 24 to 32 provinces). There may therefore be a need to distinguish between factors that led to the emergence and the consolidation of the drug economy. Drawing upon Snyder, the chapter has analyzed the institutions of extraction that evolved during different periods of Sheghnan's history in order to understand the relationship between drugs, political (dis)order and the role of the border.

For peripheral elites, drugs have enabled them to accumulate resources and build a power base. This in turn gives them a stronger fallback position in the bargaining game with the center. Drugs generate the funds to lubricate political relationships, buy votes or government positions and maintain fighters. Drugs also play an important role in attracting the state outward toward its borderlands. Historically, the lack of wealth and the marginal location of mountainous borderlands made these areas unprofitable for the Afghan state to administer (Barfield 2004). But for state elites today, the drug economy has transformed the border regions into high-value assets, which they aim to control, regulate or capture. On the other hand, an open frontier is likely to act as a brake on the state's capacity to make society more legible through census-making, taxation and so on.

Interest groups within the state now seek to exploit resource-rich peripheries. In a situation of parceled sovereignty, they do this through giving tacit monopolies to local strongmen. They have created networks of loyalty and complex interdependencies among peripheral elites. While in some respects the state appears to be weak and fragmented, actors within the state have considerable capacity and power and they are able to "make things happen" in the border areas and govern by remote control – a form of governance from a distance.

NOTES

This chapter is primarily based upon research conducted by the author in August–September 2006 in Badakhshan province of Afghanistan. It was funded by ESRC (RES-223-25-0071, Transformation of War Economies after Conflict) and Chr Michelson Institute/Ford Foundation (The Limits of Statebuilding in Afghanistan). I am grateful to Cooperation for Peace and Unity (CPAU) colleagues in Kabul who helped facilitate and were part of the research team, Marc Theuss, who generously shared his research data from previous trips to Sheghnan, and Finn Stepputat and Lars Burr of the Danish Institute for International Studies, who along with other participants in the "markets for peace" project provided valuable feedback on this chapter. The chapter draws on a working paper produced as an outcome of this project.

1   One may argue that if one views the Taliban as proto state-builders, their control and taxation of the poppy economy was a factor which enabled them to extend their control over the country and concentrate the means of coercion.

2   Whether or not a particular resource is defined as "lootable" depends on the extent to which it can easily be appropriated by individuals or small groups of unskilled workers, requiring relatively little investment or expertise for extraction.

3   Panj means five, a reference to the five rivers that make up the Amu Darya/Oxus River.

4   Until 2002 there was no road connecting Bashur, the district center, to Faizabad, the provincial center, a distance requiring a three-day walk.

5   These campaigns were in wars with the Ghilzai Pashtuns (1886–1888), in the regaining of control over Afghan Turkestan (1888), and in Hazarajat (1891–1893) and Kafiristan (1895–1896).

6   For example, Rahman Khan introduced new state minting machinery and increased sys-tematized taxation (Hanifi 2004). He also benefited from British subsidies throughout his reign.

7   Provinces were subdivided into smaller units and new governors were appointed who were personally loyal to Rahman Khan. Rebellious Pashtuns from the south were exiled to the north and given rich agricultural lands. They subsequently became strong supporters of the government.

8   As Roy (1990) notes, the Afghan state was never able to escape its tribal and Pashtun origins and throughout its history has been ruled by Durrani Pashtuns.

9   Due to the contested border, the Durrand line and the insurrectionary tradition of the eastern tribes, Pashtuns in the border areas received special treatment and benefits through the Ministry of Tribal Affairs.

10 The Soviet Union developed Tajik Gorno-Badakhshan by encouraging economic activity and promoting educational opportunity and infrastructure precisely because of its remote but strategic borderland status.

11 Ahmad Shah Massoud, who at the time was a key commander in the anti-Taliban North-ern Alliance, for example, had bases in Kolyab, and he and fellow Jamiat commanders were regular visitors to Dushanbe. In October 2000, Russian defense minister Igo Sergeev met with Massoud in Dushanbe to discuss the fight against the Taliban after which Russia stepped up its deliveries of military equipment and hardware (Jonson 2004:74)

12 It is estimated that 300–400 metric tonnes a year transit through Tajikistan (*Novaya Gazeta*, Dec. 11, 2003, cited in Nourzhanov 2005: 130).

13 It is reported that there has been a recent trend for a growing proportion of drug ship-ments to go to China because prices are four to five times higher than in the Central Asia route (Fenopetov 2006: 88).

14 The modes of crossing the border vary from swimming and wading across the Panj River, to crossing by boat, sometimes involving large-scale incursions of up to 120 persons with armed escorts and communications units, to crossing via legal checkpoints such as the "Friendship Bridge" in Khorag. The town of Darvaz on the Tajik border marks a clear dividing point, with the vast majority of opiates to the east of this point going via the Pamir Highway to Osh, while to the west – with the area around Moscovsky being key – most of them transit through Dushanbe (Townsend 2006: 71–73).

15 Many of the key military leaders in the US-backed Northern Alliance originated from the Panjshir, the home area of Ahmad Shah Massoud.

16 The Aga Khan program, for instance, has built several "friendship bridges" which cross the river and has initiated a number of cross-border markets.

17 Russian troops were positioned on the Tajik side of the border until 2004, after which they were replaced by Tajik forces. Fears of corruption, drug trafficking and terrorism have led to increased international aid to secure the border, including $4 million of foreign assistance toward "integrated border management." The European Union, for example, in 2003 started funding the Border Management Programme in Central Asia (BOMCA).

18 The hawala dealer, or hawaladar, is an informal money changer and lender who provides, historically and in the present, a reliable and inexpensive means of transferring funds into Afghanistan and among its provinces.

19 Interview, Bashur, Aug. 2006.

20 According to interviewees, this is at a rate of 13 kg of heroin per car.

21 The name has been changed in order to protect his identity.

22 Studies of drug smuggling networks in the UK report similar findings (Pearson and Hobbs 2001).

23 For instance, in 2003 there was a drug seizure of 400 kg of heroin in Sheghnan. When provincial strongmen tried to stop the seizure to protect their own businesses, the general overseeing the intervention threatened the strongmen with instant reprisals by American airstrikes (Theuss and Gardizi nd: 30).

24 The stable value of the new currency was an important factor in the popularity of the government and a source of national pride.

REFERENCES

Anderson, James and O'Dowd, Liam. 1999. Border, border regions and territoriality: contradictory meanings, changing significance. *Regional Studies* 33 (7): 593–604.

Baldauf, Scott. 2006. Inside the Afghan drug trade. *Christian Science Monitor*, June 13.

Barfield, Thomas. 2004. Problems in establishing legitimacy in Afghanistan. *Iranian Studies* 37 (2): 263–293.

Baud, Michiel and van Schendel, Willem. 1997. Towards a comparative history of borderlands. *Journal of World History* 8 (2): 211–242.

Byrd, William and Jonglez, Olivier. 2006. Prices and market interactions in the opium economy. In Doris Buddenberg and William Byrd, eds, *Afghanistan's Drug Industry: Structure, Functioning, Dynamics and Implications for Counter-Narcotics Policy*, pp. 117–154. United Nations Office on Drugs and Crime/World Bank.

Cullather, Nick. 2002. Damming Afghanistan: modernization in a buffer state. *Journal of American History* 89 (2): 512–537.

Cramer, Christopher and Goodhand, Jonathan. 2003. Try again, fail again, fail better? War, the state, and the "post-conflict" challenge in Afghanistan. In Jennifer Milliken, ed., *State Failure, Collapse and Reconstruction*, pp. 131–155. Oxford: Blackwell.

Duffield, Mark. 2007. *Development, Security and Unending War: Governing the World of Peoples*. Cambridge: Polity.

Emadi, Hafizullah. 1997. The end of Taqiyya: reaffirming the religious identity of Ismailis in Shughnan, Badakshan – political implications for Afghanistan. *Middle Eastern Studies* 34 (3): 103–120.

Felbab-Brown, Vanda. 2005. Afghanistan: when counternarcotics undermines counterterrorism. *Washington Quarterly* 28 (4): 55–72.

Fenopetov, Vladimir. 2006. The drug-crime threat to countries located along the Silk Road. *China–Eurasia Forum Quarterly* 4 (1): 5–13.

Foschini, Fabrizio. 2010. Campaign Trail 2010 (1): Badakhshan – drugs, border crossings and parliamentary seats. Afghanistan Analysts' Network. At http://aan-afghanistan.com/index.asp?id=833 (accessed Apr. 3, 2011).

Gallant, Thomas. 1999. Brigandage, piracy, capitalism, and state formation: transnational crime from a historical world-systems perspective. In Josiah Heyman and Alan Smart, eds, *States and Illegal Practices*, pp. 25–62. Oxford: Berg.

Giustozzi, Antonio. 2007. War and peace economies of Afghanistan's strongmen. *International Peacekeeping* 14 (1): 75–89.

Giustozzi, Antonio and Orsini, Dominique. 2009. Centre–periphery relations in Afghanistan: Badakhshan between patrimonialism and institution building. *Central Asian Survey* 28 (1) (Mar.): 1–16.

Goodhand, Jonathan. 2000. From holy war to opium war? A case study of the opium economy in north eastern Afghanistan. *Central Asian Survey* 19 (2): 265–280

Goodhand, Jonathan. 2004. Afghanistan in Central Asia. In M. Pugh and N. Cooper, with J. Goodhand, *War Economies in a Regional Context: Challenges for Transformation*, pp. 45–89. London: International Peace Academy/Lynne Rienner.

Goodhand, Jonathan. 2008. Corrupting or consolidating the peace? The drugs economy and post conflict peacebuilding in Afghanistan. *International Peacekeeping* 15 (3) 405–423.

Goodhand, Jonathan and Mansfield, David. 2010. *Drugs and (Dis)order: A Study of the Opium Economy, Political Settlements and State-Making in Afghanistan*. Crisis State Working Papers Series 2, Working Paper No. 83. London: London School of Economics.

Gootenberg, Paul. 2005. Talking like a state: drugs, borders and the language of control. In Willem van Schendel and Itty Abraham, eds, *Illicit Flows and Criminal Things: States, Borders and the Other Side of Globalization*, pp. 101–127. Bloomington: Indiana University Press.

Hanifi, Shah Mahmoud. 2004. Impoverishing a colonial frontier: cash, credit and debt in nineteenth century Afghanistan. *Iranian Studies* 37 (2): 199–218.

IMF (International Monetary Fund). 2005. Country Report No. 05/33 – Islamic State of Afghanistan: 2004 Article IV Consultation and Second Review. Feb.

Jonson, Lena. 2004. *Vladimir Putin and Central Asia: The Shaping of Russian Foreign Policy*. London: I.B. Tauris.

Mansfield, David. 2006. Responding to the diversity in opium poppy cultivation. In Doris Buddenberg and William Byrd, eds, *Afghanistan's Drug Industry: Structure, Functioning, Dynamics and Implications for Counter-Narcotics Policy*, pp. 47–76. United Nations Office on Drugs and Crime/World Bank.

Mansfield, David. 2007. Beyond the Metrics: Understanding the Nature of Change in the Rural Livelihoods of Opium Poppy Growing Households in the 2006/7 Growing Season. Report for the Afghan Drugs Inter-Departmental Unit of the UK Government. May.

McCoy, Alfred. 1999. Requiem for a drug lord: state and commodity in the career of Khun Sa. In Josiah Heyman and Alan Smart, eds, *States and Illegal Practices*, pp. 129–168. Oxford: Berg.

Newman, David. 2006. The lines that continue to separate us: borders in our borderless world. *Progress in Human Geography* 30 (2): 143–161.

North, Douglas, Wallis, John, Webb, Steven and Weingast, Barry. 2007. *Limited Access Orders in the Developing World: A New Approach to the Problem of Development*. Policy Research Working Paper 4359. World Bank Independent Evaluation Group, Washington, DC.

Nourzhanov, Kirill. 2005. Saviours of the nation or robber barons? Warlord politics in Tajikistan. *Central Asian Survey* 24 (2): 109–130

Passi, Anssi. 1996. *Territories, Boundaries and Consciousness: The Changing Geographies of the Finnish-Russian Border*. New York: John Wiley & Sons, Inc.

Pearson, Geoffrey and Hobbs, Dick. 2001. *Middle Market Drug Distribution*. Home Office Study 227. Home Office Research, Development and Statistics Directorate, London.

Reno, William. 2000. Shadow states and the political economy of civil wars. In M. Berdal and D. Malone, eds, *Greed and Grievance: Economic Agendas in Civil Wars*, pp. 43–68. Boulder: Lynne Rienner.

Roitman, Janet. 2005. *Fiscal Disobedience: An Anthropology of Economic Regulation*. Princeton: Princeton University Press.

Roy, Olivier. 1990. *Islam and Resistance in Afghanistan*. Cambridge: Cambridge University Press

Rubin, Barnett. 2000. The political economy of war and peace in Afghanistan. *World Development* 28 (10): 1789–1803.

Rubin, Barnett. 2006. Peace building and state-building in Afghanistan: constructing sovereignty for whose security? *Third World Quarterly* 27 (1): 175–185.

Rumford, Chris. 2006. Introduction: theorizing borders. *European Journal of Social Theory* 9 (2): 155–169.

Schetter, Conrad, Glassner, Rainer and Karokhail, Masood. 2007. Beyond warlordism: the local security architecture in Afghanistan. *Internationale Politik und Gesellschaft* (2). At http://www.fes.de/IPG/

inhalt_d/pdf/10_Schetter_US.pdf (accessed Nov. 2011).

Scott, James. 2010. *The Art of Not Being Governed: An Anarchist History of Upland Southeast Asia*. New Haven: Yale University Press.

Shaw, Mark. 2006. Drug trafficking and the development of organized crime in post-Taliban Afghanistan. In Doris Buddenberg and William Byrd, eds, *Afghanistan's Drug Industry: Structure, Functioning, Dynamics and Implications for Counter-Narcotics Policy*, pp 189–214. United Nations Office on Drugs and Crime/World Bank.

Snyder, Richard. 2006. Does lootable wealth breed disorder? A political economy of extraction framework. *Comparative Political Studies* 39 (8): 943–968.

Stepputat, Finn. 2001. Urbanizing the countryside: armed conflict, state formation and the politics of place in contemporary Guatemala. In Thomas Blom Hansen and Finn Stepptutat, eds, *States of Imagination: Ethnographic Explorations of the Postcolonial State*, pp. 284–311. Durham: Duke University Press.

Theuss, Marc and Gardizi, Manija. nd. Research notes from fieldwork conducted in Sheghnan and Ishkasham districts of Badakhshan, Afghanistan.

Thompson, Edwina. 2006. The nexus of drug trafficking and hawala in Afghanistan. In Doris Buddenberg and William A. Byrd, eds, *Afghanistan's Drug Industry: Structure, Functioning, Dynamics, and Implications for Counter-Narcotics Policy*, pp. 155–188. United Nations Office on Drugs and Crime/World Bank.

Thompson, Janice. 1996. *Mercenaries, Pirates and Sovereigns*. Princeton: Princeton University Press.

Townsend, Jacob. 2006. The logistics of opiates trafficking in Tajikistan, Kyrgyzstan and Kazakhstan. *China and Eurasia Forum Quarterly* 4 (1): 69–91.

UNODC (United Nations Office on Drugs and Crime). 2007. *Afghanistan Opium Survey 2007*. UNODC/Ministry of Counter Narcotics, Government of Afghanistan, Kabul.

van Schendel, Willem. 2005. *The Bengal Borderland: Beyond State and Nation in South Asia*. London: Anthem.

Volkov, Vadim. 2002. *Violent Entrepreneurs: The Use of Force in the Making of Russian Capitalism*. Ithaca: Cornell University Press.

Wilder, Andrew. 2007. *Cops or Robbers? The Struggle to Reform the Afghan National Police*. Afghan Research and Evaluation Unit, Kabul. June.

Wilson, Thomas M. and Donnan, Hastings, eds. 1998. *Border Identities: Nation and State at International Frontiers*. Cambridge: Cambridge University Press.

Wolf, Eric. 1956. Aspects of group relations in a complex society: Mexico. *American Anthropologist* 58 (6): 1065–1078.

20 Biosecurity,
Quarantine and
Life across the
Border

*Alan Smart and
Josephine Smart*

Mainstream border studies have neglected the impact of the movement of nonhuman life over borders. For centuries borders have been profoundly influenced by efforts to exclude or control the movement of animals, diseases and plants across state territorial limits. Contemporary borders are being restructured in response to new practices and ideas of biosecurity. This chapter was prompted by our work on Bovine Spongiform Encephalopathy (BSE), or "mad cow disease," a zoonotic disease which implicates both human/animal boundaries and the importance of nonhuman life crossing borders. Demonstrating the relative importance of border control over nonhuman life in comparison to the flow of humans and nonorganic goods would be difficult, and no general quantitative claims are possible given the lack of attention to the topic in the field. To begin to recuperate this past and explore the present dynamics, our approach has been to read widely outside border studies in areas where borders are acknowledged as having affected that issue. Searches for studies with border in the titles or subjects were used to identify starting points, and careful reading of these works provided for a kind of "snowball sampling." These studies were explored to see what issues arose, whether we could identify central themes that are important for borders but neglected in border studies, and what we could learn about the border by approaching it from these highly diverse specialized fields of research.

By "mainstream border studies," we refer to books and articles that address both borders and the interdisciplinary literature on borders. Outside this field, we read work that provides useful insights into borders but which is oriented to other fields of study, such as colonial medicine, the ecology of invasive species, or biosecurity. The body of this chapter discusses the more interesting patterns, processes and puzzles that emerged from our survey. While this research might benefit from atten-

A Companion to Border Studies, First Edition. Edited by Thomas M. Wilson and Hastings Donnan.
© 2012 Blackwell Publishing Ltd. Published 2012 by Blackwell Publishing Ltd.

tion to the insights of "mainstream border studies," that quickly growing field of research is failing to give a fully rounded account of borders by its emphasis on economies, ethnicities and politics and its neglect of the nonhuman. Posthumanists have in recent decades criticized the social sciences for the exclusive focus on the human, a category that cannot be understood except by reference to the nonhuman (Wolfe 2010). Humanism attributes agency to people so that human choices and practices are the central focus for border studies. But the auto-mobility, self-replication and transformational features of nonhuman life challenge these assumptions (Bennett 2010; Blue and Rock 2010: 2; Latour 2008). Building on ethnographic research that has forced us to expand the scope of our studies of bordering practices by attending to questions like BSE, avian flu and SARS (severe acute respiratory syndrome), in this chapter we try to provide a preliminary compendium, a bestiary, of nonhuman, or organic, cross-border movement. From this compendium, we isolate a few important themes, particularly quarantine, biosecurity and risk, and in the conclusion suggest some directions that a research strategy focused on life across the border might profitably pursue.

The auto-mobility and self-replication of organics create unique challenges long recognized by border managers. Controls over organic entities at borders began early because disease agents move along with people and animals, propagating independently. Their movement has endangered agriculture, environments and public health throughout history. Other border-crossing organics have enhanced human lives. Nonhuman border-crossing is pervasive but neglected. Only 10 percent of our cells contain the human genome, the other 90 percent consist of the "genomes of bacteria, fungi, protists, and such" (Haraway 2008: 3). Every human crossing a border brings a myriad of "tiny companions" upon which our life depends (Haraway 2008: 4). The distinctive challenges created by such companionship and our innovations in biotechnology have recently been joined in the concept of biosecurity. Before the term's existence, however, biosecurity concerns appeared in the management of borders for many centuries.

Zoonotic diseases, potential pandemics, and invasive species related to global economic integration and climate change are now headline issues. Biosecurity has become a major factor influencing the operation of national borders and subnational boundaries. Appointment of a United States "carp tsar" to coordinate action against the Asian carp, introduced to Arkansas in the 1970s and now threatening the Great Lakes, is one example (*Economist* 2010a). While intensifying, biosecurity and other controls over mobile organics are also routine at borders, as in exclusion of fruits and vegetables at borders or questions about visits to farms.

We divide the chapter into two main sections. The first section is historical, although many of the processes continue at present. The second section considers contemporary border crossing by nonhuman life, with primary attention to new phenomena and discourses, while acknowledging the continuities and legacies of the past. The dividing point between the two is taken as the 9/11 attacks – with the twenty-first century reversing a late twentieth-century trend, which was one toward more open borders – due to securitization, represented as biosecurity for our concerns here. Trade in inanimate goods liberalized from the mid-1970s, while for most people borders became harder (Smart and Smart 2008). Nonhuman organic entities have different border-crossing trajectories, about which much less is known (Cunningham 2010).

Some scholars have diagnosed an "animal turn" that is "comparable in significance to the 'linguistic turn' that revolutionized humanities and social sciences" (Armstrong and Simmons 2007: 1; see also Wolch and Emel 1995), arguing that humans cannot be understood except in relation to animality, and questioning research programs that separate the social and natural sciences (Ingold 2007). Our attempt here has been an empirical attempt to bring the plants, animals and microbes back in to the study of borders, always already there in the operation of borders. In the conclusion, we reflect theoretically on our findings and ask whether we need to develop a post-humanist border studies.

AN ORGANIC HISTORY OF THE BORDER

A survey of dozens of books within mainstream border studies, many of which are referenced in other chapters in this volume, convinced us that the history of the movement of nonhuman life over borders has not been written in mainstream border studies. There is substantial information available, but scattered in a vast range of different specialized fields which, for the most part, do not engage with border studies and with border theory. While the predominant theme that emerges from the litera-ture is quarantine against diseases afflicting humans, their animals or their plants, other intertwined issues arise: animal disease; responses to human plague; colonial expansion; and intergovernmental treaties on the movement of nonhuman life.

Animal disease

The agrarian empires were more likely to have gradually fading spheres of influence and frontiers than precisely inscribed borders. Early modern city-states and walled cities were arguably the first territories to have hard borders. Clear and policed borders were concerned with protection, but not only against military danger. For example, meat was put under municipal surveillance in France in the twelfth and thirteenth centuries. Ferrières (2006: 34) relates how medieval French city charters required that animals "must come on foot to the butcher or public butchery before being slaughtered." Bringing livestock into a crowded city with inadequate sanitation would today be seen as a health hazard, but was then thought to protect the public from unclean meat. It was easier to ascertain the health of the animal than the whole-someness of the meat after slaughter.

Animal diseases were a serious economic threat. In 1599, Venice and Padua pro-hibited the importation of Hungarian cattle in response to a cattle plague, possibly rinderpest. The Hungarian cattle trade was the longest distance livestock trade in early modern Europe, stretching over hundreds of kilometers and connecting two empires with borders otherwise sealed: the Ottoman and the Germanic (Ferrières 2006: 178). Around 1570, cattle were traded in a vast commercial system, stretching from "the Russian steppe to the North Sea, and from the Baltic to the Mediterranean," which handled about a quarter million animals per year and ranked among the most important commodities in international trade at the time (Blanchard 1986: 428). An outbreak in Italy of cattle plague, known as *steppe murrain* (the plague of the steppes), in 1713, introduced by Hungarian cattle, killed tens of thousands of animals. Asked by Pope Clement XI for recommendations on how to deal with it, his personal doctor suggested copying quarantine measures taken against human plague (Ferrières 2006).

Human disease

Quarantine can be traced back at least to the Byzantine Empire in AD 549 and seventh-century China but was very difficult to enforce in areas without walled and policed boundaries (Markell 1997). The entry of plague from the East created worries about trade. With advanced public health policies, Venice and the other Italian city-states responded by building the first specialized places of quarantine and treatment – lazarettos. The idea spread rapidly to other city ports (Healy 1997). At the Marseilles lazaretto, "Ships without clean bills of health were quarantined for 31 days, during which time any cargo of suspect fibres or other goods had to be laid out in the open air to be cleansed by the sun. People who could afford the expense could enter the lazaretto" (Healy 1997: 32). Prevailing ideas of disease causation are crucial in understanding these historical responses, which in this case may have been ineffective since the drying of goods may have allowed rats, not then understood as the main vector of transmission, to move ashore.

As well as clean-health documents for ships, individual health passports can be traced back at least to the Florentine Board of Health, established during the 1348 outbreak of plague (Porter 1999: 36). Health passports predate the earliest version of the passport. Torpey (2000) traces the first passports to 1669 France. Watts describes how "in addition to isolating plague victims, another technique was isola-tion of an entire town" (1997: 22). The first known cordon sanitaire was ordered by the tyrant of Milan on the town of Reggio nell'Emilia in 1374, in an attempt to seal off the town. Florence used soldiers to seal off a plague-ridden town and those who slipped away were tracked down and killed. The Florentine Board of Health "demanded that people planning to travel between one town and the next first secure a health passport from their place of origin" (Watts 1997: 23). The history of quar-antine practice is "bound up with the development of administrative government. The capacity to detain ships, goods and people from elsewhere . . . both presumed and tightened governmental authorities over commerce, health, and movement" (Bashford 2004: 115).

After war with the Ottomans ended in 1739, the Austro-Hungarian Empire created a large plague-control zone in Croatia that employed 4,000 troops. Sentry posts and patrols had orders to shoot unauthorized travelers. People coming from Ottoman lands had to submit to groin and armpit strip-searches and a quarantine of as long as 48 days. Trade goods were fumigated. In the case of suspect raw wool it was put in a "warehouse where low-status people were made to sleep; if they devel-oped plague symptoms they were shot and the wool was burned" (Watts 1997: 25).

Colonial expansion

The Columbian exchange between New and Old Worlds brought devastating diseases to populations without immunities. Trade between China and Europe facilitated the movement of plague (Kimball 2006). From its beginnings tropical medicine was an "instrument of empire" which served to "enable the white 'races' to live in, or at the very least to exploit, all areas of the globe" (Watts 1997: xiii). Public health problems in tropical colonies greatly raised the costs of colonization. Shortly after its establishment as a colony, two out of seven troops on Hong Kong Island died, an average soldier visiting the hospital five times a year (Ip 2002). A Royal Commission in 1863 calculated that a military force of 70,000 Europeans in Europe would require annual expenditure of £70,000, but an additional £388,000 while in service in tropical areas due to illness alone (Curtin 1989). An estimated 100,000 British-born soldiers died of disease in India between 1815 and 1855 (Arnold 1993). Plague outbreaks in Hong Kong from 1894 until the last episode in 1929 were devastating. Quarantines "dictated immediate action. The plague epidemic directly threatened Hong Kong's position as a premier shipping and commercial center and British interests in Asia" (Yip 2009: 1).

In Sudan, the importance of the massive Gezira irrigated cotton scheme led to border movement restrictions to preserve workers' health. The spread of sleeping sickness was blamed on porters from Uganda and the Belgian Congo, who were banned from the trade. In 1913, the government mandated that merchants use only government carts under police convoy on routes where the disease was thought to move. Colonial medicine, concerned with "boundaries and frontiers of all kinds," emphasized a "spatial conception of disease," which resulted in a conflict between the public health need for borders "impermeable to infection" and the economic need "for any such boundary to be extremely porous" (Bell 1999: 91). For pastoralists, the closing of borders could disrupt livelihoods, fostering social and economic changes through adaptation to the transformed cultural ecologies (Beach et al. 1992; Shahrani 1979). Such controls, however, were difficult to enforce. Epidemics were devastating for colonial cities dependent on trade.

International treaties

Unilateral quarantines created problems for the expansion of global trade in the nineteenth century. In this context, "infectious diseases represent the first global problem that States acknowledged could only be handled through international cooperation. Infectious disease threats, thus, predate other global concerns" (Fidler 1999: 7). From 1851 to 1900, states convened ten conferences and negotiated eight agreements on infectious diseases, primarily to prevent contagion spreading from developing countries to developed countries. Britain argued against the contagious character of cholera, emphasizing instead domestic sanitary and public health reforms, in part due to strong interest in freer trade. Poorer European countries were stronger proponents of quarantine (Fidler 1999). Opponents of quarantine attacked "the doctrine of contagion on which quarantine was based" (Harrison 2006: 203). A key issue was the burden of dealing with dozens of different quarantine systems, where arbitrariness rather than quarantine was the greater obstacle to trade (Harrison 2006). Quarantine was finally harmonized by a 1903 treaty (Fidler 1999).

The earliest treaty to use trade measures for a health purpose was an 1878 treaty on *Phylloxera vastatrix*, a louse that attacked vineyards (Riley 2005). An epidemic of powdery mildew encouraged winegrowers to introduce American vines to combat it, which brought along the plant lice, devastating European wine (Morrow 1973). The solution was to introduce more American vines, since *Vitis aestivalis* was resistant to the endemic aphids, unlike the European wine grape *Vitis vinifera*. From 1869 to 1973 a debate raged about whether lice were the cause of the disease, or simply an effect, where infestation was made possible by debilitation. Economic considerations, including the profitable export of French vines, "would suffer if *Phylloxera* were admitted to be the cause" (Sorensen et al. 2008: 138). The American vine solution, either direct planting, or grafting European vines onto American rootstock, faced opposition "from defenders of pure French vineyards," who appealed to national pride, arguing that "French vines should retain their ancient purity and not be mongrelized with American stock" (Sorensen et al. 2008: 139). Introduced plant diseases could cause more than economic devastation, such as in the case of the potato blight (from Mexico) and the Irish famine of 1845–1848. The 1929 International Convention for the Protection of Plants tried to regulate plant health problems. The Food and Agricultural Organization refigured it as the International Plant Protection Convention in 1951. Included as part of the World Trade Organization's Agreement on Sanitary and Phytosanitary Measures, it requires scientific validation for trade restrictions (Smart and Smart in press).

Migrant health inspections

The US and Canada had open borders for migrants until nearly the time of World War I, but with a number of exceptions, particularly those in the Chinese Exclusion Acts. The most important limit at US borders was mass medical screening on entry. Controls were effective because transoceanic travel funneled most immigrants into easily controlled ports of entry (Heyman 2002, 2004). Worries that the Mexico–US border offered easier entry, combined with worries about typhus and its lice vector, led to quarantine at El Paso's border crossing in 1917. Mexicans crossing the border, which was previously open, were segregated by sex, stripped naked, and examined for lice. In 1917, officials inspected 39,620 bodies per week on the Texas border, exceeding Ellis Island (Stern 1999: 48). Stripping and disinfection at Ellis Island were only required for those suspected of disease, because disinfection and vaccination were carried out by the steamship companies. Officials who were charged with failing to examine passengers could be fined $100 and return passage for each passenger rejected (Fairchild 2003). Some steamship lines in turn required the railroads to conduct immigrant medical inspections, and US requirements "exerted powerful influence on German port health measures, including construction of new pavilions for the detention of passengers and additional inspection stations with disinfection facilities along the Russian border" (Fairchild 2003: 61). On the Mexico–US border, where immigrants entered by foot, "medicalization was incorporated directly into the process of entry" (Stern 1999: 49). Stigmatization of immigrants through fear of disease was a powerful lever for anti-immigration politics, and affected respected scientific institutions as well. A 1913 report of the Rockefeller Foundation's Sanitary Commission wrote about hookworm: "Every Indian coolie already in California was a center from which the infection continued to spread throughout the state" (Farley 2004: 4).

Movement of nonhuman life across borders has had a long and important role in structuring national borders, with continuing legacies. The most important of these legacies is quarantine, which has returned to prominence due to the surge in new infectious diseases. The later twentieth century saw deployment of new medical technologies which created a widespread belief that infectious diseases were becoming a thing of the past (Lakoff 2008). The emergence of new infectious diseases in recent decades, and the development of antibiotic resistance, has challenged that belief. Agricultural inspection at the border is another legacy, and it has become so mundane as to pass almost unnoticed.

CONTEMPORARY ISSUES

Our organic history shows that hyperbole about globalization, pandemic risk and other elements of "world risk society" (Beck 1992) involves dynamics that are far from new. It is not that there is nothing new; technology and new forms of global governance have resulted in important border-related changes. But the continuities have been neglected. While the crucial keyword for life across borders in the past was "quarantine," this spatial practice is being discursively incorporated into more ambitious strategies signaled by the rise of "biosecurity." The meaning of biosecurity, however, is fundamentally contested and has been appropriated by many political agendas in the wake of 9/11.

Biosecurity

Dunworth notes that although "the *term* biosecurity only entered the legal lexicon in 1993 with the enactment of the Biosecurity Act, the *idea* of biosecurity stretches back to pre-colonial New Zealand" (2009: 157). The government agency Biosecurity New Zealand defines it as "Protection from the risks posed by pests and diseases to the economy, environment and people's health through exclusion, eradication, containment and management." The World Trade Center attacks of 9/11 focused attention on bioterrorism, while genetic engineering and other biological developments raised issues of research biosafety. All of these elements have become part of expanded definitions of biosecurity. Securitization of governance has produced rapid growth in biosecurity discourse and practice. By contrast, in New Zealand it replaced "agricultural security," extending its scope to "include ecologies as well as animal public health" (Dunworth 2009: 156). Confusion in these diverse usages is frequently noted, but many see something common, a "concerted effort to articulate a unified and universal version of biosecurity that could be the basis of a standard, worldwide approach to dealing with 'out of place' biological entities of various kinds" (Bingham and Hinchliffe 2008: 174).

Biosecurity discourse brings together diverse issues and actors concerned that new biological threats challenge existing approaches to security (Collier and Lakoff 2008). Fidler notes convergence of policies on biological weapons and infectious diseases due to the "realization by those concerned with biological weapons that public health has become critical to their mission" (2010: 290); framing infectious diseases as threats to security increases the political significance of public health. Keck suggests that biosecurity operates as a term that allows "threats to be categorized and blame to be distributed in ways that are still controversial" (2008: 197). As such, biosecurity's very polysemy and ambiguity make it useful.

Collier and Lakoff (2008) draw on Beck's ideas of risk society to explain contemporary biosecurity. Beck (1992) argued that dependence on complex systems produces radical new risks. Traditional risk management is inadequate, resulting in intensified uncertainties about technical expertise. The apocalyptic consequences for the Aboriginal populations of the Americas of the Columbian exchange of microbes, and the intense debates about the causes of plague and cholera, show that these phenomena were of great, perhaps even greater, importance in the past, although the range of issues has expanded. A more modest explanation of biosecurity might be that in the wake of 9/11 government funding provided incentives for reframing initiatives in security terms. The discourse has real-world consequences. Responses to avian flu had massive restructuring effects on the poultry industry (Bingham and Hinchliffe 2008). A logic of preparedness now supplements the logic of prevention, redefining public health as critical infrastructure and using scenario planning to protect vital systems (Lakoff 2008). American government funding has proliferated through such approaches.

After 9/11, the US unified inspection operations at its borders. A single inspector is charged with examining people, animals, plants, goods and cargo on entry. Transfer of these functions to the Department of Homeland Security marked a significant policy shift, showing that at least to some "the security of our borders is the top priority" (Wasem et al. 2004: 1). New technologies, such as handheld Pathogen Identification Devices, are being deployed. Overseas preclearance programs, paid for by importers, reduce workloads at ports of entry (Alvarez 2005; Wasem et al. 2004). In 2002, the Animal and Plant Health Inspection Service inspected 33.8 million passengers and made 890,000 interceptions of quarantine significance. Agricultural inspection employed 1,446 full-time equivalent staff in 2004 and had a budget of US$313.3 million (Wasem et al. 2004).

Invasive species

Invasive species are not new. Anthropogenic pathways have multiplied since foragers started spreading seeds of desirable plants. Some researchers distinguish between introduced and invasive species, the latter being those whose populations explode with destructive effect. Others find the distinction between introduced and invasive species just as arbitrary as the distinction between cultivated plants and "weeds." For Nikiforuk, invasive species "diminish diversity, decrease disease resistance, replace local biology with global tyrants, and generally homogenize all life" and call on us to recognize that "global trade is not just an innocent exchange of goods and gadgets but trade in every living thing. Each economic enterprise provokes a commensurate biological transaction" (2006: xii).

There are six main pathways in the introduction of alien species. They may arrive as a contaminant of a commodity; as stowaways in ballast water or aircraft wheel wells; along a corridor pathway; through natural spread across borders; deliberate release; or escape from captivity (Hulme 2009). Alien species do not always have negative effects: new crops have greatly expanded the ability of countries to support their populations. An estimated 98 percent of American food is from introduced species (Burdick 2005). Many introductions were thought to be improvements. The nineteenth-century American Acclimatization Society had the goal of bringing in birds and animals for the "ennobling influence of the song of birds" on inhabitants. One of their first projects, the English sparrow, was so successful that the birds devastated fruit trees, leading newspapers to publish recipes for sparrow potpie. A New Yorker attempted to introduce into Central Park all the birds mentioned in Shakespeare's plays (Burdick 2005: 79). Often problems caused by one introduction have led to the importing of its predators, sometimes with worse results.

Invasive species have only been seen as a problem relatively recently, beginning with vulnerable isolated islands (Elton 1958). Almost 40 percent of American endangered birds are found in Hawaii (Burdick 2005: 5). New Zealand's biological isolation helped agriculture to remain relatively free of pests and diseases found elsewhere but also left native species and ecosystems vulnerable. In fact, New Zealand has one of the world's strictest border inspection systems (Jay et al. 2003); quarantine became mandatory for imported livestock in 1893 and for plants in 1896 (Jay and Morad 2006). New Zealand imposes penalties of up to $100,000 and/or five years imprisonment for failure to declare biosecurity risk goods (e.g., cooked food or cheese). New Zealand's biosecurity policies evolved from a "narrow focus on production pests to a broader awareness of multiple economic, social and ecological objectives" (Jay et al. 2003: 121).

A study of 725,000 pest interceptions resulting from US border inspections found 62 percent associated with baggage, 30 percent in cargo and 7 percent associated with plant reproductive material. Pest interceptions occurred most commonly at airports (73 percent), US–Mexico land border crossings (13 percent), and marine ports (9 percent) (McCullough et al. 2006). The economic costs and consequences of alien species can be very great, as high as US$138 billion a year in the US alone, but most estimates are based on poor data, and often omit consequences that are not easily monetized (Jenkins 2001).

Alvarez (2001: 122) notes that while the US Department of Agriculture (USDA) and US Customs Service regulate the flow of fruit and vegetables entering the US at specific ports of entry, control "extends into agricultural production regions." Mangos are subject to US certification that requires use of complex technology to eliminate fruit flies. Fumigation with ethylene dibromide was the main treatment but was banned in 1987 and replaced with complex and expensive hot water treatment (Alvarez 2005). Processing in situ involved at first the delegation of US inspectors to Mexico, but subsequently the USDA "has deputized inspectors in all regions from which mangos are exported to the US" (Alvarez 2001: 125).

Alien invasive species are seen as one of the biggest threats to biodiversity, by displacing local species and by dominating resources. The American jellyfish, introduced to the Black Sea by the release of freighters' ballast water, has become so abundant that it now accounts for 90 percent of the wet biomass, devastating local fishing. Ballast has for centuries operated as "giant, moving aquariums that threaten to infest local waters" with exotic marine pests. The US National Invasive Species Act of 1996 called for a national ballast-water management plan (Burdick 2005: 252). For seafood, the issue has combined with the decline of many traditional fisheries and concern about the environmental effects of newer deep-sea fisheries to create a market for selectively consuming invasive species such as the Asian carp or lionfish introduced into the Caribbean. Climate change is increasing problems resulting from invasive species, as the habitable territories for the vectors of disease such as mosquitoes and ticks shift into colder countries. The mountain pine beetle has devastated large parts of western Canada's forests due to winters not cold enough to destroy infestations. Such shifts suggest that "the US should be partnering with Canada to try to preserve species that are moving into Canada" (Campbell 2010: 4).

Bioregionalism

Concerns about invasive species focus on protecting boundaries but some environmentalists worry about borders preventing crossing. Borders divide ecologies. These divisions can be environmentally disruptive. Predators that have low population densities face problems due to loss of corridors for genetic exchange. Since borders rarely correspond to natural systems, calls for transboundary conservation areas and other transfrontier conservation efforts have been growing (Büscher 2010).

These calls and concerns reflect an issue identified by political ecology, territorialization. Political territories rarely "follow the contours of nature. Thus, political entities seldom control key elements or parts of ecologies upon which they depend. As nature is carved up among administrative and territorial units, actions that may be advantageous for one entity may damage another" (Greenberg 2006: 128). Aquifers, "like fish stocks, are most at risk when they cross national borders, making property rights weaker" (*Economist* 2010b: 86). Effective management of many watersheds requires cross-border cooperation. Most postcolonial borders are "unerringly straight one-dimensional lines that define two-dimensional areas on a map. Yet on the ground, borders often create severe cultural, political, and biological effects" (Chester 2006: 2). Transnational conservation efforts started as early as 1868, with attempts to establish a bird flyway in Europe in order to protect agriculturally beneficial birds that were being exterminated on one side of a border, thereby making any efforts at protection on the other side useless. Eventually realized in the 1902 International Convention for the Protection of Birds Useful to Agriculture, it was not very effective because Italy, a key location, refused to sign (Chester 2006: 18).

Efforts to overcome "territories of chance" and "unnatural divisions" have public support, but border politics often make implementation challenging (Büscher 2010; Chester 2006). The International Sonora Desert Alliance on the US–Mexico border has faced great political challenges. Mexicans tend to interpret proposals for border peace parks as a grab for greater control of the region. Americans see biosphere reserves in the context of paranoia about the United Nations (Chester 2006). Environmental discourse along the boundary line can be used by human rights advocates as well as nativist militias for their political agendas (Cunningham 2010).

Bioregionalism expands conservation into broader environmental visions that challenge assumptions about borders. Sparke discusses ideas about the Cascadia region that seek to transform the transborder space into a "harmonious ecosystem" liberated from the "disciplinary apparatus of two industrial nation-states and the 'unnatural' boundary line . . . dividing them" (2005: 69). However, these environmentalist roots have tended to be submerged into a neoliberal vision of Cascadia as an economic zone that could grow faster with fewer border restrictions. Despite the potential for bioregionalist ideas of the integration of flows of nonhuman life and the water and other systems that underpin them, an emphasis on stopping organic movements is still much more prominent.

Pandemics

A pandemic is an outbreak of infectious disease which quickly spreads around the world. The most feared pandemics involve emerging infectious diseases, such as SARS, mad cow disease, avian flu and swine flu. Malaysia's Health Minister stated: "We must remember that we are more likely to be invaded by microbes than by a foreign army . . . the real threat to security would come not from invading armies, but from unknown microbes" (Abraham 2004: 2). More than three dozen "new high-impact infectious diseases have been identified since the 1970s" (Katona and Scheld 2010: 13). An estimated 60 percent of infectious diseases, and 75 percent of new ones, are thought to be zoonotic in origin, crossing species barriers and more virulent in the absence of immunological defenses (*Economist* 2011).

Although avian flu concerned experts and had a major impact in Asia, it was the SARS outbreak in 2003 that dramatized to the globe the new risks of pandemics. It exposed a neglected aspect of the global city as an intensely connected space of flows, with greater exposure to disease pathogens (Ali and Keil 2008). Its impact in Hong Kong highlighted the need for biosecurity-driven border controls. The Chinese officials underreported the number of infected cases and held off the World Health Organization (WHO) for over five months before international health experts were allowed into the country. By then, SARS had spread from Guangdong to Hong Kong and abroad. Hong Kong recorded 298 deaths; China 348. Most countries issued a travel advisory regarding infected countries. Surveillance and disinfection procedures were installed at international airports and border crossings. Travel to and from Hong Kong diminished to a trickle, causing major economic losses. The worldwide economic losses from SARS were estimated in the range of US$5 billion to US$10 billion (Smart and Smart 2008).

Pandemic crises have made it clear that surveillance had previously been flawed. No public health warnings had been disseminated to hospital authorities in Toronto before the first cases of SARS there, despite reports that had been appearing for months previously in Hong Kong newspapers about a new form of atypical pneumonia. Surveillance by national and international public health agencies has since expanded due in part to the WHO's influence, which has grown over the last decade. Fidler concluded that the WHO's 2005 International Health Regulations impose obligations on states "never before seen in international law on public health" (2010: 298). Whether biosecurity emphasis on pandemics is the most cost-effective expenditure of scarce public health resources, however, is questionable. In contrast to those who see newly emerging diseases as a result of technological change (travel plus increased use of antibiotics, etc.), some instead point to the collapse of basic public health systems. From this perspective "global living conditions – poverty, civil war, lack of basic healthcare – were the source of the emerging disease threat" and these social problems must be addressed to "provide security against emerging pathogens" (Lakoff 2008: 47). As Farmer (2001) has stressed, the plagues of the poor cause much more misery but receive much less funding.

Food safety

A series of tainted food scandals, going back to Chicago slaughterhouses in the early twentieth century and continuing to the recent melamine tainting of baby formula and toothpaste, have greatly increased consumer concern about food safety, particularly imports. In 1962 the WHO and the Food and Agriculture Organization (FAO) of the United Nations jointly organized the Codex Alimentarius international food standards. Nations continue, though, to be principally responsible for food safety regulation. The British Food Safety Act of 1990 was influenced by food scares in the 1980s which undermined trust in governmental regulation and heightened awareness of the many possible ways food could become unsafe. The Act let food businesses develop their own internal hazard analysis systems "but also made them legally responsible for demonstrating due diligence" if any of their products fell short of the government's standards (Freidberg 2004: 174). Obligations such as these traveled across borders, both as obligations on suppliers, and as competitive pressures on costs and perceived quality.

The food regulatory system only began to catch up with shifting public perceptions of food risks after heavy media coverage of crises. Government reform was constrained by divided responsibilities between promoting agricultural interests and protecting public health and safety. Food crises undermined this status quo. Food politics spread and deepened as distance grew between producer and consumer. Public trust in expert authority declined (Beck 1992; Lien 2004). The erosion of trust in regulatory agencies and scientific experts is particularly marked in Europe, whereas faith in technology and the system is stronger in the US and Canada (Skogstad 2006). European authorities adopted the precautionary principle for risk management, whereas North Americans prefer scientific evidence of objective risks prior to restrictions on private production methods. They suspect the precautionary principle operates as a disguised trade barrier (Noiville 2006). Differences in regulatory culture led to disputes over genetically modified organisms, antibiotics and growth hormones, still unresolved irritants in agricultural trade negotiations.

A wide variety of regulatory and technological fixes, such as the traceability of all meat through the entire production process, are being implemented and proposed. Breeze (2006) argues that there are no technological barriers to eliminating all major transboundary livestock diseases, only a failure of public policy. The FAO, the WHO, and the World Organisation for Animal Health are cooperating to develop a Global Early Warning System to facilitate a higher level of international emergency prepared-ness (Jebara 2004).

Conclusion

This chapter has argued that nonhuman movement has had a large but neglected influence on borders. A review of work outside mainstream border studies served here to support this argument but only a few of the many issues could be examined. We concentrated on several key issues. In the past, quarantine attempted to protect sovereignty and served to strengthen borders. It created problems for a more interconnected world, so early international treaties attempted to limit it. At present, the rapid growth of biological technologies, globalization and an obsession with ter-rorism have given biosecurity a prominent place in border practices. Zoonoses high-light the complicated interpenetration of human and animal lives and the risks that current practices pose for what veterinarians refer to as "one world, one health." Managing these risks requires moving beyond anthropocentric attitudes toward borders.

We need to integrate work in other specialized fields into border studies. We neglect such excellent scholarship at our peril. Integrating such work may be helped by exploring the possibilities of a posthumanist border studies. Rapid growth of posthumanist perspectives elsewhere may provide some opportunities to challenge our assumptions about borders. We finish here with an agenda for posthumanist border research.

First, we should develop a historiography of how border studies became humanist, excluding nonhuman life. How did border studies emerge as a self-referential field of research and did this influence why a posthumanist border studies has not yet been considered, despite the rapid growth of posthumanist perspectives in so many other topical areas? Second, what proportion of border resources are devoted to nonhuman life? Third, how does this allocation vary over time and place, or by the nature of the state? Fourth, is this quantity of resources enough? Should it be reallocated or rethought? Fifth, how are the risks best managed? Is inattention to nonhuman life crossing borders increasing our systemic risk? Sixth, what is the appropriate balance between flows and restrictions for border crossings? Finally, many theoretical dimen-sions are raised by issues such as zoonoses. Taking on such issues, and the complex relationships between borders and boundaries, could allow mainstream border studies to take a more aggressive stance within social theory.

We believe that mainstream border studies should incorporate the insights about the impacts on borders of the distinctive challenges of nonhuman life. First, these issues matter for the management of borders and neglecting them impoverishes the potential for a more holistic border studies. Secondly, the risks and concerns are intensifying due to contemporary changes such as the increasing centrality of biology in the economy, our greatly enhanced capacities to transform life in myriad new ways, greater incursion by growing populations into remaining natural areas with dangers of new pandemic diseases, and greater sensitivity to how we share our planet with our companion species. Thirdly, exciting work in posthumanism offers new ideas for border scholars to reduce the threat of diminishing returns, which is a likely outcome if the growing number of border scholars all work on more traditional border topics. To maintain the excitement achieved by border researchers over the last few decades, we need to challenge the boundaries that define our field. Rigorous research has continually challenged assumptions about borders and borderlands. Taking this approach further and exploring how transcending the human/nonhuman research divide can generate new insights into past and present borders may also offer the often too theoretical debates in posthumanism new ideas on how to intervene in fields that may be resistant to the charms of cutting-edge social theory.

NOTE

Research for this chapter was supported by a Social Sciences and Humanities Research Council Standard Research Grant. We gratefully acknowledge suggestions and advice from John Addicott, Gunnar Haaland, Paul Hansen, Josiah Heyman, Melanie Rock, and particularly Hastings Donnan and Thomas M. Wilson. Anne Rainville provided helpful bibliographic and editorial assistance.

REFERENCES

Abraham, Thomas. 2004. *Twenty-First Century Plague: The Story of SARS*. Hong Kong: Hong Kong University Press.

Ali, S. Harris and Keil, Roger. 2008. Introduction: networked disease. In S. Harris Ali and Roger Keil, eds, *Networked Disease: Emerging Infections in the Global City*, pp. 10–12. Oxford: Wiley-Blackwell.

Alvarez, Robert R. 2001. Beyond the border: nation-state encroachment, NAFTA, and offshore control in the US-Mexican mango industry. *Human Organization* 60 (2): 121–127.

Alvarez, Robert R. 2005. *Mangos, Chiles and Truckers: The Business of Transnationalism*. Minneapolis: University of Minnesota Press.

Armstrong, Philip and Simmons, Laurence. 2007. Bestiary: an introduction. In Laurence Simmons and Philip Armstrong, eds, *Knowing Animals*, pp. 1–24. Leiden: Brill.

Arnold, David. 1993. *Colonizing the Body: State Medicine and Epidemic Disease in Nineteenth Century India*. Berkeley: University of California Press.

Bashford, Alison. 2004. *Imperial Hygiene: A Critical History of Colonialism, Nationalism and Public Health*. New York: Palgrave Macmillan.

Beach, Hugo, Anderson, Myrdene and Aikio, Pekka. 1992. Dynamics of Saami territoriality within the nation-states of Norway, Sweden and Finland. In Michael J. Casimir and Aparna Rao, eds, *Mobility and Territoriality: Social and Spatial Boundaries among Foragers, Fishers, Pastoralists and Peripatetics*, pp. 55–90. New York: Berg.

Beck, Ulrich. 1992. *Risk Society: Towards a New Modernity*. London: Sage.

Bell, Heather. 1999. *Frontiers of Medicine in the Anglo-Egyptian Sudan, 1899–1940*. Oxford: Clarendon Press.

Bennett, Jane. 2010. *Vibrant Matter: A Political Ecology of Things*. Durham: Duke University Press.

Bingham, Nick and Hinchliffe, Steve. 2008. Mapping the municipalities of biosecurity. In Andrew Lakoff and Stephen J. Collier, eds, *Biosecurity Interventions: Global Health and Security in Question*, pp. 173–194. New York: Columbia University Press.

Blanchard, Ian. 1986. The continental European cattle trades, 1400–1600. *Economic History Review* 39 (3): 427–460.

Blue, Gwendolyn and Rock, Melanie. 2010. Trans-biopolitics: complexity in interspecies relations. *Health* 20 (10): 1–16.

Breeze, R.G. 2006. Technology, public policy, and control of transboundary livestock diseases in our lifetimes. *Revue Scientifique et Technique – Office International Epizooties* 25 (1): 271–292.

Burdick, Alan. 2005. *Out of Eden: An Odyssey of Ecological Invasion*. New York: Farrar, Straus & Giroux.

Büscher, Bram. 2010. Seeking "telos" in the "transfrontier"? Neoliberalism and the transcending of community conservation in Southern Africa. *Environment and Planning A* 42 (3): 644–660.

Campbell, Carolyn. 2010. Wild ecosystems and climate change – the seminal work of Dr. Camille Parmesan. *Wildlands Advocate* 18 (6): 4–5.

Chester, Charles C. 2006. *Conservation across Borders: Biodiversity in an Interdependent World*. Washington, DC: Island Press.

Collier, Stephen J. and Lakoff, Andrew. 2008. The problem of securing health. In Andrew Lakoff and Stephen J. Collier, eds, *Biosecurity Interventions: Global Health and Security in Question*, pp. 7–32. New York: Columbia University Press.

Cunningham, Hilary. 2010. Gating ecology in a gated globe: environmental aspects of "securing our borders." In Hastings Donnan and Thomas M. Wilson, eds, *Borderlands: Ethnographic Approaches to Security, Power, and Identity*, pp. 125–142. Lanham: University Press of America.

Curtin, Philip D. 1989. *Death by Migration: Europe's Encounter with the Tropical World in the Nineteenth Century*. Cambridge: Cambridge University Press.

Dunworth, Treas. 2009. Biosecurity in New Zealand. In B. Rappert and C. Gould, eds, *Biosecurity: Origins, Transformations and Practices*, pp. 156–170. Houndsmills: Palgrave Macmillan.

Economist. 2010a The carp tsar's struggle. Sept. 23, p. 44.

Economist. 2010b Deep waters, slowly drying up. Oct. 7, p. 86.

Economist. 2011 Hot spots. Oct. 8, p. 68.

Elton, Charles Sutherland. 1958. *The Ecology of Invasions by Animals and Plants*. Chicago: University of Chicago Press. Repr. 2000.

Fairchild, Amy. 2003. *Science at the Borders: Immigrant Medical Inspection and the Shaping of the Modern Industrial Labor Force*. Baltimore: Johns Hopkins University Press.

Farley, John. 2004. *To Cast Out Disease: A History of the International Health Division of the Rockefeller Foundation (1913–1951)*. Oxford: Oxford University Press.

Farmer, Paul. 2001. *Infections and Inequalities: The Modern Plagues*. Berkeley: University of California Press.

Ferrières, Madeleine. 2006. *Sacred Cow, Mad Cow: A History of Food Fears*. New York: Columbia University Press.

Fidler, David. 1999. *International Law and Infectious Diseases*. Oxford: Oxford University Press.

Fidler, David. 2010. Towards a global ius pestilentiae: the functions of law in global biosecurity. In Peter Katona, John P. Sullivan and Michael D. Intriligator, eds, *Global Biosecurity: Threats and Responses*, pp. 286–302. London: Routledge.

Freidberg, Susanne. 2004. *French Beans and Food Scares: Culture and Commerce in an Anxious Age*. Oxford: Oxford University Press.

Greenberg, James B. 2006. The political ecology of fisheries in the Upper Gulf of California. In Aletta Biersack and James B. Greenberg, eds, *Reimagining Political Ecology*, pp. 121–148. Durham: Duke University Press.

Haraway, Donna. 2008. *When Species Meet*. Minneapolis: University of Minnesota Press.

Harrison, Mark. 2006. Disease, diplomacy and international commerce: the origins of international sanitary regulation in the nineteenth century. *Journal of Global History* (1): 197–217.

Healy, Margaret. 1997. Highways, hospitals and boundary hazards. In Thomas Betteridge, ed., *Borders and Travellers in Early Modern Europe*, pp. 17–33. Aldershot: Ashgate.

Heyman, Josiah McC. 2002. United States ports of entry on the Mexican border. *Journal of the Southwest* 43 (4): 681–700.

Heyman, Josiah McC. 2004. Ports of entry as nodes in the world system. *Identities: Global Studies in Culture and Power* 11 (3): 303–327.

Hulme, Philip E. 2009. Trade, transport and trouble: managing invasive species pathways in an era of globalization. *Journal of Applied Ecology* 46 (9): 10–18.

Ingold, Tim. 2007. From trust to domination: an alternative history of human–animal relations. In Rhoda Wilkie and David Inglis, eds, *Animals and Society: Critical Concepts in the Social Sciences*, vol. 4, pp. 216–238. London: Routledge.

Ip, Iam-chong. 2002. The rise of a sanitary city: the colonial formation of Hong Kong's early public housing. *E-Hong Kong: Culture and Society Studies* 1 (2): 189–217.

Jay, Mairi and Morad, Munir. 2006. The socioeconomic dimensions of biosecurity: the New Zealand experience. *International Journal of Environmental Studies* 63 (3): 293–302.

Jay, Mairi, Morad, Munir and Bell, Angela. 2003. Biosecurity, a policy dilemma for New Zealand. *Land Use Policy* 20 (2): 121–129.

Jebara, K. Ben. 2004. Surveillance, detection and response: managing emerging diseases at national and international levels. *Revue Scientifique et Technique – Office International Epizooties* 23 (2): 709–715.

Jenkins, Peter T. 2001. Who should pay? Economic dimensions of preventing harmful invasions through international trade and travel. In Jeffrey A. McNeely, ed., *The Great Reshuffling: Human Dimensions of Invasive Alien Species*, pp. 79–85. Cambridge: International Union for Conservation of Nature.

Katona, Peter and Scheld, W. Michael. 2010. Emerging and re-emerging infectious diseases. In Peter Katona, John P. Sullivan and

Michael D. Intriligator, eds, *Global Biosecurity Threats and Responses*, pp. 13–24. London: Routledge.

Keck, Frédéric. 2008. From mad cow disease to bird flu: transformations of food safety in France. In Andrew Lakoff and Stephen J. Collier, eds, *Biosecurity Interventions: Global Health and Security in Question*, pp. 195–226. New York: Columbia University Press.

Kimball, A. M. 2006. *Risky Trade: Infectious Disease in the Era of Global Trade*. Burlington: Ashgate.

Lakoff, Andrew. 2008. From population to vital system In Andrew Lakoff and Stephen J. Collier, eds, *Biosecurity Interventions: Global Health and Security in Question*, pp. 33–60. New York: Columbia University Press.

Latour, Bruno. 2008. *Reassembling the Social: An Introduction to Actor-Network-Theory*. Oxford: Oxford University Press.

Lien, Marianne Elisabeth. 2004. The politics of food: an introduction. In Marianne Elisabeth Lien and Brigitte Nerlich, eds, *The Politics of Food*, pp. 1–18. New York: Berg.

Markell, Howard. 1997. *East European Jewish Immigrants and the New York City Epidemics of 1892*. Baltimore: Johns Hopkins University Press.

McCullough, Deborah G., Work, Timothy T., Cavey, Joseph F., Liebhold, Andrew M. and Marshall, David. 2006. Interceptions of nonindigenous plant pests at US ports of entry and border crossings over a 17-year period. *Biological Invasions* 8 (4): 611–630.

Morrow, Dwight W. 1973. Phylloxera in Portugal. *Agricultural History* 47 (3): 235–247

Nikiforuk, Andrew. 2006. *Pandemonium: Bird Flu, Mad Cow Disease and Other Biological Plagues of the 21st Century*. Toronto: Penguin.

Noiville, Christine. 2006. Compatibility or clash? EU food safety and the WTO. In Christopher K. Ansell and David Vogel, eds, *What's the Beef? The Contested Governance of European Food Safety*, pp. 307–325. Cambridge: MIT Press.

Porter, Dorothy. 1999. *Health, Civilization, and the State: A History of Public Health from Ancient to Modern Times*. London: Routledge.

Riley, Sophie. 2005. Invasive alien species and the protection of biodiversity: the role of quarantine laws in resolving inadequacies in international legal crime. *Journal of Environmental Law* 17 (3): 323–359.

Shahrani, M. Nazif Mohib. 1979. *The Kirghiz and Wakhi of Afghanistan: Adaptation to Closed Frontiers*. Seattle: University of Washington Press.

Skogstad, Grace. 2006. Regulating food safety risks in the European Union: a comparative perspective. In Christopher K. Ansell and David Vogel, eds, *What's the Beef? The Contested Governance of European Food Safety*, pp. 213–236. Cambridge: MIT Press.

Smart, Alan and Smart, Josephine. 2008. Time-space punctuation: Hong Kong's border regime and limits on mobility. *Pacific Affairs* 81 (2): 175–193.

Smart, Alan and Smart, Josephine. In press. (Im)mobilizing technology: slow science, food safety, and borders. *Identities: Studies in Culture and Power*.

Sorensen, Conner W., Smith, Edward H., Smith, Janet and Carton, Yves. 2008. Charles V. Riley, France, and phylloxera. *American Entomologist* 54 (3): 134–149.

Sparke, Matthew. 2005. *In the Space of Theory: Postfoundational Geographies of the Nation-State*. Minneapolis: University of Minnesota Press.

Stern, Alexandra Minna. 1999. Buildings, boundaries, and blood: medicalization and nation-building on the US–Mexico border, 1910–1930. *Hispanic American Historical Review* 79 (1): 41–81

Torpey, John C. 2000. *Invention of the Passport: Surveillance, Citizenship, and the State*. Cambridge: Cambridge University Press.

Wasem, Ruth Ellen, Lake, Jennifer, Seghetti, Lisa, Monke, James and Vina, Stephen. 2004. Border Security: Inspections Practices, Policies, and Issues. Report for Congress RL32399. At http://handle.dtic.mil/100.2/ADA457906 (accessed Mar. 22, 2011).

Watts, Sheldon. 1997. *Epidemics and History: Disease, Power and Imperialism*. New Haven: Yale University Press.

Wolch, Jennifer and Emel, Jacque. 1995. Bringing the animals back in. *Environment and Planning D: Society and Space* 13 (6): 632–636.

Wolfe, Cary. 2010. *What Is Posthumanism?* Minneapolis: University of Minnesota Press.

Yip, Ka-che. 2009. Colonialism, disease, and public health: malaria in the history of Hong Kong. In Ka-che Yip, ed., *Disease, Colonialism, and the State: Malaria in Modern East Asian History*, pp. 11–30. Hong Kong: Hong Kong University Press.

CHAPTER **21** # Permeabilities, Ecology and Geopolitical Boundaries

Hilary Cunningham

Currently the world's population faces many sobering environmental issues: air pollution and climate change; loss of biodiversity and deforestation; soil erosion, cropland loses and desertification; depleted fisheries, salination and river flow interruptions; water pollution and drought; as well as the increasing frequency and scale of natural disasters induced by human activity. Land, water, air and biodiversity – essential components of all living systems on earth – are now widely regarded as seriously jeopardized, so much so that social strife, displacement and violence owing to environmental degradation has become a salient feature of the twenty-first century. Such environmental challenges are not only daunting, but also defining of our present moment. In a recent issue of *Environmental Science and Technology*, for example, distinguished geologists argued that for the first time the human species, owing to its fundamental destruction and alteration of the earth's biosystems, is ushering in a new geological era, tentatively named the *Anthropocene*, in which humans are the major engine of geological change (Zalasiewicz et al. 2010; see also Scharper 2010).

The scale and breadth of contemporary environmental problems connect the world's biotic populations across political, economic, cultural and ecological corridors to such an extent that economic development, energy use, sewage disposal, agricultural production, species extinction and valuations of "nature" in one country can and do have lasting impacts on many other nations of the world. Nor are these impacts evenly distributed across the human landscape, given that the burden of environmental degradation is felt most keenly in nations of the south as well as among poor populations, pointing to what could be described as a global landscape of "unequal ecologies."

In geopolitical terms, ecological regions do not neatly coincide with international territorial borders, creating a set of signal disjunctures between "environment" and "political bordering." Thus, addressing ecological degradation inevitably and

A Companion to Border Studies, First Edition. Edited by Thomas M. Wilson and Hastings Donnan.

increasingly demands cooperation across national and other geopolitical boundaries. Consequently, environment and ecology are key areas of concern for border scholarship – both in terms of how political borders are conceptualized and instantiated, as well as in terms of the specific environmental issues that border regions entail. Drawing widely on recent scholarship in border studies, and the notion of *permeabilities* within this literature, this chapter explores political bordering and environment through an analytical lens that situates the cultural, political, and economic aspects of borders in an ecological context.

NATURE, BORDERS AND CONCEPTUAL FRAMEWORKS

In October 2003, after successfully completing China's first manned spaced mission, Major General Yang Liwei made a disconcerting announcement. Contradicting the long-standing claim that the Great Wall could be seen from space, he remarked that he had been unable to see the historic landmark. His statement sparked a rather lively and at times heated discussion among Chinese government officials about the implications of such an admission. And, perhaps not surprisingly, many members of the Western press were quick to pick up the story and gleefully broadcast the death of a venerable "galactic urban myth."

Yet this particular Great Wall saga did not end with Yang Liwei's comment – 13 months after the Wall's "disappearance" from space, it made a dramatic comeback when US astronaut Leroy Chiao, using a digital camera and a 180 mm lens, took a picture of Inner Mongolia from NASA's International Space station. NASA posted one of his photographs in which – it claimed – the Great Wall could indeed be seen.[1]

While no doubt there were many in China relieved to see the NASA photograph as well as receive credible confirmation of the Wall's visibility from space, the image itself is instructive. As viewed from low orbit and in the digital photograph, the contours of the alleged Wall are of course fragmented and geographically quite distant, disrupting the notion of a continuous and unifying boundary line – a line originally designed to demarcate a northern frontier, prevent foreign intrusions, and act as an "edge" to a newly centralizing polity. In high orbit, however, where Yang Liwei's naked eye strained to see it, the Wall and its human signature were entirely erased.

Yang Liwei's evident dismay that even fragments of "the line" were not visible to him as he orbited the earth, as well as the subsequent NASA photograph, are both suggestive. Just what had Liwei expected to see? What in fact did he see?

China's Great Wall delineates what once was the southern edge of the Mongol Empire and recent archaeological surveys place it at a length of 5,500 miles (8,851 kilometers). Of that amount, 3,889 miles are human constructions, that is, the remains of a built environment consisting of the "actual wall" (made largely of rammed earth and bricks); as well as 224 miles of trenches. At best, the NASA photograph points to segments of what once was an integrated system of wall and fortified settlements – or, in other words, the residual outlines of a once vast configuration. From space at least, and with the help of NASA indications on the photograph of where segments of the Wall can be discerned, it is possible to bridge conceptually the gaps in the Wall's geography – to connect the dots, so to speak – of the great line that has been described as "the ancient world's most stupendous architectural work" (Dalin 2005: 20).

Of the Walls's total length, however, so far we have accounted for only 4,113 miles – what of the other 1,387 miles? This third portion is made up of what are often referred to as "natural defensive barriers" – segments of rivers, hilled areas, mountains and rocky outcroppings. It is likely, then, that Liwei actually did see the Wall – although in terms of its "natural" barriers – but that, for him, these did not register conceptually as "visible" elements of the Great Wall.

Yang Liwei, of course, would not be alone in this oversight. Many of us would strain our own eyes to discern the built wall in the NASA photograph, and, in seeking bricks and mortar, overlook the synthesis between the human-made and the "natural" features in this famous border/wall – itself a distinctive kind of *natureculture* (Haraway 2008).

I begin this chapter on borders, permeability, and ecology with this particular example because it both highlights the highly fragmentary nature of any political line or boundary, and speaks to the limitations of conceiving political boundaries principally in *linear* terms (see Cohen 2000; Barth 2000; Newman and Paasi 1998). Despite the fact that geopolitical borders are often thought of as contiguous, unbroken lines, in reality they are never continuous or juridically self-evident – although they may be imagined, propagated, and mythologized as such. Rather, they are continually being made and remade in the context of diverse economic, political and cultural practices that are themselves historically defined and divergent.

The notion of a boundary as simply a *line* has been seriously challenged by border scholarship, and while acknowledging that borders can and often do function in very "line" and "wall"-like ways, border scholars note that boundaries are always permeable to varying degrees. Additionally, border scholarship has made a strong argument in favor of replacing the border-as-a-line metaphor with a more dynamic concept of a "borderlands" – that is, "zones" that span linear borders and are characterized by distinctive kinds of social, economic and political relationships (Donnan and Wilson 1994, 1999).

Additionally, linear representations of borders often confer a uniformity of function to political boundaries – for instance, they demarcate an "edge" to a territory in which states enjoy exclusive powers, as well as define the boundaries of a national society (Paasi 1999: 10). Yet there are significant differences in the ways in which political borders have evolved across the globe, as well as significant differences in the roles borders have played vis-à-vis nationalist ideologies. Although the world's current international borders have a common origin in the Treaty of Westphalia of 1648, they by no means reflect uniform models of sovereignty, and indeed there is striking variation among states, as well as regional groupings of states, with respect to how geopolitical borders are regarded and integrated into national agendas – and their environmental projects (Bradshaw 2005; see also Elden 2006).

As a result, many border scholars prefer to think about political boundaries more in terms of the *porous* and *permeable*, or in some cases, even the *mobile* – although with three important caveats. First, a geopolitical border is never simply or uniformly permeable but may be both "open" and "closed" across a wide spectrum of possibilities (Blake 2005). Second, a state's edges are not simply confined to its territorial limits but can and do pervade societies in a variety of forms and in relation to many structures of control. Third, political borders are differentially located in global political economies that are differentially "open and closed." Thus, while it is useful to envision borders and their proximate borderlands as fundamentally permeable and multiform, the question of *permeable for whom* is equally relevant.

As a physical structure and as a "mobility regime," then, a particular border zone may engage with many different licit and illicit permeabilities, and indeed, there has been substantial debate within border scholarship on how to problematize *border permeability*, especially vis-à-vis the ways in which it has been conceptualized as an aspect of globalization (see Cunningham and Heyman 2004). My purpose here, however, is not to review debates on border permeabilities, but to explore how a focus on an ecology-border nexus might expand understandings of and approaches to political borders and their permeable aspects. This brings me to a second point regarding the NASA photograph of the Great Wall.

In the past it has been common among border experts to focus upon the economic, cultural, social and political aspects of boundaries and boundary-making, especially in terms of permeabilities. There has been considerable work, for example, on migration, refugees, smuggling, cultural identity and border security, as well as a wide range of economic issues encompassing cross-border trade, transborder regional economies and transboundary governance, to name a few. Less noted in this scholarship, however, has been the recognition that such borders have also been implemented within a complex set of relations with "nature," including but not limited to distinctive geophysical processes and ecological systems. While nature always is – like a border or a boundary – a discursive formation produced in the context of many different kinds of human practices, natural systems themselves – as ecologists underscore – are also made up of complex kinds of boundaries, territorializations and agencies, and as such, entail many different kinds of *mobilities, spatializations and permeabilities*.

To some extent, then, the NASA photograph also speaks to the problematics of conceptualizing human-made borders as not only lines, but also as *primary* enclosures, that is, demarcations that are somehow written *over* or inscribed *on top of* natural "backdrops."[2] The Great Wall's disappearance and reappearance, therefore, does more than point to the politics of lines – imperial, national and otherwise – it also references a second conceptual map about what political boundaries are, which ones are important, as well as how natural formations are integrated into human-made barriers. Consequently, what might be called the ecological dynamics of geopolitical borders can be scripted into (or erased from) the dynamics of geopolitical borders along very different lines.

Increasingly border scholars are recognizing the importance of including ecology-related aspects of border-related activities. While such a focus does not necessarily preclude an emphasis on human activities and does not ignore the discursive dynamics inherent in terms such as "ecology," "nature" and "environment," it has, I argue, created a new conceptual and analytical space in which to think about borders.

BORDERS, BIOTIC CORRIDORS AND ENVIRONMENTAL LANDSCAPES

Nature and ecology perform diverse roles at borders and in borderlands, and yet, at a broad level, all political boundaries entail "natural" elements. Whether these natural features should be "causally privileged" is open to some dispute – it must be acknowledged, however, that biophysical processes play a shaping if not defining role at many political borders. And political borders themselves are significant loci in which different kinds of biota – both human and nonhuman – participate in natural as well as social, political and economic patterns of mobility. Through migration or trade, for example, humans can inadvertently introduce species into bioregions from across continents (as was the case with the gypsy moth in the United States during the late nineteenth century). Likewise, international health experts have long been sensitive to how the ecologies of disease intersect with the permeable aspects of geopolitical boundaries. The 2003–2004 epidemic of SARS (severe acute respiratory syndrome) in Canada is a case in point – a period when many international visitors to the country were subject to noncontact infrared thermometer screening as a preventative measure designed to "catch" the SARS at "the border." A political border, then, in this instance, is thus a unique site in which a variety of biota intersect within patterns of travel, health, commerce, production and governance – so much so that its permeability can hardly be discussed within the confines of a "border-line."

Borders can also intersect with nonhuman biota and biophysical nature in a variety of other ways. Without exception, all geopolitical boundaries cut across land-based and marine habitats – some of them, in the case of birds, insects, and fish, extending thousands of kilometers. A political border or boundary, then, may intersect with any number of other corridors of movement and the biota that utilize them: the spawning grounds of salmon located in a tributary of an extensive river system, the migratory routes of birds; the grazing trails of cattle raised by nomadic pastoralists, or the flight patterns of commercial airline jets. Geopolitical borders therefore represent a spatially based system of movement that is typically written across many forms and kinds of movement, not always with thought being given to how these other corridors work and the kinds of biota that are contingently linked to them.

In another important sense, a linear imagination further obscures the ecological aspects of political borders. As Gerald Blake has observed, the maps that many of us are the most familiar with rely on two-dimensional representations. Yet all territorial borders include rights to airspace above their land territories, and states with coastal borders have exclusive offshore rights to continental shelf resources up to a distance of 200 nautical miles (Blake 2005: 16). And linear borders are hardly conceptually effective when it comes to the ecological dynamics at these kinds of perimeters. The impacts of BP's disastrous Gulf Oil Spill beginning in April 2010, for example, most immediately affected Louisiana and Florida, but as the slick entered the Loop Current and then the Gulf Stream, it also seriously threatened other coastal areas in Cuba, the Yucatan Peninsula of Mexico, as well as the Atlantic Seaboard of the United States. Similarly, the giant dust storms generated in China's Gobi Desert are annually carried via air currents to Japan and South Korea, the more recent chemical residuals transported by these storms making them increasingly lethal even for the citizens of these sovereign states.

In both cases – and in many others – environmentally related aspects of human activity not only cross geopolitical borders in unique ways, but do so within the context of specific ecological systems, and in terms of distinctive configurations of biota and corridors of movement. These rarely coincide "naturally" with the world's current system of sovereign states and territorial boundaries. Perhaps for this reason it is best to think of geopolitical boundaries, and boundary-making processes, as inherently "permeable" and "porous," not just in terms of their own juridical contours, but also in terms of the ecological contexts in which they are positioned.

Thus, in tracing out the mobilities of different biota, in comprehending the contours of biological corridors and environmental landscapes (Pearson and Gorman 2010), and in looking at key transboundary environmental issues, border-ecology scholarship faces a key challenge: it must stay attentive to the discursive aspects of ecological boundaries while, at the same time, take "matter seriously" as a causative agent. Ecological boundaries, too, entail different "mappings," and the boundaries of a particular environmental issue are never simply materially evident.

Many border scholars now include ecology in their discussions of border dynamics, and several recent scholarly collections on border and boundary-making processes feature articles focusing on the environmental aspects of borders (e.g., Donnan and Wilson 2010; Nicol and Townsend-Gault 2005; Berg and van Houtum 2003). Here, however, I focus more directly on research that develops ecology as a central analytic. In pursuing this, I include scholars attempting critically to eschew unproductive binaries between human and nonhuman nature, but I also underscore broader efforts to look at the ways in which "nature" – as a complex set of relations among a wide variety of biotic agents – has intersections in border landscapes. Thus, while much of the scholarship outlined below explores ecology and environment in the specific context of borders and borderlands, as a whole it also reflects an important analytical shift in border studies, that is, one that questions the saliency of simple anthropocentric frameworks and considers the benefits of thinking about human boundary-making as contingently "nested" within a wider variety of ecological spatializations, mobilities and indeed, metaphysical realities (see also Brown and Todavine 2007).

ENVIRONMENT *AT* BORDERS AND *IN* BORDER REGIONS

Many geopolitical borders encompass natural features as part of their overall configuration. Several major rivers, for example, form international boundary lines: the Lower Orange River between South Africa and Namibia, the Rio Grande between Mexico and the United States, and the Mekong River between Thailand and Laos are but a few well-known examples. India, Pakistan and Nepal share three river basins (the Indus, Ganges-Brahmaputra, and the Ganges-Mahakab), and the countries of Congo, Burundi, Tanzania and Zambia all have borders on Lake Tanganyika. The vast Karakoram mountain range in the Himalayas forms a border between Pakistan, India and China. The Canada–US border bisects four of the five bodies of water that make up the Great Lakes System; the United Kingdom and France share a maritime border in the English Channel, and East Timor, Australia and Indonesia share a (disputed) water border in the Timor Sea. In a simple sense, then, "nature" is a critical feature of many border areas. Yet the role of "nature-at-the-border" is not in the least simple – as the Great Wall example above attests. Natural barriers often play complex roles. As both a "technology" and a built environment, border barriers can impact ecosystems and bioregions in a variety of ways. Likewise issues of nature loom large in resource management, in border economic development projects as well as in discourses linking borderscapes to national identity and national belonging. They have also increasingly become sources of considerable transboundary conflict and, less frequently, sources of transboundary cooperation between and among states (Westing 1993; Ali 2007).

Writing on the ecological aspects of specific kinds of boundaries, environmental historian William Cronon has suggested that partitioning be studied in terms of its ecological "ripple effects." Focusing on European agricultural practices that required the fencing in of domesticated grazing animals, Cronon details how colonial farmers made dramatic changes to New England's ecosystems, as well as to indigenous subsistence systems (2003: 127–156). Although the impacts of both domesticated livestock and fencing were ecologically manifold, one central effect related to the natural predators in the region. Once cows, poultry and sheep were barricaded, the animals became a draw to wolves, and, in turn, wolves became targeted as enemies of the New England farmer. Subsequently, bounties were placed on wolves (thus constituting wolves as a market), and swamp areas (mistakenly identified as wolf havens) were cleared and drained. Thus, one of the widespread effects of European domesticated animal agricultural and fencing technologies was the hunting and subsequent decimation of wolves, as well as the destruction of specific ecosystems such as wetlands and swamps.

Cronon's insights are useful for thinking about the ecological impacts at present day international borders and the "ripple effects" of certain kinds of fencing practices. How do certain kinds of border fencing impact specific species? How does border fencing impact regional ecosystems? What are the ecological, political and economic implications of these combined impacts? One area of border research that has explored some of these interconnections has focused on certain types of fencing technologies (such as "security barriers") and the kinds of ecological footprints these entail (see Cunningham 2010). The turn to "securitizing" borders, particularly in a post–9/11 global environment, has engendered preferences for certain kinds of border constructions and border management practices – both of which have had definite, and in many cases, devastating ecological impacts. Examples of "security fencing" (or what are sometimes called "separation barriers") include Spain's notorious Melilla and Ceuta border fences; the electrified fencing between Botswana and Zimbabwe; Israel's West Bank security "Wall"; Saudi Arabia's security fence with Yemen; Thailand's separation barrier with Malaysia; the Hong Kong–China Mainland border; India's "Line of Control" with Pakistan; as well the US's "Secure Border" with Mexico.

In rare instances heavily fortified border fencing can produce environmentally positive effects on local flora and fauna. Korea's Demilitarized Zone, erected in 1953, for example, has become a haven of sorts for northeast Asia's wildlife, including the endangered white-napped and red-crowned cranes, the Asiatic black bear, egrets, and according to some accounts, a subspecies of the Siberian tiger. In most cases, however, the ecological impacts of security barriers are less sanguine. The recent security barriers at the US–Mexico border, for example, include hundreds of miles of concrete-reinforced steel fencing, as well as the construction of extensive service roads and the increased presence of thousands of new border patrol agents. Portions of the border slice through several protected areas in the United States (including the Organ Pipe National Monument, the Cabeza Prieta National Monument, the Buenos Aires National Wildlife Reserve and the San Pedro Riparian National Conservation Area). As a result, there are a whole host of environmental issues for biota along this border: the fragmentation of habitat (particularly for endangered animals like the ocelot and the jaguar, which both require wide open spaces to survive and maintain gene pool diversity); habitat destruction through land filling, extensive service roads and invasive vehicular patrolling; and circadian rhythm disorders for nocturnal animals owing to the widespread use of stadium lighting. Additionally, poor residents in parts of the Tijuana–San Diego corridor will be likely to be more vulnerable to dangerous mud slides as a result of the dragging and rerouting of water runoff in the estuary.[3]

The ecological profile of the US–Mexico border fencing that I am outlining here must also include attention to the specific patterns of migration engendered by this security fencing. These particular "walls," rooted in a border management strategy adopted in the early 1990s, have also redirected migrant traffic from urban crossings into remote desert regions. Currently, thousands of migrants cross the Sonoran Desert on a daily basis and along corridors managed by trafficking cartels. The daily usage of the desert for illicit migration has resulted in enormous quantities of discarded plastic water bottles, food containers, and clothing, as well as other refuse – all of which contribute to harmful ecological effects. Taking a toll both in terms of human life and habitat destruction, these migrant routes are direct outcomes of particular border technologies, including the specific kind of fencing that has been widely adopted in this region. Thus, although here I underscore the ecological aspects of such fencing, this is clearly a form of bordering that encompasses far more than its ecological features. Embedded in broader efforts aimed at restricting immigrants and refugee populations, as well as exit migration, the built border is a composite not only of its physical properties, but also of the myriad political, economic, and ecological relations that constitute its reality on a daily basis.

POLITICAL BORDERS, BORDER HIERARCHIES AND THE BORDERS OF ECOLOGICAL SYSTEMS

Because political boundaries do not correspond neatly with bioregions or ecoregions, they pose distinctive challenges when it comes to the transboundary management of environmental problems.

First, the ways in which environmental issues and problems are conceptualized and classified *spatially* (e.g., as local/national/global) can be highly problematic. The labeling of an environmental problem as "local" can frequently be misleading, since the chemical effluents from a factory located at a specific international border may manifest effects not only on a city's local population, but also on several nearby cities in both countries, not to mention regions quite geographically distant. Moreover, an environmental problem in one region may manifest itself differently in another, since airborne toxins often end up being deposited in either water or land forms and water-borne toxins can evaporate to become airborne contaminants. Additionally, toxins can interact with different ecosystems in a variety of ways and generate both moderate and severe effects depending on where and how they travel. Intercontinental dust plumes – intensifying in both China and Australia as a result of desertification – are a good example of this last point. Scientific studies have confirmed that the presence of bacteria, fungi, viruses, radioactive isotopes, dioxin and toxic metals from storms originating in both these countries now encompass an increasing range of locations (including Boulder, Colorado and the coral reefs of the Caribbean) (Raloff 2001). Yet, as the plumes travel, the heavier dust particles (less likely to be inhaled into the lower regions of the lungs) are among the first elements to descend, while the lighter molecules carrying highly carcinogenic toxic particulates (much more likely to be breathed in deeply) travel to more geographically distant locations. Thus, what may be regarded as the "local" or "regional" impacts of the dust storms may in fact be quite differentially global, both in scope and in effects (see also Liu and Diamond 2005). In a very profound sense, then, ecological and political boundaries are deeply imbricated.

Second, environmental issues and problems are also often conceptualized and classified in terms of political priorities (e.g., security versus sustainability), and these in turn correspond to a set of legal jurisdictions and a structure of governance among the institutions and groups involved. The architecture of authority among these groups (both governmental and nongovernmental) is frequently, but not exclusively, hierarchical, hence the configuration of political authority can have serious conse-quences for the ways in which environmental issues are addressed.

While this is generally the case for most environmental issues, it is also specific to geopolitical borders themselves. In the US's post–9/11 "secure-our-borders" climate, for example, so-called *local conservation* considerations were subordinated to over-arching *federal security* concerns – despite the fact that federal environmental laws protected local concerns. In May 2005, the US REAL ID Act gave the Secretary of the Department of Homeland Security (DHS) the discretionary power to waive all environmental and cultural protocols in the face of overriding security concerns, and in September 2005, then DHS Secretary Michael Chertoff took advantage of this legislation to waive – "in their entirety" – the environmental restrictions contained in several US laws in order to build triple fencing through the Tijuana River National Estuarine Research Reserve outside of San Diego, California. This decision not only affected local environmental groups on the US side of the fence, but seriously undercut the efforts of binational environmental groups and projects aimed at creating protected transborder conservation areas (Sifford and Chester 2007; Cun-ningham 2010).

In summary, then, environmental problems – because they entail the pathways of organisms and chemical elements as they circulate within distinctive ecological cor-ridors – deeply challenge long-standing geopolitical maps, and link state spaces together in a set of key ecological relationships. Interestingly, while national territorializations are often seen as obstacles to addressing ecological issues (see Erskine 2005), it is clear that environmental problems too, have also generated a reterritorialization of state boundaries.

CROSS- AND TRANSBORDER ECOLOGIES

The kinds of environmental issues that are common to political borders have been well documented in several case studies, particularly in situations where two or more national jurisdictions share a common natural resource (Herzog 2000; Sturgeon 2006). Ecological issues in border regions include a long list of environmental topics: air pollution; industrial toxins and chemical waste; water pollution and water shortages; biodiversity loss, habitat loss and fragmentation; species decline; and the impacts of all of these on human populations. The list also includes "green crime" or Transnational Environmental Crime (such as the smuggling of e-waste, illegal industrial dumping and wildlife contraband), environmental security as well as bio-intelligence (see Hayman and Brack 2002; Elliot 2007); transborder environmental health (see Kahn 2004; Gushulak and MacPherson 2000; Orloff and Falk 2003), transborder environmental governance (see Ganster 2001) and transborder environmental conflict.[4] Additionally, issues of environmental and social justice are often prevalent in border regions, including the differential burden of environmental "costs" at borders as well as exclusionary ecopolitics that result in loss of livelihood and displacement for vulnerable communities (see Ranco and Suagee 2007; Larsen 2003). Consequently, in bordered areas where there are significant asymmetries between or among national populations, ecological impacts are usually more severe for certain sectors of the population, as is the case at the US–Mexico border (Vila and Petersen 2003; Heyman 2007).

The literature on ecology and borders is now a lively and active subfield within border scholarship and is notably interdisciplinary in nature. While much of this research is specific to particular borders and border regions, there are a variety of analytical foci developing out of this research that usefully problematize ecology and ecological relationships as they intersect in border areas and landscapes. Two key areas of productive analytical entanglements for border-ecology research are novel forms of economic regionalism in border areas, as well as cross-border conservation parks.

With respect to the economic regionalism, border scholarship generally shows a long and sustained interest in political borders vis-à-vis global forms of capital, the realignments of power inherent in these processes, and new spatializations of extraction, production and consumption. By adding political ecology to the picture – especially its focus on the distribution of ecology and ecological effects across structured and polarized forms of inequality (Paulson and Gezon 2005) – border-environment research in this area has highlighted the role of nation-states and other financial actors in the context of global resource flows.[5]

Some border scholars have explored global capital in terms of various kinds of transborder economic zones – especially in the context of "free trade" blocs (such as those implemented under the North American Free Trade Agreement (NAFTA) and through European integration). Many of these studies have underscored the importance of transborder environmental management (e.g., Kry and Wirth 1998; Fernandez and Carson 2007), but the analytical ways in which researchers have engaged with "environment" and "environmental issues" in such zones is quite diverse. For example, in looking at post-NAFTA ecological issues at the US–Mexico border, Clement et al. (2005) and Ganster (2001) embed "environment" in the context of economic development and security. This research argues that increased economic activity in many border regions (brought about by globalization) inevitably results in increased environmental degradation. Both studies advocate better transborder management in the areas of industrial pollution, water resources and bioresource depletion, as well as coordination of environmental legislation and policy. Eschewing "top down" approaches to environmental management, this research cautiously argues for regional transborder environmental coordination implemented via a constellation of governmental and nongovernmental groups. In this and other such studies, the binary aspects of the border are seen as recessing in relation to new forms of transboundary management.

Taking a somewhat different perspective in his study of Cascadia – a transborder region at the Washington State and British Columbia border – Artibise (2005) concludes that despite the intensification of cross-border economic interactions and substantial cross-border initiatives in the areas of trade and tourism, "ingrained barriers" that are more cultural in orientation have tended to preserve the international border as a dividing line. At the heart of this "divide" are opposing visions of Cascadia: as a trade corridor in the new global and continental economy versus a bioregion deeply connected to conservationist values. For Artibise (as well as Alper 2005 and Sparke 2005: 65–112), a border's ecology is a highly contested political issue – deeply and contingently implicated in different approaches to nature and, in this instance, the US–Canada border as a cultural partition.

Similarly, conservation issues at political borders and in border regions can reflect very different analytical trajectories as well as involve different genres of transboundary space. These include water boundaries, marine commons and marine parks, transfrontier protected natural areas and international parks. Scholarly explorations of the latter – such as transboundary protected areas (TPAs) – are perhaps at the forefront of efforts to bring political ecology and border studies into deeper engagement. These include discussions around the mixed benefits of these areas for resident populations in terms of livelihoods (e.g., ecotourism and "responsible" nature tourism) as well as the undersides of so-called consultative park management models. Much of this literature tends to critique transboundary conservation efforts in terms of the displacement and continued marginalization of already vulnerable groups, as well as explore the ways in which ecological enclosures can elevate the ethical standing of nonhuman actors while at the same time criminalizing the activities of local human inhabitants (Neumann 2004; see also Catton 1997). Lastly, as in the Cascadia example, the ways in which "nature" comes to be bordered and inscribed in a TPA can reflect different priorities and frequently conflicting visions of "nature," especially in the context of neoliberal sustainable-development policies (see Brockington and Igoe 2006; West 2006; Spenceley 2006; Dressler and Büscher 2008).

Both areas of border study – economic regionalism and TPAs – are also beginning to be studied in the context of the now voluminous literature on post-Westphalian spatialities and polities (Whitehead 2007) and the ways in which neoliberal agendas interface with environmental projects (Heynen et al. 2007; Fife 2010; Sparke 2005). Given the varied ways in which neoliberal enclosures are evolving in today's world, transboundary environmental practices and projects (including their economic management, cultural construction and politicization) clearly represent important future directions for any border-ecology analytic.

CONCLUSION: EPISTEMOLOGICAL ECOTONES, BOUNDARY ENTANGLEMENTS AND EDGE EFFECTS

In border scholarship, it has become commonplace for scholars to acknowledge that nature and geopolitical boundaries do not neatly coincide. This widespread and seemingly uncontroversial statement, however, belies a deeper set of issues and complexities – complexities that include conceptual orientations toward borders, the ecological impacts of borders, the political economical aspects of borders and the power differentials inherent in border politics. As a result, *borders and environment* is a dynamic subfield within border studies and one that is, in some respects, just beginning to walk on its own, after having ambled for many years alongside some of the more seasoned and foundational topics within the field.

Border-ecology studies have the potential to make critical and lasting impacts on border scholarship, owing not only to their uniquely and broadly interdisciplinary character, but also to the new directions in which they are taking border studies itself. Building upon scholarship that has complicated and in many cases eschewed the "linear imagination" that has dominated border research for a sizeable swath of its history, border-ecology studies opens up novel and critical questions about the nature of borders not simply as "lines" but as *boundaries themselves* – including boundaries as *zones, landscapes, interfaces, corridors, frontiers* and the like.

Environmental theorists and ecologists add to the above list of boundary types the concept of an *ecotone* – an area where two different plant communities meet to create a distinctive interface between two ecosystems. Examples include shorelines (transitional zones between sea and landform), savannas (occurring where hardwood forest and long prairie grasslands meet), as well as zones between pasture and woodlot. An ecotone usually retains some of the characteristics of each community, but will often also contain species not found in either of the overlapping ecosystems. The concept of an ecotone, then, has many resonances with the notion of a border zone or borderlands.

Boundary scholar and environmental philosopher Irene Klaver suggests that the *ecotone* is a fertile concept for recasting the kinds of intellectual work that can be done at "lines." For Klaver – like Donna Haraway, Gilles Deleuze and Felix Guattari – borders are "always places at work" (2007: 123), and hence are a viable place to interrogate conceptualizations of borders, but always within an epistemological framework that "takes matter seriously." Anthropologist Tim Ingold (2008) also challenges border scholarship to go a step further by suggesting that we cast our inquiries in terms of "fluid space" and the fundamental openness of living systems.

In such an approach, he suggests, the stranglehold of frameworks grounded not only on stable lines, but also on "relationality" can be loosened and reoriented toward the notion of "entanglement" as the primary source of interconnection.

Both *ecotones* and *entanglements* are provocative and fruitful directions for border-ecology research, especially as human interactions with nature gain more saliency across a broad spectrum of disciplines. Yet, I would like to include another concept here – that of *edge-effects*, likewise a concept borrowed from ecology and biology. Edge-effects are often linked to the dynamics unique to *ecotones* – understood not just as interfaces, but as distinctive habitats in their own right.

Edge-effects is a concept that describes the influences two bordering communities have on one another in a transitional area or ecotone. A species of plant native to one bordering plant community, for example, may grow more abundantly in an ecotone, and therefore may provide "friendly" spaces for some insects but not for others (thereby resulting both in different insect and different predator populations). While this example only touches the "tip" of the complex dynamics in an ecotone, it is useful here because in addition to fingering the complicated interconnections that these ecological "borderlands" entail, it also points to differential effects in "edge-spaces." Within human-made border zones too – such as those at political borders – there are unequal environmental impacts that often coexist with asymmetries of wealth, heath and power.

Thus, as the ideas of ecotone and edge-effects suggest, geopolitical borders, like our current ecological challenges, run along the same "faultlines" of social, economic, cultural, political, racial and gendered inequalities. Border studies that take seriously environmental concerns will remain most vital if they retain a vigorous sense of borders, not simply as geopolitical demarcations, but also as *differentially permeable* – that is, as "gates" that are both opened and closed in particular ways and which continue to play significant roles in the creation and maintenance of "unequal ecologies." While such gates, like the Great Wall of China, may not be visible from outer space, they are increasingly evident to border scholars on the ground, so to speak, and remain central guideposts on the expanding horizon of border-ecology studies.

NOTES

1 See http://www.nasa.gov/vision/space/workinginspace/great_wall.html (accessed Dec. 2011).
2 To some extent this is a fairly recent development. As Paasi notes (1999: 12–13), medieval approaches to borders privileged "natural" ones over human-made ones. The former were regarded as the more "real" since they had been inscribed in nature, either by God or by other natural forces.
3 The security fencing has also seriously compromised efforts to establish transborder conservation areas in both the Chihuahuan and the Sonoran deserts (see Sifford and Chester 2007).
4 See also Hoel 2002 for an overview of transboundary environmental issues.
5 Josiah Heyman (2007), for example, has looked at the gate-keeping aspects of global capital accumulation and details the ecological dimensions of this at the US–Mexico border in terms of what he calls "environmental disorders."

REFERENCES

Ali, Saleem H., ed. 2007. *Peace Parks: Conservation and Conflict Resolution*. Cambridge: MIT Press.

Alper, Donald K. 2005. Conflicting transborder visions and agendas: economic and environmental Cascadians. In Heather N. Nicol and Ian Townsend-Gault, eds, *Holding the Line: Borders in a Global World*. Vancouver: University of British Columbia Press.

Artibise, Alan F.J. 2005. Cascadian adventures: shared visions, strategic alliances and ingrained barriers in a transborder region. In Heather N. Nicol and Ian Townsend-Gault, eds, *Holding the Line: Borders in a Global World*. Vancouver: University of British Columbia Press.

Barth, Fredrik. 2000. Boundaries and connections. In Anthony P. Cohen, ed., *Signifying Identities: Anthropological Perspectives on Boundaries and Contested Values*. London: Routledge.

Berg, Eiki and van Houtum, Henk. 2003. *Routing Borders between Territories, Discourses and Practices*. Aldershot: Ashgate.

Blake, Gerald. 2005. Boundary permeability in perspective. In Heather N. Nicol and Ian Townsend Gault, eds, *Holding the Line: Borders in a Global World*. Vancouver: University of British Columbia Press.

Bradshaw, Roy. 2005. Redefining the nature and function of boundaries. In Heather N. Nicol and Ian Townsend-Gault, eds, *Holding the Line: Borders in a Global World*. Vancouver: University of British Columbia Press.

Brockington, Daniel and Igoe, James. 2006. Eviction for conservation: a global overview. *Conservation and Society* 4 (3): 424–470.

Brown, Charles and Todavine, Ted, eds. 2007. *Nature's Edge: Boundary Explorations in Ecological Theory and Practice*. Albany: State University of New York Press.

Catton, Theodore. 1997. *Inhabited Wilderness: Indians, Eskimos and National Parks in Alaska*. Albuquerque: University of New Mexico Press.

Clement, Norris, Ganster, Paul and Sweedler, Alan. 2005. Environment, development and security in border regions: perspectives from Europe and North America. In Paul Ganster and David E. Lorey, eds, *Borders and Border Politics in a Globalizing World*. Oxford: SR Books.

Cohen, Anthony P. 2000. Discriminating relations: identity, boundary and authenticity. In Anthony P. Cohen, ed., *Signifying Identities: Anthropological Perspectives on Boundaries and Contested Values*, pp. 17–35. London: Routledge.

Cronon, William. 2003. *Changes in the Land: Indians, Colonists, and the Ecology of New England*. New York: Hill & Wang. First publ. 1983.

Cunningham, Hilary. 2010. Gating ecology in a gated globe: environmental aspects of "securing our borders." In Hastings Donnan and Thomas M. Wilson, eds, *Borderlands: Ethnographic Approaches to Security, Power, and Identity*. Lanham: University Press of America.

Cunningham, Hilary and Heyman, Josiah McC. 2004. Introduction: mobilities and enclosures. Special issue on Borders. *Identities: Global Studies in Culture and Power* 11 (3): 289–302.

Dalin, Cheng. 2005. The Great Wall of China. In Paul Ganster and David E. Lorey, eds, *Borders and Border Politics in a Globalizing World*. Oxford: SR Books.

Donnan, Hastings and Wilson, Thomas M., eds. 1994. *Border Approaches: Anthropological Perspectives on Frontiers*. Lanham: University Press of America.

Donnan, Hastings and Wilson, Thomas M. 1999. *Borders: Frontiers of Identity, Nation and State*. Oxford: Berg.

Donnan, Hastings and Wilson, Thomas M., eds. 2010. *Borderlands: Ethnographic Approaches to Security, Power, and Identity*. Lanham: University Press of America.

Dressler, W. and Büscher, B. 2008. Market triumphalism and the CBNRM "crises" at the South African section of the great

Limpopo transfrontier park. *Geoforum* 39 (1): 452–465.

Elden, Stuart. 2006. Contingent sovereignty, territorial integrity and the sanctity of borders. *SAIS Review* 26 (1): 11–24.

Elliott, Lorraine. 2007. Transnational environmental crime in the Asia Pacific: an "un(der)securitized" security problem? *Pacific Review* 20 (4): 499–522.

Erskine, Brian. 2005. Disaster on the Danube. In Paul Ganster and David E. Lorey, eds, *Borders and Border Politics in a Globalizing World*. Oxford: SR Books.

Fernandez, Linda and Carson, Richard T. eds. 2007. *Both Sides of the Border: Transboundary Environmental Management Issues Facing Mexico and the United States*. Dordrecht: Kluwer Academic.

Fife, Wayne. 2010. Internal borders as naturalized political instruments. *Identities: Global Studies in Culture and Power* 17 (2–3): 255–279.

Ganster, Paul, ed. 2001. *Cooperation, Environment, and Sustainability in Border Regions*. San Diego: San Diego State University Press.

Gushulak, Brian D. and MacPherson, Douglas W. 2000. Health issues associated with the smuggling and trafficking of migrants. *Journal of Immigrant Health* 2 (2): 67–78.

Haraway, Donna. 2008. *When Species Meet (Posthumanities)*. Minneapolis: University of Minnesota Press.

Hayman, Gavin and Brack, Duncan. 2002. *International Environmental Crime: The Nature and Control of Environmental Black Markets*. London: Royal Institute of International Affairs.

Herzog, L.A., ed. 2000. *Shared Space: Rethinking the US–Mexico Border Environment*. La Jolla: University of California, San Diego, Center for US-Mexican Studies.

Heyman, Josiah. 2007. Environmental issues at the US–Mexico Border and the unequal territorialization of value. In Alf Hornborg, J.R. Mitchell and Joan Martinez-Alier, eds, *Rethinking Environmental History: World-System History and Global Environmental Change*. New York: Altamira Press.

Heynen, Nik, McCarthy, James, Prudham, Scott and Robbins, Paul, eds. 2007. *Neoliberal Environments: False Promises and Unnatural Consequences*. New York: Routledge.

Hoel, Michael. 2002. Transboundary environmental problems. In Jeroen C.J.M. van den Bergh, ed., *Handbook of Environmental and Resource Economics*. Northampton: Edward Elgar.

Ingold, Tim. 2008. Bindings against Boundaries: Entanglements of Life in an Open World. *Environment and Planning A* 40: 1796–1810.

Kahn, Matthew E. 2004. Domestic pollution havens: evidence from cancer deaths in border counties. *Journal of Urban Economics* 56: 51–69.

Klaver, Irene J. 2007. Boundaries on the Edge. In Charles Brown and Ted Todavine, eds, *Nature's Edge: Boundary Explorations in Ecological Theory and Practice*. Albany: State University of New York Press.

Kry, Richard and Wirth, John. 1998. *Environmental Management on North America's Borders*. College Station: Texas A&M University Press.

Larsen, Henrik Gutzon. 2003. Environmental boundaries of inclusion. In Eiki Berg and Henk van Houtum, eds, *Routing Borders between Territories, Discourses and Practices*. Aldershot: Ashgate.

Liu, Jianguo and Diamond, Jared. 2005. China's environment in a globalizing world. *Nature* 435: 179–86.

Neumann, Roderick P. 2004. Moral and Discursive geographies in the war for biodoversity in Africa. *Political Geography* 23: 813–837.

Newman, David and Paasi, Ansii. 1998. Fences and neighbors in the postmodern world: boundary narratives in political geography. *Progress in Human Geography* 22 (2): 186–207.

Nicol, Heather N. and Townsend-Gault, Ian, eds. 2005. *Holding the Line: Borders in a Global World*. Vancouver: University of British Columbia Press.

Orloff, Kenneth and Falk, Henry. 2003. An international perspective on hazardous waste practices. *International Journal of Hygiene and Environmental Health* 206: 291–302.

Paasi, Anssi. 1999. The political geography of boundaries at the end of the millennium: challenges of the de-territorializing world. In Heikki Eskelinen, Ilkka Liikanen and Jukka Oksa, eds, *Curtains of Iron and Gold: Reconstructing Borders and Scales of Interaction*. Aldershot: Ashgate.

Paulson, S. and Gezon, L.L., eds. 2005. *Political Ecology across Spaces, Scales and Social Groups*. New Brunswick: Rutgers University Press.

Pearson, Diane M. and Gorman, Julian T. 2010. Exploring the relevance of a landscape ecological paradigm for sustainable landscapes and livelihoods: a case-application from the Northern Territory Australia. *Landscape Ecology* 25 (8): 1169–1183.

Raloff, Janet. 2001. Ill winds: dust storms ferry toxic agents between countries and even continents. *Science News* 160 (14): 218–220.

Ranco, D. and Suagee, D. 2007. Tribal sovereignty and the problem of difference in environmental regulation: observations on "measured separatism" in Indian country. *Antipode* 39 (4): 691–707.

Scharper, Stephen B. 2010. We all lose in the war against nature. Toronto Star, Apr. 16. At http://www.thestar.com/opinion/editorialopinion/article/796148 (accessed Apr. 30, 2010).

Sifford, B. and Chester, C. 2007. Bridging conservation across la frontera: an unfinished agenda for peace parks along the US–Mexico divide. In S. H. Ali, ed., *Peace Parks: Conservation and Conflict Resolution*. Cambridge: MIT Press.

Sparke, Matthew. 2005. *In the Space of Theory: Postfoundational Geographies of the Nation-State*. Minneapolis: University of Minnesota Press.

Spenceley, Anna. 2006. Tourism in the Great Limpopo Transfrontier Park. *Development Southern Africa* 23 (5): 649–667

Sturgeon, Janet C. 2006. *Border Landscapes: The Politics of Akha Land Use in China and Thailand*. Seattle: University of Washington Press.

Vila, Pablo and Petersen, John A. 2003. Environmental problems in Cuidad Juarez El Paso: a social constructivist approach. In Pablo Vila, ed., *Ethnography at the Border*. Minneapolis: University of Minnesota Press.

West, Paige. 2006. *Conservation is Our Government Now: The Politics of Ecology in Papua New Guniea*. Chapel Hill: Duke University Press.

Westing, Arthur. 1993. Biodiversity and the challenge of national borders. *Environmental Conservation* 20: 5–6.

Whitehead, Mark. 2007. *The Nature of the State: Excavating the Political Ecologies of the Modern State*. Oxford: Oxford University Press.

Zalasiewicz, Jan, Williams, Mark, Steffen, Will and Crutzen, Paul. 2010. The new world of the anthropocene. *Environmental Science and Technology* 44 (7): 2228–2231.

PART IV Displacement, Emplacement and Mobility

22 Borders and
the Rhythms
of Displacement,
Emplacement
and Mobility

Pamela Ballinger

In his film *Jaguar*, French director Jean Rouch crafted an "ethnofictional" account
of the adventures of three young Songhay men traveling on seasonal migration routes
between French West Africa and the Gold Coast. Filmed between 1954 and 1955,
Jaguar captured a moment just before the relative fluidity of colonial borders began
to give way to more fixed national boundaries as independent states such as Ghana
(1957), the Mali Federation (1960), and Niger (1960) came into being. In the
movie, the three protagonists journey across a variety of environmental or ecological
border zones – desert yields to savannah to grasslands and finally to the sea and
coastline – that also loosely demarcate ethnic, cultural and linguistic boundaries.
When the heroes arrive at the tiny border post separating the British Gold Coast
from French West Africa, they are turned back because they do not possess identity
cards. As the guard looks in another direction, however, they merely walk around
the border station and surreptitiously cross into British territory. Consisting of a line
in the sand and a placard proclaiming the existence of an international boundary, the
border post here embodies both the arbitrary character of political borders and their
significance as sites at which sovereignty is declared and challenged. Furthermore,
borders prove central to what Wang (2004: 352) has termed a "regime of mobility,"
in which formal instruments of citizenship such as passports and documents assumed
increasing importance.

Capturing a moment in time, Rouch's cinematic fable depicts a world in which
illegal crossing of a border post bears no real costs, official border crossers need only
identity cards (not passports), and mobility proves a way of life (and a rite of passage)
for many young Africans seeking to become "jaguar," that is, cool and "with it" men

A Companion to Border Studies, First Edition. Edited by Thomas M. Wilson and
Hastings Donnan.
© 2012 Blackwell Publishing Ltd. Published 2012 by Blackwell Publishing Ltd.

possessed of cigarettes, sunglasses, and style (Stoller 1992: 135). Rouch's earlier Songhay films, however, tell a different story of isolated villages in which residents travel on quite restricted circuits (Stoller 1992: 131). Rouch's diverse cinematic reflections on the Songhay highlight the tensions in scholarly studies of borders between, on the one hand, sedentarist perspectives that privilege rootedness and fixity and, on the other, anti-sedentarist approaches that take movement and deterritoriali-zation as "inherent" conditions. At issue are the meanings of place, home and identity in a global terrain or regime of mobility marked by unequal access and capacities. These sedentarist/anti-sedentarist debates assume particular urgency when scholars focus on displacement – physical, emotional, virtual – across borders, the topic of this essay. Displacement generally implies a degree of forced or involuntary migration (Malkki 1995b: 495), although scholars continue to argue over the conceptual rela-tionship between displacement, refugees, and forced migration and the place of displacement studies within the broader field of migration scholarship (see, for example, the debate between Adelman and McGrath 2007; Cohen 2007; Hathaway 2007; Chimni 2009).

Regardless of how scholars locate displacement in the landscape of migration studies, or whether scholars posit movement and mobility as a rupture or the normal state of things, many studies of displacement prove too narrow, focusing on popula-tions which leave and the places they go to the neglect of the homes and neighbors they leave behind. In an influential 1995 review article on refugees and exile, Malkki outlined the limitations of such a one-sided view of displacement: "In many works of refugee studies, there is an implicit assumption that in becoming 'torn loose' from their cultures, 'uprooted' from their homes, refugees suffer the loss of all contact to the lifeworlds they fled. It is as if the place left behind were no longer peopled" (1995b: 515).

In the conclusion to her article, Malkki urged scholars to take account of emplace-ment together with displacement, as well as to question assumptions that displace-ment necessarily denaturalizes previously "rooted" populations (see also Malkki 1992). In Malkki's estimation, studying displacement thus requires asking, "What is the state of not being a refugee like? How is it denoted?" (1995b: 515). In this article, I examine a variety of ways in which scholars (myself included) have taken up the challenge posed by Malkki, suggesting how these perspectives may usefully inform critical border studies.

As this essay will demonstrate, recent scholarship on the interrelated processes of displacement and emplacement highlights how forcible migration brings with it multiple processes of "replacement," including the ways in which new populations come to inhabit spaces previously occupied by those who have left, how both those who leave and those who remain in specific territories reconceptualize place and home (re-placement), and how and the degree to which individuals who engage in return migration become re-placed or re-emplaced in their putative home(lands). Offering both theoretical and methodological innovations for the study of borders, this new work demonstrates that displacement and emplacement are simultaneously spatial and temporal processes. At the same time, however, the spatial aspects of place-making have received greater emphasis and much work remains to be done on the diverse temporalities experienced by those displaced/emplaced persons who live, draw meaning from and give meaning to borders, a topic I take up in the final section of the essay.

BORDERS, DISPLACEMENT AND EMPLACEMENT: RECONCEPTUALIZING MOBILITY

Whereas work on refugees has frequently rested on "deeply territorializing concepts of identity for those categories of people classified as 'displaced' and 'uprooted'" (Malkki 1992: 25), many border studies have suffered from an equally problematic but opposite assumption of mobility as a norm and even positive virtue. In their introduction to the special issue of the journal *Identities* devoted to the topic of mobility and borders, for example, Cunningham and Heyman (2004: 292) interrogate the conflation of "movement with mobility" that runs through many analyses of borders, particularly works of "border theory" that emphasize symbolic boundaries to the neglect of actual, political borders. Displaced persons, of course, offer a prime instance when movement should not (necessarily) be equated with mobility in the positive sense used by many proponents of a deterritorialized world. For some refugees, the ability not to move may appear as a luxury denied them, although this varies considerably from case to case, as subsequent discussion of the complexities of displacement/emplacement will make clear.

Just as scholars like Malkki have transformed the study of refugees by urging attention to the entwined processes of displacement and emplacement, so have anthropologists like Cunningham and Heyman (2004: 293) urged a reconceptualization of borders in terms of conjoined mobilities and enclosures. A number of authors have usefully taken up and empirically elaborated these insights in ways that highlight the role played by institutions like states (Chalfin 2004; Heyman 2004; Wang 2004) and legal statuses such as "citizen" or "undocumented worker" (Cunningham 2004; Wang 2004). Surprisingly, though, refugees merit little mention in these recent theoretical and empirical rethinkings of borders, underlining the ways in which debates about displacement and mobilities at borders frequently run on parallel but nonconverging tracks. Nonetheless, insights from scholars of displacement and emplacement may help point up some of the potential limitations of even the most cutting-edge border studies.

In envisioning a new conceptual framework for border studies, for example, Cunningham and Heyman (2004: 293) write of a "mobilities–enclosure continuum" based on the argument that "much of what we will say about mobility can be deduced from the fact that mobility is conceptually the inverse of enclosure" (2004: 294). In separate, individual essays, both scholars not surprisingly tend to contrast mobility with enclosure, even as they continually nod to the ways in which mobility and enclosure are intertwined – suggesting, in fact, a relationship different from that of the proposed continuum. Cunningham (2004: 346) analyzes migration along the US–Mexico border, reminding us of the need to attend to exclusion and "enclosed mobilities". Heyman (2004: 313) instead focuses on ports as a particular kind of border site, attending to "simultaneous acts of mobility and moves to enforce enclosure"; at the same time, he implicitly contrasts mobile flows of capital with variably mobile human flows through ports. Focused as they are on questioning the "mobility thesis" by highlighting borders' roles as places where movement may be obstructed or blocked, neither author recognizes that for some individuals, an *enclosed mobility* – that is, belonging to one state but being unable to migrate to another because of restrictive passport regimes – might be preferred to an *enforced movement* as refugee and/or stateless person. In some instances, then, enclosure may offer a form of protection and belonging (the right to nonmobility); it may even provide the grounds for mobility within a particular state or society that is denied to those cast out from that enclosure. To say this is not to rephrase the sedentarist bias nor to neglect the growing reality of what we might deem refugee enclosure or "preventive protection" (Hyndman 2000: 2), a strategy advocated by some international aid agencies to prevent (or contain) displacement across state borders. Rather, this suggests that, as helpful as it is, the notion of mobilities and enclosures requires further nuancing. Stronger integration of study of the displaced/emplaced within border studies offers a powerful way to do that; doing this recognizes that the dis/emplaced do not constitute "special" or unusual cases within border studies but may, in fact, represent limit cases that illustrate how far our theories and methods might take us. In turn, innovations in border studies also help reframe how we think about and study displacement.

Scholars of borders focused on the "regime of mobility" (Wang 2004) constituted by documents such as passports, for example, would do well to pay greater attention to refugees. Legal distinctions such as "citizen" or "refugee" (as opposed to internally displaced person) impact how displaced persons are received in host societies, the entitlements open to them, and (in some cases) possibilities for return. Yet as much as these statuses *constitute* the displaced/emplaced – for example, when a state denaturalizes individuals and pushes them to seek refuge across a border, or when the act of displacement itself creates a robust identity as a "refugee" (regardless of whether this status receives any official recognition) – processes of displacement and emplacement also play constitutive roles in the definition of citizenship and the creation of regimes designed to regulate state borders. In 1952, for example, Pakistan introduced passports as a means of curbing the entrance of Muslims from India into the new state. In both Pakistan and India, passports replaced a previous system of permits designed to address the perceived problems created by refugees (Fazila-Yacoobali Zamindar 2007: 161–162). A series of amendments made during the same time period to the Indian Citizenship Bill revolved around the issues opened up by migratory flows created by Partition (Fazila-Yacoobali Zamindar 2007: 176).

The issue of refugees and returnees thus proved central to the creation and consolidation of borders and citizenship regimes in India and Pakistan – not their mere "effects" or consequences. This reminds us that refugees frequently sit at the center of debates about national identity, given that they put in question the symbolic and physical boundaries of the nation and its members. For scholars, then, examining the figure of the displaced/emplaced person proves highly productive for interrogating the relationship between borders, sovereignty and citizenship. It is within this triadic relationship that individuals negotiate a sense of home in the legal, physical, and affective senses.

DISPLACEMENT AND EMPLACEMENT: NEW PERSPECTIVES

A common usage of displacement and emplacement sees them as opposite or mirror phenomena separated by borders, with emplacement denoting the act of remaining "in place." To some extent, this usage of displacement and emplacement is implied in Malkki's query about what it means not to be a refugee. Indeed, this is the primary sense in which I employed the distinction in my research on a population of "Italians" from the Istrian peninsula (today shared between Croatia and Slovenia), divided by partition and migration after World War II. In *History in Exile* (Ballinger 2003), I argued that the narrations of displacement by individuals who left Istria when it was transferred from Italy to socialist Yugoslavia had to be read in dialogue with the accounts of their kin and neighbors who stayed behind. The intersection of territorial borders with ideological ones in the aftermath of war meant that these competing narratives often contained accusations about the motivations of those on the other side. Beyond this narrative space, however, there existed a wide range of relationships with kin and former homes across the borders. At one end of the continuum were individuals who refused to cross the border and return the short distance to their former towns or villages. At the other, some exiles moved back to the Istrian peninsula after Yugoslavia's dissolution, thereby building connections with their lost "homeland." These examples point to a variety of other processes sometimes referred to under the label "emplacement," including the ways in which both those who migrated and those who remained rendered space meaningful (Jansen and Löfving 2009: 12).

Jansen and Löfving (2009: 13) note the diverse meanings attributed to the term emplacement. Some authors, for example, focus on the place-making capacities of emplacement as one of subjects/agents, whereas others see it as a process by which individuals and groups become emplaced (and sometimes immobilized) by powerful actors or processes. Löfving (2009: 157) considers definitions of emplacement across a wide range of disciplines:

> By far the most common usage of the concept today is in the field of geology. Emplacement designates the intrusion of igneous rocks into particular positions, or the development of an ore deposit in a particular place. Being emplaced could accordingly mean to be spatially fixed to degrees far beyond sedentarism . . . The other conventional usage of the term "emplacement" is military – it means a clearing on which heavy artillery is placed. If we combine these meanings, emplaced people become part of a political "battle" with very specific aims . . . Being emplaced thus means "being placed by others" and becomes a direct counterpart to displacement. Emplacement is redisplacement.

Though extensive, Löfving's exposition on the meanings of emplacement does not exhaust the ways in which emplacement might be employed as an analytic category for thinking about borders. Löfving's reading of emplacement focuses on the displacements inherent to being emplaced (often against one's will), whereas other scholars instead demonstrate how the displaced make home in new surroundings (thereby emplacing themselves) or how the "emplaced" (those who do not leave) must also re-emplace themselves as the meanings of place change around them. Running through all the variations on the usages of emplacement discussed here is the question of place-making, in particular the meanings associated with home and the feeling of being at home. Ethnographically oriented work on displacement and emplacement reveals the multiple meanings – and locations – of home, thereby challenging both sedentarist and anti-sedentarist perspectives that take one condition (fixity or mobility) as axiomatic (on this, see Stefansson 2004a: 3). Cunningham and Heyman's (2004: 295) insight that "enclosure is vital to place-making, as is mobility, not only in building up place from repeated connections, but also in defining certain movements as internal and others as external" underlines how a focus on borders can enrich empirical and analytical understanding of home in situations of dis/emplacement.

BORDERS, PLACE-MAKING AND THE BOUNDARIES OF HOME

Attention to borders and their relationship with various aspects of emplacement challenges unidimensional readings of displacement as merely entailing the act of leaving or being removed from a place. Writing of India's partition, Fazila-Yacoobali Zamindar (2007: 13) notes how border-making displaced "old ways of belonging for everyone." These displacements need not be external or visible to the eye but may also be internal ones that reconstitute individual subjectivities. Scholars of displacement have documented how those who experience the creation and imposition of new borders frequently express an interior sense of displacement, the sense of being "strangers in our own home" (Clark 2006; Čapo Žmegač 2007). This lament is heard just as frequently among those who remained "in place" as among those individuals who migrate across a border. This experience of displacement also figures prominently among those persons who migrate and later return to their "home," only to find that both they and their home have changed in the intervening period. Let us consider these various aspects of displacement in turn.

For both individuals who leave and those who do not, a border puts forms of sociality and belonging in question and transforms the everyday worlds they inhabit. Tense relationships between populations who left and their kin and neighbors who remained behind prove not uncommon. Anthropologist Ruth Behar acknowledges the ways in which her parents, Jews who left Cuba when the communist regime came to power, transmitted their paranoia to her. Just before a trip to Cuba in 1991, Behar fell ill (1995: 7). She later realized that her body had manifested an "internalized blockade – my own profound terror about returning." Behar's mother warned her of the islanders, " 'If they stayed in Cuba, it's because they're *comunistas*. Why would you want to go and meet *comunistas*?' " (Behar 2007: 14). Behar's mother thus assumed that remaining was an active choice that encoded an ideological preference. And, of course, such recriminations cut both ways, as when Cubans describe their exiled kin as "mutants" (Cámara 1995: 221). For those who leave, the presence of "stayees" may also serve as a reproach that puts into question claims about their lack of choice in leaving (Levy 2004: 104), a claim that may bring very real entitlements as victims. When the displaced find it difficult to rebuild lives elsewhere, the existence of stayees may also offer unsettling evidence of a "hypothetical biography . . . a present-day manifestation of their own past lives that took an alternate course" (2004: 104).

Many relationships do survive the emotional, physical and sometimes ideological distances imposed by displacement, however, as in the case of kin divided by the India–Pakistan border who continue to submit to considerable and costly bureaucratic obstacles in order to visit one another (Fazila-Yacoobali Zamindar 2007: 236). Likewise, the birth of new generations may offer new possibilities for relationships between the displaced and the stayees. Poet Richard Blanco recounts a trip to Cuba with his mother, who left both the island and close relatives behind. His mother complained about the degradation she sees in Havana whereas he found it lovely: "We were in Cuba, but not really, not the Cuba my mother remembers . . . Cuba had changed without her permission, though nothing had changed for me; I had no actual memories to hold up against the present, no before and after scenes flashing through my mind" (Blanco 2008: 20–21). This freedom from the past permits Blanco to "revel" in Cuba, even as he admits to envying his mother both her memories and her sense of a lost home (2008: 21). The parents who have known exile, though, may instead envy their children for their ability to enjoy Cuba without the acute pain of loss. Maria de los Angeles Torres says as much when she comments that her daughters "can reside in both spaces; they have not lost a home, they have gained a heritage" (1995: 41). For those born on the island but who departed when they were too young to form lasting memories of it, like Behar (2007: 3), Cuba may figure as a lost or "true" home, one whose reclamation lies forever out of reach as individuals find themselves "running away from home in order to run toward home."

At times the displaced may feel as or even more aggrieved by the behavior of their hosts in their new "homes" than by that of their former neighbors or families who did not take the path of migration. Many Istrian *esuli* or exiles I interviewed recalled the suspicion with which some of their fellow Italians had greeted them when they arrived in the ethnonational homeland in the decade after World War II. In some instances, the hostility had clear ideological motivations, as when members of the Italian Communist Party denounced the Istrian refugees as "fascists." In other cases, however, resentment over assistance for the newcomers in a situation of high unemployment and housing shortages gave expression to a more diffuse anti-immigrant hostility; here, assistance from the Italian state was premised upon the Istrians' status as Italian citizens, revealing the disjuncture between forms of legal and social belonging. Muslim migrants from India to Pakistan encountered similar rejections, as when newcomers were told, "Karachi is full" (Fazila-Yacoobali Zamindar 2007: 171). In such instances of return to a putative ethnonational homeland, the expectation that displaced persons will feel themselves at home – and be recognized as members of the community – may actually heighten the sense of dislocation.

Those who remain in the same ostensible place from which others depart complain that their sense of displacement is rarely acknowledged to the same degree as that of those who leave. In such situations there may arise a "monopoly of suffering" (Stefansson 2004b: 61), as the displaced and emplaced produce competing narratives of victimization. When, after the dissolution of Yugoslavia, former refugees from Istria employed the new vocabulary of "ethnic cleansing" to describe their experience, those who remained behind in what is now Croatian Istria also began to depict themselves as having suffered ethnic cleansing. For some exiles, this claim to an equal (or even greater) suffering smacked of opportunism by those who once embraced socialism and now, with the demise of Yugoslavia, sought to rewrite history. In addition, the new emphasis on the emplaced as victims accompanied the increase of quite tangible benefits from the "mother country," including possibilities for Italian citizenship.

Where Istrian exile narratives described the ways in which the departure of relatives led to persecution (such as firing from jobs or expropriations) that then prompted others to leave, those who remained countered by recalling their sense of desolation as neighbors migrated. Individuals who were young at the time possess visceral memories of these departures: the ever growing number of empty desks in the schoolroom, the icy wind that lashed their faces as they waved goodbye to those departing by ship, or the unfamiliarity of being surrounded by persons speaking Slavic variants rather than Istro-veneto (Italian) dialects. As Behar puts it, writing of the Cuban case, "Displacement has an emotional impact not only on those who leave, but also on those who stay. Back on the island, it is the responsibility of those who stay to wave goodbye and shed tears for the departed" (2008: 3). Yet the impacts extend well beyond the emotional, as those left behind may come to be viewed with suspicion by their neighbors or state authorities precisely because they are linked with those who have left (even, ironically, as those who leave may question the motives of those staying).

Individuals "emplaced" on the side of the border to which the displaced move, as opposed to those remaining in the areas from which displacees leave, may also experience a sense of displacement as the arrival of refugees alters their worlds. Feldman's (2007) research on Palestinians in Gaza highlights the dislocations experienced by both the post-1948 refugees migrating from areas that came under Israeli control and the long-term Palestinian populations residing in Gaza. The influx of refugees created a humanitarian crisis, one in which the status of refugee soon came to confer rights and benefits that "native" Gazans could not claim. In addition, refugee status "offered a recognition of this loss itself, which natives were denied" (Feldman 2007: 144). In this example, border-making processes constituted the refugee/nonrefugee category as a salient legal, social and economic boundary. In the peculiar situation of Palestinian citizenship in the absence of a state, refugeeness has become central to Palestinian claims more generally (Feldman 2007: 152–156). In many situations, factors such as whether the displaced have or may easily obtain citizenship in the land to which they migrate or whether they reside in refugee camps (see Malkki 1995a) may prove critical in determining the degree to which a sense of home may be constituted in diaspora.

For former refugees who return to a homeland, coming back can carry its own particular shocks. Those who suffered through war or other violence may resent it when those who escaped from the violence come back after hostilities cease. Stefansson (2004b) and Macek (2009) have documented the fraught relationships between

Sarajevans who returned after the Bosnian war (1992–1995) and those who stayed in the besieged city. "Natives" who remained in the city expressed their alienation from their home by referring to wartime as "imitation of life," a state in which normality disappeared (Macek 2009: 62). Natives frequently blamed those who left, as well as refugees who came to the city from other parts of Bosnia, for the loss of a "genuine" Sarajevan identity (Macek 2009: 87, 188). The emplaced Sarajevans thus attributed their own sense of interior displacement to both the literally displaced and the re-placed (the newcomers). From the other direction, Sarajevans who returned after the war often experienced survivors' guilt (Macek 2009: 93–94) and pursued strategies of invisibility (Stefansson 2004b: 65).

Returning to the place from which one was displaced is usually not just about an effort to go "home," however, but also about struggles over actual homes and properties with which identities may be intimately bound up (Brown 2004: 148; Fazila-Yacoobali Zamindar 2007: 124). Bureaucratic obstacles or the wholesale destruction of landscapes frequently make return of such properties slow and costly, if not impossible. In this situation, citizenship is often a necessary but insufficient condition for property claims. When return does become possible, family relationships may be torn apart not only by the different perspectives of the (formerly) displaced and emplaced but also by property disputes.

In her study of the border town of Kella in the former German Democratic Republic, Daphne Berdahl (1999) described a family divided for decades by the hard border between the two Germanies. In 1952, one daughter (Emma) had returned to Kella to take care of her elderly parents, while her siblings decided to stay in the West. In 1990, a year after the Wall came down, the Western relatives began to demand their share of the family house and property. This created bad feelings on all sides, as the siblings reminded Emma of the material assistance they had provided her over the years and Emma countered that her "sacrifice" in going back home ensured that the property had been preserved after their parents' death. In the end, the siblings broke off all communications. The erasure of the political border dividing Germany created an internal border within this family. Emma's husband noted the irony, "The border has disappeared but the rifts have become much deeper. We were more united with the border there" (Berdahl 1999: 166). This family's story reflects, in miniature, the dislocations brought about by German reunification.

In other instances where political changes (such as the collapse of authoritarian regimes) permit returns, however, former neighbors may greet returnees with curiosity and even sympathy. In her fieldwork among Tatars deported from the Crimea during the Soviet era, Uehling (2004: 223) reports that returnees often received assistance from former neighbors, who "confirmed who lived where, and explained which structures had been torn down or added in their absence." Tatars who squatted or seized property, however, were rarely met with such sanguine responses by local authorities or mafia (2004: 216–223).

Uehling emphasizes how her Tatar informants' understandings of their homeland involved deeply embodied experiences and memories. As Tatar repatriates walked pathways they had abandoned long ago, their bodies remembered where to go. In particular, "visiting houses triggered an unexpected flood of sensory-type memories in an environment that had been drained of other references" (2004: 224). Through the house, Tatars sought to re-emplace themselves in the homeland from which they or their parents had been deported decades earlier. Yet re-emplacement and the recreation of home through sensory memory practices may occur in a wide range of ways and environments (on this, see Hammond 2004 for Tigrayan refugees returned to different areas of Ethiopia from which they had fled).

Smith's (2003b, 2006) research on repatriates of Maltese origin who left Algeria for France after Algerian independence highlights the ways in which a distant, imagined homeland (in this case, Malta) may come to stand in for a lost homeland to which return proves impossible (Algeria). These *pieds-noirs* had no memories of Malta and rarely spoke of life in this "homeland" (Smith 2003b: 336–337). Trips to Malta by Maltese Algerian clubs, however, triggered memories of Algeria, as sights (the built environment, plants such as prickly pear cactus), sounds (the Maltese language, which resembles Arabic), and smells (the cooking of grilled sardines) temporarily emplaced these *pied-noirs* in a specific landscape (that of Malta) that they had never before experienced. In this re-emplacement, however, the *pieds-noirs* were no longer at the bottom of the colonial settler hierarchy nor viewed suspiciously by their fellow citizens of France. Rather, "Malta became Algeria and the Maltese themselves stood in place of indigenous Algerians" (2003b: 350). This example underscores the complex ways in which embodied memory may work to emplace or re-emplace the displaced, suggesting that scholars should be cautious in privileging returns to an originary space or home as more "authentically" embodied experiences or ones that restore integrity after rupture (a sedentarist perspective).

Likewise, some recent work on emplacement further challenges sedentarist assumptions that removal from a putative originary home necessarily produces alienation (Chu 2006: 396). In some contexts, emplaced subjects may experience their condition as one of incarceration in a space in which mobility is denied. In his long-term work in Southern Ethiopia, for example, Turton (2005) documents the state's increasing reduction of Mursi mobility accompanied by their own sense of marginalization. Chu's (2006) study of "competitive" house-building practices in Longyan, China, likewise reveals how house-building and senses of belonging (homeliness) are enabled by work outside of the town (elsewhere in China and abroad). In the cases studied by both Turton and Chu, dwelling (an index of rootedness according to a sedentarist perspective) becomes inextricably linked with movement. In Longyan, emplaced residents who did not have access to the resources that mobility brought felt themselves displaced within their own town as the homes of those with overseas connections eclipsed theirs in height and prestige (Chu 2006: 412). These examples evidence that physical movement/displacement need not carry with it a sense of loss; such loss may instead derive from lack of movement or enclosure, as scholars like Cunningham and Heyman have proposed. Whether movement or immobility is experienced as loss or gain frequently varies according to gender and age (Bahloul 1996; Borneman 1998). Indeed, the "groupness" of different populations should not be assumed but rather analyzed, given that experiences of displacement/emplacement may constitute powerful grounds for fashioning a sense of groupness, or alternatively, may foster new distinctions.

As my analysis suggests, the experiences of displacement and emplacement across borders bear an intrinsic relation to place-making but not in the straightforward manner we might imagine. Being at home may be the desired but impossible object of a return to a "lost" homeland, it may be achieved in a place distant from an original home, it may center on actual houses or it may be embodied by specific sounds or smells, among other things. Relationships of kinship and neighborliness may grow brittle and shatter with the distance of physical borders and time, or the removal of borders and the possibility for "returns" may instead erect new barriers between the various displaced and emplaced. The examples presented here neither prove nor refute the sedentarist or anti-sedentarist thesis but rather reveal the multiple and complex ways in which borders both reflect and shape relationships to place among the dis/emplaced.

New Directions: Borders, Migrations and Temporalities

The preceding discussion focused on spatial aspects of those place-making processes bound up with displacement and emplacement. Much of the scholarship also takes account of temporal aspects, although often in fairly limited ways that focus on displaced persons' unrealistic or outmoded views of the homeland or their future-oriented projections of return. More productive questions for future research instead revolve around the ways in which different state and economic regimes may instantiate divergent perceptions and experiences of *time* among displacees and stayees, as well as populations partitioned by a border.

Henri Lefebvre (2004) has suggested attending to both time and space by means of what he deems *rhythmanalysis*. Might Lefebvre's approach – which highlights regularities and cycles, as well as breaks ("arrhythmia" in Lefebvre's terms) – offer new ways for thinking about displacement and emplacement? Here I can offer only a brief comment but one that I hope will serve as the starting point for future research and debate. In *Rhythmanalysis*, Lefebvre contends, "Everywhere where there is interaction between a place, a time, and an expenditure of energy, there is rhythm" (2004: 15). He proposes that scholars attend to both repetition and ruptures, even as he recognizes that repetition always brings difference (2004: 6). Lefebvre further distinguishes between what he calls "brutal repetitions" such as those that capitalism exacts on the working body, and cyclical returns of festivals or rituals. In tracing out how so-called "natural rhythms" (including those of the life cycle) alter due to new political economies or technologies, Lefebvre also recognizes the ways in which time and its use may become objects of "bitter struggles" (2004: 74). For Lefebvre, the body stands as a simultaneous site at which different kinds of temporalities intersect, and as the very *instrument* of the rhythmanalyst, who "will come to 'listen' to a house, a street, a town, as an audience listens to a symphony" (2004: 19).

Can listening for the rhythms in mobilities in this manner reveal something new? Certainly, it directs greater attention to the ways in which displacement and emplacement alike may break old rhythms and inaugurate new ones as individuals inhabit diverse landscapes, economic systems, technological regimes, and so on. It also highlights the need for careful periodization of displacements, which may occur over considerable amounts of time and space. In the Istrian case that I know best, for instance, scholars and informants alike speak of an "exodus" as if it were a unitary event, despite the fact that diverse moments of migration reveal a complex rhythm of movements out of the peninsula in the decade after World War II. Similarly, some scholars of the Partition of the Indian subcontinent have urged reconsidering it within a much more extended geographical and temporal frame (Rahman and Van Schendel 2003; Fazila-Yacoobali Zamindar 2007).

Apart from periodization, we might discern different types of rhythms structuring migrations, as well as the situation of not leaving. Let me offer just a few examples here from ongoing research I am conducting on the "return" migrations of Italian nationals from the various possessions (ranging from former colonies to integral parts of the Italian state) that Italy lost after the defeat of Fascism. Although scholars have paid relatively little attention to the migrations of colonial settlers to the metropole (Smith 2003a), these flows highlight the problems with assuming that repatriation means "coming home" and the ambiguity inherent to the typology of migration as either voluntary or forced (see Brubaker 1998; Skran 1995: 15–16; Zolberg 1983: 27). Should we label Italian repatriates who came to the Italian peninsula with the juridical status of refugees as "forced migrants" displaced by the events of the war? Should those Italians who languished in the former African colonies (Ethiopia, Eritrea, Somalia, and Libya) awaiting permission to repatriate be considered as forcibly emplaced? How do we classify those Italian settlers who sought to return *to* Africa after World War II?

Given the complexity of Italian repatriation after the war, let me focus my brief discussion here on how a rhythm-analytic perspective opens up understandings of the movements of one particular group: Italian settlers in rural Libya after 1945. Following Highmore's (2002: 177) suggestion, I aim to take "mere snatches of rhythmicity and orchestrate them into more organized cadences." Visual materials may offer such glimpses of rhythms, as Highmore demonstrates through close study of photographs that reveal bodily inclinations shaped by a lifetime of rhythms. In the case of Italians settled in the villages established at the end of the 1930s under the auspices of the Istituto Nazionale Fascista della Previdenza Sociale (INFPS, after 1943 INPS), the registry cards that documented the settlers' activities make clear the intersection of various rhythms. The front of these cards recorded demographic information, such as date and place of birth for the heads of families and family members. A side column for "notes" documented when individuals (such as children) married, had offspring, partitioned land and households, moved away to other land parcels in the colonial settlements, repatriated back to Italy or reentered Libya, did military service, died, and so on. These modules can be read as a bureaucratic version of the kinship charts beloved by anthropologists. Simultaneously, however, they offer a visual representation of the intersection of various rhythms: biological rhythms of life and death, the distinct rhythms of war, and the complicated back and forth flows of repatriation during and after World War II. The impress of different pen colors, handwriting, and styles of notation also illustrates the passage of time and changes in personnel; files that continue into the 1950s (i.e. after Fascism and Libyan independence) contain roughly the same format but no longer record whether individuals were enrolled in the Fascist Party, for example. These documents thus reveal considerable continuity in the bureaucratic instruments employed by INFPS/INPS in Libya, as well as discontinuities created by the disappearance of the Fascist regime and Italian sovereignty over Libya.

Updated for those families still in Libya in 1951 when Italian authorities undertook a census, these registration cards are accompanied by a variety of documents, including requests for temporary or permanent repatriation to Italy, together with requests for family members to repatriate *back* to Libya. Health concerns (*motivi di salute*) constituted the overwhelming reason given by individuals seeking to leave Libya. Economic difficulties, such as bad harvests or reduced labor as sons started their own families and acquired their own land to work or migrated to the city of Tripoli or further afield, came in a close second. Here, the life cycle of the family and the disruptions and demographic imbalances of the war years weighed heavily on the ability of older parents to remain on their land in Libya. The INPS documents also contain a number of complaints about native pastoralists whose flocks damaged the crops; in the clash of sedentary/agricultural and transhumance cycles, settlers were no longer backed by a brutal colonial state willing and able to punish such "trespasses" by local populations.

The frequency of health problems prompts a number of speculations about rhythms. First, the Libyan climate and landscape likely disrupted the biological and bodily rhythms of many settlers, creating a host of physical irregularities (Lefebvre 2004: 74). Alternatively, health concerns may have provided the most legitimate reason for leaving in the eyes of INPS officials. This underscores the fact that even as late as 1959, Italian settlers in Libya did not enjoy freedom of movement; they could not simply leave the rural villages and move to Italy but rather had to furnish reasonable motivations for doing so and have their requests approved. Here, emplacement in the villages was accompanied by a sense of displacement as the Italian colonial regime disappeared and the settlers became merely tolerated presences within an independent Libya.

In this new context, Italian personnel knew that each parcel of land abandoned definitively would be "lost" to Libyans, given that departing Italians had to renounce their claims. Thus INPS officials frequently sought to slow the rhythms of migration, although they realized that they could not halt them entirely. Italians seeking to repatriate to Italy needed to pay for their trip on one of the ships that plied the Mediterranean; INPS personnel deliberated whether to cover the passage of those unable to do so. Those repatriates permitted to go to Italy but without housing then had to request temporary placement in a refugee camp, as many did.

The dossiers on colonial families evidence that in decisions about whether and, if so, when to leave, seasonal cycles (such as those of planting, the harvest and weather) also played a notable role. In 1954, drought prompted many colonists to seek to repatriate to Italy, despite the fact that they would arrive as refugees in the middle of winter, which would bring its own problems. In other cases, however, colonists who had presented repatriation requests then withdrew them, because they did not want to leave before the harvest or to go to Italy during the winter months, having received news about the hardships of the camps. These examples reveal how various rhythms (and "arrhythmias") influenced individual decisions about whether to become a colonial repatriate/refugee, as well as the timing of departures from Libya. In negotiating their departures with INPS and the Italian state, settlers exerted agency in whatever ways they could (for example, paying doctors to provide certificates stating they had health conditions that necessitated migration). This example highlights the potential for rhythmanalysis to raise new questions in the study of displacement/emplacement in the context of changing borders.

This case also underscores the complicated calculus of choice and constraint that informs decisions about migration, including "forced" migration. Brubaker cautions that the very label "forced migration" (or displacement) "obscures the fact that there is almost always, even in the case of flight from immediately threatening violence, a more or less significant element of will or choice involved in the act of migration" (1998: 1049). Decisions about the act of migration, such as whether to leave or stay, unfold in a global terrain crisscrossed by borders and marked out by agencies of various sorts, including states and international bodies and overlapping legal regimes of protection and legal statuses of belonging (notably citizenship).

CONCLUSION

Examples of migratory flows that unfolded in Africa as borders were being redrawn provide the bookends for this essay. Rouch's footloose Songhay travelers contrast with Italian settlers in Libya struggling to break out of carceral structures of rural colonialism that endured even after decolonization. Such images of mobile "natives" and immobilized "colonials" challenge many assumptions, including sedentarist ones that valorize emplacement or critiques that claim that cosmopolitan intellectuals promoting anti-sedentarist approaches necessarily endorse elitist visions. These examples also point to larger theoretical dilemmas about how to classify migrants. In practice, the boundary between forced and voluntary migration is often more porous than many scholars would have it, suggesting that we need to bring dis/emplacement closer to the center of both migration and border studies. Finally, these examples underscore the need to analyze mobilities and enclosures as interrelated processes, processes whose workings often become most apparent at and around borders.

NOTE

This chapter was written while a fellow at the Center for Advanced Study in the Behavioral Sciences (CASBS) at Stanford University. I am grateful to CASBS for providing the time and space in which to reflect upon the topic of displacement and borders. In this piece I draw on research conducted over many years and made possible by a variety of sponsors, in particular the Fletcher Fund and the Faculty Development Fund at Bowdoin College. I thank Hastings Donnan and Tom Wilson for their sound editorial advice in taming an unruly set of arguments. Ruth Mandel also read an earlier version and offered helpful comments.

REFERENCES

Adelman, H. and McGrath, S. 2007. To date or to marry: that is the question. *Journal of Refugee Studies* 20: 376–380.

Bahloul, J. 1996. *The Architecture of Memory*. Cambridge: Cambridge University Press.

Ballinger, P. 2003. *History in Exile: Memory and Identity at the Borders of the Balkans*. Princeton: Princeton University Press.

Behar, R. 1995. Introduction. In R. Behar, ed., *Bridges to Cuba/Puentes a Cuba*, pp. 1–18. Ann Arbor: University of Michigan Press.

Behar, R. 2007. *An Island Called Home: Returning to Jewish Cuba*. New Brunswick: Rutgers University Press.

Behar, R. 2008. After the bridges. In R. Behar and L.M. Suárez, eds, *The Portable Island: Cubans at Home in the World*, pp. 3–8. New York: Palgrave Macmillan.

Berdahl, D. 1999. *Where the World Ended: Re-unification and Identity in the German Borderland*. Berkeley: University of California Press.

Blanco, R. 2008. Wherever that may be. In R. Behar and L.M. Suárez, eds, *The Portable Island: Cubans at Home in the World*, pp. 19–24. New York: Palgrave Macmillan.

Borneman, J. 1998. *Grenzregime* (border regime): the Wall and its aftermath. In T.M. Wilson and H. Donnan, eds, *Border Identities: Nation and State at International Frontiers*, pp. 162–190. Cambridge: Cambridge University Press.

Brown, K. 2004. *A Biography of No Place: From Ethnic Borderland to Soviet Heartland*. Cambridge: Harvard University Press.

Brubaker, R. 1998. Migrations of ethnic unmixing in the "new Europe." *International Migration Review* 32 (4): 1047–1065.

Cámara, M. 1995. Third options: beyond the border. In R. Behar, ed., *Bridges to Cuba/Puentes a Cuba*, pp. 217–225. Ann Arbor: University of Michigan Press.

Čapo Žmegač, J. 2007. *Strangers Either Way: The Lives of Croatian Refugees in Their New Home*, trans. N.H. Antoljak and M.M. Stanojevic. New York: Berghahn.

Chalfin, B. 2004. Border scans: sovereignty, surveillance and the customs service in Ghana. *Identities* 11 (3): 397–416.

Chimni, B.S. 2009. The birth of a "discipline": from refugee to forced migration studies. *Journal of Refugee Studies* 22 (1): 11–29.

Chu, J.Y. 2006. To be "emplaced": Fuzhounese migration and the politics of destination. *Identities* 13 (3): 395–425.

Clark, B. 2006. *Twice a Stranger: The Mass Expulsion That Forged Modern Greece and Turkey*. Cambridge: Harvard University Press.

Cohen, R. 2007. Response to Hathaway. *Journal of Refugee Studies* 20: 370–376.

Cunningham, H. 2004. Nations rebound? Crossing borders in a gated globe. *Identities* 11 (3): 329–350.

Cunningham, H. and Heyman, J. McC. 2004. Introduction: mobilities and enclosures at borders. *Identities* 11 (3): 289–302.

de los Angeles Torres, M. 1995. Beyond the rupture: reconciling with our enemies, reconciling with ourselves. In R. Behar, ed., *Bridges to Cuba/Puentes a Cuba*, pp. 24–43. Ann Arbor: University of Michigan Press.

Fazila-Yacoobali Zamindar, V. 2007. *The Long Partition and the Making of Modern South Asia: Refugees, Boundaries, Histories*. New York: Columbia University Press.

Feldman, I. 2007. Difficult distinctions: refugee law, humanitarian practice, and political identification in Gaza. *Cultural Anthropology* 22 (1): 129–169.

Hammond, L.C. 2004. *This Place Will Become Home: Refugee Repatriation to Ethiopia*. Ithaca: Cornell University Press.

Hathaway, J.C. 2007. Forced migration studies: could we agree just to "date"? *Journal of Refugee Studies* 20 (3): 349–369.

Heyman, J. McC. 2004. Ports of entry as nodes in the world system. *Identities* 11 (3): 303–327.

Highmore, B. 2002. Street life in London: towards a rhythmanalysis of London in the late nineteenth century. *New Formations* 47: 171–193.

Hyndman, J. 2000. *Managing Displacement: Refugees and the Politics of Humanitarianism*. Minneapolis: University of Minnesota Press.

Jansen, S. and Löfving, S. 2009. Introduction: towards an anthropology of violence, hope and the movement of people. In S. Jansen and S. Löfving, eds, *Struggles for Home: Violence, Hope and the Movement of People*, pp. 1–24. New York: Berghahn Books.

Lefebvre, H. 2004. *Rhythmanalysis: Space, Time, and Everyday Life*, trans. S. Elden and G. Moore. London: Continuum.

Levy, A. 2004. Homecoming to the diaspora: nation and state in visits of Israelis to Morocco. In F. Markowitz and A.H. Stefansson, eds, *Homecomings: Unsettling Paths of Return*, pp. 92–108. Lanham: Lexington Books.

Löfving, S. 2009. Liberal emplacement: violence, home and the transforming space of popular protest in Central America. In S. Jansen and S. Löfving, eds, *Struggles for Home: Violence, Hope and the Movement of People*, pp. 149–172. New York: Berghahn Books.

Macek, I. 2009. *Sarajevo under Siege: Anthropology in Wartime*. Philadelphia: University of Pennsylvania Press.

Malkki, L. 1992. National geographic: the routing of peoples and the territorialization of national identity among scholars and refugees. *Cultural Anthropology* 7 (1): 24–44.

Malkki, L. 1995a. *Purity and Exile: Violence, Memory, and National Cosmology among Hutu Refugees in Tanzania*. Chicago: University of Chicago Press.

Malkki, L. 1995b. Refugees and exile: from "refugee studies" to the national order of things. *Annual Review of Anthropology* 24: 495–523.

Rahman, M. and Van Schendel, W. 2003. "I am not a refugee": rethinking partition migration. *Modern Asian Studies* 37 (3): 551–584.

Skran, C. 1995. *Refugees in Inter-war Europe: The Emergence of a Regime*. Oxford: Oxford University Press.

Smith, A. 2003a. Europe's invisible migrants. In Andrea Smith, ed., *Europe's Invisible Migrants*, pp. 9–32. Amsterdam: University of Amsterdam Press.

Smith, A. 2003b. Place replaced: colonial nostalgia and *pied-noir* pilgrimages to Malta. *Cultural Anthropology* 18 (3): 329–364.

Smith, A. 2006. *Colonial Memory and Postcolonial Europe: Maltese Settlers in Algeria and France*. Bloomington: Indiana University Press.

Stefansson, A.H. 2004a. Homecomings to the future: from diasporic mythographies to social projects of return. In F. Markowitz and A.H. Stefansson, eds, *Homecomings: Unsettling Paths of Return*, pp. 2–20. Lanham: Lexington Books.

Stefansson, A.H. 2004b. Sarajevo suffering: homecoming and the hierarchy of homeland hardship. In F. Markowitz and A.H. Stefansson, eds, *Homecomings: Unsettling Paths of Return*, pp. 54–75. Lanham: Lexington Books.

Stoller, P. 1992. *The Cinematic Griot: The Ethnography of Jean Rouch*. Chicago: University of Chicago Press.

Turton, D. 2005. The meaning of place in a world of movement: lessons from long-term field research in Southern Ethiopia. *Journal of Refugee Studies* 18 (3): 258–280.

Uehling, G. L. 2004. *Beyond Memory: The Crimean Tatars' Deportation and Return*. New York: Palgrave Macmillan.

Wang, H. 2004. Regulating transnational flows of people: an institutional analysis of passports and visas as a regime of mobility. *Identities* 11 (3): 351–376.

Zolberg, A. 1983. The formation of new states as a refugee-generating process. *Annals of the American Society of Political and Social Science* 457: 24–38.

CHAPTER 23 Remapping Borders

Henk van Houtum

This chapter seeks to further the discussion on the theorization of b/ordering processes. More particularly, I explore how justice can be done to visual representation
in the mapping of the b/ordering of migration. To focus on migration is not necessarily a self-evident characteristic of the border. But increasingly it has become one
of the most politically sensitive and influential factors shaping the nature and consequences of borders in our time. Constant border work is being carried out to try to
separate the wanted from the unwanted, the imagined barbarians from the civilized,
and the global rich from global poor. Especially after 9/11, we have seen more stress
on the bordering of territory and the protection of society. The desire to control and
reclaim space, power and national identity and to immunize against an imagined
threat from the illegal and/or Muslim migrant has found new nationalistic and
increasingly populist political adherents and partisans in many parts of the world. The
result is that the unwanted migrants have come to epitomize the extraterritoriality
of the exclusive state (Agamben 1998). Obviously, these practices of geo- and biopolitical control, which often coincide with fear-mongering security and migration
politics and the carving up of territorial containers and purified 'dreamlands' of identity, have a counterpart. This other world is the (dreamland of) escape into openness
and freedom, into a world of global democratic development and global distributive
justice. But it seems that the development of this other world is now much lower on
the political agenda. As a result, the ontological multidimensionality which is intrinsic
to any border is increasingly subordinated to the defensive filtering dimension of a
border (see also Reichert 1992). Put differently, the border, which is a necessary and
unfixable continuum between openness and closure rather than a line, is being interpreted chiefly as a line of security and protection, often coinciding with an inward-
looking reproduction and canonization of the history and culture it is believed to
contain The stress is on the building of a protective inner space or, in the words of
philosopher Peter Sloterdijk, "a sphere," and not on the possible consequences

A Companion to Border Studies, First Edition. Edited by Thomas M. Wilson and
Hastings Donnan.
© 2012 Blackwell Publishing Ltd. Published 2012 by Blackwell Publishing Ltd.

of overprotection and inward-looking behavior. The desire to open the border, to seize the spirit of the fall of the Berlin Wall, and to escape topo-logical thinking seems even further removed from us now than at the beginning of the 1990s (Reichert 1992).

Paradoxically, despite the growth of a rebordering ideology after 9/11, the network-like globalization of travel has further increased. Whereas in the past human migration often meant having to reborder one's own nationality and identity – almost to the extent of having to be "reborn" into the new nation – today people can travel quickly and maintain contact with several places at the same time. Mobility and migration typically consist of an ongoing series of cross-border movements in which people develop and maintain numerous economic, social and cultural links in more than one nation. Generally, this phenomenon is described as "*trans*nationalism," a term that suggests that today's migration is more than moving from and to closed entities – the nation states. In a sense, as so often argued, the world of travel, information, communication and migration has shrunk (Ernste et al. 2009). Due to cheaper travel and communication, it has become easier to stay in close touch with the country of origin while living elsewhere. Hence, it could be argued that national identities and national communities are increasingly transnational identities and transnational communities. Consequently, to conceive of the world primarily in terms of rationally organized hierarchies of sharply bounded territorial containers is no longer adequate, if it ever was (van Houtum and van Naerssen 2002; van Houtum 2005). The fact that many mobile people and migrants are crossing borders and have become transmobile and transmigrants – and thus find themselves neither only here nor only there, but mentally, virtually and digitally in several places at the same time – has therefore important consequences for the concepts of borders, nation and identities. It implies that geopolitical borders cannot be understood as discrete, fixed and dichotomous.

This insight builds on the rich debate that is involved in the turn to bordering rather than border studies. Whereas in the early 1960s the field of border studies was predominantly focused on the study of the demarcation of boundaries and the borderline, now the focus has arguably shifted to examining the continuous construction of borders: the process of bordering (see, for instance, van Houtum and van Naerssen 2002; van Houtum 2005; Newman 2006; Parker et al. 2009). A border today is dominantly understood as a belief in the presence and continuity of a spatially binding power, which is objectified in everyday sociopolitical practices. Put differently, the attention has moved away from the study of the evolution and changes of the territorial line to borders seen as differentiators of socially constructed mindscapes, identities and meanings (see also Donnan and Wilson 1999; Wilson and Donnan 1998). The observation that the making of borders is the product of people's own social practices and habitus has led to the study of borders beyond a focus on states or nations. The turn to "bordering" starts from the assumption that any border is not a stand-alone entity, detached from other territories or societies, but is a socio-spatially constructed and always dynamic configuration of social relations and networks. And as this approach also applies to territories other than states, such as (macro)regions, cities and neighborhoods, a border is now increasingly seen in the scholarly literature as less connected to states alone. The claim often heard in the 1980s that social, anthro-

pological and (geo)political studies fell into a kind of territorial trap by overemphasiz-
ing state borders is thus now much less applicable.

Borders are now typically no longer seen as given, fixed, linear or stable and are
conceptualized instead in terms of a much more open perspective on territoriality. It
is widely recognized that the interlinkages between places and people are loosening
the classic triangle between territory–identity–citizenship. In the process, these interlinkages between places, borders and people are being re-ontologized. Borders are
increasingly carried around over space by the human body and mind. They have
become dispersed and diffused. This means that in a given territorial entity the many
borders embodied in the temporary and not so temporary stay of migrants, tourists,
entrepreneurs, football players and managers, for example, are co-emerging and
coexisting. Put differently, borders can be seen as interfaces between people that
reveal themselves contingently.

What this shift in the understanding of borders implies is that the dominant representation of places and people as separate entities, and borders as two-dimensional
lines on a map, is a naive representation of the transnational complexity and multiplicity of human life. Yet here we still see a gap. For despite the turn to bordering
studies, the static visual representation of state borders still inspires most of the work
in the field, thereby reproducing dominant geopolitical practice.

In this chapter I consider what I see as a main challenge for a border studies
beyond the classic state-borderology: how to develop a more apt visual representation
of borders and migration, one that does not begin with the default option of the
nation-state border as a line and migration as an arrow crossing it. Can we represent
borders visually in a way that is intrinsically dynamic and subject to constant reproduction? Can we map the border work? And can we map the moving of and moving
across borders? In what follows I question the dominant visual representations of
migration and indicate what directions could be taken in mapping the mobility
of people and their personal linkages across state borders.

THE ART OF MAPPING BORDERS

Although looking at planet earth from a satellite makes clear that there are no
borders,[1] which immediately suggests that borders are human constructs, in an
average atlas the classic political approach of the bordered world prevails. Typically
an atlas of the world shows a globe divided into states. An average map is still used
as a cartographically ordered power-logic with lines and colors that delineate the
borders of territorially differentiated sovereignties. This point could be taken further.
I would venture that the default option when representing borders on the globe is
to show state borders. Apparently, the nineteenth-century ideal of the nation-state
has become rooted very firmly in our idea and visualization of borders. This state-grid
approach to mapping borders has had an immense impact on our daily lives. Weather
charts, school geography and history atlases, travel guides: state border maps are
everywhere, telling you where the borders of countries lie and thereby where you
are from or what your position is, by saying "you are here." This biased perspective
on what borders are or how they should or could be understood is more than merely

a representation of the world. As an image of the world it has shaped and continues to shape our (perception of our) world. I would argue that this perspective – one that sees mapping intrinsically as a political science, as a science of nineteenth-century political order, conquest and discovery – not only excludes the factual sociology, anthropology and geography of twenty-first century globalization and transnationalism, but it also excludes imagination, identifications, emotions, and beliefs outside the visible geopolitical realm. Moreover, it excludes the moving and mobile people inside what is imagined to be a fixed and static state-container. This "state-border gridism" becomes particularly evident when analyzing the maps of migration. Let us look more closely at this.

The use of static border-geometry in the case of the mapping of migration is not an anomaly but rather the dominant way of representation in the media, education, politics and the academy. Often no further explanation is given on the use of the semiotics, symbols and visual concepts of and behind the map. This implies that the map of the borders of today, although vividly and paradoxically reshaped by migration, is still taken for granted as static, untouched and fixed. Examples abound. For instance, when trying to represent undocumented migration, most "official" maps, whether of the United States or the European Union, indicate an imagined territorial container crisscrossed with thick arrows and lines supposed to indicate the routes, trajectories, and transit zones of undocumented migrants (see Figures 23.1 and 23.2). The thick lines, dots and arrows in Figures 23.1 and 23.2 are intended to represent migration flows. In presenting movement in this way, migration is explicitly represented as massive, unidirectional and unstoppable flows toward an

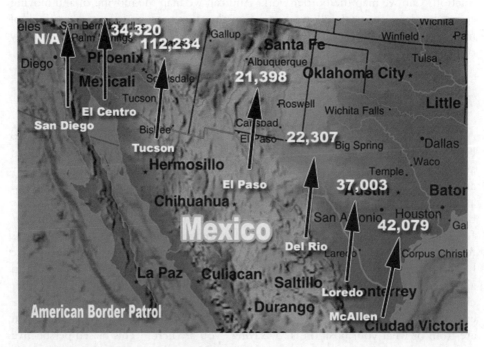

Figure 23.1   The migrant routes into the US
Source: https://segue.atlas.uiuc.edu/uploads/hancho/ImmigrationMap2003.gif.

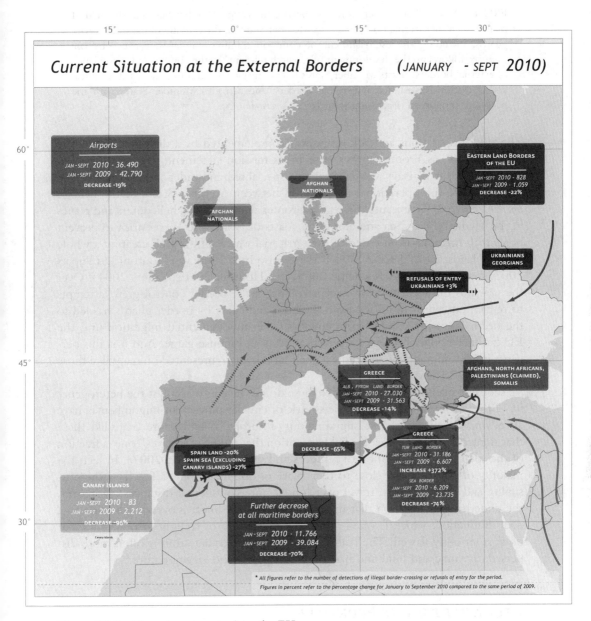

Figure 23.2   The migrant routes into the EU
Source: Frontex, 2010 (http://www.frontex.europa.eu/situation_at_the_external_border/art18.html).

imagined, reactive and vulnerable bordered fixity of the US and the EU – it is as if migration should be seen as an unfriendly invasion. For those educated in Europe like me, such maps recall the maps once shown in history class which illustrated visually successive invasions in Europe by foreign armies.[2] Fitting with this image, the EU's external border agency Frontex speaks of "risk analysis," and of "operations" in their mission, which is defined in the following way:

FRONTEX coordinates operational cooperation between Member States in the field of management of external borders; assists Member States in the training of national border guards, including the establishment of common training standards; carries out *risk analyses*; follows up the development of research relevant for the control and surveillance of external borders; assists Member States in circumstances requiring increased technical and operational assistance at external borders; and provides Member States with the necessary support in organising joint return *operations* . . .[3]

The talk of operations and risk analyses is complemented by a discourse of security and insurance, as Frontex makes clear in its mission statement: "Frontex, the EU agency based in Warsaw, was created as a specialised and independent body tasked to coordinate the operational cooperation between Member States in the field of *border security*."[4] To execute these tasks Frontex deploys boats, helicopters and planes in the Mediterranean Sea and along the coasts of North and West Africa to prevent boats with migrants from entering the territorial waters of the EU, creating a whole new EU landscape of defense and fences (see also Inda 2006; van Houtum and Pijpers 2007; van Houtum and Boedeltje 2009; van Houtum 2010; Walters 2004). Over the years, as the securitization and patrolling of the border control grew, attempts to remain unseen or to escape from the hunt and chase by border guards has led to the deaths of many would-be immigrants. The undocumented migration into the EU has increasingly become perceived as a cat-and-mouse game. And it is this perverse and for migrants often deadly game that is being represented on maps like those in Figures 23.1 and 23.2.

Yet these maps are false. Maps like these do not take into account the heterogeneity of those who move, the possible shuttle or circular movement migrants may have already made, and the people migrating out of Europe. What is more, maps like these that suggest invasions of people fail to mention that the EU "receives" only a fraction of the total global population of refugees and migrants (Walters 2007). In fact, the majority of migrants stay close to their place of origin and only a few have the possibility and/or the will to travel over longer, intercontinental distances. Moreover, the underlying assumption that migration is a one-off linear movement leading to a final destination, which is often illustrated by the use of straight arrows, lines and dots, is seriously flawed. The reality of undocumented migration is often more dispersed, dynamic and fluid and has more of a transit and zigzag nature.

CECI N'EST PAS UNE FRONTIÈRE

The misrepresentations of the dominant migration maps like those above have important consequences. Static invasion maps not only represent moral panics, they also co-construct them. Maps are and can never be neutral. A map cannot escape being productive; it fabricates an image, a lens on the world. It frames our minds and thereby our world. A mapping of migration and borders in the way described above thus not only re-presents the world, it is making Truth. As many critical cartographers have convincingly shown, the classic framing of the world via state maps predominantly serves the geopolitical goal that a bordered territory is imagined and believed to be different and distinct from other territories (see, e.g., Harley 1989; Pickles 2004; Crampton and Krygier 2006; van Houtum 2009; de Mug 2010). As Harley (1989) argues, it is no wonder then that in modern Western society maps quickly became crucial to the maintenance of state power – to its boundaries, its commerce, its internal administration, its control of populations, and its military strength. A state border is represented mainly as a strategic and intentional force, as a locus and focus of control.

What such container-like maps of borders prominently and typically re-present is a statist narration of distinctive coherence, which adds to the desired bounding of space through symbols, media, narratives and a common name for a chosen set of historically materialized social relations. Bordering and ordering territory in this way communicate the making of a place, in order to classify what is within and what is beyond. Seen through this lens, a border on the map colonizes the free and constantly ontologically reinterpreted space that truth necessarily is. The border on the map demarcates, represents and communicates truth, but it is thereby not truth itself. Put differently, the signifier of the map is not the world as we, the signified, know it, as Foucault (1982) argued when discussing the work of the surrealist painter René Magritte (*Ceci n'est pas une pipe* (This is not a pipe)). The map of a border, however shaped and curved, is *surreal*, it *is* not a border (see Figure 23.3). What a map of a border therefore actually creates is a gap, a difference. The representation of a border as a line of difference is making a difference. Or as Wood has famously argued, the map's effectiveness lies in the selectivity with which it is produced (Wood 1993). A map is an image of reality, a truth outside truth itself. Inner and external border maps are the construction of a reality and truth in a certain context, and in a certain spatial entity. What is seen as truth in one's own domain can be a lie in the space and/or eyes of an Other. And what conventional reality is in the own domain can be a doomed image or fantasy in the domains and/or eyes of the Other. A map of a state border and migration as a unidirectional, uni-versal arrow crossing that state border is therefore *active*: it represents space in such a way that it facilitates its domination and control. It communicates a truth, it actively constructs knowledge, it silences the

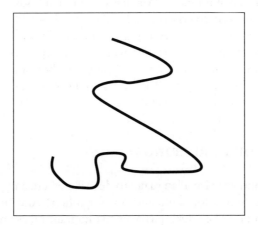

Figure 23.3   *Ceci n'est pas une frontière*

unrepresented, it visually excludes what it wishes to decline politically and it exercises geopower. The telling of the story is therefore more important than the mere visibility of the border. And stories will differ over time, over space and over people. The story and the interpretation of the border, and the reasons it is defined as it is, are matters of politics. Mapping the border in the way it is mapped is hence cartopolitics, drawing-table politics. And using that same uni-versal script of state border dominance, every cartopolitics makes its own statist maps, its own state plans, its own outer-state strangers, and its own statist u-topia – for where borderlines and dots become dominant, people are erased. Cartopolitics in its core, therefore, is cartographic cleansing. It consciously silences what is not represented and it dehumanizes the landscape.

The average geopolitical map predominantly works with the idea of state borders as a kind of unquestioned, self-evident border (see also Scott 2002). But as the present debate in border studies – or better perhaps, *bordering* studies – has learned, there are no uni-versal borders, nor is there a one-and-only original border, there is no *pre*border. The reality of the border is created by the meaning that is attached to it. A line is geometry, a border is interpretation. A gate may be a threshold for some and a passage for others. And a wall may be a "protection" against the imagined pernicious influence of others behind that wall for some and to others mostly a place to spray graffiti. A border can be drawn spatially everywhere. It is the symbolic meaning attributed to the appearance of the line which must be seen as constructor of the normative form. A border is made real through imagination. So what is important to the study of borders is not the item of the border per se, but the objectification process of the border, the socially constituent power practices attached to a border that construct a spatial effect and which give a demarcation in space its meaning and influence. So the border may communicate a truth, but this truth is crucially dependent on constant border work to make this truth real and trustworthy. In other words, a territorial border is the continuous production of a mask (see van Houtum 2011). And in this masking of reality the visual representation of borders as lines on maps and the imagined threat of those who "invade" the imagined unity of "us" play an important role. The Bordering and Ordering done in and by container-states that is communicated via maps often then leads to a persistent Othering (van Houtum and van Naerssen 2002). The world outside the domain-making border is instrumentalized by representing it symbolically as a foreign country, the competitor, the enemy, or chaos, against which the unique consistent and uniform cultural identity and tradition of our own unity will be mirrored. This may then indeed contribute to the perception that the coming of unwanted others, as argued above, is represented as an invasion.

THE RHYTHM OF BORDERINGS

How then can we find the visual language to describe where a migrant goes and how as a result a border moves for some and not for others? And how can we find the words or images to describe which passages the migrant takes and has taken, where he or she finds a shelter, or when a territory touches, pleases or teaches him or her?

And how can we map the many formal rules and informal conventions and cultural rites preventing migrants from entering certain territories, or openly using certain places, the invisible borders for migrants in a territory, the presence of "illegals," the variations in tempo, speed and rhythms in the territory, the waiting of migrants in detention centers, the different reception and appreciation of the sounds of the territories, the traveling of one's thoughts, the feeling of being at home in strange territories and the feeling of estrangement in one's "home" territory?

Can we and if so how can we represent these human borderings, human becomings, movements and migrations on a map? To begin with, it would be good to lose some of the pretensions geometry retains and realize that there is no plan, word or visualization that is *the* border or *the* migrant. For, it is humans as multidimensional and intrinsically socially sensitive beings who make the places we live in, not the lines and dots drawn on maps. A few inspiring, although still fragmented, attempts to provide alternative representations of migration patterns have been made already, mainly by what could be called a "radical cartography," such as Migmap, IndyMedia and Migreurop (see Bhagat and Mogel 2008). Until now, however, these detailed accounts and alternative representations of migration have been washed away in the highly influential mediated images of the "invasion" of unwanted migrants. What is more, despite their good intentions to form a counternarrative to the hegemony of fear-mongering migration maps, many of these alternative maps still work mainly with classic state-like maps, including bordered boxes and dots suggestive of states and humans respectively.

It is remarkable that we have still not overcome the Euclidean geometry of maps, whereas the representation of people and their relationships have gone through a revolutionary phase. I am thinking especially of the representational world of the internet (e.g., Facebook, LinkedIn, YouTube), which in contrast to classic maps, does explicitly chart human beings and their relations, yet largely without a multidimensional and spatially layered context. This poses a challenge to cartographers, anthropologists, political scientists, geographers and others to collaborate with filmmakers and image artists not only to map the urban surface on which we humans live and move but also to represent the (e)motions and physical passage of people across these surfaces, if possible interactively. Paradoxical as this may seem, the map should thus have an open eye, and visualize things that cannot be mapped, that are not re-presented, things or people that are absented, the human rhizomatic be*comings*, zigzag connections, traces, tracks and linkages, and the movements and (e)motions that cannot be universally rationalized, yet are felt, sensed and believed (Deleuze and Guattari 1987; Papadopoulos et al. 2008). A famous and striking example of a rhizomatic map is that by the composer Sylvano Bussotti, presented by Deleuze and Guattari in their book *A Thousand Plateaus* (see Figure 23.4). In this figure, spatial movement is represented as a rhythm, but then imagined as an erratic, chaotic flux. The rhythm itself is understood as a migration, an endless becoming, a constant flux of connections which together make a zigzag line. It is thus anything other than a universal, unidirectional arrow-like line. The totalitarian fixation on an essential past, a utopian future as represented by an arrow, is absent. What dominates is not the vertical or horizontal binary connections, or the uni-versal script of state border mapping, but the *transversal* network.

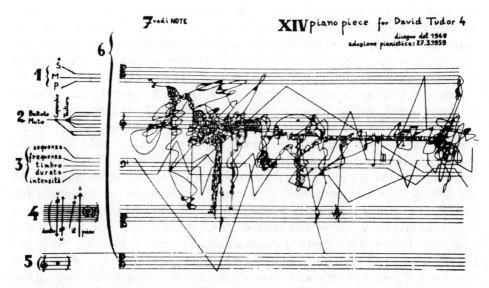

Figure 23.4 Rhizome
Source: Notation by Sylvano Bussotti, reproduced in Deleuze and Guattari 1987: 3.

Another interesting source of inspiration for the development of an ethical aesthetics of borders and migration is the documentary *Welcome Europa* by Bruno Ulmer. In this road movie one sees several young adults from various countries outside the EU without passports moving around in European spaces. They move around like ghosts, like shadow-travelers, trying to survive in the streets of different European cities without the proper documents. Again, what is striking is that the movement has a zigzag nature and includes long periods of waiting and significant immobility (see also Schapendonk 2011).

The argument that I wish to make here is that the quest for new kinds of mapping is a matter of consciousness rather than sight, of making present to the mind's eye what is visibly absent (Donald 1999). The map of the territory is or should be as dynamic as the human beings who make and give meaning to territory. The tempo, rhythm and (e)motions of people in space and not the fixity or the settling down should be central. And so the logic of being and the ontology of stasis needs to be more often and more seriously confronted, or at the least complemented with a logic of *becoming* and an ontology of the process, since what is crucial is to train our eye on the relations of movements and speeds and moments of waiting, rest and immobility (see also Schapendonk 2011). So, perhaps, instead of only *carto*graphy, we need a *choreo*graphy of space. This would mean that we would neither try to map the other immediately nor only map them as someone not-from-Here. By way of example, this persistent grounding is well expressed in the Dutch dichotomy *allochtonen* and *autochtonen* to mark the difference between Dutch and foreign-born people, in which Allos refers to other and Autos to the Self or own and Chtonos to ground. We can do without such territorial mapping of people in this time and age. A further example of this ground-politics is expressed in the question typically asked when meeting another for the first time: where are you *from*? Perhaps, following the logic of zigzag-ging and endless becoming, the emphasis should not be on the where and the belonging, which involves a fixation with mapping the other, but on the coming to be and the longing to be: where are you *coming* from? In other words, the focus should not be on the *roots*, but the *routes* of migrants.

CONCLUSION

I began this chapter by referring to how the field of border studies has developed over the last few decades. Clearly, the field of border studies has blossomed and has grown in many interesting directions. It has become clear that the philosophy and practices of b/ordering and othering, of fixing of territorial (id)entities, of purifica-tion of access, as well as of transgressions of scale, need not be restricted to states, but are valuable for theorizing and studying in their own right (see, for example, van Houtum and van Naerssen 2002; Walters 2006). Such theorizing of bordering has clearly inspired ontological and epistemological discussion about borders and bound-aries. In this chapter I have argued that despite this move to bordering studies, classic border mapping is still too easily taken for granted. And maps, as shown above, are important in co-constructing a view on and of the world. It has become clear that political forces in the US, the EU and elsewhere are keen to attract the high potential and low-cost labor migrants on the one hand, while controlling the self-defined "redundant" and allegedly non-assimilable immigrants on the other hand, in order to preserve social cohesion and regulate national labor markets within borders that they imagine as protecting their "own." It has reached the point that an increase in the mere numbers of migrants is now viewed as an invasion and a decrease as a success, which is powerfully illustrated in maps. Maps are obviously not the sole determinants in shaping the new nationalistic tendencies and increasingly militaristic border ideology, and maybe not even the biggest. Yet, border mapping does play a significant role and it is within the reach of social scientists like geographers, planners, cartographers and anthropologists to change the prevailing politically loaded inten-tionally naive maps of borders and migration into more just and multidimensional images and imaginings.

This does not mean that we should be so naive as to believe that there will ever be an end to the spatial b/ordering of our self-interest to increase our own comfort and to diminish the fear of loss of control. Nor will there be an end to classic state border mapping and the use of arrows to indicate imagined migration invasions. Borders do exist. Yet, borders exist as meaningful elements in space precisely because they are imagined, sensed, felt; because they are believed. Given this, that does not mean that we need to reproduce our own borders routinely and uncritically, or that we are forced to visualize borders and migration according to the dominant view. We are not only victims of the border, but also the producers of it. B/ordering ourselves and Othering the Other is something we do ourselves. Making a border, demarcating a line in space is a collaborative act. And so is the interpretation of it. The interpretation and meaning of borders are always open for reformation and transformation. It falls to ourselves to remap and redesign political spaces. As a start, we thus need to free ourselves from the classic geometrical thinking and open up the possibility of a dynamic line play, a choreography of the border, without the misconceiving, self-repressive or exclusionary interpretation of the border.

In sum, I would like to make a plea here that this is a path to pursue further, as this could and should have an effect, finally, on the way we visualize and represent borders and the migration across them. By focusing on the discussion of how to map b/orderings the ongoing lively and fascinating debate in border(ing) studies could be further enriched by training our eyes on what lines in spaces mean for human beings, and how we attach to and can break away from state border geometry. Drawing fixed lines on a map as a representation of borders does not help us to understand and describe the complexity and multidimensionality of borders and migration. Looking at the world, describing the world, is to a large extent also the art of learning to read space that cannot be put on a map. It is as much an intentional aesthetic design as it is a "true" representation. Space cannot be frozen, fixed and boxed into lines and colors and then be seen as the representation of the actual presence of a territory, of the actual reality. Studying the implicit ethics of the aesthetic design and suggesting alternative visualizations through video art, photography and alternative mapping forms could dismantle this taken-for-granted attitude to border mapping. When the aesthetics of borders – understood as the ways in which film, maps and video art reproduce and are reproduced by borders – is combined with the *ethics of aesthetics*, it could bring about a much-needed new route in the fascinating and blossoming field of border(ing) studies.

NOTES

I wish to thank Chiara Brambilla and Bruno Riccio for organizing a wonderful seminar on Transnational Migrations and Dis-located Borders as part of the PhD program in Anthropology and Epistemology of Complexity at the University of Bergamo at which the first seeds of this chapter were planted. The seminar provided fertile ground for transversal connections with scholars from various disciplines with multiple refreshing insights. In addition, I wish to thank Liam O'Dowd and Cathal McCall for organizing a most interesting discussion in Belfast on the theorization of borders, at which Hastings Donnan and Thomas Wilson, the editors of this book, were also present. Hastings Donnan and Thomas Wilson are also thanked for their most valuable comments on an earlier version of this chapter, which with permission substantially elaborates a paper to be published by Guaraldi Publishing.

1   See, for instance, http://www.earthmapssatellite.info/images/earth-maps-satellite.jpg (accessed Nov. 2011).
2   See, for instance, https://cac-ib-geography.wikispaces.com/file/view/800px-Invasions_of_the_Roman_Empire_1.png/45750029/800px-Invasions_of_the_Roman_Empire_1.png and http://pages.uoregon.edu/mccole/303Spring2011/maps/WWIIbattlefronts.jpg (accessed Nov. 2011).
3   At http://europa.eu/agencies/community_agencies/frontex/index_en.htm (accessed Apr. 14, 2011; emphasis added).
4   At www.frontex.europa.eu (accessed Apr. 14, 2011; emphasis added).

REFERENCES

Agamben, Giorgio. 1998. *Homo Sacer: Sovereign Power and Bare Life*, trans. Daniel Heller-Roazen. Stanford: Stanford University Press.

Bhagat, Alexis and Mogel, Lize, eds. 2008. *An Atlas of Radical Cartography*. Los Angeles: Aesthetics Protest Press.

Crampton, Jeremy W. and Krygier, John. 2006. An introduction to critical cartography. *ACME: An International E-Journal for Critical Geographies* 4 (1): 11–33.

Deleuze, Gilles and Guattari, Felix. 1987. *A Thousand Plateaus*. London: Athlone Press. First publ. 1980.

de Mug, R. 2010. Een dynamische cartografie. Masters diss., Radboud University Nijmegen.

Donald, James. 1999. *Imagining the Modern City*. Minneapolis: University of Minnesota Press.

Donnan, Hastings and Wilson, Thomas M. 1999. *Borders: Frontiers of Identity, Nation and State*. Oxford: Berg.

Ernste, Huib, van Houtum, Henk and Zoomers, A. 2009. Transworld: debating the place and borders of places in the age of transnationalism. *Tijdschrift voor Economische en Sociale Geografie* 100 (5): 567–577.

Foucault, Michel. 1982. *This Is Not a Pipe*, trans. J. Harkness. Berkeley: University of California Press.

Harley, J. Brian 1989. Deconstructing the map. *Cartographica* 26 (2): 1–20.

Inda, Jonathan Xavier. 2006. *Targeting Immigrants, Government, Technology and Ethics*. Oxford: Blackwell.

Newman, David. 2006. The lines that continue to separate us: borders in our "borderless" world. *Progress in Human Geography* 30: 143–61.

Papadopoulos, Dimitris, Stephenson, Niamh and Tsianos, Vassilis. 2008. *Escape Routes, Control and Subversion in the 21st Century*. London: Pluto Press.

Parker, Noel, Vaughan-Williams, Nick, Bialasiewicz, Luiza et al. 2009. Lines in the sand? Towards an agenda for critical border studies. *Geopolitics* 3: 582–587.

Pickles, John. 2004. *A History of Spaces: Mapping, Cartographic Reason and the Geocoded World*. London: Routledge.

Reichert, D. 1992. On boundaries. *Society and Space* 10: 87–98.

Schapendonk J. 2011. Turbulent trajectories. Diss., Radboud University, Nijmegen.

Scott, James W. 2002. A networked space of meaning? Spatial politics as geostrategies of European integration. Special Issue: *The Geopolitics of Cross-Border Cooperation in the European Union. Space and Polity* 6 (2): 147–167.

van Houtum, Henk. 2005. The geopolitics of borders and boundaries. *Geopolitics* 10: 672–679.

van Houtum, Henk. 2009. Voorbij de tekentafelpolitiek. *Geografie* 14: 14–15.

van Houtum, Henk. 2010. Human blacklisting: the global apartheid of the EU's external border regime. *Environment and Planning D: Society and Space* 28 (6): 957–976.

van Houtum, Henk. 2011. The mask of the border. In Doris Wastl-Walter, ed., *The Ashgate Research Companion to Border Studies*, pp. 49–61. Aldershot: Ashgate.

van Houtum, Henk and Boedeltje, Freerk. 2009. Europe's shame, death at the borders of the EU. *Antipode* 41 (2): 226–230.

van Houtum, Henk and van Naerssen, Ton. 2002. Bordering, ordering and othering. *Tijdschrift voor Economische en Sociale Geografie* 92 (2): 125–136.

van Houtum, Henk and Pijpers, Roos. 2007. The European Union as a gated community: the two-faced border and immigration regime of the EU. *Antipode* 39 (2): 291–309.

Walters, William. 2004. The frontiers of the European Union: a geostrategic perspective. Special Issue: *Postnational Politics in the European Union. Geopolitics* 9 (3): 674–698.

Walters, William. 2006. Rethinking borders beyond the state. *Comparative European Politics* 4 (2–3): 141–159.

Walters, William. 2007. The contested cartography of "illegal immigration." Paper presented at Royal Holloway, University of London.

Wilson, Thomas M. and Donnan, Hastings, eds. 1998. *Border Identities: Nation and State at International Frontiers.* Cambridge: Cambridge University Press.

Wood, Denis. 1993. *The Power of Maps.* London: Guilford Press.

CHAPTER 24

From Border Policing to Internal Immigration Control in the United States

Mathew Coleman

Popular and practical lenses on immigration enforcement in the US are, for the most part, border-centric. This is well illustrated by the fact that the vast majority of immigration bills considered by lawmakers during the modern period of US immigration policy, which can be dated from the Chinese Exclusion Acts of the late nineteenth century, have tackled the problem of immigration control in terms of border enforcement resources and/or practices (for an exhaustive review, see Zolberg 2006). Equally relevant, however, is the similar equivalence that humanities and social sciences research on US immigration enforcement draws between immigration control and border control. For example, much of the US immigration enforcement research revolves around what has been called the "liberal paradox" (Hollifield et al. 2008). By this is meant the selective rather than absolute openness of "globalizing" US borders – open for business, but not for bodies (for example, see Nevins 2010 on the "gatekeeper" state). This is a dominant theme across the humanities and social sciences: US immigration enforcement is nearly exclusively framed in terms of the contradictions and complementarities between US border militarization and free trade in the era following the North American Free Trade Agreement (NAFTA) (for a geographical perspective on the tension between border enforcement and trade, see Ackleson 2005; Coleman 2007a; Nevins 2001; Purcell and Nevins 2005; Sparke 2006; Wright 2006).

The often unproblematized identification traced between immigration control and border control in the US context stands in sharp contrast with European Union (EU) immigration research. The latter explicitly conceptualizes immigration enforcement as a general problem of governance and sees border enforcement as a specific

A Companion to Border Studies, First Edition. Edited by Thomas M. Wilson and Hastings Donnan.
© 2012 Blackwell Publishing Ltd. Published 2012 by Blackwell Publishing Ltd.

technology or practical subset of the former. Moreover, what counts as border enforcement has long been problematized in the EU literature. Indeed, there is a longstanding emphasis in the EU scholarship on border control as a matter of increasingly indistinct "internal" and "external" securities, such that immigration control is driven inward and/or exploded away from territorial borders (Bigo 2002; Bigo and Guild 2005; Huysmans 2000, 2006; Karyotis 2007; Walters 2002). This is in no small part due to a sustained and serious engagement between immigration scholars and critical international relations theorists regarding the nature and location of late modern "sovereign power" (well represented in Vaughan-Williams 2009, 2010), but it also in a more grounded sense reflects changes in EU immigration policy since the 1985 Schengen Area agreement. As theorized in literally hundreds of research papers, this 25-year-old reconfiguration of border control practice involves "remote control" as well as "internal control" policies which together have systematically resited immigration enforcement simultaneously "upwards" and "downwards" such that regional territorial borders are no longer privileged sites of immigration enforcement (paradigmatic statements can be found in Guiraudon and Lahav 2000; Lahav and Guiraudon 2000). This is not to detract from the importance of border enforcement per se in the EU case (see van Houtum 2010 for an account of the EU as a "global border machine"; see van Houtum and Pijpers 2007 for an account of the EU as a "gated community of fear"). My point simply is that the EU immigration scholarship has been more willing than the US scholarship to examine the spatial reconfiguration of immigration control beyond a neat inside/outside cartography, or in terms of what Walters (2006) calls a "delocalization" of immigration control into "new spaces of border control." In sum, "conventional notions of what and where borders are in contemporary political life" have been fully problematized in the EU immigration scholarship (Vaughan-Williams 2010: 1072).

There are, of course, excellent reasons for the general border-centrism in the US immigration research and to be clear my argument is not that border enforcement is unimportant. Below, for example, I sketch out how border enforcement has been, and continues to be, central to immigration control. However, what I want to argue in this chapter is that there is more to US immigration policing than border policing; US state power vis-à-vis immigration exceeds a geography of fences and walls, even if these classic sites of state authority continue to produce exceptional levels of scrutiny as well as legal and corporeal precariousness for those who try to cross them (Amoore 2006; Heyman 2004, 2008; Mountz 2010; Salter 2006). For example, perhaps the most important, yet underexplored transformation in US immigration policy in recent years, most pointedly since 9/11, has been the migration of immigration controls inwards to formally nonborder spaces – an intensified surveillance and regulation of immigrant life "on the inside" of the US state (Chavez and Provine 2009; Coleman 2007a, 2007b, 2009; Gilbert 2009; Heyman 2010; Hiemstra 2010; Nuñez and Heyman 2007; Stuesse 2010; Varsanyi 2008a, 2008b; Wells 2004). This trend can be described as immigration control away from the territorial margins of the state; involving a multiplicity of authorities, at a variety of scales; encompassing a wide range of local and federal policies, not easily classified as either domestic or foreign; and concerned with the social and political-economic pacification of a broad range of resident noncitizen populations, documented and otherwise. The upshot is that US immigration enforcement is operative across a flexible and shifting spatiality of internal controls – in addition to border enforcement, and indeed "remote" enforcement of the sort noted in the EU research.

While the migration of US immigration control away from US territorial borders may imply the growing territorial disembeddedness of US immigration enforcement, I do not also wish to imply that there is a smooth and undifferentiated domestic space throughout which state power is brought more coherently to bear on immigrant populations. If nonborder sites typically thought marginal to immigration policing are now otherwise, the topology of nonborder immigration control is nonetheless extremely patchy. This is a basic theme that I will return to in the conclusion to this chapter: that cities, counties, and states have, over the past decade, become key sites of conflict across a nascent, non-uniform, and subfederal immigration enforcement landscape (Wells 2004). In other words, the emerging nonborder landscapes of US immigration control do not adhere to a nonborder spatiality of "verticality" and "encompassment," as in a diffusion model of "police" power which reaches down into the social depths of the population as it spreads out across space (this language is borrowed from Ferguson and Gupta 2002). Rather, nonborder landscapes of US immigration control are aspects of a process of devolution that produces layered and contradictory sets of initiatives with distinctly localized conditions of possibility, which together constitute a complex landscape of differently congealed assemblages of state power (on horizontal dedifferentiation as an inadequate corrective to hierarchy, see Woodward et al. 2010). Indeed, devolution forces us to rethink an often assumed "methodological nationalism" or federalism at the heart of immigration enforcement not only on account of its recomposition of the "who" of immigration control but also on account of its uneven "regionality" (Ellis 2005; Ellis and Wright 1998; Wright and Ellis 2000).

BORDER WARS AND INTERNAL PACIFICATION

Border enforcement is undeniably a core aspect of immigration control policy in the US context. The centrality of borders to immigration control is very well illustrated by immigration enforcement spending priorities over the past 30 years. Between 1985 and 2002, the US spent $25 billion on immigration enforcement. A significant majority of this sum, some 60 percent, was allocated to border enforcement. In comparison, over the same time period only 11 percent of the immigration enforcement budget was allocated to nonborder enforcement, such as interior immigration investigations and/or workplace raids (an additional 33 percent of the budget was used to fund detention and removal operations, applying to both border enforcement and interior enforcement operations; for a discussion of immigration control spending, see Dixon and Gelatt 2005). Moreover, there has been a significant escalation in Border Patrol appropriations since the merger of the former Immigration and Naturalization Service (INS) into the newly created Department of Homeland Security (DHS) in March 2003. Since that date, the Border Patrol budget has increased some 230 percent; it now stands at approximately $3.5 billion annually (Haddal 2010; Nuñez-Neto 2008). It is worth noting that the latter figure exceeds the total annual

immigration enforcement budgets – that is, for the Border Patrol, interior enforcement, and detention and removal operations – for all years prior to 1998. This fact
should put a damper on any easy claims about the unraveling of states and the accelerated irrelevance of state borders in the cotemporary global economy (cf. Dear and
Lucero 2005).

These appropriations have not resulted in a uniform "hardening" of all US borders,
however. Historically the US–Canada border, as well as US maritime borders (with
the exception of the Florida peninsula, starting with the 1980 mass entry of Cubans
known as the Mariel boatlift) have occupied a marginal position in US immigration
control strategy. This continues to be largely the case. The US–Canada border came
under intense and unusual scrutiny in the wake of the 9/11 attacks on account of
its porosity, which in turn prompted some talk of a joint continental security perimeter (Andreas 2003; Gilbert 2005; Nicol 2005). However, ultimately the huge boom
in Border Patrol resources after 2001 did not result in a significant about-face in
terms of US–Canada border enforcement. For example, of the 12,500 new agents
hired by the Border Patrol after 9/11, 11,500 were assigned to the US–Mexico
border (there is currently a record high number of more than 20,000 Border Patrol
agents stationed at the US–Mexico border; see details in Haddal 2010). It is clear,
then, that border enforcement is a pillar of US immigration policy in light of the
substantial resources, mostly but not exclusively federal, which have been deployed
specifically at the US–Mexico border in order to regulate uncontrolled labor migration across it as well as other unrelated illicit traffic (Andreas 2010; Dunn 2010; Maril
2004; Nevins 2010).

The US–Mexico border is littered with various interdiction technologies, some
old and some new. First generation fences (recycled surplus carbon steel landing mats
from the Vietnam War), post-NAFTA triple layer border barriers (consisting primarily
of a vertical 10-foot fence with an angled extension at the top), newer generation
bollard walls (20-foot cement-filled steel tubes), permanent vehicle barriers and
checkpoints, and the recently defunded electronic fencing south of Tucson, Arizona,
which comprised a network of ground sensors and digital surveillance towers (Boyce
2011; Haddal et al. 2009; Nuñez-Neto and Viña 2006), are testament to the fact
that the US–Mexico border is an all-important geostrategic landscape for US immigration authorities. Moreover, we should note that the US Southwest border has
been a key geostrategic site since well before the formation of the Border Patrol as
a result of the 1924 Johnson-Reed Act. As Dunn (1996) has documented in extensive
detail, the use of low-intensity conflict measures to regulate border region populations has been the norm at the US–Mexico border since at least the Mexican-
American War and the subsequent 1848 Treaty of Guadalupe Hidalgo and the 1853
Gadsden Purchase, which together established what is now considered to be the
legal-territorial US–Mexico border.

In light of the above, Nevins rightly refers to US immigration enforcement as a
form of "border war" in the US Southwest (Nevins 2001). However, US immigration authorities' "border wars" have historically not been restricted to formal US
territorial borders. During the 1930s, for example, perhaps a million resident immigrant laborers, mostly Mexican nationals, were compelled to flee traditional
immigrant destinations in the US Southwest for their countries of origin. In part the

forced exodus was the result of a significant increase in immigration enforcement at worksites and across a range of spaces of social reproduction, such as residences, churches, shopping malls, parks, and so on. These raids, undertaken by federal authorities with assistance from city police and county sheriffs, and widely publicized through the print media, convinced many individuals and families to leave the US of their own accord. Simultaneous repatriation efforts undertaken by city, county and state governments were at least as important in terms of generating the decade's reverse flow of immigrant labor. Localities across the US during the Depression era, concerned about the possible fiscal burdens and social disorder associated with a growing class of destitute as well as unemployed migrant workers, enlisted government employees and nongovernmental relief organizations to compel, sometimes forcibly, immigrant laborers and their families to leave the US, often on scheduled southbound repatriation trains (in general on interior enforcement during the 1930s, see Balderrama and Rodríguez 2006; Hoffman 1974).

A similar scenario was repeated during the 1950s, during which time arguably several more million immigrant laborers, including many tens of thousands of US citizens, were deported or otherwise encouraged to depart the US. A key event during this period was the so-called 1954 "Operation Wetback", which comprised road blocks, mass immigration sweeps and worksite raids by the Border Patrol, predominantly in the US Southwest, in order to identify deportable noncitizens. It also involved strict enforcement of vagrancy laws by city and county law enforcement agencies and the subsequent transfer of suspected undocumented laborers to federal immigration authorities for deportation. Perhaps a million individuals were forced to leave the country in 1954 alone, although there is significant debate about the reliability of official statistics from this period from both the standpoint of under- and overreporting (on Operation Wetback see García 1980; Hernández 2010). Importantly, this period of mass deportations coincided with the near high point of the Bracero guest-worker program, which was started in the 1940s and extended through to the late 1960s. As Calavita (1992) argues, this was not necessarily a contradictory development. Operation Wetback compelled laborers who would otherwise have been itinerant into a captive legal labor market, which reduced overall costs and contingencies for agricultural employers specifically.

In sum, the events of the 1930s and 1950s, as Nevins and Aizeki (2008) have argued, show that US immigration enforcement has always been about the pacification of resident immigrant populations, away from US territorial borders. Another way of putting it is that working poor, nonwhite, and noncitizen populations have always lived with the ever-present threat of detention and deportation in the US interior. What I want to do below, in light of my general interest in unpacking the nonborder coordinates of immigration enforcement, or alternately the growing disconnect between immigration control and border control, is to emphasize the ongoing importance of interior pacification strategies, like those of the 1930s and 1950s, to contemporary US immigration control policy. I also show, however, that what now constitutes US immigration control in the US interior is unlike interior enforcement at any other point in the history of US immigration control. Indeed, despite the long-term importance of detention and deportation tactics in the US interior, recent changes in an era of homeland security in the way that immigration enforcement works means that now interior enforcement has taken on an unparalleled importance relative to border enforcement. Given the long-term militarization of US borders, and the US–Mexico border specifically, interior enforcement is now ground zero for US immigration control policy (see Amoore 2009 on homeland security and the spaces of daily life).

This strong claim requires at least two caveats. My first is a refutation of the argument that there has been a lull in immigration enforcement between the 1950s and the 2000s and that the present is a watershed. Indeed, the number of noncitizen laborers expelled from the US in the second half of the twentieth century increased steadily each decade until the turn of the century. The 1960s was a more modest period for removals, but throughout the 1950s Operation Wetback period, and certainly after the mid-1970s, between 700,000 and a million individuals were expelled annually from the US. Moreover, removals averaged 1.2 million cases a year in the 1990s, and peaked in 2000 at a high of 1.6 million cases. However, these numbers reflect specifically so-called "voluntary removals" or "voluntary departures." The latter refer to a specific immigration enforcement tactic whereby individuals are released on their own recognizance following apprehension by (mostly) federal immigration authorities and required to depart the country within a set time period without a formal pending immigration charge. Voluntary departure cases have historically applied overwhelmingly to Mexican nationals apprehended in the US–Mexico border region by the Border Patrol and returned more or less directly to Mexico through a border port of entry. Indeed, the various border region infrastructures alluded to in the paragraphs above have been in large measure technologies designed to funnel would-be undocumented migrants into specific areas where the Border Patrol can more easily take custody of individuals and they can be voluntarily removed back to Mexico (which should raise some questions about the extent to which this process is voluntary).

My point, though, is that the large volume of voluntary departures since the Operation Wetback period can be usefully contrasted with the relatively small number of formal deportations over the same time period. Unlike voluntary removal cases, deportation refers to the controlled removal of an individual with formal removal orders in place and with more or less continuous custody until territorial expulsion occurs. From the 1950s through the beginning of the 1990s an average of 17,000 individuals were formally deported from the US annually; some years this number was significantly smaller. Starting in the 1990s, and particularly after 1996, regularly more than 100,000 individuals have been formally deported each year. But it is the very steep increase in formal deportations since the upward trend in the 1990s – controlled deportations have averaged approximately 1,000 daily for the past four years, with a total of 1.4 million cases over 2007–2010 – that signals a decisive shift in the relative importance of interior enforcement to border enforcement. It should be stressed that over the past 10 years a record 3 million individuals have been detained and deported from the US, the overwhelming majority of whom can be classified as "removals from the interior" rather than "removals at the border." This is more than the total number of individuals deported since the Chinese Exclusion era, keeping in mind that federal deportation numbers do not include Operation Wetback cases, which are, inaccurately, treated as voluntary removals (for a discussion of the data, see Coleman 2012b; for up-to-date removals data, see US Immigration and Customs Enforcement 2011a).

My second caveat refers specifically to the mass street sweeps of the 1930s and 1950s. My argument is not that the assault on migrant labor during these two decades is now insignificant in either experiential or strategic terms, but instead that it has become normalized. In other words, my claim here is that when in the 1930s and 1950s detention and deportation became a routinized and ever-present possibility for the country's undocumented residents, this was in many ways a practical precursor to the "how" of immigration enforcement in the US today. There are at least two basic aspects to this argument. Much as in the Depression-era and Operation Wetback periods, there is an emphasis today on everyday immigration enforcement. While in many ways this is a commonsensical observation, it is nonetheless important to note that if immigration enforcement is migrating into the US interior this means that mundane spaces of social reproduction are increasingly those in which detention and deportation strategy operates.

In addition to the question of "where" enforcement is taking place, there are some important similarities in terms of who was and is detaining and deporting undocumented laborers in the 1930s, 1950s and now. As noted briefly above, the Depression-era repatriation and deportation effort, as well as Operation Wetback, were in part possible due to extensive cooperation between the Border Patrol and various city police and county sheriffs. Today we see similar sorts of cooperative immigration enforcement ventures, ranging from joint workplace raids and absconder initiatives (targeting individuals who have failed to report to federal authorities following a formal deportation order) to anti-gang and other forms of criminal operations. At the same time, we are also seeing something quite different in terms of the "how" of internal immigration control, at least as concerns the very recent formal delegation or devolution of a once exclusive federal authority over immigration enforcement to law enforcement agencies with historically very limited power to ask for immigration papers and detain individuals if immigration status was in question. Unlike during the 1930s and 1950s, nonfederal law enforcement agencies are no longer working alongside or in tandem with federal immigration authorities or in an ancillary capacity. Put slightly differently, what is going on now is not like the relaxation of the *posse comitatus* statute in the US–Mexico border region in the mid-1980s under the Reagan administration, which allowed Department of Defense officials to assist in immigration enforcement in the presence of an actual immigration officer. Rather, city police and county sheriffs, and sometimes statewide law enforcement agencies, are involved in entirely devolved immigration investigations which result in federal involvement only when the formal deportation process kicks in. In other words, devolution has prompted the development of detention and deportation regimes in the plural – a sort of patchwork of enforcement practices across the US with very little in the way of federal oversight and/or management.

NONBORDER ENFORCEMENT, PART 1: (EXTRA)LEGAL DRAGNETS

Although the extension of immigration enforcement away from militarized US territorial borders and into the US interior has been perhaps most obvious since 9/11, the stage for this process was set during the 1990s. Indeed, although the key legacy of the 1990s vis-à-vis immigration control is a militarized and walled US–Mexico border, the decade can also be characterized as having inaugurated and institutionalized a "severity revolution" in detention and deportation policy in the US interior (Miller 2003). What took place during the 1990s, on the heels of the 1986 legalization program (for a critical evaluation and contextualization, see Massey et al. 2002), was a new focus on so-called "criminal aliens" in the US interior. I hesitate to use this phrase because it is a grossly all-encompassing and slippery term, as outlined below. However, it is the case that US immigration control policy shifted during the decade before 9/11 to focus on a double-pronged "criminalization" of immigration enforcement as well as its "dejuridicalization" – which in effect produced the "criminal aliens" to whom these practices were said simply to be responding (Coleman 2007b; Kanstroom 2000; Miller 2005; Stumpf 2006). In terms of on-the-ground enforcement, criminalization and dejuridicalization meant increased federal immigration scrutiny of individuals detained by state and federal authorities on criminal grounds, as well as the beginning of a lockdown on the legal protections available to individuals in deportation proceedings.

The criminalization of immigration enforcement was brought about by a quick succession of federal immigration and counterterrorism bills, starting in 1990 and culminating in 1996. These pieces of legislation systematically merged the criminal law and immigration law systems, such that noncitizen individuals caught up in the criminal law system were, by the end of the 1990s, much more likely to face detention and deportation than had been the case in prior decades. In part this was accomplished via an array of so-called "institutional removal" and "institutional hearing" programs which initiated deportation proceedings against confirmed undocumented inmates prior to the end of their jail terms. These programs were based on an experimental mid-1980s initiative in New York in which immigration officials were sent into the state prison system to check the immigration status of incarcerated individuals. The newer programs adopted during the 1990s extended this practice to all state and federal prisons in Arizona, California, Florida, Illinois, New Jersey, New York and Texas, but also introduced derivative practices such as reinstating prior deportation orders for reentered (or never departed) undocumented inmates, in order to speed up the deportation process during incarceration. The criminalization trend also, and crucially, comprised an expansion in what crimes would count as "aggravated felonies" – an immigration-only charge which warrants mandatory detention and deportation from the country, and which was used by federal immigration authorities to point to the growing problem of "criminal aliens." By the end of the 1990s, what had started as a very narrow criminal category (related to the prosecution of "drug kingpins" for serious crimes such as drug smuggling, arms trafficking, and/or murder) was intentionally re-legislated to include a wide range of nonfelonious as well as nonaggravated offenses, including misdemeanors with a sentence (served or not) of more than one year as well as offenses such as illegal reentry to the US following deportation. The charge was also made retroactive, meaning that past convictions could be used to deport individuals in the present. The changes made to the aggravated felony charge were not based on a uniform list of crimes considered aggravated and/or felonious. As with the much longer standing "moral turpitude" basis for deportation, aggravated felony was – and continues to be – a legal term whose applicability depends on how the specific circumstances surrounding a criminal act are interpreted by the court overseeing the original, arresting offense. Accordingly, what counts as an aggravated felony varies at the scale of the courtroom within legal jurisdictions as well as between jurisdictions, especially when "crimes of violence" at the state level do not immediately translate into clear-cut criminal categories at the federal level. Indeed, the ambiguity built into the charge is in large measure responsible for its expansiveness and hence the general growth in "criminal alien" deportations over the decade (for a review, see Liem 2007).

Throughout the 1990s, in tandem with the expansion of the aggravated felony charge, lawmakers successfully dejuridicalized detention and deportation by limiting due process protections for individuals in deportation proceedings. It is important to note that noncitizens have never enjoyed access to substantive due process protections to challenge the "why" of immigration law and enforcement; this is because immigration control has been interpreted by the courts as a national security power which requires, in the last instance, an extraconstitutional advantage for the state over immigrant residents as well as visitors (Legomsky 1984). What happened during the 1990s was instead a whittling away of noncitizens' procedural due process protections regarding the "how" of immigration law and enforcement. Although a basic habeas corpus review concerning the identity of individuals held by federal authorities and awaiting deportation was kept intact, over the 1990s a wide swath of other discretionary forms of relief from removal were taken off the table. This was particularly so for noncitizens held as aggravated felons. Indeed, the aggravated felony charge was explicitly intended to have a restrictive impact on access to due process. Generally, the charge eliminated an individual's ability to petition for a deportation waiver or a cancellation of removal, regardless of the presence of dependent family members and/or long-term residence in the US; disqualified an individual from applying for asylum or adjusting status; guaranteed an individual's detention until deportation, without bail; and permanently disqualified individuals from the possibility of future legal return to the country. Moreover, aggravated felons were made subject to a newly minted administrative deportation procedure, which was essentially removal without court oversight of the civil immigration process. The legal logic here – that individuals in violation of criminal laws did not deserve a review of their deportation cases in the immigration courts – marked a definitive blurring of the immigration law and criminal law systems. In addition to aggravated felons, lawmakers also legislated "expedited" deportation practices – again, with limited court oversight – for suspected undocumented migrants who could not prove that they had established residence for more than two years at the time they were detained (Coleman 2012a; Shachar 2007).

In sum, the criminalization and dejuridicalization of immigration enforcement during the 1990s effected a strategic crossing of the criminal law and immigration law systems which contributed to a significant growth in detentions and deportations. In practice, criminalization and dejuridicalization meant that noncitizens in the US interior were increasingly subject to expansive, immigrant-only criminal enforcement categories, such as the aggravated felony charge, in order to ensure their deportation. At the same time, the legal protections that would usually kick in as a result of being detained under criminal law statute were held largely at bay during the deportation process itself, on the understanding that, unlike criminal law enforcement, immigration enforcement is a civil law matter and thus not about punishment per se. Indeed, the crossing of the criminal law and immigration law systems used the nonpunitive characterization of the immigration law system to exempt individuals from meaningful due process protections during deportation at the same time as criminal law categorizations were being literally invented so as to grow the number of individuals in civil detention awaiting deportation. The productive aspect of immigration enforcement, in other words its ability to produce the objects of scrutiny that are said to warrant enforcement in the first play, could not be clearer. In reference to the recent literature on "states of exception" (Belcher et al. 2008; Bigo 2007), the criminalization and dejuridicalization of immigration enforcement during the 1990s can be explained as a form of state power which holds bodies in relation to an expansive authority to grow the category of what counts as a legal infraction, but which at the same time and in the same place itself exempts bodies so held from normal legal protections by forsaking them to extralegal removal procedures and practices. The result is a legal dragnet that is in part constituted through the production of immigrants as illegal, or outside the law.

NONBORDER ENFORCEMENT, PART 2: DEPUTIZATION

The criminalization and dejuridicalization trends during the 1990s, however significant in terms of generating increased numbers of deportations during that decade, were nowhere near as important to the interior enforcement revolution as the deputization trend that took hold in the wake of 9/11. Deputization in the immigration context refers to the devolution of federal immigration police powers to nonfederal law enforcement agencies historically precluded from engaging in immigration enforcement under a separation of powers argument. Indeed, since the Chinese Exclusion Acts there has been a legally recognized division of labor between federal immigration authorities and nonfederal police as concerns the power to enforce the Immigration and Nationality Act (INA). Federal immigration authorities, until recently, possessed an exclusive power to enforce the INA, whereas other law enforcement agencies could enforce immigration statute only to the extent that criminal law enforcement might trigger detention and deportation. A landmark case in this division of labor was the 1983 *Gonzales v. City of Peoria* (722F.2d 468). In *Gonzales*, the 9th circuit court decided against appellants who charged that their detention by city police on immigration grounds would have been impossible without racial profiling; this reflects more or less the established role of racial profiling in immigration enforcement in the US context (Johnson 2010). However, more immediately important in the context of deputization was the court's ruling on the question of whether or not city police could apprehend undocumented aliens on account of how the city treated "illegal presence" as a local law enforcement issue. Indeed, the court affirmed that state and local police do not possess the authority to enforce civil aspects of the INA, that is, related to immigration status alone, and that state and local police are limited to criminal aspects of the INA already under their purview by virtue of their primarily criminal law enforcement duties (for early commentary, see Bau 1994;

Benitez 1994; Manheim 1995; Renn 1987; Spiro 1994; Yañez and Soto 1994). As such, the 9th circuit expressly prohibited localities' enforcement of civil aspects of the INA, that is, administrative violations like "illegal presence," or lack of legal status.

In the wake of the 1983 decision, federal lawmakers amended the INA to reflect *Gonzales*. For example, the 1996 Antiterrorism and Effective Death Penalty Act legislated explicitly that immigration violations stemming from criminal activity are subject to nonfederal police authority. However, the bulk of Congressional efforts since *Gonzales* have been about enhancing localities' criminal oversight of the INA by institutionalizing cooperation between states and localities and federal immigration authorities. The goal was to grow interior enforcement by enlisting state, county and city employees – and for the most part state and local police – as federal immigration proxies. For instance, a Senate amendment to the 1994 Violent Crime Act required that states, counties and cities with police agencies refusing to assist or cooperate with federal immigration authorities be labeled as noncooperating and be refused federal law enforcement funding. Likewise, the 1996 Welfare Act stipulated that state and local entities administering supplemental security income, temporary assistance for needy families, and/or public and assisted housing report benefits usage by undocumented aliens to the INS. Most important, however, the 1996 Illegal Immigration Reform and Immigrant Responsibility Act outlined how nonfederal agencies could directly police immigration violations. The law authorized state and local police to supplement INS activities during a mass immigration emergency, and more broadly provided for the wholesale delegation of federal immigration powers to nonfederal agencies through a new addition to the INA – Section 287(g). Section 287(g) – or simply 287(g), as it is now colloquially known – enabled state, county and city police forces to investigate criminal immigration cases, make criminal immigration arrests, take custody of immigration violators for federal authorities, as well as put together criminal immigration cases for prosecution in the courts (Capps et al. 2011; Rodríguez et al. 2010; Seghetti et al. 2006). Section 287(g) also provided for guaranteed transfer to federal custody. The 1996 changes to the INA represented a significant workaround to the *Gonzales* ruling: although *Gonzales* would still stand in the sense that nonfederal police could not in and of themselves police immigration (the perfect example here is the current federal challenge to Arizona's immigration laws, which seek precisely to usurp federal authority over the INA), 287(g) allowed federal authorities to devolve these powers under federal supervision, on a case-by-case basis and given sufficient federal training.

In the immediate aftermath of the 1996 law, no localities made use of 287(g) authority. This was largely because of the predominance of community policing, which required open lines of communication between city and county police and their resident immigrant populations. Indeed, major cities like New York challenged the federal government in court on the 1996 law on account of its impact on local police initiatives relative to its large immigrant communities. However, after 9/11, and in a general political context which emphasized enhanced local-federal cooperation over immigration enforcement and national security, localities almost immediately took up the 287(g) option (Coleman 2009).There are now approximately 70 nonfederal law enforcement agencies enrolled in 287(g) across two dozen states. The current 287(g)s consist of both jail-based models, in which officers scrutinize detainees for immigration status before there is any court action on an arresting offense, as well as "roving" models in which police are given the authority to ask for immigration documents in the course of routine policing and without any necessary criminal charge. Of the 287(g)s in effect, most are concentrated in the US Southwest and US South, and are in the majority jail-based programs operating out of county sheriffs' offices. That county sheriffs are emerging as major players in interior, nonborder immigration enforcement is an exceptionally important development because in many US counties the county jail is the primary detention center for all law enforcement agencies in the county, such as university and city police forces. What this means is that arrests by any number of agencies not formally deputized, and for a wide range of minor infractions and misdemeanors (see below), are now more or less guaranteed to trigger an immigration investigation at the county level if immigration is in question. This is no doubt one of the major reasons for the huge increase in interior deportations over the past decade. Indeed, 185,000 individuals have been put into deportation proceedings by virtue of primary contact with a nonfederal 287(g) agency since the program began in earnest in 2006. Approximately the same number of individuals have been detained by local police and put into deportation proceedings via a sister program to 287(g) called Secure Communities. Secure Communities is a 287(g) offshoot which allows for immigration checks at the county level, but unlike 287(g), does not guarantee federal custody at the end of the process. However, this last difference is tactically offset by the huge difference in coverage between the 287(g) and Secure Communities programs: by 2013 every single county sheriff's office will be enrolled in Secure Communities (for a discussion of numbers and program differences, see Coleman and Kocher 2011).

While programs like 287(g) and Secure Communities work through criminal law enforcement, this should not be taken as an indication that only serious criminals are being impacted by the programs. Indeed, emerging scholarship suggests that the devolution of immigration powers to nonfederal police works by attaching serious immigration consequences to nonserious offenses in everyday settings. For example, in their study of select 287(g) sites, Capps et al. (2011) note that a full 50 percent of deportees were checked for status as a result of being brought into local custody for minor traffic infractions, nonserious misdemeanors and on the basis of a police interrogation without an arresting offense. Their finding is corroborated by Coleman's study of 287(g) and Secure Communities enforcement in central North Carolina (Coleman 2012b; see also Coleman and Kocher 2011). There Coleman found that regularly over 80 percent of positive immigration "hits" by county sheriffs resulted from misdemeanor arrests. Coleman also found that roughly 50 percent of the charges used to book individuals into county jails for an immigration check started with a minor traffic violation, and that Latinos specifically were substantially overrepresented in aggregate traffic enforcement statistics. A recent government report on 287(g) echoes these findings and suggests that one reason devolution is disproportionately targeting misdemeanor and minor infraction offenders is because of a lack of overall management and scrutiny by federal immigration authorities (a recent internal Department of Homeland Security review of 287(g) arrives at the same conclusion, see DHS 2010; GAO 2009).

CONCLUSION

In this chapter I have argued that the frequent slippage between border control and immigration control in the research on immigration enforcement in the US context is increasingly hard to sustain, and indeed that the mass-scale interior enforcement campaigns characteristic of contemporary US immigration control policy can be compared with deportation policies in the 1930s and 1950s. This does not mean that border control is unimportant in the realm of immigration enforcement. The border building boom that characterized US immigration policy during the 1990s, and continues apace today, can in many ways be considered a strategic prerequisite for interior enforcement. For example, that the US–Mexico border region is now one of the most lethal in the world (Eschbach et al. 2003), and that resident undocumented populations are reducing travel back and forth across the border in order to avoid its hardships, suggest that border control makes resident undocumented populations spatially captive and hence vulnerable to an increase in interior enforcement. Nonetheless, the growth in interior enforcement signals an important shift in the "where" of immigration enforcement. Building on Bigo's (2002) discussion of immigration enforcement in the EU context, a fair characterization of the US case would be to understand immigration enforcement as a strategic mix of differently spatialized "management of territory" and "management of populations" tactics. The former is outward-looking and focused on stopping territorial entry; the latter is inward-looking and focused on the surveillance and regulation of resident immigrant populations.

Why are the changing coordinates of immigration enforcement in the US, which mimic longer standing immigration control policies in the EU context, important for border scholars? The transformation of immigration control into a double-pronged management of territory and management of populations means that borders are no longer adequately grasped only as spaces at states' territorial margins. Borders are of course importantly inter-national "edges," in the sense of defining the extent of states' formal legal and political jurisdictions (Casey 2011). In their strict legal-geopolitical sense, for instance as "walls around the West" (Andreas and Snyder 2000), state borders are significant in that they geographically define a space of official membership as well as pathologize unregulated mobility as a threat to strictly territorialized notions of citizenship (Cresswell 2006: 1–24; 2010). But by virtue of the way in which immigration control increasingly reaches into states' interiors, borders have also lost their specific territorial anchoring to the space between state jurisdictions. In this sense, we should think of states' ability to immobilize via borders as not specific to how borders have been conventionally located. Indeed, vis-à-vis immigration enforcement specifically, borders have become attached to immigrant bodies who are everywhere and always understood by the state as "crossing." This is most obviously the case for undocumented migrants, for whom state borders do not describe an "outside" and an "inside" but instead are literally coterminous with everyday spaces. The bottom line is that borders have lost their geographical specificity and instead are now best understood as constitutive of a territorially unanchored "society of control" (Walters 2006).

However, if both outward-looking and inward-looking, it would be a mistake to think of US immigration control as a coherent machine, as Nevins (2010) warned in his examination of Operation Gatekeeper cited above. This is so today on at least two basic counts. On the one hand, the devolutionary trend, as signaled at the outset of the chapter, has not resulted in an even delegation of federal immigration powers to local authorities. Devolutionary programs like 287(g) and Secure Communities, for example, are responsive to local policing, political, legal and economic contexts. This can be gleaned by looking at the different volumes of 287(g) arrests across the country. These arrests do not originate evenly across the states' housing 287(g) programs. The overwhelming majority of arrests originate in Arizona (50,000 cases), California (53,000 cases), Georgia (15,000 cases), North Carolina (19,000 cases) and Texas (15,000 cases); the rest of the 25 states that house 287(g) programs comprise a mere 18 percent of the total number of 287(g) arrests (US Immigration and Customs Enforcement 2010). The same sort of spatial discrepancy is visible with the Secure Communities program. Arizona (34,500 cases), California (72,000 cases), Florida (14,000 cases) and Texas (34,000 cases) together comprise 85 percent of all Secure Communities cases; the remaining 15 percent are spread across enrolled agencies in 34 states (US Immigration and Customs Enforcement 2011b). On the other hand, contributing to the patchwork-like quality of interior immigration enforcement is the fact that the devolutionary trend comprises also cities, counties and states seeking to be less involved in federal immigration enforcement. This includes localities with sanctuary laws on the books, which limit the sort of assistance that local police can give federal immigration authorities (on sanctuary, see Coutin 1993; Cunningham 1995; Ridgley 2008), as well as jurisdictions which, while not sanctuary sites, have explicitly opted out of programs like 287(g) and Secure Communities. The overall point is that interior enforcement is spatially sporadic and that moving across the US from coast to coast one will encounter zones of relatively intense local-scale immigration enforcement as well as zones of relatively relaxed immigration enforcement. One critic calls this the "thousand borders problem" and notes that the uneven enforcement of immigration law in the US interior contravenes a constitutional mandate for uniformity in the application of law (Pham 2004).

This leads to a final point about the relative unimportance of worksite enforcement, such as workplace raids, in the US today. Although worksite enforcement has never been an important component of US immigration strategy, raids against suspected mass employers of undocumented laborers were not insignificant during the 1990s. During 1996–1998, for example, approximately 27,000 individuals were arrested as a result of employer investigations by the then INS (GAO 1999). The most recent available data suggest a significant, subsequent decrease. In 2002 and 2003, for example, nationwide arrests due to workplace raids were 485 and 445 cases, respectively (DHS 2004: 157, Table 39). What this means is that the overwhelming bulk of interior enforcement operations originate with enforcement operations outside the workplace. This discrepancy between the huge increase in overall deportations and the decrease in workplace enforcement suggests another crucial aspect to the devolution of immigration enforcement: that the burden of responsibility for undocumented laboring has been definitively – and quantitatively – shifted away from those who hire and profit from undocumented labor, such that undocumented laborers face significantly greater chances of detention and deportation as a result of driving to work and changing lanes improperly, or when faced with a general policing inquiry while engaged in social reproduction activities necessary in order to work, across a range of private and public spaces. This is perhaps one of the most significant resonances with the mass deportations of the 1930s and 1950s. Now, as then, the long operative contradiction between immigration enforcement and capital accumulation in the US context is being visited directly onto the everyday of laboring bodies and families, what has been referred to elsewhere as the "fleshy, messy" sites of material life (Katz 2001; Mitchell et al. 2003). Indeed, perhaps one of the safest locations for undocumented laborers in the US today is in fact the workplace.

REFERENCES

Ackleson, Jason. 2005. Constructing security on the US–Mexico border. *Political Geography* 24 (2):165–184.

Amoore, Louise. 2006. Biometric borders: governing mobilities in the war on terror. *Political Geography* 25 (3): 336–351.

Amoore, Louise. 2009. Algorithmic war: everyday geographies of the war on terror. *Antipode* 41 (1): 49–69.

Andreas, Peter. 2003. *A Tale of Two Borders: The US–Mexico and US–Canada Lines after 9/11.* Center for Comparative Immigration Studies Working Paper 77. LaJolla: University of California, San Diego.

Andreas, Peter. 2010. *Border Games: Policing the US–Mexico Divide.* Ithaca: Cornell University Press.

Andreas, Peter and Snyder, Timothy. 2000. *The Wall around the West: State Borders and Immigration Controls in North America and Europe.* Lanham: Rowman & Littlefield.

Balderrama, Francisco E. and Rodríguez, Raymond. 2006. *Decade of Betrayal: Mexican Repatriation in the 1930s.* Albuquerque: University of New Mexico Press.

Bau, Ignatius. 1994. Interior borders: INS and police enforcement practices. *La Raza Law Review* 7 (1): 50–71.

Belcher, Oliver, Martin, Lauren, Secor, Anna et al. 2008. Everywhere and nowhere: the exception and the topological challenge to geography. *Antipode* 40 (4):499–503.

Benitez, Humberto. 1994. Flawed strategies: the INS shift from border interdiction to internal enforcement actions. *La Raza Law Review* 7 (1): 154–179.

Bigo, Didier. 2002. Security and immigration: toward a critique of the governmentality of unease. *Alternatives* 27 (1): 63–92.

Bigo, Didier. 2007. Detention of foreigners, states of exception and the social practices of control of the Banopticon. In Prem Kumar Rajaram and Carl Grundy-Warr, eds, *Borderscapes: Hidden Geographies and Politics at Territory's Edge*, pp. 3–33. Minneapolis: University of Minnesota Press.

Bigo, Didier and Guild, Elspeth, eds. 2005. *Controlling Frontiers: Free Movement Into and Within Europe.* Aldershot: Ashgate.

Boyce, Geoff. 2011. *The Rugged Border: Mobility, Inertia, and Politics on the US–Mexico Frontier.* Presented at Association of American Geographers annual meeting, Seattle, WA.

Calavita, Kitty. 1992. *Inside the State.* New York: Routledge.

Capps, Randy, Rosenblum, Marc, Rodríguez, Cristina and Chishti, Muzaffar A. 2011. *Delegation and Divergence: A Study of 287(g) State and Local Immigration Enforcement.* Washington, DC: Migration Policy Institute.

Casey, Edward. 2011. Border versus boundary at La Frontera. *Environment and Planning D: Society and Space* 29 (3): 384–398.

434   MATHEW COLEMAN

Chavez, Jorge M. and Provine, Doris M. 2009. Race and the response of state legislatures to unauthorized immigrants. *Annals of the American Academy of Political and Social Science* 623: 78–92.

Coleman, Mathew. 2007a. A geopolitics of engagement: neoliberalism, the war on terrorism, and the reconfiguration of US immigration enforcement. *Geopolitics* 12 (4): 607–634.

Coleman, Mathew. 2007b. Immigration geopolitics beyond the Mexico–US border. *Antipode* 38 (2): 54–76.

Coleman, Mathew. 2009. What counts as the politics and practice of security, and where? Devolution and immigrant insecurity after 9/11. *Annals of the Association of American Geographers* 99 (5): 904–913.

Coleman, Mathew. 2012a (forthcoming). Immigrant il-legality: geopolitical and legal borders in the US, 1882–present. *Geopolitics* 17 (1).

Coleman, Mathew. 2012b (forthcoming). The "local" migration state: the site-specific devolution of immigration enforcement in the US South. *Law and Policy* 34 (2).

Coleman, Mathew and Kocher, Austin. 2011. Detention, deportation, devolution and immigrant incapacitation in the US, post–9/11. *Geographical Journal of the Royal Geographical Society* 177 (3). DOI: 10.1111/j.1475-4959.2011.00424.x.

Coutin, Susan Bibler. 1993. *The Culture of Protest: Religious Activism and the US Sanctuary Movement*. Boulder: Westview.

Cresswell, Tim. 2006. *On the Move: Mobility in the Modern Western World*. London: Routledge.

Cresswell, Tim. 2010. Towards a politics of mobility. *Environment and Planning D: Society and Space* 28 (1): 17–31.

Cunningham, Hilary. 1995. *God and Caesar at the Rio Grande: Sanctuary and the Politics of Religion*. Minneapolis: University of Minnesota Press.

Dear, Michael and Lucero, Manuel. 2005. Postborder cities, postborder world: the rise of Bajalta California. *Environment and Planning D: Society and Space* 23 (3): 317–321.

DHS (Department of Homeland Security). 2004. *2003 Yearbook of Immigration Statistics*. US Department of Homeland Security.

DHS (Department of Homeland Security). 2010. *The Performance of 287(g) Agreements*. US Department of Homeland Security.

Dixon, David and Gelatt, Julia. 2005. *Immigration Enforcement Spending since IRCA*. Washington, DC: Migration Policy Institute.

Dunn, Timothy J. 1996. *The Militarization of the US–Mexico Border, 1978–1992: Low-Intensity Conflict Doctrine Comes Home*. Austin: University of Texas, Center for Mexican American Studies.

Dunn, Timothy J. 2010. *Blockading the Border*. Austin: University of Texas Press.

Ellis, Mark. 2005. Unsettling immigrant geographies: US immigration and the politics of scale. *Tijdschrift voor Economische en Sociale Geografie* 97 (1): 49–58.

Ellis, Mark and Wright, Richard A. 1998. The Balkanization metaphor in the analysis of US immigration. *Annals of the Association of American Geographers* 88 (4): 686–698.

Eschbach, Karl, Hagan, Jacqueline and Rodríguez, Nestor. 2003. Deaths during undocumented migration: trends and policy implications in the new era of homeland security. *In Defense of the Alien* 26: 37–52.

Ferguson, James and Gupta, Akhil. 2002. Spatializing states: toward an ethnography of neoliberal governmentality. *American Ethnologist* 29 (4): 981–1002.

GAO (Government Accountability Office). 1999. *Illegal Aliens: Significant Obstacles to Reducing Unauthorized Alien Employment Exist*. GAO/GGD-99-33. Washington, DC: US Government Accountability Office.

GAO (Government Accountability Office). 2009. *Immigration Enforcement: Better Controls Needed over Program Authorizing State and Local Enforcement of Federal Immigration Laws*. Washington, DC: US Government Accountability Office.

García, Juan Ramon. 1980. *Operation Wetback: the Mass Deportation of Mexican*

Undocumented Workers in 1954. Westport: Greenwood Press.

Gilbert, Emily. 2005. The inevitability of integration? Neoliberal discourse and the proposals for a new North American economic space after September 11. *Annals of the Association of American Geographers* 95 (1): 202–222.

Gilbert, Liette. 2009. Immigration as local politics: re-bordering immigration and multiculturalism through deterrence and incapacitation. *International Journal of Urban and Regional Research* 33 (1): 26–42.

Guiraudon, Virginie and Lahav, Gallya. 2000. A reappraisal of the state sovereignty debate: the case of migration control. *Comparative Political Studies* 33 (2): 163–195.

Haddal, Chad C. 2010. *Border Security: The Role of the U.S. Border Patrol.* RL32562. Washington, DC: Congressional Research Service, Library of Congress.

Haddal, Chad C., Kim, Yule and Garcia, Michael John. 2009. *Border Security: Barriers Along the US International Border.* Washington, DC: Congressional Research Service, Library of Congress.

Hernández, Kelly Lytle. 2010. *Migra! A History of the US Border Patrol.* Berkeley: University of California Press.

Heyman, Josiah McC. 2004. Ports of entry as nodes in the world system. *Identities: Global Studies in Culture and Power* 11 (3): 303–327.

Heyman, Josiah McC. 2008. Constructing a virtual wall: race and citizenship in US–Mexico border policing. *Journal of the Southwest* 50 (3): 305–33.

Heyman, Josiah McC. 2010. The state and mobile people at the US–Mexico border. In Winnie Len and Pauline Gardiner Barber, eds, *Class and Contention in a World in Motion*, pp. 58–78. New York: Berghahn Press.

Hiemstra, Nancy. 2010. Immigrant "illegality" as neoliberal governmentality in Leadville, Colorado. *Antipode* 42 (1): 74–102.

Hoffman, Abraham. 1974. *Unwanted Mexicans in the Great Depression: Repatriation Pressures, 1929–1939.* Tucson: University of Arizona Press.

Hollifield, James F., Hunt, Valerie F. and Tichenor, Daniel. 2008. The liberal paradox: immigrants, markets and rights in the United States. *Southern Methodist University Law Review* 61 (1): 67–98.

Huysmans, Jef. 2000. The European Union and the securitization of migration. *Journal of Common Market Studies* 38 (5): 751–777.

Huysmans, Jef. 2006. *The Politics of Insecurity: Fear, Migration and Asylum in the EU.* London: Routledge.

Johnson, Kevin R. 2010. How racial profiling in America became the law of the land: *United States v. Brignoni-Ponce* and *Wren v. United States* and the need for truly rebellious lawyering. *Georgetown Immigration Law Journal* 98 (6): 1006–1077.

Kanstroom, Daniel. 2000. Deportation, social control and punishment: some thoughts about why hard laws make bad cases. *Harvard Law Review* 113 (8): 1890–1935.

Karyotis, Georgios. 2007. European migration policy in the aftermath of September 11: the security–migration nexus. *Innovation: The European Journal of Social Science Research* 20 (1): 1–17.

Katz, Cindi. 2001. Vagabond capitalism and the necessity of social reproduction. *Antipode* 33 (4): 709–728.

Lahav, Gallya and Guiraudon, Virginie. 2000. Comparative perspectives on border control: away from the border, outside the state. In Peter Andreas and Timothy Snyder, eds, *The Wall around the West*, pp. 55–77. Lanham: Rowman & Littlefield.

Legomsky, Stephen H. 1984. Immigration law and the principle of plenary Congressional power. *Supreme Court Review* 84 (1): 255–307.

Liem, Natalie. 2007. Mean what you say, say what you mean: defining the aggravated felony deportation grounds to target more than aggravated felonies. *Florida Law Review* 59 (5): 1071–1096.

Manheim, Karl M. 1995. State immigration laws and federal supremacy. *Hastings Constitutional Law Quarterly* 22 (4): 939–1018.

Maril, Robert Lee. 2004. *Patrolling Chaos: The US Border Patrol in Deep South Texas*. Lubbock: Texas Tech University Press.

Massey, Douglas S., Durand, Jorge and Malone, Nolan J. 2002. *Beyond Smoke and Mirrors: Mexican Immigration in an Era of Economic Integration*. New York: Russell Sage Foundation.

Miller, Teresa. 2003. Citizenship and severity: recent immigration reforms and the new penology. *Georgetown Immigration Law Journal* 17 (4): 611–666.

Miller, Teresa. 2005. Blurring the boundaries between immigration and crime control after September 11th. *Boston College Third World Law Journal* 25 (1): 81–124.

Mitchell, Katharyne, Marston, Sallie A. and Katz, Cindi. 2003. Life's work: an introduction, review and critique. *Antipode* 35 (3): 415–442.

Mountz, Alison. 2010. *Seeking Asylum: Human Smuggling and Bureaucracy at the Border*. Minneapolis: University of Minnesota Press.

Nevins, Joseph. 2001. Searching for security: boundary and immigration enforcement in an age of intensifying globalization. *Social Justice* 28 (2): 132–148.

Nevins, Joseph. 2010. *Operation Gatekeeper and Beyond*. New York: Routledge.

Nevins, Joseph and Aizeki, Mizue. 2008. *Dying to Live: A Story of US Immigration in an Age of Global Apartheid*. San Francisco: Open Media/City Lights Books.

Nicol, Heather. 2005. Resiliency or change? The contemporary Canada–US border. *Geopolitics* 10 (4): 767–790.

Nuñez, Guillermina and Heyman, Josiah McC. 2007. Entrapment processes and immigrant communities in a time of heightened border vigilance. *Human Organization* 66 (4): 354–365.

Nuñez-Neto, Blas. 2008. Border Security: The Role of the US Border Patrol. Congressional Research Service, Library of Congress.

Nuñez-Neto, Blas and Viña, Stephen. 2006. Border Security: Barriers along the US International Border. Congressional Research Service, Library of Congress.

Pham, Huyen. 2004. The inherent flaws in the inherent authority position: why inviting local enforcement of immigration laws violates the Constitution. *Florida State University Law Review* 31 (4): 965–1003.

Purcell, Mark and Nevins, Joseph. 2005. Pushing the boundary: state restructuring, state theory, and the case of US–Mexico border enforcement in the 1990s. *Political Geography* 24 (2): 211–235.

Renn, Cecilia. 1987. State and local enforcement of the criminal immigration statutes and preemption doctrine. *University of Miami Law Review* 41 (5): 999–1025.

Ridgley, Jennifer. 2008. Cities of refuge: immigration enforcement, police and the insurgent genealogies of citizenship in US sanctuary cities. *Urban Geography* 29 (1): 53–77.

Rodríguez, Cristina, Chishti, Muzaffar, Capps, Randy and St John, Laura. 2010. *A Program in Flux: New Priorities and Implementation Challenges for 287(g)*. Washington, DC: Migration Policy Institute.

Salter, Mark B. 2006. The global visa regime and the political technologies of the international self: borders, bodies, biopolitics. *Alternatives* 31 (2): 167–189.

Seghetti, Lisa M., Viña, Stephen R. and Ester, Karma. 2006. *Enforcing Immigration Law: The Role of the State and Local Enforcement*. Washington DC: Congressional Research Service, Library of Congress.

Shachar, Ayelet. 2007. The shifting border of immigration regulation. *Stanford Journal of Civil Rights and Civil Liberties* 3 (2): 165–193.

Sparke, Matt B. 2006. A neoliberal nexus: economy, security and the biopolitics of citizenship on the border. *Political Geography* 25 (2): 151–180.

Spiro, Peter J. 1994. The states and immigration in an era of demi-sovereignties. *Virginia Journal of International Law* 35 (1): 121–178.

Stuesse, Angela C. 2010. What's "justice and dignity" got to do with it? Migrant vulnerability, corporate complicity, and the state. *Human Organization* 69 (1): 19–30.

Stumpf, Juliet. 2006. The crimmigration crisis: immigrants, crime and sovereign power. *American University Law Review* 56 (2): 367–419.

US Immigration and Customs Enforcement. 2010. 287(g) – Identified Aliens for Removal. Department of Homeland Security. At http://www.ice.gov/doclib/foia/reports/287g-masterstats2010oct31.pdf (accessed Nov. 2011).

US Immigration and Customs Enforcement 2011a. Immigration Enforcement Actions 2010. Department of Homeland Security. At http://www.dhs.gov/xlibrary/assets/statistics/publications/enforcement-ar-2010.pdf (accessed Nov. 2011).

US Immigration and Customs Enforcement. 2011b. Secure Communities: IDENT/IAFIS Interoperability Monthly Statistics through February 28 2011. Department of Homeland Security. At http://ndlon.org/pdf/scommfeb/nationwidestats20112.pdf (accessed Nov. 2011).

van Houtum, Henk. 2010. Human blacklisting: the global apartheid of the EU's external border regime. *Environment and Planning D: Society & Space* 28 (6): 957–976.

van Houtum, Henk and Pijpers, Roos. 2007. The European Union as a gated community: the two-faced border and immigration regime of the EU. *Antipode* 39 (2): 291–309.

Varsanyi, Monica W. 2008a. Immigration policing through the backdoor: city ordinances, the "right to the city," and the exclusion of undocumented day laborers. *Urban Geography* 29 (1): 29–52.

Varsanyi, Monica W. 2008b. Rescaling the "alien," rescaling personhood: neoliberalism, immigration, and the state. *Annals of the Association of American Geographers* 98 (4): 877–896.

Vaughan-Williams, Nick 2009 The generalised bio-political border? Re-conceptualising the limits of sovereign power. *Review of International Studies* 35 (4): 729–749.

Vaughan-Williams, Nick. 2010. The UK border security continuum: virtual biopolitics and the simulation of the sovereign ban. *Environment and Planning D: Society and Space* 28 (6): 1071–1083.

Walters, William. 2002. Mapping Schengenland: denaturalizing the border. *Environment and Planning D: Society and Space* 20 (5): 561–580.

Walters, William. 2006. Border/control. *European Journal of Social Theory* 9 (2): 187–203.

Wells, Miriam J. 2004. The grassroots reconfiguration of US immigration policy. *International Migration Review* 38 (4): 1308–1347.

Woodward, Keith, Jones, III, John Paul, and Marston, Sallie A. 2010. Of eagles and flies: orientations toward the site. *Area* 42 (3): 271–280.

Wright, Melissa A. 2006. *Disposable Women and Other Myths of Global Capitalism.* New York: Routledge.

Wright, Richard A. and Ellis, Mark. 2000. Race, region and the territorial politics of immigration in the US. *International Journal of Population Geography* 6 (3): 197–211.

Yañez, Linda Reyna and Soto, Alfonso. 1994. Local police involvement in the enforcement of immigration law. *Hispanic Law Journal* 1 (1): 9–51.

Zolberg, Aristide R. 2006. *A Nation by Design.* Cambridge: Harvard University Press.

CHAPTER **25** # Labor Migration, Trafficking and Border Controls

Michele Ford and Lenore Lyons

In the last decade there has been unprecedented international interest in addressing the crime of human trafficking. Often described as the third largest form of transnational criminal activity (cf. Jayagupta 2009), human trafficking is typically understood to involve the forcible movement of women and children across borders for the purposes of exploitative labor, usually in the commercial sex industry. This understanding is enshrined in the 2000 United Nations Trafficking Protocol which contains three key elements that in combination are said to determine whether a case of human trafficking has occurred. These are: (1) an *action* (e.g., recruitment); (2) a *means* (e.g., coercion or deception); and (3) a *purpose* (exploitation).[1] According to this definition, consent is irrelevant once it is established that deception, force or other prohibited means have been used in recruiting a "victim" of trafficking.

The issue of consent is important in distinguishing human trafficking from migrant smuggling, since smuggling is deemed not to involve exploitation of the individual at the point of destination: "Whereas the illegal crossing of borders is the aim of smuggling, the aim of trafficking is the exploitation of one's labour. In other words, the issue of smuggling concerns the protection of the state against illegal migrants, while the issue of trafficking concerns the protection of individual persons against violence and abuse" (Ditmore and Wijers 2003: 80). Although it is acknowledged that human trafficking may occur via both legal and illegal migration streams, people smuggling is defined as the *illegal* movement of people across national borders.[2] The crucial distinction between the two phenomena, therefore, is the forced labor or slavery-like conditions that always characterize trafficking, which is inherently exploitative and not incidentally exploitative as is the case with smuggling (Kempadoo 2005: xii).

International policy responses to both human trafficking and people smuggling are invariably framed in border security terms – states act to stop illegal cross-border flows, rescue "victims," detain "illegals," and prosecute evil "traffickers" and "smug-

A Companion to Border Studies, First Edition. Edited by Thomas M. Wilson and Hastings Donnan.
© 2012 Blackwell Publishing Ltd. Published 2012 by Blackwell Publishing Ltd.

glers." This criminal justice/border security framework is supported at an international level by the placement of both the Trafficking Protocol and the Migrant Smuggling Protocol within the UN Convention against Transnational Organized Crime, which aims to address other types of illegal cross-border flows such as the sale of armaments and drugs. The legal distinction between trafficking and smuggling embodied in the creation of two separate protocols reflects international concern to protect the human rights of vulnerable people (primarily women and children) who fall prey to criminal gangs and syndicates who seek to exploit them, while at the same time supporting the state's right to protect its borders from "illegals" and "queue jumpers."

While the Convention seeks to distinguish between trafficking, smuggling, and other forms of migration, in reality the boundaries are very much blurred. Individuals who have been smuggled may find themselves working in the same industries as persons who have been trafficked and may be subject to the same exploitative practices (Grewcock 2003; Skeldon 2000). Conversely, victims of trafficking may be treated as undocumented migrants if they are caught outside an obvious trafficking context. The artificial distinctions between trafficking and smuggling also overlook the temporal dimension to migration cycles. Migrant workers who cross borders for illegal work may change jobs and face exploitation (thus moving from a situation of smuggling to trafficking) many months or years after they first crossed the border; and children and teenagers, who were by definition "trafficked," become adult migrants. Moreover, these problems are not only faced by "illegal" migrants. As Wong notes in her study of labor migrants in Malaysia, "individual migrant lives constantly weave their way in and out of intersecting spheres of legality and illegality" (2005: 71), and thus, while labor migration, trafficking and smuggling are legally different, the consequences in terms of migrants' vulnerability to exploitation are often similar.

Even though scholars and policy-makers acknowledge the fluid boundaries between human trafficking, people smuggling and "legal" labor migration, these artificial distinctions remain a cornerstone of immigration laws. In a post–9/11 world, border control has become a matter of symbolic performance for many governments, who rely on the myth of its loss to justify increasingly restrictive economic and social policies (Anderson and O'Dowd 1999; Pickering 2004; van Schendel and Abraham 2005). In fact, the most common policy response to the massive movement of people that has characterized globalization is the establishment of legal frameworks aimed at restricting immigration and prosecuting illegal entries (Segrave and Milivojevic 2005). This involves increasingly punitive immigration and border control regimes and the implementation of antitrafficking laws that aim to punish traffickers and smugglers, repatriate trafficking victims and deport "illegals." In many instances, the specter of human trafficking has been effectively mobilized to legitimize the increasing criminalization of migrants and those who assist them (Sharma 2005: 92). At a policy level these ambiguities serve an important purpose, enabling compromises to be made between actors with different interests and concerns.

The blurred boundaries between human trafficking and migrant smuggling are a structural by-product of the need to accommodate different state responses to migration control and border security. The advantage of this fuzziness is that it "enables a high degree of rhetoric flexibility, which ensures an adhesion that would not be the same if policies only aimed to reduce undocumented migration" (Nieuwenhuys and Pecoud 2007: 1690). All forms of migration become confined to a narrow and restrictive security framework as a consequence of fusing migration and crime in this way. This is no more apparent than in the ways in which some states respond to the issues associated with temporary labor migration. While the capacity for individual states to regulate labor migration varies considerably, there is a remarkable consistency in the ways in which state authorities seek to manage temporary labor flows. Both sending and receiving countries have developed complex immigration and employment regimes to recruit and deploy labor migrants and most of these regimes assume a clear distinction between legal and illegal arrival and deployment. Nonetheless, most states exercise restraint and selectivity in addressing irregular labor migration, and their repertoire of responses varies according to socioeconomic and political realities (Ahmad 2008). In some cases it may suit the interests of both states and employers to have access to a large irregular workforce (Cunningham and Heyman 2004; Ford 2006a). In others, strict regulation of all migration flows is intimately tied to public debates about "law and order" and "border security" (Crinis 2005; Grewcock 2007).

Since the signing of the UN Trafficking Protocol in 2000 another dimension has been added to bordering practices as they pertain to the regulation of international labor migration. In the face of mounting evidence that documented labor migrants encounter a range of exploitative practices in destination countries, a number of international development agencies, nongovernmental organizations (NGOs) and some states have started to employ an "antitrafficking framework" in their thinking and practice when dealing with cases of labor exploitation faced by "legal" migrants. The problems that many of these workers face include confinement and restricted freedom of movement; falsified and fake documents; bonded labor and debt bondage; deception; violence and abuse; poor working conditions; and nonpayment of wages. Rather than dealing with these issues as cases of labor abuse using the labor laws of receiving countries, migrant rights activists and some states have turned to antitrafficking laws. They argue that the endemic nature of these problems, and the ease with which documented migrant workers can become undocumented, means that the vast majority of low-skilled migrant workers can quite easily be characterized as "victims of human trafficking" using the definition contained within the UN Trafficking Protocol (cf. ASI 2003; IOM 2007).

By describing "documented/legal" migrants as "victims of trafficking," this approach disrupts the categories typically used by governments to regulate temporary labor migration. This perspective has been facilitated by the massive investment in antitrafficking initiatives by international agencies and donors since 2000. Donor aid provides the resources to pursue labor abuse cases as "trafficking cases," and international pressure to ratify the Trafficking Protocol and to demonstrate compliance with minimum standards outlined in the annual Trafficking in Persons Report prepared by the US State Department provides political motivation (Chuang 2006; McSherry and Cullen 2007). Countries that do not comply are subject to sanctions, including the termination of nonhumanitarian aid and non trade-related assistance and US opposition to assistance from international financial institutions (Ould 2004:

61). In addition, trafficking and smuggling, as core subjects of the UN Convention against Transnational Crime, are linked with measures to address "global terrorism" in the heightened security environment post–9/11 and governments are encouraged to take a tough stance on irregular migration through tighter border controls (Kaur and Metcalfe 2006). In this environment, dealing with documented labor migrants under antitrafficking laws or programs can provide states with the means to demonstrate that they are "tough" on trafficking, smuggling and terrorism.

This approach should not, however, be regarded as simply a means to deal with international pressure from the United States and other donor countries. It also reflects a growing view among some scholars and activists that the legal distinction between labor migration, human trafficking and migrant smuggling should be jettisoned on the grounds that it leads to unnecessary confusion and focuses attention on the *means* rather than the conditions of recruitment and deployment (cf. Brock et al. 2000; Grewcock 2003; O'Connell Davidson and Anderson 2006): "if the primary concern is to locate, explain and combat the use of forced labor, slavery, servitude and the like, then there is no moral or analytical reason to distinguish between forced labor involving 'illegal immigrants,' 'smuggled persons' or 'victims of trafficking'" (Anderson and O'Connell Davidson 2003: 7). These concerns have led some advocates and scholars to argue that the focus should be on addressing human rights violations of *all* labor migrants, regardless of how they cross borders (Brock et al. 2000).

Once the focus of attention moves away from the means by which a migrant arrives in a destination country and shifts instead to conditions of work, strategies can be developed to address labor exploitation and promote the social and labor rights of all migrants. This approach is exemplified in the use of forced labor conventions and protocols by the International Labour Organization (ILO) to pursue the rights of migrant workers. The ILO defines forced labor as "all work or service which is exacted from any person under the menace of any penalty and for which the said person has not offered himself voluntarily" (ILO 2009: 5). In their ILO-funded research, Andrees and van der Linden (2005) describe a "forced labour continuum" in which they identify three categories of labor – trafficked victims of forced labor, nontrafficked victims of forced labor and successful migrants. They argue that trafficked victims of forced labor are subject to the worst abuses because they generally have the least freedom of movement and are the most vulnerable, while nontrafficked victims of forced labor face a range of exploitative conditions, including nonpayment of wages, retention of identity documents, long working hours and unacceptable working conditions. For Andrees and van der Linden (2005: 63), the advantage of the "forced labour continuum" over the traditional distinction between "legal labour migrants," "victims of trafficking," and "illegal migrants" is that it provides a means to examine the "varying degrees to which migrants can become victims of exploitation, routes that lead into forced labour and individual strategies to escape from coercion and control."[3]

An alternative approach within the NGO community is to argue that all migrants who face cases of labor exploitation are victims of trafficking. For example, Anti-Slavery International (ASI) includes documented migrant domestic workers as victims of trafficking, arguing that a "sophisticated system of debt-bondage and forced labour" characterizes the domestic work industry (Ould 2004: 62). Similarly, Human Rights Watch (2008: 40) concludes that trafficking is widespread among migrant domestic workers. According to Jureidini and Moukarbel, the majority of migrant domestic workers enter into employment contracts which are deliberately misleading, and "such direct and indirect deception regarding contractual security . . . places workers within the category of having been trafficked" (2004: 585). To combat the "trafficking" of migrant domestic workers, ASI recommends a three-pronged approach that includes regulation of the domestic work sector, labor organizing, and the application of the Trafficking Protocol (ASI 2003: 40).

These debates have very real consequences not only for irregular labor migrants, but also for borderlands and borderlanders, especially at highly visible international boundaries with a history of undocumented border-crossing. The increasing securitization of borders can make the process of border crossing more onerous and expensive for all individuals who seek to cross the border. As a result, borderlanders involved in routinized border crossings are subject to increasing state interest. They may be harassed, subject to a range of "fines," and even arrested as traffickers or people smugglers (Eilenberg in press). Border policing activities also disrupt the livelihoods of smugglers, petty traders, and labor brokers, especially when government officials make them the target of antitrafficking campaigns and initiatives. In contexts where borderlanders lay claim to the unique and special character of their cross-border activities as being "illegal but licit" (Abraham and van Schendel 2005), countertrafficking efforts can threaten to disrupt what many see as a traditional way of life (Ford and Lyons in press-b). Understanding the impact of the antitrafficking movement on all forms of labor migration therefore necessitates attention to the discursive and material practices of bordering that take place not only in the center and "en route," but also in the borderlands themselves.

LABOR MIGRATION, PEOPLE SMUGGLING AND HUMAN TRAFFICKING IN THE RIAU ISLANDS

The policy implications of dealing with labor migration via an antitrafficking lens are clearly demonstrated in the case of the Riau Islands, which form part of Indonesia's border with Singapore and Malaysia.[4] The complex intersections between migration flows and different regulatory regimes in the border zone reveal the slippages between labor migration, smuggling and trafficking in practice and in policy. The islands of Bintan, Batam and Karimun, which lie in the Straits of Malacca to the northeast of Sumatra and directly south of Singapore (see Figure 25.1), are part of the Riau Islands Province (Provinsi Kepulauan Riau, Kepri). Since the mid-1980s, significant numbers of Indonesians have passed through these islands in search of work abroad in Singapore or Malaysia. The islands are also an arrival point for returning international migrants, including undocumented workers deported to Indonesia by the governments of those countries. In addition, they have been identified as a trafficking "hotspot," primarily of women and girls from other parts of Indonesia into the locally based commercial sex industry but also into the international sex trade.

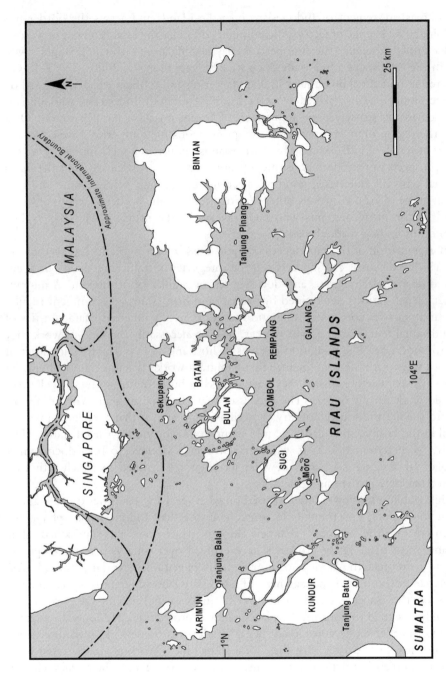

Figure 25.1   The Riau Islands

The mass movement of Indonesians into the islands and across the border was precipitated by a range of factors, including in particular the establishment of a cross-border growth triangle (the Indonesia–Malaysia–Singapore Growth Triangle, IMS-GT) in the 1990s and a free-trade zone with Singapore in the 2000s. The IMS-GT attracted international investment in manufacturing and tourism which depended on the recruitment of low-skilled workers from throughout Indonesia, who initially migrated to the sparsely populated island of Batam on short-term contracts. Over time, the region drew large numbers of spontaneous migrants who traveled to the border in search of well-paying jobs in the islands' industrial zones. Initially, employment prospects were good but, as migrant numbers grew, particularly after the Asian financial crisis hit Indonesia, good jobs became increasingly scarce. Some chose to remain in the islands. However, others decided to cross the border in search of work, joined by the many migrants who had traveled to the province with the explicit intention of finding work abroad.

An examination of the experiences of these cross-border migrants reveals the ease with which individuals can slip between the categories of trafficking victim, undocumented or irregular migrant, and documented or regular labor migrant. A migrant worker's legal status is determined by source- and host-country government regulations and practices concerning migration rather than any inherent characteristics of the individual temporary migrant worker, or even necessarily the kind of work they seek to undertake. The migration regimes of host and source countries intersect in complex ways, with the consequence that a migrant worker's status cannot simply be determined by whether or not they have entered a host country using a legally recognized work permit or visa. The processes that potential migrant workers follow prior to leaving the source country, as well as the practices that they encounter on arrival in the host country can have just as much bearing on their legal status. Ultimately, the determination as to whether a worker is deemed to be a documented "regular" labor migrant depends on which jurisdiction is invoked, by which authority, and at what time in the migration cycle.

While public attention is often focused on what receiving countries do to regulate immigration flows, governments in source countries like Indonesia also play a key role in creating the "regular" channels through which low- and semiskilled labor migrants must pass. These processes have evolved over time as a result of public pressure to protect the labor and human rights of nationals working abroad. The Indonesian government's management of temporary labor migration is enshrined in its law on the Placement and Protection of Indonesian Workers Overseas, a law ostensibly designed to improve the placement and protection of Indonesian migrant workers. In order to be considered "legal" under this framework, intending labor migrants must first register with their local labor office. Workers are recruited from this pool by officially sanctioned recruitment agents who organize their health checks, training, insurance, labor migrant passports (*paspor TKI*) and employment visas. Intending migrant workers are required to remain in holding centers for between one and three months while they await placement overseas. The complexities of the official process create ample opportunities for rent-seeking within the formal system and at each stage of the recruitment process, prospective labor migrants are faced with yet another round of paperwork and fees (Palmer in press). The time and costs involved provide many migrants with sufficient motivation to seek out an alternative migration channel (Ford 2001; Idrus 2008).

Many labor migrants passing through the Riau Islands choose to take the more cost-effective and efficient "documented but illegal" route.[5] These migrants carry what are described in Indonesian as *aspal* papers (*asli tapi palsu*, real but fake), reflecting the fact that they are genuine documents obtained without going through all the processes that define formally sanctioned channels of temporary labor migration (Ford and Lyons 2011). Migrant workers using the *aspal* route are typically delivered to the islands by middlemen or employees of agents based in Kepri. The island-based agent obtains a local identity card (known locally as *KTP musiman* or a "seasonal identity card") for the prospective worker using contacts in the local bureaucracy. The identity card is then leveraged to obtain a migrant worker passport. Alternatively, intending *aspal* migrants are issued with a standard passport which, although it does not conform to the specifications of the labor export program, is an official travel document that may be recognized by overseas governments issuing work visas. This means that a prospective labor migrant can use the passport to exit Indonesia and legally enter a neighboring country, where they are issued with a valid work permit.

The *aspal* system produces a category of migrant workers who, while "documented" from the perspective of the receiving country, are considered by the Indonesian government to be "illegal" because they have not followed official labor deployment processes for overseas workers. Although both the identity card and the passport are obtained via unofficial means and may falsify information about their bearer (including name, place of birth and residence), they are to all intents and purposes legally valid documents issued by the authorities responsible. For prospective migrant workers who have yet to cross the border, the possession of *aspal* papers does not constitute a significant source of concern – it is not unusual for Indonesians to possess multiple identity cards, often with different names or details. Furthermore, the possession of such documents rarely poses a barrier to obtaining an overseas placement or, ultimately, to leaving the country. In addition, local authorities are often reluctant to report individuals or officials involved in the production of such documents. Immigration officials who uncover fraudulent documents when they process passport applications are also reluctant to report this information because it would implicate their colleagues in corrupt practices (Government of Indonesia 2009). In countries of destination, labor attachés and other embassy officials exercise a degree of discretion when they encounter those who have not followed official Indonesian labor migration regulations abroad, with the consequence that there are few sanctions from the Indonesian government against workers who contravene its laws (Palmer in press).

Many Indonesians enter Singapore and Malaysia as "tourists" on visitor passes and then either convert their visas to work permits with the assistance of a local labor placement agent or work in contravention of the conditions of their tourist pass. The vast majority of those going to Malaysia on this basis travel the *aspal* route from elsewhere in the Indonesian archipelago. However, a significant number of temporary migrant workers – particularly of those seeking to work in Singapore – are Riau Islanders with kinship networks that stretch across the international border, or long-term residents who have forged business relationships with customers and clients on either side of the border. This subgroup, which generally travels independently of the *aspal* system, tends to be engaged in informal sector occupations that are not officially open to labor migrants such as petty trading, small-scale service provision (such as tailoring) or the commercial sex industry. The majority of short-term labor migrants cross the border with the intention of staying until their visas expire and/ or the work runs out. They then take a ferry back to the Riau Islands and, after a suitable length of time, cross the border again.

Another smaller group of migrants leave Indonesia without documents of any kind. These migrants use the services of smugglers who operate covertly, usually under cover of darkness, to drop their human cargo offshore along more remote sections of the Malaysian coastline. Attempts at landing in Singapore are much less successful because the coastline is more heavily populated and the strait more fre-quently patrolled. If they are successful in their attempt to enter illegally, these workers find work in construction sites, plantations or the informal sector. It is this group of migrant workers who most accurately meet the definition of people smug-gling and thus fall into the category of "undocumented" or "irregular" labor migrants.[6]

The channel a worker uses to get to a host country is only one possible determinant in the construction of his or her legal status – the ultimate determination rests with the receiving country. Singapore and Malaysia have complex mechanisms through which unskilled and semiskilled labor migration is managed. In both cases, a migrant worker's status is determined by (1) the issuing of a legally valid temporary work permit, and (2) the worker's compliance with the regulations that govern that permit. A host country may accommodate a source country's labor export regulations though a non-binding Memorandum of Understanding (MOU). However, such agreements are of limited effect. Although Malaysia is formally committed not to accept labor migrants who have not come through the Indonesian export labor system, anecdotal evidence suggests that it continues to accord legal status to some workers who have not emigrated in this way – provisions that have at times been of great benefit to *aspal* migrants. Malaysian officials also turn a blind eye to irregular migrants when it is politically or economically favorable to do so (Ford 2010). Singapore, which does not have a MOU with Indonesia, determines its policy on Indonesian migrant labor unilaterally, and is therefore not bound in any way to respect or enforce the condi-tions of the Indonesian labor migration system.

The more complex and arbitrary the system, the more porous these different migration categories become. They are also sensitive to changes in the political and economic climate. At times, governments actively work to increase the numbers of foreign workers and may even ignore the presence of "illegals." But at times of eco-nomic downturn or great political cost, they move to limit numbers of temporary labor migrants by closer regulation of entry and increasingly punitive sanctions against those found without appropriate documents. After the Malaysian government enacted a new immigration law on August 1, 2002, almost 400,000 Indonesians working without appropriate documentation were deported to Belawan, Batam and Dumai in Sumatra, and Pontianak and Nunukan in Kalimantan – a policy decision that resulted in a humanitarian crisis in Nunukan (Ford 2006a) and severe pressure on local authorities in other targeted ports. Since that time, there have been regular deportations: almost 17,000 deportees passed through the Tanjung Pinang holding center on the island of Bintan in 2006 alone (Ford and Lyons in press-a).

Migration status and the administrative systems designed to regulate it potentially contribute to labor exploitation. Workers can be deported if their documents are found to be fraudulent or if officials become aware that their details are falsified. With the increasing use of biometrics by immigration authorities, workers with multiple passports and/or names, or who knowingly (or unknowingly) change their personal details, can find themselves detained and deported if this information is uncovered. Underage workers may face additional problems depending on whether the host country has in place antitrafficking laws and regulations. These risks make migrant workers less inclined to stand up to an abusive employer. By the same token, migration through recognized source-country channels does not guarantee ongoing regular status or the protections that designation may appear to imply. Regular migrants can choose to enter into irregular status by breaching their visa conditions. They may also lose their regular status involuntarily because of changes within the regulatory framework or because regulations are framed in such a way as to give employers the power to jeopardize migrant workers' legal status – for example, by failing to pay a levy, by confiscating travel documents, or by forcing workers to do work that breaches their visa conditions – conditions which are set and can be changed at any time by the host state (Ford 2010).

As a result of these vagaries, for many migrant workers there is little correlation between conditions of work and legal status. Irregular workers do not always experience worse working conditions than regular migrants, but in cases where they do they have no legal recourse. *Aspal* migrants may face an additional fear that their "gray" migration status may be revealed in any attempt to address exploitative labor conditions. In contexts where work visas are tied to a single employer, even regular labor migrants often accept unreasonable conditions of work because they fear the loss of their right to stay and work in the host country. Moreover, temporary labor migration programs tend to limit foreign workers' access to jobs to sectors of the economy that are relatively poorly regulated or impose visa conditions that prevent them from accessing the same labor rights as local workers (Ford 2006b). As a consequence, documented migrants can easily find themselves victims of labor exploitation and/or subject to mandatory detention and deportation, which suggests that legal immigration status does not guarantee a successful migration outcome.

The fact that irregular labor migrants do not necessarily experience more – or even as much – exploitation as regular labor migrants either while traveling to the host country or while working there suggests that the focus on the *means* of migration rests on flawed assumptions. Nevertheless, host (and source) countries continue to cling to the legal fiction of a straightforward distinction between documented/regular and undocumented/irregular labor migration because it serves an important function in border control. Paradoxically, this preoccupation with illegal immigration and transnational crime has facilitated the implementation of the UN Trafficking Protocol and global countertrafficking measures (Kapur 2005; Turnbull 1999). The result is an elision between antitrafficking and immigration control which renders border control and anti-immigration activities more palatable to the public on the grounds that they contribute to the process of helping "innocent victims" of trafficking (Berman 2010: 89). While much of this focus has been on trafficking for sexual exploitation, the crime of "labor trafficking" is gaining increasing attention.

USING THE ANTITRAFFICKING FRAMEWORK TO DEAL WITH LABOR MIGRATION

The extent to which the abuse of labor migrants has been framed as human trafficking varies dramatically between national contexts, depending on whether or not a particular country has an antitrafficking law and, if so, whether it focuses primarily on human trafficking for the purposes of sexual exploitation.[7] While continuing to emphasize human trafficking for the purposes of sexual exploitation, Indonesian government policy has increasingly focused on labor migration since the Trafficking Protocol came into existence. Specific reference is made to the potential for trafficking within the formal labor export system in official government publications. According to *The Elimination of Trafficking in Persons in Indonesia, 2004–2005*, a publication by the Coordinating Ministry for People's Welfare (the body tasked with coordinating the countertrafficking programs of different ministries): "Labor recruitment companies, with their network of agents/brokers in many areas, are traffickers when they facilitate the falsification of ID cards and passports and illegally confine potential migrant workers at the safe house, and put them in a different job than the one promised or introduce them by force to the sex industry" (Republic of Indonesia 2005: 6). According to this view, trafficking occurs when there is deception at the point of recruitment (where deception may be interpreted as providing incorrect or false information about wages, working hours and type of work) and exploitation in the workplace (nonpayment of wages, long working hours, physical or sexual abuse and so on) regardless of immigration status. This interpretation entered Indonesian official discourse as a result of international interventions, primarily through the efforts of the International Catholic Migration Commission and the American Center for International Labor Solidarity, which jointly implemented a series of three major antitrafficking projects on behalf of the United States Agency for International Development (USAID) (Ford and Lyons in press-a). Referring to the conditions of work of *documented* labor migrants from Indonesia, a major report released by these organizations states:

> If recruitment is made through misrepresentation about earnings, and conditions of work; if there exists no clear definition of work, working hours, weekly holidays and leave; if there are unexplained pay deductions, or withholding payment of wages, confinement through confiscation of travel documents or otherwise, and/or sexual abuse . . . *then a domestic worker employed abroad can be categorized as a trafficked person.* (Sugiarti et al. 2006: 29, emphasis added)

However, for the most part, the Indonesian government has equated labor trafficking with labor migration that takes place *outside* the formal labor export system.

At the local level, the concept of labor trafficking has rapidly gained traction, particularly in transit zones like the Riau Islands. Initially, countertrafficking brought a rush of brothel raids and other measures targeted at trafficking in the local sex industry. In later years, however, the focus shifted toward labor migrants, partly as a result of pressure from – and the provision of targeted resources by – central agencies and international donors, and partly because local governments are reluctant to provide funds from their own budget to resource programs to assist deported labor migrants from other provinces to return home. Among nationally sponsored initiatives were the passing of Local Regulation No. 12/2007 on the Elimination of Trafficking in Women and Children, followed by the drafting of a Local Action Plan, the formation of a provincial coordinating taskforce and the establishment of a government-run shelter. The provincial government also initiated attempts to coordinate with provinces of origin in Java and West Nusa Tenggara (Biro Perempuan Provinsi Kepri 2009).[8] Local police established trafficking desks and use both the trafficking and labor recruitment laws to punish syndicates that deal in labor. Most of those identified as victims of trafficking in the Riau Islands are female labor migrants who have entered Malaysia without documents and have been subsequently apprehended and deported to Tanjung Pinang.

In the absence of donor support for programs that deal specifically with migrant workers, NGOs have little choice other than to try to deal with deportees through their countertrafficking programs. Over the last decade we have witnessed a fundamental shift in the ways in which NGO workers position both sex workers and labor migrants in the antitrafficking discourse. While most NGOs continue to regard trafficking as a minor problem in the commercial sex industry – for them, the main issue is the protection of sex worker rights – they are much more willing to use an antitrafficking framework to address issues faced by labor migrants. This is evident in the language used to discuss labor exploitation, which mirrors the three key elements of the UN Protocol: NGOs claim that deportees are subject to a "means" (*cara*) and "process" (*proses*) – in this case recruitment and training – which means that they were victims of trafficking. From the perspective of the NGOs involved, there are multiple advantages associated with using the antitrafficking discourse to deal with labor migrants who have been deported from nearby countries to the Riau Islands. One NGO worker explained that while government officials can be convinced to buy a plane ticket for a victim of trafficking, they would never fund the individual repatriation of a failed migrant worker, no matter how worthy the case. Selective and deliberate use of countertrafficking language can also be useful when dealing with some donors who are less committed to assisting labor migrants.

While the short-term benefits of dealing with "failed" labor migration as labor trafficking include increased donor funding and attention (the benefits of which cannot be underestimated for small NGOs), as well as repatriation assistance for "victims" of labor trafficking who wish to return home, there are also numerous disadvantages. Antitrafficking laws and regulations not only establish a victim's status but also determine the ways in which a victim will be treated. These programs have an overriding interest in returning them to their place of origin. In many cases, however, migrant workers do not want to return, especially if that involves dealing with the stigma attached to an acknowledgment of victimhood. The reality is that large numbers of failed labor migrants want to cross the border again to try their luck. With their focus on repatriating trafficking victims, countertrafficking programs not only overlook what it is that migrants themselves want out of the migration process, but how and why they become undocumented or irregular.

CONCLUSION

The nexus between human trafficking, people smuggling and labor migration is made manifest at international borders. Multiple regimes of exclusion and inclusion shaped by gender, age, ethnicity and nationality determine the politics of labor market hierarchies, which in turn shape the legal, economic and physical vulnerabilities of migrant workers. However, the power relations that underpin these migration flows and border controls are also revealed in the discursive and material practices associated with labeling different migrant populations as "documented workers," "illegals," or "victims of trafficking." It is here that the state distinction between "legals" and "illegals" becomes visible and apparent. And yet, the framing of all forms of exploitation involving temporary labor migrants as "trafficking" ignores the agency of these migrant workers and fails to acknowledge that many of them knowingly cross borders without papers and/or choose to undertake jobs deemed illegal by both sending and host societies. It also overlooks the endemic character of "gray migration" in Indonesia's labor export program, through which prospective labor migrants utilize the services of a range of middlemen to procure overseas employment. Indeed, as the prevalence of gray migration suggests, immigration status is only part of the problem – when it is a problem at all.

For many migrant workers passing through the Riau Islands to Malaysia, participation in the formal labor migration system is neither easy nor desirable, and has little impact on their experience abroad. And, except in exceptional circumstances, *aspal* and regular labor migrants experience the same kinds of problems in terms of labor exploitation, especially in domestic work or more marginal parts of the service sector, but also in mainstream formal sector workplaces where their contracts specify different working conditions from their local counterparts. The use of the trafficking discourse to deal with these issues highlights the problem of labor exploitation by emphasizing the victimhood of abused migrant workers. But at the same time it obscures ways of dealing with it by shifting the focus from host countries' failure to regulate more effectively the conditions of work experienced by migrants to the criminal actions of nonstate actors engaged in people smuggling and other forms of border-crossing. The increasing criminalization of labor migrants, and the associated use of a criminal justice/border security framework to respond to cross-border flows, has the effect of absolving host countries from having to address endemic structural exploitation of migrant workers. It also limits the ability of sending countries to protect their nationals by requiring them to deal with cases of "irregular" migration by using antitrafficking and/or other immigration laws.

The experiences of temporary labor migrants also draw our attention to the need to understand better the interactions between borderlanders and transient populations. Studies of borderlands are replete with accounts of the unique character of border life and the imposition of state border processes on long-standing border communities. The lives of transient "others" – migrants, smuggled persons, "illegals"

– rarely feature in these accounts. In contrast, studies of migration and human trafficking are preoccupied with places of destination and arrival and rarely consider spaces of transit. And yet, the bordering practices that shape border life are intrinsically linked to the security and immigration regimes that seek to manage a range of cross-border flows. This securitization of the border has transformed the physical landscape of many borderland communities, with the construction of detention facilities, repatriation desks and victim shelters. It has also irrevocably altered the ways that some borderlanders understand the nature of cross-border mobility, as the language of trafficking has entered everyday discourse and border-crossing practices themselves are subjected to increasing state scrutiny.

This global obsession with border control has recast the border as "a site of crime" (Andrijasevic 2003: 256) policed by a multiplicity of means, some material and others juridical. These practices not only "harden" the borders concerned; they also substantially change the nature of borderlands. Most important, these practices are not only played out "along the border." The border is policed by immigration officials as well as a range of state and nonstate agents, including employers, who may never visit the border regions. Borders thus have the capacity to shape the lives of temporary labor migrants (and other migrant populations) long after they arrive at their destinations, or indeed, after they return home. It is this ability of the border to reach into the heart of the nation-state that necessitates a reorientation of our gaze beyond the borderland to the political economy of labor regimes that operate within the metropole in order to understand the full extent of bordering practices in the twenty-first century.

NOTES

1 The UN Protocol to Prevent, Suppress and Punish Trafficking in Persons, Especially Women and Children (hereafter the Trafficking Protocol) defines human trafficking as "the recruitment, transportation, transfer, harbouring or receipt of persons, by means of the threat or use of force or other forms of coercion, of abduction, of fraud, of deception, of the abuse of power or of a position of vulnerability or of the giving or receiving of payments or benefits to achieve the consent of a person having control over another person, for the purpose of exploitation" (United Nations 2000: 42).

2 The UN Protocol against the Smuggling of Migrants by Land, Sea and Air (hereafter Migrant Smuggling Protocol) defines migrant smuggling as: "the procurement, in order to obtain, directly or indirectly, a financial or other material benefit, of the illegal entry of a person into a State Party of which the person is not a national or a permanent resident" (United Nations 2000: 54–55).

3 While these initiatives may improve working conditions, they are inadequate for dealing with the particular conditions facing commercial sex workers and informal sector workers, and for addressing the role played by organized crime (Bruch 2004: 27).

4 The research on which this chapter is based was conducted primarily as part of a project, From Migrant to Worker, funded by Australian Research Council Discovery Project Grant DP0880081. We would like to thank Wayne Palmer for his assistance with follow-up interviews in the Riau Islands in 2010.

5 This is also the case along the land border between Indonesian Kalimantan and the eastern Malaysian states of Sabah and Sarawak (cf. Idrus 2008).

452   MICHELE FORD AND LENORE LYONS

6   The practice of local Riau Islanders crossing the border for work, leisure or kinship obliga-
     tions without passing through immigration checkpoints is nowadays much less prevalent
     along this border than it was in the past. In other border sites, notably in Kalimantan,
     however, borderlanders regularly cross the land border to work (illegally) in Malaysia
     (Eilenberg in press).
7   See Ford et al. (in press) for in-depth case studies of labor migration and antitrafficking
     efforts in Southeast Asia.
8   Major obstacles identified by the Women's Bureau in the handling of trafficking cases in
     the Riau Islands included the problem of dealing with deported labor migrants who had
     not been trafficked and the limitations on funding for the handling and provision of services
     for victims who originate from outside the province. In addition, a lack of adequate funding
     for the shelter meant that it could accommodate victims of trafficking for a maximum of
     just 15 days, and staff have difficulty ensuring that victims are not retrafficked (Biro Per-
     empuan Provinsi Kepri 2009).

REFERENCES

Abraham, Itty and van Schendel, Willem. 2005. Introduction: the making of illicit-ness. In W. van Schendel and I. Abraham, eds, *Illicit Flows and Criminal Things: States, Borders, and the Other Side of Globalization*, pp. 1–37. Bloomington: Indiana University Press.

Ahmad, Ali Nobil. 2008. The labour market consequences of human smuggling: "illegal" employment in London's migrant economy. *Journal of Ethnic and Migration Studies* 34 (6): 853–874.

Anderson, Bridget and O'Connell Davidson, Julia. 2003. *Is Trafficking in Human Beings Demand Driven? A Multi-Country Pilot Study*. Migration Research Series 15. Geneva: International Organization for Migration.

Anderson, James and O'Dowd, Liam. 1999. Borders, border regions and territoriality: contradictory meanings, changing signifi-cance. *Regional Studies* 33 (7): 593–604.

Andrees, Beate and van der Linden, Mariska N.J. 2005. Designing trafficking research from a labour market perspective: the ILO experience. *International Migration* 43 (1–2): 55–73.

Andrijasevic, Rutvica. 2003. The difference borders make: (il)legality, migration and trafficking in Italy among Eastern European women in prostitution. In S. Ahmed, C.

Castaneda, A.-M. Fortier and M. Sheller, eds, *Uprootings/Regroundings: Questions of Home and Migration*, pp. 251–272. Oxford: Berg.

ASI (Anti-Slavery International). 2003. *The Migration-Trafficking Nexus: Combating Trafficking through the Protection of Migrants' Human Rights*. London: Anti-Slavery International.

Berman, Jacqueline. 2010. Biopolitical man-agement, economic calculation and "traf-ficked women." *International Migration* 48 (4): 84–113.

Biro Perempuan Provinsi Kepri. 2009. Upaya pembangunan koordinasi dan kerjasama antar pemerintah daerah dalam penyelenga-raan upaya pemulangan dan reintegrasi sosial [Development efforts through inter-governmental coordination and regional cooperation in provision for return and social reintegration]. In *Pertemuan Nasional Perencanaan Strategis Gugus Tugas Pence-gahan dan Penanganan Tindak Pidana Perdagangan Orang*. Bogor, Indonesia.

Brock, Deborah, Sutdhibhasilip, Mook, Gillies, Kara and Oliver, Chantelle. 2000. Migrant sex workers: a roundtable analysis. *Canadian Woman Studies* 20 (2): 84–90.

Bruch, Elizabeth M. 2004. The search for an effective response to human trafficking.

Stanford Journal of International Law 40 (1): 1–45.

Chuang, Janie. 2006. The United States as global sheriff: using unilateral sanctions to combat human trafficking. *Michigan Journal of International Law* 27: 437–494.

Crinis, Vicki Denese. 2005. The devil you know: Malaysian perceptions of foreign workers. *Review of Indonesian and Malayan Affairs* 39 (2): 91–111.

Cunningham, Hilary and Heyman, Josiah McC. 2004. Introduction: mobilities and enclosures at borders. *Identities* 11 (3): 298–302.

Ditmore, Melissa, and Wijers, Marjan. 2003. The negotiations on the UN Protocol on Trafficking in Persons. *Nemesis* 4: 79–88.

Eilenberg, Michael. In press. Territorial sovereignty and the anti-trafficking discourse in the Indonesian borderlands of West Kalimantan. In M. Ford, L. Lyons and W. van Schendel, eds, *Labour Migration and Human Trafficking: Critical Perspectives from Southeast Asia*. London: Routledge.

Ford, Michele. 2001. Indonesian women as export commodity: notes from Tanjung Pinang. *Labour and Management in Development Journal* 2 (5): 1–9.

Ford, Michele. 2006a. After Nunukan: the regulation of Indonesian migration to Malaysia. In A. Kaur and I. Metcalfe, eds, *Mobility, Labour Migration and Border Controls in Asia*, pp. 228–247. Basingstoke: Palgrave Macmillan.

Ford, Michele. 2006b. Migrant labor NGOs and trade unions: a partnership in progress? *Asian and Pacific Migration Journal* 15 (3): 299–318.

Ford, Michele. 2010. Constructing legality: the management of irregular labour migration in Thailand and Malaysia. In M. van der Linden, ed., *Labour History beyond Borders: Concepts and Explorations*, pp. 177–199. Leipzig: Akademische Verlagsanstalt.

Ford, Michele and Lyons, Lenore. 2011. Travelling the *aspal* route: grey labour migration through an Indonesian border town. In E. Aspinall and G. v. Klinken, eds, *The State and Illegality in Indonesia*, pp. 107–122. Leiden: KITLV Press.

Ford, Michele and Lyons, Lenore. In press-a. Counter-trafficking and migrant labour activism in Indonesia's periphery. In M. Ford, L. Lyons and W. van Schendel, eds, *Labour Migration and Human Trafficking: Critical Perspectives from Southeast Asia*. London: Routledge.

Ford, Michele and Lyons, Lenore. In press-b. Smuggling cultures in the Indonesia–Singapore borderlands. In B. Kalir and M. Sur, eds, *Illegal but Licit: Ethnographies of Human Mobility and Permissive Polities*. Leiden: Institute of International Asian Studies.

Ford, Michele, Lyons, Lenore and van Schendel, Willem, eds. In press. *Labour Migration and Human Trafficking: Critical Perspectives from Southeast Asia*. London: Routledge.

Government of Indonesia. 2009. Kikis Percaloan, 2009. Jakarta.

Grewcock, Michael. 2003. Irregular migration, identity and the state: the challenge for criminology. *Current Issues in Criminal Justice* 15 (2): 114–135.

Grewcock, Michael. 2007. Shooting the passenger: Australia's war on illicit migrants. In M. Lee, ed., *Human Trafficking*, pp. 178–209. Cullompton, UK: Willan.

Human Rights Watch. 2008. *"As If I Am Not Human": Abuses against Asian Domestic Workers in Saudi Arabia*. Human Rights Watch.

Idrus, Nurul Ilmi. 2008. Makkunrai passimokolo': Bugis migrant women workers in Malaysia. In M. Ford and L. Parker, eds, *Women and Work in Indonesia*, pp. 155–172. London: Routledge.

ILO (International Labour Organization). 2009. *The Cost of Coercion: Global Report under the Follow-up to the ILO Declaration on Fundamental Principles and Rights at Work*. Geneva: International Labour Organization.

IOM (International Organization for Migration). 2007. *ASEAN and Trafficking in Persons: Using Data as a Tool to Combat Trafficking in Persons*. Geneva: International Organization for Migration.

Jayagupta, Ratchada. 2009. The Thai government's repatriation and reintegration programmes: responding to trafficked female commercial sex workers from the Greater Mekong subregion. *International Migration* 47 (2): 227–253.

Jureidini, Ray and Moukarbel, Nayla. 2004. Female Sri Lankan domestic workers in Lebanon: a case of "contract slavery"? *Journal of Ethnic and Migration Studies* 30 (4): 581–607.

Kapur, Ratna. 2005. *Erotic Justice: Poscolonialism, Subjects and Rights.* London: Glass House Press.

Kaur, Amarjit and Metcalfe, Ian, eds. 2006. *Mobility, Labour Migration and Border Controls in Asia.* Basingstoke: Palgrave Macmillan.

Kempadoo, Kamala. 2005. Introduction: from moral panic to global justice: changing perspectives on trafficking. In K. Kempadoo, J. Sanghera and B. Pattanaik, eds, *Trafficking and Prostitution Reconsidered: New Perspectives on Migration, Sex Work, and Human Rights*, pp. vii–xxxiv. Boulder: Paradigm.

McSherry, Bernadette and Cullen, Miriam. 2007. The criminal justice response to trafficking in persons: practical problems with enforcement in the Asia-Pacific region. *Global Change, Peace and Security* 19 (3): 205–220.

Nieuwenhuys, Celine and Pecoud, Antoine. 2007. Human trafficking, information campaigns, and strategies of migration control. *American Behavioral Scientist* 50 (12): 1674–1695.

O'Connell Davidson, Julia and Anderson, Bridget. 2006. The trouble with "trafficking." In C.L. van den Anker and J. Doomernik, eds, *Trafficking and Women's Rights*, pp. 11–26. Houndmills: Palgrave Macmillan.

Ould, David. 2004. Trafficking and international law. In C. van den Anker, ed., *The Political Economy of New Slavery*, pp. 55–74. Basingstoke: Palgrave Macmillan.

Palmer, Wayne. In press. A labour attache's dilemma: the role of discretion in the trafficking-like practices of the Indonesian state. In M. Ford, L. Lyons and W. van Schendel, eds, *Labour Migration and Human Trafficking: Critical Perspectives from Southeast Asia.* London: Routledge.

Pickering, Sharon. 2004. Border terror: policing, forced migration and terrorism. *Global Change, Peace and Security* 16 (3): 211–226.

Republic of Indonesia. 2005. *The Elimination of Trafficking in Persons in Indonesia, 2004–2005.* Coordinating Ministry for People's Welfare, Jakarta.

Segrave, Marie and Milivojevic, Sanja. 2005. Sex trafficking: a new agenda. *Social Alternatives* 24 (2): 11–16.

Sharma, Nandita. 2005. Anti-trafficking rhetoric and the making of a global apartheid. *NWSA Journal (National Women's Studies Association)* 17 (3): 88–111.

Skeldon, Ronald. 2000. Trafficking: a perspective from Asia. *International Migration* 1: 7–30.

Sugiarti, Keri Lasmi, Davis, Jamie and Dasgupta, Abhijit, eds. 2006. *When They Were Sold.* Jakarta: International Catholic Migration Commission and American Center for International Labor Solidarity.

Turnbull, P. 1999. The fusion of immigration and crime in the European Union: problems of cooperation and the fight against the trafficking in women. In P. Williams, ed., *Illegal Immigration and Commercial Sex: The New Slave Trade*, pp. 189–213. London: Frank Cass.

United Nations. 2000. The United Nations Convention against Transnational Organized Crime, adopted by General Assembly Resolution 55/25 of 15 November 2000. At http://www.unodc.org/documents/treaties/UNTOC/Publications/TOC%20Convention/TOCebook-e.pdf (accessed Dec. 2011).

van Schendel, Willem and Abraham, Itty, eds. 2005. *Illicit Flows and Criminal Things: States, Borders, and the Other Side of Globalization.* Bloomington: Indiana University Press.

Wong, Diana. 2005. The rumor of trafficking: border controls, illegal migration, and the sovereignty of the nation-state. In W. van Schendel and I. Abraham, eds, *Illicit Flows and Criminal Things: States, Borders, and the Other Side of Globalization*, pp. 69–100. Bloomington: Indiana University Press.

CHAPTER 26

Spatial Strategies for Rebordering Human Migration at Sea

Alison Mountz and
Nancy Hiemstra

National borders are traditionally understood and policed as static (though not necessarily uncontested), identifiable lines marking territorial limits (see Nevins 2010). Contemporary borders, however, are highly mobile, diffused and always proliferating. This proliferation takes many forms, from digital information in shared databases to the offshore work of civil servants and naval personnel. The mobility of borders is always tied to human mobility. People employed by the government are often on the move in order to meet, intercept, process or exclude migrants en route. These encounters frequently entail negotiations over entry.

This chapter explores *how* and *where* borders are moving at sea. The sea constitutes one key site where borders and border enforcement are proliferating and where the policies and practices associated with proliferation can be tracked. We argue that new geographies of enforcement have taken hold and that an identifiable set of spatial strategies reverberates regionally across sites of enforcement. We map these patterns across regions where they have been spearheaded by nation-states investing in offshore interception: United States enforcement in the Caribbean and the Pacific, Australia's actions in the Pacific and Indian Oceans, and European Union member states' operations in the Mediterranean.

Nation-states aim to make their own territorial borders impenetrable by particular undesirables, but also hyperpermeable to desired groups and individuals as well as certain goods and services (Sparke 2006). Those states engaged most intensively in the securitization of migration in recent years have come to see their own national borders as elastic from within. For example, for the purposes of expeditiously designating undocumented migrants deportable, the US border can now be interpreted

A Companion to Border Studies, First Edition. Edited by Thomas M. Wilson and Hastings Donnan.
© 2012 Blackwell Publishing Ltd. Published 2012 by Blackwell Publishing Ltd.

by immigration officials as anywhere within 100 miles of any physical US border (ACLU 2006). Simultaneously, in efforts to make their own borders impenetrable, states see other countries' borders as penetrable, sending immigration control officers inside the territorial borders of other countries in attempts to prevent migrants from ever reaching their intended destination. Through such actions, borders move along with the bodily movements of authorities.

An interdisciplinary set of scholars has tracked the movement of border enforcement offshore (Collyer 2007; Hyndman and Mountz 2008; Coleman 2007a; Walters 2004) and onshore to sites internal to sovereign territory (Mountz 2010; Coleman 2007b; Winders 2007; Bigo 2000; Kocher and Coleman 2010). While building on literature that examines the movement of borders, we suggest that there is work yet to be done on where and how borders are moving. As we explore in this chapter, states also endeavor to overlay their own territorial borders on international waters through immigration enforcement actions. At sea, borders become elastic, and proliferate through their geographic dispersal. Walters (2008), for example, examines the return of marine stowaways to their places of origin and argues that scholars take more seriously the banal sites where sea meets land and technical modes of governance are carried out. Walters' work informs our own, where we seek to understand how borders become mobile entities at sea that are made to reach out strategically to populations en route (Mountz 2011c). In order to understand *how* borders are mobile at sea, we must examine not only the regions in which border enforcement operates, but the development of interception policies and practices over time and across space, the discourses surrounding them, and the legal geographies that enable border movement.

We begin by identifying three spatial strategies that undergird mobile border enforcement undertaken at sea. By employing these strategies, enforcing countries effectively relocate their borders offshore. We then explain briefly how human smuggling works, operating from the premise that smuggling and enforcement practices develop symbiotically. Next, we visit three regions where human smuggling is taking place, and enforcement authorities are moving borders at sea in efforts to disrupt smuggling routes. Our main objective is to explore ways in which these strategies are employed across distinct regions with similar patterns. In our conclusion, we examine the implications of these spatial strategies pursued by states.

Spatial Strategies Employed to "Reborder the Sea"

The strategies pursued by states that are migrants' intended destination increasingly center on a process of externalization, which entails the development of migration policies intended to prevent mobile bodies from ever reaching destination states' territorial borders (Hyndman and Mountz 2008; Collyer 2007). Externalization is typically carried out under the premise of protecting national security, in lieu of other emphases on human rights of migrants and refugees. These practices often carefully evade the provisions of international covenants pertaining to the treatment of asylum seekers (Hyndman and Mountz 2008). Externalization is accomplished through a range of practices and policies that effectively respatialize migration control. These include, for example, bilateral agreements with origin and transit countries allowing for detection, apprehension and repatriation of migrants; detention of migrants in nonstate territories; and the processing of asylum claims in states where refugees originate. Externalization raises important questions regarding the limits of sovereign territory and the mobility of national borders that inform our line of inquiry.

The concept of externalization underlies evolving immigration enforcement actions at sea, in states' policing of both territorial and international waters. Three principal spatial strategies that we observe offshore in what Walters (2008) calls 'rebordering the sea' are interception, detention and processing, and legal manipulation of territorial status. Here, we briefly introduce each strategy and its primary geographical expressions.

Through *interception at sea*, authorities from destination countries prevent migrants from entering sovereign territory, thereby precluding access to rights, services and legal procedures to which landed immigrants are entitled. As will be seen, these efforts to intercept unfold in the subsequent two strategies and themselves include a broad range of tactics, from holding migrants on boats and islands, to pressuring third countries to detain or accept migrants for resettlement. Interception at sea is often followed by offshore *detention and processing* in territory that is either foreign or holds subnational jurisdictional status as a colony or offshore territory (Mountz 2011b). Destination countries forge bilateral agreements with origin and transit countries that permit patrolling and interception activities in foreign waters or with flagged and unflagged vessels. Destination countries will often use foreign aid or other types of influence to gain these formal agreements and informal arrangements.

States have also shown success at *legal manipulation of territorial status*. These manipulations of territorial status and existing law or the forging of new laws have proven remarkable in some of the cases we review and have also been proven illegal in subsequent court decisions. These legal maneuvers tend to navigate the gray area between national security interests, domestic immigration laws, and international laws and treaties such as maritime and refugee law. After a discussion of the nature of human smuggling, we revisit these strategies in order to identify their operation across three distinct regions.

THE GEOGRAPHICAL RELATIONSHIP BETWEEN HUMAN SMUGGLING AND ENFORCEMENT

Authorities often posit the disruption of smuggling operations and apprehension of smugglers as key objectives of migrant interdiction efforts, as well as the rationale for intensifying immigration enforcement activities at sea. It is important, therefore, that we flesh out precisely how human smuggling works. Illicit migration by sea is typically orchestrated by well-organized human smuggling entrepreneurs, due to the degree of planning, cost, knowledge and equipment required.

Broadly speaking, human smuggling involves the payment of money by a family or individual in exchange for the orchestration of an illicit journey. Within this definition and its global operation there is infinite variety, in terms of the cost, difficulty and length of the journey; method and timing of payment; and sophistication of smuggling network (Kyle and Koslowski 2001). Human smuggling is generally understood to take place with the consent of the person being transported without documents, in exchange for money. Human trafficking usually implies that the person is being transported without consent or under false pretenses, solely for the financial gain of the person or network orchestrating his or her mobility. In practice, however, there can be a very fine line between smuggling and trafficking as circumstances change over time, during the trip and beyond, once migrants reach destinations. Depending on individual situations, migrants may be seeking economic opportunities that do not exist in their origin country. They may migrate to fight hunger or poverty. They may be fleeing persecution of some kind. Given this range of motivations for travel, policy-makers often refer to boats of smuggled migrants as "mixed flows," or groups of individuals traveling for a range of reasons. Some will likely fit into the category of refugee, while others will be considered economic migrants. People are drawn to a particular destination country for many reasons, such as the promise of employment upon arrival, the presence of family members, or the hope of gaining asylum. In many cases, a migrant's exact destination is chosen by the smuggler instead of the migrant herself.

Within this basic understanding, it must be emphasized that the undertaking of an *illicit journey* is central to human smuggling. Human mobility is only outside the law by virtue of the existence of laws making it so. As stated by Heyman and Smart, "State law inevitably creates its counterparts, zones of ambiguity, and outright illegality" (1999: 1). Therefore, the relationship between states' immigration policies and undocumented migration is intimate and recursive. Indeed, numerous scholars have argued that there is a symbiotic relationship between immigration policy and human smuggling as enforcement measures tighten (Salt and Stein 1997; Andreas 2001; Koser 2001; Kyle and Dale 2001). Growth in smuggling networks correlates with increased border control and migration regulation in destination countries, as heightened difficulty in making a successful journey makes the contracting of smugglers nearly essential for undocumented migrants (Kyle and Dale 2001; Kyle and Liang 2001; Spener 2001).

Immigration enforcement policies can usually be traced to particular events. For example, as discussed below, the interdiction at sea policy of the United States can be traced to the 1980 Mariel boatlift from Cuba. Australia's "Pacific Solution" can be traced to the 2001 arrival of the *Tampa* carrying 433 Afghan asylum-seekers. Policy-makers and the bureaucrats who enact policy on the ground often operate in a responsive mode when crises arise, implementing policy "on the fly" and basing decisions and actions on scant information or unverified assumptions (Mountz 2010: 20).[1] The resulting policies, consequently, are typically made without fully considering the range of possible ramifications, including the effect on human smuggling operations in the future. Frequently policies developed hastily in reaction to a particular event or crisis serve as the template for future policies and practices.

In their positions on human smuggling, states tend to mask and oversimplify both their own role and that of migrant agency (Kyle and Dale 2001). There is a tendency to view human smuggling as tightly imbricated with international criminal networks (Kyle and Koslowski 2001; Wong 2005). Certainly, there are many instances in which criminal networks are involved, but such a narrow view ignores the complexities of smuggling. For example, human smuggling can be considered a global business (Salt and Stein 1997; Spener 2004; Kyle and Siracusa 2005). There is also a wide range of actors frequently involved in smuggling, including network managers, corrupt government officials, banks and other organizations facilitating money transfers, those who house and feed migrants en route, even children hired to run errands (Kyle and Dale 2001; Ramírez and Álvarez 2009).

In addition, policy-makers tend to ignore the fact that international migration grows out of relationships of mutual dependence that develop between immigrant destination and origin countries (Sassen 1988; Bauder 2006). In the face of these relationships, the assumption that hardened migration policies deter migration often proves incorrect. In fact, scholars have found that migration policies often have little to no influence on personal migration decisions (Black et al. 2006; Collyer 2007; Nevins 2008). For instance, Nevins writes: "That many individuals choose to migrate in the face of the ever-hardening boundary between the United States and Mexico and associated risks speaks to the power of the forces driving migration" (2007: 41). The assumption that hardening border enforcement regimes will deter future immigration fails to take into account the deep-seated structural factors propelling migration (Hiemstra forthcoming).

While the hardening of immigration policy frequently fails to halt migration, it does tend to alter the spatiality of a particular migration pattern, in terms of routes, tactics, danger, cost and, as mentioned above, the necessity of hiring a smuggler. When a new policy or practice is put into place targeting a particular mobility pattern, migrants and smuggling operations adapt by changing geographical routes and methods. Smuggling routes are not coincidental. In the case of Ecuadorian migration, shifting US policies eventually led smugglers to incorporate into their repertoire a sea route between Ecuador and Central America (Ramírez and Álvarez 2009; Jokisch and Pribilsky 2002). As destination countries move to block one route, another route opens. Migrants' need to travel and smugglers' determination to continue doing business virtually ensure that this pattern repeats endlessly. Furthermore, increasingly restrictive border enforcement strategies directly correlate with rising cost and time en route for migrants. Heightened risk for mobile bodies is also a consequence (Andreas 2001; Kyle and Liang 2001; Nevins 2008). Migrants attempting to evade detection by authorities are extremely vulnerable; such migrants are subject to fraud, robbery, physical and sexual abuse, extreme physical conditions and even death (Falconí and Ordoñez 2005). For example, Ecuadorians were among the 72 migrants murdered in gang violence in Mexico in August 2010 (Agence France-Presse 2010; Archibold 2010).

We have discussed human smuggling in part to underscore the significance and dynamism of geography in the mobilization of borders at sea. While enforcement strategies may appear haphazard or ad hoc, they are generally responsive to changes in smuggling routes and enforcement policies of other countries. The perception is that smugglers will seek the "softest" entry points. As such, if one state enhances enforcement, others follow suit. This process of echoing enforcement policies reverberates throughout the three distant, yet parallel, regional examples to which we now turn.

UNITED STATES INTERDICTION AT SEA: FROM THE CARIBBEAN TO THE NORTH PACIFIC

Efforts by the United States to halt illicit migration by sea consist of a patchwork strategy of sea patrols in domestic and international waters, bilateral agreements, and diplomatic pressure on foreign governments to apprehend, detain, and deport migrants presumably en route to the United States. The development of this strategy can be traced back to a particular period of intense Caribbean migration to the US in the early 1980s. A pivotal event was the Mariel boatlift of 1980, during which approximately 125,000 Cubans entered the southern US during a seven-month period in all manner of seacraft before an agreement was negotiated to stop the movement (Miller 2003; Palmer 1997; Wasem 2009). Dire conditions in Haiti under the repressive dictator Jean-Claude Duvalier also drove 25,000 Haitians to undertake risky ocean crossings to reach the southern US during this period (Palmer 1997; Wasem 2010). These arrivals, occurring as migration from Mexico and Central America also surged, were viewed with increasing alarm among the US public in ways that provoked enforcement policies that grew incrementally more restrictive (Kahn 1996; Hernández 2008).

Under US immigration law at that time, migrants intercepted at sea were not afforded the right to present their case before an immigration judge, as were most arriving migrants apprehended on land (Palmer 1997). Therefore, the US made interception at sea a priority, carefully attaining bilateral agreements which allowed US vessels to operate in foreign and international waters in which migrants were frequently encountered. For example, in 1981, the Reagan administration put together an agreement with Haiti's Duvalier allowing the US Coast Guard (USCG) to board and search Haitian crafts suspected of carrying undocumented migrants, and then to repatriate them to Haiti (Palmer 1997; Wasem 2010). Under the program subsequently established, USCG ships patrolling waters where Haitians were encountered carried US immigration officials who would screen migrants for consideration for asylum. Of the almost 23,000 Haitians apprehended at sea between 1981 and 1991, only 11 were "screened in" and transported to the US to apply for asylum (Palmer 1997; Wasem 2010).

Throughout the 1990s, efforts intensified to avoid undocumented migrants reaching US land through the elimination of asylum screening for migrants apprehended at sea and the use of places outside US territory for migrant detention. In the six months following a 1991 coup d'état in Haiti, over 34,000 Haitian boat people were interdicted at sea. The US set up facilities at its Navy base at Guantánamo Bay, Cuba, to screen interdicted Haitians, and when capacity was reached additional Cubans were held on USCG cutters (Palmer 1997; Wasem 2010). Out of room for holding Haitians without bringing them onto US territory, in May 1992 President Bush called for the automatic repatriation of interdicted Haitians, without allowing for any type of screening process to determine if they would be in danger upon return to Haiti (Palmer 1997; Wasem 2010). He also ordered the establishment of regional refugee processing centers in Haiti, at which Haitians could make claims for asylum (Wasem 2010). Bush also declared the US exempt from its "non-refoulement" obligations under the 1951 UN Convention Relating to the Status of Refugees by stating that these obligations do not apply to migrants outside US territory (Palmer 1997).

US policy regarding Cuban migration soon approximated this new Haiti policy. Alarmed by the interdiction of almost 40,000 Cubans in 1994, the Clinton administration ordered that interdicted Cubans would no longer be brought to the US and instead would be brought to Guantánamo Bay and repatriated to Cuba, and could apply for asylum at a US outpost in Havana (Wasem 2009; Palmer 1997; US House of Representatives 2009). These changes led to the "wet foot/dry foot" practice regarding Cuban sea migration that exists today. That is, if a Cuban manages to reach US land, then she is usually allowed to remain. If she does not arrive on shore, then she is returned to Cuba. This literal reading of wet-dry has led the USCG, in cooperation with various US government agencies, to take extraordinary – and sometimes controversial – measures to prevent migrants from becoming "feet-dry." For example, in 1999, the Coast Guard employed a water cannon and pepper spray to thwart six Cubans from reaching a Florida beach. In 2006, the USCG determined 15 Cubans found on an old bridge in Key West that was no longer connected to land to be "feet-wet" and repatriated them (Wasem 2009).

These policies regarding Haitian and Cuban interdiction have served as templates for the US approach to increasing policing of migration by sea from additional countries within and far beyond the Caribbean over the last two decades. For instance, well-organized smuggling operations brought thousands of primarily Chinese migrants to the US in the 1990s (Palmer 1997; US House of Representatives 2009). In 1993 the Chinese ship *Golden Venture* ran aground just off the coast of Long Island, and the courts ruled that because these migrants did not make it to dry land, they were not entitled to an immigration hearing and could be deported (Palmer 1997). In 1999, Ecuador became a new source of migrants intercepted at sea by the US. To accommodate a sudden and sharp rise in demand, smugglers began to transport Ecuadorians by sea for the first leg of their journey, leaving from Ecuador's coast to travel north to Guatemala, Nicaragua or Mexico (Ramírez and Álvarez 2009; Jokisch and Pribilsky 2002). Anxious to head off these would-be migrants as far from US borders as possible, the USCG began to interdict Ecuadorians in the waters between North and South America and repatriate them (US Coast Guard 2010). Finally, the US has also engaged in migrant interdiction efforts in waters on the other side of the Pacific Ocean, in the Mariana Trench. In the late 1990s, large boats of Chinese migrants began arriving on Guam (unincorporated territory of the United States), and detention centers were soon operating beyond capacity. The USCG started to divert boats to Tinian, part of the Commonwealth of the Northern Mariana Island, where asylum applications could not be made because it was not US territory (Mason 1999).

These interceptions fall under a broad Department of Homeland Security strategy described as "pushing our borders out" (Finley 2004). In 2004, a USCG operations legal chief in Washington, DC stated to a reporter that the United States President has the right to take whatever actions necessary, wherever necessary, to protect US borders. Therefore, US ships will "go to the source of transnational crime and interdict it before it gets to the United States" (as quoted in Finley 2004). The USCG also works with numerous "international partners" in its migrant interdiction efforts, including the training of maritime law enforcement of dozens of other countries in interdiction tactics (US House of Representatives 2009). Today, the US has bilateral agreements with 26 countries in Central and South America which allow the USCG to board and pursue flagged vessels, patrol territorial waters with sea and aircraft and investigate suspected smuggling activities (US House of Representatives 2009). While these agreements frequently focus on counternarcotics work, migrant interdiction often occurs as a matter of course (Finley 2004; Flynn 2005).

THE AUSTRALIAN SOLUTIONS IN THE PACIFIC AND INDIAN OCEANS

Australia is an island country that prides itself on control of cross-border flows. Still, in the late 1990s, arrivals by sea increased, with smugglers operating through Southeast Asia. Asylum-seekers who arrived without visas were placed in detention in remote locations onshore. Isolation resulted in more restricted access because detainees remained distant from advocates, information, interpreters and legal counsel.

In 2001, a Norwegian merchant vessel, the *Tampa*, rescued 433 Afghan asylum seekers from an Indonesian ship. Prohibited from landing on Australian soil, the captain tried to defy orders, but was sent back and told he would only be assisted if the ship remained beyond the 12-mile zone delineating territorial waters. Then Prime Minister John Howard was up for reelection and down in the polls. By taking a hard enforcement stance toward migration at sea, he found a successful political strategy, drew his "line in the sand," and won reelection (Hugo 2001; Mares 2002). This moment signaled the beginning of the "Pacific Solution" (Magner 2004). Akin to the wet foot/dry foot policy, the solution meant that Australia would not land migrants intercepted at sea. Instead, the government invested heavily in interception at sea and outsourced detention and processing to islands north of Australia, including Manus in Papua New Guinea and the tiny island nation of Nauru (Hugo 2001). The Pacific Solution extended the isolating strategies of dispersed detention facilities internal to sovereign Australian territory. Detainees were held offshore, distanced even further away from advocates, attorneys, media, the public, and the asylum process.

Following this highly publicized, international episode, Parliament also exercised legal manipulation of Australia's own territory, retroactively excising thousands of small bits of land, declaring them to be no longer part of Australia for the purposes of migration law (Taylor 2005). Like the wet foot/dry foot policy, this system created a two-tier geography of access and protection for those seeking refuge. Those who made it to shore would accrue more rights and access, while those intercepted at sea would face more limited access. Australia's Pacific Solution thus exercised all three spatial strategies in concert: intensified interceptions at sea, detention and processing offshore, and legal manipulation of Australian territory to undermine access to asylum.

The migrants intercepted at sea during the *Tampa* incident and those subsequently intercepted were detained on Nauru, among other places, between 2001 and 2008. Australia contracted the International Organization for Migration (IOM) to run some of these facilities, including the one on Nauru. Human rights monitors, journalists, refugee lawyers and other kinds of advocates were restricted from visiting the island. This demonstrates the investment of significant resources to keep asylum-seekers away from sovereign territory, and legal advocates and information away from detainees. Migrants isolated on islands had little information about their cases. Ultimately, the UN Refugee Agency (UNHCR) arranged for many detainees to be resettled in "third countries," including Canada and New Zealand. Still others remained on islands even after the policy officially ended in 2008.

Labor leader Kevin Rudd became Prime Minister at the end of 2007. Under his leadership, detention policies shifted onshore. Mandatory detention ended and several facilities were shut down or "mothballed." Children were released from traditional detention centers and held in alternative settings in communities. The Pacific Solution also drew to a close in rhetoric, although material remnants lingered and were revived a few years later. Notably, the government continued investments in interception and construction of a A$400-million high-security detention facility on Christmas Island. The facility opened in 2008, and those intercepted at sea continue to be detained there, maintaining the two-tier system of access to asylum. At first, the numbers in the facility were small. But as conflicts continued and escalated in Afghanistan, Iraq, and Sri Lanka, the number of people trying to reach Australia to claim asylum grew. So too did Australian investments in interception, and bilateral arrangements for migrants to be returned home.

By July 2010, there were 2,600 migrants detained in three facilities on Christmas Island. There are many exorbitant costs to detention on Christmas Island, due largely to its remoteness and small size. Only one commercial flight travels to Christmas Island from Perth, some 1,160 miles away. Little food is grown and few supplies made on the island. Medical services are inadequate, even to support births among locals of the small population of approximately 1,100. As a result, all food and supplies must be flown in, along with workers who then must be housed on an island never prepared to sustain a large population. Detainees in need of services beyond the most basic medical care must be flown to the mainland, all at great cost. These investments show the length traveled by Australia not only to shift, but to sustain offshore interception, detention and processing.

Detainee populations also grew in size across Indonesia under both Howard and Rudd. This growth on foreign territory occurred more quietly. After extensive research conducted in Australian-supported facilities built on several Indonesian islands, Taylor (2009) estimated the presence of some 2,000 detainees held by the IOM and Indonesian authorities in exchange for Australian funds. Australia exchanged development aid for detention in Indonesia, which does not observe the Convention Relating to the Status of Refugees.

Critics of these practices have called these strategies the Indian Ocean Solution and the Indonesian Solution respectively (Marr 2009), because they deploy the same spatial strategies as the Pacific Solution, whilst adapting to distinct geographic terrains. In response to a challenge to the Indonesian Solution, Kevin Rudd explained why the practice continued, despite its lack of popularity: "If detention and processing in Indonesia helps prevent some of these perilous journeys, then we must support such a policy" (*Sydney Morning Herald* 2009). His response linked the assumed success of deterrence to the three spatial strategies of interception, detention and processing offshore, and use of foreign territory to block legal channels to asylum.

In July 2010, new Australian Prime Minister Julia Gillard once again shifted geographical terrain with the proposal of a new "solution": the possibility of processing asylum-seekers in East Timor (*West Australian* 2010). News quickly emerged that Gillard had not actually consulted East Timor on this proposal, sparking citizens' protests. In November 2010, the Australian high court heard a case filed by two Sri Lankan Tamil asylum-seekers who had been detained on Christmas Island. The Court decided that excision contravened domestic immigration laws. This decision threw into question the status and legal avenues to asylum of those 2,600 detained on Christmas Island, while leaving in limbo the fate of the additional 2,000 detained on Australia's behalf in Indonesia. In January 2011, the Department of Immigration and Citizenship responded, stating it would increase opportunities for appeal of decisions on asylum applications and otherwise change processing to reflect better procedures onshore. Nonetheless, plans to expand offshore detention and processing continued under Prime Minister Gillard, with talk of processing asylum-seekers in East Timor in 2010 and of reopening the Nauru facility in 2011.

Australia and the United States have emerged as global models of offshore enforcement. After Canadian authorities intercepted the MV *Ocean Lady* carrying over 400 Sri Lankan Tamil asylum-seekers to the coast of British Columbia in 2009, for example, Canadians began to debate the possibility of adapting Australia's solutions offshore and the conservative government proposed legislation to create a two-tier system of access to the refugee claimant process similar to the American wet foot/dry foot policy (Johnson 2010).

REDRAWING THE LINES AROUND THE EUROPEAN UNION

As in Australia and the US, strategies to curb migration in the European Union (EU) involved the "externalization of asylum" (e.g., Betts 2004; Schuster 2005). As EU states harmonized citizenship policies and eradicated internal borders to facilitate labor migration, they struggled to find common asylum policies. Following signals from the UNHCR to pursue "preventative" policies, throughout the 1990s and into the present EU states grew more strategic through bilateral arrangements for extra-territorial processing in the regions where migrants originate (see Betts 2004). Collaborative policies and practices have subsequently moved asylum-seekers beyond sovereign territory and closer to regions of origin (Boswell 2003; Schuster 2005). This involved construction of detention and processing facilities in transit zones in eastern Europe and northern Africa.

In the process of regionalization, the EU increasingly thought of itself as a collection of states collaborating to police an external perimeter (Salter 2004; Ceriani et al. 2009). In order to accomplish the policing of the perimeter, the EU developed an extensive series of bureaucratic and technological innovations to extend its perimeter offshore (Andrijasevic 2010; van Houtum 2010; Klepp 2010). Central to the externalization of this perimeter policing was the development of the EU border agency known as Frontex. Frontex was made operational in 2005 and coordinates joint policing and interception operations. Because of its ability to gather and invest resources, the agency influences not only enforcement operations at sea, but the ways in which smuggling industries respond to the intensification of policing in certain areas of the Mediterranean.

As processing and enforcement moved offshore, certain islands became "hot spots" where migrants frequently attempted to enter the EU by sea, and where migrants were processed following interception (Mountz 2011a). Between 2004 and 2008, Italy's Lampedusa and Spain's Canary Islands proved the most popular "backdoor" entrances to the EU from western and northern Africa, and subsequently they became sites of increased enforcement (Andrijasevic 2006). Lampedusa is a small island southwest (though administratively part) of Sicily, not far from Tunisia. Over 50,000 African migrants arrived by boat on Lampedusa between 2005 and 2007, and 6,500 more had arrived by July 2008 (*Guardian* 2008). Then, following a relatively quiet year on Lampedusa, boat arrivals once again surged during the "Arab Spring" of 2011.

Until 2004, migrants who landed on Lampedusa and made an asylum claim were transferred to a reception center on the island of Sicily (Andrijasevic 2006). In 2004, however, amid pressure to tighten security and improve enforcement, Italian authorities began to send migrants back en masse on chartered flights to Libya without processing their claims and without adequate time to establish their identities and assess their well-being if returned to and through Libya (Médecins Sans Frontières 2004).

Comparable numbers attempted to enter the EU by way of the Canaries during the same time period, with 23,000 entering between January and September 2006 (*Guardian* 2006). Migrants traveled land routes through Mauritania, Morocco and Algeria before crossing the sea (Carling 2007). Like Italy, Spain sought to balance international obligations and national agendas in relation to broader EU efforts to harmonize migration and enforcement and protect human rights. On the Canary Islands, however, asylum-seekers spent less time in detention due to national policies.

Frontex began policing the archipelago during this period of heightened arrivals in 2006, and the interceptions at sea drove human smuggling by boat east to other islands (Carling 2007: 21). The technological enhancements that enabled external border control also enhanced the spatial strategies at work there, with the development of the Integrated System of External Vigilance (Carling 2007: 21). As Carling demonstrates, the movement of enforcement outward in increments also shifted smuggling operations farther offshore, first away from the mainland, then away from the Canary Islands, and finally into Morocco.

These struggles show the complexity of detention and the complicity of local populations who are alternately employed by migrant detention operations and hostile to detainees. The games between rights monitors and Italian authorities illustrate efforts to use islands to hide asylum-seekers from view while restricting access. In the case of detention on Lampedusa (as on Nauru), not only was access to asylum inhibited, but advocates and human rights monitors were restricted or removed from the center, compounding the isolation of migrants inside.

As Frontex intensified policing of the Mediterranean, the island states of Malta and Greece experienced growth in arrivals, primarily from the Libyan coast. This enforcement intensified arrivals that had been happening since 2002 (Lutterbeck 2009: 119) and increasing on Malta once it joined the EU in 2004. Peaking at 2,775 migrants in 2008, the numbers of arrivals on Malta were much more modest than on Lampedusa and the Canary Islands (*Los Angeles Times* 2010). Malta has argued, however, that given its small territory and population, it processes the highest number of asylum-seekers of any EU member state per capita. The small country has repeatedly called on the EU to take on a greater share of "the burden." Amid intensified policing at sea and implementation of Italy's "push back policy" to prevent arrivals with increased interception and return to Libya, smuggling routes shifted again. The number of arrivals dropped precipitously on Lampedusa at this time, as smugglers moved routes, and arrivals again swelled in both Greece and Malta. As Lutterbeck suggests, "plugging one hole in the EU perimeter quickly leads to enhanced pressure on other parts of its external borders" (2009: 123).

Broader regional politics mean that burden-sharing is never perceived to be evenly distributed among member states of the EU, nor are national policies harmonized. On January 21, 2011, for example, the European Court for Human Rights ruled in favor of an Afghan asylum-seeker who had entered Europe through Greece. His counsel argued that conditions of detention in Greece were so poor that the country could not be considered a safe place to seek asylum (EurActiv 2011). This decision again raised the concept of "burden sharing," and the challenge of multiscalar governance of asylum as power struggles unfold between EU governing bodies and those countries with island territory on the periphery of the EU which argue that they face a higher share of the burden of processing. Mainland EU states want extraterritorial processing while also wishing to maintain access to asylum and protection of human rights.

As a result of the success of Italy's interception and return policies, few ships were arriving by sea by 2010. The eruption of political unrest in northern African states in early 2011 in Tunisia, Egypt, Libya and elsewhere, however, again threw Lampedusa into the spotlight. By the end of February, some 5,000 Tunisian and Egyptian migrants had landed on the island, calling attention once again to the role and ramifications of offshore interventions (Spiegel Online 2011). By June, this number had increased to approximately 42,000 (Migrants at Sea 2011). For years, migrants have traveled across multiple international borders and treacherous desert landscapes to reach the African coast. Many spent years in limbo or detention in Libya. Recent bilateral arrangements with Italy and Malta made it even more difficult for them to travel any further on their transnational journeys. As Andrijasesvic (2010) shows, Italy was increasingly policing its borders on Libyan soil, implementing deportation and detention there to prevent departure by sea. With the political crises unfolding daily in February 2011, Italy called on the EU to hold a meeting to design a concerted strategy to respond to migration. As the EU panicked about the potential arrivals and a refugee crisis developed along Libya's borders, the unsettled African states turned away from previous bilateral commitments to allow entry of European authorities to "stem the tide" (Spiegel Online 2011). In early March, Italy announced that it would set up refugee camps along Libyan borders, as both Malta and Italy were told to prepare for "unprecedented" arrivals from the African coast.

CONCLUSION

In this chapter, we have traced the diffusion of a particular set of spatial strategies surrounding border enforcement at sea. Here, we return to these strategies and review some of their implications. Across the regions discussed, destination states foreground practices based on the concept of externalization. These practices aim to prevent migrant arrivals on sovereign territory in order to preclude access to the range of legal rights, social services and economic possibilities such entry triggers. States cobble together bilateral agreements with origin and transit states that allow them to patrol foreign waters and intercept foreign vessels, carefully negotiating the limits of or working to skirt existing law. They restrict access to asylum by processing migrants at sea or in particular territories. Those intercepted are often detained at sea, on islands, or in third countries. Migrants are repatriated, usually without consideration of the reason for their attempted migration or the consequences upon their return. It is no coincidence that migration destination states in all three regions discussed here increasingly employ similar tactics. Destination states across the globe have come to understand mobile bodies as threatening. Authorities and policy-makers often watch and learn from each other, adapting other states' "best practices." This is true for the enforcement of land borders, as in the US's adoption of Israeli strategies and technologies in the building of its US–Mexico border wall; as well as in interception, processing and detention at sea, and the manipulation of territorial status.

A critical foundation of these spatial strategies is the recursive relationship between interdiction at sea and the human smuggling operations orchestrating the bulk of these migrations. Destination states' immigration policies play pivotal roles in the development of migration routes and smuggling operations. As authorities step up offshore enforcement, human smuggling operations change tactics and routes. For instance, while USCG interdiction of Asian boat migrants has greatly decreased in the twenty-first century (US Coast Guard 2010), reports indicate that smugglers have charted new routes that bring migrants (by boat and by air) to Central or South America, subsequently to travel north by land and sea (US House of Representatives 2009; Bowditch 2009). Across the globe, intensified border enforcement leads to more sophisticated smuggling networks that are more likely to engage in practices that heighten the danger and expense of migration journeys.

Interception at sea allows for the temporal as well as the geographical stretching of borders. Borders become anticipatory and mobile, and they can enclose a vessel or a body. Migrants apprehended at sea are essentially apprehended for a "crime" not yet committed; they have not yet transgressed the borders of the state that is their destination. It is the destination countries' understanding of borders as flexible and provisional that allows them to punish migrants before they have actually made an undocumented entry, with interception anticipatory of transgression.

In the three regions we have examined, migrants are increasingly criminalized and the reasons for their migration obscured in such a way that their movement toward a particular territory is construed as endangering national security. Through the deployment of these spatial strategies at sea, we see how states biopolitically produce and criminalize migrant identities in terms of threat to security. And as illicit migration is portrayed as a national and international security threat, migrant bodies on the move unpredictably at sea are positioned as risky rather than at risk. The structural and political reasons behind these migration patterns are minimized or ignored altogether. This portrayal is used to justify the exclusion of mobile bodies regardless of the cause for their migration.

Security considerations, then, come to override humanitarian ones. Consequently, international covenants regarding human rights and refugees come to be viewed as obstacles to be circumvented, instead of guidelines ensuring timely humanitarian intervention and protection. The premise of aid and rescue for migrants at sea, while still invoked, now has a guiding subtext and aim: to apprehend migrants before they reach a particular territory. Furthermore, governments often justify particularly harsh interception policies by stating that they will deter future dangerous, life-threatening sea voyages, without investigating whether these assumptions of deterrence actually play out. Offshore enforcement strategies, therefore, threaten the integrity of migrant and refugee protection.

Finally, interceptions at sea illustrate how powerful nation-states exercise sovereignty in a geographically flexible fashion, pushing their own borders offshore while infringing on the territory of others. As a result, the peripheral zones of dominant powers' sovereign territory are both ambiguous and malleable. The borders of the powerful destination state are made less permeable while simultaneously stretching across water and into the sovereign territory of other states. The borders of less powerful states of origin and transit, by contrast, are made more permeable and permeated, increasingly beyond their sovereign control. As the geographic manipulations carried out in the course of sea interdictions are practiced and accepted internationally, the concept of sovereignty is stretched to incorporate and normalize them (Hyndman and Mountz 2008). Often, the conditions under which the various forms of "cooperation" are negotiated between destination and nondestination states raise questions regarding the true sovereignty of the latter. For example, the US has threatened to withhold aid from Latin American countries in an effort to pressure them to allow the US to behave as it desires (Finley 2004; Flynn 2005). Similarly, African states and Indonesia allowed the EU to build infrastructure to detain and deter. Such maneuvers illustrate the nonnegotiability, in practice and across uneven fields of power, of many supposedly voluntary bilateral agreements.

The mapping of migrant interception demonstrates the ways in which geographic strategies have become embedded in the concept of sovereignty, as sovereignty is used as both an excuse for pushing out a state's borders and pushing in another state's borders. Sovereignty can also be understood as a tactic – for controlling mobile bodies, for extending state influence, and for normalizing intervention in both the politics and geographies of other states. Examination of sovereign border enforcement practices carried out along the margins demonstrates the increasingly transnational nature of sovereign power itself.

NOTES

The authors thank the editors for their comments on the chapter and work on the edited collection. The material presented here is based on support from the National Science Foundation, award number 0847133.

1   This phrase was used frequently by bureaucrats in Canada's Department of Citizenship and Immigration Canada who were involved in the response to human smuggling at sea from China to British Columbia (Mountz 2010: 20).

REFERENCES

ACLU (American Civil Liberties Union). 2006. Are you living in a constitution free zone? At http://www.aclu.org/national-security_technology-and-liberty/are-you-living-constitution-free-zone (accessed Sept. 20, 2010).

Agence France-Presse. 2010. Inician en México autopsias e identificación de 72 emigrantes asesinados. *El Universo*, Aug. 26. At http://www.eluniverso.com/2010/08/26/1/1360/inician-mexico-autopsias-identificacion-72-emigrantes-asesinados.html?p=1354&m=2176 (accessed Nov. 2011).

Andreas, Peter. 2001. The transformation of migrant smuggling across the US–Mexican border. In David Kyle and Rey Koslowski, eds, *Global Human Smuggling: Comparative Perspectives*, pp. 107–125. Baltimore: Johns Hopkins University Press.

Andrijasevic, Rutvica. 2006. *How to Balance Rights and Responsibilities on Asylum at the EU's Southern Border of Italy and Libya*. Working Paper 27. Centre on Migration, Policy and Society, University of Oxford. At http://www.compas.ox.ac.uk/fileadmin/files/Publications/working_papers/WP_2006/WP0627_Andrijasevic.pdf (accessed Nov. 2011).

Andrijasevic, Rutvica. 2010. From exception to excess: detention and deportations across the Mediterranean space. In Nicholas De Genova and Nathalie Peutz, eds, *The Deportation Regime: Sovereignty, Space, and the Freedom of Movement*, pp. 147–165. Durham: Duke University Press.

Archibold, Randal C. 2010. Grief across Latin America for migrant killings. *New York Times*, Sept. 1. At http://www.nytimes.com/2010/09/02/world/americas/02migrants.html?_r=2&ref=americas (accessed Mar. 1, 2011).

Bauder, Harald. 2006. *Labor Movement: How Migration Regulates Labor Markets*. New York: Oxford University Press.

Betts, Alexander. 2004. The international relations of the "new" extraterritorial approaches to refugee protection: explaining the policy initiatives of the UK government and UNHCR. *Refuge* 22 (1): 58–70.

Bigo, Didier. 2000. When two become one: internal and external securitizations in Europe. In Morten Kelstrup and Michael Williams, eds, *International Relations Theory and the Politics of European Integration*, pp. 171–204. New York: Routledge.

Black, Richard, Collyer, Michael, Skeldon, Ronald and Waddington, Clare. 2006. Routes to illegal residence: a case study of immigration detainees in the United Kingdom. *Geoforum* 37: 552–564.

Boswell, Christina. 2003. The external dimension of EU immigration and asylum policy. *International Affairs* 79 (3): 619–638.

Bowditch, Sean. 2009. Smuggling route goes through Ecuador to US. National Public Radio, Feb. 28. At http://www.npr.org/templates/story/story.php?storyId=101305866 (accessed Nov. 2011).

Carling, Jørgen. 2007. Unauthorized migration from Africa to Spain. *International Migration* 45 (4): 3–37.

Ceriani, Pablo, Fernández, Cristina, Manavella, Alejandra et al. 2009. *Report on the Situation on the Euro-Mediterranean Borders (from the Point of View of the Respect of Human Rights)*. Paper at University of Barcelona. At http://www.libertysecurity.org/article2497.html (accessed Nov. 2011).

Coleman, Mathew. 2007a. A geopolitics of engagement: neoliberalism, the war on terrorism, and the reconfiguration of USA immigration enforcement. *Geopolitics* 12: 607–634.

Coleman, Mathew. 2007b. Immigration geopolitics beyond the Mexico–USA border. *Antipode* 39 (1): 54–76.

Collyer, Michael. 2007. In-between places: trans-Saharan transit migrants in Morocco and the fragmented journey to Europe. *Antipode* 39 (4): 668–690.

EurActiv. 2011. Court exposes appalling detention conditions in Greece. Jan. 24. At http://www.euractiv.com/en/justice/court-exposes-appalling-detention-conditions-greece-news-501500 (accessed Mar. 2, 2011).

Falconí, Fabiola and Ordoñez, Carmen. 2005. Las mujeres migrantes irregulares del Cantón Cuenca. In Guiseppe Solfrini, ed., *Tendencias y efectos de la emigración en el Ecuador*, pp. 109–193. Quito: Imprefepp.

Finley, Bruce. 2004. US Takes border war on the road. *Denver Post*, Dec. 19, p. A-01.

Flynn, Michael. 2005. What's the deal at Manta? *Bulletin of the Atomic Scientists* 61 (1): 23–29.

Guardian. 2006. Immigration: West Africans are paying hundreds of pounds for a perilous, 1,200-mile trip by open boat: the D-day package from Senegal to Spain. Sept. 9, p. 27.

Guardian. 2008. Lampedusa's migrants. July 4.

Hernández, David M. 2008. Pursuant to deportation: Latinos and immigrant detention. *Latino Studies* 6: 35–63.

Heyman, Josiah McC. and Smart, Alan. 1999. States and Illegal practices: an overview. In Josiah McC. Heyman, ed., *States and Illegal Practices*, pp. 1–24. Oxford: Berg.

Hiemstra, Nancy. Forthcoming. Geopolitical reverberations of USA migrant detention and deportation: the view from Ecuador. *Geopolitics*.

Hugo, Graeme. 2001. From compassion to compliance? Trends in refugee and humanitarian migration in Australia. *Geoforum* 55: 27–37.

Hyndman, Jennifer and Mountz, Alison. 2008. Another brick in the wall? Neo-refoulement and the externalization of asylum in Australia and Europe. *Government and Opposition* 43 (2): 259–269.

Johnson, Heather. 2010. Intercepting boat arrivals: what the Australian policy model means for Canadian asylum policy. *Canada-Asia Agenda* (15) (Dec.). At http://www.asiapacific.ca/sites/default/files/filefield/australiamigrationpolicy.pdf (accessed Jan. 2, 2011).

Jokisch, Brad and Pribilsky, Jason. 2002. The panic to leave: economic crisis and the "new emigration" from Ecuador. *International Migration* 40 (4): 75–101.

Kahn, Robert S. 1996. *Other People's Blood: US Immigration Prisons in the Reagan Decade*. Boulder: Westview.

Klepp, Silja. 2010. A contested asylum system: the European Union between refugee protection and border control in the Mediterranean Sea. *European Journal of Migration and Law* 12: 1–21.

Kocher, Austin and Coleman, Mathew. 2010. Racialized policing practices and 287(g): evidence from North Carolina. Paper presented at Conference of the Association of American Geographers, Washington, DC, Apr. 14.

Koser, Khalid. 2001. Asylum policies, trafficking and vulnerability. *International Migration* 38 (3): 91–109.

Kyle, David and Dale, John. 2001. Smuggling the state back in: agents of human smuggling reconsidered. In David Kyle and Rey Koslowski, eds, *Global Human Smuggling: Comparative Perspectives*, pp. 29–57. Baltimore: Johns Hopkins University Press.

Kyle, David and Koslowski, Rey. 2001. Introduction. In David Kyle and Rey Koslowski, eds, *Global Human Smuggling: Compara-*

tive Perspectives, pp. 1–25. Baltimore: Johns Hopkins University Press.

Kyle, David and Liang, Zai. 2001. Migration merchants: human smuggling from Ecuador and China to the United States. In Virginie Guiraudon and Christian Joppke, eds, *Controlling a New Migration World*, pp. 200–221. New York: Routledge.

Kyle, David and Siracusa, Christina A. 2005. Seeing the state like a migrant: why so many non-criminals break immigration laws. In Willem van Schendel and Itty Abraham, eds, *Illicit Flows and Criminal Things: States, Borders, and the Other Side of Globalization*, pp. 153–176. Bloomington: Indiana University Press.

Los Angeles Times. 2010. Malta is a guarded gate into Europe. Oct. 10, p. A7.

Lutterbeck, Derek. 2009. Small frontier island: Malta and the challenge of irregular migration. *Mediterranean Quarterly* 20 (1): 119–144.

Magner, Tara. 2004. A less than "Pacific" solution for asylum-seekers in Australia. *International Journal of Refugee Law* 16 (1): 53–90.

Mares, Peter. 2002. *Small Frontier Island: Malta and the Challenge of Irregular Migration*. Sydney: University of New South Wales Press.

Marr, David. 2009. The Indonesian Solution: Christmas Island. *The Monthly* 49 (Sept.): 1–15. At http://www.themonthly.com.au/monthly-essays-david-marr-indian-ocean-solution-christmas-island-1940 (accessed Nov. 2011).

Mason, Jana. 1999. Where America's day begins: Chinese asylum-seekers on Guam. *Refugee Reports* (US Committee for Refugees) 20 (8) (Aug.–Sept.).

Médecins Sans Frontières. 2004. Press release. Oct. 3.

Migrants at Sea. 2011. 42,000 Migrant landings in Italy in first 5 months of 2011. At http://migrantsatsea.wordpress.com/2011/06/13/42000-migrant-landings-in-italy-in-first-5-months-of-2011/ (accessed Nov. 2011).

Miller, Teresa A. 2003. Citizenship and severity: recent immigration reforms and the new

penology. *Georgetown Immigration Law Journal* 17 (4): 611–666.

Mountz, Alison. 2010. *Seeking Asylum: Human Smuggling and Bureaucracy at the Border*. Minneapolis: University of Minnesota Press.

Mountz, Alison. 2011a. Border politics: spatial provision and geographical precision. *Political Geography* 30: 61–69.

Mountz, Alison. 2011b. The enforcement archipelago: detention, haunting, and asylum on islands. *Political Geography* 30: 118–128.

Mountz, Alison. 2011c. Specters at the port of entry: understanding state mobilities through an ontology of exclusion. *Mobilities* 6 (3): 317–334.

Nevins, Joseph. 2007. Dying for a cup of coffee? Migrant deaths in the USA–Mexico border region in a neoliberal age. *Geopolitics* 12 (2): 228–247.

Nevins, Joseph. 2008 *Dying to Live: A Story of US Immigration in an Age of Global Apartheid*. San Francisco: City Lights.

Nevins, Joseph. 2010. *Operation Gatekeeper: The Rise of the "Illegal Alien" and the Making of the US–Mexico Boundary*. New York: Routledge.

Palmer, Gary W. 1997. Guarding the coast: alien migrant interdiction operations at sea. *Connecticut Law Review* 29 (4): 1565.

Ramírez, Jacques and Álvarez, Soledad. 2009. "Cruzando fronteras." Una aproximación etnográfica a la migración clandestina ecuatoriana en tránsito hacia Estados Unidos. *Confluenze* 1 (1): 89–113.

Salt, John and Stein, Jeremy. 1997. Migration as a business: the case of trafficking. *International Migration* 35 (4): 467–491.

Salter, Mark. 2004. Passports, mobility, and security: how smart can the border be? *International Studies Perspectives* 5: 71–91.

Sassen, Saskia. 1988. *The Mobility of Labor and Capital: A Study in International Investment and Labor Flow*. Cambridge: Cambridge University Press.

Schuster, Lisa. 2005. *The Realities of a New Asylum Paradigm*. Working Paper 20. Centre on Migration, Policy and Society, University of Oxford. At http://www.

compas.ox.ac.uk/publications/working-papers/wp-05-20/ (accessed Nov. 2011).

Sparke, Matthew B. 2006. A Neoliberal nexus: economy, security and the biopolitics of citizenship on the border. *Political Geography* 25: 151–180.

Spener, David. 2001. Smuggling migrants through South Texas: challenges posed by Operation Rio Grande. In David Kyle and Rey Koslowski, eds, *Global Human Smuggling: Comparative Perspectives*, pp. 129–165. Baltimore: Johns Hopkins University Press.

Spener, David. 2004. Mexican migrant smuggling: a cross-border cottage industry. *Journal of International Migration and Integration* 5 (3): 295–320.

Spiegel Online 2011 European leaders struggle with wave of Tunisian migrants. Feb. 15. At http://www.spiegel.de/international/europe/0,1518,druck-745669,00.html (accessed Feb. 24, 2011).

Sydney Morning Herald. 2009. Go easy on boat people, Labor tells Indonesia. Oct. 27. At http://www.smh.com.au/world/go-easy-on-boat-people-labor-tells-indonesia-20091026-hgq9.html (accessed Jan. 5, 2011).

Taylor, Jessie. 2009. *Behind Australian Doors: Examining the Conditions of Detention of Asylum Seekers in Indonesia.* At http://www.law.monash.edu.au/castancentre/news/behind-australian-doors-report.pdf (accessed Nov. 20, 2010).

Taylor, Savitri. 2005. Sovereign power at the border. *Public Law Review* 16 (1): 55–77.

US Coast Guard. 2010. *Total Interdictions: Fiscal Year 1982 to Present.* At http://www.uscg.mil/hq/cg5/cg531/AMIO/FlowStats/FY.asp (accessed Nov. 30, 2010).

US House of Representatives. 2009. *Overview of Coast Guard Drug and Migrant Interdiction: Hearing before the Subcommittee on Coast Guard and Maritime Transportation of the Committee on Transportation and Infrastructure, House of Representatives, 111th Congress.* Mar. 11. At http://frwebgate.access.gpo.gov/cgi-bin/getdoc.cgi?dbname=111_house_hearings&docid=f:48204.pdf (accessed Jan. 26, 2011).

van Houtum, Henk. 2010. Human blacklisting: the global apartheid of the EU's external border regime. *Environment and Planning D: Society and Space* 28: 957–976.

Walters, William. 2004. Secure borders, safe haven, domopolitics. *Citizenship Studies* 8 (3): 237–260.

Walters, William. 2008. Bordering the sea: shipping industries and the policing of stowaways. *Borderlands* 7 (3): 1–25.

Wasem, Ruth E. 2009. *Cuban Migration to the United States: Policy and Trends.* Congressional Research Service, Report for Congress R40566.

Wasem, Ruth E. 2010. *US Immigration Policy on Haitian Immigrants.* Congressional Research Service, Report for Congress RS21349.

West Australian. 2010. Gillard's Indian Ocean solution to boat people. July 7, p. A1.

Winders, Jamie. 2007. Bringing back the (b) order: post–9/11 politics of immigration, borders, and belonging in the contemporary US South. *Antipode* 39 (5): 920–942.

Wong, Diana. 2005. The rumor of trafficking: border controls, illegal migration, and the sovereignty of the nation-state. In Willem van Schendel and Itty Abraham, eds, *Illicit Flows and Criminal Things: States, Borders, and the Other Side of Globalization*, pp. 69–100. Bloomington: Indiana University Press.

CHAPTER 27

"B/ordering" and Biopolitics in Central Asia

Nick Megoran

On September 11, 1992, the presidents of El Salvador and Honduras met on a bridge over a river that formed their common border to sign a treaty delimiting a disputed boundary over which the two countries had gone to war in 1969. The immediate spark for the short but bloody "Soccer War" was qualification matches for the 1970 World Cup, although underlying tensions were about more substantive issues, including poverty, migration and a boundary dispute. The International Court of Justice in The Hague had been asked to rule on the dispute and, although the implementation of its verdict created some difficulties with residents in exchanged territories, the Court's involvement seems to have contributed to a sustained peace between the two countries (Daniel 2002).

This vignette reminds us that international boundaries are more than simply fixed vertical planes of no material width that demarcate states off from each other in the international system. They rematerialize within and beyond the literal edge of the state, often with bloody consequences. Therefore, by studying an international boundary and the multiple borders it produces at a range of scales over time, including its varied discursive reiterations, we are afforded a unique optic on a broad spectrum of social practices in the states it conjoins. I term such studies "boundary biographies," and contend that they enable a specifically geographical contribution to the elucidation of political histories.

This chapter is divided into two sections. The first outlines this argument in more depth, briefly summarizing the boundary studies tradition in geography and critically reflecting on recent schools that view international boundaries chiefly as examples of broader social processes of bordering/bounding or as biopolitical strategies to govern mobilities in the "war on terror." The second part of the chapter exemplifies this argument with a biography of the Kyrgyzstan–Uzbekistan boundary. The chapter concludes by contending that there is a normative question at the heart of all studies of international boundaries: How do they enhance or deform the capacity to live the good life?

A Companion to Border Studies, First Edition. Edited by Thomas M. Wilson and Hastings Donnan.
© 2012 Blackwell Publishing Ltd. Published 2012 by Blackwell Publishing Ltd.

BOUNDARY BIOGRAPHIES

International boundaries provide a unique geographical optic on the political, social and economic lives of the states that they conjoin. As a historic staple of political geography – indeed, they have consistently remained on the geographer's agenda since the development of a professional academic discipline – their study also tells us a great deal about geography.

Boundary studies a century ago revealed variously the enchantment of geography with evolutionary theory and organic metaphors (Semple 1907), and the concern of imperial administrators to shore up the edges of empire and obviate troublesome frontier entanglements (Curzon 1907). A development of the work of imperial geographers was the descriptive taxonomic production of boundary typologies (Hartshorne 1936). The 1970s saw many geographers eager to turn the discipline into a rigorous social science, with some boundary scholars developing models of social and economic processes that occur at international boundaries (House 1981). Since the 1990s, geographical studies of international boundaries have drawn on social theory imported from the broader social sciences. There are various pathways in this scholarship, but this chapter will focus on two of the most influential.

The first sees international boundaries as examples of more general processes of bordering/bounding. For van Houtum and van Naerssen (2002), international boundaries are significant because "they symbolise a social practice of spatial differentiation," a process they describe as "bordering" or "(b)ordering." Likewise for Newman (2003: 134), international boundaries are examples of a more general bordering/bounding process, akin to other types of social (such as ethnic and religious) and spatial (geopolitical and substate) boundaries at a range of scales.

A second major pathway in this scholarship is interested in the biopolitics of governing mobilities as a strategy in the "war on terror." Amoore proposes the concept of the "biometric border," using a Foucauldian account of how biometric border controls are an "exercise of biopower" that inscribes "the body" with "multiple encoded borders" (2006: 337). For Vaughan-Williams, who also begins with Foucault, new border control practices in the United Kingdom have moved away from a preoccupation with "a single physical frontier located at a fixed site designed to hinder movement," to "a biopolitical apparatus of security" (2010: 1078), predicated on governing mobilities, that transforms the border into a continuum extending offshore and within the state.

These two pathways have enriched geographical studies of international boundaries in a number of ways. They have connected the study of international boundaries to wider (inter)disciplinary debates about territory, identity, sovereignty, and citizenship, have emphasized that international boundaries are not static lines but rather permeate the fabric of nation sates, and have produced critiques of politically disturbing practices of territoriality in the "war on terror."

However, there are three significant drawbacks of the bordering/bounding and governing mobilities approaches. First, they risk losing sight of what O'Dowd (2010) terms the "distinctiveness" of international borders. Newman and van Houtum and van Naerssen, as we saw above, reconceptualize international boundaries as one example of more general bounding/bordering processes. Agnew is right, however, to insist that international borders are not "simply just another example" of boundaries in general, but are "qualitatively different in their capacity to both redefine other boundaries and to override more locally-based distinctions," and also have "a specific historical and geographical origin" (2008: 181).

Second, these two approaches restrict the historic scope of international boundary studies. Newman and Paasi seek to discipline their study by calling for "the creation of a suitable framework which can bring much of this traditional research into line with the emphasis on social constructs and identities which is central to contemporary social science research" (1998: 201). But this framework finds little space for important aspects of the literatures on international boundaries, including their legal formulation, their physical demarcation and maritime boundaries.

The third weakness is a failure to think through the political ethics of border controls in a comprehensive and consistent way. The "governing mobilities" literature is particularly prone to this weakness. In a classic essay, Smith observes the paradox that "Geographical space must simultaneously be shared and divided": people "must come together to facilitate survival and prosperity, yet they may also be obliged to exclude" (1990: 1). As Agnew writes, we need to go beyond thinking of international borders as either fixed facts on the ground that serve essentially useful purposes, or as being "simply about a security-identity nexus" that is in need of overcoming (2008: 185). Instead, he argues, we need to recognize their equivocal character and reframe our understanding of borders by the overarching normative question of how far they "enhance or restrict the pursuit of a decent life" (2008: 183). The work of Amoore, Vaughan-Williams and others leans heavily on Foucault's biopolitics, and herein lies the difficulty. Foucault's primary intellectual concern, grounded in reflections on his own mental health and sexuality, was how institutional power creates subjectivities. Scholarship that builds upon his work has an inbuilt (although not necessarily insurmountable) tendency to overlook the larger ethical and political questions that Agnew insists are unavoidable and to elide questions about the state's role in enhancing human life.

The above three criticisms should not be understood as a rejection of the value of these approaches. Rather, they are to insist that theories are to be evaluated by identifying which aspects of social life they illuminate and which they obscure (any theory will do both). Each approach to boundary studies identified above both reveals and obscures. This applies, too, to those approaches that currently have significant traction in the study of international boundaries: bordering/bounding, and the biopolitical governing of mobilities.

My concern is not with the limitations of either of these approaches per se, but that in producing new research frameworks they risk limiting the historic scope of boundary studies. The challenge is to develop an intellectually generous framework for boundary studies that draws on as many theoretical and methodological approaches as possible without constricting the breadth of work in the field. Drawing upon the growing interest in human geography in producing what Naylor calls "biographies of objects and places" (2008: 265), I suggest that a solution to this puzzle is to write *boundary biographies* (Megoran, forthcoming). These explore how specific boundaries materialize, rematerialize and dematerialize in different ways, in different contexts, at different scales and at different times. Such biographies enable us to grasp the complexity in form and function of international boundaries and the borders they produce. They diverge from standard historical accounts of the wars, political negotiations and legal wrangling that created a particular boundary (for example Maxwell's 2007 history of the Sino-Russian boundary). They would include such information but, beyond that, in turn use the boundary to tell a range of stories about changing social and political processes in neighboring states and regions. International boundaries thus become a powerful geographical lens through which to make visible a range of social processes that might otherwise be overlooked. In the remainder of this chapter I illustrate this argument with a brief biography of the Kyrgyzstan–Uzbekistan boundary.

A BIOGRAPHY OF THE UZBEKISTAN–KYRGYZSTAN BOUNDARY

The Ferghana Valley, through which much of the Kyrgyzstan–Uzbekistan boundary winds, has been conquered and settled by numerous different groups, from Greeks and Arabs to Mongols and Turks, all of whom left a greater or lesser imprint on the social and political geography of the valley (see Figures 27.1 and 27.2). By the nineteenth century, it would appear that people identified themselves with, or differentiated themselves from, others in a range of registers and at a variety of scales. As Northrop contends, "Indigenous identities were complex, multifaceted and changeable" (2004: 17). Effective Bolshevik control of Central Asia was secured by the early 1920s, after which the nascent Soviet state embarked on National Territorial Delimitation (NTD). In 1924, the Central Committee's Central Asian Bureau pro-

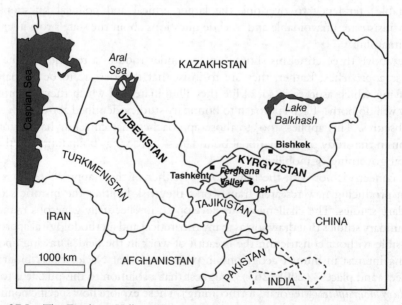

Figure 27.1 The Ferghana Valley in its regional context

Figure 27.2 The Ferghana Valley

posed that Uzbek Soviet Socialist Republics (SSRs) be created as full constitutive members of the USSR, and that present-day Kyrgyzstan be incorporated into the Russian Soviet Federative Socialist Republic as the Kara-Kyrgyz Autonomous Region (it eventually attained full union status in 1936 as the Kyrgyz SSR). This division was created in line with Stalin's concept of the nation as "a historically constituted, stable community of people, formed on the basis of a common language, territory, economic life, and psychological make-up manifested in a common culture" (1994: 20). The proposal was formally approved at a meeting of the Central Committee of the Russian Communist Party in October 1924. The nascent Kyrgyzstan–Uzbekistan boundary thus materialized in the ideological, political and executive spaces of Bolshevik power in Moscow and Tashkent.

The materialization of the boundary on maps and on the ground was performed by party functionaries of the region (Radjapova 2005: 180). The main criteria used in the division of the territories was that the new republics should have *geographical* unity, an *economic* rationale and be *ethnically* homogenous (Bergne 2007: 43). It was impossible to satisfy these requirements fully, because ethnicity was indistinct and fluid. Boundary surveyors reported confusion about how to classify people who used ethnonyms in ways that did not match their census categories (Brower 2003: 180).

NTD involved fierce political battles between the leaderships of the nascent states for control of disputed areas. In making submissions to a parity commission established to settle ethnoterritorial disputes, leaders of the nascent Uzbek and Kyrgyz polities argued over whether groups in economically important locations be considered "Uzbek" or "Kyrgyz." The boundary thus materialized in spaces of group affiliation and individual identification.

By a process driven by ideological vision and pragmatic accommodation, actualized through political struggles over ethnographic interpretation and local geographies, the highly complex Uzbek-Kyrgyz boundary, with its numerous anomalies and contested enclaves, materialized. As settlements such as Isfara, Uch-Korgan and Sokh were ceded first to one state and then the other, the boundary dematerialized and rematerialized in new places.

Hirsch's (2005) research on delimitation demonstrates that the process of making submissions to the commission taught people to participate in a new political sphere, learning to articulate linguistic, economic and ethnic differences as "national." Thus the boundary itself was not a mere product of the Soviet Union: it helped *produce* the Soviet Union. It was not a more precise realization of imprecise frontiers between Uzbek and Kyrgyz peoples: it helped *create* Soviet Uzbek and Kyrgyz peoples. Its materialization in the imaginative and applied cartographies of 1920s Soviet planners, and in numerous local disputes between existing and new elites, was entangled in the production of a whole new political geography in Central Asia, that of territorialized nationalism.

The materialization of a borderland

The period following NTD until the independence of Central Asia from the Soviet Union in 1991 saw multiple and varied rematerializations of the boundary between the Kyrgyz and Uzbek Soviet Socialist Republics. One significant process was the formal attempt to ensure that the boundary that materialized in the meeting rooms and discussions of the Central Committee of the Russian Communist Party in October 1924 rematerialized in more orderly, scientific and visual formats. The Parity Commission was wound up on Stalin's orders in 1927 without completing its work, and two years after his death in 1953 a joint Uzbek-Kyrgyz SSR border demarcation commission was established to resolve outstanding interrepublican disputes. The boundary line was readjusted in some places, dematerializing and rematerializing. Some progress was made but, again, and for reasons that will not be properly understood until further archival work is done on the topic, this commission never completed its work.[1]

This Soviet (re)materialization of the boundary in an attempt to make it more distinct occurred at the same time as it dematerialized in border processes of regional planning overseen by the Soviet authorities. As the boundary was never intended by its architects to be an international one, Soviet economic planning designed borderland electricity, gas, irrigation, transport, educational and economic networks, if not on an integrated basis, then at least on an interdependent one. This had numerous specific impacts on cross-boundary dynamics. Daily works buses ferried workers from the Kyrgyz SSR to factories in the Uzbek SSR. Ethnic minorities crossed the republican borders relatively freely for higher education in their own mother-tongues, creating new social networks as former classmates maintained contact after graduation. The more populous Uzbek SSR rented tracts of land from the less densely populated Kyrgyz SSR for use in agricultural and industrial developments. These were intended to be fixed-term contracts but frequently rents were left uncollected and land unreturned when the period of tenure expired. In January 1982, the governments of the Kyrgyz and Uzbek SSRs concluded an agreement to construct a reservoir at Sokh, flooding Kyrgyzstani land, for the use of Uzbekistan. The Uzbek SSR's Ferghana Valley cotton crop was largely irrigated by this and other such reservoirs constructed in upland Kyrgyz SSR territory; in turn, some raw cotton was taken for processing to factories in O'sh[2] as well as in the Uzbek SSR.

The transport networks designed to support these economic and demographic flows were developed with apparent disregard for republican boundaries: road and rail links in the valley crisscrossed the boundary. Likewise, the industrial, urban, agricultural and transport planning projects of one state spilled freely over into the territory of its neighbor. The legacy of NTD was the materialization of a highly complicated borderland mosaic of land use that paid scant regard to the administrative boundary between the two republics. This legacy bequeathed many difficulties to planners and populations of the independent republics that would emerge in 1991 as the successors of Soviet rule.

After independence: an international boundary?

In the early years of independence, the boundary barely materialized in either the imaginative or tangible geographies of the borderland and its inhabitants. True enough, some border and customs posts were established but control checks were minimal and easily evaded. Social and kinship cross-boundary links were very strong, and border-area shrines continued to precipitate significant flows of pilgrims at set seasons, facilitated by the Soviet-era bus routes plied by the same vehicles in the same liveries.

In the same way, this borderland was still marked by the complicated and uncertain boundary geography that was heir to the Soviet-era patterns of land use that wantonly transgressed the administrative boundaries of the Ferghana Valley republics. Uzbekistan's Marhamat region remained, utilizing 6,885 hectares of land from Osh's Aravon region. Uzbekistan paid nothing for its oil and gas plants in Kyrgyzstan's Kadamjoy region, and in 1994 took the decision to build a carbide production plant in Kyrgyzstan's territory, allegedly without seeking Kyrgyzstani permission. The January 1982 agreement to construct a reservoir at Sokh, which flooded Kyrgyzstani land, for the use of Uzbekistan, stipulated that residents of the flooded Kara-Tokoy village would be properly compensated and relocated; however, this was never implemented. Although a new international boundary had materialized on world maps, its presence barely materialized in the practices and imaginations of borderland dwellers.

Nonetheless, between 1991 and late 1998 a gradual divergence of political and macroeconomic trajectories in Uzbekistan and Kyrgyzstan led to the emergence of a more tangible borderland. As the two republics slowly "drifted apart," they became increasingly differentiated. Macro-scale political and economic changes led to a gradual emergence of a new boundary landscape. Economically, Uzbekistan maintained Soviet-style production and procurement of cotton and wheat, while the application of more neoliberal economics in Kyrgyzstan led to the breaking up of collectives and a greater diversification into cash crops such as tobacco. Agricultural landscapes thus gradually diverged. In 1993 Uzbekistan formally closed its border with Kyrgyzstan to prevent Russian rubles flooding the Valley, in response to Kyrgyzstan's exit from the ruble zone as it introduced its own currency (Olcott 1994: 39–41). This was a brief disruption and this heavily policed border quickly dematerialized, but nonetheless it anticipated the shape of things to come. Uzbekistan subsequently introduced its own currency and border landscapes became peppered with exchange booths. The economic crisis precipitated by the collapse of the Soviet Union's central economic planning created other opportunities. It pushed many professionally skilled people to make use of emerging price differentials by engaging in cross-border shuttle trade.

As well as these macro-scale political and economic changes, more symbolic indicators highlighted the divergence of the two states. Uzbekistan moved to a one-hour difference daylight-saving time scheme, whereas in the Soviet period both states were in the same time zone all year long. Valley residents had to factor this change into bus timetables and work and school times. The movement to a Latin alphabet in Uzbekistan in 1995 meant that highway signs and roadside slogans were printed in different scripts. Uzbekistan maintained its stretch of the O'sh–Andijan border in a better state of repair than Kyrgyzstan did its stretch, a difference that could be felt when driving through the border.

The gradual materialization of a distinct border landscape was suggestive and productive of new senses of citizenship; however, for most people in the 1990s Uzbekistan and Kyrgyzstan still did not *feel* like different countries. In fact, a fuller consciousness of nationality and independence did not impinge upon many inhabitants of the Ferghana Valley until the events of the late 1990s.

The "border crisis" of 1998–2000

The gradual change in border landscapes was accelerated dramatically by a number of events from the late winter of 1998 through to the summer of 1999. The winter had witnessed Uzbekistan's intermittent halting of cross-border gas supplies to Kyrgyzstan due to unpaid bills. This resulted in a double hardship, because not only did gas become more expensive and scarcer, but as people switched on their electric cookers instead of using gas, electricity supplies regularly failed. On February 13, 1999, Uzbekistan's President Islam Karimov confirmed that the major Osh–Andijon cross-border bus service, along with many other routes in the Ferghana Valley, had been suspended. He explained the moves by stating that "Kyrgyzstan is a poor country, and it is not my job to look after the people. Every day five thousand people come from O'sh to Andijon – if each of them buys a loaf of bread, there will not be enough left for my people."[3]

The suspension, which actually began in January, concluded a process that had commenced with a reduction in services the previous summer (*Mezon* 1999). It was ostensibly designed to protect the more state-run economy of Uzbekistan where it abutted economic spaces such as Kyrgyzstan, whose leaders had adopted more neo-liberal economic policies (Megoran 2002). At the same time, Uzbekistan had embarked upon other policies designed to secure greater control of flows over its border.

Closure of the border was accelerated three days later when a carefully orchestrated series of bomb blasts rocked the Uzbekistani capital Tashkent, killing 16 and plunging the state into crisis. The authorities blamed "religious extremists" and "terrorists" backed by outside powers, a reference to Islamists whose intellectual inspiration or practical support was drawn from movements and governments in neighboring states and the wider Islamic world. Their putative heartland was the socially and religiously conservative Ferghana Valley. Uzbekistan immediately sealed its border and after a partial reopening later in the week, security was dramatically tightened up. Many more soldiers, border guards and customs officers were drafted to the state borders and special units were deployed to sensitive border areas. New control posts were built and existing facilities upgraded and in many places crossings were closed, roads dug up and bridges demolished. These measures were widely reported on Uzbekistani television to bolster the project of official nationalism that portrayed Uzbekistan as a united and prosperous historic homeland of the Uzbek people, wisely governed by a strong president, standing up against the insidious threats posed by its neighbors (Megoran 2004, 2005).

The effects of these materializations of the boundary were keenly felt by Kyrgyzstanis. Daily life for many citizens was hampered by the interruption in bus services. Conditions were especially difficult for those living in remote areas of Osh and Jalal-Abad provinces, where border closures to Kyrgyzstani traffic forced often significant detours: travel times from O'sh to outlying mountainous regions such as Leylek and Batken increased up to threefold.

Uzbekistan's tighter border regime impacted national as well as local transport systems in Kyrgyzstan. The country's major rail artery, the Bishkek to Jalal-Abad rail link, ground to a halt, rendered uneconomical by Uzbekistan's decision to forbid Kyrgyzstani trains to halt en route. Traffic using the Uzbekistan sections of the major Osh-Uzbekistan highway was frequently subject to severe restrictions and delays. The economic effects were felt in the form of higher food prices, as longer journey times and corruption on the part of the increased number of officials ate into the profits of the small traders who depended on access to local markets (*Zaman Kïrgïzstan* 1999).

Initially, Kyrgyzstan's president, Askar Akaev, barely reacted to these events. There was neither money nor political will either to copy or to respond to the kinds of measures that Uzbekistan was implementing. The political opposition within Kyrgyzstan, however, was incensed by what they perceived as Akaev's inaction. Parliamentary deputy Dooronbek Sadïrbaev depicted the events as a military invasion of Kyrgyzstan, alleging that Uzbekistani forces were advancing on border posts and seizing huge swathes of Kyrgyzstani territory (*Asaba* 1999). By this, he meant nominally Kyrgyzstani territory that Uzbekistan had inherited from the SSR's unreturned temporary tenures, and omitted to mention ongoing Kyrgyzstani use of Uzbekistani and Tajikistani land from the same period. Nonetheless, the language of military invasion was stark. Sadïrbaev interpreted the border issue as indicative of Uzbekistan's arrogant attitude to Kyrgyzstan and Akaev's failure to stand up to Karimov. He advocated strong action to reclaim lost territory and suggested that Kyrgyzstan start charging Uzbekistan for the water in retaliation for Uzbekistan's halting of gas supplies. Materializing in the hard-fought power struggle between President Akaev and nationalist opposition movements (Megoran 2004), "the border" became one of the most discussed issues in the Kyrgyz press, both as a political topic and in terms of the impact on border communities.

In August 1999 an already tense situation was plunged into a crisis as the so-called Islamic Movement of Uzbekistan (IMU), a group of dissident Islamist guerrillas headed by Ferghana Valley exiles linked to militant Islamist groups in Tajikistan and Afghanistan, invaded Kyrgyzstan's southern regions of Batken and Chong-Alay from Tajikistan. Their declared intent was the establishment of an Islamic state in the Ferghana Valley. The attackers poured through a virtually undefended border, took hostages and battled with the ill-prepared Kyrgyzstani military, before melting back into the mountains of Tajikistan by November. Uzbek jets mistakenly bombed the Kyrgyz village of Kara-Teyt as claims and counterclaims flew (*Erkin Too* 1999). Uzbekistan sealed its borders, while numerous internal checkpoints sprang up within Kyrgyzstan.

In the aftermath of the Batken crisis, Uzbekistan took ever greater measures to insulate the state and its borders. Factories were instructed to shed nonessential Kyrgyzstani laborers. Poorly marked minefields were laid along vulnerable stretches of the border, including the Sokh enclave. In a decree of March 1, 2000, President Karimov introduced a mandatory visa regime for all noncitizens spending more than three days in the country. The authorities began erecting a barbed wire fence 2 meters high around large sections of the Ferghana Valley border. Breaches of the border in cat-and-mouse games played by Uzbekistani border guards and petty smugglers were frequent, sometimes leading to fatalities. An undetermined number of people and livestock died after wandering onto Uzbekistan's minefields. Occasionally, even agents of state security forces clashed. In Kyrgyzstan, President Akaev unveiled plans to create no fewer than 70 border posts on the hitherto unguarded 470-kilometer Kyrgyzstan–Tajikistan border (*Jamestown Monitor* 1999). The boundary was rematerializing in new and, for borderland inhabitants, dangerous ways (Megoran 2006).

These dramatic events accelerated the bifurcation of the political trajectories of the Ferghana Valley's principal states, Uzbekistan and Kyrgyzstan. Their joint border became, as Fumagalli (2002) said, an "alienated border," whose two populations were characterized by reduced interaction and high tension. The net result of these events and incidents was neatly summed up by Tabyshalieva (2001), who described this "new fragmentation of Central Asia" as "a painful and unpleasant lesson for the local population. The imaginary borders of Soviet times have become real."

The Uzbekistan–Kyrgyzstan boundary, 2001–2010

Subsequent to the 1998–2000 Ferghana Valley border crisis, the Kyrgyzstan–Uzbekistan boundary has rematerialized in ways that represent continuity with that period, dematerialized in ways that are breaks with it, and materialized in new ways and spaces.

International imperatives in this period, such as the US "global war on terror," reinscribed the boundary's place in "security" discourses of both states. Border control was not therefore simply a bilateral issue but became embedded in wider campaigns against supposed terrorist networks and narcotics smuggling industries that became increasingly articulated as threats to be addressed at the international scale through multilateral bodies. This new international security agenda, which coincided with the aftermath of the 1998–2000 Ferghana Valley border crisis and built on concerns in the 1990s about the flow of drugs to Europe through the region, meant that Central Asian boundaries became the locus of new flows of international aid. The US and Russia both financed significant transfers of military technology, ostensibly to combat smuggling over the two republics' boundaries. Substantial support from the US and the European Union, with assistance from actors such as the International Organization for Migration, was also provided to upgrade check-points on the Uzbekistan–Kyrgyzstan boundary. The European Union's BOMCA (Border Management in Central Asia) has been a major donor of such aid, seeking to implement an "integrated border management" system of patrolling Central Asian boundaries, providing infrastructure, equipment and training.[4]

Thus, the materialization of the Uzbekistan–Kyrgyzstan boundary in domestic politics, which occurred initially during the 1998–2000 Ferghana Valley boundary crisis, not only continued after this period, but the boundary materialized in new spaces and in new ways due to the regional and international politics of securitization. But it was in the ongoing potential for violence at the boundary that it arguably cast its longest shadow over the valley.

Continuing the ugliest aspect of the 1998–2000 crisis, the border rematerialized in the twenty-first century through frequent incidents of violence that continued to be well reported by media in both countries, often leading to diplomatic exchanges. Occurrences of violence generally related to pastoralists herding livestock in border areas who strayed into unmarked minefields or were subject to heavy-handed polic-ing, to poor petty traders trying to eke out a living by taking advantage of the opportunities created by economic differentials between the two republics, and to conflicts between the two states' border guards. Injuries and deaths were frequent, but far more numerous were reports of intimidation and minor police aggression, an everyday occurrence for border dwellers.

While the boundary materialized in spaces of conflict, cooperation between Uzbekistan and Kyrgyzstan during this period led to multiple dematerializations of the boundary through the reversal of some of the most insidious legacies of the 1998–2000 border crisis. In March 2002 Uzbekistan and Kyrgyzstan concluded their first agreement on the joint distribution of water resources and energy. In August 2004 Uzbekistan began clearing the minefields that had killed and wounded numer-ous Kyrgyzstani citizens and whose presence so irked Bishkek (RFE/RL Newsline 2004a). At the culmination of an official visit of President Bakiev to Uzbekistan in October 2006, he and his Uzbek counterpart, President Karimov, announced to much fanfare in the media of both countries an agreement to reintroduce 60-day visa-free travel for all citizens of both countries. The occasion resulted in a warmer demonstration of fraternal relations than had been seen for some time, with President Bakiev switching into Uzbek to declare: "Our air is one, our water is one, our God is one, our language is one. Therefore, the Uzbeks and the Kyrgyz will never be separated. I think that they should live together as well as grow and develop together."[5]

The question of delimitation and demarcation of the Uzbekistan–Kyrgyzstan boundary is one further concrete example of the product of engagement between the governments of the two states. While from 1998 onward, political actors in both Kyrgyzstan and Uzbekistan sought to use the boundary in domestic struggles for control, a bilateral commission formed in 2000 quietly began to seek to resolve ongoing disputes. In spite of spats between the two countries going public from time to time, the commission's work appears to have progressed steadily. By 2009, around 80 percent of the 1,375-kilometer boundary had been delimited (*Central Asian News Service* 2009).

Therefore, while the boundary was materializing through the deaths of petty traders and the politics of nationalism, it was also materializing in the diplomatic spheres of the work of a boundary commission, and dematerializing as visa regimes were relaxed and minefields cleared. These two processes of conflict and accommodation occurred simultaneously. It is not that one was real and the other illusionary or insignificant. Both were genuine and were demonstrations of how the same boundary can rematerialize and dematerialize in different spaces and ways at the same time.

The domestic political effect of boundary materializations cannot be underestimated. In May 2002 Kyrgyzstan's parliament ratified an agreement on delimitation of the country's border with China, which would transfer some 95,000 hectares of land to Beijing. However, the issue did not die with the successful passage of the bill agreeing delimitation,[6] but instead was seized on by nationalist opposition movements which used the supposed loss of sacred Kyrgyz territory to galvanize the public to their cause. The imprisonment in 2002 of southern Kyrgyzstani member of parliament Azimbek Beknazarov, who had become a vociferous critic of the boundary deal, led to demonstrations in his home district of Aksy, near the southern town of Kerben. In a clumsy attempt to dispel the protest, the police shot dead six protestors, and a subsequent inquiry led to the resignation of the government, including Prime Minister Kurmanbek Bakiev. Bakiev became an opponent of the regime, and used the shootings to galvanize an opposition movement based in the Ferghana Valley part of Kyrgyzstan that would eventually topple Akaev, who fled the country as demonstrators stormed the presidential administration in Bishkek in 2005, installing Bakiev as the new leader (Cummings 2008).

It was not the Uzbekistani but rather the Chinese section of Kyrgyzstan's boundary that raised such passions and played a significant part in the tumultuous struggle for leadership of the republic and the fall of first the government and then the president. Nonetheless, nationalistic discourse in Kyrgyzstan referred commonly to "the border" as a single, organic entity and the furore over the Chinese boundary built on the fervor excited by politicization of the Uzbekistan boundary during the 1998–2000 period (Megoran 2004). The boundary was a factor in what up until that period was arguably the most tumultuous and dramatic political drama in post-Soviet Central Asia. The overthrow of Akaev, however, was not to prove the revolutionary new beginning for Kyrgyzstan for which many had hoped. His successor, Kurmanbek

Bakiev, proved more corrupt and authoritarian than his predecessor, and was himself overthrown in violent protests in 2010. That year has arguably been the most disastrous thus far in Kyrgyzstan's brief period of independent history and is thrown into stark relief by examining it through the lens of the border.

June 2010 Tragedy and Its Aftermath

On April 15, 2010, President Bakiev fled Kyrgyzstan after street protests around the country culminated in his violent overthrow. An interim government assumed control but, lacking both effective power and political legitimacy, was unable either to make its writ run widely in areas loyal to the former regime, or to control growing lawlessness in the streets. On June 11, horrendous violence erupted between Kyrgyz and Uzbeks in the southern cities of O'sh and Jalalabat. Over the next three days some 2,000 homes were burnt down, businesses were looted and destroyed and hundreds of people lost their lives. Kyrgyz and Uzbeks suffered but Uzbeks were apparently disproportionally affected.

The Uzbekistan–Kyrgyzstan boundary took on new significance as it indexed Osh Kyrgyz and Uzbek fears. For O'sh Kyrgyz, these were fears of the very dismemberment of Kyrgyzstan. For Osh Uzbek, fearing for their lives, the border became a refuge from the Kyrgyz gangs and security forces.

For many Kyrgyz, "the border" told a story in 2010 of an extreme threat to the state's existence, which it only narrowly survived through the courageous and bloody struggle of the Kyrgyz nation and through the decisive action of Uzbekistan. This fear is encapsulated by criminal charges brought by the General Prosecutor's office, claiming that several Uzbek "separatist" leaders intentionally stirred up ethnic tensions in order to rend O'sh and Jalalabat from the Kyrgyz state and join them to Uzbekistan (*Daily Times* 2010). As Trilling noted in a commentary on these statements, "convincing publicly available evidence has been scant" (Trilling 2010). Nonetheless, it was widely believed by Kyrgyz people. One person told me he believed that Uzbek leaders had previously gone to Uzbekistan and spoken to a "high level criminal leader" who promised to help effect this change of the boundary.[7]

Thus for many Kyrgyz the violence of June 2010 was a grave plot that threatened the very territorial integrity of Kyrgyzstan by seeking to redraw dramatically the Ferghana Valley's boundary and sheer off Uzbek-populated swathes of Kyrgyz territory to Uzbekistan. This threat was only – and properly – thwarted by the combined responses of Kyrgyz counterviolence and Uzbekistan's sealing off of the border. In 2010, "the border" indexed both the extreme existential threat to the state and its ultimate bloody survival.

If Osh Kyrgyz feared that the intention of Uzbeks in both Kyrgyzstan and Uzbekistan was to exploit a moment of political crisis in Kyrgyzstan to redraw radically the two republics' mutual boundary and to annex much of southern Kyrgyzstan, they might have been reassured by the actions of Uzbekistan's President Karimov. Addressing a meeting of the Collective Security Treaty Organization in December 2010, he reported that he had had a lengthy conversation with Kyrgyzstan's interim president Rosa Otunbaeva on the morning of June 11. He said: "In response to her request, I assured her that no one from our side under any circumstances would cross the border of Kyrgyzstan. And I kept my word." If this had not happened, he explained, he was convinced that "the inter-ethnic conflict in the southern Kyrgyzstan could have turned into an interstate conflict" like that between Armenia and Azerbaijan (Karimov 2010).

Nonetheless, as what was reported in some Uzbekistani media outlets as Kyrgyz "genocide" against O'sh Uzbeks continued (*Eurasianet* 2010a), some 80,000–100,000 ethnic Uzbeks – largely women, children and the elderly – fled from Osh and were temporarily housed in refugee camps (*Eurasianet* 2010b). In describing the terrifying journey to sections of the boundary where barbed-wire border fences had temporarily been removed, trampling over fellow refugees who slipped into the mud, climbing over ditches and afraid of Kyrgyz snipers, one elderly Uzbek woman who fled to Uzbekistan evocatively summed it up as being like *qiyamat qayim*, the Day of Judgment and resurrection at the end of historical time in Islamic eschatology.[8] It would be easy to push the soteriological analogies beyond that intended by my interlocutor, but she expressed enormous gratitude to President Karimov for rescuing and sheltering her until the immediate crisis passed. The barbed wire and ditches that for O'sh Uzbeks had long been a hated symbol of rejection and separation were temporarily cleared so that the border became a gateway to salvation from apocalyptic dramas unfolding in their homeland.

But this sanctuary was to prove temporary. Uzbekistan did not grant refugee status to those who had fled but, as a measure of order was restored in Osh, encouraged them to return home. They had thus to cross the border back into a city where Uzbeks reported daily fears of intimidation, robbery, attack, verbal abuse, kidnappings and ransom demands, and retaliatory arrests by state security officials. As one of the few remaining visible female Uzbek street vendors in Central O'sh put it to me in a whispered conversation in December 2010:

> This was organized by the Kyrgyz leaders, the mayor, 100 percent, they wanted to completely wipe the Uzbeks out. Where can we go? We can go to Russia, and become citizens, but we'd have nowhere to live; we can't go to Uzbekistan, the border is closed. Our men are staying at home, not working. They are afraid to go out in the streets, they will get beaten up or kidnapped.

The woman's sense of the virtual immobility of Osh Uzbeks, of their entrapment in space, is poignant, and her expression "the border is closed" is telling. It did not mean simply that border crossings had been temporarily closed, or that it was not possible to enter the territory of Uzbekistan through a well-placed bribe. Rather, the closed border indexed the unwillingness of the Uzbek government to accept proper responsibility for its kinfolk, either to exercise leverage in Kyrgyzstan to protect them or to show hospitality and welcome them when existence became untenable.

As asserted by Goble (2010), many "ethnic Uzbeks in southern Kyrgyzstan feel that they have been betrayed by Tashkent which has failed to support them." This is because, Goble argues, Tashkent sees O'sh Uzbeks as a threat. Among them Islamism, political activism, and critical journalism have been less controlled and thus stronger than in Uzbekistan. The border for Tashkent represented, as we saw above, a bulwark against lawlessness and chaos that endangered Uzbekistan and needed sealing to prevent that engulfing the country. Refugees could be temporarily accommodated while the violence raged but thereafter Tashkent continued to protect its border against would-be migrants to disabuse O'sh Uzbeks of the notion that they had a home in Uzbekistan.

In January 2011, a commission of inquiry established by the government of Kyrgyzstan reported its findings on the causes of the June violence. Two of its recommendations are of particular relevance for this chapter. Recommendation 6 calls on "The President and government of the Kyrgyz Republic to activate work on delimitation and demarcation on borders with Uzbekistan and Tajikistan." This recommendation betrays an insecurity about the future territorial integrity of Kyrgyzstan and a belief that this can be safeguarded (and, presumably, the supposedly separatist Uzbek minority tamed) by shoring up the border through bilateral agreement and actual demarcation. Recommendation 7 calls on "The President of the Kyrgyz Republic to consider an award to the President of Uzbekistan I. Karimov for his enormous personal influence in solving interethnic conflict in the Southern Kyrgyzstan and prevention of large-scale regional war in Ferghana Valley in 2010."

The Commission's calls for both a renewed effort to delimit and demarcate Kyrgyzstan's boundary with Uzbekistan, and its honoring of President Karimov, spotlights a fundamental ambiguity about the relationship between the two states. Among Kyrgyz elites Karimov's Uzbekistan is often reviled for allegedly bullying smaller Kyrgyzstan and holding it to ransom over gas and electricity supplies. Uzbekistan's unilateral moves to fence and control its border with Kyrgyzstan have, as we saw above, been interpreted as encroachments on the sovereignty of Kyrgyzstan. Yet at a moment of deep crisis in the Ferghana Valley it suited both Tashkent and Bishkek – for very different reasons – to see the border sealed. Just as the Uzbekistan–Kyrgyzstan boundary is a cipher for the fears and hopes of Uzbek and Kyrgyz communities in southern Kyrgyzstan, so its recent biography shows that the interests of two very different state political systems can converge.

CONCLUSION

International boundaries are not "permanent fixtures for all time" (Blake 1994: xii), but rather they proliferate, unfold, move, shift, metamorphose, edge, retract, emerge or retreat (Soguk 2007: 283–285). In recent years, social theory has inspired a number of ways of reflecting on this dynamism. Two particularly productive examples are theorizing international boundaries as examples of more general processes of bordering/ bounding, and as biopolitical tools to govern mobilities in the "war on terror."

These two approaches offer valuable contributions to making visible certain aspects of social life that might otherwise be obscured. However, their provenance means that they also obscure others. They lose sight of the distinctiveness of international boundaries, restrict the scope of international boundary studies, and are insufficiently rigorous in thinking through broader political ethical questions about the place and role of international borders in our age. To address these limitations, I propose what I term the production of "biographies" of international boundaries. These explore how specific boundaries materialize, rematerialize, and dematerialize in different ways, in different contexts, at different scales and at different times.

Using the Uzbekistan–Kyrgyzstan boundary, I have shown what such a biography might look like. This chapter has outlined some of the materializations, dematerializations and rematerializations of this remarkable boundary: in Moscow committee rooms; the maps of surveyors; the imaginations of national statehood; the landscapes of border regions; the politics of nationalism and authoritarianism; domestic power struggles to overthrow entrenched elites; elections and revolutions; interethnic violence and refugee flows; and the daily practices of the rural and urban poor who live alongside it. In so doing, this boundary biography makes a distinctly geographical contribution toward a broader understanding of post-Soviet Central Asian political processes. It demonstrates the importance of geography to state-building, international relations, foreign aid, nationalism, economics, and power struggles. It makes visible aspects of social life that might otherwise be obscured in accounts that are less sensitive to space.

In an insightful intervention, Agnew writes that "the overarching normative question in re-framing the understanding of borders is how much borders enhance or restrict the pursuit of a decent life" (2008: 183). This biography suggests that the balance sheet for the Uzbekistan–Kyrgyzstan boundary, at least in its recent history, is far from positive. To be sure, independence has afforded new possibilities for many in Uzbekistan and Kyrgyzstan: a postcolonial recalibration of the value of national languages and cultures within new boundaries, plus the capability to grant themselves permission to cross those borders, whether for study, pilgrimage or emigration abroad. Yet the boundary became a biopolitical and discursive tool in Uzbekistan's politics of authoritarianism; an index for the supposed strength or weakness of the nation and state in Kyrgyzstan's politics of nationalism; a squeeze on the livelihoods of the borderland's poor; a restriction of mobility within the Ferghana Valley; and both symbol and enactment of the double exclusion of ethnic minorities – ultimately with very bloody consequences. This chapter began with a positive episode from the biography of the El Salvador–Honduras boundary to remind us that violence is not the inevitable outcome of international boundaries. Peace, however, occupies only a marginal entry in the recent biography of the Kyrgyzstan–Uzbekistan boundary.

NOTES

This chapter substantially develops and extends ideas mooted in Megoran (forthcoming). Elements of the third section of the chapter are used with kind permission of the Association of American Geographers. Research for this chapter was made possible by the UK's Economic and Social Research Council for funding my doctoral research at Sidney Sussex College, Cambridge, and the British Academy for providing me with a Small Research Grant to conduct post-doctoral work on "The impact of the Ferghana Valley boundary closures on border communities" (SG:38394). I would like to express my gratitude to all three institutions for supporting this research.

1   Interview with Azim Karashev, member of bilateral Kyrgyzstan–Uzbekistan border demarcation committee, Osh, June 12, 2000.

2 To reflect the overlapping but politically loaded differences in the naming of places, and
   to refuse to prefer one over the other, this chapter will variously use both Kyrgyz (Osh,
   Jalalabat) and Uzbek (O'sh, Jalal-Abad) variants of the two main cities of southern
   Kyrgyzstan.
3 News broadcast, Tashkent TV1, Feb. 13, 1999.
4 Interview, Tamas Kiss, BOMCA/CADAP Programmes in Central Asia, Project Manager,
   Kazakhstan and Kyrgyzstan, Bishkek, Apr. 24, 2006.
5 Uzbek Television first channel, Tashkent, "Uzbek leader urges fighting Islamic group" (in
   Uzbek), Oct. 4, 2006. BBC Monitoring CAU 041006 nu/atd.
6 Professor Salamat Alamanov, director of the Kyrgyz president's Regional Problems Office,
   reported in September 2004 that demarcation of the Kyrgyzstan-Chinese boundary was
   completed. See RFE/RL Newsline 2004.
7 Conversation, Bishkek, Dec. 9, 2010.
8 Interview, Osh, Dec. 4, 2010.

REFERENCES

Agnew, John. 2008. Borders on the mind: re-framing border thinking. *Ethics and Global Politics* 1 (4): 175–191.

Amoore, Louise. 2006. Biometric borders: governing mobilities in the war on terror. *Political Geography* 25: 336–351.

Asaba. 1999. Tübüng bütünbü, tübölük dostuk? 12. Mar. 19–25, pp. 6–7.

Bergne, Paul. 2007. *The Birth of Tajikistan.* London: I.B. Tauris.

Blake, Gerald. 1994. Preface. In C. Schofield, ed., *World Boundaries 1: Global Boundaries*, pp. xii–xvii. London: Routledge.

Brower, Daniel. 2003. *Turkestan and the Fate of the Russian Empire.* London: Routledge/ Curzon.

Central Asian News Service. 2009. Kyrgyzstan, Uzbekistan agree on 80% of total length of state border – PM Chudinov. Apr. 22. At http://en.ca-news.org/news/50331 (accessed May 2009).

Cummings, Sally, ed. 2008. Domestic and International Perspectives on Kyrgyzstan's "Tulip Revolution": Motives, Mobilization and Meanings. Special issue, *Central Asian Survey* 27 (3–4): 221–378.

Curzon, Lord. 1907. *Frontiers.* Oxford: Clarendon Press.

Daily Times. 2010. Kyrgyzstan charges Uzbek leaders over ethnic violence. Sept. 2. At www.dailytimes.com.pk (accessed Sept. 2010).

Daniel, Tim. 2002. After judgement day. In C. Schofield, D. Newman, A. Drysdale and J.A. Brown, eds, *The Razor's Edge: International Boundaries and Political Geography: Essays in Honour of Professor Gerald Blake*, pp. 269–286. London: Kluwer Law International.

Erkin Too. 1999. Bomba jaryldy, birok . . . Sept. 17, p. 3.

Eurasianet. 2010a. Conflicting narratives add to tensions in Kyrgyzstan. June 15. At http://www.eurasianet.org/node/61310 (accessed Nov. 2011).

Eurasianet. 2010b. Tashkent's response to Kyrgyz crisis boosts Karimov's image. July 15. At http://www.eurasianet.org/node/61534 (accessed Nov. 2011).

Fumagalli, Matteo. 2002. Re-thinking borders and border security in Central Asia: the Uzbek-Kyrgyz borderland and the case for "de-securitization." Manifestations of transformation in Central Asia: ten years of independence. MS.

Goble, Paul. 2010. Tashkent fears southern Kyrgyzstan unrest could spread into Uzbekistan. *Kiyev Post*, June. At http://www.kyivpost.com/news/opinion/op_ed/detail/81576/ (accessed Nov. 2011).

Hartshorne, Richard. 1936. Suggestions on the terminology of political boundaries. *Annals of the Association of American Geographers* 26 (1): 56–57.

Hirsch, Francine. 2005. *Empire of Nations: Ethnographic Knowledge and the Making of the Soviet Union*. London: Cornell University Press.

House, John. 1981. Frontier studies: an applied approach. In A. Burnett and P. Taylor, eds, *Political Studies from Spatial Perspectives*, pp. 291–311. Chichester: John Wiley & Sons, Ltd.

Jamestown Monitor. 1999. New measures to quell Kyrgyz insurgency. 5 (188). Oct. 12.

Karimov, Islam. 2010. Statement of the President of the Republic of Uzbekistan Islam Karimov at the meeting of the Collective Security Treaty Organization, December 15, 2010. At www.jahonnews.uz (accessed Jan. 2011).

Maxwell, Neville. 2007. How the Sino-Russian boundary conflict was finally settled: from Nerchinsk 1689 to Vladivostok 2005 via Zhenbao Island 1969. *Critical Asian Studies* 39 (2): 229–253.

Megoran, Nick. 2002. Contested geographies of globalisation in Kyrgyzstan: de-/re-territorialisation? *Journal of Central Asian Studies* 6 (2): 13–29.

Megoran, Nick. 2004. The critical geopolitics of the Uzbekistan–Kyrgyzstan Ferghana Valley boundary dispute, 1999–2000. *Political Geography* 23 (6): 731–764.

Megoran, Nick. 2005. The critical geopolitics of danger in Uzbekistan and Kyrgyzstan. *Environment and Planning D: Society and Space* 23 (3): 555–580.

Megoran, Nick. 2006. For ethnography in political geography: experiencing and re-imagining Ferghana Valley boundary closures. *Political Geography* 25 (6): 622–640.

Megoran, Nick. Forthcoming. Rethinking the study of international boundaries: a biography of the Kyrgyzstan–Uzbekistan boundary. *Annals of the Association of American Geographers*.

Mezon. 1999. Osh-Andijon chegarasi passajir transporti nega uchun yopiq? Feb. 13–20, p. 1.

Naylor, Simon. 2008. Historical geography: geographies and historiographies. *Progress in Human Geography* 32 (2): 265–274.

Newman, David. 2003. Boundaries. In J. Agnew, K. Mitchell and G. Toal, eds, *A Companion to Political Geography*, pp. 123–137. Oxford: Blackwell.

Newman, David and Paasi, Anssi. 1998. Fences and neighbours in the postmodern world: boundary narratives in political geography. *Progress in Human Geography* 22 (2): 186–207.

Northrop, Douglas. 2004. *Veiled Empire: Gender and Power in Stalinist Central Asia*. New York: Cornell University Press.

O'Dowd, Liam. 2010. From a "borderless world" to a "world of borders": "bringing history back in." *Environment and Planning D: Society and Space* 28: 1031–1050.

Olcott, Martha Brill. 1994. Ceremony and substance: the illusion of unity in Central Asia. In M. Mandelbaum, ed., *Central Asia and the World: Kazakhstan, Uzbekistan, Tajikistan, Kyrgyzstan, and Turkmenistan*, pp. 17–46. New York: Council on Foreign Relations.

Radjapova, R.Y. 2005. Establishment of Soviet power in Central Asia (1917–1924). In M. Palat and A. Tabyshalieva, eds, *History of Civilizations of Central Asia*, vol. 6: *Towards the Contemporary Period: From the Mid-Nineteenth to the End of the Twentieth Century*, pp. 153–183. Paris: UNESCO.

RFE/RL (Radio Free Europe/Radio Liberty) Newsline. 2004a. Kyrgyz-Chinese border fully demarcated. 8 (178), Part 1, Sept. 17.

RFE/RL (Radio Free Europe/Radio Liberty) Newsline. 2004b. Uzbekistan begins mine-clearing along Kyrgyz border. 8 (155), Part 1, Aug. 16.

Semple, Ellen. 1907. Geographical boundaries I. *Bulletin of the American Geographical Society* 39 (7): 385–397.

Smith, David. 1990. Introduction: the sharing and dividing of geographical space. In M. Chisholm and D. Smith, eds, *Shared Space, Divided Space: Essays on Conflict and Territorial Organization*, pp. 1–21. London: Unwin Hyman.

Soguk, Nevzat. 2007. Border's capture: insurrectional politics, border-crossing humans, and the new political. In P.K. Rajaram and C. Grundy-Warr, eds, *Borderscapes: Hidden Geographies and Politics at Territory's Edge*, pp. 283–308. London: University of Minnesota Press.

Stalin, Joseph. 1994. The nation. In J. Hutchinson and A. Smith, eds, *Nationalism*, pp. 18–21. Oxford: Oxford University Press.

Tabyshalieva, Anara. 2001. Central Asia: imaginary and real borders. *Central Asia-Caucasus Analyst* 12/19. At http://www.cacianalyst.org/?q=node/158 (accessed May 2009).

Trilling, David. 2010. Kyrgyzstan: official pins blame on anti-Karimov Uzbek separatists. *Eurasianet*, Dec. 14. At http://www.eurasianet.org/node/62569 (accessed Nov. 2011).

van Houtum, Henk and van Naerssen, Ton. 2002. Bordering, ordering and othering. *Tijdschrift voor Economische en Sociale Geografie* 93 (2): 125–136.

Vaughan-Williams, Nick. 2010. The UK border security continuum: virtual biopolitics and the simulation of the sovereign ban. *Environment and Planning D: Society and Space* 28: 1071–1083.

Zaman Kïrgïzstan. 1999. Bazarlarga-Tashkenttin taasiri. Mar. 2, pp. 1, 5.

28 # Border, Scene and Obscene

Nicholas De Genova

The social degradation and even fanatical castigation of deportable noncitizens (and undocumented migrant labor, in particular) require as a crucial condition of possibility the perpetuation of discursive formations that repetitively and persistently incite us to believe in the reality or truth of migrant "illegality." All discussions of the sociopolitical condition of migrant "illegality," even those that purport to be critical of it, are inevitably implicated in this larger discourse and the reproduction of its vexed premises. It is for this reason that this essay insists that the terms associated with the dubious distinction between migrant "legality" and "illegality" be signaled with quotation marks, as persistently and repetitively as the discursive formation itself renders these with the semblance of ready-made "facts." Such discursive formations must be understood to be complexes of both language and image, of rhetoric, text and subtext, accusation and insinuation, as well as the visual grammar that upholds and enhances iconicity. They may be understood to be an integral part of the larger sociopolitical production of migrant "illegality." These languages and discourses of "illegality" supply both the rationale for, and also the incessant and truly insatiable response to, what I have previously depicted as the Border Spectacle (De Genova 2002; 2005: 242–249). The Border Spectacle is a spectacle of *enforcement* at "the" border, whereby the specter of migrant "illegality" is rendered spectacularly visible. The material practices of immigration enforcement, then, must be understood to be enmeshed in a dense weave of discourse and image, and furthermore generate a constant redundancy of still more of these discourses and images. Through this same operation, the law, which has in fact produced the "illegality" of the migrants in question, is utterly naturalized and vanishes from view. In place of the social and political relation of migrant labor to the state, therefore, the spectacle of border enforcement yields up the thing-like fetish of migrant "illegality" as a self-evident and *sui generis* "fact," generated by its own supposed act of violation. An ever-increasingly militarized spectacle of apprehensions, detentions, and deportations lends migrant "illegality" the commonsensical air of a "natural" fact, to accom-

A Companion to Border Studies, First Edition. Edited by Thomas M. Wilson and Hastings Donnan.

pany the banality of a continuous *importation* of undocumented migrant labor. Thus, the Border Spectacle relentlessly augments and embellishes the mundane and diminutive human mobility of migrants with the mystique of an obnoxious and unpardonable transgression of the presumably sacrosanct boundary of the state's space.

The Border Spectacle, therefore, sets the *scene* – a scene of ostensible exclusion, in which the purported naturalness and putative necessity of exclusion may be demonstrated and verified, validated and legitimated, redundantly. The *scene* (where border enforcement performatively activates the reification of migrant "illegality" in an emphatic and grandiose gesture of exclusion) is nevertheless always accompanied by its shadowy, publicly unacknowledged or disavowed, *obscene* supplement (the large-scale recruitment of illegalized migrant labor). In light of what the scene presumes to reveal and the obscene that it simultaneously conceals, the frail ideological dichotomy of "exclusion" and "inclusion" utterly collapses.

This formulation of border enforcement as spectacle derives crucial theoretical and analytical force from the 1967 work of Guy Debord, regarding what he deemed to be the society of the spectacle (Debord 1995). Significantly elaborating upon and extending Marx's immanent critique of the fetishism of the commodity under capitalism (Marx 1976: 163–177), Debord identified the overwhelming and unprecedented hegemony of image and appearance mediating all social relations, by which "the whole of life . . . presents itself as an immense accumulation of *spectacles*" (1995: 12, emphasis in original). For Debord, the ascendancy of the society of the spectacle ensured that "all that once was directly lived has become mere representation" and tends to reduce all social life from its already estranged and atomized condition to the sheer passivity of utter spectatorship. Debord, following Marx, emphatically privileged the *visual* dimension of such spectacular representation (1995: 12), elaborating further: "The spectacle is not a collection of images; rather, it is a social relationship between people that is mediated by images." Nonetheless, Debord's theses were also abundantly concerned with the *language* of mass-mediated discourse. The spectacle is "the self-portrait of power" (1995: 19), quintessentially characterized by an incessant monological tyranny and garrulous redundancy, "a sort of eternity of non-importance that speaks loudly" (Debord 2005: Thesis VI; cf. 1995: 17, 19). With recourse to both image and discourse, the spectacle achieves "a concrete inversion of life," "a weltanschauung that has been actualized, translated into the material realm – a world view transformed into an objective force" (Debord 1995: 12, 13). It manifests itself as a specious totality, a unified self-representation of the world of estrangement, prevailing over that world (1995: 22). For Debord, the spectacle perfects the alienating isolation and separation of human energies and endeavors through a debilitating onslaught of images and abstractions to be passively contemplated, and works to induce "a generalized autism" (1995: 18, 22–23, 153).

The spectacles of migrant "illegality" thus rely significantly upon a constellation of images and discursive formations, which may be taken to supply the *scene* of "exclusion." And yet, the more noise and heat generated from this sort of anti-immigrant controversy, the more that the veritable *inclusion* of those incessantly targeted for exclusion proceeds apace. Their "inclusion," of course, is finally devoted to the subordination of their labor, which can be best accomplished only to the extent that their incorporation is permanently beleaguered with the kinds of exclusionary and commonly racist campaigns that ensure that this *inclusion is itself, precisely, a form of subjugation*. What is at stake, then, is a larger sociopolitical (and legal) process of inclusion *through* exclusion, "integration" as compulsory "assimilation," labor *importation* (whether overt or covert) premised upon protracted deportability. If the Border Spectacle supplies a *scene* of ostensible "exclusion" – indeed, if it fashions "the" border as a veritable *mise-en-scène* of the larger dramaturgy of migration as a site of transgression and the reaction formations of (law) "enforcement" – it nonetheless conceals (in plain view, as it were) the public secret of a more or less permanent recruitment of "illegal" migrants as undocumented labor. This we may comprehend to be the *obscene* of inclusion.

My notion of the coupling of the scene and obscene of borders is inspired by Slavoj Žižek's more general elaboration of this conceptual scheme. As Žižek contends, "Power is always-already its own transgression, if it is to function, it has to rely on a kind of obscene supplement" (1997: 34). In order for power "to reproduce itself and contain its Other, it has to rely on an inherent excess which grounds it" (1997: 34). In this regard, he insists upon "the ideological and political significance of *maintaining appearances*" for power discourses "whose efficiency depends on the mechanism of self-censorship" (1997: 33, emphasis in original). The Border Spectacle enhances the efficiency of its own power precisely through this sort of obscene intimacy, whereby the "dirty secret" concerning migrant "illegality" – as its inherent and defining excess – may be occasionally revealed but must be generally guarded through sanctimonious acts of self-censorship and dissimulation.

The scene of exclusion and the obscene of inclusion therefore are inextricably and dialectically linked. Yet, like the peculiar inversion in which human affairs more generally appear as "material [thing-like] relations between persons and social relations between things" (Marx 1976: 166), so the thing-like (reified) reality of migrant "illegality" – as a social, political, and juridical fact – pervasively and perniciously assists in the *object*-ification of undocumented or "irregular" migrant workers. However, these mass-mediated operations of discursive separation – producing people as "illegal" in utter isolation from and with total disregard for the legal production of "illegality" itself – systematically disorient and disarticulate the scene and the obscene with the superficial and incomplete language of "inclusion" and "exclusion." It is here that the critical procedure that seeks to identify the *spectacles* of migrant "illegality," and to elucidate their fundamental dynamics, provides a vital analytical tool for the sort of scholarship that may itself avoid finally becoming merely one more contribution to the larger discursive formation which fetishizes "illegality" as a "natural" fact.

SOCIETY OF THE SPECTACLE AND THE SPECTACULAR STATE

The Border Spectacle may be most extravagantly illustrated in the classic examples that cluster around the patrolling and policing of geographical borders, the physical frontiers of nation-state territoriality. Perhaps the most iconic of these is the vast land border between the United States and Mexico (to which my own original formulation of this concept explicitly referred), or to the increasing prominence of images of the patrols of the high seas or rugged landscapes that are pressed to serve as the elusive and increasingly virtual (externalized) borders of the European Union (see Andrijasevic 2010; Karakayali and Rigo 2010). It is instructive to note, however, that there is nothing about the Border Spectacle that requires its choreography of images to be so literally affiliated to the *geography* of border enforcement. In strict legal terms, "the border" encompasses a much more variegated spectrum of spaces, and inevitably also includes the airports (or seaports) where migrants undergo inspection by immigration authorities, commonly with visas that later may be overstayed or violated. Passport controls in the United Kingdom's international airports, for instance, make this point rather flamboyantly, announcing repeatedly in imposing lettering that one is indeed positioned at the United Kingdom's Border in spite of one's physical location deep within the geography of the country's interior. The same is true of the international high-speed rail transit stations where passengers, located physically in France or Belgium, are informed of their paradoxical presence at the UK border and subjected to the authority of British immigration officials. It is not any specific constellation of enforcement practices (such as the admittedly more sensational militarized patrols of land and sea frontiers) that constitute the conditions of possibility for the spectacle of immigration enforcement at "the" border, so much as the mere fact that borders are indeed enacted (and thus performed) through such practices.

Indeed, it is possible to go further and say that borders are truly *activated* through such practices of enforcement and thus are animated in the first place by the mobility of the travelers and would-be migrants themselves (Karakayali and Rigo 2010). Therefore, a mundane inspection of documents, accompanied always by the interlocking threats of detection, interception, and detention, may similarly generate a proliferation of spaces for the production of the Border Spectacle. Indubitably, the fetish of migrant "illegality" assumes the semblance of something most palpable and resplendently verifiable when activated through surreptitious, seemingly devious acts of "unauthorized" border *crossing*. But the grandiose, exquisitely visible spectacle at territorial borders is widely accompanied by a rather more prosaic multiplication of more discrete and relatively individualized occasions for law enforcement and "transgression." In this respect, the proliferation of heterogeneous forms of border enforcement supplies a crucial site for the renovation of diverse technologies of government, more broadly (Rumford 2006).

To the extent that the entirety of the interior of the space of the state becomes an unmitigated regulatory zone of immigration enforcement, and as borders appear to be increasingly ungrounded and internalized, the efficacy of the Border Spectacle in fact is merely intensified. Borders that seem increasingly diffuse are not thereby diluted but rather reconfigured in ever more condensed and potent forms. As the border is effectively everywhere, so also is the spectacle of its enforcement and therefore its violation, rendering migrant "illegality" ever more unsettlingly ubiquitous.

In *The Society of the Spectacle* of 1967, Debord insistently clarifies that the spectacle is more than a mere apparatus comprised of the "mass media" as means of communication, and contends that these are "only its most stultifying superficial manifestation" (Debord 1995). Nonetheless, Debord argues (again, following Marx 1976: 165) that "the social requirements of the age . . . can be met only through their mediation," and that "the administration of society . . . now depends on the intervention of such 'instant' communication." In this respect, we may infer from Debord that *state power* itself has come to rely, both intensively and extensively, on the propagation of mass-mediated public discourse. This is fundamentally so because all such instantaneously circulated mass mediation is "essentially *one-way*" (Debord 1995: 19, emphasis in original). Yet, if it is "a visible negation of life" – indeed, a negation that "manifests itself as an enormous positivity" which "*has invented a visual form for itself*" – the spectacle is effectively the culmination of a capitalist social formation predicated upon estrangement and separation, and remains "a product of real activity" (1995: 14, 15, emphasis in original). Thus, "at the root of the spectacle lies that oldest of all social divisions of labor, the specialization of *power*," and "the social cleavage that the spectacle expresses is inseparable from the modern State, which . . . is the general form of all social division" (1995: 18, 20, emphasis in original).

In his *Comments on the Society of the Spectacle* in 1988, Debord retrospectively provides a concise summation of the society of the spectacle, as he had originally depicted it in 1967: "the autocratic reign of the market economy, which had acceded to an irresponsible sovereignty, and the totality of new techniques of government that accompanied this reign" (Debord 2005: Thesis II). In this subsequent reformulation, Debord further elaborates "five principal features: incessant technological renewal; fusion of State and economy; generalized secrecy; forgeries without reply; a perpetual present" (2005: Thesis V). In order to theorize adequately the society of the spectacle, therefore, we are invited to comprehend its rampant fetishism as, in effect, a fusion of the fetishism of the commodity with the fetishism of the state.

Like the commodity itself (in its mundane and ubiquitous heterogeneity), the state (in its sovereign and homogeneous singularity) assumes the form of an alien power. As Marx demonstrates, with regard to the commodity, "What on the side of the worker appeared in the form of unrest now appears, on the side of the product, in the form of being, as a fixed, immobile characteristic" (1976: 287). Likewise, state power institutes itself as "an imaginary sovereignty . . . infused with an unreal universality" (Marx 1978: 34), and may appear as "power" in general (or in any case, as the final and decisive power) only by gathering together and objectifying the innumerable and diverse potentialities of living labor's restless subjectivity (cf. Bonefeld 1995; Holloway 1995). The multiplicity of specific forms of concrete laboring activities only achieve a semblance of universality – as "abstract labor" – through their generalized commodification and the materialization of their value-form as money (Marx 1978: 125–163). Likewise, the state acquires its own illusory universality only as a similarly alienated and fetishized reification of precisely the real universality of the abstraction of human labor (once it has been subsumed within the effectively global regime of capital accumulation).

The very existence of "*the*" (modern) "State" (and likewise, of each and every particular one) derives from the effective hegemony and apparent universalization of relations of production that assume the general form of a voluntary contract between two ostensibly free, equal, and rightful owners of distinct commodities, engaged in a simple act of exchange whereby one (the owner of the means of production) purchases the peculiar commodity being sold by the other (who owns nothing but her capacity to work, her *labor-power*) (Marx 1976: 270–280). In this defining feature of capitalist social relations – "the juridical relation, whose form is the contract," itself a "legal fiction" – all coercion appears to be absent (Marx 1976: 178, 719). Overtly *political* relations of domination and subordination in the labor process itself are ordinarily secured as "the silent compulsion of economic relations," and "direct extra-economic force" is reserved only for "exceptional cases" (Marx 1976: 899). A separate and specialized state power arises as an effect of precisely this separation and abstraction of "the political" from "the economic," ultimately allowing for an effectively *global* market to be fractured systemically into a political order of *territorially delimited* ("national") states (Holloway 1994, following Pashukanis's *Law and Marxism* of 1929 (Pashukanis 1989). In this regard, the state is an instrumental feature of capital, and in usurping for itself the elemental and generative (productive) power of living labor, it manifests precisely the "political" dimension of the capital-labor relation itself. Whereas the sheer vitality of human life manifests itself diminutively as an infinite plenitude of particular instances of labor-power in the marketplace, it acquires a rarefied yet spurious unity – as "Power," seemingly pure and simple – only when it is gathered and reified in the state (De Genova 2010). The organized means of violence must be kept apart, systematically held in reserve as a separate and apparently impersonal recourse for the maintenance of the Rule of Law.

And so it is with the routinized violence of border policing, whereby the sovereignty of the state and the superintendence of nation-state space are enforced by means of a permanent state of exception (Agamben 2005). In this regard, borders operate as filtering mechanisms for the unequal exchange of value (Kearney 2004) – filters that differentiate, sort, and rank between those to be excluded in fact (deported), and those to be included (even if only as "illegal" migrants). These inclusions of migrants and other noncitizens likewise proceed only differentially, but they almost universally impose terms that range from the immediate and categorical deportability of "illegal aliens," to the conditional and contingent deportability that remains nonetheless a defining and enduring feature of the "legality" of those noncitizens who have been "authorized," along with the requirements of unforgiving surveillance and subordination. Hence, beyond the purview of the Border Spectacle's scene of exclusion, the inclusion of migrant labor is profoundly normalized. Even if the spectacle of enforcement is a persistent and pernicious reminder of the extraordinary vulnerabilities that suffuse the migrant predicament, workplace immigration raids and deportations remain in fact "exceptional." The machinations of state power and the compulsions of the law are rendered effectively invisible by the spectacle's fetishization of "illegality" as individual transgression. Even under the relatively extraordinary circumstances of undocumented migrant workers' "illegal" status, therefore, the more coercive (and plainly political) dimensions of their particular condition as *migrant* labor generally achieves the commonsensical banality of a merely "economic" "fact of life."

Indeed, what predominates in the everyday life experience of undocumented migrants is precisely the "silent compulsion of economic relations" (Marx 1976: 899). Once within the "interior" of the space of the nation-state (however obscene their inclusion), undocumented (or previously documented and subsequently illegalized) migrants are presumed (like all other workers) to deliver their "unauthorized" labor to market – freely, voluntarily, and with no evident coercion. But this normalization occurs only after they have either successfully navigated the militarized obstacle course of the Border Spectacle or passed quietly from a prior status of tentative or tenuous "legality" to one of peremptorily disenfranchised and almost instantaneously precarious "illegality." For those who can elude detection and evade apprehension and deportation – and especially for those who can withstand the severities of an "illegal" border crossing – there awaits as their thankless reward a protracted and indefinite social condition of deportability, and its attendant deprivations, which will supply the distinctive qualification of their labor-power.

THE BORDER SPECTACLE, THE NATIONAL FRONT(S) AND RACIAL ABJECTION

The brazenness of the spectacle relies upon unrelenting mass mediation, publicity, and exuberant display to manifest itself as a specious unity, "an enormous positivity, out of reach and beyond dispute" (Debord 1995: 15). Yet, as in Marx's classic account of the thing-like reification of relations between people, the spectacle remains inevitably accompanied by the *invisibility* – again, hidden in plain sight – of the real social relations of (alienated, exploited, and subjugated) life. The exclusionary brashness of the Border Spectacle, similarly, is inextricable from its "dirty secret," its obscene underbelly – the real social relation of undocumented migrants to the state, and the public secret of their abject inclusion as "illegal" labor.

The persistent humiliation, compulsive denunciation, and exquisitely refined rightlessness of deportable noncitizens (and "illegal" migrant labor, in particular) supplies both the rationale for, and also the constant and truly insatiable response to, the Border Spectacle. The spectacle of border enforcement conjures up the fetish of transgression at the ever multiplying points of interception in an amorphous border zone where migrant trajectories may be interrupted and produced as occasions for apprehension – literally and figuratively – which is to say, as arrest and deportation, but also as fear and loathing. Thus, the Border Spectacle works its magic trick of displacing "illegality" from its point of production (in the law) to the proverbial "scene of the crime," which is of course also the *scene* of crime-fighting – indeed, the scene of exclusion. Yet, migrants' trajectories – and human mobility, generally – prevail in spite of the accumulated pressures and violences of borders traversed en route or more expansive border zones inhabited indefinitely (and this is so for the great majority of migrants). Indeed, what is *normal* is the movement itself, the mobility of migrants, as well as the concomitant routine illegalization of them, but this requires the spectacle of law enforcement that transmutes every migration into a putative violation and transposes the border zone (which finally encompasses the full extent of the space of the state) as an ostensible crime scene. Hence, the seeming paradox that the greatest theaters for the staging of border enforcement and immigration law enforcement are in fact the real sites of a massive inclusion of migrants. Their illegalization supplants and displaces their putative exclusion with their obscene inclusion.

In place of the palpable social and political relation of migrant labor to the state (a relation that is precisely obscene), border enforcement delivers the public and spectacular verification of the migrants' ostensible "illegality," a fetish which appears to be a self-generating, self-evident and thing-like fact. Indeed, if there were no border patrols or inspections, no border policing or passport controls whatsoever, there would still be migrant "illegality." We can only be made to believe in that "illegality," however, and to take it seriously, once it appears as a thing-in-itself, reified, fetishized, as the deliberate acts of a spectacular mass of sundry violators of the law, rather than what it truly is: *a transnational social relation of labor and capital*, an antagonistic relation of conflict in the process of being fixed as a relation of subordination. Indeed, the phantasm of exclusion is essential to that process of subordination, which is always inherently a matter of inclusion and incorporation. Nevertheless, the task of labor subordination is always and inescapably preconditioned by the sheer *subjectivity* of labor. Labor subordination, in Žižek's (1997) terms, is grounded precisely by the inherent excess that is the creative capacity and productive power of labor. The requirement for subordination is occasioned in the first instance precisely by human labor's distinctly subjective vitality (Marx 1976: 284). Thus, it is instructive to recall that the autonomy of migration and its politics of mobility *precede* and provoke the state's politics of control and the spectacle of border zones depicted as deplorably "out of control."

Even as the state produces migrant "illegality" as an obdurate and seemingly incorrigible "problem," however, these enforcement spectacles nonetheless reaffirm repeatedly, if obscenely, that there is indeed a subordinate reserve army of deportable "foreign" labor, always-already *within* the space of the nation-state, readily available for deployment as the inevitably overemployed working poor. Therefore, in a manner that in fact *dissimulates* state power, the Border Spectacle is also a spectacle of the state's dutiful, diligent, more or less energetic, but ever beleaguered "response" to the fetishized image of a "crisis" of border "invasion" or "inundation." The phantasmagorical invasiveness, relentlessness, and ubiquity of undocumented migration then serve to prefigure and summon forth the ever more intense and expansive irradiation of everyday life by the state as our self-anointed savior and redeemer. Moreover, the corollary discourses of "human trafficking" and "migrant smuggling" even authorize the state to gratuitously fashion itself as a paternalistic (indeed, patriarchal) "protection racket" (Tilly 1985) not merely preserved for its own "rightful" citizens but even for some of its migrant denizens, particularly women who must be rescued from the presumably intrinsic criminal excesses of "illegal" migration itself (Andrijasevic 2003, 2007; Aradau 2004, 2008; Chapkis 2003; Sharma 2003; cf. Nyers 2003). Given the sleight of hand by which the gendered discourse of "trafficking" displaces the onus of "exploitation" on nefarious "foreigners" and the opportunistic infrastructure of undocumented migration itself, undocumented migrants are deemed to be in need of "protection" – from one another! Moreover, the pitiful and helpless (feminized) "victims" of this flesh trade likewise serve to further corroborate the image of a shadowy population of docile and infinitely tractable migrant denizens. In this respect, the scene of exclusion compulsively discloses and thereby exuberantly affirms, yet again, the obscene fact of subordinate inclusion, as if subtly to reveal or expose its own ostensible "dirty secret." Thus, it enhances the efficiency of its own most elementary gesture whereby migrants are figured as menace, hereby complementing that spectral threat of their opportunistic agency with an allegation of their irredeemable incapacity or incompetence for veritable (manly) self-determination. The exploitation of "illegal" migrants is itself now refigured as merely the certification of what is alleged, if only by implication, to be their inherent and odious exploitability, their subjugation merely an index of their essential slavishness.

In light of this transposition of the politics of citizenship into an essentialist politics of difference, every question of migration and migrant deportability and their securitization more or less immediately presents the concomitant question of their *racialization*. There is no way to comprehend adequately contemporary formations of transnational migration (and hence, also deportable labor) apart from their relation to an effectively global regime of capital accumulation, which is itself inseparable from the histories of nineteenth-century European and Euro-American colonialism, and the twentieth-century eclipse of that colonial world order with the ascendancy of an ostensibly anticolonial US imperial formation. One of the key features which these apparently disparate configurations of protracted planetary inequalities of wealth and power share, all the same, is the persistence of a global sociopolitical order of white supremacy. Thus, the protracted political crisis of subordinating migrant labor only exacerbates further – indeed, reconfigures anew – the already dire postcolonial vexations of race, national identity, and citizenship throughout "the global North," and increasingly, well beyond. In this regard, it is crucial to consider Balibar's proposition that the management and policing of borders serves a "*world-configuring* function" (2002: 79, emphasis in original; cf. Hindess 2000; Walters 2002), as "instruments of discrimination and triage," globally differentiating individuals for capital in class terms as those who alternately circulate "upwards" or "downwards," while simultaneously establishing and maintaining "a world *apartheid*," which institutes a "color bar" that no longer now merely separates "center" from "periphery," or North from South, but runs through *all* societies (Balibar 2002: 82; emphases in original).[1] Indeed, new dynamics of racialization and new formations of racism increasingly become inextricable from the social production of migrants' "differences" in ways that, as often as not (or rather, *more* often than not), dissimulate their racisms and disarticulate "race" and "immigration," through a politics of *nativism* – the promotion of the priority of "natives," on no other grounds than their *being* such (De Genova 2005: 56–94).[2]

The generic figures of "immigration" and the diffuse politics of "foreignness" suffice to reanimate *race* in terms that commonly, and perhaps increasingly, are articulated as *nation* – in terms of the "national" identity of the "natives." Hence, racist far-right parties increasingly tend to articulate their reactionary anti-immigrant populism in the idiom of the purportedly legitimate politics of *citizenship*, which promotes the national priority of "natives" under the overt rubric not of racial supremacism but rather of the presumptive birthright entitlements of "the nation" or "the people." And so we have the British *National* Party, the *National* Front in France, the *National* Alliance in Italy, the *National* Democratic Party in Germany along with the German *People*'s Union, and similarly, the Swiss *People*'s Party, the Danish *People*'s Party, the *Popular* Party in Portugal, among others.[3] In Belgium, the *Flemish* Interest (or Bloc), which combines fierce hostility to migrants and Jews with advocacy for Flemish self-rule, predictably makes its subordinated national identity explicit.[4] In the United States, the Minuteman Project deploys the parallel strategy of adopting an identity that signals a historical analogy inseparable from its US patriotism. Although some of these nativist movements may officially disavow their racism against migrants, however, many are quite crass and unabashedly racist: the emphatically "national" gesture is transparently and unapologetically equated with belligerent anti-immigrant racism. Their nationalism, therefore, is not so much a screen that conceals their racism (although it may function in that fashion, in some instances); rather, their nationalism is itself overtly and unabashedly exclusionary. In this respect, they are merely the howling dogs prowling along the margins of the Border Spectacle's scene of exclusion. Indeed, they are an integral part of that scenery. But their frenzied barking and rabid growling simply enhance the efficiency of the obscene inclusion of migrants as "illegal" – and racially branded – labor.

CITIZENSHIP, SCENE AND OBSCENE

In an important sense, "foreign" (and commonly, also racially subordinate) deportable labor nonetheless presents a striking analogy to racially subjugated "minority" citizens. In their analysis of the Watts rebellion of 1965, Debord and his Situationist collaborators posited that impoverished African-Americans served as "a perfect spectacular prod," supplying the spectacle of a loathsome "threat of . . . underprivilege [that] spurs on the rat race" (S.I. No. 10, December 1965, in Knabb 1981: 157). In contrast to this sort of threat of permanent marginalization and the subordinate status enforced through protracted un- and underemployment, however, the spectacular prod of the figure of the "illegal alien" is that of a predicament of unrelenting and unforgiving overemployment, superexploitation. What the two have in common, of course, is excessive misery. What they further have in common is the stigmata of racialized *difference*, reassuring the racial "majority" (or, alternately, the racially heterogeneous but still unequal polity of proper "citizens") that their own misery is not so bad after all, while also simultaneously unsettling the presumed certitude that such excesses of suffering could ever be reserved only for someone else, the "others," a population condemned – be it as an effect of their "natural" (racial) inheritance, their "alien" (juridical) status, or both – to an inferior social station. The commonplace racial branding of migrant "illegality," in this respect, sutures the "exclusionary" work of the Border Spectacle to a vertiginous spiral of inequalities that are deeply imbricated within the obscene fabric of citizenship itself.

Deportable (migrant) labor, therefore, conceals within it – and yet, simultaneously *reveals* and proclaims – the universal disposability of *all* labor. And inasmuch as, under capitalism, labor is but the most commonplace and ubiquitous objectified, alienated, and fetishized form of *life* itself (in its active practical expression as open-ended creative capacity and productive power), so must the "irregular" and *deportable* labor of global capitalism's multifarious transnational migrant denizens signal the ultimate disposability of human life in general, on a planetary scale (De Genova 2010). The deportability of migrant denizens re-invokes the always-already established fact of an at-least potential relegation of the world's "citizens" to their properly abject condition as "bare life" (Agamben 1998), and thus their abandonment to one or another status as de facto refugees, whether stateless (i.e., at the mercy of local formations of coercive violence as well as the global administrative regime of "the world community") or state-*ful* (i.e., exposed to and utterly unprotected from the recriminations of state power).

If, for Marx, the commodity assumes the appearance of "an *alien* power" to those who have produced it (1965: 115; emphasis added), then, for Debord, in the thoroughly commodified universe of the society of the spectacle, "all time, all space, becomes *foreign* to them" (1995: 23, emphasis in original). Indeed, "the spectacle corresponds to the historical moment at which the commodity completes its colonization of social life" (Debord 1995: 29). The Border Spectacle's specter of an invasive "foreignness" thus enhances and intensifies the degree to which all labor and all of life is rendered "alien" and estranged, whereby the citizenry experiences its own condition of colonization. In a devious and pernicious inversion, however, the figure of "the alien" is mobilized as an alarming signal of alienation and supplies the proxy for reactionary populist paroxysms of exclusionary animosity (directed against the always-already included). Reflecting upon slavery in the United States, Marx famously asserted that "labour in a white skin can never emancipate itself where it is branded in a black skin" (1976: 414). Today, given our global postcolonial condition, it has become increasingly common that labor "in a black skin" presents itself also as labor in "foreign" clothing. Hence, a contemporary corollary to Marx's axiom would seem to be: labor in the prison inmate's uniform of citizenship can never emancipate itself where labor in the migrant's garb of "foreignness" is branded as "illegal."

NOTES

An earlier version of this essay was presented to the conference The Language of Difference: Mechanisms of Inclusion and Exclusion of Migrants, 1945–2005 (January 14, 2010), sponsored by the Department of History, Leiden University (Netherlands). I am grateful to Marlou Schover for the invitation to share my work, to Willem Schinkel and Sarah van Walsum for their critical insights and thoughtful suggestions on this occasion. Later versions were presented at the seminar of the Migration and Diversity Centre at the Vrije Universiteit (VU University, Amsterdam) and the Department of the History and General Theory of Law, at the University of Rome III. I owe a note of appreciation to Maybritt Jill Alpes, Juan Amaya, Galina Cornelisse, Enrica Rigo, Thomas Spijkerboer, and Maria Vittoria Tessitore for their various engaging comments and criticisms on these occasions.

1 For related invocations of global "apartheid," see Nevins 2008; Richmond 1994; Sharma 2006.
2 In this manner, the promotion of the priorities of "natives" may even masquerade as an avowedly "antiracist" politics of redress for "native" (racial) "minorities" – a nativism, so to speak, "from the left"; for an extended elaboration, see De Genova (2005: 68–79; cf. Balibar 1991: 15).
3 The most prominent exceptions to this trend are the Progress Party in Norway, the Freedom Party in Austria, the Republican Party in Germany, and in the Netherlands, Pim Fortuyn's List and the Party for Freedom.
4 Similarly, the separatist Northern League in Italy promotes a subnational politics of regional identity in concert with a broadly xenophobic agenda.

REFERENCES

Agamben, Giorgio. 1998. *Homo Sacer: Sovereign Power and Bare Life*, trans. Daniel Heller-Roazen. Stanford: Stanford University Press. First publ. 1995.

Agamben, Giorgio. 2005. *State of Exception*, trans. Kevin Attell. Chicago: University of Chicago Press. First publ. 2003.

Andrijasevic, Rutvica. 2003. The difference borders make: (il)legality, migration and trafficking in Italy among Eastern European women in prostitution. In Sara Ahmed, Claudia Castañeda, Anne-Marie Fortier and Mimi Sheller, eds, *Uprootings/Regroundings: Questions of Home and Migration*, pp. 251–72. Oxford: Berg.

Andrijasevic, Rutvica. 2007. Beautiful dead bodies: gender, migration and representation in anti-trafficking campaigns. *Feminist Review* 86: 24–44.

Andrijasevic, Rutvica. 2010. From exception to excess: detention and deportations across the Mediterranean space. In Nicholas De Genova and Nathalie Peutz, eds, *The Deportation Regime: Sovereignty, Space, and the Freedom of Movement*, pp. 147–65. Durham: Duke University Press.

Aradau, Claudia. 2004. The perverse politics of four-letter words: risk and pity in the securitisation of human trafficking. *Millennium* 33 (2): 251–277.

Aradau, Claudia. 2008. *Rethinking Trafficking in Women: Politics out of Security*. Basingstoke: Palgrave Macmillan.

Balibar, Étienne. 1991. *Es Gibt Keinen Staat in Europa*: Racism and Politics in Europe Today. *New Left Review* 186: 5–19.

Balibar, Étienne. 2002. What is a border? In *Politics and the Other Scene*, pp. 75–86. New York: Verso. First publ. 1993.

Bonefeld, Werner. 1995. Capital as subject and the existence of labour. In Werner Bonefeld, Richard Gunn, John Holloway and Kosmas Psychopedis, eds, *Emancipating Marx*, vol. 3 of *Open Marxism*, pp. 182–212. East Haven, CN: Pluto Press.

Chapkis, Wendy. 2003. Trafficking, migration, and the law: protecting innocents, punishing immigrants. *Gender and Society* 17 (6): 923–937.

Debord, Guy. 1995. *The Society of the Spectacle*, trans. Donald Nicholson-Smith. New York: Zone Books. First publ. 1967.

Debord, Guy. 2005. *Comments on the Society of the Spectacle*, trans. NOT BORED! At www.notbored.org/commentaires.html (accessed Nov. 2011). First publ. 1988.

De Genova, Nicholas. 2002. Migrant "illegality" and deportability in everyday life. *Annual Review of Anthropology* 31: 419–447.

De Genova, Nicholas. 2005. *Working the Boundaries: Race, Space, and "Illegality" in Mexican Chicago*. Durham: Duke University Press.

De Genova, Nicholas. 2010. The deportation regime: sovereignty, space, and the freedom of movement. In Nicholas De Genova and Nathalie Peutz, eds, *The Deportation Regime: Sovereignty, Space, and the Freedom of Movement*. Durham: Duke University Press.

Hindess, Barry. 2000. Citizenship in the International Management of Populations. *American Behavioral Scientist* 43 (9): 1486–1497.

Holloway, John. 1994. Global Capital and the National State. *Capital and Class* 52: 23–49.

Holloway, John. 1995. From scream of refusal to scream of power: the centrality of work. In Werner Bonefeld, Richard Gunn, John Holloway and Kosmas Psychopedis, eds, *Emancipating Marx*, vol. 3 of *Open Marxism*, pp. 155–181. East Haven, CN: Pluto Press.

Karakayali, Serhat and Rigo, Enrica. 2010. Mapping the European space of circulation. In Nicholas De Genova and Nathalie Peutz, eds, *The Deportation Regime: Sovereignty, Space, and the Freedom of Movement*, pp. 123–144. Durham: Duke University Press.

Kearney, Michael. 2004. The classifying and value-filtering missions of borders. *Anthropological Theory* 4 (2): 131–156.

Knabb, Ken. 1981. *Situationist International Anthology*. Berkeley: Bureau of Public Secrets.

Marx, Karl. 1965. *The Economic and Philosophic Manuscripts of 1844*. New York: International. First publ. 1844.

Marx, Karl. 1976. *Capital: A Critique of Political Economy*, vol. 1, trans. Ben Fowkes. New York: Penguin. First publ. 1867.

Marx, Karl. 1978. On the Jewish question. In Robert C. Tucker, ed., *The Marx-Engels Reader*. 2nd edn. New York: W.W. Norton. First publ. 1843.

Nevins, Joseph. 2008. *Dying to Live: A Story of US Immigration in an Age of Global Apartheid*. San Francisco: Open Media/City Lights.

Nyers, Peter. 2003. Abject cosmopolitanism: the politics of protection in the anti-deportation movement. *Third World Quarterly* 24 (6): 1069–1093. Repr. in Nicholas De Genova and Nathalie Peutz, eds, *The Deportation Regime: Sovereignty, Space, and the Freedom of Movement*. Durham: Duke University Press, 2010, pp. 413–441.

Pashukanis, Evgeny B. 1989. *Law and Marxism: A General Theory towards a Critique of the Fundamental Juridical Concepts*. Worcester, UK: Pluto. First publ. 1929.

Richmond, Anthony. 1994. *Global Apartheid: Refugees, Racism, and the New World Order*. Toronto: Oxford University Press.

Rumford, Chris. 2006. Theorizing borders. *European Journal of Social Theory* 9: 155–169.

Sharma, Nandita. 2003. Travel agency: a critique of anti-trafficking campaigns. *Refuge* 21: 53–65.

Sharma, Nandita. 2006. *Home Economics: Nationalism and the Making of "Migrant Workers" in Canada*. Toronto: University of Toronto Press.

Tilly, Charles. 1985. War making and state making as organized crime. In Peter Evans, Dietrich Rueschemeyer and Theda Skocpol, eds, *Bringing the State Back In*, pp. 169–187. New York: Cambridge University Press.

Walters, William. 2002. Deportation, expulsion and the international police of aliens. *Citizenship Studies* 6 (3): 265–292. Repr. in N. De Genova and N. Peutz, eds, *The Deportation Regime: Sovereignty, Space, and the Freedom of Movement*, pp. 69–100. Durham: Duke University Press, 2010.

Žižek, Slavoj. 1997. Multiculturalism, or, the cultural logic of multinational capitalism. *New Left Review* 225: 28–51.

PART V

Space, Performance and Practice

CHAPTER 29

Border Show Business and Performing States

David B. Coplan

Border Brujo,[1] the first generation: In 1971, I was a graduate student at the University of Ghana, Legon, determined to spend my holidays in neighboring Lomé, Togo, a cheerful *grand marché* of a coastal town where all sorts of goodies such as French wine and shaving cream, overtaxed or unavailable in Ghana, were on sale duty free. Obtaining a Togolese visa was both time-consuming and relatively costly, so I determined to make my way to Lomé and back via the sandy tracks inscribed across the border by smugglers. One night I set off on my motorcycle, breezing along the back road in the total darkness and thinking myself terribly clever. Then up ahead there appeared a set of headlights dipping and weaving toward me over the uneven ground. Well, a fellow traveler should be no problem, but why was he so far over to the left? And so we approached straight on, until finally coming to a halt, face to face in each other's headlights. Balanced on my one-eyed Honda I could make out clearly the terrified and quizzical faces of two Togolese police officers. Well, I knew immediately I must be in Togo, not just from their uniforms, but from the instant realization that of course in Togo one drives on the right-hand side of the road, not on the left as in Ghana in those days. Waving and bowing in both happy greeting and deep apology, I swung my cycle to the right and disappeared into the night. Of all my disingenuous performances at African international borders over the years, that was among the most transgressive and incompetent. Yet it illustrates the uses of astonishment and incredulity: if I should not, indeed could not have been there – being white, I would not be a smuggler nor even have known of that road's existence – then I simply was *not* there, as anything more than a hallucination.

   Border Bruja, the second generation: In 2010 my daughter Anna, aged 18, decided that a three-month spell of travel and work in Brazil would be the highlight of her "gap year" between high school and university. All arrangements complete, she arrived at São Paulo only to be turned away because, as officials complained, she had not enough money in her pocket. Having done their prescribed duty, they

A Companion to Border Studies, First Edition. Edited by Thomas M. Wilson and Hastings Donnan.

proceeded to forget her presence entirely: there was apparently, no official next step. Sitting crestfallen in a molded plastic chair in the arrivals hall, Anna noticed that Brazilian citizens, having passed through their own queue, were simply walking through an unattended glass door into the domestic flights section of the airport. Joining this entitled category, she proceeded to the domestic ticket counters, where she bought a ticket to Rio de Janeiro and flew with a bunch of happy Cariocas to the fabled city, where she arrived safe and happy at her backpackers' hostel and joined friends already in residence. Months later, on the way back to South Africa, no official at São Paulo either noted or cared that she had no stamp in her passport admitting her to Brazil in the first place. That's my girl (from Ipanema).

Over the years, many of my colleagues and I have experienced borders between African countries as a kind of hallucination in return, accompanied by astonishment and incredulity as well. Yes, there should be an official post: this concrete embodiment ought to be there both to mark and to signify the border's actual existence. But then why is there, courtesy of the state at its attenuated margin, all the pomp and circumstance? The demand for unobtainable stamps, documents, and permits? The unpacking and repacking of bedraggled personal possessions and petty traders' sad array of (sometimes living) goods? The loose-cannon irritability of officials – sometimes even including strip searches and beatings – not of me or mine of course: in Africa it remains a privilege to be white. Surely this was gilding the uncultivated lily of state control. Unbelievers as we were, after bowing and scraping, we made snooty jokes at the officials' expense, once safely out of earshot and on our way again. What we did not understand was the first theatrical rule of border management: that the panoply and ceremony of symbolic interaction and formality is in inverse proportion to the sense of security of the state and authorities in question. It is rather the same at university graduations, where the pomp and circumstance are in inverse proportion to the value of the degrees being awarded. Alternatively, in Africa, as elsewhere in the world-formerly-known-as-Third, the difficulty of officially negotiating a border is in surprisingly inverse proportion to the attractions offered by the country in question. In some cases, bribes may be demanded simply because officials or police assume that, for reasons of your own, you have to cross the border, for if you had a choice you would not be there. Overall, the less credible the state in question, the more performative effort is invested at its borders.

The performative dimension of bordering long precedes the formation of national states, or even multinational empires. Early on, simply encountering the Other was evidence of a border enough. Indeed, outsiders required special status and immunity simply to avoid violent attack, which is why in so many languages the word for "hello" means "peace." Later, with territorial expansion, the effort to turn influence into power and power into control in the face of the distant absence of those who believed they were or should be *in* control became the foundation of bordering itself. One met the border when a settlement asserted loyalty to a different potentate or power than the settlement just behind. Nonliterate, horseless polities such as the Zulu or the Inca were thus limited in both their ability to expand and control, and spent a good deal of time and effort attempting to terrorize subject peoples into voluntary, hegemonized submission. Elsewhere borders arose where or when one first encountered the troops and tax collectors of a different authority, or when rulers and their (often armed and dangerous) legatees arrived in your district. In medieval Europe, the kingdom existed wherever the king's person, property, decrees, or forces might be located at the time. In many cases the kingdom arrived in a subject town with the ruler and his entourage and disappeared with the dust from their hooves when they left. In medieval Mali in the African Sahel, the empire literally waxed and waned with the seasons, as the rains made travel by horseback impossible due to tse-tse fly, while the dry season was the time for imperial expeditions. On such royal *tours d'horizon* or confrontations with rebellious subjects or rival lords, the monarch and his retinue quite physically embodied and performed the state and its claims to authority, which we see now most prominently displayed at border posts. The border was then but a traveling, often rapacious, circus or theatrical event. This was very much the case with the largest land empire – not perhaps strictly speaking a state – ever to exist, that of Genghis and Timur Khan, which used the theater of genocidal terror to enforce a *pax mongolica* to enforce allegiance when there simply were not enough Mongols to enforce it by any other means. Genghis Khan's grandson, Zahiruddin Mohammad Babur (1483–1530), the first emperor of what became the more secure Mughal dynasty in Afghanistan and India, expressed his suzerainty rather more effectively with Islamic *ghazal* poetry, a unique royal autobiography, the *Baburnama*, and unparalleled architectural magnificence (Ghosh 2002: 90–108).

The reality and by extension the contestation of territorial borders was formalized with the emergence of the European monarchical nation-state, at least as a sovereign political imaginary, at the Treaty of Westphalia in 1648. Of course, on the ground and in subsequent treaties the Westphalian principles of territorial integrity and exclusive sovereignty over internal affairs were subject to the enactments in the theater of war. "Nation" conceived in the sense of *ethnos* had nothing necessarily to do with state boundaries but rather with imperial adventurism. Regrettably, such adventurism remains codified in international law as "right of conquest." Today, the ability to bring disparate "peoples" and localized regimes together under the banner of empire (the "Habsburgian" model) remains, if only wistfully, somewhere at the heart of the notion of "closer union" that motivates the European Union (Spener and Staudt 1998). But to begin at the beginning, one might view the process of "nation" building as proceeding from the installation of mythic, then legendary events, deities, ancestors (often overlapping), and ritual representations and performances. Nothing less than divine authority seemed adequate to achieve the parallel objectives of territorializing and hegemonizing history through the erasure of internal frontiers and the establishment of external ones (Zúñiga 2005: 35). Borders became key to this process because the meanings and forms of belonging arise from and depend on a socialized political-geographic space and must reference traditions of narrative that are nameable and memorable (Raymond Williams, in Zúñiga 2005: 44). Like divine authority itself, bordering is never complete, and border demarcation has proven exasperatingly impermanent. All that one can be sure of is that it always requires a performative maintenance of markers of "them" as distinct from "us."

Fast-forward to the twenty-first century and nationality has been multiplied and deterritorialized. Nationalism and its fictions are nearing bankruptcy, as they cannot maintain economic sovereignty, or erase or assimilate local or immigrant identities. The United Nations Organization, a simulacrum of world order based on performative "national" states,[2] sends "peacekeepers" who intervene clumsily around the world, attempting to enforce peace only where opposing interests seem not to want any and state sovereignty where it is irretrievably absent. Internal borders are being reborn while international capital runs roughshod over external ones and national politics has become a melodramatic sideshow (Zúñiga 2005: 46–51). "[N]ow the border stands at the center and offers us a front row view of History's drama unfolding" (Spener and Staudt 1998: 88). This is why, rather too eagerly, cosmopolitan scholars write of processes of "debordering." As Albert and Brock state, "Under the pressure of debordering processes within the world of states, territorial determinants of social life and the political process are beginning to break down" (1998: 217). This process is reflected in a growing literature on nonstate brokers as the pivotal actors in many borderlands, where one finds "the institutionalization of 'governance without government'" or the creation of "multilevel systems of govern-ance consisting of trans-governmental and trans-state networks that link parts of governments and substate actors across borders" (Rosenau and Czempiel 1992). Yet, as Albert and Brock are quick to point out, in response states initiate countervailing (and largely unavailing) appeals to economic nationalism and the performance of borders, including rebordering by coercive means (1998: 227). Indeed rebordering cannot help but engage with the multidimensionality of borders in contestation (1998: 236–237). As for subjects themselves, in the contemporary world, individual identity is increasingly self-constructed from multiple sources and references of belonging (Saez 1995: 25). The role of the state is to mediate these identities, man-aging and tolerating (or, cynically, demonizing) diversity (Saez 1995: 50–51). Claims to status through such identities are legitimated through stories, and the passionate senses of self that are forged, recreated and contested therein (Price 2004: 28).

The nationalistic European wars of the nineteenth century, culminating in World War I, both destroyed Europe's imperial states and starkly outlined the need to enshrine Westphalian principles in secure agreements and even international organiza-tions – the League of Nations. Versailles brought to the fore a newly influential American insistence on the legitimacy of a third principle discussed at Westphalia, the "self-determination of nations." Nation here was conceived as some sort of self-identified ethnos, with a common language, history and cultural values, contained within naturalized territorial borders. In a macabre festival of unanticipated conse-quences, this notion caused far more conflict than it resolved, with Ireland, South Asia, Indochina and even colonial Africa inquiring audibly as to when their turns would come. Nazi Germany's attempt to reverse totally the entire process finally demonstrated to Europeans the futility of imperial nationalism, leading to the effec-tive disappearance of extracontinental empire as well. But the bordering process resumed with a vengeance, a result of a new ideologically based imperial conflict between the United States and the Soviet Union and the need to invent and legiti-mize boundaries for newly independent postcolonial states.

And so the Broadway show of state sovereignty was duly sent on tour from the Great White Way of distant capitals to the tryouts of provincial state margins. In the case of the hyperbolically named German Democratic Republic (GDR), the new borders were based on the fortification of a foreign military occupation zone. Now demarcating a line of confrontation between hostile superpower alliances, the border in the midst of Germany was indeed a serious business and it may strike many as fatuous to emphasize its theatricality. It may be no coincidence, however, that among the most penetrating portrayals of life in twilight GDR is the 2006 Academy award-winning film *The Lives of Others* (*Das Leben der Anderen*), which was directed by Florian Henckel-Donnersmarck and in which the protagonist is a playwright and theatrical director. Berlin was of course 110 kilometers inside the GDR. It was a microcosm and micro-focus of the Cold War, with its NATO-defended enclave providing the tyrannized and abstemious East with a sparkling beacon of Western capitalism. Obligingly, East German Communist Party Secretary Walter Ulbricht built the famous 203-meter tower in the Alexanderplatz (now the state TV tower), dubbed St Walter's Tower by East Berliners, so they could enjoy a bird's eye view of the enticing glitter of the West. More significant perhaps, even the part of the border secured by the infamous wall – with its pitiless *volpos*,[3] victims crucified on barbed wire and Checkpoint Charlie – was under certain circumstances crossable, negotiable. It depended not only on who you were or pretended to be and on what your ostensible or real mission was, but also on how you behaved; how you performed. I will return to this point.

It has become clear from the contributions of many scholars that borders and border posts, whether on land, in territorial waters or at airports, are sites for the display and performance of state sovereignty. It is there at its territorial and cognitive margins that residents may be as much suspected of undermining this sovereignty as are foreigners only crossing over. Where indeed, then, is such performance more required or more opportunistically enacted, with flags, uniforms, forms, documents, interrogations, even guns and gunboats, bugles, loud-hailers and marching feet than at these official doorways to and from the outside world? Approaching a border post, one is left in no doubt that one is beseeching entry to some other domain. And so too does the seemingly peremptory arbitrariness of some border officials play a part in the demonstration. No matter how complete and valid one's documentation, or well-meaning one's mission, running the gauntlet of the border, first out of one zone of control, then into another, brings sweat to the palms, palpitations to the heart, awkwardness to the encounter. Indeed, at some borders in less developed countries, marginal traders who cannot afford inflated customs duties or significant payoffs to officials are abused, degraded, partly despoiled and beaten (Carling 2007: 315, 343). This is not for their putative "crimes," since border police know such trading is their only means of livelihood and are often personally familiar with them. It is to demonstrate an immediacy of power and extract a show of subservience that will serve as an object lesson to those who might plan to challenge the state's (uncertain) capacity for control, not by chance at the very point of entry.

The point is not to retail such extreme examples but to emphasize the need to review types of performance at borders, whether on the part of officials or travelers. These include the manipulation or simply the display of ethnicity and citizenship: strategies, not only for deceiving border control, but also for enacting attitudes that border officials wish to see and to approve as legitimation and recognition of their powers. Like the state, border operations are enacted by people; each of them not simply has their own instructions (often contradictory or inoperable) but also self-interests that may vary widely from official regulations promulgated in the capital.

To return to the point about dyadic interplay (between border official and traveler) above, consider this case, which actually occurred but whose actors it would be imprudent to identify – many such encounters, of course, occur at borders and airports around the world: A young Iranian woman flees the crackdown that follows the election of hardline conservative Mahmoud Ahmadinejad as President in 2005. Child of an active political family, she drifts through several countries, never safe or secure, without rest, trying to settle in the West. Along the way, she is assisted by small groups of activists, using forged or fake documents of varying quality, with varying success. Finally, she receives an invitation to Sweden from a local women's support group. She must rely upon some stranger's old and tattered but nationally appropriate passport, less likely to impress than others she has sported. At Stockholm airport she is questioned by a blond giant of an immigration officer, who frowns at her passport, looks her in the face, stamps her passport and lets her go. Today, after many "negotiations," she is a Swedish citizen. What happened here? The Swedish official, while not impressed by her passport, or perhaps even by her "story," looks at her weary, diminutive figure and slumping shoulders, senses the attitude of reserved supplication, notes her gaze of hopeful resignation: a *gemein* refugee. His job is to apply a legal regime, but in its performance, his power encompasses mercy. On the woman's side her performance, with its pathetic passport "prop" and lack of artifice, has succeeded where deception would not. In all such border vignettes, performance plays some, sometimes even a crucial, part.

The importance of understanding the identity performances that instantiate both regimes and strategies of border crossing led in the 1980s to a dramatic shift in the attention of border studies away from politics, law, international relations and the regulation of trade. The opposing, experiential concepts of the border led to more fluid, constructivist notions of borders as sites of social interaction where outcomes were more a product of the deployment of rhetorics of identity and personal agency than of regulatory regimes. The rules, it appeared, were made not so much to be broken as to serve as a framework for creative play. Writer and literary philosopher of *mestizaje*, Gloria Anzaldúa (1987), and border performance artist Guillermo Gómez-Peña (1996) have so described the Mexico–US border in metaphorical terms. It is a landscape where the ebb and flow of social and economic interpenetration is informed by mythic ceremonies of purity and danger, poststructuralist notions of hybridity, states of border crossing, the "third country" of borderlands, multiply emergent, ambiguous cultural and linguistic zones, and the existential deployment of fragmented identities. Mex-American governments, both local and national, join in by sponsoring grotesque, overbaked monuments to mark their border crossing points, including outsize flags, statues of national heroes, bronzed maps, pre-Columbian caricatures, streets named for heroes of the Mexican revolution (1910), and – on both sides – McDonald's restaurants (Price 2004: 107). Indeed, it is Gómez-Peña who has most consistently over many years turned "his" border and borderland (US–California) into a performance space. In Gómez-Peña's writings (2000, 1996, 1993), plays, demonstrations, museum exhibitions, lectures, performance art and endlessly transformative "blurred genres," he and his collaborators have satirically but ruthlessly interrogated every identity representation and paranoid myth or fantasy that "Anglos," "Mexicanos/as" and "Chicanos/as" cherish about one another. In that sense, Gómez-Peña has invented an art of border performance that transgresses and translocates borders of every kind, from the political and economic to the cultural, cognitive and nightmarishly psychological.

But opposing any "mentalist" conception of borders as sites of serious play are social scientists such as Pablo Vila (2000, 2003) who have described the constructions of actual border identities among people living on the Texas–Mexico border. Vila describes the ways in which border people view their identities in relation to groups they come to define as "others," often setting boundaries among Anglos, Mexicans and African-Americans living on the border. What is most significant about Vila's research is that he came to understand the US–Mexico region as one that consisted of several borders, which cannot be explained simply as an outcome of hybridization. He argues that "each [border region] is the locus of very different processes of internal and international migration, ethnic composition, and political identities on both sides." Lugo (2000: 356) makes the obvious distinction between the border as a metaphor and imposed concrete borders: the concepts of "borderlands," "border crossings" and "the border" are after all hardly synonymous. There is a difference between borderlands and border crossings conceived as a kind of interior landscape of identity and as mandated and sanctioned by nation-state policy-makers and officials. International borders are actively enforced by an immigration or customs officer, border patrol agent or policeman, in uniform and "with a pistol in his hand" (Paredes 1993). Borderlands studies as poststructuralist theory can mean dwelling in ever decentered metaphorical borderlands while losing touch with located communities and the place-specific concerns of real people. Depersonalized theory must not "deterritorialize" specific borderlands. The border is more than metaphor, it is a political economy with real material conditions (Price 2004: 109–110). Identity is performative, socially constructed and contingent. Yet this understanding is tempered by the realization that the ability of subjects to resist, subvert or redefine dominant paradigms and institutions is always historically situated and enmeshed in webs of power. For historically marginalized subjects, political agency is always simultaneously unlimited and partial (Beltran 2004: 603).

While delinking culture from geography, as culture becomes deterritorialized in global flows, poststructuralist border studies still must have a territorial focus (Spener and Staudt 1998: 16). As Truett puts it, we need "to track historical border crossers along their own, local pathways. For only then can we appreciate how ordinary people emerged from the shadows of state and corporate control to reshape the borderlands on their own terms" (2006: 9). Seeking to slip past what Gómez-Peña calls "The border guards of identity" (2000: 12), border crossers with reason to worry are often well versed in the suppression of significations of their "actual" (!) identity and the performance of one more acceptable on the spot. So, despite the suspicion and exclusionary measures directed at Mexican nationals at US border stations, migrants from Central America, who are even more subject to such suspicions and measures, frequently negotiate and contest the border by enacting Mexican identities, familiarizing themselves with the social geographies of Mexican towns and cities (Ruiz 2006: 46).

As Walters has suggested, "Border control is like antivirus software, not just because it aspires to filter and secure its interior, but also because its fate is to toil in the shadow of the restless hacker" (2006: 187). No matter how intimidating border fortifications and controls, and no matter how consistent and rigid the regulations are supposed to be, border-post formalities are still in some respect an encounter between persons. Precisely because officials need to reinforce their own *personal* authority among supplicants, they make representations and decisions in a contextual setting where anything from all things to hardly any things are considered. What gets considered is often a function of the enactment, effective or not, of scripts and routines that satisfy narrative expectations and categories of the interlocutors performing these representations of authority and control. We might even go as far as Aretxaga, who asserts that "rational technologies of control [are necessarily] animated by a substrate of fantasy scenes" (2003: 402–403). And as Chalfin writes in reference to customs officials at Accra's Kotoka International Airport:

> the systems and symbols of authority that constitute sovereign statehood are as much structures of feeling as they are structures of force: congeries of affect as much as of action. Indeed, in states such as Ghana, given the confluence of multiple and fluid regulatory registers occurring in official spaces of mobility as a result of neoliberalism's unbridled advance, affective exchange emerges as a primary means of expressing and experiencing sovereign authority. . . . These interactions and accompanying imaginaries, hence, represent a domain in which the tenuous yet ever-powerful boundary between state and society is objectified . . . in spaces of transit and transition such as Kotoka International Airport, beset by incompatibilities and ever-shifting agendas, subjective states – narratives, identifications, moral judgments, fantasies, and fears – offer an unparalleled archive of the multiplex registers of sovereign authority and transformation for state agents and subjects alike. (2008: 532–533)

Such examples show that all borders (even geographical ones) are a "construction." The construction of boundaries at all scales and dimensions takes place through narrativity (Newman and Paasi 1998: 195). The boundaries of the national imagined communities and the narratives that constitute their collective cultural discourses are also changing continually (Bhabha 1990). The construction of identity narratives is itself political action and is part of the distribution of social power in society (Somers 1994; Newman and Paasi 1998: 195). These boundary-related narratives also constitute contested frontiers, inasmuch as they exist by virtue of the boundary. Within these frontiers, the contest for identity socialization takes place, as institutions and agencies attempt to create exclusive "us" identities and, by definition, outsider images of the "Other." Local experience and folklore mediate the national forms of identity, and it is impossible to understand the latter without knowledge of the former. The iconic characters of one border may even reappear as a kind of leitmotif on another, so that Texas Rangers, Mexicans, Native Americans and the US Cavalry can be readily, even uncannily, substituted by the Boer settler commandos, African Basotho, Khoi-San and British colonial troops of South Africa/Basutoland (Coplan 2000, 2001): the classic "western" transformed into a "southern."

The implication of these realizations is that borders are as variable as the stories though which they are constructed and we have to know not only the stories, but also who the storytellers are and what their common experiences have been. Borders are made as part of a process of telling and retelling stories from which identities emerge. As times and places change, narrative plausibility varies in relation to such identities (Eder 2006: 257). So, there is something behind cognitive identity claims that determines their force (or weakness), their plausibility or their implausibility. Put another way, drawing a boundary is embedded in a series of communicative acts which involve the circulation of stories. Thus we have to analyze stories and the social relations that are constituted by shared stories in order to make sense of the embeddedness of cognitive projects of constructing boundaries and collective identities. The type of social relation varies with the type of the story told; in any case they produce boundaries, define the borders of a communicative space of shared stories. Boundaries emerge in social interaction in which people constantly check whether they share stories to be told about the world they live in (Eder 2006: 257–258). The social distance between different or opposed groups across a border or within a borderland can be measured or at least portrayed effectively through a comparison of their divergent, convergent, or parallel narrations of the borderland and its history (Coplan 2000).

An extension or rather a socialization of such bordering narratives is found in media spectacles dwelling on the xenophobia and/or xenophilia created around immigration, spectacles central to the dramatization of questions of exclusion and inclusion in "national" (putatively autochthonous) communities (Vukov 2003: 336). The affect generated around immigration in media culture plays a critical and mobilizing role in articulating the popular frames that shape the formation of immigration policy, whether through mediated panics or celebratory portraits of desirable immigrants. So, to use the United States as a self-contradicting example, the mythic status of Ellis Island as a gateway to the American Dream (when so many of the descendants of those who arrived there are now the unemployed denizens of the industrial rustbelt) contrasts with the draconian racial anti-Asian immigration laws of 1924 and with the deportation of so many US Chinese immigrants to Mexico from 1916. In Los Angeles, the 1943 *pachuco* or *zoot-suit* riots brought conservative, war-anxious US servicemen into violent conflict with the flamboyant, overdressed *boulevardiers* of Mexican-American youth gangs. It was not so much anything the young chicanos did that brought violent public attacks from the soldiers as how they theatrically represented their own styles of popular culture in defiance of Anglo-American wartime mores and strictures.

Yet the United States is in some real ways a "nation of immigrants" as advertised, and can claim to have assimilated new arrivals from almost everywhere far more effectively and peacefully than has any member of the European Union. The fact that the victims who were killed in the September 11, 2001 destruction of the World Trade Center hailed from 56 countries, and represented many different religions and national identities, attests to this claim. The ongoing irruption of media spectacles around migration speaks to the ways in which immigration evokes strong political affect around commonsense imaginings of national belonging, of who should be included and excluded in the national community. The affective amplification that news media discourses engage in (what Hall et al. (1978) call the "amplification spiral") plays a crucial role in articulating immigration, criminality and fear together by means of affective resonance (Vukov 2003: 340). Yet as Gómez-Pena (2000: 194) reminds us, journalists rarely realize that what they are doing is performance.

Nor are journalists the only public interlocutors who retail performances focusing on issues of borders and border crossers. Politicians seeking to overcome their own obscurity or unpopularity (and cynically aware in some cases of Samuel Johnson's adage: "patriotism is the last refuge of the scoundrel") often turn to attacks against immigrants or transnational residents as a way of garnering support. Western Europe, of course, currently produces more than its share of such political campaigns and campaigners. To cite but one example perhaps less known than those of Pim Fortuyn and Geert Wilders of the Netherlands or Nicolas Sarkozy of France, there is that of Roland Koch of Germany. Koch was elected Minister-President of Hesse in 1999 based on his opposition to federal plans to make dual citizenship easier for foreigners to obtain and citizens to hold. Koch's mobilization of anticosmopolitan as well as antiforeign popular sentiment kept him in power until August 2010, when he suddenly resigned. Performing German identity in this old way was not, as Koch claimed, some sort of loyalty test, but an attack on transnationalism on a more global plane, as Koch himself well understood. Its effect was not simply to make it more difficult for German nationals to do business internationally. Those who thought the campaign might somehow deter immigration were also deceived, for it meant that many of those who had come to Germany with the idea of remaining only temporarily for purposes of employment would hang on indefinitely, rather than risk losing access to the German economy by visiting their countries of birth. Such campaigns point to the most powerful contradiction of border politics globally, which is the frantic and unrelenting attempts by increasingly insecure national states to reinforce their borders and reborder themselves in response to global flows of just about everyone and everything that threaten to deborder them at every turn. Even the European Union's Schengen Treaty that in practice abolishes border controls within its compass (excluding member United Kingdom but including nonmember Switzerland!) is also an attempt to make it far more difficult for travelers from outside the EU to enter any of its member states.

Of course, neither the European Union nor the United States can be held entirely at fault for what cosmopolitans regard as an immensely damaging but still rearguard reinforcement of border restrictions. International terrorism and transnational crime syndicates have made common cause with reactionary Euro-American politics in providing credible justifications for performing state borders with draconian defensiveness. Against such justifications, which have their own domestic political utilities, the "reasonable," internationalist and even economistic arguments of more liberal commentators and political figures have diminishing effect. Turning this whole equation upside down (inside out?) is the phenomenon of Wikileaks, whose founder Julian Assange has gone to such lengths to obstruct the performance art called international diplomacy, particularly by the United States. In a bizarre display of megalomania, Assange has been quoted as arguing that far from Wikileaks promoting greater transparency in international relations, the diplomatic insularity that would be forced on the United States by the Wikileaks revelations would make global intelligence coordination more difficult, so helping to "bring the empire down." Even those who would that this were so cannot rationally credit such self-promotional misrepresentation. Putting aside that so few of the Wikileaks revelations so far have proved either properly damaging, surprising or even new (Russia is a mafia state? Surprise surprise.

The US armed forces were little concerned about civilian casualties in Iraq? Who knew?), the whole quixotic enterprise begs the question as to just what the role of professional, "station" diplomats is in the twenty-first century. Cyber communications and supernumerary "special envoys" would seem to have obviated this role and, far from effecting policy or international negotiations or agreements, professional diplomats appear to have been reduced to the performance of cocktail party espionage. The paranoid response of the United States Department of State to Wikileaks appears more a face-saving exercise dealing with an embarrassing breach of cyber security. But Wikileaks had not even the capability or initiative to hack into State Department computers: the leaked communications were supplied by a minor American foreign-based employee of the Department itself. Most recently, big Capital has itself found a use for Wikileaks, as the Swiss banking regulator handed over the names of foreign tax evaders hiding their funds in numbered Swiss bank accounts to the "crusading" website in order to avoid local legal complications.

Perhaps the most exciting and even potentially subversive arena of border performance is border performance art itself. On the adversarial side stands the work of Mexicano/Chicano Guillermo Gómez-Peña and his merry band of artistes, whose extraordinary literary works, performances and public installations are described and analyzed in such works as *Dangerous Border Crossers: The Artist Talks Back* (Gómez-Peña 2000), *The New World Border* (Gómez-Peña 1996), and *Warrior for Gringostroika* (Gómez-Peña 1993). Gómez-Peña, originally from Mexico City, has spent his adult life principally in Los Angeles and other North American and world cities, providing his mobile cultural perspectives on the dilemmas of being taken as Mexican in the United States, Chicano in Mexico, and posing a threat to ingrained ideas of identity, nationality and political attitude wherever he lives, travels and performs. His first performance was a "Spanglish" poetry reading in a public bathroom at the California School of the Arts in 1979: "I sat on a toilet and read aloud epic poetry describing my journey to the United States. Whoever happened to come into the bathroom – for whatever reason – experienced the piece."

Gómez-Peña's latest project, *El Mexterminator* (in collaboration with Roberto Sifuentes), is not a single text, event or performance. In its New York incarnation, it consisted of a month-long series of actions, appearances, performances and interventions that ranged across the geographical and virtual spaces of the city. Adopting "ethno-cyborg" personas, collaborators Gómez-Peña and Sifuentes participated in a live internet chat and a radio call-in show. Potential audiences were also invited to visit and contribute to the *El Mexterminator* "Temple of Confessions," an interactive web site. Together with Sara Shelton Mann, they roved the city's public spaces on several occasions in their roles as El Mexterminator (Gómez-Peña), Cyber-Vato (Sifuentes) and La Cultural Transvestite (Shelton Mann). Finally, anchoring these various events was the installation at El Museo del Barrio titled *Techno-Museo de Etnografía Interactiva*, featuring the performers as "live Mexicans on display."

The images, characters, narratives and actions that make up *El Mexterminator* animate and recirculate myths, cultural beliefs and stereotypes about Chicano and Latino culture, the US–Mexico border, immigration and the relation of art to politics. For over two decades, Gómez-Peña has been working both alone and in collaboration with various artists to produce performance pieces that share many elements with

518   DAVID B. COPLAN

the current one. For example, the complex and hybridized personas of *El Mextermi-nator* recall the 1989 performance piece *Border Brujo*, described by Gómez-Peña as "a ritual, linguistic, and performative journey across the United States/México border." In 1992, Gómez-Peña appeared with Coco Fusco at the Whitney Museum and other major museums around the United States as "Two Undiscovered Amer-indians," "primitives" from the fictional island of Guatinaui. As in *El Mexterminator*, the audience was positioned as the source of the anthropological gaze: audiences visiting the "Amerindians" were invited to ask for an "authentic dance," a "story in Guatinaui" or a souvenir photo. In recognition of the significance of this body of work, Gómez-Peña has been awarded a MacArthur Fellowship as well as a National Book Award for *The New World Border* (1996), a collection of performance texts, essays and poetry.

In these projects and performances, the Mexico–United States border is the spe-cific and explicit site of criticism and interrogation. At the same time, the conflicts, contradictions and complexities of the geographical border zone become metaphoric materials through which to explore cultural, political, sexual, artistic and intellectual borders as well. For Gómez-Peña, who is not only a performer and artist but also a poet and theorist of cultural borderlands and multicultures, the artist must be rede-fined: "not just an imagemaker or a marginal genius, but a social thinker/educator/counterjournalist/civilian diplomat/human rights observer" (cited in Kawash 1999). Gómez-Peña views himself as a "border artist" for whom experimental techniques and performance-derived practices become a means to intervene in, and impact on, the emergence of new cultural formations. The aim, as Gómez-Peña puts it, is "a project of redefinition, which conceives of the border not only as the limits of the two countries, but as a cardinal intersection of many realities. In this sense, the border is not an abyss that will have to save us from threatening otherness, but a place where the so-called otherness yields, becomes us, and therefore becomes comprehensible" (cited in Kawash 1999).

Like all of Gómez-Peña's work, *El Mexterminator* probes the politicized spaces of difference and desire. In this sense, it might be viewed as another salvo in the ongoing "culture wars." Indeed, what is most immediately evident in *El Mexterminator* is the way in which its thematic or theoretical concerns – ideas of hybridity and the border zone, of the cultural construction of the "other," of the body of the other as a site of projection for both desires and fears – echo and amplify issues that have been reflected in a range of "multicultural" and "postcolonial" thought and practice over the past decade (Kawash 1999).

In the course of this narrative we have learned that the fraught encounters between travelers and border officials are more often than supposed a matter of prestidigita-tion. In this dialogic magic show, with its illusions created through signs, symbols and portents, it is often unclear who is fooling whom; who is the magician and who the (sometimes willing, even knowing) "dupe." "Hey presto!" and the traveler, the border guardian, even the border itself may disappear, only to reappear on the far side or at the next crossing. No border, not even the Warsaw Pact borders of yester-year or the United States–Mexico border of today, can be policed with even modest success unless the majority of would-be border crossers "police themselves" by playing along voluntarily, at least most of the time, with the legal regime of control imposed by at least one bordering state and its agents. Securing such cooperation or at least pressing travelers who have not or cannot meet the necessary legal requirements for entry to at the very least go to inordinate lengths to circumvent them is to an important extent a matter of embedded performance. Performance by state agents must instill in border crossers discipline, respect, fear and a willingness to both recognize state sovereignty and submit to its projections of power at its territorial margins. In this elaborate field of play, it is often citizens of the very states whose territories comprise the border who have the most cynicism and the least trepidation with regard to state regulation and alternative strategies of cross-border movement.

Of course, border performance is more than a matter of enactments involving travelers, state officials and other no less important mediators, "service" providers, and assorted hangers-on. It is also a theater in which neighboring states represent and play out, often enough in hyperdramatic fashion, their bilateral relations. Today, there is surely no more performative border in the world than that between Amritsar in India and Lahore in Pakistan, at the Radcliffe Line at Wagah. The ceremony that is staged every evening at the closing of the gate for the night compresses in a short and not uncordial few minutes not only the most militant panoply of sovereign statehood, but the bitterness, anger and sorrow that is the inevitable residue of war between brothers. Meantime the hundreds of people who unfailingly gather to watch the ceremony each evening constitute themselves into an "audience," seated on bleachers provided for their convenience by the authorities. And not merely an audience: this being India/Pakistan, a general atmosphere of festival prevails, as singing, dancing, eating and hawking always enliven the proceedings. The border guards, too, dance in military style, expressing with hard-stamping precision the snarling animosity that characterizes Indian-Pakistan official relations. Formerly, there was no better example of border performance than that of the German Democratic Republic and the Federal Republic of Germany at the Berlin Wall, with its shoot-to-kill border police, growling, barely restrained Doberman Pinschers, barbed wire filigree, and no-man's land on the east, and multinational uniforms and grimly colorful graffiti decorating "Checkpoint Charlie" on the west. Some will observe that there was real *force majeure* and not just its representation involved in the East Germans' display on the thoroughfare of the Unter den Linden. That point taken, an impressive enactment of ruthless aggression was certainly a primary product of such a border regime. Not so the script through which the border was, as in a magic show, made to disappear. The Deputy Prime Minister of the GDR simply announced on radio that henceforward, the *volpos* (border police) would be withdrawn from duty at the Wall. Incredulous, those on both sides who understood this coded statement, not just in Berlin but throughout both East and West Germany, rushed to the Wall and, in a joyous festival of destruction, smashed it down. So then too is the unmaking of borders a performative engagement with our desire to remove everything that obstructs human consciousness and aspiration. Increasingly in the twenty-first century, citizens are coming to understand that it is not they who are being reassured and protected by the theater of borders.

NOTES

1 This phrase, meaning border "shaman" or "medicine man" in Spanish, is taken from Gómez-Pena (1993: 75–96).
2 Since so few of its member states are by any definition "nations," perhaps the United Nations Organization ought to be renamed the "United States Organization."
3 East German border police. Walking in Manhattan not long after the fall of the Berlin Wall, I encountered a clothing stall with a hat rack and among the items on sale was an unmistakable light blue four-muff *volpo* winter hat. "Don't you know the very sight of these struck terror into the hearts of East Berliners?" I admonished the vendor. "Well," he said in a thick Russian accent, "times change."

REFERENCES

Albert, Mathias and Brock, Lothar. 1998. New relationships between territory and state: the US–Mexico border in perspective. In David Spener and Kathleen Staudt, eds, *The US–Mexico Border: Transcending Divisions, Contesting Identities.* Boulder: Lynne Rienner.

Anzaldua, Gloria. 1987. *Borderlands/La Frontera.* San Francisco: Aunt Lute Press.

Aretxaga, Begoña. 2003. Maddening states. *Annual Review of Anthropology* 32: 393–410.

Beltran, Cristina. 2004. Patrolling borders: hybrids, hierarchies and the challenge of mestizaje. *Political Research Quarterly* 57: 595–607.

Bhabha, Homi, ed. 1990. *Nation and Narration.* London: Routledge.

Carling, Jørgen. 2007. Migration control and migrant fatalities at the Spanish-African borders. *International Migration Review* 41 (2): 315–344.

Chalfin, Brenda. 2008. Airport anthropology and customs regimes in neoliberal Ghana. *American Anthropologist* 35 (4): 519–538.

Coplan, David. 2000. Unconquered territory: narrating the Caledon Valley. *Journal of African Cultural Studies* 13 (2): 185–206.

Coplan, David. 2001. A river runs through it: the meaning of the Lesotho–Free State border. *African Affairs* 100: 81–116.

Eder, Klaus. 2006. Europe's borders: the narrative construction of the boundaries of Europe. *European Journal of Social Theory* 9 (2): 255–271.

Ghosh, Amitav. 2002. *The Imam and the Indian: Prose Pieces.* New Delhi: Ravi Dayal.

Gómez-Peña, Guillermo. 1993. *Warrior for Gringostroika.* St Paul, MN: Graywolf Press.

Gómez-Peña, Guillermo. 1996. *The New World Border.* San Francisco: City Lights, 1996.

Gómez-Peña, Guillermo. 2000. *Dangerous Border Crossers: The Artist Talks Back.* London: Routledge.

Hall, Stuart, Critcher, Chas, Jefferson, Tony et al. 1978. *Policing the Crisis: Mugging, the State, and Law and Order.* New York: Holmes & Meier.

Kawash, Samira. 1999. Interactivity and vulnerability. *PAJ: A Journal of Performance and Art* 21 (1): 46–52.

Lugo, Alejandro. 2000. Theorizing border inspections. *Cultural Dynamics* 12 (3): 353–373.

Newman, David and Paasi, Anssi. 1998. Fences and neighbours in the postmodern world: boundary narratives in political geography. *Progress in Human Geography* 22 (2): 186–207.

Paredes, Américo. 1993. *Folklore and Culture on the Texas-Mexican Border.* Austin: University of Texas Press.

Price, Patricia L. 2004. *Dry Place.* Minneapolis: University of Minnesota Press.

Rosenau, J.N., and Czempiel, Ernst O. 1992. *Governance without Government: Order and Change in World Politics.* Cambridge: Cambridge University Press.

Ruiz, Olivia. 2006. Migration and borders: present and future challenges. *Latin American Perspectives* 33: 46–55.

Saez, Jean Pierre. 1995. *Identités, cultures et territoires.* Paris: Desclée de Brouwer.

Somers, Margaret. R. 1994. The narrative constitution of identity: a relational and network approach. *Theory and Society* 23 (5): 605–649.

Spener, David and Staudt, Kathleen, eds. 1998. *The US–Mexico Border: Transcending Divisions, Contesting Identities.* Boulder: Lynne Rienner.

Truett, Samuel. 2006. *Fugitive Landscapes: The Forgotten History of the US–Mexico Borderlands.* New Haven: Yale University Press.

Vila, Pablo. 2000. *Crossing Borders, Reinforcing Borders: Social Categories, Metaphors, and Narrative Identities on the US–Mexico Frontier.* Austin: University of Texas Press.

Vila, Pablo. 2003. Processes of identification on the US–Mexico border. *Social Science Journal* 40 (4): 607–625.

Vukov, Tamara. 2003. Imagining communities through immigration policies. *International Journal of Cultural Studies* 6 (3): 335–353.

Walters, William. 2006. Border/control. *European Journal of Social Theory* 9 (2): 187–203.

Zúñiga, Victor. 2005. Nations and borders: romantic nationalism and the project of modernity. In Víctor Zúñiga and Rubén Hernández-León, eds, *New Destinations: Mexican Immigration in the United States.* New York: Russell Sage.

<table>
<tr><td>CHAPTER **30**</td></tr>
</table>

Performativity and the Eventfulness of Bordering Practices

Robert J. Kaiser

Recent research on borders has moved decisively away from static depictions of borders as things existing in space that impede or facilitate movement and toward more dynamic explorations of the ways in which bordering discourses and practices shape and reconfigure our understandings of the places and/or social communities with which we identify/differentiate one another. This more process-based under-standing of bordering shifts the focus from existential research questions (i.e., borders are this or that; borders are things that function like this or that) to studies of borders' processes of emergence or becoming. Not only that, more nonrepresentational approaches emphasize the ongoing nature of these processes that are always in the midst, without beginning or end, so that the research agenda is not to study what borders were and what are they about to become, but rather to study borders as continual processes of becoming that are neither linear nor unidirectional, but that are in many ways event-driven. Earlier volumes by Wilson and Donnan (1998) and Donnan and Wilson (1999), as well as a series of recent works in geography (e.g., Jones 2009; Newman and Paasi 1998; van Houtum et al. 2005), have significantly contributed to this body of work.

In an earlier paper that contributed to this emerging field of border studies, Elena Nikiforova and I argued that borderlands are spaces of becoming (Kaiser and Niki-forova 2006), and used Brah's (1996) concept of "diaspora space" to consider how the process of bordering was narrated and enacted by a variety of stakeholders in the Estonian-Russian borderlands. In this chapter, I develop these arguments further by exploring the ever-present eventfulness embedded in the performative process of borders' becomings. To do this, I open with a discussion of performativity and the power of border performatives, and then explore the relationship between performa-tivity and events. It is here that the chapter makes its most significant contribution to border studies, since most of the border research to date that takes a more post-structural, performative approach emphasizes the ways in which power works to

A Companion to Border Studies, First Edition. Edited by Thomas M. Wilson and Hastings Donnan.

stabilize, naturalize and essentialize borders so that they come to appear as existing things rather than socio-spatial practices. Here, I identify the ever-present potentiality of change and elaborate on how to be eventful with performativity. As part of this exploration of the relationship between performativity, events and bordering practices, I use an event from 2007 in Estonia to work through the performative eventfulness of bordering practices.

PERFORMATIVITY, EVENTS, BORDERS

Performativity is a spatial as well as social set of repetitive practices through which socio-spatial categories or signifiers (e.g., identity, place, scale) materialize as things in the world, as essences "out there" (Kaiser and Nikiforova 2008; see also Butler 1993, 1999; Brubaker and Cooper 2000). For Butler, performativity is the iterative and citational practices through which discourse produces that which it names. Performatives in turn "are statements that, in the uttering, also perform a certain action and exercise a binding power . . . statements which not only perform an action, but confer a binding power on the action performed" (Butler 1993: 225; see also Butler 1997). One of the most efficacious and ubiquitous types of such "action statements" or discursive practices are bordering performatives: they naturalize and essentialize socio-spatial categories by materializing borders and separating interior from exterior. This is so because categories are constituted not by what is inside so much as by what is exteriorized, and especially by the exteriorized interior or constitutive outside without which the signifier itself could not exist (Butler 1993, 1999; Natter and Jones 1997; Kaiser and Nikiforova 2006, 2008). The maintenance of this paradoxical relationship between socio-spatial categories and their constitutive outsides requires continual guarding and policing at the borders, to prevent the gaps and fissures performatively produced from becoming ruptures that threaten to expose the unnatural, nonessential, contingent conditions of the signifier's becoming. The gaps, fissures and ruptures are the events through which borders – and the socio-spatial categories they stabilize and transform – emerge.

In this way, the constitutive outside and the bordering practices which continually work to exteriorize it provide the conditions for social and spatial change. Because no socio-spatial category can ever incorporate its exteriorized interior or constitutive outside without itself dissolving, it also "fails to secure the very borders of materiality" that produce it, and so can never be completely and permanently closed or sealed off (Butler 1993: 187–188). It is always open to change as it is performatively enacted. Although enactments of place-identities are "repeat performances" that cite past socio-spatial norms which regulate and regularize practices, they are not – and never can be – fully determined in advance, even for the most naturalized and sedimented of signifiers.

Indeterminacy empowers enactment, since no matter how constraining socio-spatial norms are, no matter how essential place-identities and their borders appear, they only ever materialize in the doing, and do not precede the deed (Gregson and Rose 2000; Kaiser and Nikiforova 2008). Futurespace is an open potentiality, and "[t]he performative is the gap, the rupture, the spacing that unfolds the next moment allowing change to happen" (Dewsbury 2000: 475). Gaps, fissures and ruptures continually open the borders of categories through such discursive practices; performative "reiterations are never simply replicas of the same" but rather are repetitions that produce differences (Butler 1993: 226; Deleuze 1994: 286–287). In this way, borders are "events of becoming" (Woodward and Jones 2005: 239):

> Bordering describes a vast array of affective and transformative material processes in which social and spatial orders and disorders are constantly reworked . . . The bordering event . . . does not sit inertly between sets of ideational categories (Ideas, Subject, and Nature), but rather is active at the event-limit of multiplicities constituted by the affects exchanged between subjectivity and milieu. (Woodward and Jones 2005: 239–240)

Since a political signifier can never deliver on the identificational unity it promises, a dis-identification will always occur, and this dis-identifying moment is the future potentiality opened up by the signifier that can be politicized. Rather than guarding and policing the borders against those socio-spatial relations to be excluded, enforcing a never-to-be-achieved identity or unity through covering over, patching up and sewing together the gaps and fissures performatively created, Butler (1993: 219) along with Haraway (1990) and Laclau and Mouffe (1985) advocates embracing and politicizing such dis-identifications, that is, turning the gaps and fissures performatively produced into ruptures that create new or transformed political signifiers. This is how to be eventful with performativity.

This is not to suggest that agency is to be found either in individual actors or in singular acts. Human and nonhuman agents are both enabled and constrained by the categories that they in turn performatively produce. For Butler, "there is no power, construed as a subject, that acts, but only . . . a reiterated acting that *is* power in its persistence and instability" (1993: 225). Siting power in the persistence and instability of reiterated acting focuses attention not only on border policing and guarding (naturalizing, essentializing, sedimenting), but also on breaching socio-spatial borders.

> "Agency" would then be the double-movement of being constituted in and by a signifier, where "to be constituted" means "to be compelled to cite or repeat or mime" the signifier itself. Enabled by the very signifier that depends for its continuation on the future of that citational chain, agency is the hiatus in iterability, the compulsion to install an identity through repetition, which requires the very contingency, the undetermined interval, that identity insistently seeks to foreclose. (Butler 1993: 220)

Bordering practices – and so the political signifiers that they capture and partially stabilize but never fully close – are performative events. In the present moment of their socio-spatial becoming, they produce border effects as virtual bordering practices recalled from the past articulate with the open potentiality of desired future borderings. Mountz provides an exceptional example of this process – and the gaps and fissures it produces – in the case of the emergence of the "embodied nation-state" through the performative practices of Canadian immigration officers exteriorizing unauthorized immigrants as the constitutive outside. While high-level state officials produced smooth, simple narratives – frequently retrospectively – through which a natural and essential nation-state border separating us from them could be imagined, the immigration officers on the front lines – as embodiments of the nation-state border – acted not only on these narratives, along with the rules, regulations and procedures that help to stabilize "stateness," but also on the basis of their own pasts, feelings, and emotions as they encountered the unauthorized immigrants and engaged in the everyday discursive practices that embodied the nation-state (Mountz 2003, 2004). In one particularly telling example, Mountz highlights how the nation-state's border enactment by immigration officers becomes blurred or breached in practice: "One employee who worked closely with the migrants was herself smuggled to Canada as a child many years ago. She described being overcome with emotion in her initial interactions with the migrants. She characterized her experiences as 'very painful,' particularly when relating to the women and children from the boats, with whom she empathized" (2003: 635). As a socio-spatial creation that materializes performatively, "the state does not exist outside of the people who comprise it, their everyday work, and their social embeddedness in local relationships" (Mountz 2003: 640).

This presenting of future-past borderings is the time-space moment when virtual events are actualized (Deleuze 1990; Massumi 2002). A new encounter or situation serves as a catalyst or "trigger" that changes resonances or vibrations, transforming the potentiality of co-present (human and nonhuman) bodies to affect each other (Deleuze and Guattari 1987; McCormack 2007: 367; Woodward and Lea 2010: 160). Sensations, which directly affect bodies by "contracting vibrations" among them (Grosz 2008: 78–80), channel "potential into local action" (Massumi 2002: 75). The affective intensification of force relations among bodies from this contracting, channeling and concentration reaches a threshold, breaches a border, and actualizes the event. Once actualized as gaps, fissures and ruptures in the normative order of things, events create surprises (Dewsbury 2007), make differences (Stengers 2000), and produce deterritorializing lines of flight (Patton 1997). Event actualizations alter space as well as time. Rajchman provides a vivid depiction of event-effects on time:

> [The event] is not defined by a fixed beginning and end, but is something that occurs in the midst of a history, causing us to redistribute our sense of what has gone before it and what might come after. An event is thus not something one inserts into an emplotted dramatic sequence with its start and finish, for it initiates a new sequence that retrospectively determines its beginnings, and which leaves its ends unknown and undetermined (Rajchman 1991: xi, as quoted in Anderson and Harrison 2010: 22).

Event actualizations produce socio-spatial changes, particularly making differences in bordering practices as naturalized categories are destabilized and deterritorialized. Event-spaces materialize as deterritorializing lines of flight transgress the border that regulates and regularizes who may do what where. Events travel from their originating time-space moment of actualization, producing secondary intensities, resonances, actualizations and event-spaces in what Massumi (2002) refers to as "event transitivity." The longer the effects of an event last, and the farther the event travels, the more "historic" or "revolutionary" it becomes.

Reterritorialization refers to the capture of events after their actualization. This capture amounts to the suturing back together of the gaps and fissures produced by performative events as they are actualized. When this happens immediately after an event's actualization, it is frequently narrated after the act as if "nothing happened," as part of an effort to restabilize the borders circumscribing socio-spatial categories, thus restoring their naturalized, essentialized appearance. *Repetition* is produced through those events whose transformative potentiality is captured and contained during the initial moments of the event's actualization; the power unleashed by the event is harnessed to produce stability. *Incremental change* is produced when/where the actualized deterritorializing line(s) of flight are sufficient to challenge socio-spatial norms, such that reterritorialization requires a rewriting of the associated rules, regulations and procedures, as well as rebordered sets of discursive practices in order to accommodate the changes wrought by the event as actualized. *Revolutionary change* occurs when the deterritorializing lines of flight continue on, escaping capture, opening up new event-spaces that cannot readily or easily be reterritorialized. Through such change socio-spatial norms and the discursive practices through which they are enacted are successfully upended and denaturalized, creating the conditions for entirely new ways of seeing and understanding the relevant socio-spatial problems, relations and processes for which new bordering practices are required. Repetition, incremental and revolutionary change are all emergent properties of events, and should be seen as differences in degree, not as differences in kind.

ESTONIA'S BRONZE NIGHT

Estonia and Estonian-ness performatively materialize through a series of iterative and citational bordering practices that present Russia and Russian-ness, as well as the USSR and Soviet-ness, as its exteriorized interior or constitutive outside. Self-identifying Russian bodies and Russian/Soviet spaces were placed in a precarious, paradoxical position as the exteriorized interior or "Other within" after Estonia's independence, and anomalous places like Tonismagi Square emerged as powerful sites where such performative bordering practices were enacted.

The bronze soldier statue was created in 1947 to commemorate the Red Army's liberation of Tallinn from fascism during World War II. The monument – along with the bodies of a dozen Soviet soldiers – were located in a public square near the center of the city, and served as a site of Sovietization during the postwar period. The bronze soldier statue and dead soldiers' bodies buried there deterritorialized the nationalized, stately space that Tonismagi Square presented prior to World War II, and reterritorialized it as an event-space of the USSR, Soviet-ness and Russian-ness. Discursive practices that enacted a "liberation from fascism" narrative at the site stabilized its status as a border post of Russian-ness and Soviet-ness; and so for self-identifying Estonians as a space of the Other within.[1]

Independence and the dissolution of the USSR came on a wave of exclusionary territorial nationalism that was nowhere more powerful than in the Baltics (Kaiser 1994). The bronze soldier statue and dead soldiers' bodies, along with Russians living in post-Soviet Estonia became an exteriorized interior, as those discursively enacting Estonia as the exclusive homeland of the Estonian nation performatively glorified and valorized the interwar period of independence and the pre-Soviet and pre-Russian eras in Estonia's past, while at the same time vilifying the periods of Soviet and Russian domination (Kaiser and Nikiforova 2008).

As part of this effort to exteriorize, residents of Estonia who had arrived during the Soviet period – overwhelmingly Russians and Russian-speakers – were denied automatic citizenship in independent Estonia (Chinn and Kaiser 1996). This was primarily an exclusionary tactic to deprive Russian residents of legal standing in the state. Because the country in which they had citizenship (USSR) no longer existed, they became stateless overnight,[2] and this problem of statelessness was one of the mobilizing factors bringing people out to the bronze soldier statue.

Efforts were made prior to 2007 to remove the monument and bodies from Tonismagi Square, which paralleled attempts by state authorities to increase pressure on Russians living in Estonia to leave (Kaiser 1995, 2007). In addition, in 2003 the Museum of the Occupations opened just across the street from the bronze soldier statue, materializing the occupation side of the liberation/occupation discursive border.

Bordering practices on the liberation side of this discourse sought to re-emplot the bronze soldier statue and soldiers' bodies into the post-Soviet nation-state of Estonia as a site of resistance. Self-identifying Russians who were stateless and/or who otherwise felt themselves discriminated against in the nationalizing state of Estonia saw the bronze soldier statue and soldiers' bodies buried at Tonismagi Square as symbols of Russians' sacrifice in liberating Tallinn and Estonia, and so as evidence of their right to live and be treated equitably in Estonia. Increasing numbers of such Russians began to congregate at the square not only to commemorate Victory Day and Liberation Day, but also to protest against what they perceived as Russians' second-class status in Tallinn and Estonia. This heightened the post-Soviet significance of the site as a border post separating Estonia and Estonian-ness from Russia and Russian-ness.

The bronze soldier statue's affective power intensified during the mid-2000s, as it was increasingly cited by both sides in the discursive practices through which the border between Estonia/Estonian-ness and Russia/Russian-ness materialized. The size and intensity of Victory Day celebrations grew between 2004 and 2006, as did the reactions against these events and in opposition to the site, which culminated in a skirmish as young nationalistic Estonians sought to drape the Estonian flag over the statue during Victory Day celebrations on May 9, 2006. An Estonian nationalist event was staged at Tonismagi Square later that month, and following this Estonia's Prime Minister Andrus Ansip both blamed Russia for all unrest surrounding the site, and also called for the monument's removal as the only solution to the problem (Ansip 2006):

> I see the solution to this problem in the relocation of the monument to the cemetery . . . It has become all the more clear that the monument cannot remain in its old place. The question arose: whose word has authority in Estonia? The word coming from the Kremlin or the word from Old Town? We cannot say to our people, that Estonia is after all only a union republic, and our word in this country is not worth a "brass farthing."

This was also the moment when Russian activists created Nochnoy Dozor (Night Watch), an organization to mobilize support for and protection of the bronze soldier statue and to prevent its removal.[3]

Affective intensities surrounding the site continued to increase during the following year, as the Reform Party led by Andrus Ansip used removal of the bronze soldier statue and soldiers' bodies from Tonismagi Square as a political vehicle that they rode to majority status in the Rigikogu (Parliament) in March 2007. Night Watch activists organized nightly vigils in Tonismagi Square to protect and defend the monument and bodies during the same period. In all these performative ways the bronze soldier statue was becoming by early 2007 one of the most powerful borders in all of Estonia.

The intensity had reached a fevered pitch by April 2007, and the government now led by the Reform Party committed to removing the bronze soldier statue and the dead soldiers' bodies prior to Victory Day (May 9), in an attempt to prevent what many expected to be a serious ethnic confrontation from occurring. The Bronze Night event actualized on April 26, 2007, as workers presenting the nationalizing state arrived early in the morning, erected a fence around the square and a tent over the area where the monument and dead soldiers' bodies were located. This work of reterritorialization – seeking to capture and remove this remnant socio-spatial node of Estonia's constitutive outside – transited quickly and widely throughout Tallinn via news reports and word of mouth. Through this first wave of event transitivity the event that was unfolding entered homes, offices, schools, and so forth, producing secondary events as people who were affected by the news left their normal everyday activities to join the protest against the removal at Tonismagi Square.

The affective intensity of the assembled crowd swelled as the number of agitated demonstrators grew throughout the late afternoon and early evening. As the police made a futile attempt at crowd control, participants and police reported a surge of energy from the crowd. The threshold of intensification had been breached, and the Bronze Night event actualized.[4]

Intensive potential energy among the demonstrators at the site was converted into extensive kinetic energy, as demonstrators left Tonismagi Square and entered Old Town as rioters, turning it from a peaceful scene of touristic consumption into a chaotic space of violence and vandalism.[5] This deterritorializing line of flight that ruptured the normative socio-spatial practices through which Old Town Tallinn materialized lasted for two days, during which time over 1,000 arrests were made, and over 150 injuries and one death were reported. The event also traveled to Estonia's border with Russia, as well as to Russia, the United States and the European Union (EU), where reiterative and citational practices threatened to materialize a new Cold War (Kaiser 2007). Finally, the event deterritorialized cyberspace, as attacks launched against Estonian governmental, banking and financial websites effectively disrupted political and socioeconomic life in the state.

After-the-act reterritorializations sought to suture together the border ruptures produced by the event. Initial efforts by state officials and news media sought to portray the riot as the work of young, drunken, violent Russians, with the stereotypical narrative that this is just "how Russians are, what Russians do." This was followed by depictions of the demonstrators as a fifth column operating in the interests of the Russian state – a return to the post-independence discursive practices which favored the removal of members of Estonians' constitutive outside from the state. For example, Defense Minister Aaviksoo declared on May 9, 2007:

> We revived our republic in a situation where we acquiesced to granting permanent residence to a very great number of people who had arrived [in Estonia] during the [Soviet] occupation; we allowed [Soviet] reserve officers to stay behind on the territory of the Estonian Republic; and perhaps we underestimated the corresponding risks. The riots two weeks ago are partly a consequence of those decisions . . . perhaps we are seeing today what it really means to have in Estonia a great number of people who are not reconciled to the independence and sovereignty of the Republic of Estonia. (Aaviksoo 2007)

A second set of performative reterritorializations that sought to repair the ruptures produced by the Bronze Night worked to place all blame for the event on Russia, thus exteriorizing the cause. In the words of President Ilves (2007a): "I turn to Russia, Estonia's neighbor, with a clear message – try to remain civilized! It is customary in Europe that differences are solved by diplomats and politicians, not on the streets or by computer attacks. Those are the ways of other countries, somewhere else, not in Europe." Here, widening and deepening the discursive border between "civilized" Europe and "barbaric" Russia was critical to the internal suturing together of the ruptures produced by the Bronze Night, especially those related to the materialization of Estonia and Estonian-ness. In a speech later in the month, Ilves elaborated further on this theme, linking the 2007 events with the Soviet Union's takeover of independent Estonia, the deportations that followed, and even to the charges that the Kremlin was behind the polonium poisoning of former spy Alexander Litvinenko (see Fenton et al. 2006):

> This spring, Estonia was hit by a serious onslaught. True, no howitzers were used and we could track no traces of Polonium. But our Embassy and our diplomats were attacked, and thus also the principles of the Vienna Convention ignored . . . If we shall not pull ourselves together, if we shall not stand more efficiently on guard of our hard-won success, it may all vanish once again. This time, perhaps, without bayonets, or shots in the back of the head, or cattle cars with barred windows, but by means of stealthy destabilisation and subversion, poisoning of the tolerant atmosphere of our country. (Ilves 2007b)

Prime Minister Ansip, who earlier had claimed that Tonismagi Square was a space that Russia sought to utilize in order to undermine Estonia's sovereignty, now narrated the event as an attack not only on Estonia's sovereignty, but on the European Union itself, and called on the EU to come to Estonia's defense. "The European Union is under attack because Russia is attacking Estonia . . . The attacks are virtual, psychological and real . . . We believe it to be essential that the European Union react in full strength against the behavior of Russia. This might result in the suspension or cancellation of negotiations between the European Union and Russia" (Ansip 2007).

These discursive practices of bordering Russia as "not Estonia" and "not Europe" also entered cyberspace. As noted above, a series of cyberattacks were launched shortly after the Bronze Night event actualized, first forcing governmental and then banking and financial websites to shut down. These attacks were especially crippling in Estonia, which had moved very rapidly to conducting governmental and economic business online. Rather than presenting these attacks as the work of technologically savvy individuals who were upset over the removal of the bronze soldier from Tonismagi Square, Estonian state officials declared that the Russian state itself was engaged in a cyberwar against Estonia (*Guardian* 2007). This was the first open declaration that one sovereign state had launched a cyberwar against another state, and it has had a transformative effect on the performativity of national security ever since.

During research into the border effects materializing from the Bronze Night, I expected to find a similar hardening of bordering practices at the political border between Estonia and Russia in Narva, a city of Russian-ness and so another paradoxical exteriorized interior social space. During the Bronze Night event, Estonian state officials did hurriedly erect a border between Narva and Tallinn, by preventing buses from leaving Estonia's northeastern region for the capital.[6] Additionally, Russian state authorities used creative bordering practices to register Russia's displeasure over events. Most significantly, Russian officials declared the "Bridge of Friendship" (the main border crossing point between Narva and Ivangorod) unsafe, and would allow only one vehicle on the bridge at a time. Slowing border traffic to a crawl, Russian border guards produced a 10 kilometer-long line of trucks and cars waiting on the Estonian side of the border, and an average wait time to cross into Russia of nearly 100 hours. This lasted throughout much of the summer.

Surprisingly, Estonian border guards did not respond in kind. According to the head of the northeast regional border security office, this was because Estonia's border guards were preparing for Estonia's entry into the Schengen zone later that year, which was deemed an even more important event than the Bronze Night.[7] Entering the Schengen zone would standardize visa protocols with Russia, and if anything make entry from Russia into Estonia easier than it had been up to that point. The tension between the hardening of official border narratives and the softening of border practices vis-à-vis Russia can clearly be seen in a speech given by President Ilves on May 29, 2007 to mark the opening of the Narva 2 border-crossing station which had been renovated with Schengen funds: "The border must hold. Must hold back those who have evil plans. For others the border should be a friendly gate, which says, 'Welcome to Estonia! Welcome to Europe!'" (Ilves 2007c).

A third set of discursive practices reterritorialized Tonismagi Square as a space of Estonia and Europe. Following the removal of the bronze soldier statue and the dead soldiers' bodies, the square was planted with blue and yellow flowers in an effort to materialize the European Union in this space. At the same time, the monument and bodies were re-placed within Siselinna military cemetery on the outskirts of the city. This relocation was temporal as well as spatial, as the bronze soldier left the time-space of post-Soviet Estonia and entered the time-space of World War II. With these two moves, Tonismagi Square ceased functioning as a space of Estonia's exteriorized interior or constitutive outside, although the "bronze soldier" did reappear on one occasion (BBC 2009).

These initial reterritorializing efforts to suture together the ruptures produced in the regulated and regularized bordering practices that materialized Estonia and Estonian-ness on one side and Russia and Russian-ness on the other were only partially effective. Remaining fissures were most readily apparent in relation to the problem of what to do with Russian-ness as it performatively materialized in Estonia following the Bronze Night. Two questions in particular dominated the performative enactments associated with these bordering practices: (1) could/should Russians be integrated into the Estonian state and society, and (2) could/should Estonia do away with officially sanctioned statelessness and extend citizenship to all stateless Russians? In the final sections of the chapter, I explore changes in the discursive practices of integration and citizenship, as Estonian state authorities sought to stabilize the border between Estonian-ness and Russian-ness in Estonia.

THE PROBLEM OF INTEGRATION

The original Integration Program (2000) was not designed to eliminate the bordering practices producing Estonian-ness and Russian-ness in Estonia. Rather, it was structured both to stabilize the cultural hegemony of Estonian-ness, and also to "domesticate" Russian-ness as the constitutive outside by teaching Russian speakers the Estonian language, Estonian history and Estonian culture (Kaiser and Nikiforova 2008; see Hage 1996 on the concept of "domesticating" ethnic others in nationalizing homeland states). At the same time, the Integration Program worked to produce discursively one cohesive non-Estonian identity, even though the population so-labeled tended to enact much more fractured, localized identification practices. Nonetheless, the Integration Program was an important element in Estonia's accession to the European Union, and so it was also necessary to demonstrate that relations between the two communities were improving; that minority rights were being observed, and that "non-Estonians" were becoming a more integral part of the social and political life of the state (Kaiser and Nikiforova 2008).

For many, the Bronze Night was an indictment against the Integration Program, and certainly in the wake of the event more extreme nationalistic identification practices predominated on both sides of this discursive divide. The rupture that the Bronze Night created in the socio-spatial imaginary of Estonia and Estonian-ness as a "civilized" European nation-state that upheld Western values and standards with regard to minority rights required serious and immediate attention.

As noted above, early efforts by Estonian state officials to suture this rupture back together consisted of exteriorizing the cause for the Bronze Night – blaming Russia and a fifth column of Russians living in Estonia for the demonstration and riots. The event and these reterritorializing discursive practices materialized a new border within "the Russian" community, which potentially reconfigures the constitutive outside. While those who engaged in the protests and riots were proclaimed a fifth column, the enemy Other within (i.e., the true constitutive outside), those who stayed away from Tonismagi Square and who did not participate in the event's actualization emerged after the Bronze Night as "Our Russian-Speaking Compatriots," a domesticated minority that was capable of being integrated. In the words of President Ilves (2007a):

> Most of our Russian-speaking compatriots have been on Estonia's side during the troubled nights and days of the past week. You were with all of us, on the side of order and public safety, and I thank you for that . . . It is to you I turn, saying – learn Estonian, be successful, be happy! And the state will help you. The state has a duty to you, just as you have a duty to the state.

The discursive practices that materialized "our Russian-speaking compatriots" as a performative border effect both opened greater opportunities for integration, but also closed off potential enactments of Russian-ness in Estonia, since "our Russian-speaking compatriots" do not engage in antistate demonstrations and certainly do not riot. These became practices of the constitutive outside.

New bordering practices within the second Integration Program (2008–2013) reimagined integration as a two-way street which needed accommodations from Estonian as well as Russian communities. As presented by officials at the Office of the Population Minister, as well as by the director of the Integration Foundation,[8] it was necessary to create a new community of "Estonian-landers" to integrate all those residents who are loyal to Estonia as their homeland. Integration would have to happen not just through the workings of the Integration Program, but through the activities of each and every ministry and branch of government.[9] Beyond this, Tallinn city government drafted its own integration program, targeting each of the social, cultural, political and economic factors that were said to contribute to the Bronze Night (Volokhonskaya 2007). However, many of the specific activities funded through the second Integration Program looked very similar to those that took place during the first Integration Program, leaving unanswered the question of how seriously Estonian state officials have taken their own rhetoric.

THE PROBLEM OF STATELESSNESS

Although many of the self-identifying Russians who were made stateless at the time of independence had either opted for Russian citizenship or become naturalized Estonian citizens between 1991 and 2007, over 125,000 remained stateless by the time of the Bronze Night, and this condition of statelessness was one of the critical factors catalyzing the event. Following the Bronze Night, calls to resolve this situation increased in number and intensity. Demands for an end to statelessness came not only from those with "alien passports" in Estonia and from state authorities in Russia. They also came from within the Estonian social scientific and political communities, as well as from within the European Union and the Council of Europe (Integration Program 2007; Council of Europe 2007; *Baltic Times* 2007).

Although some rules regarding naturalization were eased, Estonian state officials have been unwilling to confer citizenship automatically on the stateless residents. In fact, during interviews at the Estonian Citizenship and Immigration Board, workers there contested that there was a problem of statelessness in Estonia, preferring to define this population as "residents whose citizenship is currently undetermined." Additionally, officials claimed that the population that held gray or alien passports derived some benefit from this status, that this population had many rights, that it was easy to become a citizen of Estonia, that they could do so anytime they wished, and that there was therefore nothing the state could or should do. In other words, officially there was no acknowledged "problem of statelessness" in Estonia.[10]

In follow-on interviews conducted throughout the summer of 2007, it became clear that the principal reason Estonian state officials would not eliminate the problem of statelessness had to do with domestic party politics. The conservative Reform Party had just wrested control of the government from the Center Party – a party that had much stronger support among the country's self-identifying Russians. A law that would end statelessness would also provide a large number of Russians with the right to vote in national elections, and would almost certainly lead to the return of the Center Party to power. For this reason more than any other, political forces in Estonia demanded that the border between stateness and statelessness must hold, despite the pressures for change that emerged from the Bronze Night event.

However, the conditions of statelessness in which this portion of Estonia's constitutive outside found itself were radically altered. Even before the event's actualization, in January 2007 European Union officials passed legislation allowing for visa-free travel for alien passport holders (European Union 2006). After the event, in June 2008 Russian officials passed similar legislation (President of Russia 2008). Suddenly, the new bordering practices in the EU and Russia had transformed statelessness from a condition of abjection to one of privilege, and in interviews conducted with alien passport holders in summer 2008 the status of statelessness was presented to us for the first time as something desirable, rather than as a problem to be solved.[11]

CONCLUSION

The Bronze Night event was a surprise that made differences in the performative bordering practices that materialized Estonia and Estonian-ness, Russia and Russian-ness, and also Europe and European-ness. Some of the deterritorializing gaps and fissures produced by the event were captured or sutured together fairly quickly (e.g., the discursive practices that blamed the event on Russia and a fifth column of disloyal Russians within, thereby stabilizing the border between Estonia/Estonian-ness and its constitutive outside). The power unleashed by the Bronze Night in these cases of repetition was harnessed to produce stability. Other deterritorializing breaches continued, eluding or evading reterritorialization, and produced incremental changes to these bordering practices (e.g., rebordering Russian-ness in Estonia, and opening up more widely the understanding of and potential for integration for "our Russian-speaking compatriots"). Still other ruptures produced deterritorializing lines of flight, event transitivity and secondary event actualizations that continue to evade capture and to make differences. One of the most noteworthy transformations produced by the Bronze Night is that it was the first time that officials of one sovereign state charged another state of waging "cyberwar" against it, and this continues to make differences in the bordering practices associated with securitizing cyberspace against attacks coordinated and launched by one sovereign state against another.[12] Second, the potentially most revolutionary transformation in bordering practices emerging from the Bronze Night is the revaluation of statelessness from a position of abjection to one of privilege. This deterritorializing line of flight provides, perhaps for the first time, a performativity of statelessness, a set of iterative and citational practices that naturalizes and sediments statelessness as a positive, radical dis-identification with the nation-state system, and which posits statelessness not as a problem to be solved, but as the solution to the problems of nationness and stateness. The Bronze Night's transformative effect on statelessness – in producing a potentially revolutionary moment of rupture in our naturalized and essentialized understandings of how place-identities are bordered – provides a brilliant example of how to be politically eventful with performativity.

NOTES

The author gratefully acknowledges the support received from the National Science Foundation, as well as the gracious openness of all those who agreed to be interviewed for this project. I also wish to thank Ms Piret Vaher for her timely and professional translation of the Estonian-language transcripts from the Integration Foundation conference of 27 June 2007. Most importantly, I owe a special debt of gratitude to Elena Nikiforova, whose assistance with the fieldwork and analysis of the materials collected for this chapter was – as always – priceless.

1   Many Estonians fought alongside Nazi Germany in what they perceived as a national liberation struggle against the USSR and its occupation of their homeland, making the monument and identification practices enacted at the site particularly powerful border performatives.
2   Latvia followed the same exclusionary practices. All other former union republics that gained independence in 1991 implemented a "zero-option" policy regarding citizenship, which meant that if you were a citizen of the union republic at the moment of independence you were automatically made a citizen of the independent state.
3   Interview with organizers of Nochnoy Dozor, conducted in Tallinn, July 2007.
4   I have reassembled the actualization of the event through in-depth interviews conducted in Tallinn by Elena Nikiforova and me between June and July 2007. Film footage of the event was also analyzed. For the latter, see Bronze Night 2007.
5   The feeling among participants in the riot as conveyed during interviews was that this destructive pulse was retribution for the destruction and desecration of what many perceived as a sacred site. At the time, rumors of the "dismemberment" of the bronze soldier statue were widespread. Of course, this rationalization for the riot was an after-the-act justification for what was a much more spontaneous and chaotic event.
6   Interviews conducted in Narva and Johvi, July 2007.
7   Interview conducted in Johvi, July 2007.
8   The Integration Foundation – a quasi-independent organization that ran the Integration Program – merged with the Migration Foundation and as of January 1, 2010 was renamed the Integration and Migration Foundation "Our People."
9   Interviews conducted at the Integration Foundation and the Population Minister's office, July 2007.
10   Interviews conducted at the Estonian Citizenship and Immigration Board, July 2007.

11   Interviews conducted by Elena Nikiforova and me in Narva, Estonia, July-Aug. 2008.
12   Although officials and foreign policy experts had used the term cyberwarfare earlier, this is the first time that a charge of cyberwar waged by one state against another was officially lodged.

REFERENCES

Aaviksoo, Jaak. 2007. Estonia: Defense Minister says bronze soldier had to go. Radio Free Europe/Radio Liberty, Russia, May 9.

Anderson, Ben and Harrison, Paul. 2010. The promise of non-representational theories. In Ben Anderson and Paul Harrison, eds, *Taking-Place: Non-Representational Theories and Geography*, pp. 1–34. Aldershot: Ashgate.

Ansip, Andrus. 2006. Press conference, Office of the Prime Minister of Estonia, May 25.

Ansip, Andrus. 2007. Speech of Prime Minister Andrus Ansip to the Riigikogu. Office of the Prime Minister of Estonia, Speeches, May 2.

Baltic Times. 2007. Estonia blasts UN, PACE for "propaganda" and "lies." Oct. 2.

BBC (British Broadcasting Corporation). 2009. War "statue" reappears in Estonia. May 10.

Brah, Avtar. 1996. *Cartographies of Diaspora.* London: Routledge.

Bronze Night. 2007. Bronze Night (film footage during the event shot by Estonia's Channel 2, coupled with follow-up interviews with participants in the events). Uploaded to YouTube, Sept. 18–19.

Brubaker, Rogers and Cooper, Frederick. 2000. Beyond identity. *Theory and Society* 29 (1): 1–47.

Butler, Judith. 1993. *Bodies That Matter.* New York: Routledge.

Butler, Judith. 1997. *Excitable Speech: A Politics of the Performative.* New York: Routledge.

Butler, Judith. 1999. *Gender Trouble: Feminism and the Subversion of Identity.* 2nd edn. New York: Routledge.

Chinn, Jeff and Kaiser, Robert. 1996. *The Russians as the New Minority in the Soviet Successor States.* Boulder: Westview.

Council of Europe. 2007. Memorandum to the Estonian Government: Assessment of the Progress Made in Implementing the 2004 Recommendations of the Commissioner for Human Rights of the Council of Europe. CommDH(2007)12, Strasbourg, July 11.

Deleuze, Gilles. 1990. *The Logic of Sense.* New York: Columbia University Press.

Deleuze, Gilles. 1994. *Difference and Repetition.* New York: Columbia University Press.

Deleuze, Gilles and Guattari, Felix. 1987. *A Thousand Plateaus: Capitalism and Schizophrenia.* Minneapolis: University of Minnesota Press.

Dewsbury, J.D. 2000. Performativity and the event: enacting a philosophy of difference. *Environment and Planning D: Society and Space* 18: 473–496.

Dewsbury, J.D. 2007. Unthinking subjects: Alain Badiou and the event of thought in thinking politics. *Transactions of the Institute of British Geographers* 32: 443–459.

Donnan, Hastings and Wilson, Thomas, eds. 1999. *Borders: Frontiers of Identity, Nation and State.* Oxford: Berg.

European Union. 2006. Council Regulation (EC) 1932/2006 of 21 December 2006 amending Regulation (EC) No 539/2001 listing the third countries whose nationals must be in possession of visas when crossing the external borders and those whose nationals are exempt from that requirement. *Official Journal of the European Union* L405 (Dec. 30): 23–34.

Fenton, Ben, Steele, John and Gardham, Duncan. 2006. Spy poisoned by radiation. *Telegraph*, Nov. 25.

Gregson, Nicky and Rose, Gillian. 2000. Taking Butler elsewhere: performativities, spatialities and subjectivities. *Environment and Planning D: Society and Space* 18: 433–452.

Grosz, Elizabeth. 2008. *Chaos, Territory, Art: Deleuze and the Framing of the Earth*. New York: Columbia University Press.

Guardian. 2007. Russia accused of unleashing cyberwar to disable Estonia. May 17.

Hage, Ghassan. 1996. The spatial imaginary of national practices: dwelling-domesticating /being-exterminating. *Environment and Planning D: Society and Space* 14: 463–485.

Haraway, Donna. 1990. A manifesto for cyborgs: science, technology and socialist feminism in the 1980s. In Linda Nicholson, ed., *Feminism/Postmodernism*, pp. 190–233. London: Routledge.

Ilves, Toomas. 2007a. My smozhem postroit' nashe obshchee budushchee. *Narvskaya Gazeta*, May 2.

Ilves, Toomas. 2007b. President of the Republic on Victory Day, 23 June 2007, in Rapla. President of the Republic of Estonia, Speeches. At http://www.president.ee/en/official-duties/speeches/index.html (accessed Nov. 2011).

Ilves, Toomas. 2007c. President Ilves: Every bridge has two ends. President of the Republic of Estonia, Press Release, May 29. At http://www.president.ee/en/media/press-releases/1412-president-ilves-every-bridge-has-two-ends/ (accessed Nov. 2011).

Integration Program. 2000. *State Programme: Integration in Estonian Society, 2000–2007*. Tallinn: Estonian State Government.

Integration Program. 2007. The Analyses of the Current Ethnic Relations and Integration Policy. Conference Sponsored by the Integration Foundation, Tallinn, June 27.

Jones, Reece. 2009. Categories, borders and boundaries. *Progress in Human Geography* 33: 174–189.

Kaiser, Robert. 1994. *The Geography of Nationalism in Russia and the USSR*. Princeton: Princeton University Press.

Kaiser, Robert. 1995. Nationalizing the work force: ethnic restratification in the newly independent states. *Post-Soviet Geography* 36: 87–111.

Kaiser, Robert. 2007. Estonia: the mouse that roared? At http://www.ssrc.org/features/view/estonia-the-mouse-that-roared/ (accessed Nov. 2011).

Kaiser, Robert and Nikiforova, Elena. 2006. Borderland spaces of identification and dis/location: multiscalar narratives and enactments of Seto identity and place in the Estonian-Russian borderlands. *Ethnic and Racial Studies* 29 (5): 928–958.

Kaiser, Robert and Nikiforova, Elena. 2008. The performativity of scale: the social construction of scale effects in Narva, Estonia. *Environment and Planning D: Society and Space* 26: 537–562.

Laclau, Ernesto and Mouffe, Chantal. 1985. *Hegemony and Socialist Strategy*. London: Verso.

Massumi, Brian. 2002. *Parables for the Virtual*. Durham: Duke University Press.

McCormack, Derek. 2007. Molecular affects in human geographies. *Environment and Planning A* 39: 359–377.

Mountz, Alison. 2003. Human smuggling, the transnational imaginary and everyday geographies of the nation-state. *Antipode* 35: 622–644.

Mountz, Alison. 2004. Embodying the nation-state: Canada's response to human smuggling. *Political Geography* 23: 323–345.

Natter, Wolfgang and Jones, III, John Paul. 1997. Identity, space, and other uncertainties. In Georges Benko and Ulf Strohmayer, eds, *Space and Social Theory*, pp. 141–161. Oxford: Blackwell.

Newman, David and Paasi, Anssi. 1998. Fences and neighbours in the postmodern world: boundary narratives in political geography. *Progress in Human Geography* 22: 186–207.

Patton, Paul. 1997. The world seen from within: Deleuze and the philosophy of events. *Theory and Event* 1 (1).

President of Russia. 2008. Dmitry Medvedev signed a decree on a visa-free regime for non-citizens, that is former citizens of the Soviet Union now living in Latvia and

Estonia. June 17. At http://archive.
kremlin.ru/eng/text/news/2008/06
/202640.shtml (accessed Nov. 2011).

Rajchman, John. 1991. *Philosophical Events:
Essays of the 1980s*. New York: Columbia
University Press.

Stengers, Isabelle. 2000. *The Invention of
Modern Science*. Minneapolis: University of
Minnesota Press.

van Houtum, Henk, Kramsch, Olivier and
Zierhofer, Wolfgang, eds. 2005. *B/ordering
Space*. Aldershot: Ashgate.

Volokhonskaya, Evgenia. 2007. Tallinnu
Nuzhna Nezavisimaya Programma Integrat-
sii. *Eesti Rahvusringhääling*. July 2.

Wilson, Thomas and Donnan, Hastings, eds.
1998. *Border Identities: Nation and State at
International Frontiers*. Cambridge: Cambridge University Press.

Woodward, Keith and Jones, III, John Paul.
2005. On the border with Deleuze and
Guattari. In Henk van Houtum, Olivier
Kramsch and Wolfgang Zierhofer, eds, *B/
ordering Space*, pp. 235–248. Aldershot:
Ashgate.

Woodward, Keith and Lea, Jennifer. 2010.
The geographies of affect. In Susan Smith,
Rachel Pain, Sallie Marston and John Paul
Jones, III, eds, *The Sage Handbook of Social
Geographies*, pp. 154–175. London: Sage.

31 Reconceptualizing the Space of the Mexico–US Borderline

Robert R. Alvarez, Jr

The anthropology and interdisciplinary study of borderlands has advanced in the last 20 years. New research on international borders and in continents that were less studied than the Mexico–US border has rapidly materialized (see Alper and Brunet-Jailly 2008). This is especially true of European and African scholarship (Anderson et al. 2003a, 2003b; Donnan and Wilson 1999; O'Dowd 2010; Feyissa 2010; Lentz 2003; Mbembe 2006; Nugent 2002; Wilson and Donnan 1998). The intense changes in the world's global system have altered processes on international borders and intensified how border study is conducted. In the twentieth century, European borders, for example, underwent tremendous change. Since 1989, approximately 8,000 miles of new state borders have been established in Central and Eastern Europe (O'Dowd 2003: 15). The collapse of the Berlin Wall and the creation of the European Union have created new borders, territories, frontiers and integration there. European borders manifest new forms of flexibility, cooperation and importance throughout the European states. As in Europe, crossings of the Mexico–US border – human as well as commercial and technological – have multiplied, and with them border complexity. The anthropology of borderlands, as in other disciplinary and interdisciplinary foci, has become global. Internal and external borders, boundaries and frontiers are part and parcel of the globalized world. This continuing surge of interest, however, raises important questions about how border scholars define and frame investigations and incorporate new imaginaries of borders – and in particular state borders. In this chapter I ask: How can we develop new types of methodological approaches – particularly utilizing ethnography – in border studies? How can the ethnographic encompass global processes and the contemporary lives of people while maintaining a local, ground-up perspective? How does the scholarly conceptualization of the border enact and forge our study? Rather than review the current state

A Companion to Border Studies, First Edition. Edited by Thomas M. Wilson and Hastings Donnan.
© 2012 Blackwell Publishing Ltd. Published 2012 by Blackwell Publishing Ltd.

of the anthropology of borderlands, I focus in this chapter on the Mexico–US border and assess how it has been studied and defined most recently. The goal of this preliminary gesture is to disrupt our border thinking and encourage discussion about border studies, specifically in relation to the Mexico–US border.

I argue here that border studies, and especially those of the Mexico–US border, would profit from a rethinking of the spatial imaginary of the border, a geopolitical cartography that is captured by the nation-state boundary. The metaphor I suggest is that of bridging. Bridging emphasizes connections and contrasts, spans and range to inform questions and scholarship. Bridges are not new to border studies, but as discussed below the current use of the metaphor of bridges relates primarily to cross-border cooperation, connection and integration. What I have in mind is a deeper and more multilayered concept of bridges and their processes than has previously been used in Mexico–US border studies. For example, Moraga and Anzaldúa's revolutionary *This Bridge Called My Back* (2002) evokes a meaningful alchemy of connection that is especially relevant to the Mexico–US border. The book focuses on the revelations of the experiences of a United States-Third World feminism and illustrates a relational and multilayered complexity. Through their gendered, racial, sentient and political crossings, the contributors invite a critical scrutiny of the status quo. As in Anzaldúa's (1987) earlier treatise, the border becomes a myriad of experience, a new imagining. Moraga and Anzaldúa ask: "How is connection actually separation?" (2002: 63). *This Bridge Called My Back* is based on a relational and comparative interpretation. It speaks of passages *through* not over, where multiple contradictions are bridged in an interdependence that spans and unites, yet replicates division. Similarly, our rendering of the horizontal line that is the Mexico–US border often misses the interconnections and the interdependence, and replicates divisions in the actual strip of towns and places, as well as beyond that cartography we call *la linea*. How are border towns, places and extended regions and their inhabitants connected? How, for example, might comparisons of Tijuana, Mexicali, El Paso, as well as geosocial points north and south, query social division, reciprocity and the ambience of the border itself?

Two principal interrelated arguments underlie this discussion. The first is that the geopolitical focus on the Mexico–US border frames scholarly investigation, and has also reproduced the border (and border studies) as state-centric. Border scholars have indeed challenged the power of the state's enactment of commercial and security measures (Andreas 2002; Dunn 1996, 2010; Nevins 2002; Palafox 2000). However, the focus on immigration controls, antiterrorism and the state's actions and policy have reinscribed the nation-state on the border and in border studies. This is made particularly relevant given the vast contrast of border studies in Europe. While the European Union, for example, exhibits a changing flexibility, systemic cooperation and connectivity of borders, the Mexico–US border maintains a strong geopolitical separation of the two nation-states. The permeability and changing nature of European borders is a stark contrast to the continuing image of the Mexico–US border as both symbol and marker of division, separation and difference. The second argument applies more generally to borders. Although representations of border crossings include connection, this connectivity is often not multidimensional, isolating sociological process, historical depth, and both relational and comparative understanding.

I suggest here that current border studies depend on a specific epistemology that conditions a particular way of seeing. This is especially relevant for ethnography.

CONDITIONED AND EMERGING RENDITIONS OF THE MEXICO–US BORDER

A variety of excellent research has provided new insights into the complexity of the Mexico–US border. The work of Heyman, for example, has focused specifically on the border in diverse ways and includes mobility, ports of entry, consumption, the border wall, entrapment and resistance, all ethnographically informed (e.g., Heyman 2008, 2009; Campbell and Heyman 2004, 2009). His earlier studies of the US Border Patrol, as well as labor, have also been germane (Heyman 1991, 1995, 2000, 2002).

Border scholars have also challenged the stereotype of Mexico–US border cities. Tijuana (like El Paso, see below), for example, is no longer tied exclusively to the "black legend" of its being a sin center of prostitution, gambling, drugs, and the peripheral hybrid that was depicted as marginally between Mexico and the United States. That is the Tijuana and border city of the past. Today, Tijuana is a vast metropolis, cosmopolitan, and very much a part of the Mexican nation. Yet there are new stereotypes. Muriá (2010) refers to the "Border Panopticon" – a controlling gaze that focuses on the zones and peoples of Tijuana. I would suggest that there is yet another "Border Panopticon" – the bounded gaze with which we scholars define and see the Mexico–US border.

Border scholarship has constructed a specific discourse that speaks to and of the border. Where once border studies were isolated investigations in the tradition of classic ethnography, broader genres are now defined. Maquiladoras are a good example. Fernandez-Kelly's watershed *For We Are Sold* (1983), as well as works by Peña (1997), Salzinger (2003a, 2003b) and Lugo (2008) (see also Wright 2003; Biemann 2002; Navarro 2002), illustrate a deepening and wide-ranging discourse on border industrialization, economy, labor and the changing face of late capitalism. Militarization and border control (Nevins 2002; Andreas 2002; Dunn 1996, 2010; Palafox 2000) are other sound examples of deepening themes and understanding of the Mexico–US border. Border literature has produced a richly textured canvas of border life that has begun to illustrate the vast diversity of the Mexico–US border range.

Yet, even with these positive developments, I have come to a rather odd conclusion: the scholarly rendition of the Mexico–US border itself produces specific frameworks that have also inhibited interpretation and understanding of current border society, culture and people. Over 15 years ago I argued that the US–Mexico border was the icon of the anthropological study of borders (Alvarez 1995). Today I would say that it has been the template of how most US-based scholars study and interpret this border. There is a difference. The iconic border revealed and questioned the complexities that are borders, the template becomes the manner in which we study and reproduce the border.

In the quest for understanding, border epistemology has produced a cartographic template of the geopolitical line. The Mexico–US border is viewed as a horizontal line and zone between nations in which crossings become the focus. It is a geopolitical boundary and barrier created by war and conquest. The Mexico–US border exhibits mobility but the emphasis, like all borders, is on separation and closure (Cunningham and Heyman 2004).

In this view, the 2,000-mile demarcation divides and creates conflicts and contradictions for the people who live there. Just as the studies of the early twentieth century defined the Mexico–US border as irrelevant (for example, it did not appear in the ethnographic record), our current scholarly emphasis on division, boundary and barrier continues to characterize the people and places of the border.

The Mexico–US border exhibits a diverse range of geography, cities, towns and populations along both of its sides. The emphasis has been on how the Mexico–US border defines the nation-state, yet the many boundaries that frame that expanse are often omitted. The state of California, for example, where I make my home, is (like other regions and US states) bounded and defined by numerous types of borders. It is not solely the Mexico–US border that defines the boundaries of the state. The Mexico–US geopolitical boundary frames the south, but California is also bordered and bounded by the Pacific and other US states – Nevada, Arizona and Oregon. California's border to the south is defined as a national border that abuts against Mexico. Yet the southern border also represents a global condition. The global here refers not only to the intense processes and human mobility of the current period but also to a deeper identification with the Americas. The global-border connects the US to the global south. This is a crucial aspect of the lives of people in Mexico and the hemisphere, as well as of those communities that stretch across the borderline to both the north and south, and also to the east and west.

Connections have been instrumental in descriptions of the Mexico–US border, yet it is not the border that connects. These connections and crossings are what much border work is about. But studies of the Mexico–US border continue to be tied, even when discussing crossings, to the horizontal line, that particular cartography, that edge, periphery and limit that extends west to east from the Playas of Tijuana to the Gulf of Mexico for 2,000 miles.

This "bounded-horizontal" gaze is emphasized by a decades-long persistence of particular texts that have defined border studies. Border studies are guided by a fundamental sociological and historical interpretation that might be viewed as a border trope. For example, Anzaldúa's (1987) now famous book continues to be the most referenced and staple reading and imagination of the border. It is rare to find a border study without Anzaldúa. The repercussions of Anzaldúa's *La Frontera* – that "open wound" – reverberate in even the most empirical of studies.

Gilmore introduces an interesting concept that, although aimed at political activism, is applicable to the notion of bridging presented here. Gilmore explores the concept of *desakota*, a Malay word meaning town-country "in which settlement, economic activity, politics, demographics and culture . . . belie categorization as 'either /or' – ambiguous places in the dominant typology of settlement and sector" (2008: 35). The goal of this kind of thinking is to compare "political, economic, territorial and ideological valences that *distinguish* and might *unite* disparate places shaped by external control or located outside particular developmental pathways" (2008: 35, emphasis in original). *Desakota* becomes a "mix, a region composed of places linked through coordinated as well as apparently uncoordinated forces of habitation and change" (2008: 36).

Although at one time "the border" was relatively undifferentiated in social science and historical scholarship, wherein towns, people, life, culture and society were seen to share "border" attributes, today border studies have illustrated the great variety and diverse processes of border life and society. However, there is a certain *desakota*, an ambiguity in our metaphor that is missing. What are the political, economic, territorial and ideological valences that both distinguish process and understanding, and unite (bridge) these disparate places outside of the border framework? Whereas the usefulness of border metaphor and the need for empirical reality was once debated (Heyman 1994; Vila 2003), today there is agreement that the border is real, but that it is also symbolic and metaphorical (Vila 2003). However, the embodiment has constructed a different type of barrier, one that constricts the imagination, the interpretation and the understanding of social process. The Mexico–US border scholarship has broken out of the realms of the folkloric and of isolated national-community studies. Where once we studied border sites and displaced "Mexican" and Native communities and social problems as cultural misunderstandings, there is now a realization that the borderlands are complex networks of social, cultural and political-economic behavior. People live, die and create cultural and social forms on this border.

Studies of musical genres are exemplary of a new reach and bridging across the border and illustrate the creative connections of cultural production and social activity. Simonett (2001), Hutchinson (2007), Ragland (2009), Lipsitz (2007) and Madrid (2008) focus on important cultural expressions that connect not only the border but also the cities of the north such as Los Angeles and Chicago. Madrid's *Nor-tec Rifa! Electronic Dance Music from Tijuana to the World* (2008) is an excellent example of this new genre. Madrid provides a Mexicanist border perspective of a hybrid musical form that was produced in Tijuana and crossed the US boundary but also the Atlantic Ocean to European audiences. The nature of this process goes beyond the Mexico–US border to connect vast regions and peoples but also bridging, let me emphasize – bridging – disparate social-cultural geographies as well as a global-cosmopolitan Mexicanness into youth culture. Youth throughout Europe, Mexico and Latin America, as well as in California, dance to the fused hip-rhythms of electronic and Mexican sounds. Here the mix of "traditional," that is, authentic musical forms of mariachi trumpets, conjunto accordion, the big bass umpah of the tuba and other riffs from banda, corrido and ranchera address identity but also a depth and range that is part of a new border age and process. Mexican authenticity in this genre is both redefined and rediscovered as border repertoire. Madrid's ethnography is fresh and nuanced, multisited, transborder, transnational and global. Nortec reaches across the border but also has a span that connects a broader range outside of our hemisphere.

Saldívar, in *The Borderlands of Culture* (2006), bridges the transnational border between the US Southwest, Texas, a "Greater Mexico" and the maritime border with Asia, through the life and work of Américo Paredes. Although focused on Texas and the US Southwest, Paredes' early career as war correspondent in Japan and his marriage to Amelia Sidzu Nagamine – (a Japanese-Mexican) evoke a broader mapping of both American and borderland studies as well as of the meaning and influence of border experience. It is clear through works such as these how border studies are generating new interpretations and sound, empirically grounded work.

One important development in the understanding of specific sites on the Mexico–US border is the long-term historical focus on connections and processes in specific places. This is especially true for Ciudad Juarez and El Paso. Beginning with Oscar Martinez (1978), Juarez-El Paso has been a place of much scholarly attention. Sadowski-Smith (2002), Vila (2000, 2003), Ortiz (2004), Lugo (2008) and Dunn (2010), among others, have provided deep and varied descriptions and understandings of society and life at Juarez-El Paso. This focus on Juarez-El Paso not only emphasizes the variety of border life in the places once masked simply as border towns, as sister cities, but also delves into the deep contrasts and connections in their history. In this depth, we see the variegated nature and complex nature of this border site.

In comparison to the range of ethnographic work on Juarez-El Paso, there is much less ethnographic depth for the San Diego-Tijuana border. The California-Baja California border boasts two of the largest cities on the border – Tijuana and Mexicali. Until recently, Price's *Tijuana: Urbanization in a Border City* (1973) was considered the only ethnographic work on that city and border. However, Muriá (2010) has reinterpreted the border region of the Californias as well as that of Mexico itself. She has inserted a specific Mexicanness into the border and illustrates how Tijuanenses were, in part, formed by their relationship to the city of San Diego across the line. Her study revolves around consumerism in the two nation-states and the centrifugal forces of national belonging in which Mexico reclaims this border city. This is not solely about crossing between San Diego and Tijuana, but about the connections and bridging across the border, and about the core of the Mexican nation.

Two decades ago the Mexico–US border was a different place, as was the region and hemisphere of which it is a part. The events post–9/11, border enforcement, the changing nature of not only the US and Mexico, but also of Latin America have compounded the complexity, realization and understanding of what the border is and represents. It is clear that the Mexico–US border is not only a barrier but a conduit, not solely to Mexico but to the Americas, to Asia and "the global south" through commerce, investment, ports of entry, immigration (Asian, African, Latin American, as well as Mexican and indigenous) and industrial transfer. These and other current processes have altered the border and "bridge" untapped sources and processes that include both land and maritime borders.

BORDERS AND THE NATION-STATE

The role of the nation-state beyond its borders raises important questions about the function and utility of "the border" as concept. Recently, many experts touted the demise of the nation-state. Yet the events of the last decade illustrate the rise, not the demise, of the nation-state. As the Mexico–US border became more prevalent and inflexible, a nascent nativism aimed at migrants as well as the power of the state reared its ugly head. Terrorism, increased immigration, border control and the emergence of the state's offshore activity in agriculture, immigration, commerce and the everyday activities of the South alert us to a state connectivity and influence that traverses the border itself. On the one hand, for example, the North American Free Trade Agreement (NAFTA) increased the dramatic and geometric growth of import/export exchange between Mexico, the US, and Canada (Chambers and Smith 2002), but on the other hand it closed and restricted human mobility along the geopolitical line, and within the US nation itself (Nevins 2002). This is evident not only in the northern range of the Mexico–US border, but also in the activity of the Mexican nation on the Mexico–Guatemala border (Galemba 2009).

Nation-state borders are the principal symbols of nation-state control but this simple conviction raises a variety of questions by border scholars (Donnan and Wilson 1999). Many of these queries have failed to materialize for the Mexico–US border. O'Dowd illustrates that borders of all types have become the fare of border studies in Europe. However, he emphasizes that state borders are "the most widely recognized and institutional dividers of world space" (2010: 1031). O'Dowd points to a significant dichotomy in the nature of state-centric studies. On the one hand, he relates a social science agenda focused on debates of a borderless world to a world of borders. In the "borderless world" view, globalization's new mobility, communication and connection created a world in which the state was no longer viable. In the "world of borders," a new emphasis, especially in Europe, is a condition of new territories, subnational regions and multiple borders, where the state is only one type of border among many (O'Dowd 2010: 1034). On the other hand, O'Dowd argues that social science (especially in Europe and the US) is symbolically tied to particular states and groups of states and to a worldview emanating from the dominant Western states. This raises important questions especially for the Mexico–US border. For example: Is the border synonymous with the nation-state? Is the border solely representative of the nation-state? Does the border define the nation-state? And if so, how and in what ways does the geopolitical border delineate the nation-state? On the Mexico–US border, the focus on the state border reproduces the state-centric focus on security and the maintenance of boundaries. There is an inadvertent recreation of the boundary that emphasizes the state and its control.[1]

There is a need not only to think beyond the Mexico–US border as an extension of the state's geographical control but also to examine how the state's offshore control influences ideology, practice and process beyond its border. What are the various dimensions of borders that relate to the larger questions of the nation-state, its influence and power? For example, how do the Canadian border, the Pacific and other maritime connections such as the Gulf of Mexico and the Gulf of California alert us to the workings of the bounded state, the definition of the nation-state? Maritime borders are part and parcel of border studies for the Baltic Sea and the Mediterranean, yet have failed to make their presence known in studies of the Mexico–US border. The challenge I believe is in how we imagine the border(s) – the line in the sand – and how we define borders. The epistemology of the border frames the methodology with which we query and ultimately interpret and represent the border. How do we encompass a wider range of border processes? In what ways do border studies shed light on the broader economic and social processes that are now part of hemispheric and global process? How do border studies engage the dramatic changes of the new millennium that have altered the globe, changed social and cultural expression and instilled new forms of hierarchy and structure in which the nation-state is central?

BORDERS AND BRIDGES

In 2009 I participated in a conference in Australia on food and the postcolonial city. The conference focused on Asian and Australian sites and provided a forum to exchange and compare divergent and parallel interests about food topics, agriculture, eating, and of course, borders (they are omnipresent!). The ensuing conversations turned to how Australian and Asian epistemologies contrasted with Western, that is, US and particularly Californian/Mexican, interpretations and experience. Immigration, ethnic diversity, agriculture, fair trade, culture and other themes provoked discussion and possibilities for new areas of research. These intellectual bridges connected similar areas of discourse and interest and they also provided valuable contrasts and comparisons. The discussion turned specifically to the notion of borders and bridges.

The metaphor of borders and bridges provides a refreshing cartography and architecture for border studies. The notion of bridges (and connection) is not new to border studies. Bridging, however, has primarily been defined by cross-border cooperation, integration and systemic policy (Anderson et al. 2003a, 2003b). Similarly, the idea of bridging has encompassed crossings in immigration, transborder communities and commodity chains. The concept of bridges invoked here introduces other variables and dimensions that challenge the horizontal vision of the borderline. It is not solely the crossings or cooperative ventures that are important, but the disparate connections, a *desakota*, the nodes, and the intervening process involved in the possible focus of study. Connections are not necessarily harmonious (see Grimson and Vila 2002). Bridges span turbulence and the underbelly, the subaltern. Borders and bridges connect contrasting venues and control crossings in varied manners. What I am suggesting is a different analytic to disrupt (not replace) the entrenched epistemology of the Mexico–US border. We are in need of a new architecture that builds on the studies and epistemology of the past; but that helps to break the cartography we have created to produce new analysis and understanding. The actuality and the metaphor of borders and bridges might help query both the restricted notion of the border and the study of specific processes that include entrance and closure, connectivity and contrasts, construction, historical depth and range in border thinking and empirical study. Rather than be restricted to the horizontal line in the sand and its constitutive imagining, let us be attentive to the broader spans and depth of process and human dimensions in our border lands/spaces/places.

This requires more than simply a provocative terminology; it also needs new conceptual tools. Like Gilmore's *desakota*, Anzaldúa introduced the useful notions of *nepantla* and ambivalence. These concepts challenge the idea of the "fixed line" and expand our perception of the border zone. Liminality becomes the in-between space of *nepantla*, "the space most of us occupy" (Anzaldúa 2002a: xxxvii). *Nepantla* recognizes our life in many worlds. "We do not inhabit un mundo but many" (2002a: xxxvii). Ambivalence as concept also provides a deeper sense of the negotiation of multiple worlds:

> You say my name is ambivalence? Think of me as Shiva, a many-armed and legged body with one foot on brown soil, one on white, one in straight society, one in the gay world, the man's world, the women's, one limb in the literary world, another in the working class, the socialist, and the occult worlds. A sort of spider woman hanging by one thin strand of web. (Anzaldúa 2002b: 228)

Nepantla in this sense expands the concept of bridges from the dimensions of crossing as connection, cooperation and integration. *Nepantla* evokes the multidimensional complexities of the border connecting disparate locations, social behavior and expression. Like *desakota*, *nepantla* evokes a varied and relational cartography that connects new and disparate perspectives. The state, for example, is released from the frontier and inhabits multiple venues.

THE ETHNOGRAPHIC CHALLENGE

My primary interest with borders and bridges is with the ethnographic, not solely as a method to study local human behavior but also as a conceptual parameter to address broad and complex spans of activity. The ethnographic is often synonymous with the local, the qualitative and the construction of everyday life. But the ethnographic lens also provides insight and query into broader institutional and structural influences that condition human behavior and societal process. Take, for example, Lugo's (2008) study of maquiladoras. Lugo begins by illustrating the deep place and connection of Juarez-El Paso with Mexico's colonial past, while illustrating the constructed border and its generative control through inspections in the entire Juarez-El Paso range. Utilizing a border narrative, Lugo exposes the racial, gendered and class connections among Mexicanos and Mexicanas of Juarez, people who live the border, labor in its industry and maneuver in the stronghold of the state and its economy. The maquilas are structural entities that are constructed by economic, commercial processes, but they have dramatically conditioned social forms and local relations, communities, the role of the nation-state, as well as society on both sides of the Mexico–US border. In the end, people's lives have changed dramatically not only along the border but also in the broader range and depth of the borderlands and mobile frontiers of the nation-state.

When I first began this essay, I found it useful to examine the reality of bridges on the border. In California there are no actual bridges that span the geopolitical line. In fact, where there is land on the border no bridges exist. Yet all the border crossings from Juarez-El Paso to Brownsville-Matamoros are bridges. Like all bridges, they are built over obstacles and are by design constructed to carry traffic of one sort or another. They all cross the "border," the Rio Bravo. They all differ not only in construction, but also in the flows of goods, histories and people. There are a total of 27 bridges that span and connect Texas to Mexico. The bridges themselves provoke important questions. In a recent study, his second on the border brick industry, Cook (2011) describes the sociocultural richness of the bridges in Starr, Hidalgo and Cameron Counties in Texas and the folks who use them. The historical rendition of changing commerce, as bricks, their producers, transporters and others cross the Pharr-Reynosa International Bridge and the Camargo-Rio Grande City Bridge, among others, illustrates a deep humanity in these connections. These are rich renditions of crossing strategies and of the obstacles faced on both sides of the Rio Bravo. They contain stories of Tejanos and Mexicanos who utilize, strategize, and mobilize on these bridges. This is a far different perception than that of the desert crossers who risk their lives in Arizona or the Juarez Range of Baja California, or of those of us who line up at the San Ysidro crossing to drive into San Diego. Yet, the mobilization, strategies and obstacles entailed in these land bridges are no less dramatic.

Another excellent example of bridges is the Danish-Swedish Øresund region (Bucken-Knapp 2003; O'Dell 2003). In 2000 a bridge was built to help integrate the economy and communication of the region. O'Dell, focusing on transnational mobility, illustrates the various nuances inherent in both the real and the conceptual notion of bridges. "Bridges can be understood as conduits of passage, points of support, facilitators of resonance, platforms of control and . . . streams of influence" (2003: 35). The Øresund Bridge became both symbol and physical manifestation, a social mechanism that produced tension between union and separation. According to O'Dell, bridges "treacherously steer us and limit our movement . . . They reference the perception of disjuncture in space as though the two points we now see as being unified had once been separated. The bridge tyrannically and exclusively prioritizes only two points of connection; it offers the appearance of freedom, while simultaneously shackling our potential of free movement" (2003: 38). This constructed frontier was fraught with uneasy tensions between juncture and disjuncture, freedom and constraint, harmony and discord. Rather than working to unify two territories, the Øresund Bridge reified the border between Sweden and Denmark. Hence, rather than "crossing" and "connecting," the bridge created a cacophony of disparate venues and processes along the border and between the two nation states.

The actual focus on transport bridges provides a comparison of another type. In a paper in which I focused on truck crossings at the Mexico–US border, I attempted to make sense of the current moves to negate that aspect of the NAFTA agreement that allows Mexican trucks into the US (Alvarez 2008). I began my inquiry into the perception, as argued by the US Congress, the Teamsters Union and the Sierra Club, that Mexican trucks were unsafe and would endanger US roads. Rather than focus on the border and the crossing of trucks, my investigation spanned the border and forced me to query the transportation infrastructure in Mexico. I discovered the deep tie of border trucking to an infrastructure that contains the longest privatized toll road system in the world, funded by the World Bank, and leads, as did the railroads in the early twentieth century, from the heart of Mexico to the US border, to US roads and highways.

The query on "border truck crossings" and the US policy banning Mexican trucks on "the border" led to a comparison with Canadian truck crossings at the

Canada–US border. In 2006 Canada crossed 6,650,000 trucks at the Canada–US border, almost 2 million more than Mexico, which had 4,750,000 (Bureau of Transportation Statistics 2011). However, it appears that to some at least only Mexico and its trucks will place the US nation in danger. This suggests a nativist and racialized sentiment toward the Mexicanness of trucks that was evident in a number of blogs discussing Mexican trucks as ethnic and race constructions (CBS News 2007). These "bridges" of comparison connecting the US's Canadian border to its Mexican frontier reveal insightful and important contradictions that also bridge commerce, nativism, ethnic identity, a neoliberal structure and the broad and deep contradiction of the nation-state in the North and the South in general, and of the US nation-state at its northern and southern borders in particular. These are connections of a different sort that reveal disparate but actual links and relations.

Applying the notion of borders and bridges to my own border repertoire, family migration, commerce, commodity chains, trucking, the nation-state and comparative borders (US–Mexico, southern Mexico, Canada) may help to illustrate how borders and bridges can add depth and understanding to the current border and nation-state social process. I do this cautiously as a re-analysis to emphasize not just the border and crossings, but also to illustrate how the geopolitical border is a natural part of larger contexts. These queries went "beyond the border" (see for example Alvarez 2006) and included my personal history and experience as a "Californio." This includes Baja California, Baja California Sur and the western Pacific Mexican states – it is a specific co-joining (bridging) of California and Mexico that relates to a certain *desakota*, a history, specific political-economy, regional memory and personal cartography of the border and borderlands. The "border" here is not about the fixed barrier and inspection site(s) that we cross between nations (see Lugo 2008). Events and experiences on the "line" are just that – isolated events. In my repertoire, "the border" means specific places in Baja California: Tijuana, Tecate, Ensenada, Mexicali, the Valle de la Trinidad, the company mines of the Southern Mexican Peninsula; places from which my folks emerged. It conjures up the deep sentiment and meaning that is place with embedded memory (Basso 1996). It is my grandmother who was PaiPai from El Real del Castillo, my grandfather who was a "Smith" from Comondú; it is the Coahuila (Tijuana) of my youth and the Mexican packing sheds of chilis and markets of my "frutero" market life along the Rio de Tijuana (Alvarez 2005). It is Mexico, Lemon Grove and Logan Heights in San Diego, and the array of *parientes* and friends who make up this cartography of life. It is the deepened territory, a *desakota* and *nepantla*, of personal history, and a belonging that connects and bridges – not crosses – the border range.

These genres are often classified as border studies because of the crossings of and immediacy of the Mexico–US border. Yet a central aspect of this work has not been the "border," not the geopolitical line, nor the metaphorical hybrid of the borderlands. It is not about territory, territorialization (as in control), reterritorialization (reclaiming land and identity), or deterritorialization (losing them). This is about the deep belonging and identifying with place, a bridging and continuous connection of everyday life, of social and cultural activity. I am reminded here of Flynn (1997), where the folks along the Nigeria–Benin African border controlled the meaning, practicality and everyday use and life of the border.

In 1987 when the United States Department of Agriculture (USDA) enforced an Environmental Protection Agency change in the processing and distribution of export mangos, I began studying the US-Mexican mango trade (Alvarez 2005). I focused on Mexican entrepreneurs: mangueros and their adaptive strategies in producing, distributing and complying with USDA initiatives. My initial interest was not the border, but broader connections, in market control and participation. The question was a simple one: How do mangueros like other fruit exporters get their product to market? Because the market is in the United States (Los Angeles, California), the question included: How do mangueros maneuver the border as a complex process that is tied to production and distribution, where control and the border were links in a deeper matrix created by the institutions of the nation-state? Eventually this query led to a focus on the power of the state – not on the border – and on the deeper historical relevance of mango discovery, hybridization and transfer. The sociohistoric tracing of mangos across the Mexico–US border links deep social-cultural dimensions of cross-border hierarchy (Alvarez 2005). Mangos exemplify the enactment of current trade policy in global/transnational process, with the twentieth-century initiation of nation-state power, as well as the institutional connection to current trade relations and control. The cross-border mango commodity chain exposes a complex array of people who are linked between and across social networks, power and history. Mangos reveal a larger scenario that extends beyond the fruit and vegetable global market. The mango commodity chain, like the Mexico–US border itself, is more than a linear one-dimensional phenomenon. There is a deep and vertical structure here that exposes social complexity, hierarchy and dominance, that *desakota* of "political, economic, territorial and ideological valences that *distinguish* and *unite* disparate places" and venues (Gilmore 2008: 35).

Take for example that the USDA, through the Office of Foreign Plant and Seed Introduction (Alvarez 2007), not only introduced mangos to the US, but also hybridized them in Coconut Grove, Florida, and ultimately introduced specific commercial varieties of mangos to the global South. More than an interesting quirk in fruit history, this plant transfer illustrates the vast control of the US nation as an offshore entity, with a range that includes the nineteenth-century global exploration and introduction of vegetable and fruit crops for economic purposes and the twentieth-century responses of Mexican entrepreneurs in rural Mexico. The border comes into play here because mangos, like other Mexican export commodities, must cross the border. These "connections" entail a complex matrix of nation-state processes that includes plant transfer to the south, as well as importing the fruit back across the border. A deep history of USDA plant exploration, introduction and hybridization was fundamental in the creation of the Mexico–US mango market. From the perspective of market control, the border was only a part of this larger process. Nation-state control has spanned the border and linked the economic, territorial and ideological, uniting these places and processes. The point here is that this "border" process has historical antecedents and is tied to the societal changes incurred by the strategic plans and policy of the nation-state. The complex social construction of this specific market activity – mangos – is lost if we concentrate on separation, difference and the border crossing. The ethnographic here aims at understanding the conditions and power of the nation-state and its representative institutions.[2]

The nation-state is a defining entity of border studies yet its nonlocal character and complex nature has eluded much ethnographic research. Although it is easy to see the state as a marker of control and power, it has been less easy to take the nation-state in its many dimensions as a border crosser and connector of social behavior. This may strike the reader as a misnomer, because borders themselves have been the defining parameters of the nation-state. The conflicting and complex relationships of the abutment of the US and Mexican nation-states, cultures, politics and commerce are measured and defined in relation to the border as a condition of contrast and separation. Nation-states are defined territorially by that boundary. Even when the border or borders are viewed as membranes and a hybrid, it is the boundary that is utilized as the referent.

The US-Mexican border is more than a geopolitical line. Border activities extend into the maritime borders of the gulfs of Mexico and California, the Pacific and Atlantic. However, "the border" as we define it represents a specific geography as it co-joins, mixes, separates, and creates, on that line. This framework has harnessed border studies and the interpretation of the borderlands themselves. More importantly, it narrows the broader reality of the sociopolitical, economic and social order enacted between the nations and the way in which people live today. Transnational processes, in the new intensity of global activity and engagement, are crucial for understanding and reinterpreting transborder settlement, history and border sites. My intent is not to dismiss these processes but to reconfigure and create new imaginations and investigation of the border itself, to encompass both a broader and deeper cartographic and contemporary border reality.

In retrospect, I see how my own research revolves around processes in which the border becomes meaningful, but realize that the border itself was not a central focus. My book *Familia* (Alvarez 1991) focused on migration and the US settlement of Baja Californianos but aimed to salvage human social process and agency in the immigration debate that at the time was captivated by a purely economic interpretation. It was not about the process of crossing borders. In the chili trade and among *chileros* (Alvarez 2005), the border was part of the commercial activity influencing markets in Los Angeles and Mexico as well as people on both sides of the border. But it was the broader bridging of the personnel and commercial system that made up this trade, including the processes of the control and the engagement of distributors in Los Angeles, producers in the Mexican south, and folks at all social levels and on both sides of the geopolitical line, that were paramount. The ethnohistorical research I conducted on Lemon Grove (Alvarez 1986) was contextualized and framed by what we might call border studies. Lemon Grove is about immigrant Mexicans, with strong ties to family and places across the border. These border settlers utilized their Mexicanness to challenge US-California law, yet the border itself was tangential to the process of their successful settlement and long-term association with Mexico.

Each of these themes can be viewed as bridges with particular flows of personnel and process. Like all bridges, these activities carry a certain type of traffic. The questions that emerge are not about the border but the range of transborder connections and the depth of their influence, meaning and reach. Rather than maintain the tropes of the border might we not ask what types of bridges do borders build and what do they connect? How can we explore the complexity created by bridges and connections without relying on the crosscutting, horizontal edge that separates and maintains that panopticon of control over how we see and define the nature of our studies?

The Recurrent Themes of the Anthropology of the Borderlands

In the last two decades the Mexico–US border has continued to be the focus of strong ethnography and interdisciplinary research. The existing themes of immigration, contraband, commerce, militarization and labor continue to be highlighted in border studies. Gender, citizenship and other themes reveal the complex engagement of people on both sides of the Mexico–US border and a growing trend to engage the complexity of life and society in the bordered zones of the geopolitical line. However, there remains a variety of areas that have not been engaged. Although borders, as in the world in general, have become closer because of media, technology and international trade pacts such as NAFTA, the Central America Free Trade Agreement, Plan Panama and others, there has been very little comparison of national borders, and the influence of the connected processes (bridges) inherent in these areas. This is especially evident with the borders of the United States. Although we realize that Canada and Mexico define the limitations of some aspects of US geography, these entities are rarely brought into conversation concerning the role of the state, or the contrasts of settlements, cities, communities or social-cultural behavior that illustrate similarities and linkages in border and social processes (see Sadowski-Smith 2002). And although there is an increasing focus on the southern border of Mexico (Basail Rodriguez 2005; Fabrigas-Puig 1996; Galemba 2009; Hernandez-Castillo 2001; Villafuentes Solis and Garcia Aguilar 2005), comparisons of the Mexican nation-state's northern border with the US and the Guatemalan border are extremely rare. This is especially important considering the growing interest in Mexico's southern border. What might such comparison and bridging tell us about the Mexican nation? About the US? The hemisphere? About the people who live on and cross these borders?

As stated above, the maritime borders of the nation as part of the "borderlands" have yet to be included in Mexico–US border studies. On the Mexico–US border, we appear to be stuck with the notion that it is only in the landed range of the frontier with the Americas that the borderlands are realized. The export fruit trade in Mexico, for example, is a venture that is not solely oriented toward the Mexico–US borderlands, it is also realized through maritime borders. Limes, mangos and other export produce are shipped east in great quantity to Europe as well as west to Asian markets. Maritime borders and their ports of entry are utilized not only for commerce but also for human immigration and traffic. Border scholars need to address these other borders that aim east and west and contrast them with the north–south axis.

Curiously, although the border is marked as a principal gauge in the controlling parameters of the state, we have yet to determine where the border and control end. The metaphorical uses of boundaries and control are invoked for places and regions throughout the US, yet this analytic is not applied outside of the US nation-state. Border mobility and place-making, in sites on both sides of the border cartography, warrant a broader investigation. Mobility, in addition, goes beyond the crossing of people. In a recent review of transport in Dallas, Kemper et al. (2007) document not only the volume of human traffic carried by mini-vans and motor carriers from Dallas into Mexico but a sophisticated network of resources, complex transport and human capital that has evolved as a result of immigrant and place networks that span the geopolitical line.

The focus on the border process replicated away from the border – as in Homeland Security raids in Iowa (Duara et al 2008), or in immigration law such as Arizona's 1070 (the broadest and strictest US immigration measure in generations, that would make the failure to carry immigration documents a crime and give the police broad power to detain anyone suspected of being in the country illegally) – explicitly expressed as "border control," relates directly to the nation and state power. As I have argued above, much scholarship on the nation-state revolves around issues of militarization, immigration policy and neoliberal models of trade, but with little attention paid to how the nation-state functions as a border (writ large) agency that crosses both the geopolitical boundary and polices the interior range of the state, while influencing offshore process and relationships, exercising control over human bodies throughout the hemisphere. The nation-state is not tied to its borders.

I suggest the notion of borders and bridges to raise questions and queries that might help dislodge the particularistic framework and reproduction of the Mexico–US border. Rather than maintain the epistemology of a horizontal line and separation, the notion of borders and bridges places emphasis on the connections, links and contrasts, the broad and deep range that is brought together by border processes and actors and institutions that include the nation-state. Bridges are built to be crossed and they span obstacles. They are connectors of the diverse and disparate, as well as of the history and meanings of people and places.

NOTES

I am very grateful to Pal Ahluwalia for suggesting the notion of "borders and bridges," Elana Zilberg, Hastings Donnan and Thomas Wilson for helpful comments that greatly improved this chapter. I also thank R. Aída Hernández Castillo and the *Journal of Latin American and Caribbean Studies* in which an earlier version of this chapter appeared and which this version substantially develops and extends.

1   O'Dowd argues that border studies have inadvertently neglected the importance of state borders, yet discusses how they are deeply embedded in the manner in which social scientists "think about social change, mobility and immobility, inclusion and exclusion, domestic and foreign, national and international, internal and external, us and them" (2010: 1034).

2   O'Dowd (2010) makes a strong argument for the inclusion of historical analysis of borders and boundedness especially as it relates to state and nation formation.

REFERENCES

Alper, Donald and Brunet-Jailly, Emmanuel, eds. 2008. Rarely studied borders. *Journal of Borderland Studies* 23 (3).

Alvarez, Robert R., Jr. 1986. The Lemon Grove incident: the nation's first successful desegregation court case. *Journal of San Diego History* 32 (2): 116–136.

Alvarez, Robert R., Jr. 1991. *Familia: Migration and Adaptation in Alta and Baja California*. Berkeley: University of California Press. First publ. 1987.

Alvarez, Robert R., Jr. 1995. The Mexico–US border: the making of an anthropology of borderlands. *Annual Review of Anthropology* 24: 447–470.

Alvarez, Robert R., Jr. 2005. *Mangos, Chiles and Truckers*. Minneapolis: University of Minnesota Press.

Alvarez, Robert R., Jr. 2006. The transnational state and empire: US certification in the Mexican mango and Persian lime industries. *Human Organization* 65 (1): 35–46.

Alvarez, Robert R., Jr. 2007. The march of empire: mangos, avocados and the politics of transfer. *Gastronomica* 28: 28–34.

Alvarez, Robert R., Jr. 2008. Roads, trucks and drivers: neoliberalism and distribution at the Mexico–US border. Paper presented at Society for Applied Anthropology meeting, Santa Fe, New Mexico.

Anderson, James, O'Dowd, Liam and Wilson, Thomas M., eds. 2003a. *Culture and Cooperation in Europe's Borderlands*. Amsterdam: Rodopi.

Anderson, James, O'Dowd, Liam and Wilson, Thomas, eds. 2003b. *New Borders for a Changing Europe: Cross Border Cooperation and Governance*. London: Frank Cass.

Andreas, Peter. 2002. *Border Games*. Ithaca: Cornell University Press.

Anzaldúa, Gloria. 1987. *Borderlands/La Fronter: The New Mestiza*. San Francisco: Aunt Lute Press.

Anzaldúa, Gloria. 2002a. Foreword. In Cherríe L. Moraga and Gloria E. Anzaldúa, eds, *This Bridge Called My Back*, pp. xxxiv–xxxix. Berkeley: Third Woman Press.

Anzaldúa, Gloria. 2002b. La Prieta. In Cherríe L. Moraga and Gloria E. Anzaldúa, eds, *This Bridge Called My Back*, pp. 220–223. Berkeley: Third Woman Press.

Basail Rodriguez, Alain, ed. 2005. *Fronteras desbordadas. Ensayos sobre la frontera sur de México*. Chiapas, Mexico: Universidad de Ciencias y Artes.

Basso, Keith. 1996. *Wisdom Sits in Places*. Albuquerque: University of New Mexico Press.

Biemann, Ursula. 2002. Performing the border: on gender, transnational bodies, and technology. In Claudia Sadowski-Smith, ed., *Globalization on the Line*, pp. 99–120. New York: Palgrave.

Bucken-Knapp, Gregg. 2003. Shaping possible integration in the emerging cross-border Øresund region. In James Anderson, Liam O'Dowd and Thomas M. Wilson, eds, *Culture and Cooperation in Europe's Borderlands*, pp. 55–80. Amsterdam: Rodopi.

Bureau of Transportation Statistics. 2011. US-Mexican border land-freight gateways: number of incoming truck or rail container crossings. At http://www.bts.gov/publications/national_transportation_statistics/html/table_01_54.html (accessed Dec. 2011).

Campbell, Howard and Heyman, Josiah McC. 2004. Slantwise: beyond domination and resistance on the border. *Journal of Contemporary Ethnography* 36 (1): 3–30.

Campbell, Howard and Heyman, Josiah McC. 2009. The study of borderlands consumption: potentials and precautions. In Alexis McCrossen, ed., *Land of Necessity: Consumer Culture in the United States–Mexico Borderlands*, pp. 325–332. Durham: Duke University Press.

CBS News. 2007. Court: Mexican trucks can drive in US. Sept. 3. See http://www.cbsnews.com/stories/2007/09/01/national/main3227439.shtml (accessed Dec. 2011).

Chambers, Edward J. and Smith, Peter H. 2002. *NAFTA in the New Millennium*. Edmonton: University of Alberta Press.

Cook, Scott. 2011. *Handmade Brick for Texas*. Lanham: Lexington Books.

Cunningham, Hilary and Heyman, Josiah McC., eds. 2004, *Movement on the Margins: Mobilities and Enclosures at Borders*. Special issue of *Identities: Global Studies in Culture and Power* 11 (3).

Donnan, Hastings and Wilson, Thomas M. 1999. *Borders: Frontiers of Identity, Nation and State*. Oxford: Berg.

Duara, Nigel, Petroski, William and Chutte, Grant. 2008. Claims of ID fraud leads to largest raid in state history. DesmoinesRegister.com. At http://www.desmoinesregister.com/article/20080512/NEWS/80512012/Claims-ID-fraud-lead-largest-raid-state-history (accessed Nov. 2011).

Dunn, Timothy. 1996. *The Militarization of the US–Mexico Border: 1972–1992*. Austin: University of Texas Press.

Dunn, Timothy. 2010. *Blockading the Border and Human Rights: The El Paso Operation that Remade Immigration Enforcement*. Austin: University of Texas Press.

Fábrigas-Puig, Andres. 1996. Desde el sur. Una revisión del concepto de frontera. *Fronteras* 1 (1): 10–15.

Fernandez-Kelly, Maria Patricia. 1983. *For We Are Sold, I and My People: Women and Industry in Mexico's Frontier*. Albany: State University of New York Press.

Feyissa, Dereje. 2010. *Borders and Borderlands as Resources in the Horn of Africa*. London: James Currey.

Flynn, Donna K. 1997. "We are the border": identity, exchange, and the state along the Bénin–Nigeria border. *American Ethnologist* 24 (2): 311–330.

Galemba, Rebecca. 2009. "We Are Crossed": The Politics of Nationality and Citizenship at the Mexico–Guatemala Border. Paper presented at Harvard University Social Studies Colloquium. Oct.

Gilmore, Ruth Wilson. 2008. Forgotten places and the seeds of grassroots planning. In Charles R. Hale, ed., *Engaging Contradictions*, pp. 31–62. Berkeley: University of California Press.

Grimson, Alejandro and Vila, Pablo. 2002. Forgotten border actors: the border reinforcers. a comparison between the US–Mexico border and South American borders. *Journal of Political Ecology* 9: 69–88.

Hernandez-Castillo, Aida R. 2001. *Histories and Stories from Chiapas: Border Identities in Southern Mexico*. Austin: University of Texas Press.

Heyman, Josiah McC. 1991. *Life and Labor on the Border: Working People of Northeastern Sonora, Mexico, 1886–1986*. Tucson: University of Arizona Press.

Heyman, Josiah McC. 1994. The Mexico–United States border in anthropology: a critique and reformulation. *Journal of Political Ecology* 1: 43–65.

Heyman, Josiah McC. 1995. Putting power into the anthropology of bureaucracy: the immigration and naturalization service at the Mexico–United States border. *Current Anthropology* 36 (2): 261–287.

Heyman, Josiah McC. 2000. Respect for outsiders? Respect for the law? The moral evaluation of high-scale issues by US immigration officers. *Journal of the Royal Anthropological Institute* 6 (4): 635–652.

Heyman, Josiah McC. 2002. US immigration officers of Mexican ancestry as Mexican Americans, citizens and immigration police. *Current Anthropology* 43 (3): 479–507.

Heyman, Josiah McC. 2008. Constructing a virtual wall: race and citizenship in US–Mexico Border policing. *Journal of the Southwest* 50 (3): 305–334.

Heyman, Josiah McC. 2009. Ports of entry in the "homeland security" era: inequality of mobility and the securitization of transnational flows. In Samuel Martinez, ed., *International Migration and Human Rights: The Global Repercussions of US Policy*, pp. 44–59. Berkeley: University of California Press.

Hutchinson, Sydney. 2007. *From Quebradita to Duranguense*. Tucson: University of Arizona Press.

Kemper, Robert V., Adkins, Julie, Flores, Mario and Santos, José Leonardo. 2007. From undocumented camionetas (minivans) to federally regulated motor carriers:

Hispanic transportation in Dallas, Texas and beyond. *Urban Anthropology* 36 (4): 381–423.

Lentz, Carola. 2003. This is Ghanaian territory! Land conflicts on a West African border. *American Ethnologist* 30 (2): 273–289.

Lipsitz, George. 2007. Banda: the hidden history of Greater Mexico. In George Lipsitz, *Footsteps in the Dark*. Minneapolis: University of Minnesota Press.

Lugo, Alejandro. 2008. *Fragmented Lives, Assembled Parts*. Austin: University of Texas Press.

Madrid, Alejandro L. 2008. *Nor-tec Rifa! Electronic Dance Music from Tijuana to the World*. Oxford: Oxford University Press.

Martinez, Oscar. 1978. *Border Boomtown: Ciudad Juarez since 1848*. Austin: University of Texas Press.

Mbembe, A. 2006. At the edge of the world: boundaries, territoriality, and sovereignty in Africa. In P. James and P. Darby, eds, *Globalization and Violence*, vol. 2: *Colonial and Postcolonial Globalizations*, pp. 148–171. London: Sage.

Moraga, Cherríe L. and Anzaldúa, Gloria E., eds. 2002. *This Bridge Called My Back*. Berkeley: Third Woman Press.

Muriá, Magalí. 2010. Enforcing borders: globalization, state power and the geography of cross-border consumption in Tijuana, Mexico. PhD. diss., Department of Communication, University of California, San Diego.

Navarro, Sharon A. 2002. Las voces de esperanza/voices of hope: la mujer obrera, transnationalism, and NAFTA displaced women workers in the US–Mexico borderlands. In Claudia Sadowski-Smith, ed., *Globalization on the Line*, pp. 183–200. New York: Palgrave.

Nevins, Joseph. 2002. *Operation Gatekeeper*. New York: Routledge.

Nugent, Paul. 2002. *Smugglers, Secessionists and Loyal Citizens on the Ghana–Togo Frontier*. Athens: Ohio University Press.

O'Dell, Tom 2003. Øresund and the regionauts. In James Anderson, Liam O'Dowd and Thomas M. Wilson, eds, *Culture and Cooperation in Europe's Borderlands*, pp. 31–53. Amsterdam: Rodopi.

O'Dowd, Liam. 2003. The changing significance of European borders. In James Anderson, Liam O'Dowd and Thomas M. Wilson, eds, *New Borders for a Changing Europe: Cross Border Cooperation and Governance*, pp. 13–36. London: Frank Cass.

O'Dowd, Liam. 2010. From a "borderless world" to a "world of borders": "bringing history back in." *Environment and Planning D: Society and Space* 28: 1031–1050.

Ortiz, Victor. 2004. *El Paso: Local Frontiers at a Global Crossroads*. Minneapolis: University of Minnesota.

Palafox, José. 2000. Open up borderlands studies: a review of US–Mexico border militarization discourse. *Social Justice* 27 (3): 56–72.

Peña, Devon G. 1997. *The Terror of the Machine*. Austin: University of Texas Press.

Price, John. 1973. *Tijuana: Urbanization in a Border City*. South Bend, IN: University of Notre Dame Press.

Ragland, Cathy. 2009. *Música Norteña: Mexican Migrants Creating a Nation between Nations*. Philadelphia: Temple University Press.

Sadowski-Smith, Claudia, ed. 2002. *Globalization on the Line: Culture, Capital, and Citizenship at US Borders*. New York: Palgrave.

Saldívar, Ramón. 2006. *The Borderlands of Culture: Américo Paredes and the Transnational Imaginary*. Durham: Duke University Press.

Salzinger, Leslie. 2003a. *Genders in Production: Making Workers in Mexico's Global Factories*. Berkeley: University of California Press.

Salzinger, Leslie. 2003b. Reforming the traditional Mexican woman: making subjects in a border factory. In Pablo Vila, ed., *Ethnography at the Border*, pp. 46–72. Minneapolis: University of Minnesota Press.

Simonett, Helena. 2001. *Banda: Mexican Musical Life across Borders*. Middletown, CT: Wesleyan University Press.

Vila, Pablo. 2000. *Crossing Borders, Reinforcing Borders: Social Categories, Metaphors and Narrative Identities on the US–Mexico Frontier.* Austin: University of Texas Press.

Vila, Pablo, ed. 2003. *Ethnography at the Border.* Minneapolis: University of Minnesota Press.

Villafuentes Solis, Daniel and Garcia Aguilar, Maria del Carmen. 2005. Las fronteras de la frontera sur. In Alain Basail Rodriguez, ed., *Fronteras Desbordadas. Ensayos sobre la frontera sur de Mexico*, pp. 123–52. Chiapas, Mexico: Universidad de Ciencias y Artes.

Wilson, Thomas M. and Donnan, Hastings, eds. 1998. *Border Identities: Nation and State at International Frontiers.* Cambridge: Cambridge University Press.

Wright, Melissa. 2003. The politics of relocation: gender, nationality, and value in a Mexican maquiladora. In Pablo Vila, ed., *Ethnography at the Border*, pp. 23–45. Minneapolis: University of Minnesota Press.

CHAPTER 32

Border Towns and Cities in Comparative Perspective

Paul Nugent

Border towns, taken here to include smaller urban settlements as well as very large conurbations, have dominated borderlands research during the past half-century. The reasons why they have attracted such attention are many, but for the purposes of this article they can be reduced to five. First, whereas international boundaries are, at one level, abstractions located at the sometimes clumsy interface between international law and cartography, their concrete manifestations are all too readily apparent in the tensions and contradictions embodied in border towns. There is an immediacy about everyday realities in these settlements that has rendered them especially intriguing for researchers. Secondly, border towns provide a telling insight into the geographies of wealth and power. The most studied border regions are those where the disparities between one country and the next manifest themselves in contrasting physical aspects – gleaming towers that rise upwards versus simple brick structures that sprawl outwards (Arreola and Curtis 1993) – and differential levels of state presence on opposite sides of the line. Hence, neighboring towns often stand as symbols for other kinds of unequal relationships. This is graphically illustrated along the United States–Mexico border, but also along the borders between South Africa and its neighbors (e.g., Lesotho and Mozambique) and on the external boundaries of the European Union (EU).

Thirdly, for those researchers who are interested in urbanism in its own right, a paradox resides in the disjuncture between the universalism that cities are supposed to embody and the parochialism of everyday border regulation. This matters for urban anthropologists, sociologists and others seeking to engage with the everyday life of international boundaries. Fourthly, for those more interested in the state and its attendant effects, border towns provide an excellent insight into how states seek to promote their agendas and how their advances are received, appropriated and very

A Companion to Border Studies, First Edition. Edited by Thomas M. Wilson and Hastings Donnan.

often thwarted. In the case of smaller entities, an additional anomaly often resides in a level of state presence that appears disproportionate to the size of the towns in question. Finally, border towns often function as social laboratories in which international protocols are given practical effect (or not) through the application of novel technologies of border management – what Tony Payan (2006b), with reference to the US, refers to as the "Panopticon Border." In many cases, the pursuit of cross-border cooperation, typically within the framework of regional integration, and the tighter regulation of border flows – focusing on narcotics, conflict resources, human trafficking and firearms – compete for attention. In other words, it is within border towns and cities that it is possible to discern the emergence of new and hybridized forms of governance. In some cases, what is apparent is an attempt by the state to impose its will in traditional fashion, while in others what is more striking is the emergence of powerful nonstate actors who derive their wealth and influence from their strategic position in transnational networks and whose operations set limits on the exercise of sovereignty. The latter is especially apparent in conflict zones where high volumes of trade can coexist with endemic violence.

While there are very many reasons why research on border towns has flourished, the trajectory is clear enough. There is more research being conducted on borderlands than ever before, with a noticeable resurgence in Asia and Africa, and this is likely to concentrate heavily on border towns in the future. In view of the fact that the majority of the world's population is now officially urban, and given the transboundary implications of climate change scenarios, it can safely be assumed that borderlands research will continue to invest heavily in this particular area. In addition, the fact that changing patterns of sovereignty are often most readily apparent in border zones means that border towns and cities provide a window onto unfolding patterns of governance in the contemporary world.

What Are Border Towns?

The answer to the question of what border towns/cities are might seem so obvious as to scarcely need articulation. However, the commonsense answer that they are population centers located on either side of an international border has not found universal favor with borderland scholars. In the words of Jan Buursink: "A *border city* is, in our opinion, a place that is more or less dependent on the border for its existence. That is to say, it's not just a city located close to the border, but it also came into existence because of the border" (2001: 7–8).

It is perfectly possible for towns to face each other across the line, but to have fairly minimal mutual interaction, either because the border is relatively impermeable or because the towns in question are orientated toward their respective centers and have their backs turned to each other. Buursink also questions the tendency to refer to towns that are located on opposite side of a border as "twin cities," which implies that they enjoy a reciprocal relationship, whereas historic settlements have often been in competition with one another, or have evolved separately.

Another reason for deploying terms with some care is that appearances can be deceptive. If two towns face each other across a border, that implies nothing about the underlying causalities. It may be that the towns in question existed prior to the demarcation of an international boundary, or were indeed the same town that was subdivided. Given that some of the most important urban centers have historically developed out of the commercial advantages conferred by waterways – with cities often straddling rivers – and given also that so many international borders have been made to follow bodies of water, it is not too surprising that border towns have ended up facing each other across rivers and lakes. This is true of many European border cities. A similar logic is apparent in the case of towns that have been established at either end of a mountain pass. Like rivers, mountains have often created convenient dividing lines, creating border towns of a particular subtype. Nevertheless, the act of drawing a border may also lead to the sprouting of entirely new settlements in response to the dynamics that borders create. Where different economic regimes are installed, which may translate into separate customs duties and prohibitions on specific trade goods, this tends to create an incentive to engage in trade – whether of the legal or the illicit variety. The importance of cross-border shopping in stimulating new hotspots of economic activity has been recognized in a number of different contexts (Donnan 1999; Timothy and Butler 2005). Again, where there are acute income inequalities on either side of an international boundary, border settlements may become a focus for would-be migrants seeking to enter the land of greater opportunity. The so-called trampoline towns on the Mexico–United States border are a classic illustration of this phenomenon. Border crossings may also take the form of selective use of social amenities, such as health and educational facilities, on the more richly endowed side of the line. Although the relationship between the towns/ cities may seem to be very close, the "twin" relationship may be categorically denied by the side that sees itself as the net loser.

The rest of this chapter seeks to map out some of the variations in the historical evolution and contemporary dynamics of border towns through comparisons drawn from three continents: namely, North America, Europe and Africa. In each case, the intention is to contrast both the historical processes that have led to the emergence of border towns and to explore the different ways in which they have related to each other. The underlying contention here is that while border spaces have operated in significantly different ways in the three regions, comparisons can nevertheless be highly instructive because they alert us to the contingency of phenomena that may be taken for granted. The act of comparing forces us to think more critically about what is meant by a borderland culture and whether the geographical peripheries should necessarily be considered marginal.

NORTH AMERICAN BORDER TOWNS: TACTICS OF EXCLUSION AND REALITIES OF INTEGRATION

The relationships between border towns/cities along the US–Canada and US–Mexico borders are significantly different from each other for a combination of historical and structural reasons. Whereas the former border was negotiated between the British rulers of Canada and their American counterparts, the second was the product of war between Mexico and the US that led to the cession of a vast expanse of Mexican territory in 1848. This land seizure forced many ordinary Mexicans southwards, thereby reconfiguring settlements in proximity to the redefined boundary. Perhaps the most striking feature of this border is the existence of pairs of towns running from the Atlantic to the Pacific coasts. There is a total of 14 pairings, yielding a total of 28 towns/cities in all. Some of the pairs are large cities such as San Diego and Tijuana in the far west, which are estimated to have populations of 1.3 million and 1.5 million respectively. Equally, El Paso has a population of 614,000, while Ciudad Juárez has mushroomed to an estimated 1.5 million. In the intermediate category would be Brownsville (est. 139,800) and Matamoros (est. 422,700) on the eastern seaboard. Finally, on the small side would be Nogales in the US (20,800) and Nogales in Mexico (190,000). Although these are often described as "twin" or "sister" towns (e.g., Romero 2008: 60), such terminology obscures a history of conflict and ambivalence that both the Mexican and American border populations are only too well aware of – even taking account of the heavy Mexican-American presence in the US border states. The United States–Canada border is relatively lightly populated except in the region of the Great Lakes, where a series of large cities exist, but these have grown up more or less independently of one another.

Secondly, whereas there has been relative economic parity between Canada and the US, northern Mexico has always been demonstrably poorer than the American side – even if the US border areas have been deprived relative to the hinterlands of the states concerned (e.g., California or Texas) and the rest of the US. The relationship between Canadian and American border cities has often been characterized by outright competition or mutual disregard. Moreover, the phenomenon of paired towns, which is such a feature of the US–Mexico border, does not really exist (Gibbins 2005: 158). Border populations have had little reason to frequent each other's towns, despite a period in the 1990s when it was cheaper for Canadians to shop in the US. A great deal of trade (worth $1.2 billion annually) and tourism takes place, but this has not tended to stick at the border. Buursink (2001: 10) provides a concrete example of the Canadian and American versions of "Niagara Falls City," where the Canadian settlement attracts most of the tourists and can afford to ignore its American neighbor, while the US authorities impose tolls on vehicles crossing to the Canadian side. There is little sense of shared identity between the towns despite the fact that they are sitting on a shared tourist attraction. In the case of the US–Mexico border, the marked inequalities have led to a different dynamic altogether, which turns on the complex relationships between the 28 pairs. A Mexican city like Ciudad Juárez has witnessed periods of boom in the twentieth century, but these have come at moments when wealthier Americans have chosen to relocate their playgrounds south of the border (Martínez 1978). The period of Prohibition in the US conferred a windfall on Juárez and Tijuana alike, but the boom ended when there was a return to normality in the US. Under average conditions, the relationship between US and Mexican border towns has been somewhat adversarial. While the US towns have been in favor of regulating the flow of migrants, it is in the interest of the Mexican authorities to maintain a constant movement of population across the line in order to relieve some of the social and political pressures at home. The remittances sent home by Mexican migrants in 2005, which were reputedly the largest in the world, were estimated to exceed revenues from tourism and to amount to more than 70 percent of earnings from exports of crude oil (Romero 2008: 104). Many Mexican border towns have a tradition of not merely providing springboards for legal and illegal immigration to the US, but also of sustaining a large population of commuters who work in the US and sleep in Mexico.

The North American Free Trade Agreement (NAFTA) that was signed between the US, Canada and Mexico in 1994 crystallizes many of the problems underlying trans-boundary relations. Although economic integration was supposed to bring benefits to all sides, following the logic of free trade, Canadian and Mexican critics maintain that the US has been the primary beneficiary. In the Mexican case, it is claimed that the economy was bound to suffer from US competition, leading to a further drift of dis-advantaged Mexicans toward the border. These negative predictions have been borne out to the extent that Mexican agriculture has been hit hard by cheaper American exports of wheat and maize. It is certainly undeniable that there has been a substantial drift of population toward the border since NAFTA came into existence. Only a small part of this demographic drift can be accounted for by the economic dynamism of the border towns themselves. The maquiladora phenomenon, whereby US industries are encouraged to relocate some of their operations to the Mexican side of the border, began as early as the 1960s, but received a boost from NAFTA. The deal is that foreign companies are permitted to import equipment and raw materials duty-free for use in assembly plants that produce goods for the non-Mexican market. The theory is the Mexican state will derive some revenue from this enclave activity, US companies will have guaranteed access to cheap labor, Mexican border towns will prosper and there will be less of an impulse for ordinary Mexicans to seek work across the border. Although the maquiladoras have created new jobs, the wages are typically low and the number of openings has not kept up with the constant stream of work-seekers. In short, the initiative has done little to stem the flow of would-be immigrants to the US, and may even have had the opposite effect.

Despite the structural tension between the US and Mexican border towns/cities, there has been some appreciation on the American side of the line that an intransigent attitude toward its immediate neighbor would be unwise. On the one hand, Mexicans spend a lot of money in US border cities. The relationship between Tijuana and San Diego has long exemplified stark differences between the respective populations, but the extent to which the prosperity of the latter depends on the market power of the Mexicans was underlined in 1976 when the devaluation of the peso had a severe impact on businesses in San Diego. In the mid-1990s, the people of Tijuana were reputed to be spending $950 million a year in the city (Puente 1996: 250–253). The same would be true of El Paso and many other border towns. On the other hand, there is a realization that environmental problems can only be dealt with in a collaborative manner. The problems arising from pollution and severe strain placed on water supplies, in what is after all an arid region, have been a source of concern for US municipal authorities. However, American maquilidoras have been accused of exploiting the weak environmental controls on the Mexican side for their own profit and at the expense of the transnational collective good. Because US border towns and cities share the downstream environmental consequences, there have been various initiatives since the 1990s to tackle common problems, involving municipal and state-level authorities. This is glossed in terms of the need for communities to do things for themselves, given that Washington DC and Mexico City are far away and allegedly unconcerned about the realities of life on the border.

However, these efforts at rapprochement have received a blow since the turn of the millennium. The US Federal authorities have been prepared to override local sensibilities in the name of US national interests, reinscribing what was already one of the world's hardest boundaries. There have been three factors driving this process. First, a strong "nativist" streak among so-called "Anglos" in the border zone has been reactivated, which is personified by the Minutemen. The latter are groups of private citizens who take it upon themselves to police the border against incursions by illegal immigrants from Mexico. The context is one in which poor Mexicans have sought to penetrate the US through the least policed and usually the most remote desert stretches of border. As of 2009, 930 kilometers of this 3,141-kilometer border was fenced in an attempt to create more effective surveillance, and the process of enclosure continues. The Minutemen see themselves as fighting the second round of the US-Mexican war, in the sense that they wish to prevent their states from being "overrun" by the very same Mexicans their forefathers defeated in battle a century and a half before. They have sought to legitimize their activities by working closely with the US Border Patrol, which uses the latest electronic sensory technology (backed up with aerial support), but is nevertheless overstretched. Disparaged as bounty-hunters by some, and venerated as defenders of the American nation by others, the Minutemen encapsulate the extent to which border crossings have become a serious political issue.

Secondly, the New York bombings of September 11, 2001 were followed by a heightened Federal government sensitivity to terrorist threats. The Department of Homeland Security was charged with closely monitoring entry through airports and land borders alike. It came up with the vision of creating "smart borders" where new technologies of surveillance and profiling would be deployed in a systematic manner. Although an Islamist terrorist threat emanating from Mexican soil was highly unlikely, the terrorist card has been played by those in favor of enforcing stricter border controls for other kinds of reasons. And finally, an escalation of violence along the Mexican border, arising out of a series of drug wars, has drawn attention to the need to prevent the contagion spreading to US soil. The perception of a threat from across the border is lent some vague credence by virtue of the serial killings of young women (amounting to more than 350 between 1993 and 2003 alone), which is ostensibly unrelated to the drugs issue. The killings have centered on Ciudad Juárez, but the repercussions have been felt across the border in El Paso, thus underlining the permeability of the border (Staudt 2008). The rumor has long been that the perpetrator(s) are connected to elements in the Mexican police, which can easily be elided with the contention that the drugs trade is supported by the same corrupt elements. Crucially, the expanding volume of drugs traded across the border seems to be related to vehicle movements, rather than pedestrian crossers, which cannot be disassociated from the effects of NAFTA itself. Given the sheer volume of commercial traffic, it is difficult to enforce thorough checks of vehicles that often have well-concealed compartments. This underlines the complexity of governance issues in border zones: even the most high-tech and highly funded border regime in the world is confounded by the effects of the trade liberalization which it purports to champion.

Ironically, the drug-related violence in Mexican border cities appears to be related to efforts by the Mexican authorities, under pressure from the American government, to deal decisively with trafficking. After the imprisonment of the key drug-lord, competing cartels carved out four separate trafficking corridors: referred to as the Tijuana Cartel, the Sinaloa-Sonora Cartel, the Juárez Cartel and the Gulf Cartel (Payan 2006a: 865). This stable equilibrium was upset by a Mexican government campaign, which weakened some cartels and led to renewed competition to take over their turf. In 2005, this was reflected in open conflict in Nuevo Laredo when around 150 people were killed, including many police officers and government officials (Romero 2008: 44). Then in 2008, the Sinaloa-Sonora Cartel moved in on the territory of the Juárez Cartel, leading to more than 5,000 deaths in Ciudad Juárez itself. US citizens, including Mexican-Americans, who used to cross the border regularly, have increasingly found it too dangerous to venture across the line. Although Juárez has long had an unsavory reputation in the US, the perception is of a qualitative deterioration of security. A hard border – as manifested by fortified fences redolent of the wall being created along the boundary between Israel and the West Bank – has been created by state action and local activism alike. But it is being further reinscribed by a mental border in which Americans associate Mexico with a series of interlocking threats, of which violent crime and drugs are the two most tangible. Whereas the US-Canadian border is characterized by indifference between neighboring populations, the US–Mexico border is defined by a climate of fear. In neither case does the imagery of "twin cities" convey an accurate sense of the realities on the ground.

EUROPEAN BORDER TOWNS: TRANSCENDING DIVISIONS

Europe is the continent where international boundaries have had the most tortured history. Here, the ruptures manifested in border towns/cities have represented both the failure of pan-Europeanism in the past as well as aspirations for a reinvigorated Europe in the present. The successive redrawing of boundaries in the twentieth century, turning chiefly on the enlargement and shrinkage of the contours of Germany and Poland, has involved border towns becoming hinterlands and hinterlands becoming borderlands in bewildering succession. Moreover, borders have always had a complex relationship with the cultural landscape, with substantial German-speaking populations being concentrated in urban centers well beyond the German heartlands. An example is the Baltic seaport of Gdansk which was 98 percent German in 1919. After 1945, at a time when many cities in Eastern Europe were purged of their German populations, they were also expelled from Gdansk. The latter was turned into a thoroughly Polish city that does not sit on a border today. Again, Bratislava (est. 429,000), which borders on to Hungary and Austria, is now an overwhelmingly Slovak capital city. In 1910, however, it was predominantly made up of Hungarians and Germans, who together accounted for 83 percent of the population. These populations were similarly expelled. In order to understand European border cities, therefore, it is important to take account of population dislocation on a massive scale combined with a history of mistrust between different nations and minorities.

In contemporary times, as the memories of the first half of the twentieth century turn to historical sediment, the makeup of border towns and cities continues to reflect the divisions of the Cold War. The lines of fracture between former Western and Eastern Europe are still apparent on the ground. They are reflected within a reunified Germany, but also on the international boundaries where West Germany, Italy, Austria and Finland meet the former Eastern bloc. The differences of economic wealth are often starkly manifested in lingering income inequalities, differential employment opportunities and uneven infrastructural provision between towns/cities on either side of the line. The many layers of complexity are brought out perfectly in the case of the dual towns of Słubice, in Poland, and Frankfurt an-der-Oder in the former East Germany. These were not border towns at all prior to 1945, at which point Poland's eastern border with the Soviet Union was shifted westwards and, in compensation, its border with Germany was moved to the Oder River. Frankfurt (Oder) was thereby turned into a border town overnight. Moreover, the Poles who were displaced from what was now Soviet territory, were resettled in the newly acquired western borderlands, including what came to be known as Słubice. The latter had always been an integral part of Frankfurt (Oder), but was now transformed into a separate Polish town, from which the German inhabitants were excised. Hence, as Andrew Asher (2005: 129) has demonstrated, dual towns were created on either side of a river where a border had not previously existed and where the German and Polish populations concerned had no history of mutual engagement. Crucially, the bridge came to stand for a sense of difference even before the reunification of Germany. To refer to "twin towns" or "sister cities" would again be singularly inappropriate. Although the progressive enlargement of Europe has led to removal of the hard boundaries between former Western and Eastern Europe, the legacy of disunity and mistrust between border populations has been less easy to erase.

The EU's dual strategy of seeking to remove internal borders and embracing enlargement has created important differences in border arrangements affecting the countries slated for inclusion and those countries regarded as external – with Turkey posing the greatest problem of definition. In the former case, the softening of the border has typically preceded the formal act of accession. But where the boundaries of Europe are thought to end, the boundaries have become somewhat harder. This would be true, in particular, of Spanish enclaves in North Africa that are considered vulnerable links in the war against illegal African immigration into Europe (Driessen 1998). In this, there are passing similarities with the US–Mexico border dynamic. In most other respects, however, European borders have assumed a completely different form from those in North America. Dual towns have not arisen in response to the pressure for migration – as in the US–Mexico case – and while some of the mutual disregard is comparable to the US–Canada instance, the wealth disparities and demographic patterns are significantly different. European border regions have generally combined dense settlement with the lack of a well-defined borderland identity.

It is precisely this combination that has led the EU to embrace border towns/cities as the key to the success of the European project. History is, as it were, to be turned back on itself and a grand political vision – that of a united Europe – is to be actualized in a myriad of local initiatives aimed at bridging divides. On a more practical level, the EU position is that border regions are typically the most neglected in terms of basic infrastructure and overall living standards. The EU promotion of Euroregions is in part designed to redress these historic inequalities, an agenda that is also rooted in important demographic realities. It is estimated that up to 30 percent of the population of Europe lives within border regions, while an estimated 10 percent live in border towns within 25 kilometers of an international boundary (Gasparini 2008). However, there are marked differences in border demography between countries. Gasparini (2008) estimates that 33.5 percent of Belgians live in border towns, whereas only 3.6 percent of Spanish and 1.4 percent of Italians do so.

By investing in border regions, the EU not only hopes to even out living standards, but to create the possibility of more productive interactions among border populations. Some interventions have been rather imaginative and productive such as the EuroAirport – which simultaneously serves Basel in Switzerland, Mulhouse in France and Freiburg in Germany – or the bridge between Denmark and Sweden (completed in 2000) that has brought Copenhagen and Malmö much closer together. While substantial European funding has gone into infrastructural development in border regions, other financing is directed at local cross-border initiatives that are typically proposed by municipal and local authorities. This includes shared hospitals, recreational facilities and cultural exchanges. The emphasis upon local initiative is partly intended to counter the perception that the European project is a top-down process. In some cases, such as along the Dutch-German border, the vision of a borderless Europe has been embraced in a proactive way by neighboring communities. This is true of the peoples of Kerkrade and Herzogenrath on the Dutch-German border, who have sought to revive memories of an older history of association that was abruptly ended in 1815, in support of contemporary efforts to create a shared municipality. Ehlers (2001: 22) wryly observes that creating a "we" identity requires a "they" as a foil, which in this case were national governments that were accused of having neglected these declining coal towns. In many other settings, such as along the Germany–France border, populations have reached common understandings without necessarily resorting to grand gestures. This is true of Alsace, whose capital of Strasbourg features prominently as a center of EU operations. And finally, there are many cases where cross-border initiatives are being funded, but where populations in border towns still perceive each other as distinct. It is at border crossings that the success of European integration can best be measured, and while the picture remains a somewhat patchy one the progress has been substantial.

African Border Towns: The Centrality of the Margins

In sub-Saharan Africa, border towns/cities have presented a still different picture to the North American and European cases that have so far been considered. As in Europe, there were instances where colonial capitals were located along international boundaries – notably Lomé (est. 737,500), Kinshasa (est. 7.8 million) and Brazzaville (est.1.5 million). The first was the capital of German Togo (and later French Togoland), while the last two were capitals of the Belgian and French Congo that faced each other across the Congo River. These were exceptional cases however, and in each instance the city in question was built virtually from scratch. In fact, most African colonial borders were drawn through relatively lightly populated rural terrain, with a preference for rivers and mountains as physical markers. A large number of colonial capitals were located on coastal seaboards (e.g., Dakar or Accra) or along rivers that did not themselves constitute borders. The colonial dispensation was, however, one that was conducive to the emergence of border towns where they did not already exist. The contrasting – and indeed competing – economic regimes of the colonial powers tended to produce variable demands in the shape of direct taxation, customs duties and labor requirements. Populations moved into border zones to take advantage of the opportunities for smuggling and to evade extractive demands. In the post-independence period, a similar dynamic contributed to the steady growth of border towns. Because the national centers were politically rather weak, and because the border zones were construed as zones of opportunity (Nugent and Asiwaju 1996), border towns never had their backs turned to each other, but were engaged in a constant dynamic interaction. This is not to suggest that relations were always harmonious, but merely that border towns derived their *raison d'être* from participating in transnational flows. In some instances, local populations have even come to regard themselves as the owners of profitable border spaces, in competition with state officials (Flynn 1997; Nugent 2002).

Two other aspects of African border towns are worth noting. First of all, in most cases, there were no great wealth disparities between communities on either side of the line. The exception is between South Africa and its neighbors. Although South African border towns are themselves poor, they are the gateway to the perceived riches of Johannesburg. David Coplan (2009) is probably the only person to have conducted a comparison between the Mexico–United States border and an African border, in this case the Lesotho border, on the basis of a shared history of dispossession and contemporary migration. Secondly, unlike in Europe and in South Africa, border towns were not necessarily poorer than their respective hinterlands. Although infrastructure often pulled up short of the border, there was good money to be made there. It was also not uncommon for border entrepreneurs to construct their own roads and bridges where the state was absent.

As the macroeconomic environment in Africa deteriorated in the 1980s, cross-border trade received a further impetus. Governments in micro-states which enjoyed the advantages of coastal ports – such as the Gambia, Togo and Benin – never had any serious pretensions toward industrialization strategies of their own. In the midst of the downturn, their ports provided entry points for consumer goods entering not only their own domestic markets, but also penetrating further afield. In effect, they undercut the state-owned industries of their larger neighbors, compounding their woes (Nugent 2010). Hence the commercial prosperity of Lomé until the early 1990s rested on the systematic reexport of manufactured goods into Ghana. The growth of the Ghanaian town of Aflao, which lay just across the line, reflected the importance of this smuggling activity to the livelihoods of many Ghanaians as well. Indeed, all along this border, there was a flourishing trade between networks of smugglers who operated from towns and villages located on either side of the line. Similarly, the Gambian port of Banjul was a point through which contraband was traded across the Senegambian subregion. The bustling Gambian town of Brikama, which is slightly set back from the southern border with Senegal, became (and remains) the hub for a vigorous contraband trade with the Casamance region of Senegal and Guinea-Bissau. Other towns and villages located on either side of the northern border with Senegal have become entry points for contraband goods into northern Senegal, many of which find their way onto the streets of Dakar. In the case of the port of Cotonou in Benin, the trade in second-hand cars has become a particular specialism. Vehicles are imported from Asia and Europe and are then illegally exported to Nigeria and throughout the subregion, using a range of border crossings. Although such entrepôt states (Igué and Soulé 1992) have a dynamic of their own, the proliferation of border towns across Africa is indicative of the opportunities associated with cross-border trade. Cameroun provides an excellent example of this phenomenon, with towns bordering on to Chad, Nigeria, Gabon and Equatorial Guinea expanding significantly on the basis of a vigorous commerce in manufactured goods and food-stuffs (Bennafla 2002; Roitman 2005). Equally, there is a vigorous trade in manu-factured imports and agricultural goods between coastal countries, notably Ghana, and commercial centers in the Sahel (Walther 2008). Finally, although the expanding West African drugs trade is conducted primarily through international airports, the narcotics are moved overland from the original point of entry to the eventual point of exit. The creation of the Nigerian Drugs Law Enforcement Agency has, for example, increased the risk of detection at Lagos airport, leading traffickers to re-route their trade through Ghana. These drugs pass through border towns such as Lomé-Aflao. Now that Guinea-Bissau has been targeted by the US as a growing hub in the narcotics trade, it is likely that more of the drugs will be transferred overland to Banjul and Dakar. This is focusing international attention on the border towns themselves.

Since around the 1990s, border towns have often grown extremely rapidly. This is related to two further developments. The first is the reality of conflict in which refugees and internally displaced populations have converged on "safe zones." The border city of Goma in the eastern Democratic Republic of Congo (DRC) is a classic case. It has more than tripled in size from 1994 to the present (the estimated popula-tion is now 600,000), as a result of persistent fighting in the Great Lakes region. The policy of humanitarian agencies has been to keep refugees as close to their homes as possible, making the border location a semipermanent home by default. The second is the reconfiguration of Africa's place within the global economy. In the period of most acute conflict from the mid-1990s to the early years of the new mil-lennium, valuable resources such as diamonds (in Sierra Leone) and coltan (in DRC) were located in border zones, which meant not only that that entrepreneurs of vio-lence had an interest in cornering supplies, but also that border towns became a focus for profitable business activity. This dynamic remains a feature of the Great Lakes Region, with towns on the DRC–Rwanda and the DRC–Uganda border representing strategically placed nodes in international networks that are connected to Antwerp, Helsinki and Shanghai. Although Africa has witnessed a return to economic growth and relative peace since around 2005, the manufacturing base of most countries has contracted. China's reengagement with Africa has witnessed not merely the penetration of Chinese goods such as textiles into African markets, but also the appearance of Chinese traders on the ground. On the Namibian border with Angola, the impact of oil money on spending capacity has created a boomtown at Oshikango (est. 43,000), where a significant number of Chinese merchants have congregated (Dobler 2009). This underlines the important point that while African border towns may be geographically peripheral, they are often economically pivotal.

At the time of writing, many African border zones are poised to undergo a transformation as a result of a series of interlocking initiatives. First, a series of overlapping Regional Economic Communities (RECs) have been created by African states to realize the objective of closer economic integration. A visa-free agreement has been signed by member states of the Economic Community of West African States, with the East African Community and the Economic Community of Central African States expected to follow suit. Most RECs have also signed agreements covering free trade and customs unions, with common currencies being the next item on the agenda. Secondly, at the continental level, the creation of the African Union Border Program in 2007 is intended to support integration initiatives in tandem with RECs, but also to pursue additional agendas. One is to complete the delineation and demarcation of all of Africa's boundaries by 2012, which arises out of the fear that the location of valuable commodities (such as oil) in border zones, together with the effects of climate change, represent a recipe for conflict. Another is to accelerate cross-border cooperation initiatives, with a focus on border towns. Although European borderlands have a different dynamic, there is an interest in learning from cross-border initiatives in the EU. Finally, the market value of Africa's primary commodities, such as copper, has risen in recent years, leading to a renewed importance being attached to infrastructural investments.

These developments are converging around new border management regimes that have a direct impact on the role and shape of border towns/cities. There is a growing recognition that a proliferation of border controls makes doing business in Africa much more expensive than elsewhere. The one-stop border post is being touted as creating an environment that will be more friendly toward regional trade. In addition, significant investments are being made in road and rail infrastructure. The West African Highway project that links the West African littoral is a case in point. In addition, three transport corridors are in the process of realization in southern Africa that have the potential to reconfigure economic spaces in fundamental ways. The most advanced is the Maputo Corridor that was agreed as far back as 1995. The aim has been to upgrade the infrastructure, facilitate the flow of traffic from South Africa's industrial hub and attract outside investment into the corridor. The latter is intended to benefit the population living in the borderlands as well as the established industrial centers. The Walvis Bay Corridor is in fact a network of four separate regional corridors linking the Namibian port of Walvis Bay with five neighboring states. Perhaps the most important of these is the trans-Cunene corridor, which, by means of improved roads and the construction of a bridge across the Zambezi River (opened in 2004), has connected the Congolese and Zambian copperbelts with the west coast. As Zeller (2009) notes, this has brought a century-old German dream to fruition. The bridge has already produced a boomtown effect on the Namibia–Zambia border, with Katima Mulilo (Namibia) and Sesheke (Zambia) expanding rapidly as truck stops – with hotels, prostitution and Chinese supermarkets providing much of the visible economic activity (Zeller 2009). Finally, the Beira Corridor connects the Zambian capital to the Mozambican coastal port, but there is a second branch that reaches into Malawi. Improvements to the railroad, and the creation of a navigable waterway along the Zambezi River are intended to unlock the potential for agribusiness inside Malawi. But it is to be expected that the border towns that lie on the various railway and river crossings will themselves experience a stimulus. Paradoxically, while the push for regional integration is designed to transcend boundaries, it is likely to have a pronounced effect on towns and cities located at the border.

The likely emergence of new boomtowns in Africa raises important questions about governance in borderlands. In the 1990s, before the proliferation of regional transport initiatives, African border towns had HIV-prevalence rates that were well above the national average. A case in point would be Francistown, a flourishing town in eastern Botswana that is both a mining center and a transport node linking Gaborone with Bulawayo and Harare in Zimbabwe. The public health issues that arise in newly emergent centers are likely to pose even greater problems in that services tend to lag behind demographic growth. Moreover, boomtowns may decline as quickly as they have taken off, although the new infrastructural revolution (largely driven by Chinese investment) is likely to create some fairly predictable patterns of urban growth. The public health issues may stand for the more general problem of turning frontier towns into livable urban spaces. Secondly, in some border regions, such as in the Great Lakes or along the Sudan–Uganda border, there are ongoing security issues. The very fact that the borderlands are zones of opportunity makes them attractive to military entrepreneurs who have an interest in controlling exchange. A comparison with the most embattled Mexican border towns is instructive. In Mexico, the drugs barons seek to defend trafficking corridors against central state intervention and each other. Their strategy turns on a combination of selective intimidation and liquidation of state officials and competitors alike. In the most troubled zones in Africa, warlords seek to take control of border spaces. Through control of private armies and militias, they seek to carve out their own territory within which they are at liberty to fleece populations, establish monopolistic control over valuable resources and tax external trade. Whereas in Mexico, the powerlessness of state institutions in the border setting may come as a shock, especially when contrasted with the level of state regulation on the US side of the border, in somewhere like the eastern DRC state control has always been rather episodic. Be that as it may, the overall trend would appear to point in three directions at once: the growing importance of border towns in transnational networks of exchange, the privatization of some state functions through public-private partnerships (especially along the transport corridors), and the reassertion of state presence in some troubled border zones.

CONCLUSION

In this chapter, I have sought to demonstrate that towns and cities located along international borders often occupy an important position in regional commerce, patterns of migration and discourses of public order. However, there are some significant differences in the ways in which these borders have operated. The sheer intensity surrounding the US–Mexico border – with its intimidating fences, legal and illegal crossings and border patrols – contrasts with the mutual disregard displayed at relatively sleepy US–Canada border crossings. In Europe, many border populations have their backs turned to each other, but here the underlying causes reside in a recent history of forced displacement and long periods of border closure between Eastern and Western Europe. Moreover, the wealth disparities between them have proved stubbornly difficult to erase. The project of the EU is to convert border towns and cities from monuments to failure into shining examples of the benefits of integration.

In Africa, there are almost none of the asymmetries of the US–Mexico border. Nevertheless, a dynamic of doubling is apparent for other reasons. Border towns have expanded rapidly because of the opportunities for profitable trade, and this has involved the emergence of matching pairs in which traders have sought to exploit the advantages of both sides of the line. In the medium term, the changing economic landscape of the continent is likely to lend a competitive edge to border settlements that are located along the emerging network of transport corridors. In the special cases where the capital city defines the border, there is additional potential for transformation. One initiative that may define the future of border towns/cities in Africa is the plan for a bridge across the Congo River that would bring Brazzaville and Kinshasa closer together.

The *World Development Report* of 2009 (World Bank 2009) underlines the importance of agglomeration economies for economic development, simultaneously championing the developmental effects of large cities and advancing the case for regional integration based on substantial infrastructural investments. The border city lies at the intersection between these agendas that arguably mark the most important paradigm shift within the Bretton Woods institutions since the early 1980s. Whereas the new discourse surrounding space carries an optimistic message about the benefits that will flow from freeing markets, transcending distance and concentrating economic activity, border towns and cities are also attracting attention for other kinds of reasons. That is, governments that seek to regulate the flow of migrants, narcotics and perceived threats to security often regard border settlements as the weakest link. For the same reason, they are often an irritant in intergovernmental relations, as in the case of India and Pakistan. The fact that expanding commerce along the Mexican-American border renders it impractical to maintain rigid border checks demonstrates that even the strongest states struggle to reconcile these competing agendas. The recent drugs wars on the other side of the line have also underlined the limits to the coercive capacity of the Mexican state. In the African case, where state authority in border zones has been seriously eroded in many regions since the 1980s, problems of governance have long been an issue. Here, a thriving cross-border trade has often gone together with an erosion of the powers of the state and the rise of what one might loosely call warlords. Ironically, whereas the security agenda of the United States government is complicated by the freedom of trade and migration, governments and international agencies in Africa look to economic integration as a way of reestablishing some semblance of sovereignty. Albeit for different reasons, border towns and cities are likely to provide an important focus of government attention and academic research for decades to come.

REFERENCES

Arreola, Daniel D. and Curtis, James R. 1993. *The Mexican Border Cities: Landscape Anatomy and Place Personality.* Tucson: University of Arizona Press.

Asher, Andrew. 2005. A paradise on the Oder? Ethnicity, Europeanization and the EU referendum in a Polish-German border city. *City and Society* 17 (1): 127–152.

Bennafla, Karine. 2002. *Le commerce frontalier en Afrique centrale. Acteurs, espaces, pratiques.* Paris: Karthala.

Buursink, Jan. 2001. The bi-national reality of border-crossing cities. *GeoJournal* 54: 7–19.

Coplan, David. 2009. Siamese twin towns and unitary concepts on border inequality. In Ulf Engel and Paul Nugent, eds, *Respacing Africa.* Leiden: Brill.

Dobler, Gregor. 2009. Oshikango: the dynamics of growth and regulation in a Namibian boom town. *Journal of Southern African Studies* 35 (1): 115–131.

Donnan, Hastings. 1999. Shopping and sectarianism at the Irish border. In Michael Rösler and Tobias Wendl, eds, *Frontiers and Borderlands: Anthropological Perspectives.* Frankfurt am Main: Peter Lang.

Driessen, Henk. 1998. The "new immigration" and the transformation of the European-African frontier. In Thomas M. Wilson and Hastings Donnan, eds, *Border Identities: Nation and State in International Frontiers.* Cambridge: Cambridge University Press.

Ehlers, Nicole. 2001. The utopia of the binational city. *GeoJournal* 54: 21–32.

Flynn, Donna. 1997. "We are the border": identity, exchange and the state along the Benin–Nigeria border. *American Ethnologist* 24 (2): 311–330.

Gasparini, A. 2008. Do border towns hold the key to cultural integration, incubation? *ASA Footnotes* 36 (9). At http://www. asanet.org/footnotes/dec08/intl_persp. html (accessed Nov. 2011).

Gibbins, R. 2005. Meaning and significance of the Canadian-American border. In Paul Ganster and David E. Lorey, eds, *Borders and Border Politics in a Globalizing World.* Oxford: SR Books.

Igué, J. and Soulé, B. 1992. *L'État entrepôt au Benin. Commerce informel ou solution à la crise?* Paris: Karthala.

Martínez, Oscar. 1978. *Border Boom Town: Ciudad Juárez since 1848.* Austin: University of Texas Press.

Nugent, Paul. 2002. *Smugglers, Secessionists and Loyal Citizens on the Ghana–Togo Frontier: The Lie of the Borderlands since 1914.* Oxford: James Currey.

Nugent, Paul. 2010. States and social contracts in Africa. *New Left Review* 53: 35–68.

Nugent, Paul and Asiwaju, A.I., eds. 1996. *African Boundaries: Barriers, Conduits and Opportunities.* London: Pinter.

Payan, Tony. 2006a. The drug war and the US–Mexico border: the state of affairs. In Jane Juffer, ed., *The Last Frontier: The Contemporary Configuration of the US–Mexico Border.* Special issue, South Atlantic Quarterly 105 (4): 863–880.

Payan, Tony. 2006b. *The Three US–Mexico Border Wars: Drugs, Immigration and Homeland Security.* Santa Barbara: Praeger.

Puente, María. 1996. So close, yet so far: San Diego, Tijuana bridging gap. In Oscar Martínez, ed., *US–Mexico Borderlands: Historical and Contemporary Perspectives.* Wilmington: SR Books.

Romero, Fernando. 2008. *Hyper-Border: The Contemporary US–Mexico Border and Its Future.* New York: Princeton Architectural Press.

Roitman, Janet. 2005. *Fiscal Disobedience: An Anthropology of Economic Regulation in*

Central Africa. Princeton: Princeton University Press.

Staudt, Kathleen A. 2008. *Violence and Activism at the Border: Gender, Fear, and Everyday Life in Ciudad Juárez*. Austin: University of Texas Press.

Timothy, Dallen J. and Butler, Richard W. 2005. Cross-border shopping: Canada and the United States. In Paul Ganster and David E. Lorey, eds., *Borders and Border Politics in a Globalizing World*. Oxford: SR Books.

Walther, Olivier. 2008. *Affaire des patrons. Villes et commerce transfrontalier au Sahel*. Berne: Peter Lang.

World Bank. 2009. *World Development Report, 2009: Reshaping Economic Geography*. Washington, DC: World Bank.

Zeller, Wolfgang. 2009. Danger and opportunity in Katima Mulilo: a Namibian border boomtown at transnational crossroads. *Journal of Southern African Studies* 35 (1): 133–154.

CHAPTER **33** A Sense of Border

Sarah Green

In the early 1990s, there were always several slightly dusty boys trying to sell cartons of cigarettes to the drivers and passengers of the slow-moving traffic around the Greek side of the Greek-Albanian border post at Kakavia, located at one of the spots where northwestern mainland Greece meets southern Albania. The cartons were all marked with familiar cigarette brand names, mostly American, and they were sold for less than half the usual price of cigarettes in Greece. Everyone knew the tobacco in them was harsh on the back of the throat, and that they contained random bits of plant material that sometimes made the cigarettes spark and crackle, or develop a thick twig of charcoal when smoked. The cartons had clearly made their way to Greece from Albania; nobody asked where the boys had come from. They were the kinds of people who always seemed to inhabit border crossing areas that were not subjected to precise, highly resourced, carefully organized and controlled policing and surveillance practices. Borders that were slightly frayed at the edges in that sense allowed spaces for people to do a bit of informal business, among other things.

Nowadays, almost 20 years later, things are different at Kakavia. The road has been widened and renewed; there is a fully fledged duty-free shop, on both sides; the queues are smaller; there are licensed businesses selling refreshments and snacks by the roadside; and the whole place has been tidied up. It has the appearance of a proper border post in the view of the residents nearby – which is to say, it looks like a place where bureaucratic procedures are orderly rather than disorderly. There is now much less random leakiness at this border: for the most part, the people and goods that are legally permitted to cross, do so; those that are not legally permitted to cross also sometimes get through, but not so openly in defiance of the rules, and not to such a degree as had occurred in earlier years. There were no more dusty boys, and the cigarettes for sale in the duty-free shop would only spark and crackle if you bought the brands that advertised themselves as no-name brands: the design of the box looks like a named brand, but they have a different name.

A Companion to Border Studies, First Edition. Edited by Thomas M. Wilson and Hastings Donnan.
© 2012 Blackwell Publishing Ltd. Published 2012 by Blackwell Publishing Ltd.

Twenty years before the dusty boys were selling cigarettes at Kakavia, in the early 1970s, there were very few people or buildings on the Greek side, other than an army post and a few shepherds. At the time, Greece was still formally in conflict with Albania, and the area around Kakavia was in a controlled zone accessible only to those with a special pass, which in practice meant the residents of the villages on the Greek side of the zone. On the Albanian side during that period, there were both more people and more soldiers, and they also lived in a specially controlled zone, which was pockmarked with concrete pill boxes into which soldiers could bunker down in the event of an attack. There was no manned crossing point between Greece and Albania here; crossing this border was not something that many people were officially allowed to do in the early 1970s. And to emphasize the point, the two sides were separated by barbed wire and other types of fencing. On the Albanian side, the barbed wire had goat and sheep bells attached to it every few hundred yards. This meant that if anybody cut the wire or tried to pass through it, the bells would ring from the vibration for hundreds of yards around, alerting the local military. All of that was removed after the end of communist rule in Albania in the early 1990s.

In the space of 40 years, then, the legal status and management of the Greek-Albanian border has significantly changed three times. There were also memories of previous changes, particularly of the period before World War II, effectively the pre–Cold War era. At that time, the border, though present, was not of great significance for people in their everyday lives, for they could pass freely between the one side and the other with virtually no controls at all. And since most people had family and friends on the other side, and from the Greek perspective the nearest big market town was in Albania (Argyrokastro/Gjirokastër), rather than in Greece, there were plenty of reasons to cross the border regularly.

Of course, the existence of the border in those pre–World War II years meant a great deal to the two governments involved, even if the border was not particularly marked or policed around the Kakavia area. For the Greek and Albanian governments, the border marked the edge of state territories that had been relatively recently hard won and legitimized by nationalist claims to their respective regions.[1] And as in many post-Ottoman areas, there had been ongoing disagreements about the precise location of the border and the nationalities and ethnicities of some of the peoples living on either side.[2] Those disagreements, along with the drawing up of political maps that marked the border, had helped to give one kind of shape to this border; they helped to provide a particular sense of its "borderness," a sense of its border-like qualities (Green 2009, 2010). In these early years of the state border's existence, that sense of border felt much more explicitly like an assertion than a practical reality; apart from anything else, that state-based national idea of border was not the only understanding of border around (Green 2005: 147–151). Moreover, as already described, the material characteristics and management of this state-defined border changed several times as well. Initially, there were no checks at all in crossing from one side to the other in the Kakavia region; later, it was virtually impossible to cross (during the Cold War period), and there was a very real danger of being shot for those who tried; then, just after the end of the Cold War, a rather makeshift set of bureaucratic border-crossing procedures was hastily put in place that was much more often ignored or flouted than obeyed; and then, most recently, a rather clean and efficient border post was built. This post allows people and goods to cross regularly and in an orderly fashion, and gives all the appearance of being what a contemporary European border post ought to be by combining surveillance, security and regulated commercial enterprise. The Kakavia border post now feels, to most, like a place where the two states' border agencies work together to control trade, migration and potential threats of various sorts (undocumented migration, disease and terrorism being three of the most frequently cited). Even though there are still some underlying disagreements about the status of the territory just north of the Greek side of the border, known as Northern Epirus in Greece and as Southern Albania in Albania (Winnifrith 2002: 24–26; Green 2005: 15), for the most part, the border no longer marks hostilities between states.

DYNAMIC AND NONDYNAMIC BORDERING PRACTICES

This shift in the main purpose of state-based border controls is quite common. Brown (2010: 21), in a study of the recent increase in many governments' habit of building walls, fences, barriers and exclusion zones in border regions across the world, suggests that the purpose of all this building is not in order to keep hostile armies out; rather, it is targeted against migrants, terrorists, smugglers and various other transnational threats that are not actually state-based. Hassner makes a similar point: in noting the rise of digital communication and neoliberal economic relations, he cites authors who have argued for "a new nomadism and . . . a devaluation of territory as well as of sovereignty and the state. This in turn has led to a new nostalgia for roots and for walls" (Hassner 2002: 40).

I will return to Brown's argument later. Here, the point is that even state borders, which are still the most familiar and recognizable sort of border around the world, are capable of taking different forms in almost every respect: in their material existence; in the way they are monitored and controlled; in their officially intended purpose and meaning; in the types of unofficial and informal practices that gather around them; and in the way they engage with, and are at least partly defined by, historically changing transnational political and economic conditions. This variability is obvious and has been noted by many,[3] and it carries an important implication: even in the case of particular kinds of border, such as state borders, there is little that could be called inherent about their characteristics as *borders*. Not even the tendency for borders to change regularly is an inherent characteristic of borders. While I suggest, borrowing from Massey (2005: 12), that borders mark the location of stories so far, which carries the axiomatic implication of historical change, that does not say anything about the pace at which such change might occur, and nor does it imply that change is ongoing, or constant. For example, during the Cold War period, nothing much at all appeared to be happening with the Greek-Albanian border. For most people on both sides, that border had all the appearance of being a permanent fixture that was a part of the landscape, like the mountains and rivers. The border was there, was being policed in a regular and predictable way that did not change from day to day, and people knew that it was virtually impossible to cross it. For that reason, many on the Greek side were astonished when the border was finally opened in the early 1990s, and also initially quite surprised that many things had changed on the Albanian side in the interim between the border being closed and then reopened almost 50 years later. It was like an earthquake had happened that had rearranged the landscape.[4]

The fact that borders are the outcome of ongoing activity (what many refer to as "bordering practices" or "border dynamics"[5]) does not necessarily mean that there is either much activity going on at any given time, or that the activity varies a great deal, or that the outcome of that activity will be a discernible change from what had existed the day, or even the year, before. The long-term maintenance of particular border configurations and dynamics is common. As van Houtum recently suggested, "No border is built for a short term: it is built for eternity" (2010: 290), even though everyone is aware that no borders have yet proven to have eternal properties. Related to this, borders are often claimed to have been built out of an eternal truth – one of the most common being the nation, which is regularly claimed to preexist the bounded territory that rightfully belongs to the nation; that is, of course, a part of asserting that the border *marks* a preexisting eternal truth, rather than itself being or generating one (Gourgouris 1996).

Furthermore, there is a strong association between borders and stopping things from happening, and also stalling things, as well as generating endless waiting. Border dynamics can be the opposite of dynamic, as it were.[6] This is not surprising, given that many borders are supposed to act as barriers, intended to control the movement of things, people, and sometimes also ideas, between one place and another. And unresolved political border issues (e.g., in Cyprus, or the West Bank) can generate a sense of waiting for those involved which feels as if everyday life itself has stopped until the issue is somehow resolved (Navaro-Yashin 2003; Rabinowitz 2001). And that sense of waiting until something happens is of course a defining characteristic of everyday life for those caught in transit across certain borders – asylum-seekers, refugees in camps, and undocumented migrants seeking official accreditation.[7] Malkki (1992) suggested many years ago in her study of Hutu refugees who had fled to Tanzania from Burundi that the refugees were simultaneously being defined by, and also actively defining, the character of the border. Refugee camps suggest a world in which everyone has their proper location, except for those anomalously displaced from that location. Those anomalies reinforce the idea that the border marks, in the case that Malkki was studying, national differences mapped onto Hutu and Tutsi distinctions. These kinds of border dynamics, which on the face of it look as if they are full of events that could change borders, in fact reinforce the preexisting borders. By acting on the idea that all people ought to belong nationally to a certain territory, a logic that justifies the building of refugee camps, the nationalist logic of the border is also reinforced. This is what Malkki calls, borrowing from Foucault (1974), the "national order of things" (1992: 25).

HISTORIES OF THE CLASSIFICATORY LOGIC OF BORDERNESS

Malkki's phrase draws out a key element in the approach toward borders that I am arguing for here: borders always involve a form of classification and categorization of the world, because otherwise, they would not be recognized as borders. Minimally, classification systems provide a means for grouping and distinguishing; and borders become recognizable when one or more distinctions are perceived and/or imposed. In Malkki's study, the classificatory logic of the border was a nationalist logic combined with what many have called a Westphalian logic of border construction, which has dominated the idea of what constitutes a political border, at least in Europe, for centuries: peoples, territories and sovereignty are ideally brought together and circumscribed by clearly marked, and internationally recognized, borders (Del Sarto 2010: 149). The contemporary passport is an iconic example of that classificatory logic: the passport both distinguishes and groups the holder according to a set of clear rules about the relationship between people and territories (Caplan 2001: 51). Many have suggested that the classificatory logic that would eventually lead to the contemporary passport was introduced by the Peace of Westphalia in 1648. This logic, at least at the official level, replaced an earlier notion of border in Europe, one that Hassner characterizes as the "empire" logic of border (2002: 43; see also Del Sarto 2010: 153). That earlier idea was based on the logic of centers and peripheries, rather than edges: the peripheries constituted transitional zones between regions, with relatively unclear locations in terms of where one place ends and another begins. Whereas the Westphalian logic generates the idea of an ideally homogeneous state that clearly and cleanly comes to an abrupt end at its neatly defined edges, the empire logic generates the idea of internally differentiated places and populations (not necessarily geographically contiguous) that become progressively more marginal the further away from the center one travels. Within the nationalist version of Westphalian logic, the people living near the borders are crucial, both because they can act as the bastions of the nation, protecting it from the threat of infiltration (e.g., Donnan 2005; Pelkmans 2006); and on the other hand, because there is a danger that these people are, or will become, mixtures or hybrids, transgressing and combining what should be kept separate (e.g., Ballinger 2003; Danforth 1995; Anzaldúa 1987). The echoes of Mary Douglas's (1966) notions of purity and pollution here are not accidental: the classificatory logic that requires a clear difference between inside and outside is a marked characteristic of Euro-American modernist epistemology.[8] Indeed, some anthropologists have noted an explicit borrowing of other Euro-American systems of classification, and particularly kinship structures, in the metaphors used to describe national and state belonging in some parts of the world, which have subsequently informed the building and maintenance of the borders of these political entities.[9] In short: Westphalian logic, irrespective of the literal significance of the 1648 Peace of Westphalia, was part of a wider, historically and socially specific form of knowledge practice. It was part of a way of understanding the world that made distinctions between one entity and another, one people and another, one place and another, using a particular theory of knowledge. The sense of border, or "borderness," that was generated by putting this theory of knowledge into practice in the construction of borders focuses strongly on binary distinction: the qualities and character of each side being defined by its diametrically opposed difference from the other side.

In contrast to this Westphalian logic of border, the logic of center and periphery does not require a clearly marked line at the edge of territories; it does not require the populations in territories to be regarded as having something in common (Anderson's famous "imagined community" (1983)); and the peripheries would not logically be more important than the center in defining or maintaining the character of the relationship between the people and the place. For example, the Kakavia area had been part of the Ottoman Empire before 1913. The region's most famous Ottoman leader was Ali Pasha of Tepelene (in power 1809–1822), who, at the height of his power, ruled a vast area that is today the entirety of Albania and all of northern Greece. Yet Ali spoke almost no Turkish, had gained control of most of those territories through the use of his own, not the Ottoman Porte's, irregular militias, and had high levels of administrative and financial autonomy from Istanbul (Fleming 1999; Plomer 1970). Life was not exactly wonderful for the many and diverse residents in the region (Ali exercised power more or less as he pleased); but they were at least able to travel across the entirety of the Ottoman territories without administrative barriers (Green 2005: 147–149). People's relation to the region that Ali controlled was not defined or marked by any distinctive line at the edges of his territory that would imply a strong distinction between those who lived inside and those who lived outside the region; it was mostly only Ali and his armed militias who were concerned about protecting the peripheries of these territories from threats by some other powerful entity. In everyday life, people could and did move freely, with the only proviso that, wherever they moved within the Ottoman region, they should sign up to the appropriate *millet*. This was a grouping based on religious affiliation that determined the laws and taxation rules that governed particular populations within the empire. There was no concept, here, that certain people were rooted or belonged in certain territories.

The same could be said of many parts of the world. In a detailed historical account of the shifting and multiple concepts of border in the Maghreb region, Fatma Ben Slimane (2010) outlines the process through which the "nation-state" logic of border was eventually, and rather uncomfortably, introduced there by the French. Before that, she suggests, there was a much less coherent or clear sense of border. At most, the frontier areas were "marches" – belts of land in which the people could, and did, switch their allegiance back and forth between the political powers. Ben Slimane draws on Robert Baudel's work to argue that the Westphalian logic of border is "a European invention dating back to the Middle Ages" (2010: 37). She suggests that this logic contrasted considerably with a preexisting logic in the Maghreb region. Under the Maghreb dynasties, there was no restriction on people or goods moving across their regions; there was a blurry understanding of where each dynasty's power ended at the edges; and they had a range of terms for these peripheral regions – limits, borders, marches, belts – which meant that there was no explicit, singular or coherent meaning for these peripheral regions. At most, this selection of words "meant a swathe of land, a more or less broad zone, separating two political entities" (Ben Slimane 2010: 39). Eventually, in the sixteenth century, some agreements with the Ottomans began to appear after skirmishes with them; but these still did not limit the movement of people or goods, and the agreements did not outline whole territories, but just the areas of disagreement. And in 1844, the French arrived, with a very different idea of border:

> The absence of any form of control over the movement of populations and goods from one country to the other was unacceptable. . . . The French attitude stemmed from a

political culture developed over the course of at least three centuries of wars in Europe followed by border negotiations, demarcation treaties, terrain surveys and cartographic techniques, all instruments used by states to fix their boundaries. This process reached a stage of maturity in the nineteenth century, with the advent of linear borders intended to close off territories which had become national. (Ben Slimane 2010: 53)

Furthermore, the French struggled to impose their particular understanding of border in the region, for "the conception of borders as barriers, and as instruments of spatial enclosure and distinction between people, was absent from the collective imagination, both among the men in power and the local populations" (Ben Slimane 2010: 53). Again, what this points to is an epistemological difference, a difference in the way a theory of knowledge is used to make sense of relations and the world. What is important here is that the *idea* of border is closely interrelated with much wider ways of knowing, and these ways of knowing vary across time and space.

These examples suggest that even at the level of official ideals, political rhetoric and administrative structures, there is nothing inherent about the character or nature of borders; there is no universal "borderness" that applies anywhere and everywhere. As Del Sarto puts it, "borders and their meanings are historically contingent" (2010: 151). The point is similar to Foucault's (1986) comment that sex is historically contingent rather than inherent, and Butler's related but rather differently constructed argument that gender is contingent rather than inherent (Butler 1990). This does not mean that borders, sex or gender are constantly changing; nor does it mean that they can be anything at all; and nor does it mean that they are somehow not real. It does mean, however, that borders, sex and gender are not things or objects that simply exist in the world and all a researcher has to do is to poke them a bit and then describe them: instead, they are the outcome of a particular way of understanding, constructing and performing them *as* border, sex or gender. Some would see the dusty boys at Kakavia, along with the residents who live near to this border, as a particular category of people, borderlanders, who have particular characteristics because of their proximity to a border (e.g., Alvarez 1995; Zartman 2010). I would suggest that the idea of borderlanders as an empirical category only makes sense if it is assumed that borders have certain inherent and preexisting characteristics as things or places. What I have outlined here implies that this is not the case. Performing border using Westphalian nationalist logic, and doing that within southern Europe in the early twentieth century, is one thing; performing border using center–periphery logic, and doing that under Ottoman law during the early nineteenth century, is a different thing. And it is different because the ways in which these performances of border classify the world are different; and the subsequent senses of borderness will be different as well.

I have labored the point because most border studies focus on the subjects and objects of bordering practices more than they focus on borders, as such, whether these studies depict borders as self-evident entities that have certain fixed characteristics (e.g., Alvarez 1995; Zartman 2010); or instead, as nothing, as almost pure abstraction (Robinson 2007); or as the historically and socially contingent outcome of bordering practices (Riles 1998; Sant Cassia 2005; van Houtum et al. 2005). The literature on bordering (or b/ordering) has demonstrated that borders are more of a verb, a practice, a relation, and also importantly a part of imagination and desire, than they are a noun or an object (van Houtum 2010); and indeed, this literature has strongly informed my approach. Here, my aim is to add to this and consider what kind of knowledge is needed to recognize borders *as* borders. As the discussion thus far has outlined, this varies across time and space; and as it is only possible to recognize any given practice as a *bordering* practice once it is known what counts as "border" in the first place, it is important to understand this variability – especially, as I will be discussing below, given that the logic of border has been apparently undergoing some significant changes in recent years. In effect, I am adding an adjective to the verb: this means a focus on "borderness," on the different senses of border that have been expressed in different places and at different times, and how that relates to the way borders are both generated by, and/or help to generate, the classification system that distinguishes (or fails to distinguish) people, places and things in one way rather than another.

BORDER ONTOLOGIES

There is another implication of this focus on borders in terms of borderness. While it is clear that borders do not independently exist as self-evident entities in the landscape, in that they are fashioned out of particular epistemologies that vary across time and space, it is also the case that once constructed (which includes all the various associated bordering practices, both formal and informal), borders can take on thing-like qualities, both in practice and in people's imaginations. That has, of course, given rise to a considerable focus, particularly within anthropology, on frontiers and borderlands, where widely diverse conditions provide a variety of spaces in which people, things, places and relations can take active roles in what goes on in such regions (Donnan and Wilson 1999, 2010; Roitman 2005). Borders provide the possibility of making different, perhaps additional, worlds – or, to use Viveiros de Castro's (2004) understanding, they could generate and reflect many possible ontologies. In that sense, borders are not only epistemological entities, they are also ontological ones – epistemologies made real, in a sense.

One could see this as the practice of theory, reversing Bourdieu's (1977) focus on the relation between thought and experience. However, that would not capture the additional point that Viveiros de Castro makes about ontology: he suggests that within Amerindian cosmology, differences exist in knowledge that are not so much a matter of different perspectives, but rather a matter of different experiences, meant in literal, sensory terms. He illustrates this by suggesting that within Amerindian cosmology, "what to us is blood, is maize beer to the jaguar; what to us is soaking manioc is, to the souls of the dead, a rotting corpse; what is a muddy waterhole to us is, for the tapirs, a great ceremonial house" (Viveiros de Castro 2004: 471–472). In Viveiros de Castro's view, this means Amerindian cosmology posits many worlds – one inhabited by jaguars; another by tapirs; yet another by people. All have the same perspective, the same capacity to perceive; it is just that they are applying that perspective to different worlds. So rather than there being many different perspectives and one world, Amerindian cosmology posits one perspective and many worlds to which that perspective is applied. If people began to act like jaguars, they would not be able to survive in the world of people, and vice versa. Viveiros de Castro also suggests that the same classificatory system as I have been discussing in terms of Westphalian logic, and which he associates with Euro-American modernity and anthropology's notion of relativism (2004: 482–483), has impoverished our understanding of ontology, and enormously overcomplicated our understanding of epistemology.

This debate is relevant in a discussion about senses of border because it points, as did Ben Slimane's research, to the potential multiplicity of worlds, knowledge practices and ontologies that can simultaneously exist, in parallel, and that might all be differently involved in making or defining senses of border.[10] And there is more: borders are often ascribed the capacity to alter the reality that they apparently mark; they can appear to facilitate the making of worlds, and they can come into relation with other relations, to borrow an idea from Strathern.[11] Once an official border has been built, using some kind of classificatory logic, many worlds could be generated thereafter, and not just one. I have limited my discussion to dominant, singular and formal border logics for the sake of clarity and brevity; but the obvious point that borderness can be multiple, even to the extent of some people recognizing a place or a thing as a border while others do not see anything except landscape, is a crucial aspect of what could be called "borderness dynamics," for lack of a more elegant phrase.

MULTIPLICITY AND CHAOS

Janet Roitman's (2005) historical and ethnographic study of a frontier region, the Chad Basin – a multiply bordered region that covers northern Cameroon, northeastern Nigeria, Chad, and the Central African Republic – provides some glimpses of multiple worlds that centrally involve different logics of borderness. Roitman's focus is on shifting fiscal relations between people and the state as one means to try to approach how postcolonial conditions, globalization and traces of past political arrangements are involved in the multiple, ambiguous reframing of political citizenship in the region. She charts the complex, mostly commercial and almost always illegal networks of relations between peoples, organizations and groups that constantly crisscross the region's official borders. Combined with the imposition of state borders that had begun with French colonial rule, the constant informal crisscrossing is part of how this region became, and is constantly recreated as, a frontier. To rephrase it in the terms I am using, it was both the separation and the relations between the French colonial logic about borders and the local people's rather different logic that, to Roitman, resulted in the particular "borderness" of this place.

In the early nineteenth century before the arrival of the French, "political relationships were for the most part established in a context of constant circulation and movement that defined nomadic and semi-sedentarized communities . . . dominion often took place through nonspatial and nonterritorial forms" (Roitman 2005: 102). This constant movement apparently both structurally and conceptually deeply disturbed the French colonial administrators. It not only meant that the authorities were unable to extract taxes efficiently, but it also challenged the "knowability" of the people in these territories: "Mobility certainly confounded the quest for the knowable civil and fiscal subject – for a census and the head tax (*l'impôt*)" (Roitman 2005: 136). The reason for this level of disturbance was that the logic and structure of colonial rule was territorially bound and the Chad Basin appeared to be chock full of people who eventually came to be defined as a "floating population" (*population flottante*; Roitman 2005: 137–146) who were anything but territorially bound. This named category emerged as a direct effect of an attempt to impose a particular territorial logic upon peoples who did not appear to be classifiable within that logic: "the generalized category of the *population flottante* was an effect of the colonial problematic of fixing demographic instability to establish the fiscal subject" (Roitman 2005: 137–146). Roitman concludes that:

> the ambivalence accorded to market boys, frontier traders, and itinerant salesmen – like that conferred upon brigand-chief tax collectors – ensued from their incessant transgression of boundaries . . . With respect to the literal boundaries of the colonial state, this activity obviously collided with the limits of territorial jurisdiction. More than that, efforts to institute colonial law and constitute the legal subject via "ordered knowledge of society" and enumeration were confounded by "unaccounted motion" (e.g., vagrancy), which, in subverting demographics, also challenged the law. (2005: 146)

The key point for my purposes here is that both the peoples and the places Roitman describes are a motley lot: to borrow from Strathern, there seems to be nothing holding them together in the center, only endless permutations and possibilities (Strathern 1991: xvii). And what makes them appear that way has parallels with the stereotypical reputation of the Balkan region as being chaotic or fractal (Green 2005: ch. 4): the overlapping coexistence of different kinds of knowledge practice and classification systems which, in both these cases, could not be fully encompassed by any one of these systems. The French authorities in the Chad Basin, it seems, attempted to encompass different logics within their own world, while these other logics continued to be played out in different worlds and not, or not only, the French one. In areas where these different knowledge practices could not be encompassed, the outcome, from the French colonial authorities' perspective, was chaos. As Roitman notes, it was only the French colonial logic of border and territory that required controlled borders and a territorially fixed way of classifying populations, so it was only to them that the inability to fix the *population flottante* in place made things appear chaotic. That last point is worth emphasizing: the classificatory logic that informs the construction of certain types of border often also informs other processes of classifying, defining and enumerating people, places, things and exchanges (e.g., as in a census).[12] In this case, French authorities expected to be able to encompass all peoples and places within the same bureaucratic logic; when that proved to be impossible, the result was described, by the French authorities, as chaotic.

Roitman's description of the Chad Basin frontier as a constantly shifting, discontinuous, incomplete, and (to some) chaotic outcome of French colonial imposition of a certain border logic, one that coexisted with, and never erased, a range of other logics and practices, brings to mind Foucault's (1986) notion of heterotopia.[13] Unlike utopias (places that do not exist), Foucault defines heterotopias as spaces that do exist but that have a strange quality or relationship with the rest of reality, one that is simultaneously both virtual and real. Foucault uses the example of a mirror: the reflection of yourself is you, and the mirror exists in reality, but in the mirror, you are located somewhere other than where you are at the moment in a physical sense. Foucault also outlines how heterotopias are historically contingent, and they have a range of qualities that seem to be particularly appropriate for situations such as the ones described by Roitman and by Ben Slimane. In particular, Foucault suggests that "the heterotopia is capable of juxtaposing in a single real place several spaces, several sites that are in themselves incompatible" (1986: 25). He adds that heterotopias also have some strange effects:

> Either their role is to create a space of illusion that exposes every real space, all the sites inside of which human life is partitioned, as still more illusory . . . Or else, on the contrary, their role is to create a space that is other, another real space, as perfect, as meticulous, as well arranged as ours is messy, ill constructed and jumbled. (1986: 27)

In short, Foucault suggests that heterotopias can act both as a challenge to the powers that be – a site where the trickery that goes into making things appear real and clear is exposed, transgressed and mixed up (the border as the possible site of radical fragmentation); and also, they can impose an apparent clarity, a reality that clears and classifies (the orderly, rather than disorderly, border). Roitman's Chad Basin frontier could be seen as an example of the former, and the new Kakavia border post could be seen as an example of the latter.

POST-WESTPHALIAN BORDERNESS

Foucault's notion of heterotopia has been picked up by some border theorists (e.g., Robinson 2007), who suggest that borders are becoming more complex, dispersed and chimerical entities than they have been before, in the light of economic globalization, the development of increasing numbers of transnational political and economic entities (the World Trade Organization, the European Union, the International Criminal Court at The Hague, and so on), and the development of new information and communications technologies. This has been particularly noted by those studying the European Union and its panoply of diverse policies on borders.[14] Del Sarto argues that the European Union region is now developing a post-Westphalian logic to its bordering practices. She suggests that "a multiplicity of overlapping and cross-cutting border regimes, entailing disaggregated functions of borders, characterizes the EU and its member states" (2010: 153). What the EU has been doing around its outer peripheries, Del Sarto suggests, is to create a heterogeneous kind of buffer zone, in which different regional agreements overlap with specific bilateral agreements, which overlap in turn with other kinds of transnational agreements to create a kind of smorgasbord of "borderness" around this region. Some examples: the Schengen Zone, within which people can travel entirely freely, does not include all EU member states (e.g., it excludes the UK), but does include some non-EU states (e.g., Norway);

the eurozone, which covers countries that use the euro as their currency, again includes some EU member states, but not all of them; and the European Neighbourhood Policy, aimed at generating certain types of political, social and economic relations with neighboring non-EU member states, includes Israel, Egypt and Georgia, but not Russia, Serbia or Switzerland. Del Sarto suggests that because of these multiple and complex arrangements, it is becoming increasingly unclear what is "outside" and what is "inside" the European Union area (2010: 163). She also suggests that this more visibly blurred character of the peripheries is moving the logic that is informing EU policies more toward the center-periphery logic that Hassner described (Del Sarto 2010: 152). Similarly, Liikanen and Virtanen's study of the European Neighbourhood Policy also outlines how the apparent intention of the EU in developing this policy is to blur the boundaries between inside and outside (2006: 129).

The idea that borders are increasingly being dispersed and made ambiguous in terms of their locations and their inside(s) and outside(s) – that is, the idea that single borders are becoming multiple in the course of becoming more loosely, or more complexly, related to states as opposed to nonstate transnational entities – has been a common suggestion in recent years. One of the more interesting concepts in this respect is the notion of the "smart border." It is a term that emerged in border security circles in North America and Europe to refer to the perceived need to develop better technical systems for allowing desirable people and goods to cross borders, but preventing undesirable ones from getting through; a kind of intelligently porous border (Salter 2004). This implies that outsiders and insiders exist on all sides of the border, and that the border must somehow intelligently control their movement; it also strongly implies that borders are entities that have agency, and that given the right kind of technology, they can develop intelligent agency. While this is understood to be something of a fantasy even in securitization circles (Aas 2009), it provides some sense of what many are suggesting is a cluster of interrelated bordering practices that are increasingly pointing toward a different, post-Westphalian, logic of border, which is generating, or at the very least making more visible, a range of different kinds of borderness.

Brown is a prominent advocate of this position, and she suggests that the idea of "smart borders" is exemplary in demonstrating what the transition means (Brown 2010: 94). She argues that over the past 50 years, the nation-state's power has been "severely compromised by growing transnational flows of capital, people, ideas, goods, violence, and political and religious fealty. These flows both tear at the borders they cross and crystallize as powers within them" (2010: 22). At the same time, there has been a great increase in the building of physical walls of a wide range of types in border regions, as if the solid physicality of these edifices would somehow compensate for the scattering of the location of borders, the dilution of clarity of what is inside or outside, and the waning of state sovereignty: "walls would seem to embody precisely the power of the 'no,' physically proclaiming and enforcing what is *interdit*. The new walls thus seem to stand as a certain kind of rebuke to every poststructuralist theorization of power as well as to every liberal hope for a global village" (Brown 2010: 81). There are other versions of Brown's argument that the world has become transnational rather than national; that it is smaller; and that states have been the persistent losers in that process. For example, O'Dowd, who describes borders as more or less self-evident entities, suggests that even where the borders have not been moved geographically, the logic informing them has changed significantly, which he associates directly, as does Brown, with the rise of neoliberal politics and economics (O'Dowd 2002: 20). All such approaches imply, in one way or another, that there has been a firm shift away from the binary and homogeneous logic that informed the creation of the borders of nation-states, and a firm shift toward something that is altogether less clear and/or more complex in terms of the relations between people, places, things and movement. Brown (2010: 21) resists the temptation to declare a new epoch or the return of a previous epoch; instead, she refers to a "post-Westphalian world" in which "'post' indicates a very particular condition of afterness in which what is past is not left behind but, on the contrary, relentlessly conditions, even dominates a present that nevertheless also breaks in some way with this past."

Tidemarks, Indexicality and Relational Locations

I have argued elsewhere that one of the shifts that has occurred around the peripheries of Europe is that the idea of border as line, which has not disappeared by any means, has gradually also been accompanied by the idea of border as place, a change that is associated with all the historical, political, and economic – but also conceptual and classificatory – shifts described here: changes in EU policies, and an increasing emphasis on various transnational relations that cross-cut the linearity of the state border (Green 2010). And I have also suggested that one way to think about these transitions in the combination of bordering practices and senses of borderness is as "tidemarks": tidemarks are traces of movement, which can be repetitive or suddenly change, may generate long-term effects or disappear the next day, but nevertheless continue to mark, or make, a difference that makes a difference (Green 2009, 2011).

I would like to make two small additional points here. First, that this distinction between border as line and border as place can also be thought of in terms of indexicality. As Gell (1985) outlined many years ago in his discussion of maps and mapping practices, it is possible to describe location in both indexical and nonindexical ways. For example, an indexical statement of location is: "London is south of here." The truth of the statement is dependent upon the location of the speaker: it is only true if the speaker is located north of London. In contrast, in nonindexical statements of location, it makes no difference where the speaker is located: "London is south of Manchester" will always be either correct or incorrect irrespective of where the person making this statement is located.

In this sense, borders thought of as places – Del Sarto's buffer zones, Roitman's frontier, Donnan and Wilson's borderlands, Ottoman peripheries – are indexical. Such places do not mark something like a line on a map; rather, they are always specific places, with distinctive characteristics that are dependent upon both their relations with other places and things, and their particular location. The Chad Basin could not be anywhere else, and its characterization as a chaotic frontier was dependent upon its particular relations with French-built borders; the Ottoman peripheries were each characterized by specific histories, relations with various centers and even particular personalities (e.g., Ali Pasha of Tepelene). And as Donnan and Wilson note

(2010: 6–7), this dependence upon distinctive historical relations and locations tends to give borders understood as places (borderlands and, somewhat differently, frontiers) immense variability. Donnan and Wilson explicitly contrast this indexical, place-based notion of border to the notion of border as line, which they suggest is regarded as simply the mark where states come together and separate simultaneously. I have suggested, along with historians such as Del Sarto, that this notion of line is informed by a historically contingent classificatory logic that initially accompanied the development of states in Europe, and later informed what came to be understood as nation-states. As I have described, this logic has also tended to be quite bureaucratic, accompanying all manner of modern statecraft, and some forms of colonial rule as well. And I would add that this idea of border as a line is a *nonindexical* concept of border: a line is an abstraction, a mathematical concept, and as such, it takes up no actual space. Of course, lines can be represented: drawn on maps, marked by walls, fences, border checkpoints and any manner of other types of bureaucratic bordering paraphernalia. In that sense, the fences, border posts, visas, passports, regulations, maps, surveillance, policing and any other form of procedural, legal, technical or material manifestation of border are all part of the same thing: they are part of turning an idea, a nonindexical concept, into some kind of reality, whether that be heterotopic or not.

Brown (2010: 25) suggests that the recent intensification of the production of all this border paraphernalia is an indication that state authorities are behaving a little like the Wizard of Oz: the more sovereign state power wanes, the more big walls and expensive high-tech security systems are put in place to make it *look* strong and real. Perhaps; but those practices are also increasingly emphasizing the nonindexicality of border as line: the line could be anywhere, and it could stand for anything; there are endless ways to measure it, ascribe it with capacities to define, mark or reflect, to *do* things in the world, to have agency. And the "smart borders" are going one step further in this nonindexicality, explicitly suggesting that the line is not only an abstraction that could mean anything, but that this means it is simultaneously the marker of many places, many worlds, and perhaps many logics too (and this is my second small point): tailor-made borders that might, if the securitization specialists can achieve their fantasy, be a unique border for each person, making one of Kafka's nightmares into a technical reality (van Houtum 2010: 285). This is where the notion of border as indexical place meets border as nonindexical line: how much more indexical can you get than to construct a border for every individual? And yet, if border can be anything, then it is also nothing, an empty signifier, with no relations to other people or to places – in short, no substance. Whereas border as indexical place is entirely reliant upon its dense historically and spatially specific interrelations for its "borderness," the fantasy end point of "smart borders" is that they become so individuated that they involve no relations at all. This takes the logic of border as nonindexical line to a bizarre, but epistemologically familiar, conclusion.[15]

Of course, and as Donnan and Wilson (2010) have pointed out, in practice, there are no borders that are just nonindexical lines; countless ethnographic studies of border areas have demonstrated that in everyday life, borders are always, in one way or another, indexical places. In that sense, there will always be some level of Wizard of Oz-idry about linear borders: official, and often unofficial, insistence on the ontological reality and fixity of the thing as a particular kind of line is somehow, when looked at closely, never entirely convincing. Much the same could be said of money, an equally abstract yet powerful entity that, when inspected closely, is not quite as "real" or straightforward as it seems (Maurer 2005). This fact of abstraction does not make borders understood as line, or money understood as value, any less powerful in people's everyday lives; what it does do, however, is to imply an autonomous existence separate from the historically specific and power-inflected relations, and the underlying classificatory logic, upon which these particular bordering practices and monetary exchanges rely in order to make sense. It also conceals the existence of other logics, different ways of knowing.

In sum: the aim here has been not to establish what borders are, but rather how different senses of border (borderness) have been the subject of ongoing ontological projects, those of empires as well as people going about their everyday lives. What borders locate, in that sense, is stories so far, which might be moving along slowly, quickly or not at all, but which are always in one way or another relational, both in terms of the classificatory logic that makes borders visible as such, and in terms of the coming together of people, places, things and ideas in historically, politically, economically and spatially specific ways. I have also suggested that only in some circumstances have borders become an explicit classification practice ascribed with agency. When border is imagined as having nonindexical properties (e.g., as an abstract line), it is also possible, within a particular theory of knowledge, to imagine it as the source of making realities rather than simply reflecting them; borders could then be understood as their own classification systems, rather than as indexical places that appear, then wax and wane as the result of people doing other things. And that matters: when borders are imagined as an indexical place, borders may not mark or "do" anything, for they are not necessarily imagined or experienced as an entity that marks, but as simply a place, within which, somewhere, different entities overlap. In those cases, the source of the distinctions that borders mark (the differences that make a difference) are not condensed into an abstract line at the edge of a place, but are located elsewhere.

NOTES

1 See, for example, Pollo and Puto 1981; Jacques 1995; Clogg 1992; Herzfeld 1986.
2 See, for example, Winnifrith 2002; Nitsiakos and Mantzos 2003; Nitsiakos 1996; Myrivili 2004; Cowan 2000.
3 See, for example, Zartman 2010; Scott 2006a; Balibar 1998; Bechev and Nicolaidis 2010; O'Dowd 2002; Hassner 2002.
4 The question of the relationship between literal and metaphorical earthquakes in the landscape in this region is something I have dealt with elsewhere (Green 2005: ch. 3).
5 See, for example, Hassner 2002; Scott 2006b; Leontidou et al. 2005; Suárez-Navaz 2004; van Houtum 2002; Zartman 2010; van Houtum et al. 2005.
6 See, for example, Navaro-Yashin 2003; Sideri 2009; van Houtum 2010; Jansen 2009.
7 See, for example Malkki 1992, 1995; van Houtum 2010; Clochard et al. 2003; Taylor and Rafferty-Brown 2010; Jordan and Duvell 2002; Monterescu and Rabinowitz 2007; Jansen 2009.

8   See Haraway 1985, 1997; Bordo 1987; Helman 1991.
9   See, for example, Borneman 1992; Herzfeld 1986, 1992a, 1992b; Povinelli 1997; Verdery 1999; Ssorin-Chaikov 2003; Sant Cassia 2005.
10 I am particularly indebted to the work of Doreen Massey (2005) in informing some of these insights, and I discuss her work at more length elsewhere (Green 2009, 2010).
11 Marilyn Strathern (2011) has recently engaged with Viveiros de Castro's approach and taken it in a somewhat different direction. She is concerned with the distinction between perspective as choice (which she suggests is a defining feature of Euro-American thought), and perspective as the outcome of relations (which she suggests is a defining feature of understandings in Mount Hagen, where she did her fieldwork). The notion of choice implies that the world is full of entities with preexisting characteristics; the notion of relation suggests that such characteristics are generated out of the relational position persons occupy with respect to one another: "In occupying different positions, then, a person switches not individual viewpoints but relationships" (Strathern 2011: 94). Where for Viveiros de Castro's Amerindian thought, a jaguar lives in a jaguar world as part of its embodied existence, for Strathern's Mount Hagen thought, worlds are made and remade in the process of occupying relational positions. Comparing Strathern's description of Mount Hagen thought to the different classificatory practices I have been outlining here would take me too far from the main concern of this chapter; but it is worth noting that Strathern suggests that the Euro-American approach, which she calls 'perspectivalist' after Law's (2004) discussion of the term, is beginning to overtake the Mount Hagen relational approach, somewhat in the way Ben Slimane argued that Westphalian logic overtook the logic of border in the Maghreb.
12 See, for example, Cohn 1990; Hacking 1991; Urla 1993; Appadurai 1996; Kertzer and Arel 2002.
13 Although Roitman makes considerable use of Foucault in her analysis, she does not mention the concept of heterotopia.
14 See, for example, O'Dowd 2002; Scott 2006a; Balibar 1998; Abélès 2000; Zielonka 2002; Rumford 2006.
15 A similar point about the ideals of separating things out and individuating them has been made by Strathern (1992) in her discussion of English kinship. Again, there is a clearly recognizable relationship here to a particular Euro-American theory of knowledge.

REFERENCES

Aas, Katja Franko. 2009. The "Interoperable body": Identity and Social Sorting at the European Border. Working Paper 6. EastBordNet Working Papers, WG4. At http://www.eastbordnet.org/working_papers/.

Abélès, Marc. 2000. Virtual Europe. In Irene Bellier and Thomas M. Wilson, eds, *An Anthropology of the European Union: Building, Imagining and Experiencing the New Europe*, pp. 31–52. Oxford: Berg.

Alvarez, Robert R., Jr. 1995. The Mexican-US border: the making of an anthropology of borderlands. *Annual Review of Anthropology* 24: 447–470.

Anderson, Benedict. 1983. *Imagined Communities: Reflections on the Origin and Spread of Nationalism*. London: Verso.

Anzaldúa, Gloria. 1987. *Borderlands/La Frontera: The New Mestiza*. San Francisco: Aunt Lute.

Appadurai, Arjun. 1996. Number in the colonial imagination. In Arjun Appadurai, ed., *Modernity at Large: Cultural Dimensions of Globalization*, pp. 114–135. Minneapolis: University of Minnesota Press.

Balibar, Étienne. 1998. The borders of Europe. In Pheng Cheah and Bruce Robbins, eds, *Cosmopolitics: Thinking and*

Feeling beyond the Nation, pp. 216–229. Minneapolis: University of Minnesota Press.

Ballinger, Pamela. 2003. *History in Exile: Memory and Identity at the Borders of the Balkans*. Princeton: Princeton University Press.

Bechev, Dimitar and Nicolaidis, Kalypso, eds. 2010. *Mediterranean Frontiers: Borders, Conflict and Memory in a Transnational World*. London: Tauris Academic Studies.

Ben Slimane, Fatma. 2010. Between empire and nation-state: the problem of borders in the Maghreb. In Dimitar Bechev and Kalypso Nicolaidis, eds, *Mediterranean Frontiers: Borders, Conflict and Memory in a Transnational World*, pp. 35–55. London: Tauris Academic Studies.

Bordo, Susan R. 1987. *The Flight to Objectivity: Essays on Cartesianism and Culture*. Albany: State University of New York Press.

Borneman, John. 1992. *Belonging in the Two Berlins: Kin, State, Nation*. Cambridge: Cambridge University Press.

Bourdieu, Pierre. 1977. *Outline of a Theory of Practice*. Cambridge: Cambridge University Press.

Brown, Wendy. 2010. *Walled States, Waning Sovereignty*. New York: Zone Books.

Butler, Judith. 1990. *Gender Trouble: Feminism and the Subversion of Identity*. London: Routledge.

Caplan, Jane. 2001. "This or that particular person": protocols of identification in nineteenth-century Europe. In Jane Caplan and John C. Torpey, eds, *Documenting Individual Identity: The Development of State Practices in the Modern World*, pp. 49–66. Princeton: Princeton University Press.

Clochard, Olivier, Decourcelle, Antoine and Intrand, Chloé. 2003. Zones d'attente et demande d'asile à la frontière. Le renforcement des contrôles migratoires? [Waiting zones and claim of asylum at the border: the strengthening of migratory controls?] *Revue Européenne des Migrations Internationales* 19 (2): 157–189.

Clogg, Richard. 1992. *A Concise History of Greece*. Cambridge: Cambridge University Press.

Cohn, Bernard S. 1990. The census, social structure and objectification in South Asia. In *An Anthropologist among the Historians and Other Essays*. Oxford: Oxford University Press.

Cowan, Jane K., ed. 2000. *Macedonia: The Politics of Identity and Difference*. London: Pluto Press.

Danforth, Loring. 1995. *The Macedonian Conflict: Ethnic Nationalism in a Transnational World*. Princeton: Princeton University Press.

Del Sarto, Raffaella A. 2010. Borderlands: the Middle East and North Africa as the EU's southern buffer zone. In Dimitar Bechev and Kalypso Nicolaidis, eds, *Mediterranean Frontiers: Borders, Conflict and Memory in a Transnational World*, pp. 149–165. London: Tauris Academic Studies.

Donnan, Hastings. 2005. Material identities: fixing ethnicity in the Irish borderlands. *Identities* 12: 69–106.

Donnan, Hastings and Wilson, Thomas M. 1999. *Borders: Frontiers of Identity, Nation and State*. Oxford: Berg.

Donnan, Hastings and Wilson, Thomas M., eds. 2010. *Borderlands: Ethnographic Approaches to Security, Power, and Identity*. Lanham: University Press of America.

Douglas, Mary. 1966. *Purity and Danger: An Analysis of Concepts of Pollution and Taboo*. London: Routledge & Kegan Paul.

Fleming, Katherine Elizabeth. 1999. *The Muslim Bonaparte: Diplomacy and Orientalism in Ali Pasha's Greece*. Princeton: Princeton University Press.

Foucault, Michel. 1974. *The Order of Things: An Archaeology of the Human Sciences*. London: Tavistock.

Foucault, Michel. 1986. Of other spaces. *Diacritics* 16 (1): 22–27.

Gell, Alfred. 1985. How to read a map: remarks on the practical knowledge of navigation. *Man* 20 (2): 271–286.

Gourgouris, Stathis. 1996. *Dream Nation: Enlightenment, Colonization, and the Institution of Modern Greece*. Stanford: Stanford University Press.

Green, Sarah. 2005. *Notes from the Balkans: Locating Marginality and Ambiguity on the Greek-Albanian Border*. Princeton: Princeton University Press.

Green, Sarah. 2009. Lines, Traces and Tidemarks: Reflections on Forms of Borderliness. EastBordNet Working Papers, WG1:1. At http://www.eastbordnet.org/working_papers/open/documents/Green_Lines_Traces_and_Tidemarks_090414.pdf (accessed Nov. 2011).

Green, Sarah. 2010. Performing border in the Aegean: on relocating political, economic and social relations. *Journal of Cultural Economy* 3 (2): 261–278.

Green, Sarah. 2011. What's in a tidemark? *Anthropology News* 52 (2): 15.

Hacking, Ian. 1991. How should we do the history of statistics? In Graham Burchell, Colin Gordon and Peter Miller, eds, *The Foucault Effect: Studies in Governmentality*, pp. 181–196. London: Harvester Wheatsheaf.

Haraway, Donna. 1985. A Manifesto for cyborgs: science, technology, and socialist feminism in the 1980s. *Socialist Review* 80: 65–107.

Haraway, Donna. 1997. Mice into wormholes: a comment on the nature of no nature. In Gary Lee Downey and Joseph Dumit, eds, *Cyborgs and Citadels: Anthropological Interventions in Emerging Sciences and Technologies*, pp. 209–243. Santa Fe: School of American Research Press.

Hassner, Pierre. 2002. Fixed borders or moving borderlands? A new type of border for a new type of entity. In Jan Zielonka, ed., *Europe Unbound: Enlarging and Reshaping the Boundaries of the European Union*, pp. 38–50. London: Routledge.

Helman, Cecil. 1991. *Body Myths*. London: Chatto & Windus.

Herzfeld, Michael. 1986. *Ours Once More: Folklore, Ideology, and the Making of Modern Greece*. New York: Pella.

Herzfeld, Michael. 1992a. Segmentation and politics in the European nation-state: making sense of political events. In Kirsten Hastrup, ed., *Other Histories*, pp. 62–81. London: Routledge.

Herzfeld, Michael. 1992b. *The Social Production of Indifference: Exploring the Symbolic Roots of Western Bureaucracy*. Oxford: Berg.

Jacques, Edwin E. 1995. *The Albanians: An Ethnic History from Prehistoric Times to the Present*. Jefferson, NC: McFarland.

Jansen, Stef. 2009. After the red passport: towards an anthropology of the everyday geopolitics of entrapment in the EU's "immediate outside." *Journal of the Royal Anthropological Institute* 15 (4): 815–832.

Jordan, Bill and Duvell, Franck. 2002. *Irregular Migration: The Dilemmas of Transnational Mobility*. Cheltenham: Edward Elgar.

Kertzer, David I. and Arel, Dominique. 2002. Censuses, identity formation, and the struggle for political power. In David I. Kertzer and Dominique Arel, eds, *Census and Identity: The Politics of Race, Ethnicity, and Language in National Censuses*, pp. 1–42. Cambridge: Cambridge University Press.

Law, John. 2004. *After Method: Mess in Social Science Research*. London: Routledge.

Leontidou, Lila, Donnan, Hastings and Afouxenidis, Alex. 2005. Exclusion and difference along the EU border: social and cultural markers, spatialities and mappings. *International Journal of Urban and Regional Research* 29 (2): 389–407.

Liikanen, Ilkka and Virtanen, Petri. 2006. The new neighbourhood: a "constitution" for cross-border cooperation? In James Wesley Scott, ed., *EU Enlargement, Region Building and Shifting Borders of Inclusion and Exclusion*, pp. 113–130. Aldershot: Ashgate.

Malkki, Liisa. 1992. National geographic: the rooting of peoples and the territorialization of national identity among scholars and refugees. *Cultural Anthropology* 7 (1): 24–44.

Malkki, Liisa. 1995. *Purity and Exile: Violence, Memory, and National Cosmology among Hutu Refugees in Tanzania*. Chicago: University of Chicago Press.

Massey, Doreen B. 2005. *For Space*. London: Sage.

Maurer, Bill. 2005. *Mutual Life, Limited: Islamic Banking, Alternative Currencies, Lateral Reason*. Princeton: Princeton University Press.

Monterescu, Daniel and Rabinowitz, Dan. 2007. *Mixed Towns, Trapped Communities:*

Historical Narratives, Spatial Dynamics, Gender Relations and Cultural Encounters in Palestinian-Israeli Towns. Aldershot: Ashgate.

Myrivili, Eleni. 2004. The liquid border: subjectivity at the limits of the nation-state in southeast Europe (Albania, Greece, Macedonia). PhD diss., Columbia University.

Navaro-Yashin, Yael. 2003. "Life is dead here": sensing the political in "no man's land." *Anthropological Theory* 3 (1): 107–125.

Nitsiakos, Vassilis. 1996. Place, locality and identity. the case of the Greek minority of Albania. *Ethnology* 4: 93–106.

Nitsiakos, Vasilis and Mantzos, Constantinos. 2003. Negotiating culture: political uses of polyphonic folk songs in Greece and Albania. In Dimitris Tziovas, ed., *Greece and the Balkans: Identities, Perceptions and Cultural Encounters since the Enlightenment*, pp. 192–207. London: Ashgate.

O'Dowd, Liam. 2002. The changing significance of European borders. *Regional and Federal Studies* 12 (4): 13–36.

Pelkmans, Mathijs. 2006. *Defending the Border: Identity, Religion, and Modernity in the Republic of Georgia.* Ithaca: Cornell University Press.

Plomer, William. 1970. *The Diamond of Jannina: Ali Pasha, 1741–1822.* London: Cape. First publ. 1936.

Pollo, Stefanaq and Puto, Arben. 1981. *The History of Albania from Its Origins to the Present Day.* London: Routledge & Kegan Paul.

Povinelli, Elizabeth. 1997. Sex acts and sovereignty: race and sexuality in the construction of the Australian nation. In Roger N. Lancaster and Micaela Di Leonardo, eds, *The Gender/Sexuality Reader: Culture, History, Political Economy*, pp. 513–29. New York: Routledge.

Rabinowitz, Dan. 2001. The Palestinian citizens of Israel, the concept of trapped minority and the discourse of transnationalism in anthropology. *Ethnic and Racial Studies* 24 (1): 64–85.

Riles, Annelise. 1998. Division within the boundaries. *Journal of the Royal Anthropological Institute* 4 (3): 409–424.

Robinson, Richard. 2007. *Narratives of the European Border: A History of Nowhere.* Basingstoke: Palgrave Macmillan.

Roitman, Janet L. 2005. *Fiscal Disobedience: An Anthropology of Economic Regulation in Central Africa.* Princeton: Princeton University Press.

Rumford, Chris. 2006. Rethinking European spaces: territory, borders, governance. *Comparative European Politics* 4: 127–140.

Salter, Mark B. 2004. Passports, mobility, and security: how smart can the border be? *International Studies Perspectives* 5 (1): 71–91.

Sant Cassia, Paul. 2005. *Bodies of Evidence: Burial, Memory and the Recovery of Missing Persons in Cyprus.* Oxford: Berghahn Books.

Scott, James Wesley, ed. 2006a. *EU Enlargement, Region Building and Shifting Borders of Inclusion and Exclusion.* Aldershot: Ashgate.

Scott, James Wesley. 2006b. Wider Europe: geopolitics of inclusion and exclusion at the EU's new external boundaries. In James Wesley Scott, ed., *EU Enlargement, Region Building and Shifting Borders of Inclusion and Exclusion*, pp. 17–34. Aldershot: Ashgate.

Sideri, Eleni. 2009. Between Motion and Stillness: Debating and Crossing Borders of Europeaness. EastBordNet Working Papers, WG4:33. At http://www.eastbordnet.org/working_papers/.

Ssorin-Chaikov, Nikolai V. 2003. *The Social Life of the State in Subarctic Siberia.* Stanford: Stanford University Press.

Strathern, Marilyn. 1991. *Partial Connections.* Savage, MD: Rowman & Littlefield.

Strathern, Marilyn. 1992. *After Nature: English Kinship in the Late Twentieth Century.* Cambridge: Cambridge University Press.

Strathern, Marilyn. 2011. Binary license. *Common Knowledge* 17 (1): 87–103.

Suárez-Navaz, Liliana. 2004. *Rebordering the Mediterranean: Boundaries and Citizenship in Southern Europe.* Oxford: Berghahn.

Taylor, S. and Rafferty-Brown, B. 2010. Waiting for life to begin: the plight of asylum seekers caught by Australia's Indonesian solution. *International Journal of Refugee Law* 22 (4): 558–592.

Urla, Jacqueline. 1993. Cultural politics in an age of statistics: numbers, nations, and the making of Basque identity. *American Ethnologist* 20 (4): 818–843.

van Houtum, Henk. 2002. Borders of comfort: spatial economic bordering processes in the European Union. *Regional and Federal Studies* 12 (4): 37–58.

van Houtum, Henk. 2010. Waiting before the law: Kafka on the border. *Social and Legal Studies* 19: 285–298.

van Houtum, Henk, Kramsch, Olivier Thomas and Zierhofer, Wolfgang, eds. 2005. *B/ordering Space*. Aldershot: Ashgate.

Verdery, Katherine. 1999. *The Political Lives of Dead Bodies: Reburial and Postsocialist Change*. New York: Columbia University Press.

Viveiros de Castro, E. 2004. Exchanging perspectives: the transformation of objects into subjects in Amerindian ontologies. *Common Knowledge* 10 (3): 463–484.

Winnifrith, Tom. 2002. *Badlands – Borderlands: A History of Northern Epirus/Southern Albania*. London: Duckworth.

Zartman, I. William. 2010. *Understanding Life in the Borderlands: Boundaries in Depth and in Motion*. Athens: University of Georgia Press.

Zielonka, Jan, ed. 2002. *Europe Unbound: Enlarging and Reshaping the Boundaries of the European Union*. London: Routledge.

Index

Note: page numbers in italics denote figures or tables

A Companion to Border Studies, First Edition. Edited by Thomas M. Wilson and
Hastings Donnan.
© 2012 Blackwell Publishing Ltd. Published 2012 by Blackwell Publishing Ltd.

externalization 456–7, 458, 464–7
extraction regimes 335, 340, 344–5, 349
   see also institutions of extraction

Fagan, Richard R. 8
Fairchild, Amy 359
Fallen Timbers battle 182
Familia (Alvarez) 550
Family Compact, Upper Canada 191–2
Fanon, Frantz 302
FAO (Food and Agriculture Organization) 359,
   365, 366
Farley, John 360
Farmer, Paul 365
Farrell, David R, 182
Fazila-Yacoobali Zamindar, V. 392, 394, 395
FDI: *see* foreign direct investment
Federal Republic of Germany 519
federalism 39, 262, 421
Feetham, Richard 44
Felbab-Brown, Vanda 341
Feldman, I. 396
fences 377
Ferghana Valley 476, 477, 479, 480, 481–3,
   487
Ferguson, James 277, 421
Ferguson, Niall: *The Cash Nexus* 128
Fernandez-Kelly, Maria Patricia: *For We Are Sold*
   540
Ferradás, Carmen 202
Ferrières, Madeleine 356–7
Ferry, Jules 238
Fidler, David 358, 359, 361
Finland 93
Finnish-Russian border 93–4, 271
First Nations 180, 181, 182, 183, 193n4
Flathead people 189
floating populations 582
Florentine Board of Health 357
Florida, Treaty of 187
Flynn, Donna K. 548, 566
Flynn, Stephen 108
Food and Agriculture Organization: *see* FAO
food safety 365–6
Food Safety Act (UK) 365
For We Are Sold (Fernandez-Kelly) 540
forced labor continuum 441
forced migration 390
Ford, Michele 19, 442, 444, 445, 446, 447, 448,
   452n7
foreign direct investment (FDI) 142, 143, 144, 147,
   151–2, 153, 154n6
foreignness 143, 500, 502
Forkhill bomb 218
Le Fort du Taureau 236
Fort Langley 186
Fort Malden 182
Fort Mcloughlin 186
Fort Nisqually 186
Fort Simpson 186
Fort Stikina 186
Fort Vancouver 186
Fortress Europe concept 130, 149, 312
Fortuyn, Pim 516
Forum for Democratic Change, Uganda 325
Foucault, Michel 232, 294, 474, 475, 576, 579,
   582–3

France
   center-periphery relations 233
   Chad Basin 582
   decolonization 35
   geography 235
   in Maghreb 578–9
   National Front 500
   Old Northwest 180
   penal colony 237, 238–9
   Roman Catholicism 190
   Third Republic 233
France-Germany border 238, 565
France-Spain border 69
Francistown 569
Frankfurt an-der-Oder 564
Frazer, George M. 73
free trade 380–1, 444
freedom of movement, denied 254–5
Freidberg, Susanne 365
French Congo 566
French Mandate, Israel 253
French World Exhibition 241–2
From Barriers to Bridges (AUBP) 78
La Frontera (Anzaldúa) 541
FRONTEX 105, 110, 113, 115n3, 409–10,
   465
frontier cities 158–9, 162, 166, 171
frontier zones
   conflict 158–9
   and core relations 165
   EU 214
   external 245
   geopolitics 164
   peopling of 197
   Roitman 585
   settlements 305, 306, 309
Frontiers (Anderson) 10–11
Frost & Sullivan 293
fruit flies 362
Fumagalli, Matteo 482
fundamentalism 249
fur trade 180, 182, 186, 193n2
Fusco, Coco 518
futurespace 523–4

G8 group 174n12
G20 group 174n12
Gabon 567
Gaborone 569
Gadsden Purchase 422
Gaelic games 223
Galemba, Rebecca 544
Gallant, Thomas 334
Gambetta, Léon 244
Gambia 566
Gandhi, M.K. 36, 37
Ganges-Brahmaputra 376
Ganges-Mahakab 376
Ganster, Paul 381
García Canclini, Nestor 48, 49
An Garda Siochána 221
Gardizi, Manija 341, 342, 344
gas supplies 479, 480–1
Gasparini, A. 565
gatekeeper states 419
Gates, Charles M, 191
gaucho culture 207, 208, 209